W9-AST-392

White Sea

Archangel

S I B E R I A

Ekaterinburg

Perm

tolbovo

Kostroma

Volga River Kazan

Nizhni
Novgorod

Suzdal

Alexandrov

Tver   Troitsk   Vladimir

MOSCOW

Borodino

Simbirsk   Samara

Orenburg   *River*

Ural

lensk

Ryazan

Kulikovo

Andrusevo

Saratov

iev

Kiev

Dnieper   R.

Poltava

Tsaritsyn   *Volga R.*

Astrakhan

Don R.

U   K   R   A   I   N   E

Taganrog

Zaporozhe

Azov

*Caspian
Sea*

ishinev

Odessa

CRIMEA

Sevastopol

GEORGIA

Black Sea

ARMENIA

uchuk Kainarji

Sinop

Bosporus

Constantinople

Sea of Marmara

T   U   R   K   E   Y

Don Pitcher

THE TRAGIC DYNASTY

A History of the Romanovs

THE TRAGIC DYNASTY

A HISTORY OF THE ROMANOVS

by John D. Bergamini

G. P. PUTNAM'S SONS   *New York*

Contents

Photographic illustrations follow page 256

MAPS

I.
Introduction

1. Prologue and Epilogue

IN 1613 a general assembly of Russians elected Michael Romanov as tsar in an effort to end more than a decade of civil war and foreign invasion known as the Time of Troubles. The old dynasty of Rurik, which had ruled since 862 A.D., had died out. Desperate men agreed to raise the popular Romanov family to royal dignity in the person of sixteen-year-old Michael, a shy and somber youth who was currently in hiding in a monastery.

Tradition gives us the story that the newly chosen tsar was narrowly saved from capture by a roving band of Polish soldiers because of the heroism of an ordinary Russian peasant, Ivan Susanin. Compelled to act as guide for the Poles, Susanin deliberately led astray the enemies of Russia and Orthodoxy until they found themselves hopelessly lost in a forest and blinded by a snowstorm. Susanin was cut down, but the fledgling dynasty was saved. This story is beautifully celebrated in the opera *A Life for the Tsar* by Glinka.

Three hundred and five years later, history affords another story of another Michael Romanov, a time of troubles, a national assembly, and a forest. This Michael was a gay and supercilious grand duke, a hell-for-leather cavalry officer, and the only living brother of Nicholas II, the last tsar. In a sense, the grand duke deserves the title Michael II, because in March, 1917, Nicholas II abdicated in his favor, and the best part of a day elapsed before Michael cautiously declared that he would accept the throne only if it were duly offered him by a national assembly.

The summer of 1918 found Michael II in seclusion in a hotel in Perm, a city 700 miles east of Moscow. By now the democratic revolution that toppled the tsar had been taken over by the Bolsheviks. Lenin and the Soviets ruled in Moscow. The rest of Russia, however, was an ever-shifting battlefield. The Red Guards held some cities, while White counterrevolutionaries controlled vast areas in the south and Siberia, German troops of the still-undefeated kaiser ravaged the southeast and the Crimea, and Allied and American troops were making forcible entry into key ports.

A group of soldiers traced Michael II to his hotel room in Perm, where he was staying unattended except for his English secretary. Persuading him that they were loyal monarchists, the soldiers proposed to help Michael reach the safety of the nearest White-ruled area. In high spirits Michael slipped out of the hotel with his deliverers. The city patrols were evaded. Soon the party was in the cover of the great forest outside the city. There Michael was shot as a traitor to the people.

Both these stories of 1613 and 1918 are legends. In the case of the first Michael Romanov, people craved a tradition that would identify the dynasty with the patriotism and piety of its humblest subjects, like Ivan Susanin. Exactly what happened to the grand duke in 1918 is largely conjecture. The details of his murder will probably remain unknown. This story fits its times just as aptly as the first legend, however.

The rise of the Romanovs to the position of first family of Russia, their three centuries of rule of what they considered their estate, and their decline to the status of being despised and rejected by virtually all Russians constitute the subject of this book.

2. Princely Russia Before the Romanovs

There were twenty chronicled generations of Russian rulers before the first Romanov tsar. Moreover, the history of Russia began long before the monarchy. Present-day guides in the Hermitage Museum in Leningrad will show the visitor gold bracelets and necklaces made by preliterate peoples of Russia that for beauty and craftsmanship almost make the adjacent finery of Catherine the Great suffer by comparison.

In the days of Greece and Rome, northern Russia was inhabited by primitive peoples related to the Finns of today. Southern Russia was subject to a succession of barbarian invaders, mainly peoples from central Asia, who pushed westward in search of better grazing only to find themselves confronted with the civilized riches of Europe. Such were the Scythians, whose lands helped feed Periclean Athens; such were the Visigoths, who succeeded in sacking imperial Rome in 410; and such were the Huns of Attila, who were the most ferocious and evanescent of all the conquerors. In the course of the last of these upheavals, still another mass of barbarians—the Slavs—were driven from their original home in the Pripet Marshes area of present-day Poland and pushed outward in several directions. Eventually, the Slavs differentiated themselves into three main groups: the Western Slavs, who peopled Czechoslovakia and Poland; the Southern Slavs, who invaded the Balkans and became Serbs and Bulgarians; and, most important for history, the Eastern Slavs, who took over the huge forest plain of Russia. In time the Eastern Slavs themselves were to divide into three nationalities: the predominant Great Russians; the Little Russians or Ukrainians; and the White Russians or Byelorussians, not to be confused with twentieth-century anti-Reds.

The Slavs were unglamorous conquerors. They did not smash old empires and storm citadels but were relentless infiltrators and settlers. They dug in, and they lasted, whereas the Huns and Goths are only names today. By the ninth century, when Charlemagne was reviving the Roman Empire in France and Germany, the Slavs far to the east were a semicivilized federation of tribes living, fighting, and trading from the Baltic to the Black Sea.

The historic (that is, chronicled) Russian state and the Russian monarchy date from the year 862, when the anarchic Slavs invited certain foreign princes "to come and rule over us." The invitation was taken up by a Varangian adventurer named Rurik.

The Varangians were Vikings. They were Scandinavian freebooters who turned east rather than west, and thereby they missed all the sport of burning down priceless Irish monasteries, of reducing King Alfred the Great of England to despair and burned oatcakes, of taking Normandy away from the successors of Charlemagne, of reconquering England in Norman-French costume under William the Bastard, of wresting Sicily away from the Moslems, and of discovering the New World. The Viking epic after the ninth century affords many exciting exploits but few more lasting results than the Varangian take-over in Slavic Russia.

The picture of Rurik being called upon to rule over the Slavs is blurred by modern historians who question his identity, his dates, and his actual power. Tradition has it that he came and ruled from 862 to 879, and since then thousands of Russian aristocrats, claiming princely descent from him, would not have the story otherwise.

Rurik's brother Oleg (ruling 879–912) extended the Varangian sway southward from the Novgorod area to the Slavic cities located on the Dnieper River just above where the forest zone yields to the open steppes. Two armed expeditions of Oleg by land and sea to Constantinople are confirmed by treaties of 907 and 911. The next ruler, Igor (912–45), who was said to be a son of Rurik, resided at Kiev and used the title Grand Prince in his dealings with the Byzantines. The Kievan state now comprised the water route, the system of rivers and portages connecting the Baltic to the Black Sea, and it extended eastward toward the Ural Mountains and the Caspian Sea.

Igor's eventual successor was his son Sviatoslav (964–72), whose Slavic name is an indication of the absorption of the Varangian overlords by their Slavic subjects to produce a stock known as Russians, very much in the way Norman "coronets" mingled and bred with Saxon "kind hearts" to make Englishmen. This grand prince's campaigns carried him from Russia over the Danube into the Balkans, but his imperial ambitions came to naught, and the slain Sviatoslav's skull ended up as the gold-encrusted drinking cup of one of his enemies.

The heir of pagan Sviatoslav was to be known as Vladimir the Saint, for he brought about the conversion of Russia to Christianity in 989. The legend is that Vladimir became a Christian only after first examining other faiths such as Judaism and Mohammedanism, and subsequently there were mass baptisms of his companions and his subjects, often at sword's point. That the loosely organized Russia of 989 was converted through the offices of the Patriarch of Constantinople is one of the salient factors of the history of the next thousand years, for earlier, in 966, the equally amorphous Slavic area known as Poland accepted Christianity at the hands of the Pope. The formal schism between the Roman Catholic Church and the Eastern Orthodox Church was to follow soon after in 1054, with no end of bitter consequences for Poles and Russians.

The death of Vladimir the Saint was followed by a civil war among his sons which occasioned the interested interference not only of the Byzantine Empire, but even of the Holy Roman Empire far to the west. The winner, Yaroslav the Wise (1019–54), earned his sobriquet for a reign that was victorious when not peaceful and for a law code that obtained in Russia down to 1649. The Kiev of Yaroslav was described by a Western bishop as "the rival of Constantinople." Among the surviving glories of the city is the Monastery of the Caves, an imposing magnificence on a hilltop overlooking the city named for the subterranean caves of its first zealots. Yaroslav's marriage alliances attest to the fact that Kievan Russia was in the first rank of European states in the eleventh century—a status not enjoyed again until the Romanov rulers of St. Petersburg Russia in the eighteenth century. His female relatives were established in the courts of Byzantium, Poland, Hungary, Norway, and Germany, and through the marriage of his daughter Anne to King Henry I of France the blood of Rurik is to be found in the French royal line down to Louis XVI and also, via the French, in both the Scottish and the English genealogies of Queen Elizabeth II.

Yaroslav's son Iziaslav, who journeyed to Mainz in 1075 to confer with Emperor Henry IV, was the last grand prince to visit Western Europe until 1698. Kievan Russia was falling apart because of internal dissensions and the pressure of barbarian invaders on the steppes. Division of the grand prince's domains among all his sons had become an accepted practice, resulting in a periodic reallocation of all the greater and lesser Russian provinces among senior and junior members of the dynasty. A last flicker of unity, stability, and glory occurred in the reign (1113–25) of Vladimir Monomakh (One-eyed), who successfully fought the Polovtsy invaders (celebrated in the Borodin opera *Prince Igor*) and left the famous crown defined by his name—a conical, fur-trimmed object, bejeweled with rough stones and surmounted by a cross. It is the greatest of Russian national treasures in the Kremlin to this day, although of doubtful authenticity.

Population and power were shifting to the less exposed northern parts of Russia. Eventually only prestige remained to Kiev, and even this vanished in the reign (1157–74) of Andrew Bogoliubsky (God-loving), a grandson of Monomakh, who sacked the capital and then returned, with the title of Grand Prince, to his own rich patrimony in the north.

The first Russian state was completely swept under by the Mongols, or Tatars, the last and greatest of the Asian invaders. One of Genghis Khan's forces raiding beyond the Caucasus annihilated a hastily assembled and badly led Russian army at the Kalka River in 1223, thereafter celebrating their victory by erecting a dining platform on the living bodies of their enemies. (Tatar custom forbade shedding the blood of princes outright.) In 1237 a horde of more than 100,000 Tatars crossed the Volga and ravaged central Russia. Major cities were put to the torch, as was the little fort known as Moscow. Kiev was leveled in 1240. The magnificent Russia of Vladimir the Saint, Yaroslav the Wise, and Vladimir Monomakh was virtually wiped out; it survived only in the fact that there remained Russian-speaking, Orthodox-believing peoples and that the princely bloodline flourished still in numbers, if not in individual champions.

Novgorod provided the link between the first medieval Russian polity at Kiev and the later Muscovite state. The northern metropolis also gave the harassed Russians a great national hero in the person of Alexander Nevsky, a grandnephew of Andrew Bogoliubsky and eventually holder of the title of Grand Prince (1252–63). Alexander had won his sobriquet "Of the Neva" for his defeat of a Swedish incursion on the banks of that river (quite near the site of later-day St. Petersburg), and he went on to achieve his greatest renown for his victory over the Teutonic Knights, the pick of German Catholic chivalry, in the Battle of Lake Peipus in 1242 (subject of a Prokofiev cantata and the Soviet movie produced just before Hitler's invasion of 1941). Yet in the face of the greatest enemy, the Tatars, Alexander Nevsky was helpless and made several trips to their capital to pay tribute and beg mercies. Canonized later, he passed on the royal bloodline to Moscow through a younger son.

3. The Russian Nobility, Old and New

Russia's early dynasty, the house of Rurik, is unique in producing so many descendants, who rank first in the Russian nobility to the very present. How many French aristocrats can claim descent from Charlemagne, who predates Rurik by only a century? How many English lords can adduce blood ties to the Saxon Alfred the Great, a contemporary of Rurik, or even to the Norman William the Conqueror, whose familiar 1066 date makes him a comparative newcomer in history? As of about a century ago there were no fewer than thirty-four families in Russia who counted themselves heirs of Rurik, or, in the Russian word, Rurikovich.

A compilation of 1858 lists thirty-one "descendants of Rurik from the male lineage, direct, and legitimate by the sequence of birthright." First are the princes Odoievsky, followed by such names as the Gortchakovs (number three), the Bariatinskys (number six), the Obolenskys (number seven), the Dolgorukys (number nine), the Lvovs (number eighteen), the Kropotkins (number twenty-one), and the Gagarins (number thirty). Three more families are added by including descent from Rurik in the female or indirect line, such as the Repnins (number thirty-four).

Again and again the above-mentioned families will figure prominently in history, in the Romanov era emerging as statesmen, patrons of art, writers, and military leaders. An Odoievsky, for example, was principal author of the law code of 1649. A Prince Kropotkin was one of the two or three most famous anarchist leaders of the nineteenth century. The Dolgorukys supplied several brides, usually of tragic memory, to Romanov tsars, and a Dolgoruky was one of a handful of attendants who loyally stuck by Nicholas II in his last days. A Lvov was the first Prime Minister of Russia after the tsar's abdication in 1917. Of a family which shared royal Russian fortunes over many centuries, Serge Obolensky escaped the Revolution to become *bon vivant* companion of the Duke of Windsor and a successful American hotel manager. Dispensing with the title of Prince in his new life, Serge Obolensky blithely starts off his *Memoirs* with a genealogical table beginning with Rurik, Igor, Sviatoslav, Vladimir, and Yaroslav and ending thirty-three generations later with his father, Prince Ivan Serge Obolensky. Princely forebears have even been hinted in the case of the first space pilot, Yuri Gagarin.

Sixty-five Rurikovich families became extinct before Peter the Great (1682), and by the mid-nineteenth century another thirteen had died out.

Russian princes holding their titles by right, by virtue of royal descent rather than royal dispensation, include the descendants of the first King of Lithuania, Gedimin (died 1341). The piecemeal absorption of Lithuania by Russia added to the aristocracy Gedimin's descendants the Khovanskys, the Golitsyns, the Kurakins, and the Trubetskoys. Of the Gedimin-line princes the Golitsyns (rated number thirty-six) are rivaled only by the Dolgorukys for the frequency with which they crop up prominently in Russian history.

Added to the thirty-four Rurik-line families and the four Gedimin descendants (in 1858) were ten families who claimed the title Prince from foreign sources. The most famous of these are the Yusupovs, who begin with no less than a descendant of the Prophet Mohammed's cousin Ali and end with the assassin of Rasputin.

Created princes, rather than born princes, appear in Russia only after Peter the Great, and between 1707 and 1841 a mere twelve families were so elevated. Menshikov, Peter's lowborn lieutenant, was the first to be so honored. The list also includes Prince Suvorov, who rose from the ranks of the army to become Russia's greatest general during the Napoleonic era. The title of Count was another innovation of Peter the Great, and in the given period fifty-nine families received the less-than-princely rank. All male descendants of a prince or count inherited the title. The only other title of nobility in recent Russian history, Baron, is considered of very little account.

The term "boyar" is important in medieval Russian history as a link between the era of Rurik and the era of the Romanovs. The grand prince at Kiev had his immediate companions or bodyguard (known as the *druzhina*), and from them developed the boyars. In the first centuries of Muscovite Russia the grand princes (later tsars) depended for support entirely on their own boyars, making them leading officials and endowing them with vast estates and serfs. Princely families, holding title by right, found that influence and wealth came to them only if they were also boyars in the service of the grand prince, and indeed, being in state service remained the prerequisite of being received at court during the last days of the monarchy in the present century.

4. *The Triumph of Moscow; the Arrival of the Romanovs*

After the Tatar invasion Russia lay in pieces. Much of the former realm of the Grand Princes of Kiev came under the rule of foreigners: the Tatars on the southern steppe and along the Volga in the east; the Lithuanians in the western provinces; and the Teutonic Order on the Baltic coastlands. The north of Russia was under the loose control of the great and free city of Novgorod, a republic ruled by merchant oligarchs who were more concerned with the fur trade than with the fate of race and religion. Central Russia, the backwoods area to which many had fled from the south, resolved itself into a welter of small principalities torn by petty dissensions, at desperate odds over the succession to the title of Grand Prince, and united only in the burden of paying heavy tribute to the Tatar khans. The city which succeeded in picking up the pieces of Russia seemed an unlikely contender, Moscow. The rise and triumph of Moscow happened to coincide with the ascent toward power of the Romanovs.

Not until 1147 did the Chronicles even allude to the little wooden fort of Moscow, surrounded as it was by such venerable princely citadels as Vladimir, Suzdal, and Tver. In 1272, Moscow went to a younger son of Alexander Nevsky as his "portion." A fortuitous succession of strong princes in this offshoot of the line of Rurik proceeded to take full advantage of Moscow's favorable geograpical position: The city was near the sources of rivers leading to all three of Russia's seas, yet it was removed from the brunt of renewed Tatar attacks.

The first of the masterful princes of Muscovy (1325–41) was Ivan Kalita (Moneybags)—so nicknamed not for tightfistedness but for his clever use of limited resources to attract settlers and to acquire real estate. His great coup in 1327 was to receive the title of Grand Prince at the hands of the khan and to gain the power to collect tribute for the Tatars from the other Russian princes. The year before, the removal of the metropolitan, the head of the Russian Church, to Moscow added a spiritual glory to the city that counted as much as the title. The son and successor of Ivan Kalita, Simeon the Proud (1341–53), earned his sobriquet because the khan put all the princes in his hands and he behaved accordingly. His brother, Ivan II (1353–59), was invested with the right of justice throughout Russia. These honors accrued to Moscow not as a result of heroic defiance or even of sturdy independence but because of sheer subservience to the Tatars, with the so-called grand princes tolerating a permanent Tatar mission or court in their capital and their frequently making the long journey to the khan to prostrate themselves before their overlord.

Ivan and his successors were farsighted enough to attract to Muscovite service refugees from elsewhere in Russia, foreign nobles, and even Tatar adventurers. Land and the title of boyar were given to the newcomers, and soon this aristocracy of favor came to rival in influence the old Rurikovich nobility in and about Moscow who held their titles and estates hereditarily. Such a boyar family of Tatar stock were the Godunovs, arrivals of the mid-fifteenth century. Also parvenus were the Romanovs, who made their way from the "land of Prus," an unknown area referred to in the Chronicles.

The earliest reference to a Romanov was for the year 1346. During that summer "Grand Prince Simeon Ivanovich, grandson of Daniel, was married for the third time; he married Mary, the daughter of Grand Prince Alexander Mikhailovich of Tver; and those who went to Tver after her were Andrei Kobyla and Alexei Besovolkov."

It was this Andrew Kobyla, a boyar entrusted by his master with the most important kind of mission, who was the progenitor of the dynasty. The line involved several changes of name. The fifth son of Kobyla was known as Fedor Koshka, and his sons in turn were known as Koshkins. The branch of the family descending from Zachariah Koshkin were called the Zacharin-Koshkins and later simply Zacharins. In the sixteenth century Roman Zacharin had a son named Nikita Romanovich, and after him the family were the Romanovs.

Not much is known about the first several generations of the family. They made money. They held their own against the other new arrivals in the boyardom, and they were not outfaced or outdone by the great princely families like the Shuiskys.

Dmitri Donskoy (1359–89) was a truly renowned ruler of Moscow for shifting from the defensive to the offensive against the Tatars. His success owed much to the solid support and good counsel of his brothers, of the church, and of the Russian nobility, including the boyar Fedor Koshkin. Twice the great walls of Moscow served to shatter major incursions of the Prince of Tver assisted by the Lithuanians, and here now rallied regiments from all the Russian principalities to cheer Dmitri and cry defiance of the Tatar yoke. In 1380 Dmitri's forces smashed a great Tatar punitive expedition at Kulikovo on the banks of the upper Don River 150 miles south of Moscow, and for this victory Dmitri was ever after hailed as "Of the Don." Although the Tatars continued their depredations and sporadically exacted tribute, Dmitri had challenged them at Kulikovo and had won the right of national leadership.

Basil I (1389–1425), Dmitri's son, had to make only one trip of homage to the khan. The reign of Basil II (1425–62) saw Muscovy cruelly beset by civil intrigues and foreign interventions, including the kidnapping and blinding of the ruler, but the fact that in the end Basil the Sightless sat securely on the throne was a tribute to the tenacity of the dynasty and even more was an avowal of the necessity of unity by a harassed church and people. To his eldest son was bequeathed a full two-thirds of the royal domains, with the brothers receiving only one-third, indicating that oldtime family politics had been superseded by an awareness of larger state interests.

Ivan III (1462–1505) was to be known as Ivan the Great for his tremendous territorial conquests, his new titles, and his cultural pretensions, ranking him with Peter the Great and Catherine the Great and for the same reasons. Actually devious in character and even cowardly, this grand prince owed much to his predecessors' setting the stage for great events. The first major achievement was the annexation of Novgorod, the metropolis itself, plus stretches of land in the Russian north that more than doubled the size of Muscovy. In fear of its rising neighbor in the East, Novgorod had turned West and put itself under the protection of Catholic Lithuania, providing

Ivan with an excuse to wage a crusade against traitors to Russia and apostates. Submission came in 1478, at which time Novgorod's merchant and boyar families were deported and its great bell—symbol of democratic independence—carried off to Moscow. To annex Novgorod meant to gain a small empire; to seize Tver, which Ivan succeeded in doing in 1485, meant to eliminate the greatest surviving rival among Russian princely cities. These and other conquests have been referred to as the gathering together of the Russian lands, for Ivan proclaimed himself successor to the grand princes of Kiev, saying that "the Russian land from our ancestors since antiquity has been our patrimony." The greatest stumbling block to such ambitions became Poland-Lithuania, but Ivan did not shrink from the challenge, and he initiated three centuries of warfare to regain the western provinces, declaring that in this national cause there could be only truces in order to draw breath.

The definite end of the Tatar yoke also occurred during the reign of Ivan the Great, more in the manner of farce than of heroic epic. The khan made a last effort to prove his power and marched north to demand tribute in the spring of 1480. Ivan's army stationed itself across a river from the Tatar horde, but then the grand prince himself left the scene in terror, so outraging Moscow, especially the clergy, that he dared not return to his capital. The Tatars played for time, too, hoping vainly for Lithuanian reinforcements, and finally in the fall of the year both armies fled in mutual panic.

Ivan was forward about assuming titles to match his conquests, to commemorate the Tatar default, and to satisfy his fantasies of imperial glory. His taste for grandeur was excited in 1472, when he succeeded in marrying the niece of the last Byzantine Emperor. Constantinople had fallen to the Ottoman Turks in 1453, and the heiress of the Palaeologues had found herself a refugee in Rome, where the Pope promptly enlisted her support in the project of reuniting the Orthodox to the Catholic Church. The union of the faiths against the infidel ceased to interest Ivan once he had brought Zoë Palaeologue to Moscow, renamed her Sophia, and wed her, having disposed of his first Russian wife. Ivan's aim was not religious; rather he sought international prestige for an unknown dynasty.

After his remarriage Ivan adopted the Byzantine double eagle for the royal coat of arms, and Byzantine ceremonial was deliberately made the daily routine. But if Byzantine stiffness was to dominate the atmosphere of the court for centuries, its architecture owed less to Constantinople and more to Renaissance Italy. Italian members of Sophia's train were soon followed by architects from cities like Bologna and Milan, whom Ivan commissioned to build an opulent citadel. The sheer strength and magnificence of the stronghold that rose up in the 1480's and 1490's made Ivan's titles seem other than grandiloquence. The Italian builders were also responsible for bringing Russia two persistent curses: vodka and venereal disease, which was called the Latin sickness.

The imperial pretensions of the Muscovite prince were handily reinforced by the bookmen of his day. A fanatically Orthodox monk came up with the theory of the three Romes, a theory much elaborated upon over the centuries: The first Rome of the Caesars had flourished and then fallen because of the heresy of papal supremacy; the second Rome at Constantinople lasted for a glorious millennium, only to go under in 1453, ostensibly because of Turkish conquest but actually because of a belated compromise with the Pope; Moscow was the third Rome, "and the third stands, and a fourth will not be." Another antiquarian conveniently discovered that Caesar Augustus had given the lands of Eastern Europe to a brother named Prus, of whom Rurik was a descendant in the fourteenth generation and Ivan III kin in the forty-fifth generation. Still another allegation was that a Byzantine emperor had presented to Grand Prince Vladimir Monomakh the treasured crown bearing his name and pledged to share the rule of the world with him.

However fanciful the Roman and Byzantine claims of Ivan, it was perfectly logical for him after the end of Tatar overlordship to take the titles Gosudar (sovereign or lord) and Samoderzhetz (self-ruler or autocrat). Toward the end of his reign the full signature was Ioann, by the Grace of God, Sovereign [Gosudar] of all Rus, and Grand Prince of Vladimir and of Moscow and of Novgorod and of Pskov and of Tver and of Yugria and of Viatka and of Perm and of Bolgary and of others." An earlier offer from far-off Germany to designate Ivan king—an honor very rarely bestowed over the centuries by the Holy Roman Emperors—was haughtily refused as unnecessary in view of the titles he held by right.

It is a provoking fact of history that the rule of Ivan the Great in Russia, coming at the end of the fifteenth century, coincided in time with the reigns of noted rulers who were to consolidate similarly powerful national monarchies in Western Europe: Henry VII of England brought an end to the Wars of the Roses and created the brilliant Tudor monarchy; Louis XI of France was known as the Spider for the cleverness and persistence which brought the collapse of the rival kingdom of Burgundy and which produced a united France near in size to that of today; and Ferdinand and Isabella joined contentious Aragón and Castile by means of their marriage and expelled the Moors from all Spain by means of their armies. The surge of nationalism in every instance was the force behind the solid new states with their nearly absolute rulers. Yet in other respects Russia developed completely differently from the Western powers, for it remained cut off largely from Western contacts. Russia had missed so much and was destined to miss more of the great movements which caused the West to advance: the Crusades, the founding of universities, the development of free cities, the growth of capitalist enterprises, the voyages of exploration, the Renaissance, the Reformation, and the Counterreformation.

It was not the destiny of Ivan the Great to thrust Russia into the mainstream of Europe. Nor was the task undertaken by his son, Basil III (1505–33), who confined himself to rounding out the realm with a few more cities and to adding flourishes to Moscow. Fully two centuries would elapse before a Romanov successor made Russia a European power.

5. The Kremlin

The focal point of the newly emerged and expanding principality of Muscovy was the Kremlin of Moscow. In the reign of Ivan I, when the Romanov family first came to try their fortunes in Russia, the Kremlin was still a citadel of wood—just a huge stockade of oaken timbers enclosing many churches and mansions, some also of wood, some of masonry. By the time that Romanov boyars stood in the inner councils of the grand princes—that is, during the reigns of Ivan III and Basil III—the Kremlin had been reconstructed into a great fortress of stone and brick, surviving in its essentials to this day. The first Romanov rulers of Muscovy merely embellished the prize they had gained.

From a distance the Kremlin of the sixteenth century appeared to be both formidable and dazzling. The high battlements and sturdy bastions surrounded an array of buildings constructed of red brick, white stone, rich marbles, varicolored tiles, and shining metals. Roofs were decorated with colorful tentlike structures and fanciful steeples. Everywhere rose gold and silver bulbous cupolas, the familiar Russian onion domes, which gleamed in the sun like a hundred tongues of flame. Within the picturesque ensemble were Byzantine motifs, Oriental touches, and extensive borrowings from the Italian Renaissance, as well as traditional Russian forms.

The Kremlin took the shape of a rough triangle, the base of which faced the Moskva River on the south. Each side of the triangle was about half a mile long. The walls of red brick, from 12 to 16 feet thick, rose straight up 30 or 40 feet, ending in embrasures or narrow slits, from which archers could shoot. Interspersed along the battlements were nineteen bulky towers, reaching upward over 100 feet in some cases. At the three corners of the triangle were distinctive round towers, each an impregnable fortress unto itself with entry possible only through a slot in the roof.

There were the five massive gate towers of square design—two on the east, two on the west, and the Secret Gate on the south. A small river joined the Moskva on the west, and a moat 120 feet wide was dug along the east wall, so that the Kremlin became an island citadel. Drawbridges from the gate towers east and west connected with additional barbican fortifications built beyond the natural and artificial water barriers.

Several of the Kremlin towers had their own secret water supplies; some of the springs still function today. Two of the bastions were used as prisons and contained elaborate dungeons and torture chambers underground, notably the circular Beklemishev Tower on the southeast, named for a boyar executed on that spot for "being overly smart" to Ivan III. The mysteries of the Kremlin fortifications included numerous secret passage-ways, one of which, for example, ran all the way from the southwest tower to the gate on the northeast and on into the city.

The main entrance to the Kremlin was the Saviour's Gate, on the east side facing the area which later became Red Square. Its name derived from the large icon set over the archway before which candles were always kept burning. It became the custom for all Russians entering the Kremlin to doff their hats and cross themselves. The Saviour's Gate was erected by Ivan's Italian architects, as were all the other towers and walls on the perimeter of the citadel. Accordingly, the externals of the Kremlin looked strikingly similar to, say, the Sforza Castle in the heart of Milan. At the end of the fifteenth century the towers had squared-off tops with battle-ments and embrasures. The peaked roofs and spires were seventeenth-century additions by an English architect. The original Saviour's Gate, for example, rose seven stories to a height of about 100 feet, and its walls were thick enough to contain stairways. When show replaced military security as the main consideration, the tower gained 140 feet of fanciful superstructure, including a large clock and a set of chimes. These were the main chimes of the Kremlin, and in one era they played the imperial anthem of the Romanovs daily and in a later time "The Internationale."

The route of grand Kremlin processions ran from the Saviour's Gate in the direction of the gate near the southwest corner. This main cross axis actually coincided with the brow of a hill rising 130 feet above the Moskva River.

Ivan III intended that visitors to his capital, whether Orthodox, infidel, or heretic, should be impressed by the number of churches within and by their magnificence. In point of size the Russian shrines seem small by Western standards. Some of the structures were called churches, such as the tiny Church of Our Saviour of the Forest, the only survivor from the Kremlin of Ivan I. Several of the new shrines were called cathedrals, notably those of the Assumption, of the Annunciation, and of the Arch-angel Michael.

The Cathedral of the Assumption (Uspensky Sobor), the largest of the three, was rebuilt in the 1470's by an Italian architect who had profitably studied native church forms. The result of his efforts was a simple, square

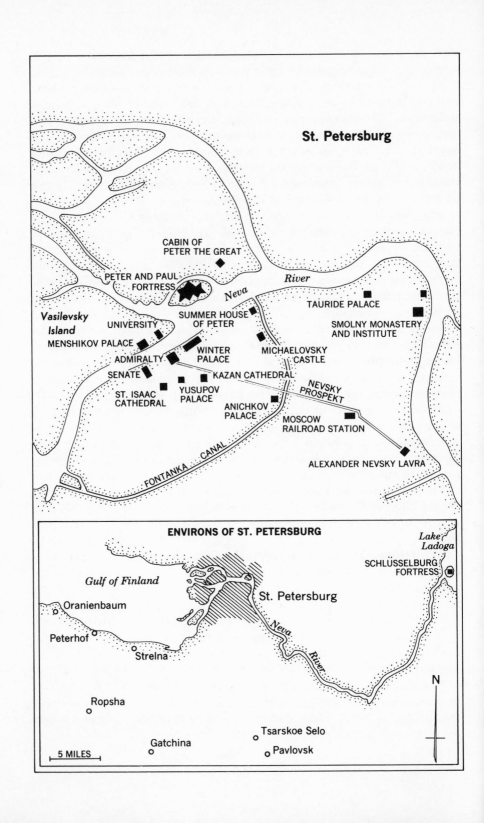

white structure, surmounted by a large central cupola and four lesser onion domes. The wall of the main façade was framed in four great arches going from ground to roof, and it contained an imposing entranceway facing south. The inside of the building was monumental and far from simple. In fact, the magnificence of the decoration was such that some visiting boyars were reported to have exclaimed, "We have seen heaven!" The foretaste of paradise was imparted largely by the paintings which covered every surface of the interior, even high up into the cupola and on the four massive pillars supporting it. To dazzle the beholder even more was the huge iconostasis hiding the altar: There were fully four tiers of life-size representations of the saints, and these icons were studded liberally with precious jewels and framed in gold and silver. Among the treasures of the cathedral were the Repository of the Robe of Christ and the reputed throne of Vladimir Monomakh (in actuality a richly carved seat built in about 1551 by Kremlin craftsmen). Every Grand Prince of Russia after Ivan the Great celebrated his coronation here, even after the capital was moved from Moscow. Napoleon, when he captured the city in 1812, had so little respect for the Rheims of Russia that he stabled horses in it, but his French soldiers did not neglect to cart off five and a half tons of gold and silver —a telling measure of the opulence of the cathedral.

To the south of the place where Russia's rulers were crowned was the shrine where the earliest of them were buried, the Cathedral of the Archangel Michael. Completed in 1505, this building had the typical cluster of Russian domes high above, but the exterior below somewhat reflected the Italian tastes of its architects, who succeeded in incorporating such Renaissance features as porches in front of the doors and great carved scallop forms in the wall of arches.

Next to it was the Cathedral of the Annunciation (Blagoveshchensky Sobor), the place where Russian rulers were wed. The small but beautifully proportioned building was erected in the 1480's by anonymous architects from Pskov, and it was a masterpiece of Russian decorative elements, including a riot of little domes. The interior was intimate as befitted its main ceremonial function. Among the treasures of the Annunciation were icons by Theophanes and Rublev, two of Russia's greatest masters of this art.

The center of outdoor ceremonial in the Kremlin was the square bounded by the cathedrals and by the palaces to the west. In the sixteenth century, Cathedral Square was further defined by the building of a series of bell towers to the east in the area in front of the Saviour's Gate. The first-built of these, the Bono Tower, was endowed with the largest bell in all Moscow. In 1600 the Belfry of Ivan the Great was finished. Two hundred seventy feet tall and the new focal point of the whole Kremlin, it contained the great bell of conquered Novgorod and thirty-two others. Nearby is preserved a bell intended to be not only the biggest in the belfry but the largest in creation; under successive tsars it suffered a series of accidents in its casting and recastings, so that today it stands on the ground minus a wedge of metal taller than a man. The bells of the Kremlin were one of its chief glories. Celebrations started with the striking of the huge bell in the Bono Tower; next, the many bells of the Belfry of Ivan sounded joyously or somberly as the occasion demanded; and finally, tumultuous reply was made by the 5,000 bells of the 400 churches of Moscow itself.

Beyond Cathedral Square rose the royal palaces, great golden-roofed structures topped with colorful and elegant domes and tents. Over several centuries the palaces were burned, demolished, enlarged, or rebuilt many times. Surviving to this day is Ivan's splendid Palace of the Facets, so called because of the diamondlike facing of its stones which gives it much of the appearance of the Pitti Palace of Florence. The aspect within was entirely Russian, especially in the main chamber, 70 feet square, which contained one massive pier that supported the vaulted ceilings. Around this pier were ponderous buffets on which banquets were served or the ruler's treasure displayed. Richly frescoed scenes glorifying the princes of Russia, real and legendary, were everywhere. On the south wall the throne stood under many icons, and high on the west side was a secret gallery for the royal women.

Alongside the Palace of the Facets arose the imposing Red Staircase, where many of the bloodiest dramas of the Kremlin were to happen. The stairway led to an entrance vestibule between the great reception chamber and the Terem Palace to the north, which contained the prince's living quarters and the secluded apartments of his women (the *terem*). Seclusion of women, a Tatar practice taken over by Muscovy and lasting through the seventeenth century, meant that the wives, daughters, mothers, and sisters of the prince were never beheld by any except male relatives, clergy, and privileged courtiers.

Near the royal palaces lay the armory, a great complex of buildings situated along most of the west wall of the citadel. This arsenal, begun in the sixteenth century, became much more than a manufactory of weapons. It developed into a great national workshop where the finest products of a whole school of Russian iconmakers, jewelers, and other craftsmen were created. The present repository on the site, called the Hall of Arms, is one of the richest museums of the world.

Elsewhere in the Kremlin were situated the mansions of the boyars close to the grand prince by virtue of blood or prestige, each with its *terem* on the upper floors. From time to time a special palace would be built for the heir of the ruler, usually when he reached the age of five. None of this succession of buildings is still standing, except for a boyar's house which was taken over as the royal Pleasure Palace—that is, theater—a unique structure because of its cantilevered chapel, which, by the rules of the church, could not be built over chambers devoted to secular activities of any sort.

The Kremlin contained the residence of the head of the church (the metropolitan, later the patriarch). This large palace to the north of the Cathedral of the Assumption was connected with the grand prince's quarters by a wondrous series of gardens, terraces, and covered passageways. In addition, the Kremlin had its monastery and its convent. The Chudov Monastery (Miracle Monastery), founded in 1365, had been proudly built near the Saviour's Gate in the very area where once stood the symbol of a subservient past, the court of the Tatar Khans. The nearby Ascension Convent, endowed by the wife of Dmitri Donskoy, was the burial place of the grand princesses, and like the monastery, this nunnery came in time to hold many secrets, especially those involving mysterious prisoners and royal revenge.

The Kremlin complex of forts, cathedrals, palaces, armories, and cloisters was at the height of its grandeur in the sixteenth and seventeenth centuries. It was abandoned and largely ignored in the eighteenth century by the Romanov rulers at St. Petersburg. Catherine the Great saw fit only to add a large triangular building in the northern corner, housing her Senate behind classical columns and under a wide low dome unlike the onion bulbs elsewhere. In the 1840's Nicholas I satisfied his need for adequate accommodations in Moscow and his taste for the distant past by building the Grand Kremlin Palace, a pseudo-Byzantine monstrosity which swallowed up the surviving medieval palaces. It contains flights of stairs and a throne room worthy of Hollywood.

The Communist regime returned the capital to the Kremlin in 1918 but disturbed the architectural treasure-house only slightly. The imperial eagles on the pinnacles of the watchtowers were replaced by huge red stars that light up at night and can be seen for miles. The two cloisters were demolished to make room for a classic-style building with the offices of the Presidium of the Supreme Soviet. In 1961 a marble and glass building in contemporary rectilinear style, called the Palace of Congresses, was added north of the cathedrals. Visitors to the Kremlin—which was completely opened to the public in 1955—might think this last addition very out of place, but the simple fact is that all the newer buildings recede into insignificance in the presence of such a profusion of reminders of the era of Ivan the Great.

Outside the sixteenth-century Kremlin on the east lay an open area once called the Fire, because it was meant to protect the fortress against the conflagrations, which reduced Moscow to ashes with regularity. Later this area under the walls was paved over and came to be known as Red Square (*krasnyi* in Russian can be translated either as red or as beautiful). Since the principal trades routes converged here, Red Square was boastfully termed by a chronicler the "umbilicus of the world," and indeed it presented a colorfully heterogeneous aspect as great boyars in caftans and rich furs rubbed shoulders with travelers of varied tongues and costumes, silk merchants, vendors of meat pies, heavy-bearded religious people of many orders, half-naked soothsayers and flesh deniers, whores, pickpockets, jugglers, and keepers of trained bears. On the east, Red Square was bounded by tradesmen's stalls (destined to become today's GUM department store), and to the south it looked up at the most famous of all Russian churches, the Cathedral of St. Basil the Happy. This fantastic array of twisted and faceted cupolas and towers of every color and size was built in the 1550's. Before it stood a stone mound called the Place of Executions, where criminals were tortured and killed, while often the grand prince looked on from a specially built pavilion on the Kremlin walls (later replaced in stone by the Tsar's Tower, the smallest of all).

The city which lay about the citadel and square was one of narrow byways and closely packed wooden houses, 41,500 of them according to an English traveler of the late sixteenth century, who concluded that Moscow was clearly larger than London and probably larger than Paris. A modern estimate of the population then is 100,000. As the city grew, various sections were ringed with battlements less formidable than those of the Kremlin, and still Moscow expanded beyond the new walls and beyond the river. One of the quarters that developed four miles to the southeast of the Kremlin was called the German Liberty—a haven for foreign mercenaries and craftsmen that was destined to hasten the demise of medieval Moscow.

The countryside around Moscow was one of forests and clearings with many villages. Wretched hovels of the peasants clustered close together on the crude highways into the city. Numerous small churches of wooden construction often boasted cupolas, cleverly angled roofs, and architectural decorations that the builders of Ivan's cathedrals were not above copying in stone. There were occasional boyars' mansions, mansions in the sense that they were wooden structures a little bigger and more solid than the peasants' huts.

A growing number of royal residences were established outside Moscow. In time these ranged in size from modest hunting lodges like those at Preobrazhenskoe and Izmailovo to the vast wooden palace at Kolomenskoe, which had 270 rooms and 3,000 windows. Kolomenskoe Palace was a convenient stopover on the way to the celebrated Trinity Monastery, 40 miles northeast of the capital and, since its founding in 1337, the frequent goal of royal pilgrimages. The grand princes could find physical security, as well as bountiful hospitality, at a huge monastery such as this, with its walls a mile in circumference, its eight great watchtowers, and its supporting population of 20,000 peasant households.

The Russian lands controlled by the old dynasty a century before its extinction in 1598 stretched up to the Arctic Ocean. The great pine forest country of the north, reaching from Finland to the Urals, was the habitat of fur trappers. In the less wooded area of the center where the peasants often had to supplement agriculture with crafts, Muscovy's territory was quite confined: There were hostile neighbors but a few hundred miles from the capital in three directions.

West and somewhat north of Moscow lay ancient Novgorod, now the grand prince's second largest city and a Russian bridgehead hemmed in by Sweden and by the lands of the Teutonic Knights on the Baltic coast (later the provinces of Livonia and Courland). Just over 200 miles due west of Moscow the fortress city of Smolensk (in Russian hands only since 1514) guarded the boundary with Poland-Lithuania, this Catholic and largely Slavic kingdom still being in control of the former Russian capital of Kiev. The claim of Ivan III to all the lands of the grand princes of Kiev was fully countered by Polish ambitions to expand eastward.

The frontier below Moscow was an ever-shifting line of small forts, a line which Russian settlers advanced cautiously southward toward the incredibly fertile open steppes. The line recoiled when the Moslem Tatars exerted themselves and swept north. The Tatars, still powerful enough to sack Moscow as late as 1571, were no longer a unified horde; they had split up into rival khanates, the most fearsome being the khanate of the Crimea on the Black Sea and the khanates of Kazan and Astrakhan on the Volga.

There came to be something of a no-man's-land between Russians and Tatars, between the farmers and the nomads, and it was here that the Cossacks came into existence. Pioneers only in the sense that they ventured beyond organized settlement, the Cossacks were more accurately freebooters who found farming and trading relatively dull and unprofitable compared to fighting and plundering. Many Cossacks were serfs run away from Muscovite landowners, and their loyalty to Russia and Orthodoxy hung lightly on them. In time two great aggregations of Cossacks established themselves in the southern no-man's-land: the Zaporogian Cossacks on the Dnieper River (their main camp near the present-day Dniepropetrovzk Dam) and the Don Cossacks on the waterway by that name.

As in the west and in the south, the frontier of Moscow in the east was a ride of only a few days. Russian settlement still clung to the upper Volga River, and Nizhni Novgorod was a bridgehead city, like its namesake all the way to the west. The rivers reaching over to the middle Urals and the great sweep of the Volga 500 miles south to the Caspian Sea were denied the grand prince by non-Christian states, the khanates of Kazan and Astrakhan. It was this area that awaited the conquests of the last great ruler of the line of Rurik, Ivan the Terrible.

II.

The Time of Troubles
and a Change of Dynasty

---

1. Ivan the Terrible and Anastasia Romanov

THE story of the Romanov family might have remained confined to the annals of the minor Russian nobility but for their link with Muscovy's Ivan IV (1533–84), better known in history as Ivan the Terrible. This dread ruler—and "dread" is a more accurate rendition of his Russian sobriquet than "terrible"—ushered in an era of unparalleled turmoil in Russia that ended only when a Romanov was placed on the royal seat.

To his contemporaries Ivan IV was Ivan Vasilievich, for Russians to this day use the patronymic after the surname in both formal conversation and writing. The elder of two sons born to the second wife of Grand Prince Basil III, who had waited twenty years before putting away his childless first consort, Ivan came into the world under a formal curse. The Patriarch of Jerusalem, opposing Basil's remarriage, had addressed these words to him: "If you should do this wicked thing, you will have a wicked son; your states will become prey to terrors and tears; rivers of blood will flow; the heads of the mighty will fall; your cities will be devoured by flames." Predictions that come true have a way of being remembered.

Succeeding as grand prince in 1533 at the age of three, Ivan was first protected by his mother, Helen Glinska, a Lithuanian woman, who made herself regent and successfully countered two throne-minded uncles and a restive aristocracy with the help of her lover, Prince Ivan Obolensky. The mother regent was poisoned in 1538 and Obolensky murdered soon after, giving control of the Kremlin and its orphaned tenant to two rival Rurikovich families, the Belskys and the Shuiskys. Several years of misery as the puppet of these contentious boyars were to be long after resented by Ivan, who bitterly recalled that they had treated his brother, Yuri, and him "as foreigners or rather as menials," depriving the princes of even food and clothing all the while the royal treasury was being despoiled. During this period Ivan was constantly exposed to the spectacle of bloodshed as Belskys and Shuiskys did each other in "like beasts" in their scramble for power. One hideous night he awoke to find his chamber full of armed soldiers, who, it turned out, were there not to murder the young sovereign but to cut down the metropolitan, the head of the church having fled his own quarters.

Ivan's own taste for violence was whetted early. He and brutal young companions took to dropping dogs from the Kremlin towers and to charging on horses into the crowds in Red Square. Real friends were denied him, for, as he later complained, anyone he developed affection for was taken from him. At age thirteen he shrilly denounced one of his chief tormentors, and to his surprise the boyars allowed Prince Shuisky to be handed over to the gamekeeper and torn to pieces by the hounds. Now treated with more respect, Ivan was content to leave the actual governing to his mother's relatives, the Glinskys, and he finished his solitary self-education with the few books available in the Kremlin: ancient histories and religious texts. Even this intellectual activity had to be accomplished by subterfuge, for his elders distrusted learning outside the pieties of the prayer manuals. In later years Ivan's ability to quote the classics and to reason on unconventional lines was one of the things which inspired terror in his boyars.

In 1546 Ivan boldly told an assemblage of notables in the palace that he intended to marry, revealing to them that he had abandoned his original idea of taking a foreign bride in favor of making a Russian match because he felt that his years as an orphan had made him a difficult person to get on with. The prospect of a royal bride hunt so excited the boyars that they almost missed the import of the concluding part of Ivan's announcement, his wish to be invested before marriage with "the ancestral rank, such as that of our ancestors the Tsars and Grand Dukes and our kinsman Vladimir Vsevelodovich Monomakh." The title Tsar was, in fact, an innovation that had burst forth from Ivan's historical research into the Byzantine Empire. The derivatives of "tsar" soon became familiar: tsarina or tsaritsa, the wife of a tsar; tsarevna, daughter; tsarevich, usually reserved for the first son or designated heir, like dauphin or infante, whereas other sons were called grand dukes. The magnificent coronation took place in January, 1547, when the metropolitan consecrated Ivan IV with the fur-trimmed crown of Monomakh as Tsar and Autocrat of All Russia.

Letters had been sent out to every locality in the tsar's domains that all marriageable daughters were to be brought to Moscow for Ivan's inspection. There would be no Cinderella ending to the drama, for only the daughters of the boyars and rich townsmen were considered fit consorts for a tsar. Several hundred eligibles were housed in dormitories set up on the Kremlin grounds, and they had to submit to rigorous tests by doctors and midwives with regard to their health and, of course, their virginity. After scores of girls had been found wanting and sent home with small gifts, the tsar himself began to tour the quarters of those remaining to judge for himself their claims to beauty, their conversational charms, and their table manners. Sometimes he would observe them secretly from behind a screen. Clandestine midnight visits were in order, too. Ivan must be sure that his intended was not a restless sleeper or, worse yet, a snorer.

Intrigue became frenzied when the choice narrowed down to ten maidens. To have a daughter married to the tsar meant not only great honor for a boyar family but also titles, preferments, and gifts for everyone from uncles to second cousins. In the past, boyars, or more likely their wives, had not been above poisoning a rival's daughter.

Ivan made his choice one day by unexpectedly sitting down next to Anastasia Romanov and presenting her with the traditional handkerchief and ring. The marriage was celebrated in February, 1547, in the gilt-laden Cathedral of the Annunciation. The service, lasting several hours, ended when the metropolitan turned to Ivan and Anastasia and said: "My lord! Love and honor your wife, and you, Christ-loving Tsaritsa, obey him! As the Holy Cross is the head of the Church, so is the husband the head of his wife. Fulfilling God's commandments, you will have vision of the blessed Jerusalem and peace in Israel." Bride and groom then presented themselves to the crowds outside. Ivan had gifts for his boyars, while Anastasia handed out alms. As the court and city banqueted, the royal pair were put to bed publicly with the greats of the land performing the duties of valet and maid.

There was a honeymoon—of a sort. The tsar and his bride set out on a devotional pilgrimage, going on foot through the snow the 40 miles to the great Trinity Monastery. After the return to the Kremlin, Ivan tended to stay in his quarters, leaving affairs still to the Glinskys. Many remarked that Ivan never seemed more at peace with himself.

The elevation of a Romanov to tsaritsa came as a surprise. Her family was well known, even popular, around Moscow, but they were nobodies compared to the Rurikovich princes and to some other boyar clans. Perhaps the very lack of influence and involvement of the Romanovs in the turbulent struggles earlier in the reign stood much in their favor. Undoubtedly, however, it was Anastasia's personality and its effect on Ivan that mainly explain the beginning of the Romanov grand march through history. Anastasia was later characterized by an English traveler as "wise and of such holiness, virtue, and government that she was honored, beloved, and feared of all her subjects. He being young and riotous, she ruled him with admirable affability and wisdom." Brought up quietly by her widowed mother, Anastasia was probably as unread and superstitious as any other sixteenth-century boyar's daughter, but she was smart enough to please Ivan by being unassuming. It is likely that she was Ivan's only love, and only friend for that matter, during his lifetime. The complete lack of any contemporary comment on the tsaritsa's looks suggests that she was plain. Ivan's own appearance was less than prepossessing: He was lanky, stoop-shouldered, and hawk-faced, with such close-set, piercing eyes that reportedly women fainted and men trembled at his glance.

The daily life of the first great Romanov lady meant seclusion in the *terem* except for rare ceremonial appearances. At best Anastasia's participation in affairs was in the realm of charity and intercession for prisoners. Her affection for the tsar's slightly dotty younger brother, Yuri, endeared her to Ivan, and at Yuri's wedding in the fall of 1547 Anastasia appeared in a gown of gold and a headdress of jewels to bless the couple, to comb their hair with wine, and to fan them with a sable. When Ivan set off on his first military campaign, he bade farewell to Anastasia on the cathedral steps, kissing her in the view of everyone and showing his complete trust in her by giving her the keys to the jails. During the banquet after Ivan's triumphal return Anastasia carried wine to the great nobles and allowed them the honor of an official kiss.

Married, Ivan became all goodness in people's minds. A zealous monk and an efficient clerk of humble estate were made his chief advisers. The church and the laws were reformed. The tsar's greatest triumph, one that brought tears to the eyes of Orthodox Russians, was the capture of Kazan from the Moslem Tatars in 1552. The fall of this fortress city on the great bend of the Volga, 500 miles east of Moscow, was followed four years later by the conquest of Astrakhan, the outlet to the Caspian Sea. It was to commemorate these victories that the riotously colorful St. Basil's Cathedral was erected on Red Square. In 1553 Ivan's empire was dramatically extended by means other than conquest. In that year the first English ships arrived in the White Sea, far to the north, and soon Russia's isolation from the West was broken by the active trade going on between the subjects of the tsar and those of Queen Elizabeth I.

Ivan's joy in 1552 as the hero of Kazan was doubled when he received the news that Anastasia had borne him a son, thereafter named Dmitri. Great unhappiness beset the royal pair the next year. Ivan fell so deathly sick that the boyars were summoned to kiss the cross to the one-year-old tsarevich and to promise support to the mother. With the exception of Anastasia's relatives, all, even Ivan's humble appointees, refused support, saying that they would rather raise Ivan's grown cousin Vladimir to the throne. In the end the tsar forced them to swear for his son, and then he himself recovered, as embittered as Anastasia was frightened. To make full mockery of their position, the baby, Dmitri, died soon afterward. In 1554, however, the loving couple were blessed with the birth of a new tsarevich, christened Ivan and destined to live into manhood. Another son, Fedor, came in 1557.

The death of Anastasia in 1560 was mysterious, if not sudden. Ivan later claimed that she was poisoned, and this idea is accepted in the Soviet movie treatment of the tsar, which includes a scene of cousin Vladimir's witch-like mother performing the nefarious deed. Actually, Anastasia had been prone to attacks of an unknown sickness, and the tsaritsa was stricken the last time during a pilgrimage, under circumstances when no medicines were available. Brought back to the Kremlin, she became hysterical because of the flames and smoke of a great fire in Moscow and was removed to Kolomenskoe Palace outside the city, but to no avail.

Ivan's grief at the loss of Anastasia gradually turned to rage and the conviction that there had been a plot against him and his loved ones. All the pent-up viciousness of his youth burst forth, and he ordered the destruction of his closest advisers. Terror provoked many boyars to flee the country; they included his leading general and confidant, Prince Andrew Kurbsky, who offered his services to Ivan's Polish rival in 1564. This event brought the tsar's paranoia to a peak, and the nightmare period of his reign ensued. Always the showman, Ivan first pretended to abdicate late that year, removing himself and his treasure from the Kremlin to the village of Alexandrov. A delegation from Moscow, who begged the tsar not to hand the country over to anarchy, found that the price of the tsar's return was unlimited power to deal with those he thought traitors. In due course Ivan proceeded to organize the monstrous oprichniks (roughly, those set apart), a group of 6,000 handpicked sadists who were outfitted in black uniforms and given a dog's head and a broom to carry on their saddlebows, the one signifying that they devoured the tsar's enemies and the other that they swept treason from the land. For the next seven years all Russia, but particularly the boyar class, was terrorized by them in a series of beatings, skinnings, fryings, drownings, impalings, and rapes.

Even Ivan's handpicked metropolitan of the church ended up on the list of traitors. He was thrown in a dungeon as a sorcerer and at length was murdered when he refused the tsar his blessing. In 1570 Ivan and his oprichniks wiped out virtually the entire population of Novgorod, reducing the second-greatest Russian metropolis to the small town it still is. The next year the perpetrators of this atrocity were themselves purged, the leading oprichniks being given an elaborately refined execution in Red Square. On this occasion Ivan forced Prince Alexis Basmanov's son to kill his father so that the son would have this sin on him when he was duly executed, an indication of the persistent religious reasoning, however sick, behind

Ivan's cruelties. Lest one conclude that this fanaticism and barbarity were peculiar to Russia in Ivan's day, it should be recalled that the Massacre of St. Bartholomew's Day in France is almost exactly contemporary.

While some historians have seen only madness in Ivan's *oprichnina,* others have perceived genius and modern statecraft in the tsar's setting himself against the feudal pretensions of the boyars and high churchmen. The oprichniks were the first officials to swear loyalty not just to the person of the ruler but to the national state (*gosudarstvo*). Like the Tudors in England, Ivan allied himself with a kind of patriotic middle class. In 1566 Ivan summoned the first Zemsky Sobor, an assembly of the land which, although not representative of the great masses of peasants, gave voice to broader interests in countryside and city than the boyar Duma, the aristocratic council traditionally consulted by the tsar. Perhaps intended as only an expedient to raise money or to overawe Ivan's enemies, the Zemsky Sobor was an important precedent for later events affecting all the early Romanov tsars.

Five years after the summoning of the first Zemsky Sobor came the sack and burning of all Moscow, except the Kremlin, by the Crimean Tatars in 1571. The failure of Ivan's oprichnik terrorists to stop the real national enemy caused their final purge and disbandment.

Near the end of his reign Ivan ordered prayers said for his victims, sending to a monastery a list of 3,470 individuals, headed by the cousin princess who was reputed to have poisoned Anastasia. Once Ivan had written his refugee enemy, Prince Kurbsky, that had they not separated him from his "little heifer," there would not have been so many victims.

In the words of one chronicler, "after the Tsaritsa's death the Tsar began to be wild and very adulterous." Ivan turned to debauchery in the grand manner, keeping a large harem in the Kremlin and, in addition, having a steady stream of virgins brought to the royal bedchambers. Oprichnik headquarters at Alexandrov, ostensibly organized as a monastery, became one vast brothel. From his Polish refuge Prince Kurbsky hurled the additional charge of sodomy against the tsar and his oprichnik cronies: "They defiled the temple of your body with various forms of uncleanliness, and furthermore practiced their wantonness with pederastic atrocities and other numberless and unutterable wicked deeds." Indeed, young Prince Basmanov, who was described as outrageously handsome, slept in the royal bedchamber over a period of years, and this fact gives some, but not much, credence to the charge that Ivan practiced homosexuality. There were countless young women in Russia who certainly believed otherwise.

Ivan had five wives in all, seven if one includes two official mistresses. His second wife, whom he married in 1561, was a half-savage Circassian princess, the complete opposite of Anastasia. Soon abandoned by Ivan, this princess died in 1569, poisoned, he said, as was his third mate, a merchant's daughter, who lasted only two weeks in 1571. Wife number four was a wench Ivan raised to glory in 1572 and banished to a nunnery in 1576, where she lived on as an ex-tsaritsa to 1626. Next, and for a time simultaneously, came the two mistresses, who were accorded many royal prerogatives. The tsar was fifty when, in 1580, he married for the fifth and last time, his bride, Maria Nagaia, being described as "a very beautiful young maiden of a noble house and great family." The wedding, by interesting coincidence, was attended by three future tsars and the father of an entirely new dynasty, only one of these men being directly related to Ivan. Like Henry VIII, Ivan, with his many wives, confused and complicated the succession to the throne.

The Tsarevich Ivan, now in his mid-twenties, was his father's pride and largely his image, both good and bad, sharing a taste for intellect (he even wrote a book) and readily joining in all the cruelties (like the Novgorod massacre). He also shared his father's virgins, perhaps even swapping wives, of which the tsarevich had already had three. Intimacy led to tragedy. One evening the tsar accosted the tsarevich's wife in her own apartments and, in a fit of puritanism, began to berate her for the immodesty of not wearing the requisite number of garments for a pregnant woman. There followed heated words with the tsarevich. In a blind fury, Ivan struck his son on the temple with the iron-headed cane he always carried. Ivan's instant remorse is movingly rendered in the celebrated painting by Ilya Repin showing the hideous-faced father clutching his dying son in his arms.

There was farce near the end of the reign, a farce closely involving the fortunes of the Romanovs. An Anglophile ever since the English ships had come in 1553 and occasionally possessed by the thought of taking refuge in England, Ivan kept up negotiations throughout his reign with Queen Elizabeth I, begging an alliance and munitions against his enemies, chiding her for being too money-minded, and secretly offering his hand in marriage. To facilitate such a match, Ivan may have poisoned his second wife. The Virgin Queen skillfully kept Ivan dangling for years until 1582, when the tsar decided that he would marry Elizabeth's niece, Mary Hastings. The Russian envoy brushed aside the objection that the tsar was already married and flatly denied the news of the birth of a new son. Failing in her stratagem of passing her niece off as too ugly for Ivan, Elizabeth ended up writing him that she could not force one of her subjects to marry, an excuse completely lost on the Russian autocrat, who seemed prepared to disinherit his own Romanov-blood children in favor of the progeny of Mary Hastings.

Crushed by his crimes and failures, Ivan died in 1584, falling to the floor in a fit while playing chess with Boris Godunov. Again the possibility of poisoning comes up. Ivan's body was recently removed from its tomb in the Kremlin, and it was announced by the Soviet Academy of Sciences that his organs contained an overdose of mercury, possibly the result of medical treatment, possibly of foul play.

The fifty-one-year rule of Ivan the Terrible, the longest reign in Russian history, has excited great interest but little agreement among historians. Some see only viciousness and destructiveness, while others emphasize the progressive aspects of Ivan's struggle with the boyars. It has been argued that Ivan was really a traditionalist and Muscovite exclusivist, as fanatic about preserving Orthodoxy as his contemporary Philip II of Spain was about maintaining Catholicism in the West. It has also been asserted that he was a Renaissance type, a Russian Machiavelli and modernist. The best, albeit easiest, interpretation of this furious tsar was that he was a schizophrenic, a ruler who was as capable of the most pious humility as of the most outrageous terrorism. An interesting case of Ivan's two minds is that some years after Anastasia Romanov's death he sponsored the printing of Russia's first book, only to allow a hysterical mob to wreck the press a few months later. One thing is sure: Ivan the Terrible has always remained a popular figure in the legends of the common people. The association of the Romanovs with Ivan counted more than anything in that family's favor.

2. *Fedor I: A Tsar with Romanov Blood*

The genes of Rurik and of Roman Zacharin were mingled in the person of gentle Fedor Ivanovich. Unfortunately, thirty-year-old Fedor was a near idiot. His short reign (1584–98) initiated a dynastic crisis and a struggle for power that eventually reduced Russia to complete chaos and near ruin.

Born in 1557, Fedor had lost his mother at the age of three. His youth was spent amid the indecencies of the mock monastery at Alexandrov. Fedor had been weakly from birth, and he grew up to be white-faced, undersized, sickly from dropsy, and unsteady on his feet because of a disease that affected his legs. Unlike the Tsarevich Ivan, who had hunted and whored at his father's side, the younger heir was despised by Ivan the Terrible, who called him "a sacristan, not a Tsar's son" or a creature fit only for ringing monastery bells, which indeed was Fedor's greatest delight. Alternately goaded and ignored by Ivan, Fedor now sat on the throne of his ancestors, his unhappy past revealed in his expression of bewilderment.

The second Tsar of Russia hardly inspired awe. Fedor was described in these words by an envoy from Poland:

> The Tsar is short of stature and meager withal, and has a gentle voice like one who suffers and likewise a simple countenance. Of mind has he but little or . . . none at all, in as much, when seated on the throne and

receiving an ambassador, he refrains not from smiling nor from gazing first upon his sceptre and then upon his orb.

It was reported back to Sweden that Fedor was virtually an imbecile, who ran about the Kremlin cathedrals ringing all the bells for hours on end and who varied this pleasure with pilgrimages to the holy places around Moscow at the rate of one a week. For Russians, however, such a ruler was not the object of contempt or laughter, but rather he was treasured as one of God's "devout idiots" (*urodivi*). Fedor, it was said, "did all his life shun the baubles and vanities of this world and think of things heavenly," resembling thus the many holy beggars and soothsayers who enjoyed a special place in Moscow streets and homes.

Fedor's coronation was celebrated with all due pomp, his 200 pounds of gold robes requiring the assistance of several boyars, who were otherwise preoccupied with the question of who would actually rule Russia. An immediate attempt to seize the Kremlin by Prince Bogdan Belsky and his retainers was blocked by the others.

The natural person to act as regent for Fedor was his uncle, Nikita Romanov (actually Romanovich Zacharin), a man both able and popular. Nikita Romanov had been associated with the oprichnik regime following the death of his sister, the beloved Tsaritsa Anastasia, but his role was not that of terrorist but of intermediary between the people and a grief-maddened Ivan. A popular song of the time mentions Nikita as the only boyar of the whole century who deserved the people's love. Nikita did, accordingly, become regent but in a matter of months was removed from the scene by illness and death.

The able father left an even abler son, Fedor Nikitich Romanov, who was almost an exact contemporary of his namesake and first cousin, Tsar Fedor. This Romanov was something of a dandy, a handsome and high-spirited young man, whose kindheartedness and democratic ways won him the hearts of the mob and whose genuine erudition earned him the respect of the few learned men around. The English envoy related that Fedor Romanov was so progressive in his thinking that he requested the compilation of a dictionary so that he could learn Latin. His youth and inexperience prevented him from succeeding his father as regent. Instead, he went off to gain considerable distinction both as a military commander and as a diplomat, and he was destined for the greatest things in due time.

The man who gained ascendancy in the first years of the reign of Fedor was Boris Godunov, whose Tatar ancestors, like the Romanovs', were parvenus to the Muscovite boyar class. As one of the chief advisers and confidants of Ivan the Terrible, Boris Godunov owed his rise to two marriages. He himself married Maria Skuratov, daughter of a hated but all-powerful oprichnik leader. Like Nikita Romanov, Boris married his sister into the royal house: Irene Godunov became the consort of Tsar Fedor.

Soon it was said of Boris that he was "hearkened to like unto the Tsar" and that he was "honored with no less homage than was rendered to the Tsar himself." Fedor was left to his prayers and charities while Boris ruled, gaining the acquiescence of the boyar Duma because of the wisdom and competence of his regime. He brought a welcome peace after the last serious Tatar attack on Moscow was turned back with great hurt to the Khan of the Crimea. Boris did fail in an attempt to secure Fedor's election as King of Poland, but he achieved a great triumph and a fitting memorial to pious Fedor when he pressured the four existing patriarchs of the Eastern Church into raising the Moscow metropolitan to their rank.

For all his good policy, Boris Godunov was still just an upstart with too much power in the eyes of many great boyars, and before long an attempt was made to overthrow the Godunov family. The Moscow mob was stirred up into a howling riot, demanding that Tsar Fedor put aside the Tsaritsa Irene for failing to give him a son. No nunnery was in store for Irene at this time, however, and it was not Boris who was driven from Moscow but rather the troublemaking princes.

The succession was becoming a grave problem with Fedor, sickly and lacking a male heir. The only direct-line prince left was the Tsarevich Dmitri, born to Ivan the Terrible by Maria Nagaia and considered by some illegitimate because she had been his fifth (or seventh) wife. When the pretensions and intrigues of Tsaritsa Maria and the Nagaia family became too great, Boris persuaded Tsar Fedor to send them off to the great royal estate at Uglich. Here the tsarevich started to grow up as disturbed a child as his father had been. In 1591, at the age of nine, Dmitri killed himself while playing with some boys in the courtyard; he fell on a knife he was carrying, probably as a result of one of the epileptic fits to which he was prone. Hysteria gripped the witnesses or near witnesses of the tragedy: The mother started thrashing Dmitri's nurse; servants accused his playmates; his uncle took up the cry that the murderer was the son of Boris' agent in Uglich, despite the fact that the boy had not even been at the scene. When the rioting was over, the mangled bodies of some thirty boys lay about the town. The government sent Prince Basil Shuisky to take depositions, and the conclusions of his investigation were that the tsarevich was unquestionably dead and that it was death by accident.

Fedor and Irene did produce a tsarevna, Feodosia, but she died mysteriously in 1593. The pathetic tsar himself finally expired in 1598, leaving the real world he comprehended so little in the expectation of finding the world of his pious dreams. According to the Chronicles, his death represented the "withering away of the last flower of the land of Russia." The dynasty of Rurik, the direct line of the grand princes of Kiev and Muscovy, was extinct.

3. Boris Godunov: A Parvenu on the Throne

While Russia's first patriarch guided the rulerless nation, a Zemsky Sobor was convened to begin discussion of the crisis. The boyars, gentry, and clergy deliberated unhurriedly for weeks, observing all the religious and genealogical protocol despite the mounting tension in the city, the growing frenzy of intrigue, and the deepening suspicion among the superstitious that Russia was due to be punished mightily for its sins.

Fedor Romanov, nephew of Ivan the Terrible, was a leading contender for the throne in 1598, and his cause was aided by the rumor that he had been named successor in Fedor's will, as well as by his reputation for openhandedness, for heroism in battle, and for learning. There were many princely boyars pitted against him: Prince Fedor Mstislavsky, premier boyar, was a grandson of Grand Prince Ivan III; Prince Shuisky claimed descent from the royal line going somewhat farther back; Prince Basil Golitsyn had *his* bloodline put forth for all to admire, while Prince Belsky relied more on his ability to bribe the civil servants. Although these men were sure the throne belonged to one of their class, they could never agree on which one.

Boris Godunov's humble origin seemed to disqualify him. His first move was to have all take the oath to the tsaritsa, but his sister pleaded illness and refused to be Russia's first female ruler. In the end, Boris' control of the army enabled him to become tsar himself. It all was stage-managed in the best manner of Ivan the Terrible. Soldiers and the city mob forced the patriarch and boyars to go in procession to the Novodevichy Monastery in Moscow, where Boris was in self-imposed seclusion. There they begged him to be tsar, again and again. He refused, again and again. The drama went on for days, with people kneeling in the snow and wailing that Russia was to be ruined, a scene effectively realized in the Moussorgsky opera. Boris consented at last "in deep humility, with great reluctance, his heart heavy within him." His coronation was celebrated with all the style of his genuinely royal predecessors.

The Romanovs took their revenge on Tsar Boris in the history books over the next three centuries, just as the Tudors did with Richard III. Boris Godunov is, in fact, the same sort of historical riddle as Richard York: Both men were superbly enlightened for their times; both were misunderstood; and both were accused of monstrous crimes, for which they paid dearly, whether guilty or innocent. The popular conception of Richard III was fixed by Shakespeare. The standard version of Boris Godunov is the Pushkin poem, on which Moussorgsky's opera was based, depicting him as a strong and clever ruler driven to hallucinatory madness and bitter death because of his guilt as perpetrator of the murder of the Tsarevich Dmitri. In Boris' own day rumors spread by enemies such as the Romanovs credited him with a list of crimes against the royal family, including not only the murder of Dmitri but also responsibility for the untimely deaths of Ivan the Terrible, Tsar Fedor, the Tsarina Irene, and the Tsarevna Feodosia.

Be that as it may, Boris Godunov was better fitted to rule Russia than any other man—with the possible exception of Fedor Romanov. Boris was the first tsar to send selected young boyars to study abroad. Unfortunately for Russia only two of thirty ever bothered to come back. Although illiterate himself, Boris was open to Western ideas, actively encouraged Western modes like shaving, and was successful in attracting foreigners into Russian service. The building of a Lutheran church for the benefit of the foreigners scandalized the Orthodox, but Boris' piety was never questioned, and he was strong enough to show tolerance. The tsar even dreamed of a college or university, Moscow's first, to be staffed perforce by Westerners. The building funds, however, were needed as usual for strengthening fortresses on Russia's ever-extending but shaky frontiers.

Like Ivan the Terrible, Boris promoted foreign trade and dynastic ties abroad. There were new inquiries to the court of Queen Elizabeth about merchandise and marriage. All the foreign courts recognized Boris, who seemed intent on establishing a Godunov dynasty forever. He had an exceptionally gifted and healthy son, Fedor, who was still in early adolescence, and his daughter, Xenia, of marriageable age, was a ravishing creative of unusual intelligence and amiability. Her first suitor was a son of the King of Sweden, but he brought his mistress with him to Moscow and proved himself to be a lout with few prospects. There followed a Prince of Denmark, a handsome, dashing, storybook prince, but unfortunately for Xenia, he died during the course of the prewedding celebrations, probably before she even saw him.

Added to the frustration of Boris' plans for his family were his fears for his own position, arising from a paranoiac distrust of the boyars. If Ivan was the Stalin of his era, Boris was the Khrushchev who followed, ruthless in eliminating potential opponents but not usually murderous about it. Prince Belsky, the perpetual conniver, was the first to be humiliated, and later the Shuiskys were rendered harmless. In 1601 the Romanovs' turn came. Boris' agents found allegedly poisonous herbs in the storehouses of Alexander Romanov, the brother of Fedor. Moreover, Boris suspected that the Romanovs were behind the increasing volume of rumors that the Tsarevich Dmitri had miraculously escaped death. After a trial in the boyar Duma, all the Romanovs and connected families were sent into exile. Three Romanovs died in prison. As for the talented Fedor, an end was seemingly put to his political prospects by having him shorn as the monk Philaret, the name he bore throughout his subsequent career. At the same time his wife was forced to take the vows as the nun Martha. Michael Romanov, their sole surviving son, was considered so young and unimportant that he was suffered to live in mild confinement.

To compound Boris' troubles, famine swept Russia. The year 1601 was very bad; 1602 was even worse; and 1603 was completely frightful. The tsar responded to the crisis with energy and exceptional generosity, opening food distribution centers, curbing speculators, and giving tax relief. His openhanded compassion for his people earned him the sobriquet Boris the Bright-souled. In the end his efforts backfired, and many of his once grateful subjects began to revile his name. Thousands of peasants had uprooted themselves and flocked to the cities for the free food, causing the supplies to run out and upsetting the whole economy. Now Boris was forced to issue decrees forbidding peasants to leave the land and giving more control over them to the large landowners. The whole system of serfdom was given its major reinforcement under Boris. Just as the enclosure of the commons by the great landowners was, in the main, foisted on the English countryside during the confused years after the death of Henry VIII, so in Russia bondage was clamped on the peasants by piecemeal and obscure enactments in the troubled times after Ivan IV.

In 1603, when it seemed that Boris had no enemies at large and also no friends, rumor became reality with the appearance of a Tsarevich Dmitri, outside Russia and the reach of Boris' agents. This Dmitri first came forth on the estate of the Polish magnate Prince Adam Vishnevetsky, who was a descendant of both Rurik and Gedimin and who had recently had two of his many estates stolen from him by the Muscovites. In the course of taking his bath one day, Prince Adam found occasion to slap his valet and curse him. On his knees, the valet suddenly blurted out the fact that in reality he was the tsarevich, in hiding from Boris' police. Prince Adam did not let his disbelief last more than momentarily. Within hours his astonished wife and friends found themselves doing obeisance to the Grand Prince of Muscovy, and Dmitri was duly furnished with gorgeous robes and expensive accouterments.

The following year Dmitri was escorted to the court at Krakow, stopping on the way at the estate of Pan George Mniszek, a relative of Prince Adam's by marriage but essentially an upstart in the Polish aristocracy, who had thrown away one family fortune and was greedy to make another. Dmitri fell wildly in love with Marina Mniszek, the inevitably beautiful daughter, a little slim by Russian standards but really handsome, with dancing eyes perfectly setting off a chiseled face. (A good portrait of her is to be seen in Wawel Castle in Krakow.) The love was one-sided, and

Pushkin was onto this when he gave his Princess Marina these lines to sing after Dmitri's passionate declarations:

> . . . As God is my witness, till your feet
> Are resting on the dais of the throne
> Till Godunov is overthrown by you
> I will not hear more monologues on love.

Dmitri promised her and her father much indeed. At Krakow he got a noncommittal reception from King Sigismund III, but he soon enlisted the ecstatic support of the Roman Catholic Church by secretly converting to that faith and promising to further its fondest desire, the reunion of the Western and Eastern churches.

In the east of Poland Dmitri rallied around him an army of Polish hot-bloods, Russian refugees, and the usual Cossacks ready to join any wild cause. While the Polish authorities looked the other way, Dmitri invaded Russia in October, 1604, proclaiming Boris a usurper. The first battle was won handily, and many towns started ringing their bells and opening their gates for Dmitri, who, it was rumored, was going to be a "Good Tsar"—that is, a tsar who would favor the people as opposed to the aristocracy.

In the Kremlin Boris first scoffed and then armed. After an investigation, the patriarch solemnly proclaimed that Dmitri was an impostor, in reality Gregory Ostrepev, son of Bogdan Ostrepev, a former menial on the estate of one of the Romanovs, later a monk of the Chudov Monastery in the Kremlin, and most recently a runaway. Boris had Prince Basil Shuisky publicly reavow that the real tsarevich had died at Uglich. The great boyars like the Shuiskys, Mstislavskys, Golitsyns and Sheremetevs threw their support to Boris, not out of any love for him but out of sheer fear of just what a "Good Tsar" might do. Another reliable supporter and an able general was Prince Peter Basmanov, son of the reputed bed companion and later victim of Ivan IV. Dmitri was soundly defeated by Boris' armies in January, 1605, and forced to flee south with a fraction of his followers.

With complete victory at hand, Boris died unexpectedly in April, 1605. At the age of fifty-six Boris was in bad health, but on the day of his death he had enjoyed a large meal just before an attack quickly carried him off. It is unlikely that Boris rolled down the steps from his throne, as most operatic bassos do, or somersaulted down them, as Siepi used to do so gracefully.

Boris had ruled Russia for seven years and had controlled it for the previous fourteen. As late as the beginning of our own century a distinguished Russian historian could put Boris down as "a parvenu converted into a poltroon with all the petty instincts of a policeman." Romanov propaganda set aside, it is more apt to say that Boris was something of a genius, one whose luck and character failed him in the end.

In the Kremlin both those who mourned Boris and those who did not took the oath to his sixteen-year-old son Fedor, pledging to protect the young tsar, his mother, and his sister, and specifically abjuring the pretender, Dmitri. Many people may well have felt that in Fedor II Russia was getting the best-prepared and most promising ruler in all its history. Fedor was uncommonly handsome, well built, and graceful. He was active, knew his own mind, and showed every sign of kindness. His education was exceptional, and he had recently finished making the most accurate map of his country ever undertaken by a Russian. History was unkind to the tsar-cartographer.

Boris' army in the south at first swore loyalty to Fedor, but during a melee with the enemy, Prince Basmanov suddenly shouted out his allegiance to Dmitri. Soon after, the Princes Mstislavsky, Golitsyn, and Sheremetev also proved to be turncoats. Even before Dmitri and his new supporters moved against Moscow, his agents were able to stage a coup in the capital. Two of his men boldly preached his cause in Red Square. Confronted by an aroused crowd, Prince Basil Shuisky announced that the Tsarevich Dmitri was indeed alive, thus reversing the oaths he had sworn on at least three earlier occasions. This was enough to stampede the mob through the Kremlin gates and into the palace, where they found Tsar Fedor sitting on the throne with all his regalia. The young ruler's hope of overawing the people was roughly crushed, and Fedor and his family were unceremoniously removed to the Godunov mansion in Moscow. Their confinement there lasted but ten days. In the middle of June, 1605, the mansion was invaded by some boyars and soldiers, who proceeded to strangle the dowager tsaritsa and then set upon Fedor. Husky as he was, Fedor grappled successfully with three soldiers until Prince Golitsyn joined in, this iron-handed veteran reaching up under the tsar's gown and foully causing him such pain as to make Fedor beg for death, which came as the result of a clubbing. The beautiful Tsarevna Xenia was spared by the assailants, spared, it was said, to suffer the embraces of the lusty Dmitri. She ended up, not as Dmitri's wife, but as the nun Olga, living on to 1622.

4. Dmitri the Self-styled: A Pretender with No Doubts

Ten days after the destruction of the Godunovs (which Dmitri may or may not have authorized) the invading hero entered Moscow in a great triumphal procession of Poles and Russians, clergy and soldiers, riffraff, and some sixty boyars. Although secretly Catholic, Dmitri observed all the forms at the cathedrals of the Kremlin, later mounted the Red Staircase, and confidently sat himself on the throne. Thereafter, one of his first acts was to summon the ex-Tsaritsa Maria Nagaia from her nunnery, and to the delight of Dmitri's supporters the mother acknowledged her long-lost son. Three days later Dmitri's formal coronation occurred amid extraordinary popular fervor for the "Good Tsar."

A true successor of Dmitri Donskoy would merit the title Dmitri II, but the young man hailed as tsar in 1605 is usually called Dmitri the Self-styled. Who was he really? It is unlikely he was, as Boris claimed, Gregory Ostrepev, son of Bogdan, once serf of the Romanovs, and defrocked monk. A man calling himself Gregory Ostrepev actually showed up in Dmitri's camp and subsequently was a great nuisance as a drunkard. One theory is that Dmitri got his royal manner as the natural son of Shephen Barthory, King of Poland. Another claim is that Dmitri was the lost child, not of Ivan the Terrible, but of his son, the Tsarevich Ivan. While it seems probable that the Tsarevich Dmitri did kill himself accidentally at Uglich in 1591, it is possible that he was saved in all the confusion, spirited away by an uncle, perhaps given to Bogdan Ostrepev to bring up as his own son, and so forth. Thus, Dmitri may have been real. An important consideration is that he never doubted himself.

In his day and in ours it has been said of Dmitri that he could not be prince of the line of Rurik because he was vulgar. Actually his vulgarity could be the lordly familiarity of someone completely sure of himself, coupled with the natural lack of snobbishness that one would expect of a border crosser and a refugee among the humble. Dmitri knew the protocol of the boyars, although he might sometimes force them to mingle with his enthusiastic Cossacks. Dmitri could overawe ambassadors with his bearing and freeze them with his glance, but other times he dispensed with Byzantine ceremony and chatted with envoys man to man.

Dmitri's lack of formality was his charm for some, but it was part of his undoing by others who saw the tsar's bluffness and rashness as threatening symbols of non-Russian thinking and of radical plans for the future that might even include religious toleration, educational institutions, equitable taxation, protection of the serfs, or an alliance with Poland. Dmitri also caused talk by taking walks unescorted, getting on his horse by himself, having music instead of chants at dinner, eating veal, dining with priests and foreigners, firing cannon with his own royal hand, staging war games and even snowball fights, and fighting bears in person. Then there were sins of omission. People were alarmed, for instance, that Dmitri did not cross himself constantly, that he did not take naps, and that he did not use the palace steam rooms. The western design of the small wooden palace Dmitri had built within the Kremlin puzzled some people, and the new uniforms and new guards companies manned by foreigners upset others. The boyars muttered that the young tsar was squandering the treasure of the father he claimed. Dmitri's expressed desire to be elected King of Poland sounded costly, and his military preparations for a crusade against the Tatars and Turks seemed like sheer madness.

Dmitri willfully fulfilled his desire and his promises when he married by proxy his Polish lady, Marina Mniszek. The bride, now called Maria, arrived in Moscow in June, 1606. Dmitri outtalked the patriarch on the matter of rebaptizing her and connived that her chrism coincide with the usual rite in the coronation ceremony. That neither of the royal couple would take communion in the Orthodox cathedral (because of secret orders from the Vatican) was the most upsetting incident on a day otherwise celebrated joyously and with clumsy fraternity by the Russians and Poles in Moscow. At the wedding banquet, a Polish mazurka was danced in the Kremlin for the first time.

Far from joining the whispered opposition to Poles and priests in the Kremlin and seemingly forgetting any claims of their own to the throne, the Romanov family came back from exile to be solid supporters of Dmitri. Philaret, once the dashing Fedor Romanov, received the important post of Archbishop of Rostov.

Among the boyars Prince Basil Shuisky was the most persistent in his intrigues against the new tsar. At the very outset of the reign Shuisky was caught and was sentenced to beheading in Red Square. There was a delay when the executioner insisted that the prince remove his bejeweled and golden robes, while Shuisky desisted, saying that he would not meet his God dressed in an unseemly manner. A messenger from the palace appeared, apparently a Shuisky hater because he walked so slowly, and in the end Shuisky was saved through Dmitri's clemency—the tsar's chief fault of virtue next to his informality.

Prince Shuisky soon resumed his whispering campaign. When it did him no good to reverse his oath again and say that the real Dmitri was dead, he embarked on a more diabolical scheme. His agents set up the cry that the Poles intended to murder Dmitri, and this served to propel a mob, including Shuisky's own men, into the Kremlin. In the tsar's apartments Prince Basmanov and the guards were cut down, while Dmitri retreated and barricaded himself in one room after another. In time Dmitri had no other recourse than to jump down into the courtyard, a drop of 100 feet. Crippled but not desperately so, Dmitri was found by loyal soldiers and carried back to the palace, only to be set upon and hacked to pieces by Shuisky's men. His corpse was thrown down once again, with a cord tied around his sexual organs, and for days it was ghoulishly desecrated by passersby. Finally, Dmitri's remains were burned, the ashes loaded in a cannon, and the cannon fired in the direction of Poland. Tsaritsa Maria hid during the killings under the skirts of an ample, tough, and fast-talking lady-in-waiting and survived without injury.

5. Basil IV: The Boyar Tsar

Any man who could engineer the downfall of a young ruler genuinely beloved by the masses could get himself made tsar. Accordingly, Basil Shuisky was acclaimed by a small crowd in Red Square, a riotous parody of a Zemsky Sobor. The new sovereign was indeed a descendant of Rurik, and he falsified his genealogy only slightly in order to make himself appear a direct descendant of the heroic Alexander Nevsky. His coronation as Basil IV in June, 1606, was modest and economical. One of Basil's first acts was to revise his oath about Dmitri for about the seventh time, now recognizing the remains brought back from Uglich as the dead tsarevich and insisting on having this Dmitri sanctified as a martyr. It was a futile effort to exorcise a ghost.

Nobody except some of the boyars expected Shuisky to be a "Good Tsar." His family's fur business did give employment to many people in the capital, but now the Russian people outside Moscow rose in anger and stayed in a state of wild ferment for the best part of a decade, threatening the traditional order, or disorder, more seriously than ever before.

The first leader of social revolt was a desperado named Bolotnikov, formerly a serf, a prisoner of the Tatars, and a galley slave who escaped back to Russia via Venice. Bolotnikov put together a ragged army of runaway serfs, Cossacks, refugee supporters of Dmitri, and even some gentry, honest soldiers who hated the greedy boyars in the Kremlin. They fought with Shuisky's troops, at times within sight of the walls of Moscow, from 1606 to the spring of 1608. At one point Bolotnikov was joined by an independent force under a man claiming to be a lost son of Tsar Fedor I. Eventually, the gentry supporters deserted Bolotnikov as too revolutionary, and he and the "tsarevich" were caught and viciously executed.

Within months after Bolotnikov was disposed of, Tsar Basil faced a new pretender calling himself Dmitri. The new ghost-in-the-flesh proceeded to set up an armed camp at Tushino, a place lying on the trade routes only a few miles from the center of Moscow. That this man could have escaped the violence both in Uglich in 1591 and in the Kremlin in 1606 might have seemed preposterous to all but for an extraordinary turn of events: He contrived to capture the Tsaritsa Maria Mniszek and she chose to recognize him as her lost husband, to remarry him, and even to bear him a son in time. The second false Dmitri became known as the Brigand of Tushino. He took himself entirely seriously and set up a royal court with full ceremonial, with "boyars" in attendance and with his own "patriarch." The man designated Patriarch at Tushino was none other than Philaret Romanov.

Not only the Romanovs but many of the nobility supported the second

pretender against Shuisky, and Dmitri's forces were swelled by the remnants of Bolotnikov's army. Together, they ranged over central Russia,
starting revolts along the Volga, besieging the great Trinity Monastery,
and nearly beleaguering Moscow itself. Tsar Basil was reduced to hiring
a Swedish army. Dmitri's fortunes shifted in 1609, however. Once again
the gentry deserted the pillage-prone rabble, and King Sigismund of Poland
decided to invade Russia in person at the head of a professional army.
The Brigand of Tushino was forced to flee with his wife and son to the
south, where in late 1610 he was murdered. Many of his forces stayed intact
under Cossack chieftains, and some swore allegiance to the infant "tsarevich."

Tsar Basil's position was virtually hopeless now that he faced the might
of Poland, as well as the ceaseless activity of the bands of freebooters.
There was a moment of success when his cousin, Prince Michael Skopin-
Shuisky, was able to stop the Polish army, but shortly afterward Basil's
one effective general died of poisoning at a banquet, possibly at the bidding
of a jealous tsar. Meanwhile, Philaret Romanov returned to Moscow to
agitate against his old enemy. The downfall of Basil IV came swiftly in
July, 1610: A mob invaded the Kremlin and dragged Shuisky into Red
Square, where he was deposed and forcibly shorn as a monk.

6. Anarchy, Foreign Invasions, and Liberation

At this juncture some people tried to get the riotous assemblage in the
square to shout in as new tsar Prince Basil Golitsyn, the assassin
of Fedor and a man apparently undismayed that the Kremlin had
had four successive masters in only five years. The attempt failed, for
nobody wanted another boyar-tsar. The leaders of the privileged classes
presently considered an extraordinary alternative. The restoration of law
and order above all required a man with an army, and the only disciplined
force available would be a foreign army. Accordingly, the boyars and
gentry solemnly agreed to offer the throne of Russia to Prince Ladislaus
(or Vladislav), son of King Sigismund of Poland, whose troops even then
were besieging the great Russian stronghold at Smolensk. Philaret Romanov
and Prince Golitsyn, in fact everybody who appeared to have any claim
to the throne, were sent off to Krakow in the delegation to negotiate the
settlement. The discussions with the Polish king dragged on over constitutional and religious issues. Finally, negotiations broke down altogether when
King Sigismund decided that he wanted the Kremlin throne not for his
son, but for himself. The Russian envoys were taken into custody in Krakow, and Philaret found himself a Polish prisoner for the next eight years.

So great was the boyars' fear that the Moscow commoners would invite in the Brigand of Tushino (the second pretender was still alive) that in September, 1610, they allowed a Polish army to occupy the Kremlin. Clashes between these Poles and the populace were inevitable, and in the course of the fighting much of the city was burned. The Poles imprisoned the old Patriarch Hermogen in the Chudov Monastery, where he was allowed to starve to death but not before he had smuggled out letters appealing to Russians to throw out the foreign heretics and to hold a Zemsky Sobor.

By 1611 all Russia was in the grip of lawlessness, plague, and famine. One-third of the population, perhaps, had already perished. Trade was at a standstill, for no merchant would brave a countryside infested with Polish regulars and irregulars, Cossack bands, and brigands of every description. The Protestant Swedes had seized Novgorod for themselves, piqued that one of their princes had not been called upon to rule Russia, as well as seriously alarmed at the successes of the Catholic crusade being waged by Poland. The Khan of the Crimea was planning to roll back the frontier northward. With no tsar in Moscow "the State appeared to be no man's property," and all Russians became "anarchists against their will," to use the words of a great Russian historian.

The liberation began late in 1611, partly as a result of the fact that one of Hermogen's patriotic appeals fell into the hands of a good citizen of Nizhni Novgorod named Kuzma Minin, sometimes described as a public-spirited butcher but more accurately seen as a substantial capitalist, a wholesale meat dealer whose business along the Volga was near ruin. Minin was able to arouse the people of his city and area to put up men, supplies, and treasure for the national cause. While he handled the money, the military leadership was taken over by Prince Dmitri Pozharsky, a Rurikovich but essentially a patriotic country gentleman. In the spring of 1612 Pozharsky's national militia moved on Moscow. A Polish relief column was beaten, and finally, in October, 1612, the Kremlin itself was captured, its Polish defenders having been reduced to cannibalism. Following a massive thanksgiving parade to the Cathedral of the Assumption the leaders of the liberation sent out letters summoning a Zemsky Sobor that would choose a new tsar. A statue to Minin and Pozharsky as saviors of Russia now stands near the Place of Executions in Red Square.

7. *The Election*

The Zemsky Sobor which deliberated Russia's future at the close of the Time of Troubles was the most representative assembly of the land that had ever met. There were more elected delegates, fewer officially designated ones. Besides the boyars, gentry, merchants, and clergy, there were for the first time representatives of the Cossacks and of the free peasants. The serfs, of course, were not heard from.

The assembly opened in late 1612 with three days of fasting to purge Russians of their sins of the past decade. The delegates were in a high-minded mood, but they moved in a leisurely way in their discussions and they were not above backstairs intrigue, deliberate stalling, bribery, and even occasional swordplay.

At the outset some still favored calling in a Polish, Swedish, or even Hapsburg prince to found a new dynasty, but soon it was agreed that a non-Orthodox foreigner would not do. Also, the notables were nearly unanimous in rejecting the claim of Tsaritsa Maria's infant son, the candidate the Cossacks clamored for.

The number of highborn Russian candidates to be considered protracted the choice. Prince Pozharsky, the idol of the nation, could probably have got himself carried to the throne by acclamation, but an old wound and his recent exertions deterred him. Many of the great boyars preferred Prince Mstislavsky, but when his name was put forward, Mstislavsky closed the issue with the words: "I do not like the throne and since you threaten to mount me forcibly upon it, I prefer turning monk." Prince Basil Golitsyn's name was raised once again, many boyars considering him the most personable and talented of the princely class, but Golitsyn was in a Polish prison, as was Philaret Romanov.

At this juncture a member of the lesser gentry proposed for tsar Michael Romanov, Philaret's sixteen-year-old surviving son. The decisive turn of events came when the Cossacks seconded the choice, having given up on Maria's son and now throwing their support to the heir of the Brigand's chosen patriarch. The boyars were reluctant to join in the enthusiasm for Michael Romanov, but eventually they heeded the general will and the reasoning behind it.

The great thing in Michael's favor was that he was the grandnephew of Ivan the Terrible. Also counting very much for him was the basic popularity of the Romanov family, which in recent memory had given the nation the sainted Anastasia, her openhanded brother, Nikita, and his son, once the war hero Fedor, now the martyr patriot Philaret. Moreover, the rumor was revived that Tsar Fedor I had bequeathed the throne to his Romanov first cousin once removed, and it was further whispered that the martyred Patriarch Hermogen had specially commended Michael to the nation. Actually, Philaret's record during the Time of Troubles was no less seamy than everybody else's: He had accepted his title of Patriarch from the second pretender, and later he took the lead in trying to give the Russian crown to Poland. These matters were covered up by the Romanovs for the next three centuries. Whatever the truth about his father, clearly Michael was blameless and innocent during the Time of Troubles, blameless to the point of being colorless, but that is what people wanted. Michael's mother was Rurikovich.

Having reached a provisional decision, the Zemsky Sobor sent emissaries (actually police agents) throughout Russia to promote Michael's candidacy, and they reported back that the country was entirely behind him. The final vote was in writing and was unanimous at a meeting in the Kremlin on February 21, 1613, after which the crowds in Red Square were informed. The commoners anticipated the choice of their betters by taking up the shout: "Let Michael Feodorovich Romanov be tsar-lord of the realm of Muscovy and the whole state of Russia."

The fact that Michael was an elected tsar might seem to put him and his Romanov successors in a special constitutional relation to the Russian people, but actually at the time men rejoiced that Michael was a "born tsar" and "the chosen of God before birth." Michael himself was always careful to stress his relationship to Ivan IV. The lesson of the years of turmoil before 1613 was that Russia simply would not tolerate a ruler who owed his position solely to the whim of the magnates or the mob. Boris Godunov was the most capable man of his day, but he was an upstart. His successor, Fedor, was even more promising, but he was an upstart's son. The Dmitris, the first possibly genuine, could be blackened as the most brazen usurpers of them all, and finally, Basil was a self-seeking fraud who fooled no one. Michael, too, might appear to come from nowhere, but it turned out he was the nearest kin and embodied the ideal of legitimacy and continuity.

Never before had the masses of the Russian people played such a large role in choosing who was to rule over them, but it did not turn out that the Romanovs were a dynasty responsive to the people. Although the boyars were the class least enthusiastic at first about Michael, the Romanovs and the aristocracy proceeded to go hand in hand through history until both were destroyed in 1917. This was presaged in 1613. Prince Sheremetev wrote Prince Golitsyn, still captive in Poland: "Our Michael is yet but young and has not come unto understanding, yet he is such as will be familiar unto us." Michael was the most convenient tsar for many reasons, and he was to reign undisturbed for thirty-two years.

III.

The Mildest of the Tsars: Michael

1. The Young Figurehead

SUCH was the chaotic condition of Russia in 1613 that the representatives of the Zemsky Sobor had some difficulty finding the newly designated tsar. Michael was located eventually at the Ipatiev Monastery, near Kostroma and about 200 miles from Moscow, living in simple circumstances with his mother.

At this point the remnants of the Polish forces around central Russia had much to gain from seizing Michael and may have tried to do so. The legend sprang up that the royal prize was kept safe by the patriotic sacrifice of Ivan Susanin, the humble peasant who guided the Polish soldiers to doom in a trackless forest. In the early nineteenth century the composer Glinka used this legend as the basis of one of his major operas, and Tsar Nicholas I was so delighted that he himself suggested the title, *A Life for the Tsar*. Since the fate of Michael and of all the Romanovs is a matter of some indifference to the Soviet regime, the Glinka opera is today performed as *Ivan Susanin*, revised so that the hero shields the whereabouts, not of the tsar, but of the resistance leaders, Minin and Pozharsky.

A great procession of people came to wait on Michael in his monastery refuge, and they begged him not to despise the tears and groans of all Russia and to accept the rulership. Michael refused and kept refusing, "with tears and great wrath." His mother pleaded that he was too young and delicate, at the same time reminding the boyar representatives that the disloyalty and treachery of their class in the past was the cause of the troubled times. They assured her that none of them wanted any further turmoil, and they informed Michael that he would be responsible to God for the wreck of Russia. After some hours, Michael at last let them kiss his hand and promised to come to Moscow. Michael's "no," then "yes" performance was made in deep humility and doubt, unlike the theatrical and deceitful actions of Ivan IV in 1564 and Boris in 1598, but it had the same effect as theirs in making him incontrovertibly the expression of the national will. The news of Michael's accession was unwelcome to one man—his father, still captive in Poland: Philaret possibly feared for his son, but more likely he wanted the throne for himself.

Tsar Michael forthwith set off for his capital. Royal reentries or returns are generally dramatic and memorable. Eighteen-year-old Mary Queen of Scots, who had been removed to France as an infant, slipped back to Edinburgh in a wee boat, and presented herself at Holyrood Palace to the initial astonishment and subsequent delight of all, except the unromantic John Knox. Charles II, restored as Stuart king after Cromwell's death, received such a tumultuous welcome in London that he remarked that he should have come back sooner. Napoleon escaped Elba, won over the troops sent against him, and reentered Paris as if nothing had changed, while at the Tuileries the court ladies worked frantically to remove the Bourbon fleur-de-lis recently sewn over the imperial bees on the palace carpets.

Michael's journey to Moscow was more a nightmare than a triumph. On the way from Kostroma all he encountered was burned-out villages and pillaged churches, thousands of unburied corpses of men and animals, and throngs of miserable and suppliant subjects, many robbed to the skin, bleeding, blinded, or maimed. The horrified young ruler ordered a stopover at the Trinity Monastery until the carnage was cleared away.

An additional reason for delay was that he had no money to equip his retinue. In patriotic response to some unroyal begging by Michael came cash, cloth, salt, grain, fish, and beef from the Stroganovs, not an old family but Russia's richest, merchants in Siberian furs, Ural iron, and Astrakhan silk and caviar. Duly outfitted, the tsar proceeded and in May, 1613, entered Moscow escorted by the entire male populace. The Kremlin stood ready to receive him, but it was in sorry shape, with burned roofs, smashed windows, and litter-heaped floors. All the treasure was gone—between the extravagant generosity of the pretender and the rapacious barbarity of the Poles. There was nothing to eat from, nothing to sleep on —no furniture at all. Such was this royal restoration.

By May the Cathedral of the Assumption had been cleared of the filth of men and horses, and the formal coronation of Michael Fedorovich took place in the tradition of the great Ivans but with scarcely the old splendor. On this occasion Michael ennobled Kuzma Minin, the meat dealer of Nizhni Novgorod who had started the liberation movement. Titles were all that Michael had to give. A portrait of Michael made by an unknown artist soon after the coronation shows his gentle and serious young face staring out from beneath the furred, caplike crown of Vladimir Mono-makh. His big eyes appear dreamy.

So near complete social dissolution and ruin, Russia in 1613 seemed to need an exceptionally strong and energetic ruler. Instead, it had as tsar a shy and inexperienced youth, who was weak physically because of an ailment in his legs. As things turned out, Michael's deficiencies were out-weighed by the fact that all the stable elements of the nation rallied around the throne as never before, offering steadfast obedience and good counsel. The boyars' Duma managed affairs from day to day decisively and justly, and the Zemsky Sobor met annually for the next decade to provide the support of the whole land. Eschewing conspiracy, the boyars allowed themselves only the old luxury of quarreling over family precedence. Once, for example, Tsar Michael was compelled to order Prince Pozharsky, the war hero, to walk on foot to the house of Prince Sheremetev and to offer his apologies for trying to outplace him.

The prime task of the government was obviously the restoration of law and order and the removal of rival claimants to power, both domestic and foreign. One immediate threat was the Cossack chief Ivan Zarutsky, who controlled the whole Astrakhan area and threatened to sweep north up the Volga. Zarutsky, holding as his wife the incredible Marina Mniszek, was the third pretender calling himself Tsar Dmitri Ivanovich. In 1614 boyar generals succeeded in capturing the self-styled tsar, and he was executed by impalement. The ex-Tsaritsa Maria was brought to Moscow under heavy guard and died soon after seeing her four-year-old son hanged in front of the Serpukhov Gate. This latter act of state expediency was an atrocity in a reign notably free from violence against individuals. As for the other remnants of royalty, the Shuiskys became extinct as a family soon after ex-Tsar Basil Shuisky died as a monk in Warsaw in 1612. Ex-Tsaritsa Anna, the fourth wife of Ivan IV, and ex-Tsarevna Xenia Godunov both did obeisance to Michael and lived on as nuns into the 1620's, the latter being granted her wish to be buried next to the unhon-ored graves of her royal father and royal brother.

The King of Sweden, in possession of Novgorod since 1611, was on the point of receiving the allegiance of all the north and intended to move his capital from Stockholm to the Baltic coast of Russia. This threat was ended when the citizens of Novgorod declared for Michael and Orthodoxy and the boyars Boris Morozov and Ivan Buturlin heroically defended Pskov against Gustavus Adolphus, the greatest warrior king of the age. By the Treaty of Stolbovo concluded in 1617, Novgorod was restored to Michael's realm and his title as tsar recognized by Sweden, which con-tented itself with the annexation of territories blocking Russia from the sea.

The same year central Russia was invaded once more by a large Polish force under Prince Ladislaus, who asserted his claim to the throne and proposed to unite the two Slavic nations. Many Russian towns opened their gates to him, and he confidently offered amnesty to all, including Michael, the son of Philaret. The Polish army actually tried to storm the walls of Moscow in late 1618, but it was thrown back with huge losses. Russian peasants were wont to bury captured Poles up to their necks and then behead them with scythes. With both sides too exhausted to fight further and too proud to make a real peace, Russia and Poland concluded the truce of Duelino the next year. The truce lasted for a decade and a half and left Poland in possession of much Russian land, including the fortress city of Smolensk, only 200 miles from Moscow. Prince Ladislaus continued to style himself ruler of Muscovy.

Russian diplomatic efforts backed up Tsar Michael's feeble armies. Close relations and trade with England were revived. The Ottoman Empire was successfully bought off, although the rapaciousness of two grand viziers in quick succession necessitated huge shipments of sable skins as gifts. Recognition by the Holy Roman Empire was achieved only after a contretemps. Emperor Matthias refused to rise when the Russian envoy first brought Michael's salutation, and in turn the envoy bowed only to the waist, not to the ground. The envoy was held captive, but his stubbornness won out in the end. At a subsequent interview the emperor blamed his gout for his not rising and went so far as to offer Michael the hand of a Hapsburg archduchess, to which the envoy grandly replied that "the Tsar's intentions are in the hands of God and are known to God alone." Less sophisticated apparently were the envoys Michael dispatched to Denmark. Of them the king had this to say: "If these people come again, we must build them a pigsty, for nobody can live in any house that they have occupied until six months afterwards because of the stench they leave behind them."

2. Dutiful Son, Dutiful Husband

The truce with Poland had one significant outcome: the release of Philaret from detention. The head of the Romanov family was greeted outside of Moscow by huge crowds, and Michael and his father fell to their knees, embraced, and wept for many minutes after their separation of nine years. In the summer of 1619 the monk Philaret was enthroned as Patriarch of the Russian Church, the Patriarch of Jerusalem officiating.

Having been many things in his day, Philaret now had his chance to fulfill the political ambitions of the former Fedor Romanov. For his part, the twenty-two-year-old tsar, out of duty or out of diffidence, was content not only to share power with his father, but even to efface himself. Officially now, there were two gosudars, and they sat side by side in equal magnificence, each receiving ambassadors' credentials and each replying to them separately. Michael's name took precedence on public documents, but often Philaret conducted state affairs without consulting him.

Philaret returned to Russia embittered and hardened in his ideas. His lofty demeanor and dictatorial actions made him many enemies, but his power went unchallenged until his death. His harsh rule was enlightened and just, as time proved, and it restored Russia to the disordered prosperity and showy grandeur it had had in the sixteenth century.

In the economic field Philaret's measures bore down on all segments of the populace to some degree: tax reform, curbing of corruption, exemptions for foreign merchants, and reinforcement of serfdom. Taverns were made a government monopoly, and state-promoted drunkenness was so profitable that shortly all of Russia's grain export surplus was needed for the distilleries. In cultural affairs Philaret was conservative but not entirely isolationist: A few heretics were burned, but the doors were opened to Greek and Latin scholars. He founded the nucleus of the famed patriarchal library and took a hand himself in the publication of books. As for foreign policy, Philaret simply kept the peace at a time when Russia's need was survival, not aggrandizement.

Dynastic considerations obviously dictated that mild-mannered Tsar Michael should become husband and father. Even before Philaret's return the boyars decided to confront the young ruler with their daughters, and in due course Michael was betrothed to a Maria Khlopov. Just before the wedding, however, it was announced that Maria had a sickness that was both incurable and infectious, and she and her family were sent to one of the farthest new settlements in Siberia. Subsequently, Philaret determined on a foreign consort to raise the dignity of his house, but Denmark was insulting about the matter, and Sweden said its princess would not sacrifice her soul's salvation even for all Muscovy. Falling back on a native match, Philaret suspected trickery in connection with Maria Khlopov, and a new health examination led to the discovery that her vodka had been spiked on the earlier occasion. This time it was the Saltykovs who were banished, for "interrupting the Tsar's wedding and pleasure." *That* Maria got handsome gifts for her trouble, but not the tsar, for Michael now decided to please his mother and marry Princess Maria Dolgoruky, of one of the highest Rurikovich families in the land. The wedding took place in 1624, and within a year *this* Maria was dead in childbirth. Thus Michael was the first of several Romanov tsars to experience unhappiness over a Dolgoruky princess.

Michael's second and lasting marriage took place in 1626. His bride was Eudoxia Streshnev, daughter of a family of the minor gentry. Ten children were born in the course of the reign. Six died in infancy, but the succession was assured. There was no sign that Michael was in love with his wife, as Ivan had been with Anastasia Romanov, but he was dutiful and faithful to her, and he was an affectionate parent.

3. The Shadowy Lord of the Kremlin

Philaret died in 1633 after ruling Russia in peace for fourteen years, and Tsar Michael, now thirty-six, found himself head of the Romanov family and master of his own house politically. He chose to remain shut up in the Kremlin, an unapproachable, ceremonial figure, almost entirely hidden from ordinary people's view and colorless in all but his amusements.

The citadel and city of the tsars had been fully restored by the 1630's, and growing revenues allowed the acquisition of new marvels. An English architect built Michael a fine stone palace, and lesser mansions were erected for his heir and for boyars close to the tsar. Another Englishman, Christopher Halloway, built additional stories on the Saviour's Gate, causing this main entry of the Kremlin, with its combination of Renaissance and Gothic styles and with its great clock and chimes, to become one of the architectural masterpieces of Russia. About the same time as this first Kremlin clock (1625) weather vanes were added atop the crosses of the towers: Thus was Western precision superimposed on Muscovite other-world lines. In 1634 a Swedish engineer started construction of a stone bridge over the Moskva River. Ten goldsmiths were brought in from Holland, followed by coppersmiths and a bellmaker.

The tsar's delicate health permitted him to leave his palace only on ceremonial occasions such as New Year's Day (celebrated on September 1), when there was a great concourse on the square between two of the cathedrals. On December 21 was the festival of the patriarch, and the court went in procession to his palace. The tsar played host to the patriarch four days later after long religious observances. At Epiphany the tsar left the Kremlin for the famous "blessing of the waters" ritual. At these events the public saw Michael only at a great distance, a crowned figure so laden down with gold cloth and jewels that two boyars supported him, one on each arm. A contemporary print of one of these royal processions across Red Square shows all the onlookers, including the soldiers in ranks, prostrated on the ground.

The normal court routine began with the morning assembly outside the palace. The older boyars arrived in sledges, ponderously climbed the Red Staircase, and took their positions in a richly frescoed antechamber, the tsar's chief advisers (the *blizhnie*, or near boyars) standing closest to the inner chambers. The younger nobles, including some 500 chamberlains, rode to the assembly on horseback and stayed below. Michael then limped into the antechamber and sat down in a large armchair, above which hung many icons. Nearby was an ornate silver casket containing the most precious of Romanov documents, "The Act of Election of Michael Fedorovich." After all had done obeisance, the tsar noted any absences, whispered to a few favored nobles, and then allowed petitioners to come forward and prostrate themselves. The most frequent request was for permission to leave the court for family business, and if granted, the petitioner and tsar exchanged small gifts, Michael always inquiring after each member of the noble's family.

On some days the reception was held in the inner Golden Room, with Michael enthroned, the nobles seated on benches according to rank, and the clerks standing. The opinions of each of the boyars were sought on these occasions, but many just sat and stroked their beards, "as the Tsar graciously makes many to be boyars, not because of their learning but because of their high birth, wherefore many boyars are ignorant of letters." The Golden Room was also famous for its Petitioners' Window from which a basket was lowered to the ground so that the humblest of the tsar's subjects might deposit their petitions therein.

After the reception Michael and the whole court dined in state. The tsar ate and drank sparingly, but just as he delighted in giving presents, he took much pleasure in providing sumptuous feasts, sending down to his guests sixty or seventy separate dishes. A nap always followed, and after that, public business was transacted, each *prikaz* (governmental bureau) being allotted a different day. The *prikazi*, with their hundreds of clerks, were a medieval, not modern, machinery of government, a muddled and overlapping collection of offices for privately royal or public purposes. There was a *prikaz* to handle certain of the tsar's estates, another to provide specified delicacies for Michael's table, and another to manage the royal broods of 100,000 pigeons (somehow it turned out that this last *prikaz* became the secret police office, the forerunner of the MVD). Foreigners most often dealt with the envoys' bureau (*posolsky prikaz*).

Much of Michael's private life was as rigorously circumscribed as his public conduct. Religious devotions accounted for at least one-third of his day. Not only were such things as fasts prescribed for certain periods, but church rules governed even the times when the tsar could have sex with his wife. (Devout Russians still count things up and then affect shock if children are born in certain *wrong* times of the year.) The tsar visited his family ceremoniously each day, entering the *terem* with a retinue of relatives and privileged courtiers. Michael's wife and children hardly knew of any other world than the dark, low-vaulted rooms, the candles, the icons, and the incense of their palace quarters. When the tsaritsa and her children did venture out, on a pilgrimage, for example, they traveled in windowless carriages, and in Kremlin processions they walked surrounded by guards carrying large screens to confound the curious.

Largely bored by public affairs, mechanical in his religious activities, and merely dutiful toward his wife, Michael had another side to him, a pleasure-loving side. The tsar was never seen to laugh or even smile in public, but in private he allowed himself many amusements, of which folk singing and music were his favorites. An organ brought to the Kremlin from Holland in 1632 particularly delighted Michael, who had a great penchant for foreign curiosities. The tsar did not try to conceal his joy and pride in receiving such things as clocks, carriages, perfumes, fancy textiles, and even a lion sent by the Shah of Persia. Like Ivan the Terrible, Michael had no modesty about having his growing treasure brought out and displayed. Dazzling jewels and plate and finery connoted power in the Russian mind.

The rest of Michael's pleasures still had a traditional, medieval ring to them. His private court was peopled with many jesters, brightly dressed in blue and red, and the more prized, the more idiotic they were in their speech and antics. There were sixteen dwarfs and a Negro in the group. The female fool of Michael's mother was the best known of any in this period, so cherished that a hospital was built in her memory.

4. Loser in War and Diplomacy

While the splendor of Michael's way of life in the Kremlin may have impressed the few foreign envoys who happened to see it, the first Romanov tsar enjoyed little real prestige abroad. Throughout his reign Russia stayed on the defensive and was of no account in European power politics. Russian military efforts were farcical, and Russian envoys cut comic figures.

The Time of Troubles had made it evident that the feudal type of Russian militia was no match for Swedish mercenaries or even Polish chivalry. Accordingly, right from the beginning of Michael's reign, great efforts were made to Westernize the military establishment. Foreign officers were enlisted wholesale, receiving high salaries or estates for their services. As early as 1624 there were 445 foreign officers, mostly Poles and Germans, with a number of Greeks and Italians and a flamboyant contingent of Irish and Scots. Later there were whole companies of foreign soldiers, especially among the 20,000 *streltsi* (originally archers, later musketmen) who were the royal guard in Moscow. Besides soldiers, foreign weapons were bought, and technicians, ranging from bullet casters to carpenters, were hired abroad. In 1632 a Dutchman established Russia's first modern iron mill to turn out munitions. It was all in vain.

The truce with Poland was denounced in 1632, and for a while a Russian invasion force of more than 50,000 under a general named Shein "picked up fortresses as if they were birds' nests." (This war, incidentally, was the first one in which the Russian army was provided with military maps.) Shein settled down to the siege of Smolensk, found himself besieged in turn, and ended up surrendering his whole army. It did Tsar Michael no good to order Shein to be beheaded and other generals banished, for the simple fact was that the whole army still behaved like "herds of cattle." The battle cry of the soldiers was reported to be: "God grant us some slight wound which will not hurt much, so that we may obtain a reward from the great Gosudar." Fortunately for Russia, Poland could not continue fighting either, and a new truce was signed in 1634, leaving the boundaries about the same but this time containing Prince Ladislaus' acknowledgment of Michael as tsar not "of all Russia," but just "of his own Russia."

Michael's weak position was ludicrously revealed in 1637, when, independently of Moscow, a force of fewer than 4,000 Don Cossacks sailed down their river and stormed Azov, the key Turkish fortress on the north coast of the Black Sea. After killing all the Moslems they could find, the Cossacks sent couriers to the Orthodox tsar and offered him Azov as a gift. Michael reacted not with joy, but with alarm, reproving the Cossacks for their foolhardiness and assuring the sultan that he would not protect a "lot of runaway thieves and rascals." In 1641, 10,000 Cossacks in Azov held off the sultan's army of 240,000, and once again they offered the fortress to the tsar. This time Michael praised their valor and called a Zemsky Sobor to advise him what to do. The indecisive ruler found his advisers of divided counsel: The clergy, who usually were eager to strike a blow for the faith, said that war was not their business; many of the boyars declined to fight; and the lesser gentry and townsmen, while wanting to keep Azov, spent their words attacking the selfishness and corruption of the other classes. Reminded of the sultan's threat to massacre all Christians in Turkey, reminded of the fickleness of the Cossacks, and reminded of financial problems, Michael finally ordered the Cossacks to abandon their prize, and accordingly they razed Azov in 1642.

There was one further tragicomedy in store for Michael's diplomacy. The first Romanov tsar dreamed of marrying his daughter to a foreign prince, just as the grand princes of Kiev had done centuries before. The Tsarevna Irene was said to be lovely, although no portraits of her were sent out on the ground that being painted would endanger her health. A pleasing suitor was acquired in the person of Prince Waldemar of Denmark, who came to Moscow in 1644 after being promised free exercise of his religion, "an honorable and glorious appanage, and precedence in rank over everyone except the Tsar and Tsarevich." Waldemar was given a handsome palace, but soon he found himself besieged by a whole array of high clerics urging him to give up his Lutheran faith. The tsar personally seconded their efforts. The patriarch condescended to take on himself all responsibility for the prince's soul, writing to him: "We know you *call* yourselves Christians, but you do not in all things hold the right faith in Christ." The Dane futilely reminded his hosts of their promises, adding that he had read the entire Bible five times and could argue Scripture better than any of them. At length Waldemar demanded his passports, but Michael declared it would be indecent and dishonorable to part with his "son." The prince attempted to break out of the Kremlin, first by force and later in disguise, and each time violence resulted, the killing of guards or the torture of go-betweens. Not until the next reign did Waldemar gain his liberty.

Michael suffered great bereavement in the course of the spring of 1645, when his two oldest sons died, and to this was added his increasing mortification over the failure of his daughter's marriage plans. Doctors later reported that the tsar wept so continuously that the accumulation of tears in his stomach, spleen, and liver had deprived these organs of their natural warmth, chilling his blood and producing evil humors. Michael had a fit and fell during mass on his name day, July 12. He was carried away dying. There was time for him to name and bless his successor, Alexis, and tearfully to beg that all protect his surviving son.

In people's memories, the mildest of all the tsars had been an honest and conscientious ruler, even if remote and uninspiring. No great deeds were done, but Michael served his purpose in unifying the country and, it turned out, founded one of the celebrated dynasties in the world.

IV.
Tsar of the Good Old Days: Alexis

1. Hesitant Autocrat

THERE was no question about the right of accession of Alexis Michael-ovitch in 1645. The hereditary principle had been sanctified by the great Sobor of 1613. Like his father, Alexis came to the throne at age sixteen, and also like him, he reigned serenely for just over thirty years. The second Romanov, however, was far better endowed mentally and physically to be ruler than the first. The reign of Good Tsar Alexis is remembered as something of a golden age, this despite the fact that many disasters were barely turned into great successes and despite the fact that Western influences were beginning to rock traditional Russian society to its foundations.

As a prince Alexis had been treated wisely and generously by his father. At age five he was taken away from the female world of the *terem* and given his own household within the Kremlin, including a score of companions his own age and a tutor named Boris Morozov. His childhood possessions were princely for his day, however ordinary they might seem to a Romanov boy two centuries later: toy soldiers, a miniature sleigh, a little wagon, musical instruments, a small set of books, and a suit of armor he soon grew out of. Tradition insisted that Alexis' formal clothing and his Kremlin appointments be costly beyond belief, but the tsarevich grew up to prefer the active life and less formal atmosphere of the royal country house at Izmailovo. Hunting, particularly falconing, became a lifelong enthusiasm of Alexis, as did overseeing the gardens of this palace.

A nineteenth-century Russian artist did a painting of Alexis as tsarevich and successfully rendered the whole manner of his life: The prince is shown as a clean-shaven, long-haired, lithe young man dressed in dark velvet clothes and divided in his preoccupation between the falcon on his wrist and the surrounding clutter of books and foreign gadgets. Active and curious about things, Alexis demonstrated early his two natures about people: a kindness so complete as to gain him genuinely devoted friends and a temper so explosive as to shatter the aplomb of the most exalted boyar.

Alexis' education was merely good for his times, more comprehensive and stimulating than his father's, but still narrow and traditional compared to his successors'. In Morozov he had a tutor of worldly, progressive views who was able to gain Alexis' confidence and to develop his appetite for learning. The tsarevich was taught to read and write, to do arithmetic, and to sing church music. Although he remained ignorant of foreign languages, in time Alexis managed to read everything written in Slavonic, including history books and some recent technical manuals, as well as the lives of the saints and the Bible, newly translated from the Greek. As a young man Alexis tried his hand at poetry, later set down some war memoirs, and also undertook an instruction book for falconers. Alexis' writings did not find their way onto the shelves of major Russian literature, but his taste for florid rhetoric did influence state documents of the day.

The tsarevich had been presented to the Russian public only once, during the next to last year of Michael's reign, and even following his accession Alexis preferred to stay in seclusion, more often than not on one of his hunting estates. The pupil was willing to leave state affairs to his shrewd and capable teacher, and Boris Morozov gained almost complete ascendancy in the Kremlin, especially after the Tsaritsa Eudoxia followed her husband to the grave in 1645. Alexis' self-indulgent freedom was abruptly terminated at the end of his teens by two events in 1648, marriage and a major state crisis.

The burlesque tragedies of the past notwithstanding, in early 1648 Russian high society was treated to the excitement of another royal marriage contest. The two or three hundred comeliest virgins were sent off to Moscow for interviews and health examinations, and when the choice narrowed down to just six maidens, Alexis took an ardent interest in it all. His choice went finally to a Theodosia Vsevolozsky, but he could have spared himself the effort. The bride-to-be promptly fainted, and rival families were quick to establish that this was not just a matter of girlish nerves but a case of deliberately concealed falling sickness (epilepsy). Alexis chose again, this time Maria Miloslavsky, daughter of a typically clever and unscrupulous boyar family who now found themselves very close to throne and fortune. Ten days after Alexis was wed to Maria Miloslavsky, Morozov married her sister Anna, giving himself the ultimate status of brother-in-law to the tsar.

Morozov's prospects proved to be a house of cards, and Alexis' honeymoon was short-lived. On the way back from a pilgrimage to the Trinity

Monastery that summer Alexis and his retinue were stopped by a riotous crowd. The royal bridle was roughly seized, and Alexis was forced to listen to a recital of people's grievances, mostly charges of extortion and high-handedness on the part of Morozov and two newly appointed ministers. The young tsar succeeded in calming the mob with the promise of an inquiry, but moments later he was forced to gallop from the scene under a barrage of stones because some of his young courtiers had been imprudent enough to begin cursing and whipping at the rabble surrounding them. Forthwith an orgy of violence began in Moscow itself: One of the hated ministers was lynched, boyars' houses were attacked, and the foreign quarter was sacked. A mob descended on the mansion of Morozov, who managed to hide from their fury. Not so fortunate was his wife. Her life was spared since she was the tsar's sister-in-law, but she was stripped naked, and her clothes and jewelry were grabbed up by her shamers. The pillagers saw to the destruction of Morozov's beautiful, English-made carriage, one of the two or three Western-style conveyances in Russia.

Inevitably, all the bells of Moscow cut loose, and the howling mob descended on the Kremlin, a scene so familiar and so fateful in recent memory. This time, however, the outcome was not revolution. For one thing, Alexis was guarded by several companies of foreign musketeers, who were promptly deployed menacingly in Red Square. The tsar's extremely popular uncle, Nikita Romanov, was sent out to try politeness and tact with the people, and it worked. The leaders of the crowd declared that they wished no harm to Alexis, only to his evil counselors.

After a few days Alexis saw fit to venture beyond the walls of his citadel and to address his subjects. The crowd received his thanks for revealing the presence of evildoers in the government and his promise to appoint "honest and pleasant men" as new officials. Significantly, Alexis guaranteed the end of oppression by declaring his intention to look after all state affairs himself. As for Morozov, Alexis was poignantly honest, declaring that "I cannot altogether justify him, yet . . . to give him up to death would be most grievous to me." Alexis' tears won him great shouts of allegiance and wishes for his long life. Morozov was merely banished and soon brought back as a secret and subordinate adviser.

The Moscow riots of 1648 were just the beginning of a wave of insurrectionary protest. Pskov and Novgorod each were completely taken over the next year by rioters, who opened the prisons and heaped outrage on outrage for weeks on end. Beatings, chains, torture, and death were visited, not only on tax collectors and governors, but on high clerics and foreign ambassadors. The events happened to bring to the fore the Metropolitan of Novgorod, named Nikon. Although he had been nearly murdered in his own cathedral for excommunicating the rioters, Nikon wrote to Alexis advising him to be compassionate in dealing with the situation. This cleric was also realistic enough to admit that the rebels would simply take over the whole area if the government tried to reply to violence with what small forces it had. Alexis wisely followed Nikon's advice: Amnesties were rapidly forthcoming and wholesale; punishments few and much later.

The disorders in Muscovy were matched by a great Cossack uprising beyond the border in the Ukraine, an event Alexis later turned to his profit. At the time, however, the tsar was terrified that a new Time of Troubles had begun, especially since there was a pretender to the throne on hand. This man, Timothy Ankudinov, claimed to be the son of Basil Shuisky and therefore legitimate successor of an anointed tsar. He got some attention at Krakow and at Rome, until he was revealed as a thief, arsonist, and sexual pervert.

The near anarchy, which lasted well over a year, produced one immediate result, the *uloshenie* (law code) of 1649 revising that of Yaroslav. This was rushed to completion by a fearful assemblage of the privileged classes meeting in the Kremlin, the last important Zemsky Sobor to be held. Guided by Prince Odoievsky, whose family were counted first among the Rurikovichi, the codemakers provided fierce penalties for treason to the state and dire punishments for disobedient serfs (the use of the knout was mentioned 142 times). The first major document in Russian vernacular, rather than Church Slavonic, Alexis' law code lasted until 1833.

Alexis' decision to play the active autocrat was reaffirmed by events from another quarter, oddly enough from England. A Russian envoy arrived in London toward the end of the great Civil War, and he simply could not believe that King Charles I was being held prisoner and therefore was unavailable to him. Even though the parliamentary leaders doffed their hats in the proper manner at the mention of the tsar's name, the Russian envoy refused to hand over his credentials and allowed himself to be confined. When the news of this and of the execution of the king reached Alexis, the tsar abruptly canceled all English trading privileges within Russia. His angry pronouncement said: "You English have done a great wickedness by killing your Sovereign king Charles, for which evil deed you cannot be suffered to remain in the realm of Muscovy." Some years later an envoy from Cromwell arrived in Moscow and was roundly lectured for his trouble. Alexis backed up his words with action: Royalist agents for the later King Charles II were presented with 5,000 rubles' worth of grain, which they wanted badly, and 15,000 rubles' worth of furs, which they did not want but took.

By the early 1650's state documents were using the revived styles of unlimited, divinely based autocracy. Also, Alexis felt strong enough after 1653 to dispense with the periodic Zemsky Sobors. Finally, the tsar was able to subordinate the power of the boyars' Duma using these words to describe this development to Nikon in 1652. "Now they listen to me and things get done without discussion and argument." Alexis' notes on the meetings with his boyars were later discovered: Interestingly, they contain not only the questions the tsar intended to ask, but also the answers he expected to receive; rare was the problem left for open-ended discussion.

The ouster of Morozov and the assumption of personal power by Alexis did not mean that this tsar would conduct a one-man show for the rest of his reign. Rather, one of Alexis' great strengths as a ruler was his ability to discover gifted subordinates and to allow them an almost free hand when it suited his purpose. In this way three of the most brilliant and able statesmen of pre-Petrine Russia were brought to the fore: the religious reformer Nikon, the successful diplomat Athanasy Ordyn-Nashchokin, and the cultural Westernizer Artamon Matveev. Each of these men in turn seconded Alexis in one of the three major roles the tsar would assume during his reign.

Alexis' strength as a ruler was limited not by other men, but by his own character. The man who emerged in the 1650's was a paradoxical combination of gentleness and irascibility. The nearsighted chroniclers of the day called Alexis the mildest of all the tsars, but this title surely was better deserved by his father. Usually, the second Romanov ruler was kindly, unassuming, easygoing, loving, and love-inspiring, at time so seemingly meek and eager to please that some officials wished that he were gruff and overbearing. At other times the same Alexis was in the grip of a passionate rage or tantrum, what old-fashioned historians liked to call a paroxysm. The tsar's excitability could so much get the better of him that he would curse and even assault people around him. The verbal abuse did not go much further than expressions like "son of Satan," but it flowed in torrents. One account we have of Alexis' resort to physical violence is the time he seized his uncle Miloslavsky by the beard, punched him all over, and then booted him out of the boyars' meeting. In Alexis' favor, he did not hold grudges, or, in the rhetoric of the time, "the sun never went down on the wrath of the Gosudar." To be a great ruler, Alexis was, perhaps, too ready to take the path of least resistance, too willing to placate his foolish old uncle with gifts, and too sociable and indulgent of others. The tsar was indulgent of himself, too, his devotion to his comforts often negating his conscientious desire to run things. "Amiable," without connotation of weakness or colorlessness, is the word for Tsar Alexis.

2. Reluctant Reformer of the Church

The force of events, not force of character in the tsar, caused Alexis' reign to be the time when the Russian Orthodox Church split wide open. There were two permanent results of the split: The official church became an unhealthy dependent of the state, and the heretical offshoots of Orthodoxy nurtured millions of Russian citizens essentially disloyal to the Romanovs.

In a sense, it is appropriate that it was Alexis who presided over these momentous developments, for he was a pious tsar. Most of the male rulers of Russia and all the tsaritsas without exception are described as pious. Alexis really was pious, not mechanical in his devotions like his father or rebellious about faith like his famous son. Perhaps the tsar's piety might best be defined by likening him to some familiar English kings: He had something of the I-love-God-and-all-men devoutness of Henry VI, endower of monasteries; he had something of the I-will-not-be-thwarted-in-things-religious stance of Henry VIII, expert on both heresy and wives; and finally, he had something of the I-can-argue-Scripture-better-than-any-man attitude of James I, "the wisest fool in Christendom." Alexis was perhaps unique in his wont to dictate to secretaries during mass, but he was simply demonstrating his conviction that state business was God's business.

A legal suppression of popular amusements, what we today call blue laws, was the first of Alexis' innovations in the name of religion. There is a touch of Cromwell here, and indeed, it is a great coincidence that the English Puritans banned the Maypoles and the theater at precisely the same time that new austerity swept over Russia. Joylessness under Cromwell lasted even less time than Alexis' Puritanism (a word once aptly defined as a nagging worry that somebody someplace is having a good time). Specifically, the tsar was persuaded by his chaplain and by the fanatical Patriarch Joseph that the riots and troubles of 1648–1649 were a result of the "diabolical" amusements of a people who, in actuality, had little to be frivolous about. The clerics reinforced their arguments with references from the famous *Domostroy* (Foundation of the Home), which was surely familiar to Alexis as a sixteenth-century masterpiece of literature and as the moralizing work of a very guilt-ridden, pleasure-hating, and misogynistic priest named Sylvester. The resulting decrees of 1649, which were read in every church and marketplace, banned the following things: tobacco, all musical instruments, cards, dice, jugglers, jesters, soothsayers, dancing bears, performing dogs, masks, devilish songs, dirty jokes, seesaws, boxing (the Moscow free-for-alls produced many fatalities), the taking of baths outdoors during thunderstorms, and, finally, gazing at the moon during the first night of any month. Punishments ranged from fines to prison or even mutilation. Later an effort was made to close the taverns, but drunkenness, a really great social evil in Russia that foreign observers found appalling, was a vice too dear to the hearts of tax collectors and priests alike. The tsar gave up fewer pleasures than his subjects: The jugglers and performers were not seen in the palace for twenty years, but Alexis allowed jesters on special occasions and secreted his storytellers where he could visit them anytime. Alexis did not consider giving up hunting as a sinful amusement, nor did he cease his many contacts with heretic foreigners.

The fateful and lasting religious reform of Alexis, revision of the rituals, was accomplished under the influence not of Puritanism but of enlightenment. The leader of the reform was Nikon—self-educated monk from the northeast, resourceful Metropolitan of Novgorod during the 1649 riots, patron of learning, and endower of many monasteries. Nikon, appointing himself Alexis' conscience, persuaded the tsar, for example, to send him with a memorial of apology to the Solovotsky Monastery where lay the remains of a patriarch martyred by an earlier tsar. Alexis was capable of writing his friend words like "so vile are my deeds that I am not fit to be a dog let alone a tsar."

The patriarchate became vacant in 1652, and Alexis wrote Nikon to that effect in rhetoric typical of him:

> Elect and immovable Pastor and Guardian of our souls and bodies, gracious, kind, benevolent, guileless, and well-beloved child of Christ . . . my own beloved familiar friend and yoke-fellow . . . the great shining sun, the most holy Nikon . . . it has pleased the creator to take unto himself from the false and treacherous world . . . [the Patriarch Joseph, whereby] our Mother the Holy Apostolic Church hath become a widow.

A synod duly elected the tsar's friend and only candidate, but Nikon flatly refused to be patriarch, reviving a familiar drama. The final scene was when Alexis ordered the boyars and clergy to drag Nikon to the cathedral by force, whereupon all fell at his feet and wept. Nikon wept himself and made the following speech:

> You know that in the beginning we received the Holy Gospels, the traditions of the Holy Apostles, the canons of the Holy Fathers, and the imperial laws from orthodox Greece, and thereafter were called Christians. But of a truth we have followed neither the evangelic precepts nor the canons . . . nor the laws as to religion of the Greek tsars. . . . If it seem good to you that I should be your Patriarch, give me your word, and make a vow in this cathedral church before God our Saviour and His Most Pure Mother and before the angels and all the saints that ye will keep the evangelic dogma and observe the canons.

The ultimatum to reform was delivered and accepted: Nikon was consecrated the sixth patriarch in August, 1652, at the age of forty-seven. In an unprecedented move, Alexis promised to obey Nikon in all that he taught on dogma, discipline, and custom.

The Nikonian reforms involved not theology, but details of ritual and liturgy where Russian practice over the centuries had parted from the Greek original. What became truly life-or-death issues were such things as how many fingers should be used when crossing oneself (two or three), how many iotas in the spelling of the name Jesus, or how many allelulias at some part of the service. For another example, there was the chanted phrase "the true and life-giving Holy Spirit," which Nikon restored simply to "Holy Spirit." It was not just a picky desire to be correct that was Nikon's motivation, however, but rather the most far-reaching sense of mission. Only if all signs of backwardness and unenlightenment were removed from the church could the Russian patriarch claim leadership over the other four patriarchs and thus pursue the grandiose goal of uniting all the Orthodox peoples. Only with a reformed church could Moscow truly claim to be the "third Rome."

The people stirred up by the Nikonian reforms, later known as the Old Believers, cherished the Russian practices and distrusted Greek learning as the work of crypto-Catholics, loose livers, and place seekers. Ironically, it was the Russian texts and rites they considered sacrosanct that were, in fact, relatively new and the Greek "novelties" genuinely old, but nonetheless, the Old Believers became convinced that they were keeping the faith uncontaminated and that the reformers, with tsar and patriarch at their head, represented the Anti-Christ.

Greatest of the anti-Nikonians was the priest Avvakum, at once the most fearless and sublime and the most xenophobic and narrow-minded of men. Born at Nizhni Novgorod in 1619 and raised in mean circumstances, Avvakum made himself into the most eloquent preacher of his day and, by the 1650's, had a prosperous Moscow church as a base from which to speak against the patriarch. A man who could hold his hand in the flames to conquer his desire for a woman was the kind of fanatic who would yield to no amount of reasoning, even by Alexis personally, about correct ritual. Nikon had Avvakum seized in his canonicals, put in a dungeon, banished to Tobolsk, and later sent him on a seemingly suicidal journey to the Chinese border. His many followers were persecuted cruelly, but Avvakum was by no means defeated yet.

Another leading anti-Nikonian was the rich boyarina Theodosia Morozova, sister-in-law of Boris Morozov and related closely enough to the tsar to have had the fifth place of honor at his christening. Finding herself at age thirty a widow with 30 domestics and 8,000 serfs, Morozova devoted her life to religious argument and to charity. The Morozova mansion was opened to all manner of pilgrims, orphans, and poor people, whom the owner cared for personally, and it was also the center of pro-Avvakum propaganda. "The lioness among the foxes" of the opposition, in Alexis' own phrase, Morozova, by virtue of her position, was temporarily safe from persecution.

Alexis would have done well to have read about Becket and Henry II.

Nikon had become "a ravening bear in the forest" about suspected heretics. The patriarch's concern for the true faith led him into a campaign against foreign-inspired icons, and his jumping up and down on some revered examples was so crudely sacrilegious that Alexis had to intervene in protest. The patriarch's zeal was excessive, and so was his arrogance. He had been allowed to style himself Great Lord, just like Philaret, and he made the mistake of trying really to share power. Nikon did everything possible to exalt the majesty of the church at the expense of the state with attention-getting devices such as the enrichment of clerical costumes, the reburial of relics, the entertainment of foreign patriarchs, and the embellishment of monasteries. Alexis suddenly became aware that his friend was eclipsing his tsarish dignity. And so the reformer went—but not the reforms.

The fall of the patriarch came about in 1658 after incidents such as Nikon's being left out of a state dinner, a messenger's having his head broken, and Alexis' being absent from a major ritual. Nikon, feeling unappreciated, left Moscow dressed as a simple monk to await events at the Voskresensky Monastery. Alexis ignored him, refusing to let the scene of 1652 be repeated, but fearing to go so far as to remove him. There were attempts at reconciliation, but many worked assiduously to widen the breach, notably the boyer Streshnev, who earned the patriarch's solemn curse for naming his pet dog Patriarch Nikon and teaching him to give the blessing. Late in 1664 Nikon and a large retinue made a sudden nighttime descent on the Kremlin, took over the services going on in the cathedral, and sent a lordly summons to the tsar. This crude attempt to terrorize Alexis failed, as did anathematizing the royal family (Alexis' plaint at this was: "I know I am a great sinner but what have my wife and children done to be cursed?"). A church council in 1666 finally deposed Nikon. The charges against him included reviling the tsar, illegally deposing bishops, exalting the church above the state, and abusing his servants. The sentence was banishment to a place far away. In time Alexis relented and asked the blessing of his old friend, which he got, and the tsar began to send Nikon delicacies from his own table and a sable coat in the name of the new Tsarevich Peter. The once-domineering cleric soon asked Alexis' forgiveness and wrote him that a vision of God had revealed to him his new career as healer of the sick, a role he played devotedly until his death in 1681.

Nikon's ouster was political. His religious opponents in time fared much worse than he. In 1662 the boyarina Morozova and others secured the recall of Avvakum from exile and his reestablishment in a Kremlin church. For a while Alexis was a frequent and respectful visitor of the one he called angel of God, but Avvakum's pigheadedness was merely encouraged to the point where he pontificated that babes knew more than the Greek scholars and that all Nikonians should be rebaptized. These indiscretions led to his second banishment, this time to the shores of the White Sea. In 1667 the same group that deposed Nikon declared Avvakum a heretic and condemned him, along with several of his followers, to the loss of their tongues and right arms and to exile in the northernmost village of Russia. The tsaritsa had the mutilation sentence stayed, and Avvakum's final martyrdom came only after more troublemaking in the next reign.

The death of Alexis' first wife in 1669 was a great blow to the Old Believers and the occasion of his remarriage a disaster for their leader and his kinswoman Morozova. The boyarina's absence from the wedding (pleading health, but whispering that the bride was a "heretic") infuriated the tsar, who exploded: "Would she put herself against us? She will find that one of us must give way!" Taken in chains before a tribunal, Morozova was grandly defiant, sneering at them: "It is plain ye are the followers of Nikon, the enemy of God who hath spewed forth his heresies like vomit, which filth ye now lick up." On the way back to her dungeon, Morozova caught sight of Alexis spying on her from a window: Avvakum's greatest devotee promptly crossed herself with two fingers and kissed her chains. The torture of her devoted dependents nearly broke down the indomitable boyarina, who herself silently suffered exposure half-naked before a crowd, prolonged flogging, and finally torture in the form of alternate applications of fire and ice. The ecclesiastics on Alexis' council wanted her burned alive, but the boyars were opposed on the ground of their class privilege, and the actual death of Morozova, together with her sister, came about as the result of starvation in their place of exile.

In a last letter to his fanatic and rebellious kinswoman, Alexis begged Morozova to accept the chief reform, the crossing of oneself with three fingers. "Righteous mother, for the people's sake do me this honor," he wrote. "I the Tsar render thee homage." It is hard to believe such a ruler found himself presiding over the self-destruction of the Russian Church, the degrading of the patriarch, and the departure of many of the flock.

The religious turmoil of Alexis' time saw two great movements fight each other to mutual exhaustion, with the spiritual society the loser and the secular state the winner. Nikon was a theocrat whose exaltation of the church hierarchy related him to the ideas of the Catholic Counterreformation currently taking place in the West, while Avvakum was a fundamentalist not unlike some of the evangelical Protestants of the day. Yet both men held themselves untainted by foreign influences and sought for Alexis to restore a pure "Russian" church. The tsar merely succeeded in creating an official church, in the end receiving with satisfaction the new patriarch's declaration that he was prepared to obey orders in all matters.

The schismatics were to plague the dynasty to the end. Old Believers ensconced in the Kremlin's Belfry of Ivan the Great took to raining down stones on Alexis as he took part in religious processions. Many thousands of the unreconstructed faithful barricaded themselves in the wooden country churches, and the bells warning of the approach of the tsar's troops were a signal for mass self-immolations. Russia's second greatest monastery, the Solovetsky on the White Sea, resisted the bombardment of a royal army for the eight years from 1668 to 1676.

3. Haphazard Conqueror

Tsar Alexis made large territorial annexations. His diplomatic and military efforts were complex and protracted, and they occurred simultaneously with the unfolding of the internal religious struggle, making it almost impossible to unravel Alexis' reign simply and chronologically. Yet the territorial and ecclesiastical problems were far from unrelated. The triumphant capture of Kiev was preceded by the appropriation of Kievan-Greek scholarship. The Orthodox souls of the Cossacks and of the Polish-ruled Russian peoples were as precious gains to Alexis as their taxpaying bodies.

At the outset of Alexis' reign Russia was still hemmed in on all sides and virtually landlocked but for the precarious White Sea outlet (Archangel was icebound half the year). Sweden blocked access to the Baltic; Poland-Lithuania stood firm in the center; and the Crimean Tatars, backed by the Ottoman sultan, denied Russia the southern steppes and a coastline on the Black Sea. The puzzle was first unlocked for Alexis by the independent actions of the Zaporogian Cossacks, a force of roughly 50,000 renegade Russians who were settled on the steppes on both sides of the Dnieper River and who maintained an uneasy freedom from Poles, Tatars, and Russians alike. Tsar Alexis won over these Cossacks and, even though he suffered more defeats than victories, became the first Romanov conqueror through the ill luck of his enemies.

Bogdan Khmelnitsky was a Zaporogian Cossack chieftain who had been robbed and abused by his Polish overlords. The revenge he took was monumental. In 1648 Khmelnitsky started a revolt on the lower Dnieper, stirring up first the runaways and Tatars in the area and then gaining over to his cause the Cossack settlements to the north. Three large Polish armies sent against him were ambushed and cut to pieces, after which Khmelnitsky sacked Kiev. His followers then ranged throughout Eastern Europe, massacring some 200,000 Jews, in the greatest single catastrophe for these people until Hitler. Warsaw itself seemed the next helpless victim, and late in 1648 Poland had to buy off Khmelnitsky with the title of Cossack Hetman and huge gifts of liquor. Three years later, however, Khmelnitsky's army was surprised and crushed by the Poles, ending all hope for an independent Cossackdom. Khmelnitsky forthwith turned to "the Lord's anointed," the Muscovite tsar, and by the historic Convention of Pereyaslavl in 1654 pledged Cossack allegiance to Alexis. Although Alexis offered the Cossacks his protection, his agents refused to bind him to respect their privileges, saying that it was not customary for an autocrat to make promises to his subjects. Ever since Khmelnitsky and Pereyaslavl, scholars and politicians, tsarist and Soviet alike, have argued whether the convention gave Russia binding control over what is now the Ukraine.

The allegiance of the Cossacks led to the Thirteen Years' War between Poland and Russia, which started in 1654. Although Alexis was far above rubbing shoulders with the unruly Cossacks as Tsar Dmitri the Pretender had done, he feared what would happen if the Orthodox Cossacks were overwhelmed by Poland or, worse still, seduced by the Moslems. The war also had the aspect of a religious crusade against Catholic Poland. The actual pretext for opening hostilities, however, was that the Polish government had allowed the publication of books calling Russia barbarian and unchristian and poor and also casting doubts on Alexis' title. The Poles atoned to the extent of burning the offending pages, but this was the fate Alexis demanded for the authors. The declaration of war came at an extraordinary service at the Cathedral of the Annunciation, when it was announced that Alexis had prayed long to God and the Virgin and had consulted Nikon and the boyars before asking to have the plan of campaign blessed on the altar. Alexis then adjured his generals to live pure lives and to show mercy to their own soldiers, and he served them ceremonial drink in the order of their precedence. "And this I tell you boldly," he said, "if you participate at the deathless table, the angels of the Lord will encamp about your hosts." The tsar emotionally pressed to his breast the head of the commander in chief, a man described as "wise in the Holy Scriptures and fortunate in war and a terror to his enemies." The general wept and did obeisance thirty times, after which Alexis handed out mead to the common soldiers, their pledge of devotion to the death making Alexis shed tears.

The tsar went to the front in person, an unusual and brave thing. His best general, Prince Trubetskoy, won striking victories over his Lithuanian opponent Prince Radziwill, and Smolensk fell the first year. Then came a Russian defeat, and many towns repledged their allegiance to Poland because of the plunderings, desecrations, and other excesses of the Russian soldiers. Alexis returned to Moscow to pray over the relics and to reassure the boyars. As it turned out, the Thirteen Years' War surpassed in brutality and horror even the Thirty Years' War, just barely terminated in Germany, and cost Muscovy one-third of its population, largely the result of plague. An English doctor reported that the surviving women in Moscow outnumbered men 10 to 1, but Alexis' crusade went on implacably.

The whole aspect of the war changed in 1655, when King Charles X of Sweden intervened in Poland, drove out King John Casimir, and occupied

most of the country, including Warsaw and Krakow. At first this development aided Russian armies, but then Sweden began to take away Alexis'
newly won towns. In 1656 Alexis led an army into Swedish Livonia, on
which occasion Nikon blessed the terrible Cossacks and hoped that they
would seize Stockholm. Some Swedish forts were taken, but Alexis was
forced to witness ghastly losses in the futile Russian siege of Riga.

Alexis' military troubles were compounded when a sudden national revival in Poland restored King John Casimir and drove the Swedes into the
sea. In 1660 the Poles made complete peace with Sweden, mutually freeing
their armies to strike at Russia. Previously, Khmelnitsky's successor as
Hetman of the Ukraine had gone over to Poland, and in 1659 a combined
Cossack-Tatar army had annihilated a large Russian force at Konotop.
Alexis went into mourning and fortified Moscow.

At this low point in Russian fortunes, Alexis had a major decision
to make. Should he make peace with Poland or with Sweden? Which was
the main enemy? The case for peace with Poland, even at the price of
ceding back everything, was made by the man who had replaced Nikon as
Alexis' chief adviser and friend, Athanasy Ordyn-Nashchokin. Here was a
man who had risen almost all the way from the bottom: son of a clerk in
Pskov; self-educated student of Western languages; diplomat under Tsar
Michael; hero as governor of Pskov against the rebels of 1650; and successful general in 1657. Ordyn had foreign policy ideas of world scope and
sought the thorough militarization of Russia, but his great contention was
that Russia needed the Swedish Baltic ports far more than it needed Polish
real estate. For this conception Ordyn was later hailed as a forerunner of
Peter the Great, while Alexis was called shortsighted for eventually giving
in to the national hatred toward Poland and deciding against any concessions. "It is indecent to feed dogs with a single scrap of Orthodox bread,"
Alexis once declared. In 1661 Alexis made peace with Sweden, restoring
everything held in Livonia and on the Baltic, and Ordyn was allowed to
resign.

The 1660's saw great disasters for Alexis somehow turned into ultimate
success. The Poles won a huge victory at Zeromak in 1661, causing a Russian loss of 19,000 men, ten cannons, and the "Miraculous Icon of the
Mother of God," the last "especially lamented by Tsar Alexis." All Lithuania was regained by the enemy, and after Prince Sheremetev surrendered
a whole army in 1662, Kiev and Pereyaslavl were once again out of Russian
hands. There were widespread desertions in the army, particularly over the
matter of their payment in debased copper coinage. The coinage fraud,
whereby the government would not accept back its own money, implicated
several of Alexis' relatives and produced riots in Moscow, followed by
7,000 executions. (Alexis cleverly, if tactlessly, turned the situation to

some profit by having the worthless money melted down to make a splendid railing for one of the Kremlin terraces.)

Ordyn-Nashchokin came back into favor, but his offers to negotiate were at first curtly rejected by the seemingly unbeatable Poles. In time, however, Poland found itself once again under attack by the fickle Cossacks, and the republic returned to its usual state of feudal anarchy. Peace negotiations with Russia were begun at Andrusovo, and in 1667 Ordyn was able to report back to Alexis that he had won gains "contrary to all human expectations." Russia received the Cossack lands east of the Dnieper, the city of Kiev (technically for two years only but never given up), all territories lost by the 1618 truce, notably Smolensk, and more besides in Lithuania. Additional revenues of 10,000,000 rubles were in store for Alexis, while Ordyn was rewarded with the title of near boyar and posts equivalent to making him chancellor. In the following years Alexis presented himself as candidate for the Polish throne, but this was asking too much of the hereditary enemy.

In the same year that the Peace of Andrusovo confirmed Alexis' control of the Zaporogian Cossacks of the West, there was an uprising against the tsar by the Don Cossacks of the East, an upheaval that shook the Russian state almost as badly as the Time of Troubles. If there had been foreign interference at this juncture, Russia might have gone the way of Poland, but Alexis was fortunate again.

The revolt began in 1667 along the Volga River under the leadership of a truly magnetic, singularly unscrupulous, and atrociously cruel Cossack adventurer named Stenka Razin. Caravans were the first targets. Then a government post suffered massacre—after Razin gained entry disguised as a pilgrim. The marauders were next emboldened to sail out into the Caspian Sea in 1668, and Razin spent a year ravaging Persia, bringing back a Persian princess and later receiving the tsar's pardon for everything. In 1670 Razin, in a ceremonial act, decided that he owed more to the Volga than to his princess, whom he threw overboard, and that he enjoyed rebellion more than the good wishes of the tsar, whose envoy he murdered. With a new army of Don Cossacks he seized the city of Tsaritsyn (later known as Stalingrad) and defeated two armies sent against him. After pondering an attack on Moscow itself, Razin sailed south to capture the great port of Astrakhan, the city letting him in without resistance. At Astrakhan Razin slaughtered hundreds of boyars who had taken refuge in a church and destroyed the *Orel,* Russia's first warship, which had taken three years to build at the cost of 9,021 rubles. After proclaiming a republic, the Cossack chief went on a three-week drunk.

Razin later moved north again and handily captured the cities of Saratov, Samara, and Simbirsk. His proclamation of a social war caused thousands of serfs throughout the region to rise up and do violence to the landowners and clergy. "I do not want to be your tsar," Razin declared. "I would live among you as a brother." Just in case people did have any old loyalties left, however, Razin made it known that his entourage included none other than the Tsarevich Alexis (in reality recently dead) and Patriarch Nikon (in exile, of course).

There was no question of apathy among the boyars in the face of such a threat, and the tsar found able commanders. Razin was first checked at Simbirsk in 1671, and his flight became a rout in which more than 100,000 Cossacks and serfs were killed. In the end it was the jealous elders of the more settled Don Cossacks who had Razin handed over to the tsar's agents. Brought to Moscow, the man of the people endured with bravado the ultimate in torture, having his ribs unjointed by red-hot pincers, and was quartered, still alive, in June, 1671.

To Alexis, Razin was simply a bandit, an "outlaw from God," and a traitor. To many of the tsar's subjects however, here was a bold champion, and Razin's legend grew apace to lend precedent to other revolts against the Romanovs. The last tsar, for example, might profitably have pondered the celebrated huge canvas by Repin showing a powerfully built Razin glowering from the midships of his small boat.

4. Gentle Innovator

Tsar Alexis married a second time in January, 1671, the year of Razin's capture and only four years after the glorious outcome of the war with Poland. A measure of peace was achieved also on the domestic religious front, for it was the tsar's wedding which led to the destruction of the out-spoken boyarina Morozova. At the age of forty-two Alexis almost deliberately began a new phase of his reign, one given over to pleasure and the promotion of Western innovations.

The tsar's remarriage came after the traditional assembling of socially eligible virgins, sixty on this occasion, but the boyars and their wives did not need to brace themselves, for the contest had been decided long before by Alexis. The bride was Natalia Naryshkina, ward of the royal councilor Matveev, who, with his Scots wife, had given the girl an education both careful and unusual by Russian standards. (Natalia was the daughter of a Scots royalist refugee from Puritanism.) Alexis was completely captivated when he first met the beautiful, vivacious, and seemingly intelligent young girl at the Matveev mansion, and he coyly reassured her that "little pigeon, I will find thee a suitable mate." The royal ring was presented the next day. Following the marriage ceremony, it was observed that Alexis seemed more a lovesick youth than a middle-aged husband.

Significant changes in court life followed. Ordyn-Nashchokin, who presumed too much on his indispensability as a diplomat and complained too much of his enemies, was nudged out of power to useful retirement as a monk in Kiev, the city that was his greatest gain for Russia. It was no surprise that his successor as near boyar was Matveev, a man less ambitious and more tactful with the prejudices of the powerful and the stupid. Matveev —following Morozov, Nikon, and Ordyn—was the last and also the greatest of the Westernizers of Alexis' reign. Of obscure background, he entered the royal service an accomplished scholar, one imbued with the newest ideas, one free of old superstitions, and one creative in his own right. Matveev wore Western-style clothes, and his house was an oasis of contemporary Western decor set down, as it were, in another country and another age. A complete novelty for Moscow were the at homes the Matveevs gave: There were paintings to look at; there was smart conversation; and the women entered into things freely (Matveev's wife even dared drive about in a carriage). Missing from the scene was the dead drunkenness, so much a Russian ritual.

Royal sponsorship of theater, beginning in 1672, symbolized the end of the austere phase of Alexis' reign and the hastening of his advance on the path of Western culture, a progress which sometimes surprised the tsar himself. Spectacles of any sort had been condemned in the *Domostroy,* a position fiercely defended by Alexis' first tsaritsa, although as early as 1664 Alexis encouraged the production of a "handsome Comedie in Prose" by the first ambassador to be sent by Restoration England. Now Alexis chose openly to patronize playwriting in order to please his new young bride. With the consent of the tsar's confessor, the first theater was built at Preobrazhenskoe, the wooden country palace, and winter weather soon dictated the construction of a second hall of comedy in a boyar's mansion within the Kremlin itself.

The German Liberty was the source of many changes. During the Puritan reaction of 1652 Alexis had been advised by the patriarch to expel all the foreigners in Moscow, their presence causing frequent popular outbursts, but the tsar decreed merely that the aliens be kept confined to one section in the southeast of the capital. The German Liberty soon overflowed its bounds physically, and its influence reached the court, causing Alexis to develop a passion for such things as gilded carriages, brass bands, and mechanical toys for his children. The pastor of the Lutheran Church went so far as to address an ode to "the incomparable tsar . . . who loves our German people more than the Russians."

There developed a bizarre mixture of the old and the new at court, notably in the case of music. A novelty at Alexis' second wedding, music became an essential feature of the great banquets held with the traditional style and sumptuousness of Tsar Michael. Baroque, polyphonic singing and instrumentation were allowed to mingle with the Russian forms of chant, the resulting cacophony, according to an English observer, being like "a flight of screech owls, a nest of jackdaws, a pack of hungry wolves, seven hogs on a windy day, and as many cats."

In art and architecture, too, innovations came apace. Alexis ordered the painting of a "Book of Titled Figures," a work striking not only for the naturalism of the pictures but also for the fact that rulers other than the Russian tsars were represented. It took considerable argument by the scholar Simeon Polotsky to bring about change in the stiff and stylized forms of icon painting, but Alexis gave in and the Russian icon masters, transferred to the Kremlin armory, were encouraged to experiment. Illustrations from the German Piscator Bible soon adorned the walls of the tsarevich's apartment. Alexis went so far as to hire an official portrait painter, who, with others, produced panels which were to give later generations some notion of the human characteristics of Alexis, his bride, Matveev, and leading boyars of the day. In the later years of Alexis' reign architectural endeavor in the Kremlin was centered not on church building but on the envoys' *prikaz,* the director of which had a greater taste for clocks than for icons.

Innovations in architecture were to be found at Alexis' favorite summer residence at Izmailovo. Here a new Baroque entrance led to a layout of gardens which included windmills, canals, cages for animals, and pavilions designed for nothing more serious than relaxation. At Izmailovo Alexis showed that his devotion to hunting was rivaled only by his passion for gardening. Again the lover of the curious and the luxurious shows through, since the tsar was proud to be the producer of such things as Bokhara melons, Hungarian pears, figs, almonds, pepper, cotton, and mulberries. It could hardly be said that the tsar was conducting an agricultural experiment station in order to uplift the peasants. Rather he had been made envious by a report of the magnificence of certain gardens in Florence.

During the late 1660's Alexis had rebuilt yet another palace outside Moscow, Kolomenskoe, and this wooden marvel also had its great gardens and its incongruities. Seen from a distance, Kolomenskoe appeared a huge fairy-tale assemblage in the Russian manner with hundreds of onion domes, tent roofs, horseshoe arches, and spires. But close at hand it was startlingly new: Three thousand mica windows dispelled the memory of Kremlin gloom and frescoes and portraits instructed the visitor in the classical, rather than the Biblical, glories. There were many mirrors—a shocking novelty in themselves—Western-style furniture, and such mechanical devices as a throne flanked by a pair of ferociously performing metal lions.

Alexis' enthusiasms were spread thin, and his admiration for things European was often confined to gadgets, but it is undeniable that his reign did much to secularize Russia and to hasten the end of its isolation from the rest of the world. For example, a sort of postal service abroad was opened by Ordyn in 1665, and even if Russian censors opened all the letters without fail, it was a step forward both commercially and spiritually. A great embassy was sent to the Western capitals in 1672 to announce the birth of the tsar's son Peter, a move indicating the desire for wider contacts and prefiguring that very person's famous continental tour less than twenty years later. New interest was also shown in the other direction, the Far East. The first great trade caravan to China in 1667 brought back not only exotic goods, including tea (destined to become the Russian national drink), but also reports on Confucianism. In 1676 an interpreter from the envoys' *prikaz* was sent as an ambassador to Peking; there were immediately Russian-Chinese recriminations over titles, the celestial emperor not being able to conceive of the tsar as other than his tributary.

It was under Alexis that Russian secular intellectuals first became acutely aware of the problem of the *Russian* versus the *Western*. Simeon Polotsky, a monk, a poet, and the most learned man of his times, brought Kievan scholarship to Moscow in the 1650's. He became the influential tutor of Alexis' children, male and female, and was secure enough in his position to make a wholesale denunciation of the ignorance of the Muscovite clergy. Not so fortunate was Gregory Kotoshikhin, an undersecretary in the envoys' *prikaz,* who chose to flee Russia after such incidents as being flogged for making a mistake in inscribing Alexis' title. Abroad, Kotoshikhin set down his hurts in *Concerning Russia in the Reign of Aleksei Mikhailovich* and made quite explicit his belief that Western civilization was far superior to that of his native land. Russian ineptness in trade, the boyars' general fear of education, and the harsh penalties for unauthorized travel abroad were singled out by Kotoshikhin as evidence that this society should be drastically changed. Still another intellectual of the era was an immigrant Serb, Yury Krizhanich, who at one point enjoyed the position of Alexis' librarian only later to find himself banished to Siberia. Unlike Kotoshikhin, Krizhanich believed that Russian culture was unique and basically valuable, that Alexis' full autocracy was a desirable thing, that Orthodoxy had a great mission among the Slavs, that the borders should be kept closed, and that borrowings from the West were necessary only in limited areas. Krizhanich thus took an intellectual stand somewhere between the emulators of the West and the benighted mass of Russian society who were inordinately proud of themselves and feared "cleverness from beyond the seas" like the plague.

At the very end of his reign Alexis had some second thoughts and reinstated the penalties for foreign dress and for shaving. The tsar died peacefully in early 1676, genuinely mourned by all his family and associates. His demise, coming but a few days after the surrender of the Old Believer hold-outs at the Solovetsky Monastery, was taken by some as a portent, and as Alexis' punishment for giving in to foreign ways so much.

Alexis Michaelovich Romanov had been an easygoing man called to preside over a turbulent era. Hesitant at first and somewhat lazy about ruling later, nonetheless, he felt compelled to use the full powers of the autocracy, the law, and the army to curb the social disorders of 1648 and Razin's powerful bid for anarchy in 1669. The tsar, who once had treated Nikon as an associate and Avvakum as a saint, ended up firmly prosecuting both parties in the church schism. The reign of a man horrified at blood-shed and inept at strategy saw great slaughters and great annexations. The final paradox was that the Russian frontiers were opened to revolutionary Western influences under the regime of a tsar who was later made the symbol of traditional etiquette, Russian piety, and such feudal virtues as love of the chase.

V.

A Struggle of Brothers and Sisters

1. Fedor III

A T the time of the death of Tsar Alexis in 1676 the Kremlin apartments were generously populated with Romanovs and Romanov kin. Unfortunately, however, Alexis' two marriages, first to a Miloslavsky and then to a Naryshkin, meant two bitterly rival factions within the dynasty. The backbiting and intrigues that began among the variously related females in the *terem* soon involved the whole Moscow court in violent coups and countercoups. The ultimate arbiters of power, the *streltsi* and the mob in Red Square, made the most of the turmoil for two decades. It was almost a full century before Russia and the dynasty put behind them the last complications caused by the two Alexievich families.

There had been thirteen children by the first wife, Maria Miloslavsky. The sons were sickly without exception, and of them Alexis, Dmitri, and Sergius had predeceased the father. Alexis the younger (born 1654) had been an exceptional tsarevich, remembered for his bookishness and for his sweetness. The best minds in Russia—like Polotsky and Ordyn-Nashchokin —had been appointed his tutors, and he grew up the master of several languages, a devotee of Aristotle, and a keen observer of state affairs. Hunting was not for this Romanov. But three years after Alexis Alexievich had been presented to the people he was dead of chest trouble: the year, 1667. Of his surviving brothers, Fedor (born 1661) was also learned but in extremely bad health, while Ivan (born 1666) was called a sad head, meaning that he was a gentle imbecile and suffered from epilepsy. Five of the Miloslavsky daughters of Alexis were as robust as the sons were weak, and the tsarevnas had the benefit of the same tutors as their brothers. Of these daughters Sophia Alexievna turned out to be as power-thirsty as she was gifted; she became a great Romanov heroine for some, a villainess for others.

Alexis' second marriage, to Natalia Naryshkin in 1670, produced three more children, a vigorous and precocious boy, Peter (born 1672), and two daughters. The new wife meant a stepmother whose hand the other children in the *terem* had to kiss, and it meant that Naryshkin uncles outplaced Miloslavsky uncles. The family feud was well on before Alexis died at forty-seven, having named Fedor his successor, belatedly and, perhaps, reluctantly.

The natural leader of the Naryshkin party was Matveev, Tsaritsa Natalia's old mentor and Alexis' last chancellor. This accomplished statesman was not above passing a few bribes around among the *streltsi* before he spoke to the mourning boyars on the matter of the succession. Matveev's arguments were that Fedor could scarcely stay alive, let alone rule; that Ivan was an idiot and should be passed over; and that Natalia's four-year-old Peter was sturdy, promising, and the logical heir. The boyars demurred. It was not difficult for the Miloslavskys to stir up grumbles against the upstart and unconventional official, and there was dismay that the tsaritsa would perforce be regent for her son. The patriarch reminded them of Alexis' deathbed consecration of Fedor and of the past troubles attendant upon elected tsars. In the end the assemblage proclaimed Fedor Alexievich tsar, the fourteen-year-old ruler having such swollen legs at the time he could not stand for the allegiance ceremonies. As of January, 1676, the Miloslavsky clan had gained their first victory, and they followed it up by the banishment of Matveev (to Pustozersk, where the heretic Avvakum still plotted) and the virtual exclusion from court of Tsaritsa Natalia and her children.

Fedor was an unlucky name for tsars. The son of Ivan the Terrible had ruled in a holy trance for fourteen years. The talented Fedor Godunov had lasted but a few weeks. The third Fedor was on the throne only six years, his reign a tragic race between the ambitions of a fine mind and the aches of a failing body. Educated by Polotsky, the leading Slavonic scholar of the age, Fedor startled the traditional Russians by his knowledge of Polish and Latin. The tsar was pro-Western in his outlook, noble of inclination, and conscientious. It was a cruel thing for him that he frequently could not attend councils and was often obliged to direct state business lying on his back. A mysterious scurvylike disease had left Fedor half-paralyzed and hideously disfigured.

Fedor's six years were epoch-making and reveal the great potential for change in late-seventeenth-century Russia, a potential that Fedor's famous half brother was to speed up and dramatize. The whole atmosphere at the court was deliberately relaxed. Petitioners were forbidden to do scores of obeisances before the throne and were cut short in their expressions of servility. The ban on foreign dress and shaving was removed, even though the patriarch fulminated against imitating "pagans and heretics, Lutherans and Poles." The crowning effort to remove medieval and Byzantine vestiges was Fedor's ukase of 1682 abolishing *mestnichestvo,* the system of place among the aristocracy, whereby not only precedence in court but also the important military and civil commands were awarded according to the ranks held by a man's remote ancestors. The old books of genealogical rankings were destroyed, and the army and bureaucracy opened to people on the basis of merit. This landmark ukase showed the growing self-confidence of the Romanov autocracy, for the abolition of *mestnichestvo* meant that both the great and the small live by the sovereign's favor. It was a damaging blow to excessive pride and family rivalries.

One incident of the reign, essentially a legacy of the previous reign, indicated the quality of the opposition that a reforming tsar like Fedor faced. The celebrated leader of the Old Believers, Avvakum, chose to write Fedor from exile in Pustozersk to disclose that Christ Himself had revealed to him that the late Tsar Alexis was suffering the torments of hell because of the Nikonian changes in ritual. The tsar's firm response to the priest's gratuitous taunt was to condemn Avvakum to being burned alive. Avvakum met his long-sought martyrdom in the Pustozersk marketplace with "joyful composure," according to his supporters, crying out to the people: "There is terror in the stake until thou art bound to it, but once embrace it and all will be forgotten. Thou wilt behold Christ before the heat has laid hold upon thee, and thy soul released from the dungeon of the body will fly up to heaven like a happy little bird, along with angelic choirs." Avvakum died in 1682 after crossing himself with two fingers. His great foe, Nikon, partially pardoned, had made the sign with three fingers and had rejoiced in Fedor's blessing when his end had come a few months previously on his way back to Moscow.

Hopelessly crippled as he was, Fedor III yet married twice for the good of the dynasty. His first consort was Agatha Grushevska, daughter of a Polish nobleman from Smolensk. It was not a brilliant match, but it was a happy one, for Agatha was in full sympathy with her husband's efforts to transform Russian traditionalists. The tsaritsa was sufficiently charming to induce many of the Kremlin courtiers to crop their hair and wear Polish-style clothing (Fedor himself compromised with Ukrainian costumes). The marriage lasted less than two years, for in 1681 Agatha succumbed during childbirth, her son, Ilya, living on for only six more days.

After a prolonged illness, Fedor was strong enough to marry again in early 1682, the bride, Martha Apraxina, coming from a boyar family dating from the fifteenth century. This was not to be the moment of glory for the Apraxins, however—that would come in the next century—because the unfortunate Fedor died a few months after the wedding. He left no issue and had appointed no successor.

One incongruous monument of Fedor III is the 40-ton Tsar Pushka, the largest cannon in the world at that time. Cast in 1586, it was designed to take a ball one meter in diameter, but it was never operative, and it never left the Kremlin grounds.

2. The Coup of 1682: Sophia

Every new Romanov ruler so far had been under age. The situation in April, 1682, was no exception, but now there were two boys to choose from: Ivan, sixteen years old, a Miloslavsky, and an imbecile, or Peter, ten years old, a Naryshkin, and a charmer. The boyars' council deliberated gravely and decided the choice was too difficult for them. Thereupon the patriarch had the bells of the Kremlin rung, and an informal *sobor* of the Moscow people assembled before the porch of the Cathedral of the Assumption. Asked whom they wanted for gosudar, the crowd did not hesitate to shout, "Peter Alexievich"; the bearded dignitary blessed the child then and there. Natalia Naryshkin assumed the regency for her son without anyone's protest, and her first order was to summon back from exile the able Matveev. The Naryshkin party prepared to assume the choice state jobs and to revenge themselves on the Miloslavskys for all the humiliations endured during the last reign. They grossly underestimated, however, the ambitions and abilities of Sophia Alexievna, Peter's half sister.

Tradition dictated that a tsar's funeral be attended not by all his relatives but only by his consort and by his successor. At Fedor's obsequies Natalia Naryshkin decided to accompany the new child tsar and joined the funeral train in a discreetly covered litter. Her break with precedent was nothing compared with what then ensued. The excited murmurs of bystanders caused Natalia to look back and behold a strange spectacle: Sophia and all the ladies of the *terem,* on foot and only partially veiled, had joined the procession. Natalia quickly lost her composure and withdrew from the ceremonies. There later came a brief opportunity for Sophia to address the onlookers and to lament the fate of herself and her family.

Next, Miloslavsky supporters began to stir up Moscow's 20,000 *streltsi* with bribes and promises of a pay increase. Usually ineffectual against foreign armies, the Russian musketeers could turn from indolent braggarts to ferocious beasts on their home grounds in defense of their privileges and prejudices. The first march of these Janissaries against the Kremlin three days after Peter's accession brought them money concessions from the terrified regent, whose great hope was Matveev's rapid return from exile. This strong-minded official finally did reach the capital and vowed: "I will put down the rebellion or lay down my life for the Tsar."

A rumor spread by the Miloslavskys that Ivan Alexievich had come to grief at the hands of the Naryshkins sufficed to bring the *streltsi* charging into the Kremlin once more in mid-May. There was a confused confrontation at the Red Staircase between the soldiers and the royal party, which included Peter, Ivan, Natalia, Matveev, and the patriarch. Ivan was held up to stammer reassurances about his safety, and Matveev succeeded in calming the throng with promises. The situation turned to madness only because the commander of the *streltsi*, Prince Michael Dolgoruky, saw fit to begin cursing out his men. Promptly Dolgoruky was seized, and his body was hurled onto the pikes of the soldiers below. Then Matveev was torn from Peter's embrace and was hacked to pieces before the young tsar's eyes. Natalia caught up her son and withdrew in safety to the *terem,* but the rest of the Kremlin was given over to an orgy of torture and murder for three days. All the Naryshkin supporters the *streltsi* could lay hands on were cut down. Peter's Uncle Ivan Naryshkin managed to hide successfully, but at length the *streltsi* demanded his life, too. Natalia cried, whereupon Sophia said brutally, "Come, come, the Streltsi must have your brother. We cannot all perish because of him." Ivan's place of concealment was revealed, and he met a hideous end. One of the last victims of the mayhem was the court doctor, a German who kept preserved snakes in his study, thereby qualifying as Tsar Fedor's poisoner in the imaginations of the rioters.

The *streltsi* eventually tired of their bloody fury and declared their satisfaction at having rid Moscow of traitors. The court remained panic-stricken until the Tsarevna Sophia openly took charge. Sophia not only granted the *streltsi* complete amnesty but also arranged to caress their self-esteem with such things as increased pay, the pretty title of Court Infantry, and the promise of a triumphal column to be erected in Red Square to honor their recent epic of brutality. Proclaiming it the people's will that the country have two tsars, Ivan and Peter, Sophia in late May, 1682, secured the boyars' consent to this, to herself being declared regent, and to her own brother being designated the senior of the co-tsars. The clergy was quick to come up with Biblical precedents for the dual rule—Pharaoh and Joseph, for example. Actually all real power was being gathered up in the hands of a remarkable female, an unusual thing, indeed, for Russia.

Still further confrontations in 1682 with the mutinous *streltsi* revealed the steely character and modern mind of Sophia Alexievna. Two fresh complications had emerged, one religious, the other romantic, of a sort. The first problem was that many of the *streltsi* had taken up the cause of the Old Believers and were beginning to clamor angrily against the official church. The second new development was that a Prince Ivan Khovansky had made himself leader of the *streltsi,* and this handsome, wealthy, and confident man sought nothing less than the throne itself, making no secret of his desire and intention to marry Sophia in order to get it.

Sophia handled the revived religious crisis masterfully. A delegation of *streltsi* and monks who had come to the Palace of the Facets to protest Nikon's novelties of ritual were treated to a really staggering novelty: The petitioners were brought before a court group in which sat not only the patriarch and the boyars but also Sophia herself, her Aunt Tatiana, her sister, the Tsarevna Martha, and the Tsaritsa Natalia. For the first time the great ladies of the *terem* presided at a public meeting. It was a wrangle-some session, to which the patriarch had come tearfully, fearing for his very life. Sophia let the Old Believer monks read through their complaints and polemics until they reached a passage reviling Nikon as a heretic. At this point she rose and sternly cried: "I have heard enough. If Patriarch Nikon were a heretic, then so were my father, Tsar Alexis, and my brother Tsar Fedor, and the reigning tsars are no tsars, and the reigning patriarch is no patriarch, and we have no right to rule this realm. Exposed to these affronts, it were better for the tsars to leave Moscow." Turning to the *streltsi,* she proceeded to mock them for being beguiled by the pseudo-learned. The ever-volatile *streltsi* forthwith protested their loyalty, proving their devotion by cutting off the head of the monk who had been their spokesman just before.

Since the *streltsi* leader continued to stir up subversion, Sophia carried out her threat and took the whole court away from Moscow. Like her great predecessor, Ivan the Terrible, the regent declared her intention to stay absent until she got her way. In time the boyars secretly consented to the execution of Sophia's rival and would-be husband, and the ever-confident Khovansky was then lured to a cruel death at the hands of the guards outside Sophia's gates at Vozdnozhenskoe. The leaderless *streltsi* milled about the empty Kremlin. They succeeded in receiving royal forgiveness only after publicly confessing to all their crimes and sheepishly giving up their new title and new column. Sophia returned to Moscow in November, 1682.

Russians had had little occasion in the past to inform themselves about what went on in the *terem,* but now there was every reason to find out just what kind of woman it was who had made herself undisputed mistress, or really master, of the Kremlin. Sophia, born in 1657, was the third daughter of Alexis. She was brought up as a child by three of her aunts: Irene Michaelovna, once the frustrated betrothed of Waldemar of Denmark and later the sternest disciplinarian of the *terem;* Anna, a pious and lovable mouse of a woman; and Tatiana, a fairly learned and amiable eccentric. From the aunts Sophia appeared to have gained such characteristics as self-control, religious conviction, and a love of books, but her upbringing would not have been unusual for a Romanov tsarevna if her brother and confidant,

Alexis, had not insisted that she become a pupil of Polotsky, the poet-scholar who was his tutor. Polotsky found Sophia not just an apt student but a brilliant one, capable of mastering three foreign languages, translating Molière at length, and imitating the verse of Horace. The pupil absorbed discussions on the European state system with much more enthusiasm than she had ever shown for Aunt Irene's needlework lessons. Sophia Alexievna was a prodigy with a will.

Sophia developed a marked interest in masculine affairs. Her uncle, Ivan Miloslavsky, who was privileged to visit the *terem,* was subjected by her to a stream of queries, as was the English doctor on hand who found himself obliged to explain the intricacies of his country's political and religious institutions. When her brother Fedor became tsar, Sophia received permission to attend the boyar Duma and to raise questions. Sophia further broke precedent during her brother's illnesses by insisting on accompanying him in public, pushing aside his attendants, and ministering to his needs.

After Fedor died, she proved herself an adept intriguer. Not only had this Miloslavsky daughter outmaneuvered her stepmother and the Naryshkin party, but she also had brought an abrupt end to the ambitions of Prince Khovansky, reduced the *streltsi* to blubbering children, and confounded the Old Believer clergy. Emerging as regent, Sophia was supreme in terms of hers being the only decisive voice, but she was vulnerable in terms of existing male traditions and the continued physical existence of many of her adversaries.

The regent made quite clear her interest in continuing in power. Seclusion in a husband's *terem* or honorable retirement in a nunnery were not for a woman of Sophia's spirit. During the nominal rule of her brothers, she soon saw fit to style herself autocrat and sovereign princess of all Russia. Steadily she promoted the feeling that she was ruler in her own right, going so far in the late 1680's as to have published engravings of her sitting regally alone, with accompanying inscriptions praising her above the great queens of history.

Although the regent's intellect, temper, and position stood well in her favor, her looks did not. Contemporary accounts of Sophia's physical aspect vary wildly, for the adage of beauty's being in the eye of the beholder seems to apply doubly in politically unsettled times. Admirers of Sophia described her as tall and dignified. Enemies of the woman ruler reported that she was dumpy and had hairs on her face. One observer allowed that Sophia was the ugliest woman that ever lived, while another compared her favorably to Elizabeth of England. The comparison with the famous Tudor queen suggested qualities of spirit and bearing outweighing superficial charms. There are no authentic portraits of Sophia that have come down from her time, even though many of her contemporaries, male and female, were braving the scrutiny of painters. Perhaps the refusal to be painted was indicative. "Imposing" is probably the best word for Sophia, meaning regal to some, sexless to others.

A breaker of precedents, Sophia could, or would, go only so far. She wore rouge and went unveiled, but not at church services. She came out in public, but she did not attend the traditional great banquets. The *terem* retained enough hold on the regent so that she felt obliged to rule from a distance and let men take the public honors. She allowed herself lovers, but she could not resolve her marriage status. To wed would go against the tradition of centuries that the daughter of a tsar was too good for anyone except, perhaps, a foreign prince: To wed would mean at best sharing power, at worst surrendering it. In time Sophia linked her fortunes to those of two men, Prince Basil Golitsyn and Fedor Shaklovity.

Prince Basil Golitsyn was more than just the scion of an illustrious princely family descended from Gedimin; he was of the new breed of Muscovite boyars, who set greater value on European ways and ideas than on medieval privileges. Educational reforms, religious toleration, and amelioration of serfdom were among the things Golitsyn talked of. His abilities and farsighted plans earned him from Sophia the title of Keeper of the Great Seal, the equivalent of foreign minister, and his prospects seemed more than princely. Unfortunately for Sophia, Golitsyn was married.

There was not rivalry but friendly cooperation between Golitsyn and Shaklovity, the other man with whom Sophia was linked romantically. Shaklovity's courage, cunning, and ruthlessness won him a position in the regime like that of a chief of police (he alone could manage the *streltsi*), but his origins were obscure. *Mestnichestvo* might no longer exist, but all the old prejudices remained. Sophia could have Shaklovity as her lover, but she could not marry a man of so little social standing. The regent stayed unmarried.

Sophia and her accomplices brought measures of enlightenment but no great milestones. The position of women in Russian society was alleviated by legislation, as well as through the regent's example. Taxes were made more equitable. Street brawling and drunkenness were curbed, and sanitation measures adopted.

In foreign affairs there were grand hopes but meager results. Russia found itself for the first time taken into the councils of Europe, but the Russian military response proved laughable. The crisis and opportunity that arose involved the seeming collapse of the Ottoman Empire, following hard on its high tide in 1683, when Turkish armies besieged Vienna and Louis XIV of France sought to block any opposition to France's infidel ally. The Austrian capital was saved by the intervention of the heroic Polish king John Sobieski, and forthwith Poland, Austria, Venice, and the Pope formed the Holy League to bring about the complete downfall of the Turks. The league invited "the Most Serene Tsars of Muscovy" to join. Prince Basil Golitsyn got a good price for Russian participation: A new treaty of perpetual peace was signed by Poland confirming all the provisional Russian annexations of 1667, including Kiev. Sobieski was said to have wept when he signed the pact, and indeed, it became evident in future decades that Poland's power to thwart Russia ended at this time.

Golitsyn was a better diplomat than a soldier. In 1687 he led an army of 100,000 Muscovites south against the Khan of the Crimea, ally of the Ottoman Empire and controller of the Black Sea coast. Grass fires on the steppes halted the campaign abruptly, and Golitsyn retreated. It was small satisfaction to accuse the Russians' Cossack allies of treachery and to dictate the election of a new Cossack hetman, Mazeppa—a name that would be remembered later. Golitsyn had gained nothing in a year when Russia's European allies were scoring dazzling successes.

A new effort against the Crimean khan was mounted in 1689. Delegations from the Patriarch of Constantinople and from Balkan towns had assured Golitsyn that the whole Moslem world was about to fall to pieces. There were some doubters of success in Moscow. A grave was dug in front of Golitsyn's house with a sign on it saying: "For the Commander in Chief if the second campaign fails." Once again a huge Russian army moved down the steppes, reaching the very gateway to the Crimean peninsula. Then supplies began to give out, and another retreat was ordered. Endeavoring to act as though the desultory campaign was a victory, Sophia rejoiced that the light of her eyes had escaped injury at the hands of the wicked Tatars, and she rewarded her "little Basil" liberally. The disgust of the public was ominous.

Despite its failure to gain new lands and glory, the regime of the regent seemed stable and competent. One memoirist of the period was effusive in his praise, writing:

> . . . never had there been such a wise reign in the Russian realm.
> . . . So much were augmented commerce and all sorts of crafts, and
> the learning began to be restored in the Latin and Greek languages, and
> also good manners were established among the great nobility and the
> other courtiers after the Polish custom—as well evidenced in carriages,
> and in housebuilding, and in attire, and in dining. And there triumphed
> then the great contentment of the nation.

These words were written by the brother-in-law of Sophia's greatest enemy, her half brother, Peter.

3. *The Rival Court at Preobrazhenskoe*

During the years of Sophia's sway in the Kremlin there existed another center of attention for Russians, the household of Tsaritsa Natalia and her son, Peter, at Preobrazhenskoe. This palace, a favorite hunting residence of Alexis, was a large, rambling country house located by the Yauza River a few miles west of Moscow's German settlement. Puzzling and unpredictable things were going on at the court at Preobrazhenskoe. The tsaritsa, surrounded perforce by Naryshkins and other disgraced courtiers, felt herself humiliated to the extreme, not just for being ignored by her stepdaughter but for being spitefully denied, often as not, the essentials of her maintenance. The important news from this quarter, however, was not of the mother's impotent dreams of revenge; the startling rumors concerned play forts and play ships. The son was extraordinary to start with, he was brought up in an extraordinary way, and he gave promise of being the most extraordinary Romanov of them all.

The birth of a robust son in 1672 to his beloved second wife had been an event of great joy for Tsar Alexis, who celebrated it in such ways as commissioning special theater performances and sending off extra delicacies to the exiled Nikon. Peter Alexievich as an infant was shown marked favor by his father and his godfather, Matveev, both of whom vied to heap the prince's nursery with all the latest foreign toys and curiosities, noisemaking gadgets being the child's favorites. All precedent was broken when at the age of three Peter was presented to the public: On this occasion he rode out amid a grand procession in his own miniature gold and jeweled coach, which was drawn by special small ponies and attended by five dwarfs. The spoiled storybook princeling was but a brief phase, however, for after the death of his father Peter became a pawn in the struggle of Naryshkins and Miloslavskys.

During the reign of his half brother Fedor, Peter fared comfortably and received the beginnings of a formal education—all he ever got. The tutor assigned him, Nikita Zotov, was a modest, kindly clerk of the civil service who had been warmly recommended to the post by Fedor's tutor, Polotsky. Zotov taught Peter how to spell out the usual devotional books and how to chant. The pupil gave evidence of a good memory, natural curiosity, and a short attention span. Rather than burden his young charge with formal lectures and readings in the humanities, Zotov was inspired to expose him to picture books and found in the Kremlin libraries both old religious manuscripts and exciting new German volumes of illustrations showing animals and natural scenery, monuments and cities, and kings and battles the world around. Subsequently, it was charged that Peter's enemies in court, like Sophia, had deliberately put him in the hands of a pseudo-learned, lazy, and drunken tutor, but these charges were largely unfair to Zotov, whose learning and whose devotion to drink were considerable without being excessive. Many years later Peter showed his own lack of rancor about his schooling and his continued affection for his old tutor by appointing Zotov "the Most-Exalted Mock Patriarch of Moscow" in his court of drinking companions.

Peter's formal training ended at the age of eight, when Zotov was sent off on a diplomatic mission. Two years later Peter was acclaimed tsar, and in the first few weeks of his reign he was given a lifetime's worth of lessons in human perversity and cruelty, culminating in his being witness to the slaughter of Matveev and most of the people dearest to him. The frightful memories of 1682 never let Peter alone: He admitted years later that he was disturbed by constant nightmares as a youth and could not sleep without an attendant to cling to. His subsequent proneness to fits of hysterical fury and convulsions fully attest to the shocks sustained in his early years.

The upshot of the turmoil of 1682 was that Peter became a tsar in name only, a co-tsar with his half brother Ivan. The regent Sophia saw to it that Peter spent most of his days at Preobrazhenskoe away from affairs, having him escorted to Moscow only for unavoidable ceremonies of state. It was on such an occasion, a reception for ambassadors from Saxony, that people were able to take some measure of Peter when he had reached the age of twelve. For the audience the two boy rulers sat side by side surrounded by the dignitaries of the realm and guarded in front by twelve giant men dressed as Roman soldiers (a whim of Fedor III's) and armed with gleaming battle-axes which they held up menacingly. The throne was a specially made double seat, all gold and gems; it is one of the great treasures of the Kremlin museum today and a special source of delight to the guides because its back reveals the secret slot through which Sophia whispered instructions to her brothers. The Saxon ambassadors presented their credentials before this throne, and later they recorded their reaction to the two tsars. Ivan appeared half-asleep and was so nearsighted that he had to be held up by his uncle for the hand kissing. On the other hand, Peter was fidgety and curious, taking the credentials to eye the workmanship, later extending his hand on his own accord, and at the right moment giving forth a gracious smile. It was duly reported that Peter was uncommonly handsome and intelligent, his natural gifts being held more estimable than even his royal birth.

Young Peter being charming and regal in the Kremlin throne room was a very atypical picture of him at the time, however, for the adolescence of the tsar was largely spent as a joyous, uproarious, and down-to-earth boy of the streets, whose royal position served only to allow him unconventional experiences and escapades on a grand scale. The Tsaritsa Natalia was too silly-minded or too preoccupied to control the activities of her son, who, for his part, did everything he could to get away from the dreary court at Preobrazhenskoe with its pervading self-pity and boredom. Peter was put entirely on his own and took to the byways around Moscow to become the rollicking leader of whatever other boys came along. His associates were mostly of the lower classes, urchins who found Peter more active, devilish, and riotous in his sense of fun than any of them. The people of the Kremlin began to hear of Peter's pranks, but no one made any effort to curb the royal delinquent. Sophia openly muttered about Peter's companions and secretly hoped that her half brother would grow up to be an uneducated wastrel.

Playing soldiers was the favorite sport of Peter and his gang. In time, however, toy noisemakers, makeshift uniforms, and wooden swords began to give way to the real thing. The arsenal at the Kremlin was soon pressed with orders for bugles and band instruments, for armor and boots, for pikes and sabers, for muskets and artillery, and for horses and wagons. To meet the royal requests, the arsenal virtually emptied itself of some items, and the Kremlin artificers were kept busy repairing articles Peter sent back. When he was not yet twelve, Peter was allowed to construct a good-size wooden fortress on the grounds of Preobrazhenskoe, complete with bastions, towers, earthworks, and a moat. Peter worked right along with the laborers sent to dig and build the play fort he called Pressburg. When the tsar's birthday came, there was a grand battle. While half of Peter's cronies defended the position, Peter led the charge against it and proved victorious, earning him a triumphal entry through the gates. Peter promoted himself only if he felt worthy of a new rank; he was not the kind of leader who kept all the best medals for himself. In time the war games at Pressburg became so well equipped and so intense that there were fatalities among the casualties, but Peter was spared injury.

Peter's band of soldier playmates evolved into something far more serious than the original casually-come-together gang. For one thing, the young tsar found that he had no patience with hunting—his father's favorite activity—and he decided to find better employment for the many falconers and huntsmen maintained at the royal country palaces. In due course several hundred of these joined the forces at Pressburg. For another thing, many young boyars came to realize where the action was and presented themselves at Preobrazhenskoe, often bringing their numerous grooms along and suffering to be treated as their equals while raw recruits. Such young aristocrats as Prince Ivan Buturlin and Prince Michael Golitsyn graduated from what Peter called his merry company at Preobrazhenskoe to become national war heroes and field marshals.

The nobles among Peter's companions caused less notice and outraged comment than the presence of persons like Alexander Menshikov, who, it was rumored, first attracted the attention of one of Peter's friends as a clever-talking vendor of meat pies in Red Square and was recruited for Preobrazhenskoe then and there. Actually, Menshikov was the son not of a pastry cook but of a minor civil service clerk; he was illiterate but very smart, unpolished but good company, and above all loyal. In the course of Peter's life Menshikov made himself his closest companion and gained the reputation of being the number two man of authority and the number one thief.

As for Peter's merry company as a whole, it became in the late 1680's two companies of about 300 soldiers who wore distinctive green uniforms and drew regular military pay. The young tsar's soldiers turned out to be the most effective military force in the nation and the nucleus of the Preobrazhenskoe and Semenovskoe Guards regiments, the elite units of the army right down to the end of the Romanov dynasty.

When he grew tired of banging on drums or setting off explosions—and he never really did for long to the day he died—the youthful Peter found any number of other activities to interest him, as he ranged about the palaces and monasteries and towns near Moscow. On one of his expeditions he came upon something that was to influence him all his life as much as the play fort at Pressburg; rummaging through the junk stored in the attic of his rich and long-deceased cousin Nikita Romanov, Peter came upon a small boat of real size and strange aspect. Someone was able to explain to the excited lad that the boat was of English workmanship (most likely a gift of Queen Elizabeth to Ivan the Terrible) and that it was unique because it could sail against the wind. Previously, Peter had played with models of the ill-fated *Orel* (destroyed at Astrakhan by Razin), and he was familiar with ordinary Russian pleasure boats, but here was a craft that really challenged him to become a sailor. The young tsar first experimented with the English boat on the Yauza River, later transferred activity to the pond at Izmailovskoe Palace, and ended up sailing on the large lake at Pereyaslavl, 80 miles away, where a German shipmaster built him an even larger ship. For the rest of his life Peter was happiest as sailor and shipwright; on his own merits he would have been Russia's greatest admiral.

His apprenticeship as soldier and sailor was but the most dramatic of Peter's experiences during the seven years of gloriously free vacation around Preobrazhenskoe. Any kind of constructive physical activity engaged Peter, and he eagerly set about learning such trades as carpentry, masonry, horseshoeing, and printing. Years later Peter could boast that he was proficient in fourteen manual skills, of which the most fearsome from his courtiers' point of view was dentistry. The more sophisticated mechanical and scientific pursuits were largely barred to the young tsar in the 1680's because of Russia's backwardness, but Peter developed a keen curiosity about the technical arts. One big step in this direction came when Prince Jacob Dolgoruky, about to leave on an embassy to France, told Peter of an instrument they had in the West that could measure distances without the observer's moving. The tsar begged for one to be sent him, and in due time Russia received its first astrolabe. It required some searching before Peter found a Dutch sailor named Franz Timmerman who could teach him how to use it. In a sense the second tutor of Peter, Timmerman also instructed the fifteen-year-old in the rudiments of geometry with special reference to fortification and ballistics.

It is doubtful if Peter ever opened a book during his adolescence, with the exception of technical manuals. His self-education was extraordinarily rich in practical matters, but Peter was sorely lacking in communicative skills, reasoning power, and feeling for people. His handwriting for the rest of his life was only somewhat less crude and ludicrous than his command of Russian syntax and spelling. Unlike his half brothers and Sophia, Peter had not been taught Latin and Polish, and his knowledge of foreign languages was limited to what he picked up enthusiastically but erratically from German and Dutch companions. His intellect would greatly develop in time, but when he was a young man, his mind was a strange collection of primitive prejudices and new ideas. His great interest was in things, not human beings.

Inevitably the time came when Peter abandoned adolescent high jinks for the boisterous debauchery of a young man. Since he was naturally attracted to foreigners for their technical knowledge and their worldliness, the German Liberty of Moscow naturally became his favorite haunt. At the homes of various expatriates Peter found sympathy and, better yet, informality, good conversation, and emancipated women. The only thing Russian about the nightly carousing in the foreign quarter was the sheer amount of drunkenness. In particular, Peter was attracted to the house of General François Lefort, a Swiss adventurer whose hospitality, wit, and broad intelligence made him Peter's mentor and closest friend for a decade. It was at Lefort's that Peter became attracted to a German girl named Anna Mons, daughter of a vintner. Brazenly sexy and unrestrained by Russian standards, fair-haired Anna became a mistress who could match Peter drink for drink and joke for joke. Her brother, William Mons, did everything in his power to promote the liaison for the sake of his own advancement, a side plot which had an ironic denouement thirty years later. Meanwhile, the pious people in the Kremlin shook their heads over Peter's association with foreigners and heretics and orgiasts.

In 1689, when Peter had reached seventeen, the Tsaritsa Natalia roused herself from her lethargy and made her one great attempt to direct her son's life, a mistaken and fateful step: She persuaded him to marry a Russian girl. Part of the mother's motivation was simply to change Peter's unroyal and unseemly habits. Another factor involved the old Naryshkin-Miloslavsky rivalry: Peter's half brother, Tsar Ivan V, had left off his prayers and slumbers long enough to be married, rather well married at that, to Praskovia Saltykov; moreover, the "sad head" Ivan proved quite capable of siring children (four daughters eventually). Fear for her son's chastity and fear for the future of the Naryshkins combined to impel Natalia to seek a marital union, preferably with one of Russia's best old families. The regent Sophia, who had secured a princely match for her own brother, was able to thwart her stepmother's similar social aspirations, but she could not altogether stop Peter's being married.

On January 27, 1689, Peter was duly wed to Eudoxia Lopukhin. The Lopukhins were a numerous and well-connected family of small squires who had failed over several centuries to attain top rank in the Russian nobility. It was the best Natalia could do. The boisterous son had given way to his mother's wishes tamely, although Peter sulkily refused to bother to see his intended beforehand. According to Alexis Tolstoy, whose biography of Peter is based on private family sources since destroyed, the following scene briefly interrupted the wedding formalities. Sensing that the bride was fretful at one point in the long ceremonies, Peter pulled aside Eudoxia's veil to find tears on the face he had never seen. It was ascertained that she had not eaten in many hours, and Peter therewith remedied the situation by producing a roast chicken, tearing off a piece, and thrusting it at the astonished girl. Youthful subterfuges are the stuff of many a romance, but it was not to be so for this royal pair.

Eudoxia Lopukhin had only good looks to offer Peter. Since she was a typical boyar's daughter, her horizons went no further than the routine of the *terem*. Her arrival in the household brought the descent on Moscow of about thirty Lopukhin relatives, the men as greedy and uncouth as the women were petty and quarrelsome. The tsaritsa developed an intense dislike for Eudoxia and her family, and she was secretly pleased when her son simply took off. Within three months Peter had virtually abandoned his bride and was back with his boats, his fortifications, his friends in the German quarter, and his Anna Mons.

One time shortly after his marriage Peter suddenly presented himself in the Kremlin, took his place on the throne, listened silently to the deliberations of the boyars, and then hurried off as abruptly as he had come. To Sophia and other witnesses of such behavior, Peter at seventeen appeared a boor, pure and simple. Not only did he lack the old-fashioned regal dignity of his father and grandfather, but he also seemed to be without modern polish, the poise and assertiveness associated with those Russians exposed to Western ways. How could such a lout expect to rule Russia?

4. The Showdown

As of 1689 each of the co-tsars was of age and was married, and there seemed no legal basis for the continuance of Sophia's regency. Nonetheless, her regime had been strong and progressive, and there was reason, some thought, to perpetuate it, even if it was necessary to change a few titles and render a few personages harmless. Other people, supporting legitimacy and male rule, waited for Peter Alexievich to assert his rights. All realized that Ivan V was too softheaded to shape his own destiny or to play any positive part. The uneasiness grew in and about Moscow, but there was a long standoff between Sophia's and Peter's supporters before plots and incidents boiled over into a confrontation.

Sophia herself made no overt moves, and Prince Basil Golitsyn shrank from drastic action, but both countenanced the tireless efforts of Shaklovity to subvert the *streltsi*. This plotter sought to have the regent acclaimed tsaritsa, even if it were necessary to remove "the old she bear and her cub" from affairs—that is, to confine Natalia and Peter.

There were also signs that Peter and his party were becoming restless. In July during a religious procession out of the Kremlin the young tsar suddenly protested his half sister's taking part, although she had done so for years, but Sophia marched on with her icon, and Peter left the scene in confusion, causing the pious to mutter that he had sold out to the German faith. Peter found a more popular issue later when he protested the honors given Basil Golitsyn for the Crimean campaign and refused to receive him.

In August rumors produced a real crisis. Shaklovity mobilized the Kremlin *streltsi* and tried to stir them up over a report that the force at Preobrazhenskoe was coming to murder Ivan V. *Streltsi* friendly to Peter made their way to Kolomenskoe Palace with exaggerated news of Shaklovity's preparations. It was the night of August 12, and Peter responded to the report by jumping out of bed and fleeing naked to a nearby wood. After clothes and horses had been brought him, he and a handful of friends rode off at a gallop and never stopped until they reached the Trinity Monastery at dawn on the thirteenth. The young tsar was sobbing and shaking. He had given no thought to the safety of his mother and wife, so intense were his fears of the *streltsi* as a result of his childhood. It was the right move, however, for Peter to take refuge in the national shrine rather than in his beloved German quarter. Very shortly he was joined by his family, by the two companies of soldiers from Preobrazhenskoe, and by some loyal *streltsi*. The military force was put under the command of Prince Boris Golitsyn, the able and energetic cousin and rival of Basil Golitsyn.

Back in the Kremlin amid general dismay and hesitation, only Shaklovity crowed about Peter's running away. Messengers went back and forth to the Trinity. Sophia refused to let a *streltsi* deputation go forth, but she was afraid enough to send off the Patriarch Joachim to mediate. This proved to be a mistake, for the patriarch was only waiting his chance to side with

Peter. Fresh ultimatums from the Trinity to the *streltsi* finally persuaded Sophia to go herself and have it out with her half brother. At Vozdrozhenskoe, the scene of Sophia's triumph over Prince Khovansky seven years previously, her carriage was turned back by a messenger from Peter, who declared Sophia "would not be treated honorably" if she proceeded.

On her return to the Kremlin Sophia took heart and made a rousing speech to the *streltsi* and people, reminding them of her past services and begging their protection against untold present dangers. Ivan V was sent down to pass out vodka among the soldiers. Shaklovity was all defiance, threatening to behead a new envoy from Peter but relenting before a sword was found.

The turning point came on September 4, when the *streltsi* companies of the German quarter decided to obey final orders to report to the Trinity Monastery. Basil Golitsyn now fled the city, and on the sixth everyone in the Kremlin deserted Sophia, her once-loyal *streltsi* handing Shaklovity over to Peter's men to save themselves.

Shaklovity was promptly tortured and during a whole night of agony confessed to several pages' worth of plots and crimes, but he never admitted to more than the intent to dethrone Peter, and he would not name accomplices. On September 11 Shaklovity and other *streltsi* leaders were publicly executed. Prince Basil Golitsyn was seized, but his life was spared on the intervention of his cousin and other boyars. Charged with abetting Sophia's usurpations and with mismanaging the Crimean campaigns, Golitsyn was banished to the remote north, where he remained in disgrace until his death in 1714—a great misuse of the talents of a man whose outlook ironically was so close to that of Peter in his maturity.

Sophia might easily have left the country, but she refused lest flight be used to compromise her further, all the while protesting her innocence and patriotism. It was ordered that the ex-regent be confined in the Novodevichy Cloister in Moscow, together with her sister, the Tsarevna Martha; Peter at this time shrank from requiring Sophia to take the veil, a fate utterly hateful to that worldly woman. Ambitious and domineering as she had been, Sophia had not indulged in the murder of her relatives when she could have. So Peter too spared his fellow Romanov. He referred to her as "that shameful third person" in a kindly letter to her brother, Ivan V, who was left undisturbed with his regalia and daydreams.

VI.
Greatest of Russia's Tsars and First Emperor: Peter I

1. Boozer and Bombardier

THE drama of Peter's long reign to 1725 was all action, with drastic changes in the mood and lighting and with unrelenting noise for the sound effects. There were only the briefest moments of repose. Darkest disaster alternated with brightest victory, tragedy with joy. Above all, there was noise, noise that awakened medieval Russia and noise that alarmed modern Europe. To imagine the days of Peter the Great, one must listen for the laughter and roars of three-day binges; the pounding of hammers and the creaking of timbers when Peter worked in shipyards abroad; the wails and groans of the Russian soldiers following the Battle of Narva; the crash of new guns and the huzzahs after the triumph at Poltava; the moan of men and materials while St. Petersburg was being built from nothing; the shrieks and curses of Peter's opponents and victims, including his own son; and finally the never-ceasing rumble and clatter of the tsar's coach-and-six as he relentlessly inspected and reordered every corner of his dominions. It is appropriate that from the time he was a small boy to his last days Peter Alexievich had a passion for fireworks.

With Sophia deposed, Peter Alexievich would now be tsar in fact, as well as name; this outcome was the logical but mistaken assumption of the notables who journeyed in their sledges to and from Moscow on the first snows of late 1689. The new master of the Kremlin appeared full grown at seventeen, and his physique was truly awe-inspiring. Unlike his stoutish and mild-eyed father, Peter stood nearly seven feet tall; his muscular body seemed about to burst from his clothes; and his eyes were large and penetrating, their intensity accentuated by a nervous twitch on his face. The active intelligence of the young tsar was immediately apparent to any visitor, and all knew that in his recent contest with Sophia, Peter had shown himself decisive and confident, once his fright of the first hours had passed. Peter was surrounded by loyal and forward-looking supporters. The recent events must have taught him lessons about the need to abandon youthful excesses. Yet for all that, Peter refused to assume his responsibilities for another six years.

Tamely giving over power to his relatives had been the choice of Ivan IV a century and a half before, when at thirteen he had rid himself of his persecutors with one bold act. Peter's predecessor, remarkably like him in the experiences of his youth and in his later fame, returned to his reading and brooding. Peter in 1689 went back not to books, but to play soldiering and debauchery.

Control of state affairs was duly taken up by Peter's mother, the Tsaritsa Natalia. Natalia was assisted by the reactionary Patriarch Joachim, and by her empty-headed Uncle Leo Naryshkin, who tried to fill the place of Basil Golitsyn as director of foreign affairs. The able Boris Golitsyn was pushed aside because court gossips were able to exaggerate his ties to his disgraced cousin. The cessation of Sophia's reforms and the widespread corruption of the new regime made it appear that the ways of old Muscovy had triumphed. The co-tsar, Ivan V, in his feeble way maintained Byzantine court etiquette. Accordingly, Peter, who had a fondness and trust for his half brother, was freed of many of the demands of ceremony and was able to run wild again.

The chief victim of Peter's irresponsible willfulness was his bride of a few months. Together with her mother-in-law, the Tsaritsa Eudoxia had triumphantly taken over the *terem* apartments in 1689, and the Lopukhin clan joined the Naryshkins in dividing the spoils. His boorishly provincial in-laws disgusted Peter, and the whole idea of his wife in seclusion offended his modern sensibilities. Eudoxia was a lovely and loving woman three years older than Peter; she was modest, unassuming, and brought up in the fear of the Lord. Probably she would have been a model tsaritsa of the old type since she expected no more than the pleasures of ceremonial visits from her husband, care of his children, hours with her illuminated prayer books, and chitchat with the other women over embroidery or sewing.

Peter's increasingly long and frequent absences drew from Eudoxia letters pleading her love for him. He failed to write assurances about his health, and she begged him not to despise her yearning for his company. The birth of an heir, Alexis, in early 1690, did not affect the couple's relations, and soon after a second son, Alexander, was safely delivered (only to die in a few months), Peter deserted his wife altogether.

Preobrazhenskoe, with its out-of-doors life and informality, was one place that attracted Peter away from the Kremlin, but more and more he sought out the foreign quarter, where Anna Mons and other women redoubled their efforts to please. At his own expense Peter had a large hall added to Lefort's house and saw to it that his host and closest companion made full use of it. In time there were duly recorded tales of three-day drinking orgies behind locked doors at which some of the great names of the land gave up not only their dignity but even their lives. As for Peter, perceptive people noted his fantastic capacity for drink, his capacity for anger, and also his capacity for sobering up, forgetting, and turning to serious matters.

Peter's merry company felt no reluctance to cavort in the streets, and the manner of these celebrations revealed much about the new tsar. A typical public carousal was the marriage of Peter's favorite jester to a sexton's daughter in January, 1694: On this occasion the couple rode to church in the tsar's fanciest coach, and they were followed by a bizarre procession of officials and boyars sporting outlandish costumes and riding on an assortment of oxen, asses, pigs, and big dogs. Another royally sponsored wedding revealed Peter's lifelong penchant for people with physical deformities: The invitations were conveyed by four stutterers; the running footmen were the fattest people that could be found; and the priest was blind, deaf, and just as drunk as everybody else.

The tsar's companions often staged moving tableaux on sledges, comically depicting such figures as the Pope, but the Russian patriarch and his venerables were not immune either. Peter's inconoclasm, although intellectually deliberate, was largely an expression of a basic delight throughout his life in the coarsest buffoonery and the roughest horseplay. A touch of brutality was evident in the fact that the most feared man in the realm, both politically and physically, forced his companions to exaggerate even their own tastes for deviltry.

In 1693 Peter forsook revelry in Moscow and journeyed far north to Archangel, where he saw the open sea for the first time. Tsaritsa Natalia exacted a promise from her son, "my life and my hope," only to look and not to sail. Peter sailed with gusto, and he countered the inevitable reproaches with sophistries about his mother's having committed him to God's care. On this occasion Peter picked up the lore of the foreign mariners on hand and departed with the self-bestowed title of skipper. A year later he was back in Archangel and had the satisfaction first of launching a Russian-built ship and then of giving receipt for a Dutch-constructed forty-four-gun frigate.

The dowager died in 1694 in the period between Peter's two ventures to the White Sea. The loss of his mother affected the tsar variously: She had given him all her love; she had controlled him but little; and she had relieved him of duty. A prolonged drinking bout followed Natalia's funeral.

Peter felt free that same year to stage the greatest yet of the sham battles. A force under Prince Fedor Romadonovsky, who was to be addressed as "Fedor, King of Pressburg," attacked a company under Prince Ivan Buturlin, "King of Izmailovskoe." More than twoscore men were killed in the exercises. Peter, who exchanged the rank of skipper for that of bombardier on this military occasion, distinguished himself in the melee by capturing an officer of the *streltsi,* thereby heaping further humiliation upon the Moscow musketeers.

The image of Peter and his cronies remained less than heroic six years after the downfall of Sophia. Accordingly, in 1696 Lefort persuaded the tsar to undertake a serious campaign. Projects on various frontiers were discussed, but the one that most recommended itself was the capture of Azov, the Turkish fortress on the Black Sea that Michael Romanov had once feared to accept from the Cossacks. Such an enterprise would serve many ends: keeping the restless Cossacks occupied; outflanking the Crimean khanate; redeeming Golitsyn's failures; overawing the sultan himself; and furthering Peter's newfound dream of penetrating to India and China. An army of 30,000 was hastily put together and, with Lefort in command, proceeded by land and river to the mouth of the Don, Peter serving as an officer of a bombardier force. Bombardment failed, as did two attempts to storm Azov after the Turks captured all the siege equipment. Peter's return to Moscow that year was without fanfare.

The next year the Azov campaign was recommenced with new ideas and energy. Foreign engineers and Dutch ship models served as the initial means for constructing a fleet on the Don River. Storms, fires, sinking, and desertions by impressed soldiers and serfs failed to halt the launching of two warships and twenty-three galleys. Peter labored and lived with the workmen. Despite the generous liquor supply laid in, Lefort and the rest of the entourage set to their tasks unstintingly. During the attack Peter, who gave himself the rank of a mere captain, commanded eight galleys. The Turks surrendered in July, finding themselves unable to relieve the fortress by water. Peter kept up his earlier masquerade of honors by writing Romadonovsky: "My Lord King ["Min Her Kenich," in his peculiar Dutch], I beg to report that the Lord God hath blessed your Majesty's Arms."

The news of the fall of the great stronghold of the infidels released a fervor of weeping and chanting in Moscow, led by the new patriarch, Adrian. The triumphal reentry of the army was not in the traditional manner, however. There was a welcoming arch agreeably inscribed IF GOD IS WITH US, WHO SHALL BE AGAINST US? but the procession was dominated not by Orthodox dignitaries and their icons but by Lutheran General Lefort riding in a gilded carriage. Behind him walked Peter with a pike on his shoulder. The tsar's effacement and his German-style uniform caused some consternation, of course, but thinking Russians could hardly mistake the intended message about merit and hard service.

The death of the pathetic Ivan V in 1696, following closely on that of the Tsaritsa Natalia, left Peter with no apparent recourse but to assume all the duties of rulership. His apprenticeship had seemingly reached a successful conclusion. Yet there was to be another great adventure.

2. Grand Tourist

In 1697 Peter came up with the dramatic decision to travel through Europe. The victory at Azov rekindled Russian interest in the Holy League against Turkey, operative since Sophia's time. The inadequacies of past Russian performances persuaded Peter, and he in turn convinced two state councils, that the military establishment needed a major infusion of Western arms and techniques. Accordingly, Russians were to be dispatched to Europe no longer singly as envoys or connoisseurs but in droves as students and recruiters. Peter chose to go himself, incognito, listed as a volunteer sailor in the entourage of Lefort, who headed up the most important embassy of 250 persons. Lefort's mission, which combined the seeking of alliances with the enlisting of mechanics, turned out to be Peter's grand tour. There were 2,000,000 rubles on hand to finance the expedition, but Peter's wants, it turned out, could usually have been satisfied on the basis of Europe on 5 rubles a day. Peter seemed confident that ordinary officials could run Russia in his absence.

The grand embassy left Moscow in March, 1697, and proceeded via Novgorod to the frontier of Swedish Livonia. There were difficulties at the port of Riga, when the Swedish commandant, who was scarcely fooled by the royal incognito, refused to let the party inspect the fortifications. Peter's experience in "this accursed hole" was later to serve him as a *casus belli*. Crossing Swedish Courland, the party embarked at Libau and sailed the short distance to Königsberg, the territory of Elector Frederick of Brandenburg (later to be first to assume the title of King of Prussia). The elector entertained Peter lavishly, monarch to monarch, and talked anti-Swedish combinations. Peter was more excited by earning a master gunner's certificate from a local artillery expert.

From Königsberg Peter traveled by land to Berlin and reached western Germany in July, 1697. Near Celle he had a formal encounter with two sharp-witted princesses, Sophia, Electress of Hanover, and Sophia Charlotte of Brandenburg. The former was the progenitor of the Hanoverian dynasty in England; at the meeting with her Peter had occasion to kiss her grandson, the future King George II, then sixteen. The latter princess left letters detailing her generally favorable impressions of the stranger from the East. In one she wrote: "The Tsar is very tall, his features are fine, and his figure very noble. He had great vivacity of mind, and a ready and just repartee. But with all the advantages nature has endowed him, it could be wished that his manners were a little less rustic. . . ." Sophia Charlotte continued: "I asked him if he liked hunting. He replied that his father had been very fond of it, but he himself, from his earliest youth, had had a real passion for navigation, showed us his hands, and made us touch the callous places that had been caused by work." The princess concluded: "He is a very extraordinary man. . . . He has a very good heart and remarkably noble sentiments. I must tell you, also, that he did not get drunk in our presence, but we had hardly left when the people of his suite made ample amends."

That Sophia Charlotte was charmed by the meeting was unmistakable. Yet six years later a book was circulated in Germany purporting that Peter had appeared before the princesses in a wild-eyed state, dressed in animal skins, and intent on raping the nearest young woman.

When the Rhine was reached, Lefort and the main group were left behind to conduct diplomatic negotiations, while Peter and ten companions hurried on to Holland, the country which the tsar had heard so much about. In a short time one "Peter Michaelov" was working in the shipyards of Saardam as a laborer and boarding with an old carpenter he had known in Archangel (the house is today preserved as a museum). The tsar's disguise served him only about one week: His height, his twitch, and a wart on his cheek gave him away, and it did him no good to turn his back on officials who called him your Majesty and on the crowds of the curious.

In August Peter went on to Amsterdam. Much of the five months spent there was devoted to the launching of a frigate for Russia, to inspecting other ships, and to watching naval maneuvers, Peter amazing his hosts by his habit of running, jumping, and climbing over everything.

Later Peter journeyed to Utrecht to meet the Stadholder of Holland, who was also King of England, as William III. At Leiden he was fascinated by the anatomical theater, and, when he noticed that his Russian companions were squeamish about the bodies, he forced them to tear apart the muscles of corpses with their teeth. There were rounds of banquets everywhere to honor the royal visitor, but Peter was not to be deterred from seeing all he could in the way of factories, museums, hospitals, and military establishments. A visit to a paper mill was not complete until Peter had made a sheet himself. In Amsterdam Peter patiently learned the art of engraving so that he was able to produce and send off to the Patriarch Adrian an elaborate illustration of the victory of Christianity over Islam.

From Holland the tsar sailed to England on the *Royal Transport,* a gift from his new friend William III and the newest in naval yachts. Most of the stay in England was spent working at the royal docks at Deptford. After watching a sham naval battle, Peter declared that the life of an English admiral was the finest on earth. Probably untrue is the English navy legend that the tsar wanted to see a keelhauling demonstrated and, on being told that there was no English seaman at the time deserving of this gruesome punishment, offered one of his Russians. There is on record, however, a bill for 350 pounds' damage submitted to the king by Sir Christopher Wren on behalf of the owner of the mansion where Peter's suite was housed: 300 windowpanes broken; the walls and floors ruined; the paintings riddled with bullet holes; the furniture smashed; and the hedges wrecked (in the last instance, because Peter had happily practiced trundling a wheelbarrow).

While in England, Peter visited such places as the Tower of London, the Observatory at Greenwich, and the Royal Society. The tsar went to a ball and attended the theater, enjoying a liaison with an actress afterward. His favorite public house on Tower Hill was afterward renamed the Czar of Muscovy. There was a trip to the House of Lords in session with the king presiding. Peter diffidently insisted on watching from a high window outside, prompting a wag to say that he had seen two monarchs that day, one on his throne and one on the roof. The constitutional arrangements in England, as in Holland, interested Peter a fraction as much as technical things. Peter sat still long enough to have his portrait painted by the celebrated Sir Godfrey Kneller (the canvas still hangs at Hampton Court), and he allowed himself to be interviewed by a delegation of bishops. One of the bishops later put down these observations about the tsar:

> He is a man of very hot temper, soon inflamed, and very brutal in his passion. He raises his natural heat by drinking much brandy. . . . He wants not capacity and has a larger measure of knowledge than might be expected from his education, which was very indifferent. A want of judgment, with an instability of temper, appears in him too often and too evidently.
>
> He is mechanically turned and seems designed by nature rather to be a ship carpenter than a great prince. . . . After I had seen him often and had conversed often with him I could not but adore the depth of the providence of God that had raised so furious a man to so absolute an authority over so great a part of the world.

Peter did not go to France to dally at the most magnificent of European courts, the Versailles of Louis XIV: The deterrent was that the French, besides being the inveterate enemies of William III, were the chief supporters of the sultan in Europe as well as of the anti-Russian party in Poland. Back in Holland, the tsar found that the efforts of his diplomats had come to naught. It was easier to make ships than alliances. England

and Holland were much less excited about the Turkish menace than about the dangers inevitably thrust forward by the Spanish succession, and moreover, there was obvious relief that Russia, the unpredictable giant, would get bogged down in the east.

In July, 1698, Peter made his way to Vienna, where he was cordially received by Emperor Leopold I, but here again his promotion of the Holy League fell on deaf ears, for indeed, the Austrians were just about to conclude an exceptionally favorable peace with the Ottoman Empire.

There remained only Venice as a possible ally, but Peter never reached Italy. At Vienna he received the news of a major revolt of the *streltsi* in Moscow. Hurrying back to Russia, the tsar did find time for an interview with Augustus II of Saxony, who had recently been elected King of Poland with the aid of Russian bribes and threats. After gratefully presenting the tsar with a magnificent sword and a dress suit, Augustus talked to him not of the Turkish menace but of the possibilities for action in the north against Sweden, the Baltic empire which had just a year before received a young and untried ruler, Charles XII.

The tsar's grand tour had kept him away from Russia for more than a year. His once secondhand admiration for the West was broadened by firsthand views of English naval power and of Dutch prosperity, the appearances of which he appreciated more than the underlying causes. His taste for technical projects, rather than social systems, was further exaggerated. As for Russia, the grand embassy had failed to recruit allies but had succeeded in enlisting upward of 1,000 foreign technicians, ranging from Greeks to Dutchmen, from carpenters to engineers, and from a ship's cook to a vice admiral.

3. Royal Terrorist

Peter returned to his capital in September, 1698. Ignoring the dignitaries awaiting him at the Kremlin, he spent a riotously drunken first evening with Anna Mons. He then retired to Preobrazhenskoe to sober up, and there, the morning after, he set about the regeneration of Russia, inflamed by drink, by old hatreds, and by the new convictions of one who had just seen a superior civilization.

The tsar's first action was a symbolic drama for which he has remained famous ever since. Peter emerged from his quarters with a huge pair of shears, and instead of greeting the great men of the realm ceremoniously, he went about cutting off their beards. General Shein and Prince Romadonovsky were the first victims of the royal barber. Of the men present only the clergy and two of the most elderly boyars were spared. Beards were the pride of the old-fashioned Muscovite, and it was believed that allowing them to grow to natural length was mysteriously connected with getting into heaven.

Beard cutting was followed by sheering off the floor-length sleeves that many of the nobility affected. Peter quipped that such sleeves often got into people's soup and caused things to be broken, but his real concern was with the whole image of the begowned, besleeved, and bewhiskered boyar, examples of which caused infinite amusement at European courts. Sumptuary laws were forthwith decreed: German or Hungarian styles of dress were prescribed for the upper classes, meaning cocked hats, wigs, shortcoats, knee breeches, and buckled shoes. It would be two full centuries before Russian aristocrats again felt chic and comfortable in the national dress of Alexis' day (such was the rage at parties in the last years of the Romanovs). The peasants were exempted from Peter's dress regulations and were allowed to keep their beards, but the tsar did come up with the clever notion of a graduated tax on beards to be paid whenever a person entered a town.

The pressing problem facing the tsar on his return was the mutinous *streltsi*. Peter's solution for these long-feared enemies was not rehabilitation but extermination. The cause for the *streltsi* revolt during Peter's absence was simply that the musketeers had been ordered to give up their lazy, parasitical existence in Moscow in favor of such activities as rigorous training, building fortifications at Azov, and mobilizing on the western frontier. Various acts of insubordination were followed by the decision of several *streltsi* companies to march on Moscow, raze the German quarter, and restore Sophia Alexievna. There was considerable panic in Moscow for a while, but Prince Boris Golitsyn took charge and sent off a punitive force of 4,000 foreign soldiers with twenty-four cannons under the command of General Shein. The mutineers' resistance collapsed after three volleys of Shein's guns. Peter advised from abroad that the harshest punishment was in order "since nothing but severity can extinguish this fire." The ringleaders of the *streltsi* were tortured to death in their own camp and their mutilated bodies hanged along the roads to the capital.

Peter was scarcely back at Preobrazhenskoe when a two-month orgy of terror was started against the rank-and-file *streltsi* prisoners, numbering more than 1,000. Day after day groups were killed with every refinement of cruelty. Their limbs were broken on wheels, and then they would be carted off to Red Square to have their backs broken and to be left to slow expiration, unless they were fortunate enough to be shot at the tsar's express order. The corpses were exposed for months. The continuing horror finally moved the patriarch and his clergy to appear at Preobrazhenskoe with a miraculous icon and pleas for mercy. But the tsar merely became more infuriated, shouting: "Take that icon back to its proper place. . . . Perhaps I do greater honor than you do to God and His Most Holy Mother by defending my people against evildoers. Take it away, I say!"

The climax of the terror was a day in October when Peter ordered his entourage to compete in decapitating the survivors, already mutilated and buried up to their necks. He cursed out Prince Boris Golitsyn for a bad performance and applauded Prince Romadonovsky for the way he dispatched five. Menshikov ingratiated himself by killing fifteen. Lefort and the other foreign officers excused themselves from the proceedings, saying that their rank precluded the duty of executioner. According to the reports of the Austrian ambassador, who had every reason to exaggerate these Muscovite barbarities, Peter was the most active participant in the beheadings.

One minor incident in the destruction of the *streltsi* deserves notice. A sergeant among the mutineers named Ivan Orel (Orlov) kicked aside the head of a comrade, cursing it for getting in the way of his own execution. Peter admired the man's bravado and saved him for the army. More than sixty years later Orlov's sons were to make an empress.

The tsar now found the excuse fully to revenge himself on his half sister, Sophia, who in her cloister had done no worse than to wish success to the *streltsi*. The former regent and her sister Martha were shorn as nuns, put under heavy guard, and treated to the spectacle of dead *streltsi* hanging outside their cells. Sophia lived on peacefully as the nun Susannah until 1704.

Peter's wife, Eudoxia, was completely innocent in this situation, even if some of her relatives were accused as plotters, but Peter took the opportunity to rid himself of an unwanted wife. Even while in London, Peter had replied to Eudoxia's loving letters with requests that she retire voluntarily into a cloister, and in late 1698 she was unceremoniously sent off to Suzdal. After a delay of nine months a terrified patriarch and his clergy, some of whom had been tortured, consented to making the tsaritsa a nun against her will. She became Sister Helen and was destined to experience more trials and an eventual triumph in the course of the next three decades. Her eight-year-old son was put in the charge of Peter's sister, Natalia.

Ivan the Terrible had interspersed his acts of violence with prayers and fasting. Peter killed *streltsi* by day and dined festively by night. It was at one of these banquets in the fall of 1698 that Peter revealed himself as near the brink of madness. An argument over a trivial point so aroused the tsar that he drew his sword and berserkly struck out at the surrounding company, including Lefort, Shein, Romadonovsky, and Zotov. Their lives were saved only by the intervention of Menshikov. This was the most extreme of Peter's outbursts at a time of great fear and tension, but the resort to physical violence against his subordinates was to remain a part of Peter's makeup. His rages were volcanic, and there were tremendous fists to back them up.

During the bloody bacchanalia Peter had occasion to write a newfound Dutch associate: "The shadow of doubt crosses my mind. What if the fruit of my labor be delayed like the fruit of the date palm, the sower of same seeing it not." Peter the terrorist was also Peter the creator, the ruler in a hurry. The first steps toward the deliberate Westernization of Russia came along with the executions, notably the regulations on dress. The seclusion of women was banned, meaning the end of the *terems* and curtained litters. Soon followed laws standardizing the coinage and introducing municipal self-government. There was a decree changing the Russian New Year from September 25 in the year 3016 to January 1, 1700. This measure to put Russia in tune with the Julian calendar was actually a miscalculation since all Europe, except England, had already changed to the Gregorian calendar, which was ten days ahead of this. Still another reform was made by inadvertence: In late 1700 the Patriarch Adrian died, and Peter was reluctant to name a successor to the man who had shown himself so averse to new ideas. It ensued that Peter never chose a new patriarch, nor did his Romanov heirs for the next two centuries, and in this manner the Russian Church lost much of its already dwindled independence.

Like the cutting off of beards, the cutting down of *streltsi* was symbolic, however ferociously, of Peter's intent to break with the past. The dream of reform was to be given precision by sudden new needs of war and diplomacy.

4. Learner from Defeat

The eighteenth century in Europe opened with two major wars, which were fought simultaneously in the West and in the East. The War of the Spanish Succession (1701–14) found the Western countries supporting rival Bourbon and Hapsburg candidates for the throne at Madrid, with France on one side and England, Holland, Prussia, and Austria on the other. Russia was affected by this conflict only indirectly. The Great Northern War (1700–21) was an effort to partition the Baltic empire of Sweden by its neighbors. Russia was the most active participant and, as it turned out, the main beneficiary of this prolonged struggle.

Sweden had been one of the most powerful nations in Europe ever since the victories of Gustavus Adolphus in the Thirty Years' War. At the turn of the century, however, the Swedish state appeared weak and divided under the uncertain leadership of King Charles XII, a young man of seventeen, a showoff, and a spendthrift. Denmark now saw the opportunity to regain the mainland provinces opposite Copenhagen, as well as to contest the extensive Swedish possessions in northern Germany. Augustus II of Saxony-Poland declared hostilities against Sweden with the idea of reconquering Livonia. Peter coveted the Swedish territories north of Livonia—Estonia, Ingria, and Finnish Karelia—which would give Russia access to the sea. A pretext for war was the insult at Riga at the beginning of his grand tour.

Russia let her newfound allies march without her until a truce was secured from the Ottoman Empire, since a two-front war was unthinkable. The usual bribes sent to Constantinople in the form of thousands of sable furs were now reinforced by the appearance at the Golden Horn of a fifty-six-gun frigate, the fruit of Peter's efforts to build a navy on the Black Sea. The resulting treaty provided that Russia retain Azov, that tribute to the Crimean khan cease, and that a permanent Russian mission reside at Constantinople. The sultan refused free navigation on the Black Sea for Russians, saying he would as soon open his seraglio.

The day the news of the truce with Turkey reached Peter, in August, 1700, the Russian army was flung over the northwestern frontier, its object to capture the Swedish fortress at Narva. The tsar was unaware of the fate of his allies, which was even now ignominious: Charles had knocked Denmark out of the war altogether, and other Swedish forces had crushed Augustus' invasion of Livonia. Peter's troops before Narva were delayed by the fact that their siege artillery was not in position before October. Suddenly the news came that Charles XII had appeared from nowhere. Peter simply abandoned his army—wisely it turned out. The ensuing Battle of Narva in November saw 8,000 Swedish veterans annihilate the Russian force of more than three times their number. The Russian infantry, many of them raw recruits, fled like cattle, the cavalry scattered without engaging, and all the precious guns were lost. Only the two Guards regiments gave a good account of themselves.

Europe laughed over Peter's humiliation at Narva. Peter was called a barbarian justly punished for trying not to be one. Peter himself wrote of the "terrible set-back" and feared that his country lay exposed to invasion. Indeed, advisers to the Swedish king proposed a march on Moscow and the restoration of Sophia. Charles XII, however, declared that "there was no glory in winning victories over the Muscovites; they could be beaten at any time." The young king, who was proving himself to be one of the greatest warriors of his day, turned his forces against his most hated enemy, Augustus II, and was to find himself bogged down in the Polish morass for the next six years.

Peter was quick to realize that he had been blind to expect an easy success and a short war. "Necessity now drove away sloth and forced us to labor and devise night and day," he reported. The tsar set about a threefold task: to make small conquests at the head of the Baltic; to keep hostilities in Poland going; and, above all, to establish a permanent, well-equipped, and first-rate army. The Swedes were acknowledged as his masters in war, but he would learn from them.

The chief military reform was the replacement of temporary feudal levies by a standing army of men conscripted for twenty-five-year service on the basis, roughly, of one man from every twenty households (this system lasted until 1874, when it was replaced by universal short-term service). Whereas only a fraction of the peasantry was thus made professional soldiers, all the nobility without exception were now obliged to serve the state for life in the army, or navy, or civil service. New training manuals were imported to acquaint Russia with the latest European tactics. The use of improved flintlock guns began with the purchase of 40,000 English models after the 1698 trip and was made universal when production of them in Russia itself achieved the rate of 30,000 a year soon afterward. Peter outdid his European masters by establishing two Russian military traditions: the use of the bayonet as an offensive weapon for the infantry and the same with the saber for the cavalry. The tsar was not at all interested in fancy uniforms that made troops look like "dressed-up dolls"; moreover, the import of cloth from abroad was a drain that had to be resolved. Realistic training was decreed, for Peter did not want soldiers who "play the fencing master with their muskets and march as if they were dancing." To replace the artillery lost at Narva, the tsar peremptorily ordered the melting down of many church bells, but Peter relied more on the establishment of heavy industry in the Urals. No fewer than seven ironworks were built in four years, largely by the state. Within a few years foreign experts pronounced Russian iron better than the Swedish and Russian artillerymen the equal of any.

The main legacy of Peter was the thoroughgoing militarization of Russian society. Most of his reforms, but not all, were related directly to the needs of his soldiers and sailors. Such, for example, was the establishment of schools of mathematics and navigation in 1702, albeit a landmark in the development of secular education. Also, with education in mind, Peter had a German theater company brought in to play in a wooden theater erected in Red Square. His sister, the Tsarevna Natalia, helped this cause by writing plays in Russian. Another novelty was Peter's *Russian Gazette,* the first native newspaper. It was designed largely to keep lesser officials abreast with developments.

Peter's military efforts paid off quickly. In late 1701 Prince Boris Sheremetev overwhelmed a Swedish holding force in Ingria, and Peter, exulting that "Narva is avenged," ordered the surviving church bells rung and made Sheremetev a field marshal and first recipient of the Order of St. Andrew. Peter himself was occupied with building a galley fleet on Lake Ladoga to aid him in an assault on Noteborg, the Swedish fort guarding the eastern end of the Neva River. Captured, Noteborg was renamed Schlüsselburg, and its forbidding fortress was destined to become a famous political prison.

The capture of the western end of the Neva in May, 1703, enabled the tsar to found a Russian port on the Baltic Sea, a port that was named St. Petersburg for Peter's patron saint and was so prized by him that in eleven years it became the capital of Russia. It was an act of sheer will, daring, and imagination to plan a great city on enemy territory, to say nothing of building a metropolis on the inhospitable marshy islands of the Neva Estuary.

The first visit of foreign merchant ships to Peter's new window to the West saw gala fireworks and handsome presents given. That Peter was building more than just forts and shipways was attested to by the orders sent out in the first months for flowers and decorative trees by the thousands.

In that same year Peter made a more personal conquest than the head-waters of the Baltic Sea: He acquired the mistress who was destined to be his beloved the rest of his days. Born to Lithuanian peasants sometime in the 1680's, Martha Skavronska had been orphaned at age three and was brought up as a servant in the household of a Lutheran pastor in Marien-burg, where she learned such things as doing laundry, baking bread, and making pickles—simple skills she did not forswear even after she became an empress. It was possibly the pastor's fear of her seducing his own son that led to his betrothing her to a Swedish dragoon named Johan. Whether this marriage was consummated or not is uncertain, but in any case Johan abandoned her when the Swedish garrison evacuated Marienburg. Martha became the luscious prize of a Russian soldier, until Field Marshal Count Boris Sheremetev heard of her and, perhaps, paid as much as a ruble for the prisoner of war. Legend has it that she was brought to Russian head-quarters clad only in a shift, whereupon the Russian commander had a soldier's cloak thrown around her. Some time later the bachelor Menshikov noticed the new adornment among Madame Sheremetev's household staff, and the tsar's crony bullied the marshal out of his new mistress. Then Peter himself laid eyes on Martha, and it was now Menshikov's turn to yield as gracefully as he could to his master (the Soviet movie *Peter I* has a fine scene in which Martha, coming downstairs after her first private meeting with the tsar, slaps the now-too-familiar Menshikov almost senseless).

Peter and Martha were a love match ever after. The woman was practical and commonsensical, being neither a spoiled ninny like the Tsaritsa Eudoxia nor an empty-headed flirt like Anna Mons. Physically, Martha was attrac-tive indeed—extremely blond, nicely featured, and happily voluptuous. After the birth of a daughter, Catherine, the first of nearly a score of chil-dren she gave Peter, Martha was received into the church as Catherine Alexievna, and after a few years Peter married her secretly. Eventually eclipsed in history by her illustrious namesake, Catherine was an outstand-ing figure in her own day, Peter's uncomplaining companion almost everywhere he went and the one person with the power to soothe Peter's troubled head in her ample lap and to stay his tempestuous rages with her words.

The year 1704 saw two Russian successes. Marshal Sheremetev besieged and took the major Swedish fastness of Dorpat in Livonia, which Peter called "this domain of our ancestors." Another army at last captured Narva, and thereby all Ingria and St. Petersburg were secure. The tsar was active in the military operations, all the while assuming subordinate rank. Menshikov especially distinguished himself for energy and ability.

Peter was eager to make peace at this point, provided that he could keep his gains, but Charles XII was unwilling even to negotiate. Such tremendous success had crowned Swedish arms in Poland that Charles XII was able to declare Augustus II deposed and to dictate at Warsaw the election of a rival king, Stanislaus Leszczynski. Russia had little alternative but to give hundreds of thousands of rubles of subsidy to Augustus' partisans and to send troops to the battle-worn nation. So greatly had the Polish-Muscovite relationship changed since the defensive years of Michael and Alexis that in 1705 a Russian army stationed itself at Grodno, more than 200 miles over the frontier. Once again the appearance of Charles XII wrecked Russian plans. A Swedish army annihilated a combined Polish-Saxon-Russian force at Posen in 1706, and fearing treachery, Peter ordered a general retreat toward Kiev. The orderliness of the withdrawal said something for the new Russian army.

Now Peter found Charles XII intent that Russia should not only surrender its conquests but also pay an indemnity. Russian diplomacy became so frantic in 1706 and 1707 that an approach was made to the Duke of Marlborough, the English general whose renown for defeating the best armies of France on the Rhine was matched only by his reputation for taking bribes from many quarters. Peter's agent was authorized to offer Winston Churchill's famous ancestor the grant of a large Russian principality (such as Kiev, Vladimir, or even all Siberia), 50,000 thalers a year, a "rock ruby such as no European potentate possesses," and the Order of St. Andrew. The attempt to secure Marlborough's aid or mediation with Sweden came to naught.

The tsar's diplomatic discomfiture was compounded by a series of revolts in Russia itself, provoked in part by the military strains and more especially by the popular fear of innovation. The first major eruption took place in July, 1705, at the city of Astrakhan, where the governor was murdered and a provisional regime set up to win over the Volga Cossacks and serfs. The revolutionary appeal was revealing:

> We of Astrakhan have risen for the Christian faith and because of the beard-shearing and the German clothes and the tobacco, and because we and our wives and children are not allowed to go to church in the

old Russian dress and because the governors worship Kummerian idols
[the idols which they referred to were in actuality wig blocks] and would
make us do likewise and because of the taxes on our cellars and baths
and because we cannot bear our grievous burdens. . . .

Admiral Fedor Apraxin's ships served to localize the revolt, but in the end
Sheremetev had to storm the city in 1706. As usual, several hundred rebels
were sent off to be broken and decapitated.

Astrakhan had scarcely been pacified when a great insurrection of the
Bashkir tribes in the Urals broke out in 1707. Too rapid Russian settlement
of their area and disregard for their Moslem religion were the grievances.
Lacking other troops, Peter resorted to Kalmuck mercenaries for suppressing the Bashkirs, the use of one nationality against another becoming a
standard Romanov policy. The situation would have been disastrous if the
Bashkirs had been linked up with the revolt of Don Cossack fugitives begun
the same year by one Bulavin. The Bulavin Jacquerie against the serf
owners was the greatest Russian social uprising since Stenka Razin's in the
1670's and necessitated the dispatch of troops from the regular army in the
west to protect the naval base at Azov. The pitiless repression continued
until 1708.

5. *Victor on Land and Sea*

In January, 1708, Charles XII crossed the Vistula River with an army
of 46,000 Swedish veterans and marched east to annihilate Russia. He had
complete confidence that this was the best army he had ever led and that
he was divinely commissioned to punish evildoing. Nothing less was sought
than the deposition of Peter as tsar and the restoration of the old regime in
the Kremlin. In Charles' own words, "the power of Muscovy, which has
risen so high thanks to the introduction of foreign military discipline, must
be broken and destroyed."

The Swedish king rejected counsel that he begin with the reconquest of
the Baltic provinces, which were near home, and instead struck out for
Peter's main forces and Moscow. At the crossings of the Niemen River he
easily smashed through a Russian force in July (his last real victory) and
reached Mogilev in August, 100 miles from the Russian strongpoint at
Smolensk. The Russians resorted to scorched earth tactics and avoided
pitched battle. The Swedes found themselves surrounded by burning villages
and harassed by sharp hit-and-run attacks. Charles XII now decided to
winter in the Ukraine, where he expected to find ample supplies and Cossack help. Swedish reinforcements were sent to join him in the south, but
in October they were intercepted by a Russian army at Lesna and were
utterly smashed in a two-day battle in which Peter himself took part. The

Swedish losses were 8,000 men, 16 guns, 42 standards, and 2,000 wagons —a tremendous boost for Russian morale. Only a small Swedish detachment succeeded in joining Charles.

Above all, Charles XII was counting on the treachery of the Cossack hetman Mazeppa. The Russian-appointed leader in the Ukraine had been playing a double game for a long time: He once boasted, for example, that Russia's enemies had four times tried to corrupt him in vain, sending off a captured agent to Moscow to prove his case. At Peter's time of need, however, Mazeppa feigned sickness, waiting to see who the winner would be. In October Mazeppa finally threw his support to Charles XII but brought with him only 1,300 followers, not the tens of thousands the Swedes expected. Betrayed, Peter ordered a race for Baturin, the main Cossack stronghold, and Menshikov's force got there first, leaving it a gruesome ruin before the Swedes arrived. The Russian victories and Peter's propaganda in the next months largely secured the loyalties of the Ukrainian Cossacks. This was helped by the price scale the tsar set on captured Swedes: 2,000 rubles for a general; 1,000 for a colonel; and 5 for a soldier (3 for a dead soldier).

The army of Charles XII faced an unusually harsh winter, so cold that firewood would not ignite and spit froze in the air. By early 1709 the Swedes numbered only 20,000, but the king made superhuman efforts to inspire his followers and accomplished miracles during skirmishes and sieges. Reinforcements were expected. There were good prospects of aid from the forces of revolt on the Don and Volga, as well as from the Tatars and Turks.

The climax came in the summer at the town of Poltava, nearly 200 miles east and south of Kiev. Charles XII, who was besieging the fort of Poltava, was confronted across a river by the main Russian army, which Peter had joined in June. Even with a two to one superiority of numbers Peter considered a battle to be "a very hazardous affair," but events forced the issue on July 8. Charles XII was hampered by a wounded foot, and his army suffered a lack of ammunition, but the first spirited Swedish charge swept all before it. Then the well-trained Russian infantry stood their ground and let the Russian cannons pound the Royal Swedish Guards to pieces. The Swedish infantry was next to be annihilated that day, and 14,000 Swedish cavalry surrendered two days later, when they were trapped at the Dnieper River. Only 1,500 of the enemy, including Charles XII and Mazeppa, succeeded in escaping to Turkish territory.

During the Battle of Poltava Peter had been grazed by bullets three times. It was to be his greatest triumph. Modestly he wrote of it as "a very outstanding and unexpected victory," and he could not help adding, "now the final stone has been laid of the foundation of St. Petersburg."

The news of Poltava was generally received in Europe with more alarm than joy. It was admitted of Charles XII that "nothing was left of the Lion but his roar." Peter's former allies hastened to join in the kill.

The capture of Viborg, the gateway fortress to Finland, came about in 1710, a triumph for Peter's new navy where in the past purely military assault had failed. The whole Karelian peninsula was conquered, and Peter wrote Catherine that "now by God's help it is a strong pillow for St. Petersburg." The fleet of galleys, which proved so effective in the shallow Finnish waterways, was being constantly reinforced by ships of the line, such as would in time contest the whole Baltic Sea with Sweden. This prospect was further advanced during 1710 by the capture of the great naval bases at Reval (modern Tallinn) and Riga (capital of Livonia).

6. Master Diplomat

The victories of Russia at Poltava, Viborg, and Riga were followed by a near catastrophe for Peter at the hands of the Turks, but after that Russian diplomatic and military efforts were persistently gainful. Russian ambassadors were now listened to rather than laughed at, and Romanov princesses became marriageable prizes instead of pitiable spinsters.

Charles XII continued to be a redoubtable enemy during the several years he remained on Turkish territory. In 1710 he accomplished the seemingly impossible when he persuaded the vizier of the sultan—traditionally the greatest bribetaker in the world—to lend him a huge sum to equip forces. Peter rashly sent an ultimatum and then in 1711 set out to invade the Ottoman Empire. A solemn ceremony in the Uspensky Cathedral blessed his "crusade against the enemies of Christ," which was to be the first Russian invasion of the Balkans since Grand Prince Sviatoslav in the tenth century. The confident tsar counted on support from the Orthodox hospodars of Moldavia and Walachia, and agents were sent to stir up a general rising of the Slavic peoples in Bulgaria, Serbia, and Montenegro.

At the outset of the campaign Peter suffered the most severe to date of the fits he was prone to: The tsar's seizure lasted thirty-six hours, and his life was despaired for. Recovered, Peter marched south from the Ukraine but soon found that his expedition was critically short of supplies. A foray across the Pruth River revealed that Peter's hope of local support in the Balkans was the same will-o'-the-wisp that had led Charles XII to destruction, for only some Montenegrans rose against the Turks. In July, 1711, the Russian army of 38,000 entrenched itself on the Pruth, only to be surrounded by the vizier's army, numbering 190,000 Turks and Tatars with 300 cannons. It seemed just a matter of starving the Russians into surrender.

Peter's hopeless position on the Pruth led him to write a despairing letter to the Senate in Moscow, newly instituted to govern in the tsar's absence.

"In case of my death," Peter said, "elect the worthiest as my successor."
On the slimmest hope, negotiations were started: Peter was willing to surrender all gains except his darling St. Petersburg; the Baltics, Poland, and
Azov were simply written off. The unbelievable happened: The vizier
agreed to let the Russian army escape in return for a maximum bribe of
money and a minimum of political promises. The story was soon spread
that it was Catherine, accompanying her husband, as always, on his campaign, who alone had stayed calm and resolute and that it was Catherine's
jewels that bought off the Turk. The legend became as good as fact after
a grateful Peter publicly solemnized his marriage to his Lithuanian mistress
on his return to Moscow in January, 1712.

Hostilities with the Ottoman Empire were to flare on and off in the years
to follow. Peter's indestructible ambassador at Constantinople, Peter Tolstoy, was periodically thrown in the prison of the Seven Towers and made
the acquaintance of hundreds of rats, but a serious contest with Turkey
never ensued, and the tsar was free to intensify Russian pressures in the
north against Sweden.

In 1712 Peter's troops joined the Danes and Saxons in attacking the
Swedish ports in northern Germany. The Russians, wintering in Pomerania
that year, were now operating within the boundaries of the Holy Roman
Empire. The next year Russian regiments moved even farther west to join
the campaign against the Swedes in Holstein. Still unable to secure peace
terms, the tsar next decided on the conquest of all Finland, so as "to break
the stiff necks of the Swedes" and to have an additional bargaining piece.
By the end of 1714 the entire duchy was under Russian occupation, and
Peter had the satisfaction of defeating the Swedish Baltic fleet for the first
time in a major engagement at Hango.

The year of the victory at Hango the capital of Russia was formally
transferred to St. Petersburg. The new capital was a symbol of Russia's
looking forward and westward, not backward and eastward. Militarily secure, St. Petersburg was still largely a hope, however, for Peter's jewel was
quite unfinished: The fortresses were surrounded by only a handful of
mansions, despite Peter's ban on the construction of stone buildings elsewhere in Russia; the impressed laborers had to be content with the worst
sort of shanty settlements; streets existed on paper more than in reality;
and the incomplete system of canals and embankments meant that the
whole area was periodically flooded during storms. Wolves occasionally
killed people in the streets, and foreign diplomats complained that it required more than eight weeks on incredibly bad roads to regain the comforts of Moscow.

Ignoring the mud for the dream, the tsar calmly sent off orders to the
sons of Lefort and Zotov to buy art treasures in Paris, to acquire statues in

Venice, and to send 100,000 planks of the best walnut for the summer palace.

Alliance making still required Peter's attention more urgently than city planning, and the tsar spent first months and then whole years away from his realm. A number of developments changed the European situation substantially: the War of the Spanish Succession ended in 1714, freeing the Western countries to interfere in the Baltic; Queen Anne of England died and was succeeded by George I, whose great concern was the aggrandizement of his electorate, Hanover, in Germany; and Charles XII at last made his way back to Sweden from Turkey in late 1714. France began mediation attempts in favor of its traditional ally in the north, much to Peter's annoyance, while the new English king showed himself openly hostile. The Swedish king remained adamant against concessions, and Russia's Danish and Saxon allies conspired to keep all gains for themselves.

Marriageable Romanovs were one diplomatic tool in Peter's hands which he began to use assiduously, impervious often to the tears of the family members involved and unthinking about possibly tragic complications for the dynastic succession in Russia. In 1710 the tsar hastened to marry his niece Anna Ivanovna to the Duke of Courland. During three days of uproarious wedding festivities the couple was presented with a huge cake from which two dwarfs jumped out to dance a minuet, and the occasion was used for the marriage of Peter's favorite dwarf, with seventy-two other dwarfs in attendance. The duke promptly died from overindulgence 30 miles out of Petersburg. But this did not stay Peter from sending off Anna and a Russian garrison to Mitau, capital of Courland, to counter Swedish, Polish, and Prussian interests there. The next year the Tsarevich Alexis was forced into marriage with Princess Charlotte of Blankenburg-Wolfenbüttel —the first of a series of marriages that were to involve the Romanovs in petty German politics and intrigues right down to the fall of the dynasty in 1917. Another German wedding came about in 1716, when another of Peter's nieces, Catherine Ivanovna, was handed over to the Duke of Mecklenburg, a tyrannical boor and notorious wastrel. The immediate gain of this cruel match for Peter was that Russian troops were allowed to occupy Mecklenburg, where they served to menace Sweden from another quarter.

The tsar's longest trip away from Russia lasted from February, 1716, to October, 1717. After arranging the Mecklenburg alliance, Peter went on to Copenhagen, where he was warmly received by King Frederick IV and where he enjoyed the spectacle of 30,000 Russian troops and a large Russian galley fleet deployed near this Western capital. During his visit Peter's yacht reconnoitered the Swedish coast and was struck by a shell, but it was not fright, merely distrust of his allies, that persuaded the tsar to call off an invasion of Sweden at this time. Subsequently, Peter journeyed to his favorite foreign city, Amsterdam, and there took place a joyous and triumphant reunion of the tsar and his chief advisers and ambassadors.

Peter's search for aid in a knockout blow to Sweden took him on his first visit to Paris, where he arrived in May, 1717. Apartments prepared for him in the Louvre were rejected as too pretentious, and the tsar insisted on lodging at a simple private house. After being called on by the regent, Peter exchanged visits with seven-year-old Louis XV, with whom he was so delighted that he took him up in his arms and hugged him intently. There were whispers about a match with the nine-year-old Tsarevna Elizabeth. Typically Peter lingered little at the picture galleries and spent long and fascinated hours at the Gobelin lace factories. He did trouble to visit Madame de Maintenon, as a relic of the days of Louis XIV, reducing the old lady to helpless rage by pulling aside her bedcurtains and just staring at her. The upshot of the whole mission was an alliance signed in Amsterdam in August pledging French and Dutch cooperation "to bring the King of Sweden to reason."

With prospects of a complete diplomatic victory before him, Peter had to hurry back from Europe in the fall of 1717 to face a sensational domestic crisis. The Tsarevich Alexis had fled Russia the previous fall, and it had taken a year of searching and threatening to persuade him to return to Moscow. Peter's work would remain unfinished, if not in vain, as long as the problem of his successor was unresolved.

VII.
A Son Undone by His Father:
The Tsarevich Alexis and Peter

1. The Heir of Russia, Miserable Misfit

NOTHING better illustrates the sheer tensions engendered by Peter's projection of a new Russia than the fact that his firstborn son grew up to be his great ill-wisher and would-be reverser. Peter—all energy, iconoclasm, militarism, and technology—found himself with an heir who was seemingly all indolence, piety, pacifism, and love of the traditional. The outcome was not entirely a foregone conclusion. After all, the contemporary King of Prussia, a martinet of martinets, was to threaten his violin-playing son with disinheritance, even death: It turned out that the son became one of the most famous soldiers of history—Frederick the Great.

Alexis Petrovich was born in February, 1690, and was brought up by his heartbroken and embittered mother, Eudoxia. For nine years the roistering, ever-traveling tsar simply ignored the existence of Alexis in the Kremlin *terem,* with the exception of providing him with an indifferent instructor in letters when he was six.

When Eudoxia was removed to a nunnery in September, 1698, following the *streltsi* crisis, Alexis was given over to the care of his aunt and began to see more of his father. His education was now entrusted to two learned foreigners. Book learning in sheltered circumstances was not, however, Peter's ideal for the tsarevich, and as early as 1703 Alexis was ordered to follow the army as a private in a bombardier regiment.

By the time Alexis was fourteen he had been thoroughly instructed in mathematics, geography, history, and "the true foundations of politics." He had already read the Bible six times and had a good command of German and French. Essentially Alexis was a student, with a theological and an antiquarian bent, in these respects resembling but far surpassing his grandfather and namesake. His tutor Huysens had nothing but praise for Alexis' precociousness and also noted that he had a singularly amiable disposition.

Summoned to be present at the triumphant capture of Narva in 1704, Alexis was made aware that his father already had reservations about him. In a boding letter to his son Peter wrote:

> I have taken you on the campaign that you might see that I do not fear either toil or danger. I am a mortal man and I may die today or tomorrow; therefore you must be assured that you will receive little joy if you do not follow my example. . . . [If] the wind dissipates my counsels, I shall not recognize you as my son, and I shall pray to God that He punish you in this life and in the life to come.

Alexis apparently already gave his father cause to worry that he was fitful in his interests and bookish to no apparent end.

The years right after 1704 were critical, for Alexis was entering manhood just at the time his father was most preoccupied with turning defeats into victories. Huysens was needed for a diplomatic mission, and the tsarevich was left largely to his own devices, falling into the company of the clerical and aristocratic stay-at-homes in Moscow who took a jaundiced view of Peter's innovations and who hoped for better things from his heir. At this juncture Alexis was greatly under the influence of his confessor, Jacob Ignatiev, a well-read and conniving man who expounded to his charge on the miseries of the nation and was not above making dark hints of parricide. It was probably Ignatiev who encouraged Alexis to pay a visit to his mother in her nunnery in 1708, a venture which roused his father to rage and the severest reprimands. Alexis was promptly ordered to Smolensk to levy recruits and lay up provisions, and when he was sent back to Moscow in 1708, he was charged not to read and pray but to fortify the city against Charles XII.

Following the victory of Poltava, Alexis was ordered to go abroad, and at the end of 1709 he went to Dresden to begin a twelve-month course of prescribed studies in languages, mathematics, and the science of fortification. These were to be the tsarevich's finishing lessons, for his father had other plans for him—military tasks mainly and marriage incidentally. Rarely was a father so completely insensitive to the sensitivities of a son.

2. Family Complications: A Wife, a Stepmother

Following Alexis' twenty-first birthday the tsar demanded that he marry and narrowed his choice down to a few German princesses, alliance with whom would best fit Russian diplomatic needs. In vain Alexis declared his preference for a Russian wife. In October, 1711, he duly wed Princess Charlotte of Blankenburg-Wolfenbüttel. This German house was as important then as its name was long, for previous to Charlotte's match her sister had espoused the Holy Roman Emperor Charles VI.

On the personal level, Charlotte described Alexis as "sensible, upright, and amiable," while the tsarevich had to own that his bride was the most attractive princess in Germany and "a good creature." In a letter to his confessor, Alexis held himself assured that Lutheran Charlotte would accept the Orthodox faith, not through compulsion, but by the sheer splendor and appeal of the icons, priestly vestments, and rites.

The tsar allowed the couple a honeymoon of only three weeks, and then Alexis was hurried off to Poland on a military mission. Princess Charlotte, who had been promised 50,000 rubles a year, found herself reduced to borrowing money from Menshikov, and eventually sheer poverty forced her to return to her mother a year after the marriage.

Alexis at this point had another marriage to brood over, that of his father to Martha (now Catherine) Skavronska, solemnized in 1712. Actually Peter had been secretly married to his Lithuanian mistress since 1707, but he did not officially divorce Alexis' mother until 1711, the year when Catherine earned her mate's everlasting gratitude for her courage in the Pruth campaign. At the reception following the open acknowledgment of Catherine as empress, Peter joked that she came with a ready-made family, for there were two living daughters by him, Anna, born in 1707, and Elizabeth, born in 1709. Alexis had to do even more than acknowledge this lowborn foreigner as empress and pay deference to a stepmother scarcely seven years older than himself. Calculation, perversity, or even malice on Peter's part made the tsar force Alexis to stand godfather when Catherine was received into the Orthodox Church, and accordingly, she became known as Catherine Alexievna.

Although in time Catherine had her own children's interests to consider, she was too good-hearted a person to bear any ill will toward the son of her husband's first wife. On the contrary, she intervened with Peter about Alexis as she did for all unfortunates. She very kindly welcomed Princess Charlotte to St. Petersburg, after Alexis' wife finally received the money necessary to come to Russia from "your affectionately inclined father." But no woman could prevent the collision course of father and son.

At the end of 1712 Alexis had been whisked off to Finland on an inspection tour with his father, and later he was commissioned to superintend the building of ships on Lake Ladoga. On his return to St. Petersburg the tsarevich was promptly given a set of mechanical drawings to do in order to demonstrate his abilities in mathematics and marine architecture. Alexis panicked at the assignment and ended up shooting himself in the right hand, like the most cowardly recruit and like the least adept, for indeed he missed and just burned himself. The incident shocked Peter more than anything else could have. There were curses and blows, and then Peter lapsed into utter indifference toward his son, avoiding social contact and ceasing to give him jobs.

Alexis was by no means friendless as he reached his mid-twenties. The clergy were obviously for him, and a notoriously corrupt ex-official named Kikin attached himself to the tsarevich. More important were his friendly relations with such old aristocratic families as the Dolgorukys and Golitsyns, who made little secret of their antipathy to the lowborn creatures on and near the throne. Prince Basil Dolgoruky, for example, confided to Alexis: "You are cleverer than your father," hinting at future changes. Prince Boris Kurakin, who was also Alexis' relative, asked him once, "Is your step-mother good to you?" Upon getting an affirmative reply, the prince said ominously, "Well, so long as she has no son of her own she will be good to you, but when she has a son she will be different."

It was, indeed, the birth of babies—both to Alexis and to Peter—that preceded the ultimate crisis. Alexis' relationship with his wife left much to be desired, particularly after he started an affair with a Finnish serf girl named Afrosina. If the tsar expected Charlotte to be a steadying influence on her husband, he had himself in large part to blame for his failure. She was forced to live on miserly doles of money and was allowed to shut her-self up away from the court to cry and brood about her barbaric surround-ings in endless letters of complaint to her sister in Vienna. A child, the Tsarevna Natalia, was finally born in July, 1714, at which time Peter and Catherine sent gifts and felicitations, while Charlotte relented enough about the clumsiness of Russian midwives to apologize for failing to pro-duce a son. The boy did appear at last in October, 1715, and he was duly named for his grandfather, Peter Alexievich. Princess Charlotte, however, died four days after the birth as a result of a chill brought on during con-gratulatory ceremonies. Three weeks later the Empress Catherine also was delivered of a son, apparently healthy and likewise named for the tsar, Peter Petrovich.

3. Cruel Choices and Escape

From guilt or from a father's renewed affection, Alexis was beside him-self during Princess Charlotte's confinement and death, fainting on three separate occasions. His woe was capped on the very day of his wife's funeral by the following letter from Peter, in which he was given a last chance. The tsar began:

> My joy [in all the accomplishments of the past years] is swallowed up by grief when I look around me and see in you a successor very unfit

for the administration of affairs of state and above all determined not
to give any attention to military affairs, by means whereof we have
emerged out of darkness into light and have become honored and of
high repute.

Peter continued with a historical reflection:

> Nor is ill health any excuse. It is not work I want from you but good
> will, which is quite independent of sickness. Ask anyone who remembers
> my brother [Tsar Fedor], who was incontestably much sicker than you
> and, for that reason, could not ride swift horses. Yet, having a great love
> of horses, he was continually inspecting them and kept them constantly
> before his eyes, so that there were not, and to this very day never have
> been, such stables in Russia as he had.

His father turned to the Bible:

> I feel that I am leaving my inheritance to one who resembles the
> slothful servant in the Gospels, who hid his talents in a napkin. Here
> have I been cursing, and not only cursing but even striking you all these
> years, and it has all been in vain. You will do nothing but simply sit
> at home enjoying yourself, however contrary things may be going.

Sorrowful, pessimistic, but still willing to wait a little longer, Peter ended
with a threat if Alexis did not change his ways:

> If you do not, be quite sure that I will deprive you of the succession.
> I will cut you off as though you were a gangrenous swelling. . . . I have
> never spared nor will I ever spare my life for my country and my peo-
> ple. How then shall I spare a useless thing like you? For better outside
> merit than one's own rubbish.

Bereaved and bewildered, Alexis consulted his friends, such as Kikin
and Prince Dolgoruky, and finally wrote a craven reply to his father in
which he offered, on the grounds of ill health and lack of ability, to renounce the succession in favor of his newly born half brother, Peter Petrovich (thus neglecting the rights of his own son, Peter Alexievich). The
intervention of Prince Dolgoruky saved the tsarevich from being executed
then and there, after which Peter subsided into such a tremendous drinking
bout that his health collapsed and at one point he had to be given the last
sacraments.

After the recovery of his health at Christmastime Peter sent another
letter to his son, offering Alexis the choice of changing his ways or becoming
a monk: "It must be one or the other, for it is impossible for you to be
neither fish nor flesh nor fowl forever." Alexis' friends advised him to submit to tonsure, Kikin arguing slyly: "The hood won't be nailed to your
head; you can take it off whenever you like." Accordingly, Alexis asked
Peter's permission to take the vows, signing his letter "Your slave and useless son, Alexis."

On the eve of his departure for the German campaigns of 1716 Peter visited Alexis, who was ill in bed, and this time kindly urged him to reconsider and make no rash decisions. The tsar's vacillation did not allay the tsarevich's fright and desperation, and Alexis was not surprised later to receive a letter peremptorily ordering him to join the distant army if he wished to keep his title. After some delay and further ultimatums Alexis finally informed Menshikov, governor of St. Petersburg, that he was joining Peter, and he sailed from Riga in September, 1716, accompanied by his mistress, Afrosina, her brother, and three servants.

The idea of taking refuge abroad had already been suggested to Alexis at an earlier time when he was out of Russia, and his aunt, the Tsarevna Natalia, advised such a step for him on her deathbed early in 1716, a revealing assessment of the situation on the part of Peter's much-beloved sister. In the course of his journey west Alexis ran into another relative, the tsar's half sister Maria returning from the grand tour. A high-spirited old lady, this tsarevna had a Miloslavsky's antipathy toward the Naryshkin-born tsar, but she did not think much of the sniveling, self-centered tsarevich either. Her warning that "wherever you go your father will find you out" was countered only by the arrival of Kikin, who assured Alexis that it would be possible to ignore Peter's letters and to brazen it out in cities friendly to the tsar until the safety of the Hapsburg domains was reached.

In November, 1716, some weeks after Menshikov's messengers began to inform Peter that the tsarevich's whereabouts were not known, a hysterical young man presented himself at the door of the Austrian vice chancellor's house in Vienna. Introducing himself as Alexis, he proceeded to run about looking for Russian spies in every corner, raving and gesticulating until finally kindly assurances and a glass of Moselle made him collapse in an armchair. Alexis therewith recited his fears of the immediate alternatives hard labor and drinking bouts with his father in Germany or the ultimate possibility of monkhood and disinheritance by a cruel man surrounded only by evil people. With peevish pride Alexis declared that he had refrained from going over to Sweden, the national enemy. In a defiant moment he confided: "My father says I am no use for war or governing, but still I have sufficient sense to rule," adding that "God is master and disposes of the succession." Finally, he appealed to his brother-in-law, the emperor, "to protect my life and assure my succession and that of my children."

In due course Alexis was spirited off to the Tyrolean fortress of Ahrenberg. The Austrians denied all knowledge of him, but a Russian agent, Rumyantsev, tracked the tsarevich to his hideout, and his extradition was demanded. The emperor temporized, this time having Alexis and Afrosina whisked off to Castel Sant'elmo in Naples. A letter of Charles VI to King George I of England at this time explained that he was protecting Alexis from possible "poisoning or other Muscovite gallantries."

Alexis' incognito in Naples also vanished, after Peter's spy Rumyantsev was joined by Count Peter Tolstoy, the man who had an impressive record of murders and bribes as envoy at Constantinople. With an eye to the Russian troops poised in Germany, the emperor consented to Peter's agents interviewing Alexis, and Tolstoy began testing his wiles in September, 1717. There was a letter in his hands from Peter swearing "before God and his judgment seat" that he would not punish but rather would cherish his son in the future. The first interview saw Alexis simply incoherent with fear that Tolstoy had come to murder him. At the second meeting the tsarevich blankly refused to return, causing Tolstoy to report that only extreme measures would "melt the hard-frozen obstinacy of this beast of ours." In the end it was Tolstoy's threat of a Russian declaration of war that persuaded the local officials to threaten in turn to take from Alexis his Afrosina, who was now pregnant. Alexis gave in on two conditions, confirmed verbally by Tolstoy and later in a letter from the tsar: The tsarevich could live quietly on his estates, and he could marry Afrosina.

4. Return and Judgment

Alexis was hustled out of Italy immediately, being allowed only a brief visit to the relics of St. Nicholas at Bari. The emperor avoided an opportunity to see his brother-in-law in Venice, but he did instruct an official to talk with the tsarevich in private. Tolstoy insisted on being present at the interview, and the official came away with only the intelligence that Alexis was in a shockingly dirty, neglected condition. In February, 1718, after an absence of a year and a half, Alexis was brought back to the Kremlin.

Within three days of his return to Moscow Alexis was deprived of his sword and then led before his father and an assemblage of clergy and nobility. The tsarevich fell on his knees and begged mercy—this behavior, when no charge had been raised against him except flight from Russia. At Peter's stern insistence, Alexis stood before the Gospels and publicly renounced the throne in favor of the baby Grand Duke Peter Petrovich. A manifesto that same day, to allay the national alarm, began with Peter's observation that Alexis deserved death for shaming his father before the world, but it ended happily with the words: "Our fatherly heart having taken compassion on him, we promise him immunity from all punishment."

The trials of Alexis had just begun, however, for Peter suspected a widespread plot against his regime. Under orders the tsarevich began to set down on paper details of his flight abroad, naming names and revealing confidences in view of the threat that anything compromising discovered later on would result in the forfeit of his pardon. The spring of 1718 in

Moscow turned increasingly into a reign of horror, as an ever-widening circle of associates and abettors of Alexis was brought in by the police. Kikin was three times put to torture, and after he admitted advising Alexis to go to Vienna, he was condemned to death. The old tutor of the tsarevich avoided a similar fate only because he was able to prove that he got nothing but kicks and blows at the hands of his charge. Prince Basil Dolgoruky was sent over in chains from St. Petersburg, but in the end he escaped even the sentence of banishment because his fellow aristocrats in the Senate would not believe Alexis' testimony against him. The Bishop of Rostov was degraded to a monk. Eight persons in all were executed, and several suffered lesser sentences, hardly evidence of a widespread conspiracy to overthrow Peter. There were many unspoken resentments and unresolved hopes afoot, but people cannot be prosecuted for their feelings, and Peter knew it. Yet the tsar was right when he observed to Tolstoy, "If there had been no monks and nuns, Alexis would never have dared commit such an unspeakable evil."

New horrors were perpetrated when Peter used the general crisis to settle some scores within the royal family. Off to a nunnery went the Tsarevna Maria, the one Alexis had seen at Libau. Most sensationally, the ex-tsaritsa Eudoxia was arrested without warning at the cloister where she lived simply as the nun Helen, albeit the other sisters persisted in treating her as the lawful gosudaruinya. Peter's first wife was thereupon brought to Moscow, together with some relatives and associates, including a certain Major Stephen Glebov. In general, torture disclosed only that these people desired the reconciliation of Eudoxia and Peter. The major, said to be uncommonly handsome, was further induced to make a public confession of adultery with the ex-tsaritsa, although there was no corroborative evidence and Eudoxia was legally divorced anyhow. This sufficed, nonetheless, to let Peter decree Eudoxia's removal to a more remote place of banishment. As for her alleged paramour, he was impaled and left all one night to die in hideous pain on the stake. It was reported that Peter approached his victim the next morning and told him to confess and receive the sacraments. Glebov spat in the tsar's face.

There was a brief suspension of terror for Alexis after Peter left Moscow to be near the negotiations going on with Sweden. The tsarevich even hoped that his promised marriage to Afrosina would take place, gaining the backing in this of his good-hearted stepmother. Afrosina, with her newly born child, finally arrived in St. Petersburg in April, 1718, only to fall under brutal interrogation by Menshikov and Tolstoy. The friendless, untutored girl was driven to babble forth all and anything Alexis had ever confided in her. His daydreams were spoken aloud, as were boasts and fears expressed when he was not sober. The tsarevich was said to have rejoiced at news of army mutinies, and his glee on hearing of an illness of Peter

Petrovich came out in these words: "You see what God is doing? Father works, but God is working too." Poor Afrosina was induced to picture her lover as intent on moving the capital back to Moscow. On the throne, Alexis would abandon the navy and pare the army, for "he did not want to have wars with anyone and wished to content himself with the old dominion." Respect for the church, deference to the needs of the nobility, and alleviation of the taxes and levies on the people were also subjects Alexis had held forth on.

Alexis was confronted with Afrosina's hearsay and, after collapsing in tears, was taken off to confinement in June, 1718. Renewed efforts to produce documentary evidence against him were not successful. There were some four-year-old notes of his on Caesar Baronius' *Annales ecclesiastici,* but Peter, perusing them himself, could only put marks opposite his son's noting down Charlemagne's edict on dress and the killing of Childeric for expropriating the church. Two undelivered letters of the tsarevich from abroad to the Senate asked little more than that they keep him in remembrance. More serious was a report in Alexis' possession from the Austrian minister in Russia: It spoke of a conspiracy in the army in Germany to kill Peter and elevate Alexis. But Alexis persistently disclaimed knowledge of such a plot, and it required torture to make him admit later that he would have accepted the throne from the rebels if asked to. Hopes, not actions, intent only in the sense of wishing his father dead were all that really could be proved against Alexis. Alexis' mother-in-law was right when she had said of him that he preferred a rosary in his hands to a pistol.

Grim, unfinished St. Petersburg was the scene of a new summoning of notables in June, 1718, this time to consider the death penalty for the tsarevich. The prelates and nobility were instructed by Peter to weigh the enormity of Alexis' crimes against Peter's several solemn promises not to punish his son. Peter's final charge was: "Do justice, lest ye jeopardize your souls and mine likewise, so that our consciences may be clear on the terrible day of Judgment, and our country may at this present time be secure."

At this juncture the clergy failed or feared to take up the cause of their great friend. They merely set forth that there were both Old and New Testament precedents for the forgiveness of a fallen sinner. A genuinely persuasive effort to hold Peter to his oaths was neglected.

The lay notables, if no more courageous and no less unanimous, were at least more forthright than the clergy: They recommended the death penalty, declaring their conviction that Alexis had "imagined" rebellion against his father and had countenanced a revolt of the common people, as well as intervention by the country's enemies. Their report was signed by all the senators and ministers, including not only Menshikov and Tolstoy but also the Dolgorukys and Golitsyns.

Peter never replied to their recommendation. Already Alexis was undergoing torture with the knout, twenty-five strokes one day and fifteen about a week later. The knout, a whip made of parchment hardened with milk, was so heavy and sharp that some died after three strokes and few lived out thirty blows. That Alexis, sickly and hysterical as he was, survived for so long was a miracle; that he had no more to confess was less surprising. His end came at six in the evening of July 7 in the guardhouse of the Trubetskoy Bastion.

The populace of the capital recovered from their stupefaction and horror at the news and took up the wildest rumors about the manner of Alexis' death, the favored report being that the tsar had killed the tsarevich with his own hand, just as Ivan the Terrible had dispatched his son. The foreign capitals, of course, were willing to believe anything unspeakable coming out of Muscovy. Peter's official communiqué informed the world that "the Almighty . . . cut short the life of our son Alexis, by sending upon him, after the declaration of his sentence and the detection of so many of his great crimes against us and the realm, a cruel disease resembling apoplexy." Unlike his predecessor Ivan the Terrible, Peter never betrayed the slightest remorse at killing his firstborn. People would say in time that the tsar cemented the foundations of the new Russia with the blood of the tsarevich. The metaphor would not necessarily have offended Peter.

There hangs today a modest-sized portrait of Alexis Petrovich at the age of twenty for the visitor to ponder in the Russian State Museum in Leningrad. His long dark hair and delicate features immediately remind one of his grandfather Alexis at about the same age. The bright-red jacket of Western cut that he is wearing jars with the preconception that Alexis was just a bookish, psalm-singing traditionalist. His large brown eyes have a faraway look and are slightly askance, suggesting moodiness, frustration, even a touch of madness. Did he dream of returning Russia to the Kremlin? Did he dream of letting the navy sink? Did he dream of peace? Very probably, and in any event his dreams were not his father's dreams.

5. Peter's Final Victories

Following the execution of Alexis, there remained seven years for Peter to solidify his new Russia. His campaigns in the West were brought to a triumphant conclusion, and new ventures were begun on other frontiers. Major enactments thoroughly reordered the government, the church, the economy, and the social system. Only in the matter of assuring the succession did Peter leave things unsettled.

After eighteen years of hostilities, peace negotiations were begun with exhausted Sweden in 1718. The diplomacy was entrusted to Andrew Osterman, an able German taken into Peter's service and destined to figure importantly in affairs for more than two decades. The tsar was prepared to offer the enemy reasonable terms. Charles XII, however, preferred to gallop around and breathe defiance, causing Osterman to wish out loud that he would break his neck. This hope was fulfilled in December, 1718, when Charles was killed in the siege trenches during a side campaign to conquer Norway. The new Swedish regime of Queen Ulrica in turn proved obstinate, and talks were broken off.

Eventually Sweden was able to make separate peace arrangements with each of Russia's allies. All Europe seemed to fear Russian expansion and to rejoice at Russian difficulties. King George I of Britain and Hanover was particularly determined "that the Tsar should not grow too powerful in the Baltic." The threat of intervention by the British navy, however, was handily countered by Peter's entering into negotiations with the Old Pretender, the Stuart claimant to the British throne.

The Russian navy began to make armed descents on the Swedish coast, and in 1721 a force of 5,000 troops was landed. Sweden hastened to come to terms. By the Treaty of Nystad, signed in September, 1721, Russia gained the Baltic territories west, north, and south of its new capital, paying for them a money indemnity and ceding back to Sweden the main part of Finland. Free Russian trade on the Baltic was assured. What was really gained was complete hegemony in this area, for Sweden simply ceased to be considered a great power. On the news of the peace treaty Peter wrote: "Most apprentices generally serve for seven years, but in our school the term of apprenticeship has been thrice as long. Yet God be praised, for things could not have turned out better for us than they have done."

Peter's fiftieth birthday was officially celebrated in November, 1722, with a thanksgiving service in the cathedral of St. Petersburg and a great parade of the victorious regiments to the Senate Building. There the chancellor acclaimed him as "Father of the Fatherland, Peter the Great, and Emperor of All Russia." In his reply, Peter consented to the imperial title, left the accolade of "the Great" to history, and modestly attributed the victories to God, rather than to personal merit. The tsar warned his supporters against softening and going the way of the Byzantine Empire, but he was scarcely heard for the bells and trumpets and salvos and cheers. In Europe, Prussia and Holland were quick to acknowledge Peter as emperor, but the Holy Roman Emperor chafed at having an equal, and King George sulked.

Peter's horizons went beyond Europe. Hardly was the Great Northern War concluded than Russia was fighting Persia. There was Russian interest shown in Christian Georgia and Christian Armenia in the Transcaucasus area, and the first Russian expeditions were sent by Peter to probe the strength of the central Asian khanates of Khiva and Bokhara. A large mission was sent off to China in 1719 and was treated with new courtesy, the emperor declaring to the envoy: "Why should we quarrel? . . . We both have so much land that a little more or less would be of no profit to either of us." Permanent consulates and a commercial treaty were shrugged off by the Chinese, however, with the remark, irking to Peter, that trade was only for poor countries. The global scope of Peter's concern was illustrated in 1723 by his dispatching two frigates "to the illustrious King and Owner of the glorious island of Madagascar." The ultimate goal was the riches of India, but the enterprise was a fiasco. More successful was Peter's sponsorship of the explorations of Captain Vitus Bering in the Pacific, resulting in the detection of the strait bearing his name and eventually in Russian colonization of Alaska.

Peter the Great left Russia with a regular army numbering 210,000 men and a navy comprising 32 battleships, 16 frigates, and 800 other craft. The army and navy came to receive two-thirds of the state revenue, in contrast with one-half in Alexis' day, and the revenue itself had tripled to 10,000,000 rubles in just the fifteen years since the first formal Russian budget was set down in 1710. Under Peter, Russia had been at war steadily for twenty-eight years, and the costs and burdens for its people were staggering. The achievement was to end Russia's isolation and backwardness and to thrust it into international affairs—an unasked-for and unwelcome event for many, both at home and abroad, but all the same a development of the modern age comparable in importance to the rise of the New World.

6. The Petrine Reordering of Russia

A man who detested flattery and disdained unearned titles, Peter once became quite angry with his companions for glorifying him by disparaging his father, Alexis. Turning to old and unimpeachable Prince Jacob Dolgoruky, Peter demanded an honest appraisal and got this considered reply: As for diplomacy and the navy, Peter was greater than his father; as regards the army and war, much had been accomplished by both men, but a favorable conclusion to the Swedish war would tip the balance toward the son; finally, in the matter of administration and justice, Alexis was rated better, although Peter still had the opportunity to catch up with his father.

Although the autocracy remained unimpaired, considerable refashioning of the central institutions was undertaken. The Senate, already invented in 1711 as an executive body during the tsar's absence, was later given more precise functions of an administrative and judicial nature, making this institution the modern successor to the old boyar Duma. Another medieval legacy, the *prikazi,* was replaced by well-defined departments, these being set up in 1717 as the Colleges of Foreign Affairs, War, Navy, Justice, etc.

The collegiate system meant that each department was headed by a board, rather than a single minister, a system copied from the Swedish, that proved inefficient in time but was justified originally by the need to divide authority between loyal Russians and expert foreigners.

One of the new departments represented a great change in itself—namely, the Holy Synod of the Orthodox Church, established in 1721. This institution, filled with the top clergy but headed by a lay procurator, marked the formal demise of the patriarchate and the full subordination of church to state. Peter had every reason to curb the independence of a church that all along had openly sided with the Tsarevich Alexis and his reactionary dreams. Yet a calculating religious regulation of Peter's in 1718 made attendance at Sunday and holiday services compulsory for all people; part of the aim was to make sure that everyone heard the decrees of the state read from the pulpits.

Often accused in his lifetime of being antireligious, Peter was, in fact, an agnostic, but few rulers of his day quoted Scripture as liberally as the tsar, and none was more conscious of his mission as God's representative on earth. He was pragmatic about the matter of religious toleration, once ordering that a colony of Old Believers be unmolested because they were more useful to the state as ironworkers than as martyrs.

The Russian nobility also felt the strong hand of the reforming tsar. Their privileged position as the serf-owning class was not curbed in the least, however, and they could hardly complain that the basic idea of service to the state was new, since it predated the Romanovs. Lifetime service, however, meaning constant absence from their estates, was a much-resented new burden, and Peter was zealous in enforcing it. The tsar had nothing but hatred for "those who buried themselves in their villages" or those "who did not present themselves through stiff-necked sloth." The new navy represented a quite untraditional area for compulsory service, as did the civil service. The whole system was formalized by a law in 1722 that established a table of ranks, whereby there were fourteen parallel civil, army, and navy grades and each aristocrat was obliged to start at the bottom and win promotion through length of service or special merit. All military grades carried the privileges of nobility, as did the civil service from the eighth rank on. Peter was the first Romanov to create princes and counts (the latter a new title for Russia), beginning with the lowborn Menshikov, who became Prince Menshikov after 1707.

The disciplining of the nobility and the clergy under Peter was an attack on feudalism, and thus the revolutionary tsar was hailed in later times as a promoter of capitalism and the middle class. Trade and industry did, indeed, loom large in Peter's mind, but the class of merchants and factory owners remained relatively small and essentially crushed between state regulation and aristocratic privilege. Nothing comparable to the rise of the freewheeling middle class in Tudor-Stuart England or in Bourbon France took place in Petrine Russia. It was the appearance of prosperity, not its essentials, which interested the tsar.

What did occur under Peter was an intensified but still haphazard mercantilism, the promotion of economic development by a paternalistic state. There were great public works, notably the Ladoga-Volga Canal, connecting the Baltic and the Caspian, and, of course, the building of St. Petersburg itself. With the new outlet to the West, Russian trade quadrupled and showed a favorable balance—the export of raw materials bringing in more than the import of finished goods cost. Aside from general promotion policies such as the law which specified that Russian-made cloth must be used for the uniforms of both soldiers and servants, mercantilism under Peter often took the form of the most minute regulation of business activity. For example, a decree written by the tsar himself prescribed the use of train oil to prepare leather, instead of tar as of old. His belief in the need for such decrees is shown in the following observations:

> That there are few people wishing to go into business is true, for our people are like children, who never want to begin the alphabet unless they are compelled by their teacher. . . . So in manufacturing affairs we must not be satisfied with the proposition only, but we must act and even compel, and help by teaching, by machines, and other aids, and even by compulsion, to become good economists. For instance, where there is fine felt we should compel people to make hats, by not allowing the sale of felt unless a certain number of hats are made.

While the Petrine noble could at least look forward to retirement on his estates in his old age and while a successful Russian businessman could hope to end up with a fine town house in Petersburg, for the Russian peasantry there was only work and increased taxes. National security and glory were Peter's basic concerns, not the economic well-being of the masses. By them he would be remembered particularly for the institution of the passport system in 1722, making escape from serfdom virtually impossible. A portion of the serfs was for the first time forced to serve as professional soldiers, and the rest, besides maintaining their owners, were the primary payers of the head tax from which nobility in service were exempt. The head tax, levied on communities, not on individuals, accounted for three-fourths of the revenue, the rest coming from vexatious imposts on everything from oak coffins to beards. A census of sorts taken in 1718 required the use of troops to force the serf communities to reveal their true numbers.

Popular opposition to the ruler who relentlessly conscripted and taxed was widespread, and it thrived on the wildest rumors. It was reported that Peter was the son of a German girl substituted for a daughter born to

Tsaritsa Natalia. Another story had it that he was Lefort's child, and still another belief was that the real Peter had stayed abroad and sent back a foreigner in his place. The idea that the tsar was the Anti-Christ, widely accepted even in Tsar Alexis' day, seemed even more apt in the case of Alexis' son. A bishop and a printer daringly circulated the Anti-Christ view in a pamphlet, earning the one monkhood and the other cruel execution. Revolts there were and on a large scale, such as the Bulavin rising on the Volga in 1707, but Peter's new army and bureaucracy were too strong.

An admirer of Peter's once wrote: "The Tsar pulls uphill with the strength of ten, but millions pull downhill," thus characterizing not only the active opposition to Peter's reforms but the sheer inertia of old Russia as well. Peter himself on one occasion despaired of things to Catherine in the words: "How many there are to help me, you know for yourself." Yet in considerable measure, the tradition of absolutism and Peter's own dominance negated his hope for the development of an independent and responsible civil service. The tsar was often inconsistent, writing to one official that "you will pay with your head if you interpret orders again," while complaining to another of excessive cautiousness about instructions in these words: "This is as if a servant, seeing his master drowning, would not save him until he had satisfied himself as to whether it was written in his contract that he should pull him out of the water."

Corruption among his officials was a recurring problem of fantastic proportions for Peter. In 1714, for example, it was revealed that a governor in Archangel, with foreign trade going through his hands, had mulcted the state of 675,000 rubles. The tsar resorted to the institution of a set of special officials to ferret out corruption, paying informers, if necessary, and giving special attention to the affairs of senators. In 1722 the office of procurator-general was established "to be our Eye," since, in Peter's words, "it is a vain thing to make laws if they are not kept or if people play at cards with them."

In the face of such Russian traditions as corruption and parasitism, to say nothing of ignorance, Peter turned increasingly in his last years to educational reforms. The tsar declared: "For learning is good and fundamental and, as it were, the root, the seed, and first principle of all that is good and useful in church and state." The navigation school started at the beginning of the reign was followed later by several grammar schools, unique in that they were open to all classes. In 1714 Peter decreed compulsory elementary education for the children of the nobility and civil servants from the ages of ten to fifteen, providing the novel penalty that a graduation certificate was necessary for marriage. Yet by the end of the reign there were fewer than 3,000 school attendees in the secular institutions. Of all Peter's efforts, education fared worst, encountering much opposition from the very class the tsar expected to be leaders.

The unfortunate reality was that Peter not only had to provide schools for Russia but was obliged to furnish the learning materials as well. In addition to the first Russian newspaper, Peter provided even a new written language, introducing a script wherein the number of letters was reduced from forty-eight to forty. The first Russian textbook in arithmetic, printed in Amsterdam in 1699, was followed by a stream of translations, published in Russia, ranging from technical manuals to Aesop and Ovid. As in the case of business activity, Peter involved himself in this publishing with minute instructions, writing on one occasion: "Inasmuch as it is the practice of the Germans to fill their books with many useless details, in order that they may appear grand, see to it that such long-winded details be not translated. They only waste time and weary readers." In 1724 he brought about a favorite project, the founding of a Russian Academy of Sciences. This remained only on paper during his lifetime, however, except for the establishment of a library and museum (called the Kunstkammer). The museum, containing curiosities in the way of bones, rocks, and freaks of nature, is still a tourist attraction in Leningrad today, but it no longer serves free vodka, Peter's device to lure citizens there to be educated.

Little cultural activity was undertaken independently during Peter's reign. A handful of the nobility did make themselves connoisseurs of Western learning and arts, collecting libraries and embellishing their mansions. It is ironic that the most original literary production of the time, a work called *A Book on Poverty and Wealth,* was never seen by Peter, and its middle-class author Ivan Pososhkov—a mercantilist, a great admirer of the tsar, and a would-be adviser of his—was ignored, only to be arrested as a subversive in the next reign and left to die in prison.

It is entirely typical of Peter's concern for Western appearances that in 1717 he caused the translation of an etiquette book, a German pamphlet called *The Honorable Mirror of Youth.* In this it was set forth that those seeking preferment should avoid such gaucheries as cleaning their teeth with a knife, spitting in the midst of a group, wolfing down their food, and wearing heavy boots when dancing. The tsar further decreed that persons of means should entertain in the Western manner periodically. They were ordered to receive company at home between five and ten in the evening for the purpose of social intercourse and discussion of the news. The host did not have to be present always but was obliged to clear out several rooms and to provide tables and cards, candles and tobacco, and food and wine. Bowing and curtsying, done constantly according to traditional Russian manners, were limited to entrances and exits. The tsar himself was frequently guilty of cures worse than the disease—something that some people muttered was true of all his reforms for Russia. There is the story of the boyar who disdained eating salad as un-Russian; he was held by guardsmen while Peter forced lettuce and vinegar into his mouth until he bled.

Western envoys never ceased to be amazed and amused at the combination of new manners and old barbarities. They duly reported back instances where knee-breeched cotillions ended up as violent brawls. The Danish minister, after leaving a banquet at dawn, said that the land around the house looked like a battlefield, there being so many drunken bodies lying in the snow.

The veneer of the West was all Peter introduced to the favored classes of Russia, according to the observers of the time. Yet the veneer was to last and to deepen so that within a century a Russian noble could scarcely be told from a French aristocrat—not exactly the outcome wished by callous-handed Peter. In Alexis' time a boyar and a serf were so mutually ignorant and crude-mannered as to be distinguishable only by their clothes and basic wealth. After Peter, however, a great gap opened between noble and peasant—a gap with revolutionary implications. Besides the social transformation, the political, military, religious, and economic changes under Peter took root, too. The old Muscovy of the boyars, the patriarch, the *prikazi,* and the *streltsi* disappeared. Imperial Russia or Petersburg Russia —a new system dominated by government offices, barracks, and country houses—became the regime of the next two centuries. It was almost as if the first three or four Romanov rulers had not reigned, so completely was Westernized Russia identified with Romanov Russia and so persistently was Peter regarded by his successors as the founder of everything.

7. *The Passing of the Great Tsar*

As Peter reached his fifties, he traveled abroad less and turned to projects in and about St. Petersburg, enjoying a relaxed home life and holding court. His relationship with Catherine was exceedingly happy, barring one scandal and the loss of most of their children. Peter's associates were puzzled, however, that he acted so haphazardly in the matter of perpetuating his achievements by failing to regulate the succession to the throne.

The royal couple ordinarily lived in the modest Summer Palace, built from 1710 to 1712 on a canal across the river from the Peter and Paul Fortress. The house was less than 100 feet in length and contained fewer than a dozen rooms. Those occupying the first floor included Peter's bedroom done in red cloth, a study decorated with Delft tile and Dutch paintings, a dining room with a heavy square table seating no more than twelve, and a capacious kitchen. Restored and maintained scrupulously by the Soviet government, the Summer Palace is full of objects reminiscent of the great tsar: his armchair and suits of clothes, in which only a man the size of General de Gaulle might look comfortable; a snuffbox made of wood and mother-of-pearl in the shape of a ship; and a Dresden-made contraption in the form of a shield with three huge dials, showing, respectively, the time, the wind force, and the wind direction. Upstairs were Catherine's quarters, her more comfortable than pretentious bedroom, a children's room, a reception room, a throne room hung with tapestries, and a ballroom elegant for its English-made mirrors.

Catherine, too, was required to hold receptions on the European model. These usually took place in the late afternoon in the gardens of the palace, with the bands of the Preobrazhenskoe and Semenovskoe regiments providing entertainment. The former serving girl greeted her guests with simple dignity standing near a fountain in the midst of her ladies-in-waiting, attired in Paris creations or local facsimiles. Expecting the worst, foreigners were surprised at the gentility of it all and reported that Catherine's court was not inferior to the best of its small German counterparts. Somewhat incongruously, it was the tsar himself who saw to passing wine and beer, Peter all the while affecting military simplicity rather than finery or high fashion. There was dancing until midnight in a gallery overlooking the Neva, and the broad river provided a fine backdrop for displays of fireworks.

Following the execution of Alexis Petrovich, the heir to the throne was Catherine's son, Peter, born in 1715. Peter Petrovich was the darling of his parents and was proudly displayed at celebrations astride his little pony. A portrait of the tsarevich in the Summer Palace depicts a rosy-faced, chubby child with a hoop, but little Peter became sickly, and he died in May, 1719, at age three and a half. Another son was born, only to die soon after in 1723, leaving the royal couple only their two adolescent daughters, Anna and Elizabeth.

In a decree of 1722 Peter abruptly declared that the succession to the throne was henceforth to be dependent solely on the will of the reigning tsar. In one of his usual rambling explanations, he denounced primogeniture as stupid, dangerous, and unscriptural, concluding: "Thus children, or children's children, will not be tempted to fall into the sin of Absalom, and this law will be a curb on them." The dead Alexis had in the past been likened to the rebellious Absalom in the Bible, and Peter had the tsarevich's son, Peter Alexievich, in mind, too. It was ordered that the name of the grand duke follow those of his half aunts in the prayers for the imperial family, drawing protests from his relatives in Austria and causing twelve outraged Cossacks to blow themselves up in a church.

Traditionalists were further set aghast when the tsar announced that Catherine would be formally crowned empress, citing again Biblical and historical precedents. The coronation of Catherine took place in May, 1724, with extraordinary pomp and in the traditional setting, the Cathedral of the Assumption in Moscow. Catherine's crown was the most dazzling and expensive ever made. Paris jewelers fashioned it on the model of the Byzantine imperial diadem, using 2,564 precious stones of fantastic cost, among them jewels stripped from Peter's own crown and a huge ruby bought in Peking at the price of 60,000 rubles. The new empress' magnificent gold and scarlet brocade dress is still preserved.

But a few months after her coronation, Catherine faced charges of infidelity and the prospect of being discarded. She was accused of having an affair with her estate manager, William Mons, who was none other than the brother of Peter's former mistress, Anna Mons. Mons' lack of scruples was indicated by his earlier willingness to promote himself through his sister's charms. Considering the many evidences of Catherine's unbounded gratitude and devotion to her husband, it is improbable that she indulged in intimacies with Mons, although familiarities with him would not be inconsistent with her generous nature. The denouement was the kind of cruelty by Peter that people were accustomed to: Mons was horribly tortured and then beheaded, his listed crimes being somewhat beside the point—peculation and so forth. It was later reported Peter had ordered Mons' head preserved in spirits and the grisly reminder placed in Catherine's apartments—a barbarity, indeed, but the only personal punishment the tsar wished on his beloved.

By the age of fifty-two Peter had worn himself out, in spite of his originally iron constitution. The insinuations about Catherine and the obvious financial sins of Menshikov caused the tsar moments of self-doubt and despair. Attacks of ill health came with worrying frequency after his return from the Persian campaign, but Peter cursed out the doctors and recovered. In late 1724, against medical advice, he embarked on a fatiguing inspection tour of the great Ladoga-Volga Canal, followed by a visit to the ironworks in the far north, during which the tsar set an example by digging out a huge chunk of ore with his bare hands. While on his way back to St. Petersburg in November, Peter saw a boatload of soldiers foundering on the rocks of a river, and unthinkingly and characteristically, he plunged into the icy water to save them from drowning.

Back in the capital, Peter began to have convulsions, all too familiar from the past, but now with redoubled violence. A long history of syphilis was later alleged to be the truly debilitating factor. As late as January, 1725, the tsar showed himself in public, but then he took to his bed for good. When his agony became more sharp and prolonged, he alternated between having religious finalities performed and issuing pardons to imprisoned swindlers and deserters, to all but murderers and major outlaws. Catherine was at his bedside continuously, trying to soothe the great head in her arms as she had done so often in the past. In the final moments Peter gave thought to the succession and began to say: "I give all to . . ." His daughter was called to write down his wishes, but he could utter no more, and the empress closed his eyes.

"Thunderstorm," "whirlwind," "hurricane"—all these words were used to describe Peter the Great by his awed contemporaries and successors. Another term, "the first Bolshevik," was more recently invented in an effort to convey the energy and impact of his revolutionary reign. A titan Peter was, indeed, grandiose both in his visions and his accomplishments and in his outrages and cruelties. A bully and a tyrant, Peter was yet patient in defeat, modest in victory, and more demanding of himself than of others. Of all the Romanovs, he was the self-made tsar.

VIII.

The Dynasty in Disarray:
Catherine I, Peter II,
Anna, and Ivan VI

1. Family Feuds, Factions, and the Choice of 1725

As Peter the Great lay dying in his modest palace in his half-completed capital, it became apparent that the future of Russia and of the Romanovs was full of the greatest uncertainties. Thirty-six years of iron rule were drawing to a close. No successor to the throne had been named, a step seemingly especially incumbent on Peter since it was he who had recently decreed that the choice of heir was to be dictated not by hereditary right but by the will of the reigning autocrat. Unhappily, there were numerous individual candidates for the new imperial title, divided among three separate and mutually antagonistic branches of the dynasty.

The most devoted attendant of the expiring giant was his second wife, Catherine. She wanted to rule after him—perhaps, to continue his work; certainly, to protect her own position; and, above all, to safeguard the interests of her family. Her surviving children were only the tsarevnas Anna and Elizabeth, who even now joined with full devotion in the nursing and praying for a beloved father.

Already the two tsarevnas presented personal contrasts for courtiers to whisper about and alluring prospects for them to plot over, even if both, as everyone knew, were conceived out of wedlock. Eighteen-year-old Anna was brunet, statuesque, amiable, and intellectual—altogether a worthy heir of the great Westernizing tsar—but it was blond and vivacious Elizabeth, now sixteen, who had, as a child, been unsuccessfully promoted by the tsar as a bride for Louis XV of France. The younger sister was shamelessly flirtatious, and there already was gossip. Currently, the politically prized young Duke of Holstein was in St. Petersburg, paying court to each of the tsarevnas.

Some miles east of the palace where the tsar lay dying rose the forbidding prison-fortress of Schlüsselburg. Here brooded an ex-tsarina, Eudoxia, Peter's first wife, a dour and cantankerous woman of sixty. Allowed to maintain something of a court, Eudoxia surrounded herself with monks and other malcontents who opposed all the innovations of the regime and who considered their benefactress still the lawful tsarina. The ex-tsarina had much to ponder. There was the unthinkable death of her firstborn son, the Tsarevich Alexis, possibly by his father's own hand. Fortunately, Alexis had left an heir, Peter, and on this ten-year-old grand duke rested all of Eudoxia's hopes of personal vindication, of overturning the impieties of Peter, of a regency, and of revenge. The orphaned grand duke had never seen his grandmother and could have had no idea of the fervent expectations on his behalf of the antireform party. Although little Peter came not first, but last, in the official prayers for the royal family, he was brought up in honor in the tsar's household and was genuinely loved by his stepmother, Catherine, as he was by his singularly appealing older sister, Natalia. The young grand duke and grand duchess quite naturally joined their half aunts Anna and Elizabeth in the frightened group of children near the deathbed.

In one of the lesser palaces of Russia's new capital lived yet a third tsarina, Praskovia, widow of the dim-witted but fertile Ivan V, older half brother of Peter the Great and for a few years co-tsar with him. Praskovia was old-fashioned but good-natured and tremendously charitable. She was said to run her house more like a hospital than like a royal residence. Tsar Peter greatly favored Praskovia and her three daughters—the Ivanovs, as this branch of the dynasty was called—especially since marriageable princesses were very useful in diplomacy. The eldest daughter, Catherine, had been allied with the Duke of Mecklenburg, unfortunately a worthless prince hated so generally that he and his wife seemed doomed never to return to Russia. Anna, the second Ivanovna, was thirty-two and already widowed, her husband, the Duke of Courland, having died immediately after the lavish wedding festivities. The youngest Ivanovna, the somewhat sickly and stupid Praskovia, was unmarried and still at home. Praskovia, the mother and tsaritsa of unblemished background, might well reason that her daughters had excellent, even prior, claims to Russia's throne. The fortunes of the Ivanovs and their adherents would certainly flourish if a stalemate arose between the claims of the Empress Catherine and her daughters and those of Peter's first wife and her heirs.

The existence of such a large number of possible successors to the Romanov throne, all of them women except for a ten-year-old boy, offered great opportunity for intrigue. The play of factions was encouraged by the tremendous social cleavages and political antagonisms brought about by the revolutionary works of Peter the Great. No tsar before or after Peter so completely divided Russia's ruling classes into two camps—two ways of looking at the past, two modes of present existence, and two programs for the future.

The chief lieutenant of Tsar Peter in the past and natural leader of the pro-Western faction was Prince Menshikov. Although the prince's palace in St. Petersburg was grander than the royal residence itself, no one was likely to forget Menshikov's humble beginnings. Possessing now the most resounding titles in Russia, Menshikov had one of the greatest fortunes in Europe and an insatiable thirst for graft. Several times the tsar had angrily forced Menshikov to make restitution to the state of sums like 200,000 rubles. Even now he was in disgrace and under house arrest with a Senate judgment for corruption facing him.

Prince Tolstoy was allied with Menshikov in interest, even though this hard and unscrupulous man was of the old aristocracy. At an early age Tolstoy had linked his fortunes to those of the reforming tsar and had performed countless tasks for him, including luring the Tsarevich Alexis back to his execution, a fact which ex-Tsarina Eudoxia and her supporters would not be likely to forgive.

Another major figure in the new establishment was the German Osterman, who had made the College of Foreign Affairs his domain. Astute as he was to be in guessing which way political survival lay, Osterman was singularly uncorrupt, kindly, and sober in an era notorious for viciousness. The dying tsar appreciated the qualities of the man who had started as his private secretary, calling him "indispensable" as the only one who had never made a diplomatic blunder.

Elsewhere in Petersburg gathered the men who hated the Menshikovs, the Tolstoys, and the Ostermans. Here were many of the fabled names of Russia, the Trubetskoys, the Repnins, the Golitsyns, and the Dolgorukys, noble families who mostly traced their descent from Rurik's Viking companions of the ninth century and who could well regard the Romanovs themselves as come-latelies. Many of them occupied high posts in Peter's regime, but it rankled that their genealogies counted so much less than hard work and ability.

The most learned and eloquent of the old aristocracy was Prince Dmitri Michaelovich Golitsyn. Honest, upright, haughty to extremes, Golitsyn had been educated abroad and remained a cultivated man when he returned to his great boyar's inheritance. It was not ignorance of the modern world but the conservatism of conviction that had made him again and again question innovation.

Of the old nobility the Dolgorukys made up in numbers what they lacked in ability. The several princes Dolgoruky were born intriguers, and they had marriageable daughters and sons. Their chief desire was to return to their Moscow estates, where they could hunt to their hearts' content and influence the Kremlin at the same time.

Long before Peter's death was announced, plots and rumors of plots grew apace. The clergy was openly blessing the cause of Grand Duke Peter, the candidate of the Golitsyns and Dolgorukys. Menshikov and Tolstoy were purportedly bribing the Guards regiments.

An open confrontation took place the night of January 28 in the Senate chambers. Prince Golitsyn declared that the Grand Duke Peter was the natural, lawful heir. Prince Tolstoy countered that Catherine had experience in ruling and had already been crowned empress. A compromise to let Peter reign in name under a temporary regency of Catherine and Menshikov was not accepted. Golitsyn hinted that the aristocracy should permanently limit the powers of the autocracy, but other great nobles opposed him, as did the reform party. One of Peter's secretaries proposed in vain that a decision be postponed until the summoning of a Zemsky Sobor, a parliament of all the land such as had chosen the first Romanov in 1613.

There were drum rolls in the courtyard as the Preobrazhenskoe and Semenovskoe Guards regiments drew up in formation. The commander of the Petersburg garrison, Prince Anikita Ivanevich Repnin, flew into a rage and demanded to know by whose authority the troops had been called out. A subordinate officer announced that it was by command of the Empress Catherine herself, adding ominously that Repnin, like every Russian subject, had better swear allegiance. All the dignitaries complied, and a delegation took the news to Catherine, who was still weeping at her dead husband's bedside.

The drama of January, 1725, was to be repeated, with only slight variations in cast, a dozen times in the course of the century. Each of the three branches of the Romanov family was to occupy the throne at one time or another. Both the reform party and the antireformers were to taste power. In all the crises, as in this one that brought Catherine to the throne, the role of the Guards regiments was to be decisive. To foreign observers it often seemed that the destinies of Russia and the Romanovs reposed in the barrack rooms of the Preobrazhenskoe Regiment, rather than in the old Kremlin or even in the new Winter Palace.

2. Catherine I: A Peasant and a Parvenu Rule in Petersburg

When the Senate in St. Petersburg proclaimed that all should render faithful service to Catherine, autocrat of all the Russias, it was making fantastic breaks with tradition. Russians were asked to pay homage to a ruler with no Romanov blood, a commoner, a foreigner, and a woman. Yet no effort was made by the numerous heirs of Romanov name and blood to challenge the authority of Peter's consort. No protest was voiced publicly by the great noble families of Russia against the fact that a former peasant ruled over them as successor to Rurik and the Ivans and Alexis. Only some of the' common people were puzzled and obstreperous. On the day for swearing allegiance many of the humble men of Moscow refused to take the oath, saying that since a woman had become tsar, only women should kiss the cross to her.

The empress and her supporters were careful to consolidate their position. Every effort was made to please the Guards regiments: Money for their back pay was found; work by the soldiers on the Ladoga Canal was abolished; and new uniforms were issued. Catherine herself found many occasions to visit her Guards officers, flattering them by serving them wine with her own hand. There were also measures taken to allay any possible outbreak on the part of the common people. Menshikov, who realized that the burdens on the serfs were at the point of being intolerable, persuaded the empress to reduce the head tax by one-third and to cancel all arrears. But generally, the new regime simply continued the projects and policies of the old; in Catherine's position she had no choice. Peter's cherished Academy of Sciences, for example, came into being during the reign of his unlettered wife; at first, all the academicians were perforce foreigners.

Catherine's court remained in the raw new capital on the Baltic. This was not yet the place for a brilliant and sumptuous royal court, and foreign ambassadors regarded it as a dreary post of exile. Yet Catherine I laid the foundations for the grandeur that would come forty years later under her great namesake. Her personal extravagance became a byword. The cost of maintaining the court increased to 6,500,000 rubles, several times what it had been in the frugal days of Peter. Observers also noted that the tone of the court changed, and for the better. Gone were the crudities of Peter's day—the vulgar pranks and the bacchanalian feasts, where the women were expected to drink glass for glass with the men.

Catherine herself, at thirty-eight, hardly cut a brilliant figure. Once buxom and vivacious, she was now fat and spent. A visiting German princess described her hostess as a short, squat, graceless, slatternly woman who waddled like a duck and who wore unfashionable and unclean dresses bedecked with a jangling array of religious medals and patriotic emblems.

None of the several portraits of Catherine I to be seen in Russia suggests that she was really a peasant in disguise, but the preaccession ones do indicate a little diffidence and discomfiture. The paintings of her as empress show a somewhat puffy-faced woman, but her features remained good and her look direct, imperturbable, and kind.

No longer beautiful and still illiterate, the empress was shrewd, commonsensical, and extremely even-tempered. Her generosity to her friends was unbounded. She gave herself no airs and openly reminisced of her lowly past in Lithuania. Some of her peasant relatives of the Skavronsky family were brought to Petersburg, the prettiest young girl, Sophia, being made a lady-in-waiting, while two brother were created counts.

The empress had little inclination or ability to deal with affairs of state. In the first month of her reign, at Baron Osterman's suggestion, a new institution was established: the Supreme Secret Council "to lighten the heavy burden of government for her Majesty." This Privy Council was also a guarantee of the future for the reform group. Only six men were designated privy councilors: Menshikov, Tolstoy, Osterman, two other reliables, and Prince D. M. Golitsyn. The first meeting of this exalted new arm of government was preceded by a banquet, and it is reported that when the ailing Osterman arrived for the transaction of public business, he found the others not at the council table but literally under it.

Drunk or sober, Menshikov emerged as the real ruler of Russia. One of his first acts was to quash the legal proceedings instituted against him in the previous reign, and then he proceeded to use his position shamelessly to increase his properties and hoards, setting an example of venality which was soon imitated by all the lesser bureaucrats.

Foreign policy was under the firm hand of Osterman, and the abilities of this astute Westphalian were sorely needed at a time when the European powers hopefully expected Russia to lapse into anarchy. Two crises, involving not only diplomacy but the family affairs of the dynasty, were successfully surmounted. The first stemmed from the marriage of the empress' elder daughter, the stately and intelligent Anna, to the Duke of Holstein, in Petersburg in May, 1725. This duke was a claimant to the Swedish throne, and his position in Holstein involved him in the complicated politics of Germany—that is, the Holy Roman Empire. The upshot of an international game of nerves was that King George I of England, feeling his position as Elector of Hanover menaced, sent the English navy to the Baltic to overawe the Duke of Holstein's chief protector, Russia. An English ultimatum was rejected by Osterman in the name of Empress Catherine with such vigor and pride that George I soon withdrew his ships.

The second crisis concerned Russia's interest in the duchy of Courland, where Anna, a Romanov princess of the Ivanov branch of the family, resided unhappily and uneasily as the widowed grand duchess. In 1726 there suddenly appeared at the grand ducal capital, Mitau, a brilliant and unscrupulous adventurer, Maurice of Saxony, an illegitimate son of the

King of Saxony. Maurice proceeded to bribe and cajole the estates of Courland into electing him grand duke. Far from acting to prevent this turn of events, Anna Ivanovna begged to marry the dashing newcomer. Osterman reasoned, however, that it was not at all in Russia's interest to have an independent-minded duke in Courland, which was only 400 miles from St. Petersburg. Forthwith, Menshikov was sent with an army to teach the Mitauers a lesson. Maurice escaped capture by jumping out of a window, and Grand Duchess Anna was left once more to her empty title, her memories, and her boredom.

In December, 1726, the empress' health began to fail markedly. Catherine's physical condition had been greatly weakened by her habit of banqueting with her Skavronsky relatives until five in the morning. She caught a severe chill when she was forced to flee her apartments in the middle of a winter night because the waters of the Neva River had risen suddenly and flooded the palace.

Once more the court seethed with intrigue over the question of the succession. The Dolgorukys and Golitsyns again had the clergy saying special prayers in the cause of the Grand Duke Peter Alexievich. Count Tolstoy, who had the most to fear from this quarter, persistently worked on Catherine to name one of her own daughters, both of whom were coached by Tolstoy to shed tears of fright for their future. Which daughter was the problem. The more moral and intellectual Anna was ideal, except that her accession would give a dominant position in affairs to her husband, the Duke of Holstein, and his foreign entourage. Tolstoy accordingly promoted the candidacy of the younger daughter, the gay and flirtatious Elizabeth. There would be a regency, Holstein could be army chief, and Grand Duke Peter would be got out of the way by sending him abroad to complete his education. When Tolstoy's scheme failed to find favor, the wily Osterman suddenly suggested the startling compromise of marrying the eleven-year-old grand duke to his seventeen-year-old aunt, but his proposal was opposed as incestuous, and the empress would not countenance it.

The situation was resolved in an unexpected manner: Prince Menshikov deserted Tolstoy and threw his support to Grand Duke Peter. This switch was brought about largely by the secret efforts of the Austrian ambassador in the name of the Hapsburg emperor, who was Peter's uncle through marriage and who promised Menshikov the first vacant electoral seat in the Holy Roman Empire. Although Catherine preferred to name one of her own, she desired peace above all and acceded to Menshikov's solution.

The empress died on May 28, 1727, after a reign lasting a few months more than two years. Although her ignorance of public affairs had been laughable and her extravagance outrageous, there was a dignity to this woman of common origins and tastes. Catherine did her drinking in private. She kept the peace abroad without appeasement, and she soothed the factions of the dynasty and nobility at home. Deservedly revered as the devoted consort of the great Peter, Catherine as ruler had demonstrated that her husband's reforms might survive without his strong hand.

3. Peter II: Four-legged and Two-legged Dogs Supreme

The will of the late empress was read to the dignitaries of Russia in a great hall of the Winter Palace, and then the young grand duke was proclaimed sovereign autocrat as Peter II. Everyone in turn kissed the great cross of the metropolitan. The new tsar descended to the courtyard of the palace, and the area rang with the shouts of the assembled Guards regiments. Later Peter presided ceremoniously over a solemn meeting of the Privy Council. The first day of his reign ended with a banquet in Menshikov's mansion, where the greatest magnates of the land vied with one another to serve the boy monarch on bended knee.

At age eleven Peter was a handsome lad. Tall and well built, he was high-spirited and active, although occasionally he seemed to withdraw into himself and observers claimed to detect a trace of melancholy in his face. The boy's underlying character was still a mystery.

Peter's mother, Princess Charlotte of the obscure German state of Blankenburg-Wolfenbüttel, had died giving birth to him, and he was orphaned by the time he was three, when the Tsarevich Alexis was executed. Instead of being given over to the care of his relatives such as his grandmother, Eudoxia, the child was brought up by a succession of strangers in the back rooms of the court of Tsar Peter and his second wife. His first governesses were respectively the wives of a vintner and of a tailor, foreigners in Petersburg, and it is said they treated him very harshly. Later he was put in the charge of an ordinary sailor who taught him such accomplishments as playing the hornpipe. Then his grandfather entrusted the young Romanov's education to a Hungarian refugee. This tutor was reasonably capable, and, at the time of his accession, Peter was credited with an understanding of German, French, and Latin, an accomplishment of which his predecessors could hardly boast. Precocious was the word for Peter, his tutor reported, for he appeared to be naturally lazy.

Within a week of being hailed Tsar of Russia, Peter was taken from the royal apartments and installed by Menshikov in his own great mansion on Vasily Island, which was the suburb across the Neva from the Winter Palace where the nobility were erecting their town houses. Menshikov treated Peter with paternal solicitude, surrounding him with an entourage of young people, mostly sons of staunch adherents of the prince. Maria

Menshikov, two years older than the tsar, was in this group, and in a very short time she was betrothed to him in a formal religious ceremony followed by a gay party.

Peter's education was now entrusted to no less a personage than Osterman himself, who also apparently was a permanent house guest of Menshikov. The foreign affairs director laid down an elaborate plan for the royal instruction that would occupy four hours every day. First came courses that Osterman felt had immediate utility: modern history, especially of neighboring states; general political economy, or what would be called comparative government in a later day; and the science of war. Of lesser or supplementary use was a second group of courses: ancient history, mathematics, geography, astronomy, natural science, archeology, heraldry, and genealogy. Whenever possible, biographies would be introduced to teach the tsar the virtues of great monarchs and the works and fate of evildoers. Peter was not required to read and report himself; the method of learning was listening to declamations by Osterman and other instructors. He was encouraged, however, to keep a diary. Whatever Peter may have thought of this regimen of study, he quickly developed a great fondness for the kindly German, and it is said that the first thing the boy did each morning was to run down the halls, still wearing his nightclothes, to greet Osterman in his rooms.

Peter's confidant was his sister, the twelve-year-old Natalia, who had shared all the difficulties of his early years. Everyone associated with the court found this girl to be the most lovable of royalty. She was not beautiful, and there was something pathetic in her bearing, but Natalia was all heart and mind, wise beyond her years. She was readily enlisted by Osterman to counter the indolence and frivolity that often seemed to take hold of her brother.

Another close companion of the not-yet-adolescent tsar was his fourteen-year-old aunt, Elizabeth, perhaps not altogether a good influence. Elizabeth was a laughing and lively blonde. She apparently had no regret that her side of the family had lost out in the game of capturing the throne. A great horsewoman and devotee of dancing, she "always had one foot in the air," according to the Spanish ambassador, who was offended by the giddiness of the tsarevna but who could not help reporting that Elizabeth was the most exquisite creature in court.

With the tsar and his young companions relegated to studies and amusements, Menshikov ruled Russia. The prince acted swiftly to make his position unassailable by exiling his enemies to remote posts. To the White Sea whale fisheries went Count Tolstoy, once Menshikov's ally but now abruptly dismissed as privy councilor for backing the tsarevna. The Privy Council, initially the stronghold of the reform party, was filled with Golitsyns and Dolgorukys, Menshikov's new associates. The ultimate sop to the sensibilities of the old aristocracy came when Menshikov authorized the transfer of ex-Tsarina Eudoxia from Schlüsselburg Prison to a nunnery near Moscow.

The Duke of Holstein, considered a rival, was asked to leave the country. He eventually took up residence in his ducal seat at Kiel, enjoying a liberal pension from Menshikov's government. This development led to an important event in the affairs of the dynasty. Happy in her new country, the Duchess of Holstein—Anna, the older sister of the Tsarevna Elizabeth—gave birth to a son in February, 1728. This boy, named Peter, was a distinguished prince to behold when he was presented to cheering crowds in Kiel, for he was the first male Romanov born in more than a decade and he was a grandson of two of the major figures of the century, Peter I of Russia and Charles XII of Sweden. But his birth was attended by tragedy. There was a great ball with fireworks afterward, which the young duchess insisted on watching. As she stood in the chill air on her balcony, she turned aside warnings, saying she was Russian and used to a worse climate. She was dead in ten days. In accordance with her wish, the body of Tsarevna Anna was brought back to Russia to be laid at the side of her beloved parents, Peter and Catherine. Her baby remained in Holstein, until as a young man he caught the fancy of a Russian empress—unfortunately for everyone concerned.

In Russia, as the year 1727 wore on, the Menshikov regime ruled efficiently and energetically, however corruptly. The French ambassador to the court of Peter II reported that not even the late Tsar Peter the Great "was so feared or obeyed" as Menshikov, and "God help him that resists." One enlightened act of Menshikov's government was to remove the stone columns from the capital and Moscow where the heads and limbs of executed criminals and traitors were exposed to the elements, the birds, and, presumably, the conscience of the populace.

It became evident, however, that Menshikov had overreached himself as far as the young tsar was concerned. The first nasty scene was over money, a strange thing for Menshikov to be particular about. The city fathers of St. Petersburg had made a present of several thousand rubles to Peter, who with boyish enthusiasm presented it to his beloved sister. Learning of this, Menshikov intervened, took the money, and lectured Peter on the value of things. Enraged, the tsar shouted in a voice which was just beginning to break: "I will see whether you or I am the Emperor." The young tsar began to mutter about Menshikov's familiarity, including his custom of referring to himself as "your father."

Late in the summer of 1727 Menshikov fell so sick as to require extreme unction at one point. The tsar, the Tsarevna Natalia, and the Tsarevna Elizabeth absented themselves from the capital, as did Osterman, the royal party holding court at Peterhof, the new summer palace being built on the breezy shores of the Gulf of Finland. The management of affairs seemed to proceed quite serenely without Menshikov. When the prince recovered his health, he proceeded to destroy his status entirely. In a drunken interview, he brought about a rupture with Osterman, accusing him of being an atheist. Then Menshikov presented himself at Peterhof with other complaints. There was no meek surrender. Peter turned his back on his exalted guardian and said to his astonished entourage, "You see, I am at last learning how to keep him in order."

The fall of Menshikov dated from September, 1727, when the Privy Council denounced him for treason and levied a fine of 500,000 rubles against the master grafter. His execution was recommended, but Menshikov's daughters softened the young tsar's heart in a tearful interview. Menshikov was allowed to depart to his estates in the Ukraine, and it is reported that his move from the capital required four six-horse carriages and sixty wagons of baggage. The tsar's betrothal to his daughter was, of course, annulled.

Peter, now twelve, fell easily into other self-seeking hands. Of the members of the old nobility now entrenched in the Privy Council, the Golitsyns deserved well of Peter II, since they had been unswerving in their loyalty to his father and to him, but their leader, Prince D. M. Golitsyn, was simply too imperious and aloof, and he had been compromised by his recent close relationship to Menshikov. Into the vacuum of power thus created came the Dolgorukys, that numerous and muddleheaded clan of the ancient Muscovite aristocracy. The three Dolgorukys now in the Privy Council first consolidated their position by establishing fifteen-year-old ivan Dolgoruky as chief companion of the tsar. Young Ivan, a strapping, good-natured, and idle-minded product of the boyar class, was installed in the same room Peter slept in and soon distracted the tsar from any thoughts of ruling or even learning to rule. To no avail Peter's sister, Natalia, warned him of "bad companions." Osterman chided him about his neglect of his studies, but Peter ended this interview haughtily with the words, "My dear Andrei Ivanovich, I like you and . . . you are indispensable, but I must ask you not to interfere in the future with my pastimes."

Peter's personal development and the future history of Russia were at stake when the Dolgorukys secured the removal of the royal court to Moscow in January, 1728, ostensibly only to hold the coronation there as sanctified by four centuries of tradition. With Peter in the Kremlin, the Dolgorukys were bold enough to secure the release of Tsarina Eudoxia from her nunnery and to talk of her assuming a regency. Even Osterman hastened to write ingratiating letters to the first wife of Peter the Great.

But the ceremonial interview between Peter II and the grandmother he had never seen proved to be pathetically unaffectionate and halting. Everyone was relieved to see the senile Eudoxia return to her nunnery forever, with a pension of 60,000 rubles.

The coronation of Peter II on February 25, 1728, recalled all the Byzantine splendor of old Muscovy, despite the Western clothes and uniforms of the Petersburg people. The young tsar spent a whole week in prayer and fasting. On the day of the ceremony in Uspensky Cathedral he was paraded around Moscow in a carriage drawn by eight horses, Ivan Dolgoruky at his side. The festivities ended with a banquet given by the Spanish ambassador.

Shortly after the coronation, some mysterious letters from Menshikov to Tsarina Eudoxia were brought to light. The Dolgorukys talked of plots on the part of the reform party and brought about Menshikov's complete ruin. The great prince and his family were exiled to Berezov, a little village in the tundra zone of Siberia, where the mean annual temperature was four degrees above zero. One of the most celebrated of Russian historical paintings, by Repin in the nineteenth century, shows this corrupt but capable minister of three rulers as a haggard old man, broken by the completeness of his fall and inconsolable in the midst of his three faithful daughters, one of whom was almost a tsarina.

The court stayed on in Moscow, despite the grumblings of the Petersburg civil servants and military. The young tsar soon made apparent his own feelings in the matter, declaring that he hated St. Petersburg with its gloomy fortresses and its ever-present sea and shipping. "What am I to do in a place where there's nothing but salt water?" he exclaimed to the foreign minister, adding grandly—and ominously for Russia's future—"I will not sail the seas as my grandfather did." Eventually, even mention of St. Petersburg was forbidden. The navy would be left to disintegrate.

Peter was becoming a tall, strong, and handsome young man, but only in those respects did he resemble his illustrious namesake. Reserved of nature, he reminded observers of the ill-fated Alexis, and he had inherited his father's aversion to strong drink. His preoccupation with dogs and horses recalled the days of his great-grandfather, Tsar Alexis. Dogs were a subject in which Osterman had little interest, and Peter began to shun his official tutor.

The last good influence on the young tsar was removed by the tragic death of Tsarevna Natalia in late 1729. Osterman was in despair at the loss of this enlightened, Western-minded Romanov. The Spanish ambassador recorded bitterly, "Thus died a Princess who was the idol of all good people, the pearl of Russia, a creature far too perfect to be left by God in the midst of barbarians." Peter had been away hunting when his sister died, and subsequently he shut himself up for three days, overcome with grief.

Shortly afterward, Peter's young aunt, Elizabeth, fell from favor. Deprived now of both her mother and her sister, the tsarevna was thrown back on her own modesty and prudence, things she simply did not have. The Dolgorukys were unwilling, however, to cast aside this royal hussy altogether and proposed that their young Ivan marry her. Elizabeth refused, preferring her freedom, and found her expense money pared down to virtually nothing.

When the Privy Council had the Government Mint transferred back to Moscow, it appeared that St. Petersburg had ceased permanently to be the capital. Osterman and the foreign ambassadors made desperate last efforts to appeal to Peter II but found that they could not even gain an audience. As a final expedient they tried passing a letter to the tsar through none other than his blockheaded crony Ivan, but even this was forestalled by the elder Dolgorukys. To assure their triumph, the new ruling group hastened to organize a grand hunting party for Peter. The tsar was absent from Moscow for a full two months, proceeding from one hunting lodge to another, accompanied by 620 dogs and a giddy company of Dolgoruky youngsters, both male and female. When Peter returned to the Kremlin, he could boast that he had killed 3 bears, 5 wolves, 50 foxes, and 4,000 hares.

The triumph of the reactionaries seemed assured with the announcement in November, 1729, of the betrothal of Peter to Catherine Dolgoruky, two years his senior and the daughter of Prince Alexis. The Golitsyns were enraged by the success of the rival boyar clan, and apparently even the Dolgorukys themselves were divided by jealousies and began fighting over future preferments. What is more, it was plain that the tsar himself was unhappy and becoming increasingly morose and withdrawn. One day at a banquet someone tried to draw Peter out on the subject of his exploits in a recent chase. The tsar muttered that he did not need to discuss the hunt when he was surrounded by four two-legged dogs all the time. As for his wife-to-be, Peter avoided seeing her.

The wedding date had been set for January 30, 1730. A week or two earlier Peter officiated at the ceremony of the blessing of the waters and caught a cold. Soon the tsar's continuing indisposition was diagnosed as smallpox. He died, aged fifteen, on the day he was to have been married.

During the final moments, Prince Dolgoruky in desperation thrust his daughter into the expiring tsar's bed. Coitus having taken place, the prince was to announce, Catherine was rightful successor to the throne. Harebrained Ivan Dolgoruky ran out of the palace sword in hand, shouting hysterically, "The Tsar is dead. My sister is Empress."

4. The Crisis of 1730: The Last Stand of the Old Aristocracy

Once Peter II had breathed his last, the royal physician slipped away and hastened to the apartments of the Tsarevna Elizabeth to urge her to make the most of the situation. Drowsy and bemused from the usual evening of revelry, she acknowledged his warnings, yawned, and went back to sleep.

All the notables of Russia had been assembled in the Kremlin for the joyous occasion of the tsar's wedding. Now, on the night of January 30–31, they confronted the task of deciding on Peter's successor, in the absence of any will or other indication from the late ruler. It soon became apparent that they would have to consider the claims of all the surviving members of the imperial house, a dynasty in rather complete disarray at this point. The possible claimants included the dowager Tsarina Eudoxia, dotty but still alive in her nunnery; two-year-old Peter of Holstein, son of the late Tsarevna Anna; the scandalous Tsarevna Elizabeth; Catherine Ivanovna, Duchess of Mecklenburg; Anna Ivanovna, Duchess of Courland; Praskovia Ivanovna, the third daughter of Ivan V; and, finally, Catherine Dolgoruky, the betrothed of Peter II.

The vital deliberations actually took place among a small group of men sitting in an antechamber apart from the hundreds of lesser dignitaries. This was the Privy Council, once the stronghold of the reform party. Now it was almost exclusively a club of the old aristocracy, for of eight members who met for this midnight conference, four were Dolgorukys and two were Golitsyns. Despite its family composition, the Privy Council promptly rejected as preposterous Prince Alexis Dolgoruky's claim for his daughter. Why, indeed, should the other Dolgorukys be ruled by their niece? The succession of the Tsarina Eudoxia was more than even these conservative boyars could stomach. The discussion dragged on until finally Prince D. M. Golitsyn took the floor.

In the critical years since Peter the Great's death Golitsyn had felt that his talents were ignored, and he had come to abhor not the Romanovs so much as the autocracy and the favoritism that went with it. Now at last Golitsyn found his leadership sought. In his speech to the Privy Council he first of all stated that the tragic death of Peter II was the punishment of God for Russia's adoption of foreign ways and vices. He then pronounced all the descendants of Peter the Great by Catherine illegitimate. Of the remaining possible claimants to the throne, Golitsyn rejected Catherine Ivanovna as the wife of an alien and worthless prince and her youngest sister, Praskovia, as a hopeless ninny. The only logical candidate, declared the prince, was the widowed, entirely Russian Anna, Duchess of Courland, the middle sister. In the face of his logic and eloquence, the other seven privy councilors all shouted, "Agreed."

At this point Golitsyn might have concluded his remarks with the familiar political adage that a bad title makes a good monarch. Instead, he put this crucial question to his fellow nobles: "Would you not do well to act now so as to ease matters for yourselves hereafter?" In effect, Golitsyn was making the dramatic proposal to limit the autocracy by making it subject to the control of an oligarchy. This would mean a constitution, for the benefit not of all the people, but of the great aristocrats, a Russian Magna Carta.

Golitsyn's proposal found immediate response. The Privy Council speedily drew up *Punkti* (Points of Government) for submission to the Grand Duchess Anna. In the future, the consent of the self-perpetuating Privy Council would be necessary in all these matters: the marriage of the sovereign; the choice of an heir; the declaration of war or conclusion of peace; the appointment of commanders of the Guards regiments; the levying of new taxes; and the depriving of a noble of life, liberty, or property. The Privy Council was seeking to freeze into law the commanding role it had frequently played under those haphazard autocrats Catherine I and Peter II.

The council's choice of Anna as successor and the *Punkti* as well gained the vocal approval of the dignitaries assembled elsewhere in the Kremlin. Certain people, however, promptly sent off messengers to Courland warning Anna against submitting to the Golitsyns and Dolgorukys. Nonetheless, when the *Punkti* were formally presented to her in Mitau, she felt that she had no choice but to sign them, along with a declaration acknowledging that failure to fulfill them would mean dethronement. This was a supreme humiliation for the Romanov dynasty.

While awaiting the arrival of the new empress, Moscow began to indulge in political speculation of a nature and degree entirely unprecedented in Russian history. Once any curb on the autocracy had been proposed, it seemed legitimate for citizens to discuss the whole political system. A French diplomat wrote to Paris that "here, in the streets and in houses alike, one hears nothing save talk of the English constitution and the rights of the English Parliament." There were even those who proposed a republic. The main undertone was one of resentment against the privy councilors for considering only the selfish interests of their class. The lesser nobility, serving in the huge army and bureaucracy created by Peter, feared for their future. One of these wrote about the events of the time: "May God grant that in place of an Autocrat-Emperor we not be given a half score of arrogant and mighty families, for then we serving gentry will be undone."

Empress Anna traveled from Mitau first to St. Petersburg, making her royal progress as grand as possible. At the gates of the new-old capital she was presented with the ribbon and Cross of St. Andrew by representatives of the Privy Council, but Anna simply took the medal and put it on with a remark to the effect that it was hers by right, hers only to give. Afterward she proclaimed herself colonel of the Preobrazhenskoe Guards, a step that immediately infringed the *Punkti,* and she personally saw to serving the officers drinks.

Nonetheless, the Privy Council largely succeeded in keeping the empress in ignorance of affairs, foiling, for example, an effort to smuggle messages to her in the bib of the baby of one of her ladies-in-waiting. Anna finally entered Moscow in the middle of February, 1730. The Privy Council felt confident enough of its strength to announce that her personal expenses would be limited to 100,000 rubles a year.

After a few skirmishes, the showdown came at a great banquet in the Kremlin given for the empress by her Privy Council in late February. A delegation of 150 of the lesser gentry burst into the hall with a petition to abolish the *Punkti.* Anna feigned ignorance, asking, "What, were not these same Punkti written with the people's will?" The petitioners shouted, "No!" The empress turned to Prince Basil Dolgoruky with the words "Then, thou hast deceived me," and before his eyes she tore up the document she had signed a month before. There was no protest, for as an observer noted, "If the Privy Councillors had uttered so much as a word, straightway the officers of the Guards would have cast them from the windows."

On March 1, 1730, a new oath was sworn in all the churches to Anna as empress-autocrat. So ended the first major attempt to curb the arbitrary powers of the Romanov monarchs and there would not be another try for a century. The issues and lines of struggle in 1730 were confused. Not all the old aristocracy were conservatives supporting the Privy Council: Many of the boyar families had divided loyalties, for they had sons serving in the Guards or otherwise involved in the system Peter had created. The struggle of classes was obscured by the struggle of institutions, with the Senate and the army, as well as the council, jockeying for power. The simple explanation of the outcome of the crisis is that people were agreed that "better one autocrat than many." Yet Empress Anna and her successors contrived to jeopardize even this negative kind of popularity, and eventually the Romanovs lost it altogether.

Prince Golitsyn wrote bitterly of his short-lived constitutional experiment: "The banquet was spread, but the guests were not worthy of it. I know that I shall pay for the failure of the enterprise." Indeed, the worst was in store for the conspirators of 1730. The principal Dolgorukys, accused of causing the death of Peter II and of deceit, were first banished to their estates. Later came confiscation of their property and exile to Siberia, ironically to that same wintry outpost, Berezov, where the Dolgorukys had sent Menshikov. Prince Golitsyn himself suffered only banishment initially, but in 1737 the regime implicated him in an alleged plot by his son to overthrow the empress. The greatest of Russian aristocrats was left to die slowly in prison. Other Golitsyns suffered torture, dismemberment, and beheading.

5. Empress Anna: Foreigners and Low Comedy to the Fore

Thirty-seven at her accession, Anna Ivanovna ruled Russia for eleven years without real drama and without distinction. "Few murkier pages in Russian history" exist than this period, according to one great historian, and "the murkiest blot was Anna herself." Actually, the reign was not all bad: There were glimmers of the glories to come for the Romanovs in diplomacy and in cultural splendor. For one thing, Anna promptly returned the court to her uncle's new capital at St. Petersburg as soon as she had undergone her ceremonial coronation in Moscow in May, 1730.

The tawdriness and frustration of Anna's early career were such that the empress may well have expected God and her subjects to forgive her for treating the throne of Russia as a means of self-gratification. As a child Anna had been subjected to the conflicting influences and desires of her old-school mother, the Tsarina Praskovia, and of tradition-hating Tsar Peter. Married off to the Duke of Courland for reasons of diplomacy when she was eighteen, Anna found herself closing the eyes of her young husband even while on the road back to Mitau after the riotous wedding festivities. Forced to take up residence as grand duchess in that dreary capital, Anna did not enjoy the substance of authority or even the glitter of prestige. Over the next nineteen years Anna sent one piteous letter after another to Peter, later to Catherine I, and finally to Peter II, begging for enough money even to set a good table. A chance for remarriage and excitement were denied her in the episode of 1726 involving Maurice of Saxony. Neglected, powerless, and impoverished, the Romanov princess found solace in love affairs, first with the Russian ambassador Peter Bestuzhev and then with the Courlander Ernst Johann Bühren. Then came the completely unexpected call to Russia in 1730.

The new empress' "terrible scowl" is what contemporaries seemed first to remark about her, a look that had withered old Prince Dolgoruky himself. Anna's general appearance was imposing but scarcely such as to inspire devotion. Swarthy, coarse-featured, and deep-voiced, she definitely had a masculine air about her, which was further emphasized by the fact that she stood higher by a head than most men. Her delicate hands and dignified carriage were inadequately redeeming characteristics in a woman who was immensely fat, as well as tall. The most enduring portrait of this virago is a bronze statue by the Italian Carlo Rastrelli which dominates a whole room in the Russian State Museum in Leningrad. Anna is presented as a determined, tough-looking amazon grasping a huge scepter and towering over a separately sculpted Negro page, who is presenting her with an orb. The total effect is somewhat vulgar, except for the fine detailing of the royal robes.

In character, Anna was serious to the point of grimness. Spiteful, harsh, neurotically suspicious and needlessly severe, she made her reign remembered as a time of gloom. She did not tolerate impiety or scandal. Unintellectual but by no means dull-witted, the empress was methodical about performing her essential responsibilities, leaving the day-to-day management of affairs to men.

The person who became the real directing force in the Russian state in the 1730's was the Empress' favorite, Bühren, a German adventurer who was to try to maintain his preeminence even after Anna's death. Grandson of a ducal groom who had later been rewarded with a small estate in Courland, Bühren had been expelled from school for riotous conduct, and he had been rejected when, in his first attempt to seek his fortune in Russia in 1714, he sought a place in the shabby, short-lived court of Tsarevich Alexis and Princess Charlotte.

Back in Mitau, Bühren gained a footing at the court of Grand Duchess Anna through the Russian ambassador, Bestuzhev, after Bühren's sister became Bestuzhev's mistress. Since Bestuzhev was supposed to be Anna's lover, Bühren was in a good position to intrigue, something he did do so successfully that he not only brought about his patron's downfall but replaced Bestuzhev as Anna's bedmate. Subsequently, Bühren married a Courland lady, and although Anna apparently ceased to sleep with him, he remained unshakably her favorite.

At Anna's coronation Bühren was made grand chamberlain and a count of the Russian Empire; he received an estate with a large annual income; and he changed his name to Biren, casually assuming the coat of arms of the illustrious warrior dukes of France. Some people came to characterize Biren as mean, treacherous, and vindictive, altogether an evil man. Other observers put him down as not really bad, just stupid and greedy. In any case, he enriched himself mightily at the expense of his new country, being in a position to receive most of the bribes that passed through the Russian court. Huge bribes in turn were paid out by Biren himself in 1732 to gain his election as Duke of Courland, a throne his family had once most humbly served. This title enabled Biren to receive royal honors at the Russian court. When, much later, the tide of events turned against him, diamonds worth more than half a million pounds were confiscated from his possession.

Anna's favorite symbolized the most hated feature of her reign: the taking over of the court, the bureaucracy, the army, and the navy by foreigners, adventurers from all over Europe but mostly from Germany. "Like a troop of cats around a bowl of milk" was one disgusted Russian's description of the horde of parasitic immigrants, whose one goal was a government job.

One particularly unpopular move of the new regime was the creation of a new Guards regiment, the Izmailovskoe Regiment, staffed by and recruited exclusively from Courlanders. The German soldiers counterbalanced the power of the Preobrazhenskoe and Semenovskoe Guards and were used for the punitive expeditions occasionally required to suppress the restiveness of the peasants and for the police activity directed against many of the best old Russian families. It is estimated that 20,000 persons were deported to Siberia during the following decade.

There were a few efforts to placate the aristocracy, as well as to frighten them. The Corps of Cadets was established in Petersburg, giving young aristocrats an inside track in education and preferment and thus reversing Peter's original policies.

Under Anna the other members of the Romanov dynasty went into eclipse. Her sister Catherine and her family remained in Germany. The young Romanov prince in Kiel was virtually ignored, his pension cut to nothing, just as Anna's had been in Courland. The Tsarevna Elizabeth remained in and around Petersburg, hunting and lovemaking, seemingly oblivious to all except her wild pleasures. Once Elizabeth overstepped the bounds by starting an affair with a sergeant in the Semenovskoe Guards. The Empress Anna had the culprit soldier sent to Siberia, minus his tongue, and threatened her cousin with a nunnery. Afterward Elizabeth simply effaced herself as much as possible.

Foreign policy remained in the capable hands of Osterman, who was now known as the Oracle. This German, a member of the Privy Council of Peter II, had survived the crisis of 1730 by pretending to be ill, so desperately ill that he could not sign his name to the *Punkti*. Under a grateful Anna, Osterman for a brief period raised Russian and Romanov prestige to such a high point that Peter the Great would have been envious. The military forces were generally revitalized, and during the War of the Polish Succession (1733–35) Russia found herself with many allies. Brilliant successes under Field Marshal Peter Lacy brought a Russian army westward all the way to the banks of the Rhine, helping persuade France to make peace quickly with Austria. The ensuing war with Turkey (1735–39) saw Russian victories far south in the Crimea and almost in sight of the Danube. A military hero arose from these events: Field Marshal Burkhard Christoph Münnich, yet another German, but a popular commander who was destined to figure briefly on the political stage. By the peace treaty with Turkey, Russia gained Azov and the surrounding Black Sea area at last. Some quarters grumbled that Osterman should have gained more for Russia, in return for the 100,000 men lost and millions of rubles spent, but thhe fact was that Russia's ally, Austria, had collapsed military at the critical juncture. But for that, Anna might have been remembered for the huge acquisitions in the south that later brought greatness to Catherine II. In any case, prestige was gained. As the British ambassador noted, Russia was beginning to have a great deal to say in the affairs of Europe.

The diplomats of all Europe, who now journeyed to Petersburg with less reluctance than in the days of Catherine I, found the court of Anna a thing of contrasts. "I cannot express how magnificent this court is in clothes," reported the British ambassador, who pleaded with London for more money in order to keep up. Yet other reports say that visitors gasped with amazement at the vulgarity they encountered.

Most of the year Anna resided at the Winter Palace, to which she added considerably. She led a reasonably regular daily life, rising at eight, usually having dinner with the Birens, supping lightly in the evening, and retiring before midnight. The Birens had adjoining apartments to hers. The Duke of Courland's Riding School, built near the palace, was a popular attraction for the court. In the summer there was the lovely Palace of Peterhof, with fountains and gardens sweeping down to the sea, where the royal party could hunt imported animals in the park.

Hunting, incidentally, became a mad passion of the empress, who proved herself adept with both guns and bows. She would have shotguns left around in many of the palace rooms so that she could take potshots at passing birds from the windows. Sometimes the large cages of birds kept in the palace were emptied in the rooms so that Anna could pursue her sport indoors.

Anna's extravagance surpassed even that of Catherine I, and the cost of the court strained the state budget to the extreme, all the while increasing the burdens on the people. The era of the 1730's was remembered as a time of revels. Champagne was introduced to Russia. So was gambling, which became a major pastime of an aristocracy that demanded only more money from the overseers of their seldom-seen estates. The empress herself came to enjoy playing banker at faro or quinze, capriciously choosing just who could place bets but generously never letting anyone lose to her. Servants in liveries were another innovation, the outfits for the royal household being blue and yellow, laced generously with silver. Two surviving personal extravagances of Anna's are an ensemble of horse fittings in solid gold decorated with many large square-cut emeralds and a gold toilet set made in Augsburg containing forty pieces weighing 50 pounds.

Much was sham in the high society of Anna's day: Gorgeous costumes ill concealed ragged undergarments; fine furnishings were laid on filth amid settling floors and cracking walls; and elegant food and wine did not hide savage manners. One particular thing noted by foreigners was the ever-present lice, even on the best people. Russian men picked them off themselves without stopping conversations, while their women resigned themselves to the consequences of their lousy servants' custom of sleeping in milady's furs while keeping warm outside parties. Yet it would not take so many years before St. Petersburg saw true civilization.

The empress herself could not rise above the coarseness of her tastes. She frequently appeared with an old kerchief on her hair while wearing a jewel-studded gown from Paris. She preferred the company of lowborn jesters and gossips. A letter of hers to a kinsman in Moscow is quite candid on this score: "Seek out for me among the poor gentlewomen of Pereslavl some who are like Tatiana Novokshchenova, for methinks she is soon to die, and I want someone to take her place. You know our ways, and that we like such as be about forty and are chatty, like N." Another time she made this demand on the same correspondent: "Pick out for us two little Persian or Lesghian girls, good, clean, and not foolish—for our amusement." Anna seems to have avoided intimate contacts with men, at least after the days of Bestuzhev and Biren.

A taste for cruelty was definitely part of Anna's makeup. One April Fool's Day, for example, she panicked the whole city of St. Petersburg by having the fire bells rung. Theater productions were reintroduced at the court, and it is typical of the empress that she wanted only the lowest sort of German and Italian comedies, especially those featuring cuffings, kickings, and beatings. In the absence of real actors, Anna delighted in making members of her entourage stage brawls. These usually consisted of a conflict with two persons on a side, one sitting on the other's shoulders. The battles ended satisfactorily only when all were on the floor, engaged in a frenzy of bloody hair pulling, scratching, and biting. It seemed to be Anna's particular pleasure to involve the high nobility in her gross amusements, humiliating them amid general hilarity by demanding that they perform such tricks as imitating hens cackling over their eggs. Drunkenness, however, was not at all favored by Anna, possibly because she remembered how she had lost her husband. People were allowed to overindulge in her presence only on the anniversary of her accession, and then, perversely, she would present each courtier with a bottle of Hungarian wine to be emptied on the spot.

The most vicious of all the follies of Anna's regime was the Ice Palace episode of 1739. Young Prince Michael Alexievich Golitsyn, having survived the terror directed against the rest of his family, incurred Anna's displeasure by marrying a Catholic woman from abroad, who subsequently died. The empress ordered him to remarry, introducing as his bride a completely hideous Kalmuck woman. The wedded couple were subsequently put in a cage on top of an elephant and paraded around Petersburg in a procession of goat carts, oxcarts, and reindeer sledges, peopled with the weirdest-looking natives that could be found in the far corners of the empire. All through her reign Anna made a practice of surrounding herself with freaks, collecting them as other rulers might collect paintings. The bizarre procession ended up at a palace constructed entirely of blocks of ice. This practical joke could not have been more elaborate, the building measuring 80 by 20 by 30 feet and costing 30,000 rubles to erect. Outside there were ice balustrades, ice trees with ice birds in them, and ice statues. Inside, the bedroom contained an ice four-poster, ice pillows, ice toilet utensils, an ice tea service, an ice card table, tinted ice cards and foodstuffs, and an ice fireplace blazing with a petroleum fire (the last, a great novelty). The luckless couple were then stripped naked by guards and kept inside their frightful igloo all night (they survived).

These sumptuous and crude amusements continued until Anna's health gave way at last. She had a fit at table and was taken insensible to bed, never to rise again. She died in October, 1740, in her forty-seventh year, scowling to the end and surrounded by her foreign entourage.

6. Emperor Ivan VI: Two Palace Revolutions in One Year

Having suffered over the course of fifteen years the whims of two dissolute women and an adolescent boy, Russia in 1740 faced the prospect of rule in the name of a three-month-old baby, titled Ivan VI. This Romanov was another descendant of Ivan V, rather than of Peter the Great. The infant's grandmother, Catherine, who was an intelligent and dignified princess, had been passed over as ruler in 1730 only because her husband, the Duke of Mecklenburg, was so energetically incompetent and dislikable. The Mecklenburgs left a daughter, Anna Leopoldovna, who in time was taken into the court of her aunt, the Empress Anna, and was married in 1739 to a German prince, Anthony of Brunswick. This last union produced the child who became Ivan VI, a Romanov who had only one-quarter Russian blood.

The Empress Anna had been at least wise enough to choose her successor two months before she died, naming her grandnephew. Above all, she was determined that descendants of her father should rule in Russia. Biren was insistent on becoming regent, saying with considerable truth to the Privy Council that Russians did not want things to be as they were in Poland where many ruled instead of one. Anna had consented to this only reluctantly, hiding Biren's petition under her pillow and tearfully prophesying: "Duke, Duke, my heart is sad, for thou art encompassing thine own ruin." Nonetheless, Biren assumed the regency the day after Ivan VI was proclaimed emperor-autocrat on October 17, 1740.

Almost immediately Biren faced a conspiracy against him on the part of Ivan's father, Prince Anthony, but the blabbings of this incompetent to officers of his Semenovskoe Guards were promptly disclosed, and the culprits were punished summarily, the tearful prince being told to confine himself to his wife's apartment.

Biren's one-man rule was to be shorter even than Menshikov's in 1727. Continued government by foreigners and heretics was becoming more than the Russian gentry could bear. The regent promptly threw away such popularity as he had by peevishly calling the Guards regiments Janissaries. He went so far as to propose that the Petersburg nobles be transferred to the line corps of the army and that officers chosen from the common people would best protect the court.

The army temporarily found a leader in Field Marshal Münnich, a veteran of battles in Western Europe and in the Balkans, who had recently been decorated for completing the Ladoga Canal project. Münnich acquired a ready ally in Anna Leopoldovna, who had hated Biren ever since, two years earlier, he had made the insulting proposal that she wait around long enough to marry his thirteen-year-old son. Now she tearfully complained to the marshal that Biren affronted her at every opportunity, including threatening to pack her off altogether. November 20 was the day Münnich's own Preobrazhenskoe Guards were on sentry duty in the city. Twice that day Münnich ate meals with Biren in the Summer Palace, observing that the regent seemed increasingly depressed, even when the marshal gaily told war stories over the wine. At 10 P.M. Münnich left his unsuspecting host and went off to rally his supporters. Anna Leopoldovna was aware of the plot but was scared to appear in the streets. With eighty men, Münnich returned to the palace and proceeded to Biren's unlocked apartments, where the regent was found asleep with his wife. The regent's screaming, kicking, and biting were to no avail. The guardsmen dragged him from bed, throttled him, gagged him with his nightshirt, and then carted him off, bound and wrapped only in a bed coverlet, in Münnich's carriage to Schlüsselburg Prison. All of the regent's acts were declared void, and the whole record was expunged. A commission condemned Biren to death by quartering, but this sentence was commuted to banishment for life to Pelin in Siberia, Münnich taking upon himself the designing of the house to be Biren's jail. The vast fortune of the Courlander was confiscated.

In the next months, the new regent, Anna, and her blithering husband, Prince Anthony, now "generalissimo," repaid Münnich with nothing but ingratitude, and in March, 1741, he resigned in disgust. Osterman had a hand in Münnich's departure, accusing him of insolence to the regent, and it was this smooth-talking diplomat who at last achieved full control of the government. Of Osterman, the French ambassador now wrote: "It is not too much to say that he is Tsar of all Russia."

The Regent Anna was entirely incapable politically, even more so than her two female predecessors in Petersburg, nor did she make any effort to enjoy her sudden prominence. Having been brought up in Germany, she impressed the wife of an ambassador as a shy, awkward, and stupid creature when she had first appeared at her aunt's court. Actually, as a round-faced blonde, she was not bad-looking, and no one ever questioned her inexhaustible good temper. The degeneracy of a dynasty was hinted, however, in her utter indolence and ignorance. Her husband, if possible, was even more insipid than Anna, making her look almost colorful by contrast. Even when he was her fiancé, she had hated him, but after their marriage, in the last days of Empress Anna and during the Biren regime, husband and wife had stuck together for reasons of self-preservation. Now freed of restraint, these two fell into accusing each other of both probable and improbable infidelities, their mutual enmity fed by intrigues on Osterman's part.

Anna Leopoldovna's personal life was scandalously messy. She had a very special woman friend in the person of a Fräulein Julia Mengden, who was set up in adjoining apartments. The nature of their relationship was suggested in a report to London by the British ambassador:

> I should give your lordship but a faint idea of the great affection that the Grand Duchess has for Mademoiselle Mengden by adding that the passion of a lover for a new mistress is a jest to it. By good luck, she has no great share of parts, nor, as they say of any malice, so that it is to be hoped that she will neither have the power nor the inclination to do much harm.

As if the two women cooing and chattering to each other in German were not enough, Julia's mother, brother, and several sisters were invited to Russia, and this new set of foreign parasites soon received their share of royal bounty.

Public functions were almost completely avoided by the regent, less out of shyness than out of dullness and inertia. She scarcely had the energy to wash or dress herself. Her preferred daily routine was to stay for hours on end in one of Julia's rooms, playing cards, gossiping, and wearing nothing but a shift and a ratty kerchief.

To make matters seedier, Anna had a passion for the Saxon minister,

Lynar, to the point that Empress Anna had once ordered him sent home. Now returned to Russia, this extremely handsome man was promptly married to Julia Mengden, who further obliged her friend by standing guard against any intrusion by Prince Anthony when Lynar and Anna made love. Just before this bizarre *ménage à trois* was established, Anna gave birth to her second child, a daughter named Catherine.

Much of the time the almost inseparable Anna and Julia spent huddled in bed, together with the infant emperor. They were so found late in the night of December 16, 1741. Anna awoke to the words "Come, my sister, it is time to rise." She called to Julia, but it was not Julia who had spoken. It was her cousin, the Tsarevna Elizabeth, her blond hair stuffed into a soldier's shako and her voluptuous figure crammed into the uniform of the Preobrazhenskoe Guards, the unit which, in fact, had pledged their undying devotion to her a few hours before.

The regent, Julia, and Ivan VI unceremoniously joined Biren in Schlüsselburg Prison. Field Marshal Münnich and Osterman were likewise dragged there. The hated regime of Germans was over, as well as the rule of Ivan VI, the most unlucky of Romanovs, whose days were to linger on to a brief flicker and tragedy two decades later.

The rapid succession of rulers and regencies for the sixteen years past now gave way to a reign of twenty-one years and to respite from palace revolutions.

IX.

The Good-Hearted Empress: Elizabeth

1. Patriotic Intriguer

ELIZABETH was the third of four empresses St. Petersburg was to know in the eighteenth century, the only crowned female rulers before or after in Russian history. With the warmth and some of the peasant qualities of Catherine I, Elizabeth was to show herself far more capable and stylish than her mother. She could be as firm and willful as Anna, but in Elizabeth there was none of the harshness and bitterness of her cousin. She would be remembered as less clever than Catherine the Great but also as less calculating; she was not as brilliant as her nephew's wife, but Elizabeth was far more lovable and beloved.

The achievements of Elizabeth's reign (1741–62) were considerable: the giving back of Russia to Russians; the smoothing out of the hostilities of factions, old and new; the encouragement of elegance and of the basic arts as well; the embellishment of St. Petersburg; and the reassertion of a major role for Russia in European affairs. As usual under the Romanovs, the vast majority of Russians were at best spectators of Elizabeth's glories.

The birth of a second, robust daughter to Catherine at Kolomenskoe Palace in December, 1709, so pleased Peter the Great that he cut short the Poltava victory celebrations in Moscow. As she grew up, Elizabeth Petrovna came to delight all for her beauty and her high spirits, being something of a contrast with her more sedate elder sister, Anna, to whom, nonetheless, Elizabeth was always deeply devoted. It was, perhaps, a premonition that led the painter Louis Caravaque to do a delicious little portrait of the tsarevna at the age of eight completely nude, for sensuality was to be her dominating trait. At a very early age Elizabeth earned herself a special place in Peter and Catherine's assemblies as the first to begin and the last to stop the dancing of minuets and quadrilles. Münnich, writing of her at twelve, declared that "she already had a beautiful figure and was full of grace, though inclined even then to fatness, and was bursting with health and vivacity."

Although not unintelligent, Elizabeth had an indifferent education, her father being too busy and her mother too illiterate to bother. Somehow Elizabeth developed a haphazard command of German and Italian, as well as of French, and she used to make it a point to speak to foreign ambassadors in their native languages. It was improbable that Elizabeth ever read a book, with the exception of devotional volumes printed in huge type and profusely illustrated, for she developed a lifelong conviction that reading was harmful to one's health, even going so far as to blame the death of her sister, Anna, on her studiousness. Of her knowledge of the world at large, it was often mentioned that Elizabeth lived out her days never quite sure whether England was an island.

Even in her mid-teens Elizabeth was considered the most eligible of Romanov princesses. Although her father was unsuccessful in arranging her marriage to Louis XV of France, it was a consolation to know that of a selection of the eighteen most beautiful princesses in Europe, the fastidious French rated the tsarevna number two. Later she was betrothed to Prince Karl Augustus of Holstein-Gottorp (uncle of Catherine the Great, it turned out), but the handsome suitor died of smallpox shortly before the wedding, to Elizabeth's genuine grief.

With the death of her father and mother and following the departure of her sister, Anna, to Kiel in 1727, Elizabeth at eighteen was very much on her own. With "eyes merry as a bird's," she became the madcap companion of Peter II, first in Petersburg and later in Moscow, until the Dolgorukys had her pushed aside for being Catherine's bastard. Nonetheless, Elizabeth contrived to continue her carefree life in the country houses about Moscow, hunting wolves at Kurgan, frolicking at Alexandrov, or planting new gardens and building chapels at Izmailovskoe. Athletic, Elizabeth was always riding, tobogganing, and boating. Easygoing and unaffected, she liked nothing better than to fill her little court with singing and dancing peasant girls.

The advent of the Empress Anna required Elizabeth to restrain herself. Expected to attend Anna's court, to sit near her demurely at entertainments, and to produce suitable gifts on occasion, Elizabeth could not help outshining her cousin. Anna was offended by Elizabeth's frivolity; she was jealous of the younger woman's irresistible sex appeal; and she was nervous about the tsarevna's popularity with people. It was said that the soldiers worshiped her for standing godmother to so many of their children and that the shopkeepers refused to take her money. That Elizabeth was potentially more than just the dizzy young thing she appeared is attested by the wife of the English minister, who wrote:

> I have a veneration for her, and fondness in my heart, that makes a visit to her a thing of pleasure, not of ceremony. She has an affability and sweetness of behaviour that insensibly inspire love and respect. In public she has an unaffected gaiety, and a certain air of giddiness, that seem entirely to possess her whole mind; but in private, I have heard her talk with such a strain of good sense and steady reasoning, that I am persuaded that the other behaviour is a feint. . . .

Elizabeth's sensual appetites were almost her undoing. Soon after an affair with the sergeant of the Semenovskoe Regiment, Elizabeth began a liason with Alexis Razumovsky, which was to become a lifelong and altogether noble relationship. Her new lover was lowborn, a Ukrainian and a musician. A year older than his mistress, Razumovsky had been born in a little village north of Kiev, his mother being a sometime innkeeper and his father a Cossack shepherd (who earned the name Razum because of his wont to sigh "muddleheaded" whenever he was drunk, a frequent thing). The sensitive, studious boy on one occasion provoked his father to chasing him around the hut with an ax, and Alexis took refuge with a sympathetic priest, who turned his charge into the finest singer in the local choir. An imperial courier passing through heard that voice, and forthwith Alexis was transported to the Empress Anna's court chapel, which is where he first came to Elizabeth's notice—a tall, lithe, swarthy, fiery-eyed, and finely featured youth. First Elizabeth's official lute player, he was then appointed to her household as *Kammerjunker,* receiving every possible mark of favor.

Passed over as successor in 1727, in 1730, and again in 1740, Elizabeth began to bestir herself politically only during the regency of Anna Leopoldovna. There were clashes with the foreign minister, Osterman, whom the tsarevna took to referring to as that "petty little secretary." Once Osterman failed to convey to Elizabeth a gift from the Shah of Persia, drawing an outburst from her: "Tell Count Osterman . . . I am aware that he tries to humiliate me on every occasion. . . . He forgets what he was and what I am!" Although basically he underestimated Elizabeth, Osterman was careful to plant insinuations about her in the regent's ear, leading on December 14, 1741, to a nasty scene between the two princesses in which Anna Leopoldovna accused Elizabeth of plotting with the Swedes (then at war with Russia) and their French allies. Threats were uttered, and Elizabeth burst into tears, after which the two women emotionally forgave each other and pledged their eternal devotion. Actually, the accusations against the tsarevna were largely true.

"Too fat to be in a plot," was the British envoy's reaction to the excited rumors about Elizabeth. The same man, however, also reported with greater perspicacity that Elizabeth did "not have an ounce of nun's flesh in her." The renewed prospect of being shorn and leading a recluse's life was, indeed, too hideous to contemplate for this tsarevna, and all doubts in her mind about a coup were removed by the simple expedient of showing her two drawings, one of herself as empress, the other as nun. To further her popularity among the soldiers, she set about buying them liquor with money lent her by the French minister, the Marquis de la Chétardie, causing him later to take great credit for events which actually caught him by surprise.

The crisis came the day after Elizabeth had pledged her eternal devotion. The Guards regiments were alerted to be ready to leave for the war front in Finland within twenty-four hours. At 10 P.M. in Elizabeth's little house at Smolny there was a feverish conference involving Razumovsky and friends of the tsarevna, notably one Michael Vorontsov and the Shuvalov brothers, Peter and Alexander. The discussion ended when Vorontsov convinced Elizabeth with the flattering words "Truly, Madam, the affair demands no little daring but where shall we find it if not in the blood-kin of Peter the Great?" Twenty guardsmen, previously bribed, were brought in and chorused: "Yes, little Mother, we are ready to die for you." Elizabeth emotionally took up an icon and swore that if she were successful, she would never as empress sign a death warrant for a soldier. The tsarevna, having spent an hour in prayer, was urgently summoned and then decked out in a mailed cuirass with the Order of St. Catherine to wear and a silver cross to carry.

Elizabeth and her friends silently made their way on a sledge the short distance to the Preobrazhenskoe barracks at 2 A.M. on December 16. After ordering the drums to be slit to prevent warnings, Elizabeth struck a pose in the mess hall and stirred up the 200 men assembled there with these words: "My children, you know whose daughter I am. It is my resolve this night to deliver you and all Russia from our German tormentors. Will you follow me?" Twice thereafter she had to caution the enthusiastic and unruly throng that she wanted no bloodshed.

At the head of her guardsmen, Elizabeth then set off for the Winter Palace, sending messengers to the other regiments and dispatching patrols to arrest Osterman, Münnich, and others in their homes. At one point as her procession moved along the Nevsky Prospekt, she abandoned her sledge in favor of walking, but the soldiers hoisted her less than sylphlike figure to their shoulders. Reaching the palace, the tsarevna personally intervened to save five guards from being bayoneted and led the company up the grand staircase to where the regent and her friend Julia were asleep. In less than an hour Elizabeth and her prisoners were in the same sledge on the way back to her house.

Later that day Elizabeth received the dignitaries of the realm, winning all with her grace and bearing. One vital commander, Marshal Lacy, had been cornered by Elizabeth's partisans and asked, "To what party do you belong?" "To the party in power," was the quick rejoinder. The new empress declared herself colonel of all three Guards Regiments and bestowed on her person the Order of St. Andrew. Thus enhanced, she showed herself to the crowds from a balcony and was met with a pandemonium of cheers such as had not been heard since the days of Peter the Great. There was a triumphal procession through dense crowds to the Winter Palace, and a *Te Deum* was sung in the chapel, while the guns and bells of Peter and Paul proclaimed the coup to the entire city.

Elizabeth's bold action was viewed negatively by many of the foreign observers. One wrote disdainfully that in Russia, with a little money and a few barrels of vodka you can do anything. It was seriously predicted that the self-indulgent princess would return Russia to its old barbarism and indolence, all foreigners would be expelled, and the fleet would rot.

2. Beloved Ruler

The new empress was lavish in rewarding her supporters, deliberate in restoring the native nobility to favor, and firm in rendering her enemies harmless. Elizabeth's essential good-heartedness was usually evident in both political and family matters. Of the immediate promoters of the coup, the Shuvalov brothers were created generals by their grateful sovereign, while her adored Alexis Razumovsky was commissioned a lieutenant colonel. A total of 12,000 rubles was distributed to the soldiers of the Preobrazhenskoe Regiment, who also got new uniforms and the title of Imperial Body Guard. All officers were promoted, and even Guards privates found themselves lieutenants, members of the nobility, and estate owners. Elizabeth and the army were forever as one.

The old Russian nobility were no longer held in disgrace, and Golitsyns and Dolgorukys found important places in Elizabeth's government alongside her newly created aristocrats. Prince Vasily Dolgoruky, for example, was released from his dungeon at Narva to become head of the College of War. Another victim of past turmoil, Biren, was freed and allowed to live on his estates in comfort, although this German of hated memory in Anna's day was forbidden to come to court. Elizabeth's determination to give her regime a broad base was indicated by a ukase revitalizing Peter's Senate as a replacement for the cliquish council favored in previous reigns. Russians were named chiefs of all the government colleges. The nobility as a class were later flattered by being given additional legal authority over their serfs.

The leading lights of the last regime were promptly subjected to farcical trials. Osterman, accused of suppressing the will of Catherine I and of other improbable intrigues, fell back on the plea that all he had done was for the good of the state. Field Marshal Münnich was alternately resigned and defiant: He first asked the court to dictate his answers, as well as the questions, but when his conduct of the Crimean campaign was impugned, he declared that his only regret was not to have hanged the president of the court for cheating on supplies during the very same campaign. The personal sentences handed down to the foreigners, dismemberment and beheading, were outrageous, although no one was surprised that their estates were confiscated to provide easy rewards for Elizabeth's supporters. The empress had conveniently absented herself in the country when the scaffolds went up in January, 1742, and the prisoners were brought to their fate. Gouty and whimsically cross at hearing the tedious and ungrammatical charges read against him, old Osterman laid his head on the block only to hear an official cry, "God and Her Majesty give thee back thy life." Münnich, powdered and dressed to the nines for the occasion, rewarded his would-be executioners and joked all the way back to prison. The marshal may also have appreciated the irony of his new sentence, banishment to the very house in remote Siberia he had designed for Biren; The two enemies passed each other on the road without stopping their sledges or even speaking, as the one began his exile and the other returned. As for Osterman, the once-powerful diplomat was exiled to Berezov, where he died six years later.

Regarding her deposed Romanov cousins, Elizabeth showed little compassion and took no chances. Anna Leopoldovna, her pettish husband, and their two-year-old child, the erstwhile Ivan VI, were sent to Dünamünde Prison near Riga. In 1743 a plot in their favor and threats to the life of Elizabeth were revealed by a French diplomat. Anna and her family were transported to the Solovetsky Monastery on the White Sea, and Elizabeth's fears were such that her royal rivals were made to travel secretly, by night and in a closed carriage, little Ivan being renamed Gregory for the occasion. Despite ill fortune, tawdry Anna Leopoldovna did not cease producing new Romanov heirs. A second son, Peter, was born in 1745, and a third, Alexis, in 1746—both destined to oblivion. The latter childbirth caused Anna's death. Rather unpredictably, Elizabeth had her cousin's body brought back to St. Petersburg and buried in state in a monastery, the empress shedding many tears as she laid her wreath on the tomb. As for Ivan VI, he was left to grow mad and rot in solitary confinement, a new punishment for Russia and an unmerited one, Elizabeth forgetting that at the time of her coup in 1741 she had whispered to him, "Poor child, it is not you, but your parents who are to blame."

A promise Elizabeth did not forget was her pledge the night of the coup never to sign a death warrant for one of her soldiers. In fact, she went so far as to have a decree drafted abolishing capital punishment, and although her advisers kept her from ever promulgating it, she took pains to commute every death sentence passed in her reign. She rejected a law project brought to her by Peter Shuvalov with the words that it was "written not with ink but with blood," all the while neglecting, however, to take positive steps to help the downtrodden people. Elizabeth's genuine horror at bloodshed and suffering did not prevent her, weeping and praying, from sending off great armies to war year after year, but it was said of her that her concern for the soldiers' clothing reduced casualties from exposure to the minimum. Her spontaneous feelings of pity and kindness showed themselves in her precipitate offer to aid earthquake-wrecked Lisbon in 1755, even though she had no idea where Portugal was.

The chief object of Elizabeth's affection continued to be Alexis Razumovsky, her darkly attractive Cossack musician. He was always established in apartments near those of the empress, who visited him daily and personally saw to nursing his gout. The recipient of much wealth from the state treasury, Razumovsky was presented with several estates so that he could entertain Elizabeth. It was because of him that Ukrainian music and Ukrainian dishes became the vogue at court. Created a count in 1744, Razumovsky also found himself made a field marshal, an honor which drew this modest response: "Your Majesty may create me a Field Marshal if you like, but I defy you to make a decent Captain of me."

It is altogether probable that Elizabeth and Razumovsky were privately married in the fall of 1742, at the insistence of her confessor (two village churches still claim the distinction of being the site of the secret ceremony). The couple may have had as many as six children, but none of them survived childbirth, although, as so often in Russian history, pretenders to this parentage immediately popped up in the next reigns. At the end of Elizabeth's days, according to one story, Razumovsky tore up the evidence of the marriage before the eyes of the chancellor, acting out of feelings of honor.

Razumovsky was, perhaps, the most admirable and deserving royal favorite in all history. Nobody in his day faulted him. He was all nobility, generosity, honesty, and level-headedness. In the opinion of the woman who was later Catherine the Great, no one was more "universally beloved" at court than he. Rated by the same observer as "one of the most handsome men I ever saw," Razumovsky let nothing "turn his head" or "spoil his heart," remaining "cool-headed and sober-minded in the midst of every whirlpool of intrigue and not very decent delights." The secret of success for Razumovsky was that he simply did not meddle in politics, he was not self-seeking, and he had enough sense not to let others use him. Actively religious, he did see to the building of several churches, and he is credited with sending the first Russian missionaries to the far reaches of Siberia and the Caucasus. Although largely unlettered himself, Razumovsky may be considered one of the first notable Russian patrons of literature.

Razumovsky's family benefited from his fortune. The amusing story went around concerning the one and only visit his old mother made to the capital: Newly bedecked in the finest clothes and jewels, she caught sight of herself in a palace mirror and straightaway fell to her knees, thinking that the gorgeous reflection could be none other than the empress. Alexis' brother, Cyril Razumovsky, born in 1728 and thus nineteen years his junior, was given a magnificent education which took him to Königsberg, Berlin, and Paris, and he returned to Russia with all the latest in French mannerisms. A determined dandy for the remainder of his life, Cyril Razumovsky was loaded with favors by the empress, including the inevitable ranks of count and field marshal. Remembered for his works as president of the Academy of Sciences, Cyril was as generous and beloved as his brother. At the age of only twenty-two, this son of a Cossack shepherd received the high distinction of being designated Hetman of the Ukraine, to which post Cyril repaired with a huge retinue, including an acting troupe and six French chefs, one of which was reportedly better than the famous Duval of Frederick the Great.

At the urging of Alexis Razumovsky, Elizabeth made a state visit to the Ukraine in 1744. She traveled with her whole court, including 230 major personages, some of whom were detached along the way and sent off to Siberia for allegedly plotting against the empress' life. Everywhere the reception was enthusiastic. Elizabeth impressed the populace by her graciousness, by her liberality, and especially by her prolonged devotions at religious shrines. At the gates of Kiev the theological students turned out costumed as Greek gods, and after being presented with the keys to the city by an old man dressed as St. Vladimir, Elizabeth rode into the Ukrainian capital amid great cheers on a large, fanciful conveyance. Later she was to describe this visit together with her Alexis as the two happiest weeks of her life, exclaiming: "Do but love me, oh my God, in thy heavenly kingdom as I do love these gentle and guileless people."

Without surviving children of her own, Elizabeth let her natural motherliness find many other outlets. In addition to her willingness to stand godmother to everyone's children, nothing delighted the empress more than to play host to sixty or eighty children, throwing full-scale banquets for them in high style. Moreover, the empress was an inveterate matchmaker, the confidante of her young ladies-in-waiting, the persuader of difficult parents, and the provider of dowries to the dowryless.

A sensible desire to confirm the succession, combined with family feeling, led Elizabeth to hasten the coming to Russia of her beloved sister's son, Karl Peter Ulrich, an orphan of thirteen. Peter arrived from Kiel in February, 1742, just three months after his aunt's accession, and within a year was received into the Orthodox Church and proclaimed heir. Despite every mark of affection shown the nephew, he turned out to be as ungrateful as he was unbalanced. Elizabeth hoped to improve him by marriage, and one of the most sumptuous events of the reign was the wedding in August, 1745, of Peter to Sophia of Anhalt-Zerbst, who was renamed Catherine. For Peter the marriage proved in time to be his undoing. It gave Russia a potential new Romanov heir in the person of the Grand Duke Paul, born to Catherine in 1754 and immediately appropriated by Elizabeth as her own. The empress' smothering Paul with too many blankets and too much affection unfortunately helped make the son as neurotic as the father. As for Catherine, she was destined to become empress in her own right, Russia's greatest, having had her strong character tempered in the court of Elizabeth, a woman whose bumbling interference Catherine resented but whose basic good-heartedness she never doubted.

It was said of Elizabeth that she inherited her warm heart from her mother, while to her father was attributed her quick and violent temper. She could curse in the language of the least of her subjects, she boxed ears and clouted people, and she often threw things. Elizabeth storming was impressive indeed, and so was her willingness to forgive and forget. More than one soldier or courtier melted her simply with the words "I am guilty, little Mother." There was no vengeance in Elizabeth, for she wanted people to be as joyous as she herself usually was.

One of Elizabeth's great gifts was her capacity to judge human nature and to deal with people. She was successful in choosing able advisers and in making ambitious rivals work in harmony. The play of factions never assumed the harmful proportions it did in the previous reigns simply because Elizabeth would not have it, imperiously, yet gently. Often she employed simultaneously and otherwise protected from each other a pro-French-Prussian set headed by Vorontsov and a pro-English-Austrian group led by Alexis Bestuzhev-Ryumin who emerged as the greatest of the statesmen who came to the fore under Elizabeth. He was to keep her confidence for eighteen years.

Descended far back from an English yeoman named Best (who came to Russia in 1403), Bestuzhev had complete admiration for things English, and it was to be his ultimate undoing. He had been well educated abroad in languages and science (his experiments in biochemistry were still the pride of his middle age), and in 1712, at age nineteen, he was employed in Peter's diplomatic corps. His career alternated between triumphs and disgraces because of the complicated intrigues among his father (Anna Ivanovna's first lover), Biren (the elder Bestuzhev's replacement), and Osterman (rival to both). Made a vice-chancellor after

Elizabeth's coup and Osterman's downfall, Alexis Bestuzhev became grand chancellor in 1744. A Russian of Russians and as cunning as he was patriotic, Bestuzhev developed a superb spy system that suborned everyone from ladies-in-waiting to chambermaids, according to the British ambassador, and that decoded foreign-sent confidences with a huge efficiency, to the distress of Frederick the Great, who also pouted that Bestuzhev was his imitator. Absolute incorruptibility was another Bestuzhev boast, a unique one in his day. Once the chancellor did accept 50,000 rubles from the British, his official salary being modest and the mansion provided by the empress (Osterman's) being unfurnished. Bestuzhev's sardonic twist, however, was to have fifty certificates of indebtedness guaranteed by fifty picked Russians, notably his enemies. Bluff, moody, dictatorial, and with a touch of both paranoia and hypochondria, Bestuzhev was a man eager for power and altogether capable in its use.

The grand chancellor bemoaned Elizabeth's inattention to affairs and the need to coax her to work, citing the fact that important documents often lay in her apartments unheeded for days on end. It was said, for example, that two handwritten letters from the august Louis XV of France never did get a reply from her. The empress was indeed lazy and haphazard in her schedule. Although willful and determined to govern, she was often ill informed and slow to inform herself. However, Elizabeth was often deliberately irresolute, avoiding precipitous actions and letting time solve the problems which seemed pressing.

Immediately following her accession, Elizabeth received a proposal from La Chétardie that she end the war in progress with Sweden and cede back all Russian gains in order to please France and Prussia, Sweden's friends. The empress' indignant reply to the man who had lent her conspiracy 10,000 ducats was to say that the daughter of Peter the Great would not give up an inch of ground won by the blood of Russian soldiers. The war was intensified until the enemy forces in Finland capitulated at Helsinki. By the Treaty of Abo signed in August, 1743, Russia annexed an additional southern Finnish province, but not the whole duchy as Bestuzhev demanded, because Elizabeth feared French-Prussian intervention.

During the Russian-Swedish conflict, Western Europe was engaged in the War of the Austrian Succession (1740–48), which pitted Austria (Maria Theresa) and Britain (George II) against France (Louis XV) and Prussia (Frederick the Great). Elizabeth briefly drew close to Prussia, at one time calling Frederick the Great the most perfect monarch in the world. Then Bestuzhev secured a reversal of Russian policy and friendship with Prussia's enemies. La Chétardie was unceremoniously dismissed as French ambassador, after Bestuzhev produced letters of his calling Elizabeth "frivolous and dissipated" and "abandoned to voluptuous lethargy." Forthwith, Elizabeth made up with her fellow empress, Maria Theresa, and Russian diplomacy became increasingly concerned about the progress of French and Prussian aggrandizement at Austria's expense. After formally allying with Austria and receiving British subsidies, in January, 1748, the Russian army was ordered to march to the Rhine. This move caused the French-Prussian side hastily to conclude a peace treaty—the second time in fifteen years that Russian troop deployment thwarted all-powerful Louis XV. French and Prussian diplomats, who first put down Elizabeth as stupid and easily swayed, had learned otherwise.

In 1749 Elizabeth's love life threatened to intrude into affairs with the appearance of a new favorite, Ivan Shuvalov, a man young enough to be her son. Ivan was the nephew of Alexander and Peter Shuvalov, who were upstarts in the Russian aristocracy but close to Elizabeth for their leadership in the 1741 coup, if not for more personal reasons. Made a count, Alexander Shuvalov was remembered as a harsh and avaricious director of police activities. His brother, Count Peter, equally cruel and covetous, was all the same gifted and able as director of the War College and promoter of economic reforms. The Shuvalovs further tried to make themselves indispensable by prostituting Nephew Ivan with their all-too-susceptible sovereign. To the surprise of all, the favored Ivan Shuvalov turned out to be as studious, modest, unambitious, and amiable as he was handsome, refusing to interfere in affairs any more than to encourage the arts.

Initially, however, Bestuzhev felt his position endangered by the turn of events and sought to counter the Shuvalovs' influence by putting an even prettier and younger man in the path of Elizabeth, a fellow named Nikito Beketov, who hitherto had been familiar at the court only as "first lover" in the Cadets' theater productions. Briefly and conspicuously Beketov enjoyed the finest clothes, apartments near Elizabeth, and the title of Colonel. Then it became evident that in fact, a strange *ménage à quatre* was going on, for it pleased Elizabeth to keep all her men around, including Shuvalov, Beketov, and the original and agreeable Alexis Razumovsky, who blithely made Beketov his adjutant. After a year of this, Beketov was the first to go, ousted by a diabolical maneuver by Ivan Shuvalov's Uncle Peter. The elder Shuvalov gave Beketov an ointment to give Elizabeth, and the all-too-innocent young man unhesitatingly repeated to her the assurance that it would restore the beauty of her complexion. Elizabeth fled the court in tears, forbade Beketov her presence, and then gently sent him off to be governor of Astrakhan.

The bemused court discovered from all this that Elizabeth's lovers were just emperors of the night. She did not mix romance and politics. Razumovsky remained the old lover, Shuvalov the new. The elder Shuvalov

brothers kept their important jobs, but so did Bestuzhev, supreme in diplomatic affairs. Secure in the hearts of many men and able to make them
work together, Elizabeth was free to pursue her pleasures.

3. Extravagant Hostess

"The eternal debutante" is an apt description of an empress devoted
almost entirely to self-display in terms of clothes, jewels, parties, and
spectacles. Only one generation removed from the peasant class, but all
the same autocrat of Russia, Elizabeth first of all indulged herself by
ignoring routine. She ordered, or disordered, her daily life according to
whim. Instead of regularly dining at 12 and supping at 6, as Anna had
done, Elizabeth got up when she felt like it, often put off the main meal
until 5 or 6, might then nap, take supper as late as 2 or 3 in the morning,
and finally retire at 7 A.M. Frequently she stayed awake in bed after sun-
rise, gossiping with her ladies, who were commissioned to take turns
tickling the soles of her feet. Only two things could be counted on to make
the empress bestir herself—religious devotions and parties.

There is something of the traditional Russian gentlewoman in Elizabeth
lazing about, often in dishabille, surrounded by her chattering, idlebrained
ladies and maids. The chief women claimed nobility for being the wives
of the men in power, notably the countesses Vorontsov and Shuvalov.
Elizabeth's Skavronsky relatives, like Countess Hendrikov, held their own
against old aristocrats. A somewhat disreputable and mysterious female
favorite of the empress was known simply as Elizabeth Izmailovna; her
backstairs missions won her a wit's appelation as *le ministre des affaires
étranges* (in contrast with the official *le ministre des affaires étrangères*).
Elizabeth's informality of manner was also evident in her treatment of
her chamberlain, a man raised to that honor from his job as stoker of
the palace stoves. He slept like a watchdog at the foot of her bed, and she
often had to tickle him into wakefulness.

While Elizabeth was capable of wallowing in hair-down seclusion, she
was neither plain nor dull, and she did not hide herself perpetually in her
rooms, as her predecessor had done. In fact, Elizabeth's vanity about her
charms drove her more than anything else to play the grand hostess.
Described as exquisite and ravishing in her teens, the empress in her late
thirties still had beauty and magnetism worthy of the admiration of the
whole world, according to the English ambassador. Her large blue eyes,
brilliant and friendly, set off a cherubic face, with its broad forehead and
small, firm mouth. A defect was the small, bulbous nose, but Elizabeth
saw to it that this was neither mentioned nor portrayed. Her hair was a
particular triumph, luxuriant and richly auburn, capable of any number

of stylings and just right for her fine, rosy complexion. Relatively tall, Elizabeth always tended to the voluptuous, but even so she was well proportioned, and her grace and agility dispelled any impression of excessive fatness.

Elizabeth was not above displays of vanity. There was the incident with Madame Lopukhina, who appeared at a ball in the exact same getup as the empress, a pink gown and roses in her hair. Pink was so much Elizabeth's favorite color that she had forbidden others to wear it. Whether her mistake was one of forgetfulness or defiance, Madame Lopukhina promptly found herself on her knees before Elizabeth, who took some large shears and proceeded to cut off the offending flowers together with much hair, and slapped the lady soundly, causing her to faint. "She only got what she deserved, the little fool," announced Elizabeth, resuming the dance.

Dancing gave Elizabeth the best opportunity for showing off her face and figure, and it became a passion with her. It was, in fact, the greatest expression of her whole nature, from the time she was a young girl remembered for always having one foot in the air. Now the empress, Elizabeth would summon for her company in this activity as many as 400 couples, and huge balls were often held more than once a week. The minuet, just about a century old in the West, was a favorite means of displaying Elizabeth's grace, but she also flung herself into English country dances, polonaises, Ukrainian measures to please Alexis, and even the wild native Russian dance known as the plyaska. When the empress tired of disporting herself, usually not soon, she turned choreographer and organized elaborate quadrilles.

Most of Elizabeth's balls were masquerades, and here she indulged another idiosyncrasy, her delight in appearing in men's clothes. Her success in this role is well attested to in the following statement by Catherine, her nephew's wife:

> A masculine habit suited the Empress marvellously well. She had the finest legs I have ever seen (far finer than any man's) and a foot of admirable symmetry. She danced to perfection and was equally graceful whether dressed as a man or a woman.

Catherine's continuation is also revealing of its author:

> One day, at one of the Court balls, I was watching her dance a minuet. She approached me when it was over, and I took the liberty to say to her that it was very fortunate for us poor women that she was not a man, as, dressed as she then was, even her portrait would be sufficient to turn all our heads. She replied in the most gracious manner in the world, that if she were a man, it would be to me that she would give the palm.

A smiling exchange of compliments is certainly the way Elizabeth wanted life to be.

Elizabeth delighted in all kinds of costumes, except those of pilgrims, considered impious, and those of harlequins, thought scandalous. Most dear to the empress, however, was her getup as a Dutch sailor, which brought out all her pride in her father and his Amsterdam days, and so attired, she would acknowledge no address other than Michaelovna.

Many of her masquerades were specifically decreed metamorphoses. At these all the women had to dress as men and all the men as women. Foreign diplomats came to regard this official transvestism as one of the greatest burdens of service in St. Petersburg. Although the empress might shine, the others felt both laughable and uncomfortable, particularly the men wearing hoopskirts.

The variety and pace of the entertainments were impressive and exhausting for those less vigorous and party-mad than the empress. The grand fetes in the imperial palaces were customarily followed by elaborate suppers, and often there were lengthy displays of fireworks afterward. It was not unheard of for Elizabeth to insist that all her guests at a masquerade stay on to witness a full-length opera or the latest French play. Those on the guest list had no choice but to arrive at seven and stay to three. Moreover, Elizabeth expected her courtiers to use their own resources to the utmost, giving favorites like Razumovsky the settings and the means to surprise her with particular singing, dancing, or acting groups.

Outdoor activities were also essential for the spirited empress. The whole court would set off in a fleet of colorful yachts or gondolas, with bands of musicians also afloat, and proceed to an island in the Neva, where they might find in readiness an array of Chinese tents, or a dancing pavilion, or an open-air theater, or, perhaps, just swings and merry-go-rounds. There were also hunting fetes, for Elizabeth was a devotee of both hunting and hawking, having boasted of her riding and shooting abilities since her youth.

Setting a good table played a large role in Elizabeth's entertaining. She paid an Alsatian chef 800 rubles and raised him to the fifth rank of court nobility. Her representatives abroad vied to send her special delicacies, Périgord pâtés and truffles and the like. Peter Shuvalov brought about the introduction of pineapples to Russia. In her efforts to please her guests —say, at a supper for several hundred—Elizabeth would offer dishes of all nations, even having special servants inquire of foreigners what particular native treats they would like prepared. The pursuit of *haute cuisine* on a lavish scale was limited, however, by two eccentricities of the empress: her love of cooking for herself and her taste for traditional Russian foods. The despair of her foreign chef was her frequent demand for things such as buckwheat cakes, cabbage soup, and pickled pork and onions.

Travel was another of Elizabeth's luxurious whims. She journeyed with a large personal staff and enjoyed the comfort of a selection of huge conveyances, including a sledge fitted with a stove and a card table and a golden carriage made in Paris and decorated entirely with panels by Boucher. The whole court was often required to travel with the sovereign, including the personnel of all the government offices, the Guards regiments, and the foreign representatives. As many as 19,000 horses were needed to transport perhaps 24,000 persons and their belongings on one of Elizabeth's visits to Moscow. Once every three years was about the frequency of the empress' stays in the old capital. On such occasions St. Petersburg would be emptied of society and of society's furnishings as well, for even the best families could not maintain their accustomed style in Moscow without the presence of their fine French and English pieces. Lesser gentry were frequently reduced to taking the necessities of eating, sitting, and sleeping.

Even if Elizabeth's pleasures were to make her court the most splendid in Europe, her extravagance was cause for criticism. Notably, old Prince Michael Shcherbatov muttered forth in his memoirs about the English racehorses and the pineapples, decrying the perversion of the supposedly Spartan virtues of old Muscovy, to say nothing about the abandonment of Petrine frugality. There were, of course, no critics from the masses, who were vouchsafed only an awestruck glimpse of the fairy-tale empress who spent their taxes with such happy abandon.

The result of Elizabeth's hedonism was not entirely negative. Not only did she import French dresses and paintings at fantastic expense, but she brought in French craftsmen and artists as well, thus laying the foundation for the rapid flowering of a native culture. Russian art, ballet, theater, and literature were largely born out of Elizabeth's caprices.

During a major fire in Moscow in 1747 one of Elizabeth's new palaces went up in flames, and with it no fewer than 4,000 of her dresses. Yet this was but a small and temporary loss, for it was discovered after her death that she had left 15,000 dresses in the wardrobes of various residences, in addition to two chestfuls of silk stockings and several closetfuls of shoes. Most of the dresses had been worn only once. The costs of all this are unknown, but it was reported abroad that French couturiers eventually cut off the credit of her Russian Majesty

Elizabeth found it becoming to wear jewels in quantity as well as quality, wholly aside from the imperial set pieces. Usually her hair would be done in diamonds or pearls, her neck would be laden with lavalieres, and her whole bodice would be ablaze with gems as well. The visitor to Leningrad may see today exquisite artificial flowers in jewels and brilliants created for the empress' coiffure. Also striking are a number of wristwatches, mostly Paris-made, including three similar in design and in glittering brilliance but differentiated by their predominant blue, green, and red coloring —sapphires, emeralds, and rubies.

Her courtiers were quick to imitate her extravagance, disregarding their origins and sometimes their solvency. Alexis Razumovsky was responsible for the male fashion of diamond buttons, epaulets, and shoe buckles. His brother, Cyril, on one occasion bought up 100,000 bottles of French wine, including 6,800 of the best champagne, much of which he distributed freely among his friends. The younger Razumovsky's income reached into the five figures annually, but he left enormous debts. Count Peter Sheremetev, descendant of the original Romanov ancestor, Andrew Kobyla, displayed his wealth by dressing his servants in as much gold and silver as he wore himself, and he kept such an ample table that if the entire imperial entourage happened to drop by his palace at Ostankino, they would be entertained just as easily as if expected days in advance. Field Marshal Stephen Apraxin, only a generation removed from the bluff sea dog by that name beloved by Peter, won his military fame fairly enough and also the reputation of a great dandy. A snuffbox for each day of the year was one boast of Apraxin, a man who went off on campaigns with several hundred wagonsful of personal baggage and a man who once refused a gold-hilted sword from King George II because it did not have any jewels.

Native extravagance was spurred by imperial sumptuary decrees. On the occasion of the wedding of Peter and Catherine in 1745, Elizabeth ordered that the two highest degrees of the military and civil nobility appear in carriages, each attended by a minimum of two footmen and eight lackeys. Her own conveyance was, in Catherine's words, *un vrai petit château,* drawn by eight horses, but Sergius Naryshkin managed to top the empress by arriving in a carriage, including the wheels, inlaid completely with crystal mirrors. It had cost him 7,000 pounds in England, something less than the value of his costume, which featured a tree trunk up his back done all in diamonds with appropriately jeweled branches reaching out on his limbs.

The harsh fact of Russian social structure in Elizabeth's day was that a favored aristocrat like Cyril Razumovsky could blithely order out a few thousand serfs to construct a dam and pond so that nightingales would sing for the entertainment of his guests.

Elizabeth was a patron of art on a grand, if somewhat indiscriminate, scale. Paintings were essential for the decor of her many new palaces, and she spared no expense to get French or Italian artists to execute them. Portraitists were popular, for the empress was a more than willing subject. There are scores of canvases of Elizabeth to be seen, ranging from her nakedness at eight to royal dignity in gold and ermine, or from portrayal as the goddess Flora to a fetching figure in male attire. Imperial vanity was such that Elizabeth ordered wholesale quantities of her likeness for presentation abroad; the French master Caravaque was said to have got 1,200 rubles per twelve export portraits. The courtiers were not far behind the sovereign, and the Russian State Museum in Leningrad today affords the historian opportunities to ponder at will a large selection of likenesses of Razumovskys, Shuvalovs, Vorontsovs, Bestuzhevs, and Apraxins—men, women, and children. Many of these were by French ex-patriates, but the number of Russian names increases with time. It was the favorite Ivan Shuvalov who brought about the founding in 1757 of the Russian Academy of Fine Arts, which received little attention at first but laid the way for a later flourishing. The first director of the academy was the French painter Louis Joseph Le Lorrain, whose Russian experiences were unfortunately short and unhappy: He was robbed of every stitch of his belongings by pirates during the sea voyage and then died within a few months of a respiratory ailment contracted in St. Petersburg.

The purchase abroad of talent, not just of articles, held also for some of the applied arts. For example, the Imperial Porcelain Factory dates from Elizabeth's reign, production beginning about 1750 under the direction of a German named Christoph Konrad Hunger, whose predilection for drink turned out to be a greater obstacle than Russian clumsiness. Hunger was greatly influenced by Meissen designs, and he used the Chinese asymmetrical leaf and scroll and shell motifs then fashionable as part of the Rococo style (later, under Catherine, Sèvres and geometric classic style became the fad). Little jugs, cups, and a proliferation of snuffboxes were the first things turned out. By the end of her reign Elizabeth was able to give banquets on specially made tables in the shape of the script *E,* all garlanded and flowered, with the tableware as frivolous and fragile as the guests, but Russian-manufactured all the same (one of these whole settings is exhibited in the Tsarskoe Selo Museum).

Opera, ballet, and theater were no longer novelties by the time of Elizabeth's accession, but her reign saw the firm establishment of these arts and the first Russian claims on them as their own. The empress' passion for music and her desire to please Razumovsky led to the coming of *opera bouffa.* The chief singers were highly paid, having been lured away from Italy, France, and Germany. A choral group from the Ukraine was sometimes heard along with them. As for the ballet company, it was drawn largely from the Imperial Corps of Cadets, the young nobles gaining the reputation of being superb dancers, as well as of excelling in female theatrical roles.

A man named Fedor Volkov was so carried away by the opera he saw in the capital that he returned to Yaroslavl and built his own complete theater seating 1,000. Volkov was author, actor, director, decorator, and carpenter. His quick fame in the provinces brought him in turn an imperial summons to St. Petersburg, and Volkov's company found itself the darlings of the Winter Palace. Elizabeth was promptly generous in supplying elaborate and costly costumes and jewels from her own wardrobes, and she did not disdain helping with the makeup and dressing, especially when the ubiquitous Corps of Cadets became involved in the productions. Full attendance was aided by the 50-ruble fines Elizabeth assiduously levied on aristocrats who stayed at home. From these beginnings Prince Boris Yusupov and others brought about the foundation of a permanent national theater in 1756, performing Russian comedies and tragedies at the Golovin mansion on Vasilevsky Island and offering a native repertoire of fifty plays within a few years.

The first original Russian libretto to accompany an opera was the *Clemency of Titus* written by Volkov in 1751. The most prolific Russian writer of plays, all so bad as to be forgotten within a short time, was an ex-Cadet actor named Alexander Sumarokov, who became known as the father of the Russian literary profession for his pioneer dabblings in poetry, criticism, and journalism. It was at Sumarokov's tragedy *Khorev,* concerning the legendary days of Kiev, that Elizabeth was smitten by the pretty bejeweled star performer, Nikita Beketov, who became her partner in the most foolish of her amorous intrigues. In general, native texts, productions, and actors could still not hold their own against foreign competition, but by the end of Elizabeth's reign there were few gilded youths in Russia who were not well conversant with the whole range of Molière, Corneille, and Racine.

The greatest single intellectual figure of the time was Michael Lomonosov (1711–65), a man who was less a recognized glory of the reign, however, than a promise of great things to come. Of peasant stock but self-educated, Lomonosov was given the opportunity to study in Germany and returned to Russia to pursue both science and literature. As a professor of chemistry, he reached astounding heights in his theoretical investigations into thermodynamics and physical chemistry, anticipating by decades the discoveries of Lavoisier, Dalton, and Joule. His works in these fields remained unpublished in his lifetime, however. About all that Elizabethan Russia was ready for from this genius was his establishment of a mosaics factory in the old Menshikov Palace at Oranienbaum, the first of its kind and the source of many strikingly original vases and portrait panels (Oranienbaum has accordingly been renamed Lomonosov by the Soviet government).

Lomonosov was, however, justly famed for a distinguished work on Russian grammar, a history of Russia, and numerous sacred and patriotic odes—all of which made him a founder of the classical Russian literary language. Many of his odes and panegyrics were for the occasion of Elizabeth's anniversaries or other celebrations. Probably the empress was unaware that Lomonosov had similarly honored her predecessor, Anna. Lomonosov was to find that the court had little real use or appreciation of his efforts. He might well complain, in the words of another writer of the day, that his poems were treated "like the fruits and sweets which appeared on the tables of the rich." In time he turned to drink and died a ruin.

It is Lomonosov's name, not Elizabeth's, which is now attached to the University of Moscow. Its founding in 1755, which owed much to Ivan Shuvalov, was an incontestably great achievement of her reign. (The full title currently is the Moscow Order of Lenin and Order of the Red Banner of Labor State University Named for M. V. Lomonosov.) This was Russia's first institution of higher learning, excluding the Polish Academy at Kiev and the University of Dorpat, which were gained through territorial annexation, not creation. The faculty was entirely foreign at first, the languages of instruction being French and Latin. The formal boast was the three schools of law, medicine, and philosophy, but such was the inadequacy of Russian schooling at the time that it was necessary to attach preparatory facilities, two Gymnasiums, one for nobles and one for others. Even thirty years after its founding, Moscow University had only eighty-two students.

Only religion claimed as much devotion from Elizabeth as disporting herself indoors and out and playing the lavish hostess. Probably she spent as much of her leisure time at her prayers as at anything else. She was rigorous to the point of fanaticism about observing holy days and keeping fasts. Elizabeth was unquestioning and altogether Old Russian in her piety.

Like her father, she was to burn herself out by the age of fifty. Already as she entered her forties, the marvelous complexion was gone, and it took hours of camphor and ice and layers of cosmetics to re-create the illusion. Yet even the discriminating eye of the French ambassador was still impressed, and he reported back to Paris quite frankly: "She could not look better or combine, at her age, a greater appearance of freshness with a life more designed to banish it." Serious illnesses took their toll. Elizabeth would then make solemn vows to intensify her devotions and would visit this or that religious shrine, taking her entire suite on pilgrimages, most frequently to places situated 60 or 70 miles from Moscow. Insistent on walking, but no longer able to accomplish more than 6 or 7 miles a day, the empress might spend more than a week fulfilling her duty in stages. The courtiers and ambassadors grumbled incessantly at this imposition on their patience and purses, but Elizabeth pursued this whim just as serenely as when she made the men dress as women for her metamorphoses.

4. Foe of Frederick the Great

Ambassadors' dispatches to the Western capitals might report that Elizabeth's life was frivolous and that Petersburg's new palaces were barbarous, but the more telling news in the 1750's was that the armies of the Russian empress were marching up and down Germany making themselves the arbiters of Europe. Elizabeth's military and diplomatic successes consolidated the work of Peter the Great and made her the wrongly forgotten forerunner of Catherine the Great.

As of the middle of the eighteenth century there seemed to be three basic givens in European great power politics: British-French antagonism, going back centuries and now intensified by the race for empire in America and India; French-Austrian hostility, likewise of ancient origin and in its current phase a Bourbon-Hapsburg dynastic rivalry; and, finally, Austrian-Prussian enmity, a relatively new factor but a highly volatile one in view of the Hohenzollerns' recent aggrandizement at Hapsburg expense. The resulting sorting out of friends and enemies meant Britain and Austria on one side, France and Prussia on the other. Then, abruptly, the groupings reversed themselves. By the Diplomatic Revolution of 1756 Britain and Prussia became allies, and even more surprisingly, so did France and Austria. Fighting promptly broke out on the Continent, to be known as the Seven Years' War (1756–63), matching the struggle in the New World called the French and Indian War. As the fifth and newest member of the club of great powers, Russia's position naturally was of crucial concern to both sides.

The diplomatic choices available divided the court of St. Petersburg. The chancellor, Bestuzhev, was stubbornly pro-British, no matter what they did. The Francophile party, including the Shuvalovs, was considerable, however, and profited from the current popularity of things French. Grand Duke Peter, the heir to the throne, was pro-Prussian to a pathological degree, while his wife Catherine's attitude was more opportunistic, even if she had been sent to Russia virtually to be a Prussian spy. Only the empress appeared unwaveringly pro-Russian, instinctively keeping the main chance in view and skillfully surmounting the play of factions. Elizabeth did have something of an anti-Prussian bias, stirred up by King Frederick's bon mots about her love life and intensified by his reported threat to aid the restoration of Ivan VI.

King Frederick's first victories against the French and Austrians were reported in the summer, and court opinion swung sharply against British money and Prussian soldiers for upsetting the whole European balance of power. Fear of Prussia, particularly, led to Russia's joining the French-Austrian side in the fall, all this negotiated behind Bestuzhev's back. The war preparations went slowly, however, and the army did not move that year. Elizabeth had been severely ill, and the commanders feared a complete reversal of policy if Grand Duke Peter became ruler.

Field Marshal Apraxin finally got his forces under way in May, 1757, and invaded East Prussia in August. A sharp engagement soon took place at Gross-Jägersdorf, with Prussia's fearsome military reputation being matched for the first time against Russian numbers (55,000 to the enemy's 24,000). On the right wing Peter Shuvalov's newly invented howitzers helped repulse the full force of the famous Prussian dragoons. In the center the Russian infantry was attacked unexpectedly, reeled in chaos, but then by sheer courage recovered the situation. On the left the Cossack horsemen enticed their pursuers to a general massacre. It was a haphazard thing but in the end a stunning victory for the Russians. When the news was brought to Elizabeth, she joyfully ordered a salvo of 101 guns from the citadel, while Catherine tactfully gave an entertainment, as Peter sulked. The capture of Königsberg seemed imminent, and Frederick wrote of his situation: "If this lasts through the winter, I am lost." Apraxin, however, found excuses to order a retreat, and the army, demoralized, returned to the frontiers. At this juncture Elizabeth suffered a collapse, variously attributed to her shock at the war casualties and to high living. She fell senseless outside a church and for days did not recognize people or talk intelligibly. Recovered, she promptly dismissed Apraxin, attributing his dilatoriness to his speculating on her death.

At the insistence of the empress a winter campaign was undertaken, and in January, 1758, Russian troops captured Königsberg and most of East Prussia. Satisfaction with this achievement was interrupted by a sensational event at court in February, the fall of Bestuzhev from power after eighteen years. The chancellor was suddenly arrested in the middle of a conference of the ministers, at which time Prince Nikita Trubetskoy ripped off Bestuzhev's Order of St. Andrew. He was accused of plotting with Field Marshal Apraxin and Catherine to ease up on Prussia and to bar Peter's succession to the throne. Protesting his innocence, Bestuzhev nonetheless burned all his papers. Torture was avoided only after he swore on the sacraments to Elizabeth's satisfaction. A tribunal condemned him to death anyhow, charging him willy-nilly with usurping the royal power, revealing state secrets, and intriguing in general. Elizabeth's good sense and good heart prevailed over his enemies, however, and Bestuzhev was merely exiled to his estates, to ponder how a man once so clever and indispensable could become so superfluous. Field Marshal Apraxin died of apoplexy, without ever getting the exoneration he begged. Catherine survived by combining abject appeals to the empress with insouciance toward her ill-wishers (at a party, when she still feared the worst, she gaily addressed Trubetskoy: "Well, your Excellency, have you discovered more crimes than criminals or more criminals than crimes?").

The internal crisis over, the Russian army that summer invaded Pomerania and reached the frontiers of Brandenburg itself. At the Battle of Zorndorf, in August, 43,000 Russians confronted 33,000 Prussians under none other than the great Frederick. Frederick later admitted that he expected complete defeat three different times, but in the end both armies clung to their positions on the battlefield. Then the Russian commander decided to retreat and eventually retired behind the Vistula River, even though reinforced. Elizabeth was furious, but helpless, writing her commander stern lectures, such as one where she ordered: "Avoid in the future . . . all such expressions in your dispatches as 'if time, circumstances, and the movements of the enemy permit.' " The talk in St. Petersburg was that Austria and France were letting Russia do their fighting for them, but the empress remained doggedly loyal to her allies and determined in her crusade. For his part, Frederick wrote in wistful discouragement: "So our campaigning is over, and nothing has come of it for either side, but the loss of many an honest fellow, the distress of many a poor soldier crippled for life, and the ruin of several provinces."

In 1759 the Russian army moved down into Saxony to join up with the Austrians. The new commander, Peter Saltykov, proved courageous in skirmishes when he showed himself to his men flailing at bullets with his whip. Frederick at this point saw a great chance to annihilate his enemies separately and suddenly confronted the Russian army at Kunersdorf in August. By late afternoon the Prussians had completely smashed Saltykov's left wing, taken 182 of his cannon, and reduced him to prayer on his knees. Then the miracle happened: The Prussian knockout blow miscarried, and the Russians fell on their exhausted enemies, eventually causing 19,000 casualties to the Russian 16,000. After Kunersdorf, Saltykov wrote Elizabeth that she "must not be surprised at our serious casualties," for "another such victory, your Majesty, and I shall be obliged to plod staff in hand myself to St. Petersburg with the joyful news, for want of messengers." While the Russian court was delirious with thanksgiving services and salvos, Frederick rued his "horrible catastrophe" and swore "I will not survive the ruin of my country." Once again, however, lack of supplies and disputes with allies saw the Russian army retire when complete victory seemed at hand. War weariness was growing among the courtiers, but Elizabeth remained unshakable.

When the Austrian ambassador presented his congratulations to the empress for the new year of 1760, she took the occasion to make this spirited response: "I am always a long time making up my mind but once I have decided what ought to be done, I stick to my opinion. I mean to continue this war in cooperation with my allies, even if I am compelled to sell all my diamonds and half my clothes." Only the master of the royal wardrobe could have made the calculation from this that Elizabeth might be leaving herself only 7,000 dresses. Moreover, her crusade to stop Prussian aggrandizement was losing some of its moral force, for Russian diplomats now had their hopes firmly set on the annexation of East Prussia. The financial strain of the yearly campaigns was becoming desperate; it was a guns-or-parties dilemma in a sense, something Elizabeth dimly appreciated. But once again, in early 1760, the Russian army moved westward into Germany, only to retreat back to Poland, this time because of news of Frederick's victories elsewhere. It did Elizabeth little good to change commanders or to declare that she for one had no fears of "hazarding our army in an engagement with the King of Prussia, however desperate and bloody."

Cossacks in Berlin! It happened in October, 1760, and was a bitter reminder for Germans over the nearly two centuries separating this event from the fall of Hitler. Actually, a Russian raiding force occupied the Prussian capital for only four days, their main intent being less military than the beating out of Russia's allies in exacting financial tribute from the Berliners while Frederick's armies were engaged elsewhere.

The new year, 1761, came, and the illuminations before the Winter Palace stressed the theme of peace, but the empress still clung to her aims of crippling Prussia and of getting compensations. The French and Austrians favored a peace of mutual exhaustion, negotiating behind Russia's back but to no avail. The initiative in diplomacy, as well as in war, remained with Elizabeth. Alexander Buturlin, the new commander and reputedly a former lover of the empress, moved his army deep into Germany and, after joining with the Austrians, had 132,000 men to the Prussians' 50,000. Frederick for once was forced to hole up in a fortified camp, but Buturlin was as cautious as his predecessors, refusing to assault and then retreating. Elizabeth wrote sorrowfully, yet defiantly:

> We will not conceal from you that the news of your retreat has caused us more sorrow than the loss of a battle would have done. . . . Without wasting any more words, we command you to proceed forthwith to Berlin. . . . If anyone in the future dares to say that our army is not fit for attacking strongholds, he is instantly to be arrested and sent hither in chains.

Although Buturlin failed to move on Berlin, the empress' firmness began to have its effect. A subordinate commander named Peter Rumyantsev showed great skill and persistence in gaining the key Prussian fortress of Kolberg in the first days of 1762. Previously considered too impetuous,

Rumyantsev stood likely to become the new commander in chief, one who would not repeat the mistakes of the past—the cautious strategies, the unexpected victories, and the failures to follow them up. The prospect of continued Russian pressure drove Frederick of Prussia to complete despair. His magnificent efforts to snatch victory from repeated defeats had come to naught, and he vowed to seek a soldier's death, leaving whatever fragments of his domains to his heir. Then the unexpected came: The fighting stopped, the Russians mysteriously disengaged, and finally the news arrived of the empress' death, which had occurred the very day of Rumyantsev's victory.

Since her attack of 1757 Elizabeth's health had been a problem, but she persisted in her disorganized life. Her legs eventually became so painfully swollen that she could not walk. Yet she would have herself conveyed on a litter to the apartments of Razumovsky or Shuvalov and try to revive the past over an intimate little supper. Pathetically, she might order several hours' worth of costuming, coiffure, and makeup and then, viewing herself in a mirror, decide to go back to bed again. Her worries were many and the unfinished war and the unfinished Winter Palace especially—and there was cause for anxiety over her unpredictable successor and his whispered-about wife. On December 23 she had a terrible coughing fit and hemorrhaged persistently, but once again the fifty-two-year-old woman recovered and then ordered the doctors away to attend her sick jeweler. A relapse on January 3 led to her receiving the last rites, during which she repeated favorite passages from the prayers. In the end she was attended by most of her intimate friends, Catherine, and Peter, the last being made to promise that he would protect the Razumovskys and Shuvalovs. At four in the afternoon of Christmas Day (Old Style; January 5 by the New) the senior Senator Trubetskoy announced to the weeping dignitaries in the antechamber: "Her Imperial Majesty Elizabeth Petrovna has fallen asleep in the Lord. God preserve our Most Gracious Sovereign, the Emperor Peter III."

There was cause to weep. Few rulers had been so genuinely beloved. Elizabeth was remembered as kind, motherly, and, above all, fun to be with. Her temper and her follies were easily forgotten. Moreover, the empress had real majesty, her twenty-year reign bringing great relief from the tawdry era preceding. Elizabethan St. Petersburg was a sparkling city. The tinsel was Frenchified, perhaps, but the foundations for a true Russian culture were laid. Finally, there were the victories at Gross-Jägersdorf and Kunersdorf, things for Russians to boast of and for Europeans to ponder.

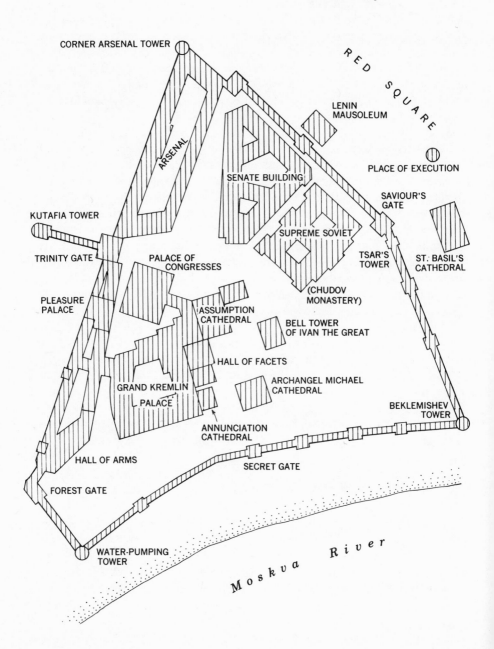

The Moscow Kremlin
as it is today

CORNER ARSENAL TOWER

RED SQUARE

LENIN MAUSOLEUM

ARSENAL

SENATE BUILDING

PLACE OF EXECUTION

KUTAFIA TOWER

SAVIOUR'S GATE

SUPREME SOVIET

TRINITY GATE

PALACE OF CONGRESSES

TSAR'S TOWER

ST. BASIL'S CATHEDRAL

PLEASURE PALACE

(CHUDOV MONASTERY)

ASSUMPTION CATHEDRAL

BELL TOWER OF IVAN THE GREAT

HALL OF FACETS

GRAND KREMLIN PALACE

ARCHANGEL MICHAEL CATHEDRAL

BEKLEMISHEV TOWER

ANNUNCIATION CATHEDRAL

HALL OF ARMS

SECRET GATE

FOREST GATE

WATER-PUMPING TOWER

Moskva River

X.

Romanov St. Petersburg and Rastrelli's Palaces

1. The Northern Side of the City

EVEN if the Empress Elizabeth spent 1,000 rubles on her transitory pleasures for every 100 spent on the permanent enhancement of St. Petersburg, she did leave behind her a transformed city, a worthy—indeed, admirable—European capital that even today is a source of delight for the student of Baroque-Rococo style. At her death St. Petersburg had attained the same population as Moscow—about 150,000—and there would no longer be any doubt that it would remain the seat and symbol of the Romanov dynasty.

The phrase "citadel of Peter's," which Pushkin used in a poem eulogizing the city, is a true attribution, for the fortress metropolis was deliberately thrust forward at the extremities of Russia through the exertions of the great tsar. Peter created a Russian "window to Europe," to use a phrase, not of Pushkin, but of an Italian visitor in 1739. A unique feature of the new capital was that it was the first planned city, excluding Versailles as something less than an urban concentration, and this, too, was Peter's doing. It was "the most abstract and contrived city on the entire earthly sphere," in the words of Dostoievsky. Still another special quality lies in the fact that today's Leningrad remains the northernmost large metropolis and, accordingly, is subject to the hauntingly beautiful bright nights of summer —for Pushkin "the marvelous brilliance of the light . . . neither lamp nor candle needing."

The Empress Elizabeth's contributions or, better, those of her great architect Bartolomeo Francesco Rastrelli, consisted of visual delights, specific buildings notable for their imposing size, brilliant colors, and lavishness of decoration. Above all, the colors are Elizabeth and Rastrelli's legacy: the oranges, the yellows, the pinks, and especially the many greens —emeralds, turquoises, and pistachios. The bright walls set off and are set off by the white columns, the silver domes, the golden cornices, and—as Pushkin wrote—the "traceried iron of gate and railing." Heavy snow and the gloom of winter only enhance the effect; actually this is the season when St. Petersburg is meant to be seen. If it was Peter the Great who imposed the basic plan on St. Petersburg and Catherine the Great who gave the city block after block of Neoclassic grandeur, it was Elizabeth who provided architectural zest and exuberance.

The city arose on the score of marshy islands in the Neva River estuary and later earned the name Palmyra of the North for its picturesque canals and waterways. The endless embankments were still largely crude pilings in Elizabeth's time, to be replaced by granite walls soon after. Peter began his dream in 1703 on the small Zayachy Island, where the river is widest, with the Peter and Paul Fortress, which was developed into a large citadel with V-shaped bastions and curtain walls. No longer needed as a defense position by the mid-eighteenth century, Peter and Paul became a political prison. The Commandant's Wharf, where prisoners were transferred, and the Trubetskoy Bastion, where they were kept in not incommodious cells, were grim memories shared by the Tsarevich Alexis, the first prisoner, and by the members of the provisional government of 1917, the last.

The central feature of the citadel was the Peter and Paul Cathedral with its 400-foot spire—a Germanic, Protestant-looking spire, perhaps conceived by Peter as a symbolic break with Byzantine-Russian church architecture. The spire was all out of proportion to the squarish building beneath it, but the gilded, sun-catching needle became the trademark of the city. The inside of the cathedral was dominated by a traditional and hugely costly iconostasis ordered from Moscow by Peter, who also contributed a massive candelabrum of ivory carved by his own hand. It was here, not the Kremlin, that Peter chose to be buried. Elizabeth and all of Peter's successors, except Peter and Nicholas II, lie nearby in row on row of catafalques, mostly unadorned white marble boxes. Elizabeth ordered Peter's first little boat brought to Peter and Paul and placed in a special pavilion near the Government Mint, one of the important buildings within the walls. Another Elizabethan addition was the great clock imported from Cologne, which after 1760 chimed out the hours across the river.

Near the fortress was the little cottage occupied by Peter in the first days of the city. The 60- by 20-foot building, whose logs were painted to look like brick, was put up in three days by the labor of the tsar himself and others, and it contained only two rooms and a kitchen (since Catherine, the cottage has been protected within another building). Generally, however, the area directly above Peter and Paul and the Neva was not built up until the late nineteenth century. In Elizabeth's time there was just a crude road leading to the country estates of the courtiers, which she was very fond of visiting. For example, Kammenoy Ostrov (the Stone Island celebrated in the Rubinstein music) was the summer residence of Chancellor Bestuzhov. An island still farther beyond was known as Apothecary Island, the site of the original medicinal plantations of Peter which later became the extensive botanical gardens of the city. In the last devil-may-care days of Romanov grand dukes, gypsy entertainments took place on these northern islands. West of the Peter and Paul Fortress and still on the north side of the Neva was Vasilevsky Island, largest of those in the estuary. This is where Peter expected to establish his geometrical New Amsterdam, and accordingly, the island was cut through with parallel *lineki* (lines) or narrow canals bordered by streets. In time the center of the city moved across the river, the unused canals were stagnant ditches that had to be filled in, and the numbered lines became streets that grew increasingly less fashionable as their digits progressed. In Elizabeth's day there were lighthouses at the tip of the island. These navigational aids, which served for a century and a half, were large rostral columns decorated with sculptures commemorating Russia's great rivers. Nearby were warehouses and also the customshouse with its underground gold stores room (now the repository of Pushkin's manuscripts). Farther along the embankment was the bluish Kunstkammer, one of the oldest buildings in the city, begun in 1718 as the repository for Peter's curiosities of nature and later used as the seat and library of the Academy of Sciences. Russia's first observatory was on the upper floor, and here Lomonosov did some of the scientific researches that Elizabeth's hedonistic court chose to ignore.

A dominant building on the eastern end of Vasilevsky Island was the Menshikov Palace, a three-story structure with projecting wings, which the parvenu put up in 1710, when the tsar was still living in a cabin. The Italianate building was covered with iron plates that were painted red and surmounted by outsize emblems of Menshikov's princely rank. From Menshikov the palace passed to Elizabeth's enemy Osterman, and once in power, the empress hastened to confiscate it and present it as the center for the Corps of Cadets. Originally, Peter had given all of Vasilevsky Island to Menshikov, but he took it back five years later in order to use it for government offices. The celebrated Twelve Colleges arose between 1722 and 1732 as barrackslike edifices intended to house the government departments with rectilinear precision. Even under Elizabeth the trend had started to move the bureaucracy to the more convenient side of the river, and the Twelve Colleges became the university buildings, where students still pant up and down the half-mile-long corridors designed by Peter. The Academy of Fine Arts, founded under Elizabeth, was the next major edifice along the embankment, but its present building, like the Naval College and the Mining Institute beyond, dates from Catherine's time. Under Elizabeth these areas were gardens merging into virgin forest.

The Neva at the juncture of Zayachy and Vasilevsky islands is sufficiently wide and sufficiently open to gales from the Gulf of Finland to make communication hazardous between the northern and southern sides of the city. Once Peter almost lost his life in a wildly choppy crossing, and the ferry boatmen were the bane of the foreign representatives. In the reign of Empress Anna a bridge on boats was built for summer use, the ice serving as a natural highway in the winter (in the early twentieth century it yearly supported a streetcar line). There was no permanent bridge over the Neva until the 1840's, when Elizabeth's great-great-nephew, the grim Nicholas I, rewarded an engineer with one rank of nobility for each supporting pier he built successfully and then made him test his finished work by accompanying the first huge load drawn across by twenty oxen.

2. The Southern Side of the City

Almost directly across from the Peter and Paul Citadel stood the Admiralty. Originally developed as a strongpoint with moats, earthworks, and guns, it was intended primarily as a shipyard, and here the first vessel of Russia's Baltic fleet was launched by the sailor tsar in 1706. This establishment on the south bank was known to Elizabeth as a huge, ramshackle, U-shaped wooden building of one story enclosing ten covered shipways. Surrounding it were warehouses for naval materials and shanty settlements. Not until the early nineteenth century did the Admiralty get a 1,340-foot façade in the Classical style. Great yellow wings were added, as was a gilded spire 236 feet high, which came to rival that of the cathedral. In Elizabeth's day the Admiralty was already the focal point of the whole city, standing as it did at the head of the broad Nevsky Prospekt, the central avenue cutting south and east toward the interior of Russia.

Eastward from the Admiralty was the Winter Palace. Actually, over a period of half a century there were four Winter Palaces, each more spectacular than the last. The surviving one is Elizabeth's great monument. The first building, Peter's headquarters on the south bank, was little better than the workmen's hovels about it. It was succeeded by a structure erected in 1716 that was still modest; in the view of an English envoy's wife, it was "small, far from handsome" with a "great number of little rooms, ill-contrived and nothing remarkable either in architecture, painting, or furniture." The third Winter Palace was more pretentious. Built under the Empress Anna between 1732 and 1736, it was a huge but irregular quadrangle of four stories incorporating Peter's palace and two nobles' mansions nearby. Anna and Biren lived there in adjoining apartments, but it offered little to dazzle the eye, except, perhaps, for the grand salon decorated with paintings by Caravaque. Bartolomeo Francesco Rastrelli, the architect of this patchwork, soon-to-crumble monstrosity, was capable of far greater things.

The circumstances of Rastrelli's Florentine origin and his birth in Louis Quatorze Paris about 1700 are less important than the fact that he was brought to Russia at age sixteen by his father, who made something of a mark in the decorative arts and earned the title of count. B. F. Rastrelli's earliest architectural contributions date from the last years of Peter's rule. He was in Europe during the reigns of Catherine I and Peter II, only to return under Anna to build her triumphal arches and palaces. The Italian not only kept in favor in the first months of the new regime but emerged without rivals as the architectural mastermind of Elizabeth's whole reign. One has to recall Bernini and Rome to find a comparable example of one man who had such a free hand to exercise his genius as Rastrelli did in and about the Russian capital.

Although no one is certain just where and what Rastrelli studied while abroad, it is clear that he came to Russia young and impressionable enough to be influenced by the atmosphere of his adopted country. There is little of the Italian Baroque or of Versailles in this supremely individual architect, although some see in him the overdecorativeness of the German Baroque and Rococo. Rastrelli evidently absorbed much from his long sojourns in Moscow and Novgorod: He could design a five-domed church effortlessly.

Little marble was available to him in the early days, but lumber was in endless supply, as were good brick and plaster. Rastrelli made the most of these humbler materials, which, together with paint imaginatively applied, produced movie-set miracles. Just as Hollywood designers who win Oscars are convention-bound to acknowledge their many assistants, Soviet guidebooks are quick to point out that Rastrelli's creations were achieved by armies of Russian craftsmen, who contributed skills, as well as blood. The hand of a single genius, however, shows in the enormous scale of the buildings, in the sure sense of proportion, in the daring massing of large forms, and in the use of rich and flamboyant decorative effects.

The first major creation of Rastrelli for Elizabeth—and one of the most astonishing—was the Summer Palace. It was built more than a mile to the east of the Admiralty—past Anna's Winter Palace, beyond the huge parade ground known as the Field of Mars, and across the Fontanka Canal. Here at one corner of the Summer Garden stood the modest mansion where Peter and Catherine gave their first assemblies in the 1720's, a building that is still preserved.

Completely extravagant and not to survive was the grandiose structure by Rastrelli at the opposite corner, where once stables had stood. Actually begun during the regency of Anna Leopoldovna, the Summer Palace was finished in 1744 and was the scene of many of the merry entertainments of Elizabeth's court. Engravings of the period show a massive three-story central structure with lateral galleries and jutting wings, all facing a parterre at the juncture of the Moika and Fontanka canals; there are gondolas filled with people arriving, companies of soldiers doing drill, and bystanders lolling about elegantly. The building featured richly columned porticoes, massive outside staircases, hundreds of windows elaborately molded and carved, and everywhere statues and urns. A tremendous façade on one side overlooked the gardens, and behind there were extensive buildings for the staff. This exuberant fancy of Rastrelli served Elizabeth's successors only to 1797, when her slightly mad and spiteful great-nephew, who was born there, had it pulled down and replaced with an ugly castlelike palace.

From the very first days of the city Peter had spared no expense to make his Summer Garden better than that of the French king at Versailles. The rectangle of about 37 acres was laid out in the textbook patterns of the day by the Frenchman Alexander Leblond. Trees were imported from all over: thousands of limes to form avenues; oaks and elms from Moscow and Kiev to make scenic groves; and cypresses and fruit trees to provide curiosities. The engineer was allowed to construct numerous grottoes, cascades, and basins, all supplied with water from the Fontanka, the canal taking its name from its function. A flood in 1777 led to the abandonment of the fountains but Elizabeth knew and loved them, as she did the other delights of the Summer Garden, such as the rare fishes in pools, the aviaries shaped like pagodas, and the monkey cage. Surviving to this day are the hundreds of statues Peter imported from England, Holland, and Italy, including a specially ordered allegorical group called "Peace and Plenty" to commemorate his victories. Closed to the general public until the present century, the Summer Garden had its many privileged enthusiasts, Pushkin and Moussorgsky being among them.

Proceeding east from the Summer Garden toward the bend of the Neva, where it turns south, one comes to the famous Smolny buildings, so named for the taryard that Peter had once built there. A palace was later built on the site, and this became the residence of Elizabeth in her perilous days as tsarevna and was the starting point of her coup in 1741. This building, like so many others of the period, went up in flames in 1744. Elizabeth then commissioned Rastrelli to build a nunnery at Smolny, and the resulting fairy-tale building in blue with intricate white trim was considered by some to be the architect's masterpiece. Included in the ensemble was a cathedral rising 230 feet, with four onion towers and a large central cupola, a Rococo adaptation of the style of old Russian monasteries. In short, Smolny displayed a striking combination of piety and luxury in its conception that seemed to be the common bond between Rastrelli's work and Elizabeth's life. The empress once actually considered retiring to the new nunnery as a penitent. Her practical-minded successor, Catherine, established at Smolny a society for the education of young ladies of noble birth, and the resulting buildings of jarring Classical style and of a size to dwarf the nunnery come down in history as the Smolny Institute, from which Lenin and the Bolsheviks were to launch their revolution.

On the west side of St. Petersburg—that is, beyond the Winter Palace in the other direction—arose another religious monument of the reign of the Empress Elizabeth. This was the Cathedral of St. Nicholas, built between 1753 and 1762 by the Russian architect Sava Chevakinsky, who was almost completely under the spell of Rastrelli. Known as the Sailors' Church, St. Nicholas was another brilliant combination of traditional and Baroque elements, offering, on the one hand, the five gilded domes and, on the other, a delicate and unusual belfry detached from the main two-story structure. This cathedral still functions as a place of worship, and the icon kissing, obeisances, and alms begging that occur amid its dark pillars and chapels cause bewilderment, even terror to the young Soviet guides. Near the cathedral arose a major theater district, including today the Kirov Opera-Ballet and the Conservatory. The theatrical companies were familiar enough to Elizabeth, but the first wooden house of drama was not erected until four years after her death.

Going northward toward the river, one comes upon the area of St. Isaac Cathedral, the Astoria Hotel, and the Senate Building. There was a St. Isaac here for Elizabeth to worship in, but the building finished in 1725 proved too large for its foundations, and it was replaced in the nineteenth century by the massive landmark with its 40-ton marble pillars and great gold dome. The Senate Building, which faces the west façade of the Admiralty, was built after the Senate was moved from Vasilevsky Island in 1763. Senate Square is dominated by the "Bronze Horseman" statue of Peter the Great, executed by Étienne Maurice Falconet late in the century.

The main axis of St. Petersburg, its Broadway and Fifth Avenue combined, was the broad boulevard stretching three miles from the Admiralty to the Alexander Nevsky Monastery and connecting thereafter with the Great Novgorod Road of medieval times. Likened on maps to a bowstring drawn to the arc of the Neva River, the avenue, stone-paved from the first, was known as Great Prospect Road in Elizabeth's time but since then is more familiar by the name Nevsky Prospekt. At its head developed the financial district, the nucleus of the state and private banks being Elizabeth's Nobles Bank of 1754.

The Nevsky was originally a choice location for aristocratic town houses, and still preserved, for example, is Number 17, the mansion of the Princes Stroganov. This bright-green corner palace, erected in the 1750's, was considered one of the finest examples of Rastrelli's work. Farther along the *prospekt* come several non-Orthodox churches, such as the Dutch Reformed, dating from after Elizabeth, for she was not quite *that* tolerant (it is a fact, however, that Rastrelli left a design for a Catholic church in the capital). Since Peter's time there have been elaborate trade arcades along the west side of the avenue as one goes south, and today's main department store is located here.

The original boundary of the city was placed at the intersection of the Fontanka Canal and the Nevsky Prospekt. Here was built the Anichkov Bridge, a narrow drawbridge with granite towers constructed by the sentry company of a Commander Anichkov. The large Anichkov Palace was added at the corner of the avenue and the canal. This was one of Elizabeth's favorite city residences and her most handsome gift to Razumovsky. The palace, begun in 1741 by a Russian architect, was taken in hand by Rastrelli, who compensated for the dullness of the first floor by adding a whimsical array of cupolas and porticoes, plus a lavish assortment of statues, crowns, and trophies. The interior was equally lavish, with a grand curving staircase and with many of its 300 rooms done in various colored marbles and hung with crystal chandeliers. Apparently Elizabeth was so determined to use this palatial wonder to the utmost that she even hired it out for parties. Not until 1756 was it deeded to "little Alexis" in hereditary possession. The Romanovs repossessed the Anichkov later on, and it contained the playrooms of the last tsar before becoming the gloriously untouched mecca of Soviet children as the Palace of Young Pioneers.

Near the Anichkov stood the Cathedral of the Transfiguration, completed for the use of the empress and her favorite in 1754. (It burned in 1825.) The western façade of the palace looked over a pavilion for Razumovsky's collection of paintings and extensive gardens along the canal. At the margin of the gardens (along what is now a major cross thoroughfare) was the Vorontsov Palace, built by Rastrelli for Elizabeth's self-important but capable vice-chancellor. It has been called perfect Rastrelli style for its delicate interplay of white columns and pilasters set against bright-orange walls, and it is now the seat of the Institute of Botanical Studies.

The Nevsky Prospekt after the Fontanka Canal was a line of suburban residences surrounded by wasteland. The royal fowlyard and kennels became the site of the Moscow Railroad Station, in front of which began the Revolution of 1917. Here is also the present-day October Hotel, the second largest in the country. At the very end of the great avenue rose the Alexander Nevsky Lavra (*lavra* meaning a specially hallowed monastery). Founded in 1716 by the agnostic Peter, the monastery was erroneously thought to be located on the exact site of St. Alexander Nevsky's famous victory over the Swedes in 1240. The buildings, including colorful towers and chapels built over gates, were rambling and extensive in the Russian manner, but they lacked the elegance of Rastrelli's not altogether dissimilar creations, such as Smolny. The empress used the monastery as a stopover on her way to her country estates, and Elizabeth's aunt, Peter's beloved sister, Natalia, was buried here in the Lazarus Cemetery, later the resting place of poets and artists.

Other roads led westward out of the metropolis. The so-called Moscow Prospekt began at the Sennaya Square, which was laid out in the 1730's as a market area but was destined to become the center of the city's worst slums, which would be immortalized in the writings of Dostoievsky.

3. The Palaces Outside St. Petersburg

Just a few miles outside the city limits was Strelna, one of Peter's first country retreats. Its origins were a cabin constructed by the tsar himself and a treehouse, where he could sit and smoke and watch his ships. In order not to be outdone by the huge palace Menshikov was building 12 miles away at Oranienbaum, Peter ordered Leblond to build a proper palace. The resulting structure, a central pavilion with wings containing a theater and an orangery, was torn down in 1844. Strelna, however, was a mere prologue to Peterhof, 5 miles down the Gulf of Finland, which emerged as Russia's Versailles and is still a glittering and grandiose architectural array including a long Grand Palace, several lesser pavilions, acres of formal gardens, and an incomparable series of fountains and pools.

Peter had as many as 4,000 laborers working at Peterhof, simultaneously draining the area and bringing in everything from soil to trees. An anecdote typical of Peter was that he found the upper gardens too formal, lacking in educative value. Accordingly, scores of statues illustrating Aesop's fables were added, and to be doubly sure of his aim, the tsar had metal plates with explanatory inscriptions attached. The central structure of the palace was built by Leblond and still contains the tsar's study whose solemn carvings are out of character with the succeeding Elizabethan additions.

Elizabeth had loved Peterhof since childhood, but she could only agree with the foreign visitor who said that "the house is of no great matter . . . the apartments are extremely small and low." Simplicity was the last thing the empress had in mind when she ordered Rastrelli to reconstruct and extend the building in 1746. The ensuing Grand Palace, predominantly dark pink with touches of white and metal colors, stretched for several hundred feet. It included a heightened center and two wings, one ending in a five-cupola church and the other known as the Coat of Arms Wing for its 600 pounds of gilt decoration. The interior was breathtaking, with room after room of the most ornate woodwork, tracery, and scrollwork on the doors, windows, and ceilings. Often only one room wide, the palace offered many stupefying vistas of lavish doorways seen through doorways seen through doorways. Perhaps the most stunning of all the Elizabethan rooms was the Cabinet of Modes and Graces, which contained 328 portraits of the empress' young ladies-in-waiting, all smiling, dainty, and rosy-cheeked. The whole palace was meant only for receptions, not for living in.

The upper terrace of Peterhof stood 40 feet above the sea and looked down past one of the world's greatest hydraulic displays to the Lower Park. In the center the Grand Cascade was a rush of water down seven high steps of colored marble, lined with Tritons and other figures blowing jets of water. Beyond was the fountain known as the Wicker Basket, which was a perfectly geometrical pyramid created by hundreds of varying sprays. Next was a pool with a huge statue of Samson wrenching open the jaws of a lion, an allegory of the Poltava victory over Sweden. From the pool a canal flanked by more fountains and statues and trees led out to the Gulf of Finland, and this was how foreign representatives were first brought to Peterhof from the city. The water for the fountain was brought from the heights of Ropsha 13 miles away, the original wooden pipes being replaced by metal ones during Elizabeth's reign. The empress was not limited to the brief displays of the fountains that Louis XIV could afford at Versailles. Soviet engineers estimate that even at 7,500 gallons of water a second the Peterhof fountains can run for half the day.

The Lower Park of Peterhof was laid out in severely symmetrical patterns, as required by the French and Dutch models for it. It contained other major fountains such as the Chessboard Cascade, as well as a number of trick fountains casually placed for the unwary, notably the Little Oak and Little Mushroom, which douse or trap people who step or sit in the wrong place.

Three considerable pavilions in the Lower Park are part of Peterhof's glories. One of the three, the Hermitage, is a pleasantly light and airy building that was surrounded by a moat and reached by a drawbridge. Among its features were 119 paintings done by Dutch, Flemish, and French masters and a special table for twelve that could be lowered to the kitchen by a lift and reset there, obviating the presence of curious servants among the diners. Nearby was Marly, a quiet building set on an island in a pond. Bearing no resemblance to its Mansard-built namesake that Peter saw in France, Peterhof's Marly pavilion endeared itself to Elizabeth for its Dutch kitchen, done in Delft tiles, which she used when she herself cooked.

A few miles beyond Peterhof on the gulf was Oranienbaum, the first modern palace in Russia, built not by the tsar but by Prince Menshikov and distinguished more by the bulk of its horseshoe design than by any decorative appeal. Later used as a naval hospital and then as a mosaics works by Lomonosov (for whom the place is currently named), Oranienbaum was presented by Elizabeth to her nephew Peter, who, typically, added a toy fortress and barracks for his Holstein Guard. Equally typically, his wife, Catherine, had built for her an elegant twelve-room mansion on the ridge where graceful willows replaced the heavy oaks below.

Inland from the shore palaces was Ropsha, which Elizabeth also bestowed on Peter, a lonely but pleasantly situated country house of stone surrounded by a gracious park. Here is where the water for Peterhof's fountains originated, and it was here that a famous royal murder was to occur.

One might think that the palaces mentioned hitherto might have satisfied an empress even as extravagant and extroverted as Elizabeth. After all, there was Peterhof for sheer exquisiteness; Ropsha and Oranienbaum for a change of scene; the Summer, the Winter, and the Anichkov palaces for city entertainments; and royal residences, old and new, large and small, in and about Moscow, to say nothing of the facilities of Kiev and other centers. Yet Elizabeth's name and that of Rastrelli are also intimately connected with another huge complex of architectural luxury, and a historically famous one, Tsarskoe Selo (now Pushkin). This was a country palace like Peterhof but 15 miles southeast of the capital and thus well inland. Indeed, if sea breezes and fountains were the main joy of Peterhof, Tsarskoe Selo is memorable for its highland fresh air and broad expanses of green lawn. The original buildings were willed to Elizabeth by her mother, and even in her lean days as tsarevna she invested in additions. As empress she spared nothing. The epitome of Rastrellian architecture was the immense Catherine Palace, named by Elizabeth for the first, but mistakenly associated with the second, Catherine. It was completed in 1756 and became the scene of imperial balls, fetes, and banquets.

Facing a vast court and semicircle of servants' buildings, the Catherine Palace had a colossal façade 326 feet long interrupted only by shallow protuberances and had little variation in elevation except the usual cupolas at the very ends. The seeming monotony of the front, which was painted bright blue, was relieved by rhythmic arrangements of columns and pilasters, and the whole upper two stories seemed to be supported by a series of giant male caryatids, whose twisted muscular forms were repeated in smaller sculptures enlivening the roundheaded French windows. "The completest triumph of barbarous taste I have ever seen," declared an English visitor, who added that "all the capitals of the pillars, the statues, and many parts of the external structure are gilt." The local populace apparently was under the impression that the balustrades were solid gold.

The word "barbarous" recurs among many critics of Rastrelli's masterpiece, most of whom were captivated by late-eighteenth-century classic simplicity. "The interior of the building," wrote one, "presents a number of spacious and gaudy rooms, fitted in a style combining a mixture of barbarity and magnificence which will hardly be credited." Contemporary observers and those of later eras when exuberance was again in vogue, could not help being dazzled, however, by the palatial offerings. Inside, the enfilade of doorways, each extravagantly carved with shields and figures, was repeated from the Peterhof Grand Palace. The chapel was the most costly Russian Baroque imaginable. Elizabeth's bedroom was sheer loveliness, with a painted ceiling and the alcove surmounted with cherubs, goddesses, and her monogram. The picture gallery was overwhelmingly profuse, although foreign esthetes were disturbed by the fact that paintings were sawed up in order to fit every space between the carved moldings. There was the fantastic Amber Room, 55 square meters of decor in this material, originally bartered by Frederick William to Peter in exchange for fifty-five soldiers more than 6 feet 6, to fill out the eccentric king's favorite grenadier company (this treasured room, valued currently at $50,000,000, has disappeared since the Nazi occupation). Finally, the most munificent room of the Catherine Palace was the Great Hall, 180 by 52 feet in extent, thirteen windows running two stories to a side, and equipped with endless mirrors and 696 lights; many thought this at least the equal of, if not the superior to, the Galerie des Glaces at Versailles.

Elsewhere at Tsarskoe Selo were scores of lesser architectural diversions, many of them Rastrelli's. There was the elegant pavilion called the Grotto, the Concert Hall on the Island, the Ruined Kitchen, an exquisite hunting box named Mon Bijou, and the inevitable Hermitage, an exceptionally ornate building with sixty-four columns. A large part in the annals of the later Romanovs was played by the Alexander Palace, built in 1792 and used as a residence by sober-minded tsars like the last one.

The imprint of Elizabeth's pleasure-bent reign remained in most of the architecture of Tsarskoe Selo, however, and there are records of extravagant fancies that have since disappeared. Such was the Sliding Hill, where Elizabeth and her court pursued the persistently favorite Russian winter sport of tobogganing. Rastrelli put up a central building 150 feet long and 80 feet high to its gilt cupola, from which extended slides and switchbacks to the length of 900 feet. Apparatus driven by animals brought the sleds to the top. The whole construction with its marble pillars, gilded balustrades, statues, and parquet floors survived its royal patron by only forty years.

4. The Winter Palace

Having accomplished among other things two such grandiose projects as Peterhof and Tsarskoe Selo, Rastrelli might well have considered his reputation made for all time, but the surprising fact is that he went on to gain his greatest renown for the tremendous Winter Palace built in the very center of St. Petersburg—not the "third" Winter Palace as originally patched together by Rastrelli in the 1730's, but a completely new, all-of-a-piece, dream-of-a-lifetime creation that his patron Elizabeth missed enjoying as a residence, but only by one year.

Anna's Winter Palace was pulled down in 1754, a ukase at that time inviting the populace to scavenge and cart off what materials they would. Construction on the new and final palace lasted for eighteen years. The human costs as usual were excessive. Reminiscent of Peter's day, a whole army of impressed laborers was settled around in makeshift quarters, and the toll from disease and exposure was in the thousands. (It was truly said that St. Petersburg was built on the bones of a multitude of Russians.) The finished building contained more than 1,000 rooms, 1,945 windows, 1,768 doors, and 117 staircases.

The front façade was 450 feet long and only 70 feet high, although the original turquoise color, restored now, lends an airier feeling than the dark red by which the building was known for more than a century. A French critic dismissed the exterior as *"un décor d'opéra,"* complaining of the overelaborate windows, the too-frequent columns, and the 176 statues on the roof gesticulating among an even greater number of urns. Rastrelli made each façade quite individual. The main façade on the south had Ionic columns at the base and Corinthian ones for the top two stories, and there was a generous interspersion of cupids, lions' heads, and fanciful scrolls. Here three great arched entrances overlooked the huge Palace Square past an elaborate iron fence (torn down since the Revolution). The square was defined after Rastrelli's time by the erection of a wide semicircle of classical buildings and an archway leading to the Nevsky Prospekt. The western façade, described as a "panoply of pylons," gave onto a park and was directly opposite the east wing of the Admiralty. The side facing the Neva was quieter in decoration, but its sheer length and the play of light and shade among its columns were truly impressive viewed from the Peter and Paul Fortress. To the east the façade was obscured by additions, notably Catherine's famous Hermitage, of whose collection of paintings she boasted only she and the mice could enjoy. The collection formed the nucleus of the fantastic array of art, ranging from Rembrandts to Matisses, which is now exhibited throughout the entire Winter Palace and is the chief tourist attraction of Leningrad. Much of the Rastrellian-Elizabethan interior of the palace was destroyed by fire in 1837.

Just as Elizabeth was never to live in her greatest monument, so Rastrelli was to enjoy little appreciation or renown in his last days. Pensioned off by Catherine and later made to feel virtually in disgrace, he traveled abroad on two extended trips, returning to die in St. Petersburg in 1771.

XI.
A Husband-Wife Scandal:
Peter III and Catherine

1. The Hapless Groom

UGLY, gauche, and unbalanced; married to a woman determined to make the most of her looks, her charm, and her intelligence, Peter III was the tragic successor to his Aunt Elizabeth. He had been born in Kiel in February, 1728, his mother Anna dying immediately afterward. The child was formally christened Karl Peter Ulrich: first, after his paternal great-uncle, Charles XII of Sweden; second, after his maternal grandfather, Peter the Great of Russia; and third, after Ulrica Eleonora, reigning Queen of Sweden. Peter's father, the Duke of Holstein, was the son of an older sister of Charles XII and thus not a direct male heir. His claims to the Swedish throne were passed over, and he spent a lifetime denouncing his enemies, begging subsidies, and putting up a front of royal extravagance and military prowess. His interest in his son, Peter, was as fickle as his fortunes.

For the first few years of his life Peter was brought up as heir to the crown of Russia, but the accession of the Empress Anna Ivanovna in 1730 seemingly dashed the hopes of the Petrovich line. As Peter grew older, things Russian came increasingly under ridicule as his prospects of succeeding to power in civilized Stockholm seemed to improve. Accordingly, his religious training was strictly Lutheran, and Swedish became his natural language. Efforts to teach him Latin as a child revealed his stubbornness: His hatred of that language became a lifelong obsession. On the other hand, a kindly French governess (who outlived him) gave Peter a considerable command of French. Physically, the little prince proved prone to illness and suffered from convulsions.

The militaristic posturing of his gruff father left a lasting imprint on Peter: The worst punishment conceivable to the child was to have his windows overlooking the parade ground closed up. Later Peter was to confide to a tutor that the happiest day of his life was on his ninth birthday, when the older duke promoted his son from sergeant to lieutenant, with appropriate change of uniform, and allowed him to sit at the adults' banquet table.

Neglect gave way to mistreatment after his father died in 1739 and Peter came under the guardianship of his uncle, the Prince-Bishop of Eutin. This uncle was more interested in the revenues of the duchy of Holstein than in the education of his nephew, and Peter was resigned to the care of an *Oberhofmarschall,* or military governor, named Brummer. A sadistic bully was the worst possible tutor for an orphaned prince who was already abnormally sickly and highly strung. Brummer and his mistress subjected Peter to an inexplicable regimen of being thrashed, tied up, and otherwise tormented. A favorite form of punishment was to have Peter kneel upright on a scattering of hard beans. A searingly humiliating memory of these years was the time Brummer made Peter sit on a stool with the effigy of an ass around his neck, suffering in silence, while through a doorway his supposed gentlemen-in-waiting regaled themselves at dinner. "A small hunted animal" were apt words applied to this young Romanov in his teens.

The security of steady misery was suddenly replaced in January, 1742, by the shock and uncertainty of a new environment—Russia. Peter, still in the charge of the brutal Brummer, had been whisked out of Kiel, as abruptly and secretly as if he had been kidnapped, and shortly found himself in St. Petersburg—the object of an unknown aunt's tears of joy, the recipient of profuse congratulations from hundreds of strangers, and the cause of a great thanksgiving service in an unfamiliar style and language. Only the magnificent fireworks seemed like home. The young duke made an odd impression on his new well-wishers. He had long, lank blond hair and the stance of a wooden soldier. His pallor, thinness, and air of fragility were alarming. He was painfully nervous and shy, speaking, or better squeaking, in a shrill mixture of French and German. Yet here was Elizabeth's chosen heir, and the empress was resolved to gain his trust and love by being profuse with her own. Peter's known passion for soldiering was immediately catered to by naming him lieutenant colonel of the Preobrazhenskoe Regiment and colonel of the Body Guards, in which capacity the thirteen-year-old solemnly countersigned orders brought to him each day by Field Marshal Lacy. Peter's fourteenth birthday, which fell in February, was made the occasion of a journey to Moscow and elaborate celebrations.

Peter's education was an immediate concern even to his unlettered aunt. The empress chose as his tutor a German-Russian named Stehlin, who was more a dilettante than a scholar, but likable and patient. The introduction was made by Elizabeth, too tactfully perhaps: "I see that your Serene Highness has still a great many pretty things to learn, and Monsieur Stehlin will teach them to you in such a pleasant manner that it will be a mere past-time for you." The pupil proved to be a challenge indeed. He was found to be extremely childish for his age and ignorant of all useful things except French. The book Stehlin kept for Elizabeth's infrequent perusal often noted that Peter was frivolous and unruly. The tutor's efforts were also disrupted by the fact that the dancing master, at Elizabeth's express order, had first call on Peter's time. Furthermore, Peter's illnesses, including a nearly fatal bout in 1744, meant many lost months in the three years that Stehlin had him in his care.

The schooling had to be keyed to Peter's military bent. Miscellanies of history were woven into studies of warfare, and military models offered opportunities to discuss general science. A book of Russian fortresses was the basis of geography lessons. Peter was encouraged to draw plans of his own apartments and later a map of the Kremlin. Attempts to interest Peter in the general arts and literature were fruitless, however, nor did he profit from seeing the diplomatic dispatches generously supplied by the Chancellor Bestuzhev. Even the Russian language met with princely obstinacy. He made a point of not speaking the language unless required to and of not bothering with grammar when he did, although his good memory enabled him to master a large Russian vocabulary. Likewise, Peter resisted training in the Russian Orthodox Church. He learned the conventional religious formulas but enjoyed parodying them in a singsong way, all the while volunteering snide comparisons in favor of Lutheranism.

The petulant prince was formally received into the Orthodox Church in November, 1742, and proclaimed heir to the throne. The empress herself led him to the Gospels, where he recited the creed and received the traditional symbols, after which he prostrated himself three times before the archbishops, took communion, and received the allegiance of the court as the Grand Duke Peter Fedorovich. On his return to his apartments Peter found a gold plate with a draft for 300,000 rubles on it, a gift from his aunt. With newly acquired assurance in his position Peter began to order around his old governor, Brummer, now marshal of the grand ducal court, even threatening his life on occasion. He also saw fit to make a scene when a delegation arrived from Stockholm, shortly after these events, to offer him the throne of Sweden for sometime in the future. Elizabeth declared grandly that she had other plans for her nephew and ordered him to refuse. Refuse he did at a public reception for the Swedish envoys, but in the most halting and ungracious manner possible, virtually implying that the Russians were cheating him out of his true heritage. The grand duke lost no opportunity to remind listeners of his Western inclinations and tastes.

After three years of putting up with Peter's willfulness, Elizabeth realized that the grand duke was some sort of dreadful mistake, but one she could not disavow. Her efforts to gain his trust and love invariably met with hostility, and in time the self-centered empress lost patience. She could barely maintain a front of affability with her nephew for fifteen minutes at a time. The charmer of men and the fondler of children simply could not deal with an adolescent so different from herself. Peter was brittle, while she was easygoing; he was full of half-formed ideas and prejudices, whereas she was the soul of practicality; and above all, his plainness and clumsiness clashed with her beauty and grace. Elizabeth probably could have forgiven Peter almost anything if only he could have danced a proper minuet, but the sorry fact was that he could not even enter a room without falling over himself physically and verbally. There seemed no further recourse for the empress than to find her heir a wife and to hope. The resulting match was one of the strangest and most consequential in Russian history.

2. *The Ambitious Bride*

The girl destined to become Russia's most famous empress was then and later accounted an obscure German princess—Sophia of Anhalt-Zerbst. Why she was matched to the Grand Duke Peter presented no problem from her point of view, one of sheer ambition. Why Sophia was found suitable for Peter was a more complex question. The choice of a bride had been debated in the Senate and preoccupied the chancelleries of Europe. No less than a daughter of Louis XV was the union favored by Elizabeth, but the French were reluctant to sacrifice a Bourbon lovely on a prince rumored to be personally degenerate and the heir to a country considered politically unstable at best, barbaric at worst. Frederick II of Prussia likewise declined the hand of one of his sisters for Peter, but the Hohenzollern king's interest did not end there. It was Frederick who blocked the choice of Princess Mary of Saxony, for political reasons; she was the favored candidate of Chancellor Bestuzhev, likewise for reasons involving international diplomacy. The choice finally fell on Sophia of Anhalt-Zerbst, a political neutral. A timely sent portrait of Sophia pleased both Elizabeth and Peter.

She had been born in May, 1729, and christened Sophia Augusta Frederica. Her father was eventually to reign as co-Prince of Anhalt-Zerbst, but the actual possessions of this minor German dynasty had been so fragmented in the course of history that Christian Augustus had no alternative but to pursue a full-time career as a professional soldier in the service of the King of Prussia. Military governor of Stettin when Sophia was born, he rose to the rank of general and was, indeed, just what was expected of a Prussian officer—methodical, conservative, and pious. Sophia's mother was twenty-seven years younger than her husband and of a better family. As Joanna Elizabeth of Holstein-Gottorp, she was closely related to the Grand Duke Peter's Swedish relatives, but she came with no dowry and so was fated to the less than brilliant match. The young wife was genuinely pretty, somewhat flirtatious, and socially ambitious. It was later rumored that she had a liaison with none other than Frederick of Prussia and that he was the real father of Sophia, but this is unlikely in the light of her strict upbringing and her set-lipped loyalty to her husband. Joanna Elizabeth did enjoy enough family connections to have entrée to the Prussian court, and she took advantage of her yearly dinner with the queen to promote her family's fortunes.

In later years Sophia was to remember of her parents how different they were in age and disposition, old Papa being "extremely thrifty," while giddy Mama was "very extravagant and generous." Nor was she to forget that Joanna Elizabeth had badly wanted a boy for her first child and that when a son was born some years later, the mother doted on him completely. This brother was tragically delicate and died in early adolescence. A sister also died young, but another brother, Frederick, who was five years younger than Sophia, survived into adulthood and enjoyed his sister's affection. Of her parents, Sophia was to write: "My father, whom I did not see so often, considered me to be an angel; my mother took very little notice of me. I was merely tolerated and I was often cruelly snubbed and not always justly."

"The little girl is impertinent," exclaimed King Frederick William. Little Sophia had just been presented to the martinet King of Prussia but failed to kiss the hem of his coat as she had been taught, explaining out loud: "His clothes are too short. I can't reach them." As a child Sophia trailed in her mother's wake to parties and receptions, and someone later recalled her as a little brown-haired doll in elaborate hoopskirts. The ceremonial life, however, was no more typical for her than it had been for Peter the Great as a boy. Sophia, or Figchen as she was called by her family, was left to her own devices and took to the streets of Stettin, much as Peter had taken to the byways of Preobrazhenskoe. For a period she was known as something of a tomboy, a natural leader among children of all classes. By her own admission, she became willful and obstinate, and her unpredictable actions and carefree attitude led to frequent scenes with her mother, increasing Sophia's feelings of neglect and rejection.

A succession of inconvenient nurses finally gave way to a beloved governess named Babet Cardel, the daughter of a Huguenot refugee from

France, who persuaded Sophia to behave in front of her parents, to try to be pleasing, or, in effect, to become deceitful. "Mlle. Cardel's pupil" was the way the celebrated empress of a later day signed her letters to Voltaire.

Sophia's youthful habit of asking questions had proved embarrassing in social situations, but it was also the mark of a good student, and this is what she became under the guidance of Mademoiselle Cardel. Both French and German were thoroughly mastered, and Sophia was to be an accomplished writer all her life. Although French fiction failed to interest her, the princess' inquiring mind made her a lover of books in general, her taste for serious reading remaining undiminished after the schooling was over. She was a graceful dancer, but music was a complete loss; for the rest of her life it was just so much noise to her. As for interest in religious teachings, Sophia went from alarming intensity to untroubled acquiescence. When she was eight, she spent whole afternoons whimpering and sobbing in a dark corner, all in reaction to her pastor's expositions on the Last Judgment. Her governess persuaded the religious worthy to desist, and in adolescence Sophia developed a conventional and, as it turned out, rather flexible piety.

In point of number of ailments, Sophia might have been described as a sickly child, but she had great recuperative capacities and her good health in time became a boast. A spinal disorder necessitated her wearing a ghastly iron corset when she was between seven and ten.

As Sophia entered her teens, she was ugly by her own evaluation, and her willful nature reflected itself at times in an unpleasant expression. Resigned to being less than a beauty, Sophia decided to acquire merit instead. The pursuit of intelligence, charm, and worth in other people's eyes was the preoccupation of an ambitious girl, who was to remain quite as calculating as a woman.

Sophia was not yet fifteen when the summons to St. Petersburg came in January, 1744. The invitation did not take her by surprise. She had met Peter, who was in fact her second cousin, at a party in Kiel, when they were ten and eleven respectively. The boy, actually a miserable creature at this time, she remembered as "good-looking, well-mannered, and courteous," as well as being the object of great expectations. Sophia in her fantasies willingly had "bestowed herself on him." There was marked lack of enthusiasm for the match on the part of Sophia's determinedly Lutheran father, but this was more than compensated for by the delight of his employer, King Frederick, at the thought of having a friend of Prussia so close to the Russian throne.

Berlin was a major stopover before the journey to Russia. Joanna Elizabeth, who was closeted at length with Frederick and emerged a proud spy for Prussia, seemed strangely reluctant to show him Sophia, fearing, perhaps, that her daughter's looks were not up to Frederick's standards. The excuse of Sophia's not having a court dress was eliminated by the king's sending one belonging to his sister. She dined at the king's own table, while Mama had to content herself with sitting at the queen's. Frederick, then ruler for only four years and still in his thirties, already had the reputation of being the finest soldier in Europe and the head of a court quite un-Prussian for its glitter. The impression he made on Sophia could not have been more favorable, for he knew how to put her at ease and then proceeded to win her completely by treating her as an adult. They talked of "opera, comedy, poetry, dancing" and a "thousand things," the king taking the lead, but Sophia responding with increasing assurance and animation. Such was the first encounter of two members of royalty who were to be rivals in the later eighteenth century but also common owners of the sobriquet "the Great" and joint practitioners of the concept of enlightened despotism.

The winter journey that took Sophia away from Germany forever was by carriage and sledge. Her mother's complaints about the hardships of the trip lasted only until the party reached Riga, where the empress put a large train and scores of gentlemen at their disposal. Thereafter, Joanna Elizabeth was captivated by it all, fully enjoying being the center of attention, while the less impressionable Sophia at times felt neglected. On the road they passed a tightly curtained carriage going the other way; it was taking Anna Leopoldovna and Ivan VI to a harsher place of confinement, serving as a sharp reminder of the possible fate of German princesses in this country. St. Petersburg was finally reached in February, and here Sophia was shown the route of Elizabeth's coup of 1741, leading her to observe: "It is incredible that her Majesty could have endured so long a walk and that she was not betrayed."

The court happened to be in Moscow, forcing Joanna Elizabeth and Sophia to make another arduous journey, but affording them a view of Muscovy, which became increasingly medieval and semi-Oriental as they traveled farther from the self-consciously European new capital. The arrivals were greeted joyfully by the empress, who had to retire from them in tears when she perceived Joanna Elizabeth's resemblance to her brother, Elizabeth's dead betrothed of years past. Elizabeth's sentiment was moving, and her diamonds down to the waist were striking, to say the least.

As for Peter, Sophia found him "very childish" but openly friendly and happy to have a contemporary to talk to. Almost immediately the grand duke, whose tact was never to be a strong point, allowed to Sophia that he was infatuated with the younger Lopukhina (daughter of the woman who had but recently suffered such a painful disgrace). "I blushed as I listened to him," Sophia wrote, "but I rejoiced that I had at least won his confidence." Later she could avow that "the Grand Duke loved me passionately." There were other obstacles to her success than Peter, however.

The matter of religion was important. Sophia's father hoped that, at best, his daughter could keep her Lutheranism (as did the Tsarevich Alexis' wife) or, at least, fall back on some unspecific peasant faith. The empress would hear of no compromise, however, and Sophia perceived that this was the person she had to please. Accordingly, the princess threw herself into Orthodox studies with the greatest dedication. Her zeal, late on cold nights, was so great that she contracted pneumonia, causing her detractors at court to write her prospects off for lost. In this crisis Elizabeth personally took over, attended to all the nursing, and gave Sophia a memory of a kind motherliness that she had never known and was never to forget, even in later times when her relations with Elizabeth were at their most trying. For her part, Sophia, even in sickness, showed herself far more clever than the hysterical Joanna Elizabeth. She weakly refused the comforts of Lutheranism and called for the presence of her Orthodox confessor, an action which could not help impressing the empress and court. By the time of her birthday in April Sophia had recovered sufficiently to appear in public, and her favored status was evident in the gift of a diamond snuffbox.

Following the illness Sophia wrote her father of her intent to convert: "Since I can find almost no difference between the Greek faith and the Lutheran, I am resolved (with all the regard to your Highness's gracious instructions) to change, and shall send you my confession of faith on the first day."

Late in June Sophia was formally received into the church. She was to be known as Catherine Alexievna. Sophia Christianovna would have been proper, but the one name upset Elizabeth on account of her father's half sister, and the other smacked of more recent bad memories of Germanic royalty. Catherine it was and unforgettably so. After her conversion she received a necklace valued at 150,000 rubles and portraits of Elizabeth and Peter set in brilliants.

The betrothal of Peter and Catherine occurred the following day, after a dazzling procession down the Kremlin's Red Staircase, in which Elizabeth appeared under a canopy of solid silver carried by eight major generals. The ceremony in the cathedral saw Catherine created a grand duchess, giving her precedence right after the empress and grand duke. Joanna Elizabeth wrote back to Germany: "My daughter conducts herself very intelligently in her new status; she blushes each time she is forced to walk in front of me."

A terrible crisis came after that summer of 1744, when the whole court had accompanied Elizabeth on her joyous pilgrimage to Kiev. On the return journey from Moscow to St. Petersburg in December, Peter caught smallpox and was again given up for dead by the doctors. Catherine's mother simply ordered her to abandon her fiancé and continue the journey.

As usual, Elizabeth rose to the occasion, hastened to the scene, and took over the nursing herself, even at the great risk involved. Her copious tears and fervent prayers were answered. Peter was left badly disfigured, however, his face swollen and deeply pockmarked. Catherine wrote that he was "unrecognizable" in a big wig over his shaved head and that "he had become quite hideous," so much so that she could scarcely bear to look at him.

Unhappy as his childhood had been, Peter's real tragedy probably dated from his smallpox. Far from loving or really even pitying her unfortunate playmate, Catherine took to ingratiating herself with other people, although, as she wrote later, "I decided to humor the Grand Duke's confidence in order that he should at least consider me as a loyal friend to whom he could say anything without risk."

The wedding took place in August, 1745, in grand style, for this was the first proper Romanov wedding since Peter the Great's, and the empress sent for information from Versailles and Dresden to make sure that it would match or even excel the highest Western standards. Early in the morning Catherine was brought before Elizabeth, who helped dress her, making the decision to leave the princess' dark hair unpowdered. The wedding dress, which is one of the Kremlin treasures today, was shimmering silver, richly bejeweled and embroidered, with a very small waist and a wide skirt, the whole thing dreadfully heavy, as Catherine recalled. Peter, also dressed richly in silver, joined the two women for the ride to the cathedral. Elizabeth led the couple into the sanctuary, where the traditional gold coronets were held over their heads, the Gospels read, and their wedding rings blessed by the archbishops. After the ceremony the couple did obeisance to the empress, who quickly raised them to their feet, weeping and laughing with emotion. A great banquet followed and then a ball, but the dancing was cut short by Elizabeth, intent on organizing the procession to the bedchamber. The empress saw to Catherine's attiring in her dishabille, then went to bring Peter, and finally supervised the couple's lying down between the sheets on a huge bed with an orange canopy decorated with garlands and hymeneal emblems. The next day the bride was rewarded with two toilet sets, one in emeralds and one in sapphires, and a prayer book set in large type ("to save your eyes, my dear"). Then came ten days of festivities for the court, the populace at large not being forgotten in the royal bounty.

3. The Young Marrieds

On the wedding night there had been no transports of romantic passion, not even any attempts at adolescent experimentation—in fact, nothing.

The wife later credited her obviously confounded husband with the remark "How amused the servant would be to find us in bed together." Both the newlyweds probably remained virgins for the next seven years.

Children they both were, and they were not allowed to forget their helplessness for long. Peter was happy at first to have a daylong playmate, but Catherine found toys and games less than satisfying. Her mother, to whom she clung in sudden desperation, was forced to leave her, departing from St. Petersburg and Catherine forever. Joanna Elizabeth was gone abruptly, without a good-bye, thus avoiding a scene, although she still smarted from the reproaches of the empress over debts, love affairs, and pro-Prussian indiscretions. Catherine was all alone except for a husband of whom she was later to write bitterly:

> I told myself: if you love that man you will be the unhappiest creature on earth, since your character is such that you would demand your love returned. This man scarcely even looks at you; when he talks to you it is of practically nothing but dolls, and he pays more attention to any other woman than he does to you.

The young couple were allowed their own court, which, at first, was a gay and mindless assortment of their contemporaries. Catherine could dance and frolic as before. Peter's passion was his puppet theater, which the wife found the most insipid thing in the world. It was the wood drill which Peter was given to aid his stage constructions that led to the first major clash with the empress. The grand duke conceived the jolly notion of drilling holes into the door of Elizabeth's private dining room and inviting his friends to spy on the adult informalities beyond. The escapade was discovered, and Elizabeth's rage was all out of proportion but for the general doubts she harbored about her nephew's stability and promise. Elizabeth finally quieted down with the observation that Peter "was nothing but a boy and she would soon find a way of teaching him how to behave."

Catherine's turn for a personal dressing down came not long afterward and was essentially caused by Elizabeth's belief that the grand duchess was responsible for the lack of children after a score of months. Among other charges wildly thrown out by the empress was that Catherine had conspired with her mother and was all the while betraying Elizabeth to the King of Prussia. More to the point, Catherine was accused of forcing her charms on the grand duke's valets in general and of loving another man in particular, unnamed, although Elizabeth said she knew all. The thoroughly terrified girl managed to withdraw, noting afterward: "I saw that she was on the point of hitting me."

A harsh new regimen for the young couple was inaugurated with the appearance of "Instructions for the persons attached to the service of the Grand Duke and Grand Duchess," a document framed by Bestuzhev himself, who made little secret of his dislike of Peter and his distrust of Catherine. Peter was to pay close attention to the clergy and answer clearly about his health "so liable to indisposition and so slow to recover therefrom." Twice-weekly audiences were to be held, during which the grand duke was to strive to appear serious, pleasant, and courteous, avoiding vulgarity or affectation. Peter was forbidden to joke with his servants, to read romances, or to play with soldiers. To make sure he devoted himself to the higher things, it was decreed: "No drums, tents, weapons, or uniforms are to be introduced into, or used in, the private apartments of the Grand Duke by any of his domestics under pain of dismissal." It was laid down for Catherine that she was to have no unduly familiar or unbefitting intercourse with the gentlemen-in-waiting, particularly in the matter of secret letters. She was to display no "familiarity or sportiveness with any page or groom of the bedchamber or coffee server or table layer or lackey to the disparagement of her dignity." The grand duchess was to say her prayers in private, as well as in public. In particular, Catherine was enjoined not to show Peter any chilliness, and the couple were to take special care to avoid saying rude, hasty, and unbecoming things to each other in the presence of servants.

To see to the enforcement of the new regimen, Elizabeth appointed a Mr. and Mrs. Choglokov as master and mistress of the grand ducal household. Mrs. Choglokov, a first cousin of the empress, was supposed to provide the example of a loving helpmate, but Catherine from the first regarded her as a dragon and thoroughly delighted in finding out that her husband was being unfaithful to her. By a supplementary edict of 1747 the empress provided that no one could speak to Catherine or Peter without the Choglokovs' permission.

Added to the tribulations of the young couple was the systematic removal of any friends or even favorite servants. The isolation of the pair from normal friendships was more lastingly harmful for a person as unmoored as Peter than for self-reliant Catherine. This treatment brought out paranoia in the husband, cunning in the wife.

For a while the harsh regimen served to drive the couple together. Peter took to escaping into forbidden books about chivalrous knights and highway robbers, while Catherine nearby read more serious fare. The forbidden toys were procured, too, and hidden under Catherine's bed. The wife related how at night, after the Choglokovs and the other attendants had withdrawn, Peter would grin, pull out the box of soldiers, and devise games with them until one or two in the morning, when he finally tired of play. "Methinks, I was good for something else," she wrote.

Once Catherine returned to their chamber and was startled to find a dead rat hanging on the wall. Peter arrived to provide an explanation. The rodent had been caught in the act of eating up two stuffed soldiers, not just any soldiers but sentries assigned to guard Peter's fort, and the seriousness of its crime merited the fullest penalties of military law. Then later came his passion for hunting dogs, which were also kept in Catherine's room in an alcove where their sniffing and smell drove her to distraction. Resigned, Catherine confessed that the unparalleled insipidity of her husband made the dullest of books seem like the most delicious of entertainments.

As the couple grew older, if not wiser, the stringent regimen was relaxed. Peter was given the estate of Oranienbaum to spend summers at, and there he was able to play the reigning Duke of Holstein with appropriate court officials and real soldiers, in time numbering 5,000. In fact, he put his establishment entirely on a military footing, while Catherine played chatelaine of a stylish house she had built. The youthful bickering between the two eventually gave way to more decorous behavior together and the pursuit of separate interests apart. Catherine made a point of visiting her husband one or two hours a day and discussing his affairs with him. She did have a head for business and for keeping out of trouble, so that "Madame la Ressource" became Peter's admiring, affectionate epithet for her.

Peter held very dearly his status as Duke of Holstein. A model of the city of Kiel was displayed in his apartments, so that he had a conversation piece for telling his visitors that he treasured the city of his birth more than the whole Russian Empire. Peter's pride on this matter was treated indifferently, if not contemptuously, by Elizabeth, who casually gave away some of his hereditary possessions by the 1745 peace treaty with Sweden and once blithely suggested that Peter exchange Holstein for Oldenburg.

After seven years of marriage it was a scandal that Peter and Catherine had no children. From the point of view of a much diminished dynasty, what good were the half-foreign idiot and his all-foreign hussy? Peter boasted of romantic conquests, but Catherine knew that her husband could not be amiable with any woman. It was now her action which set them both on the path of infidelity. In 1752 Catherine met Sergius Saltykov, a dashing young roué who came to evening parties at the Choglokovs' house and so flattered Mr. Choglokov that Saltykov was able to flirt with Catherine behind her guardian's back. His protestations of love were finally returned during a hunting party on an island in the Neva. Four months later Catherine had a miscarriage. Peter at the time seemed more delighted that the Choglokovs had been fooled than upset about his own honor. Nonetheless, about this time the grand duke was finally induced to have an operation on his genitals that was considered necessary for him and forthwith he was put up to sleeping with Madame Groot, wife of the noted painter. Since nothing happened to this obliging woman, it seemed obvious that Peter was sterile, if no longer impotent, and the blame in the royal marriage was thus pinpointed. These events took place in mortal terror of the empress' finding out, but in truth Elizabeth probably had not only knowledge of them but a hand in them as well.

A great turnabout came in the attitude of Mrs. Choglokov. An interview between her and the grand duchess was so sensational that it was expurgated from Catherine's *Memoirs* as late as 1907. The good wife was said to have begun a eulogy of marital fidelity only to end it by saying "that there were certain circumstances of an overriding nature that should be made exceptions to the rule." When Catherine played innocent, Mrs. Choglokov went on to allude to Catherine's love for Saltykov and then declared: "You will soon see how much I love my country and how frank I can be." Catherine soon after had another miscarriage.

In the eyes of the grand duchess, Saltykov was "as handsome as the day, and there was certainly no one to equal him at the grand court or still less at our own." For his part, Saltykov soon got bored with the love of the naïve and demanding woman he deflowered, but nonetheless, he and Catherine were constantly kept in close association. At the same time it is probable that Peter found himself capable of taking a sexual interest in his wife. At any rate, Catherine became pregnant again during a winter visit to Moscow. In St. Petersburg the following September, 1754, she gave birth to a son. Whose?

The child, titled and christened the Grand Duke Paul, was destined to reign for only a short time, but his descendants were to number in the hundreds. Was he a Saltykov, as Catherine hinted in her *Memoirs*? Was he Peter's own and thereby a true Romanov? Or was he equally a Romanov by virtue of being the secret baby of the Empress Elizabeth by Shuvalov or another, a possibility suggested by the French ambassador? In any case, Paul was immediately taken away by Elizabeth and installed in a crib in her room, while Catherine had to get news of the child secretly and did not see him for forty days, and then only briefly at a church service. Virtually abandoned after the childbirth, the grand duchess was then brusquely rewarded with 100,000 rubles, which she later had to return because of Peter's jealousy, and "a miserable little necklace with earrings and two dingy rings which I would have been ashamed to give to my maids."

The day of Paul's birth Peter got drunk. Thereafter all cordiality to his wife vanished. He addressed Catherine coldly as Madame la Grande Duchesse, and her advice was no longer sought. Peter tended more and more to take refuge at Oranienbaum where he was surrounded by uncouth Holsteiners and a succession of mistresses of whom he was now able to take advantage. The winter of 1754–55 was the most miserable of Catherine's existence. Her husband loathed her, the empress treated her as if her useful function were finished, and on top of everything else Saltykov deserted her and was openly carrying on with others. Catherine's first reaction was to escape into her books, reading everything from Tacitus to

Voltaire. Her thoughts soon turned to revenge. Revenge required power. The way to escape being a victim of events was to dominate them, and Catherine had both the will and the ability to succeed at this, unlike her husband, who knew only how to sulk and stamp his foot helplessly. The next spring Catherine returned to court, a proud smile on her lips and steel in her heart, ready to counter intrigue with intrigue and to match insult for insult.

Catherine's peculiar position in the Russian court made her a person of great interest to foreign diplomats. In 1755 the British ambassador succeeded in gaining her attention for his protégé, Stanislaus Poniatowski, an exceptionally handsome Polish aristocrat (connected with the celebrated Czartoryskis), gentle, cultivated, Paris-educated, and something of an innocent. The grand duchess took to leaving her quarters two or three times a week, and disguised as a man, she would make her way to a friend's house where she, Poniatowski, and others indulged "in the maddest hilarity it is possible to imagine." Still hurt by Saltykov's rebuff, Catherine was less than passionately enamored of her second lover, three years her junior. Avowing that she was the first woman he had been involved with, Poniatowski then and later was the infatuated one. He left a description of Catherine at what he said was the "height" of her beauty: "She had a dazzling fairness, the liveliest coloring, very eloquent blue eyes, a rather prominent mouth that seemed to call for kisses, perfect hands and arms, a slim waist, tall rather than short, with an easy gait that yet contained perfect nobility, and a laugh as gay as her manner."

As for Peter, he confided in Catherine about his love affairs, asking her how to decorate one mistress' apartment or complaining about the demandingness of another. Then the grand duke finally settled on one woman in particular, Elizabeth Vorontsova, daughter of the vice-chancellor. The lady in question was unprepossessing in her looks and inelegant in her manner, but Peter made his choice all on his own for once and stuck by it. Vorontsova, however tawdry and uneducated, was a great drinking companion, her whole being expressed in loud singing and hearty laughter. Moreover, she was utterly attached to Peter, even if quarrelsomeness was the main way she showed it. The relationship was understandable, if one took into account how his mistress' very plainness and lack of breeding soothed Peter's inferiority complex. Gradually, Vorontsova was accepted as the heir's official companion and was to remain so to the end, although she had a more exalted status in mind.

Any furtiveness in their outside affairs was soon dispensed with by the grand ducal couple. In fact, Poniatowski related with some amazement how once he went out to Oranienbaum disguised as a tailor, only to be accosted by Peter, who then proceeded to chide him for the secrecy and forthwith hustled him right into Catherine's bedroom, saying, "Well, there he is!

Now I hope everyone will be pleased with me." Subsequently, Peter took upon himself the arranging of rendezvous between his wife and Poniatowski, and on occasion, he would play host at intimate dinners for four, at the end of which he would rise, take Elizabeth Vorontsova on his arm, and announce, "There now, my children, you don't need me any more, I think."

When Catherine was about to have her second child, her husband's actions were typically eccentric. On one occasion he told a group that "I don't know how it is my wife becomes pregnant." Catherine promptly dared him to "swear on oath he has not lain with his wife" and to lay the whole matter before the grand inquisitor of the empire. Peter did not choose to expose himself to official inquiry, as well as to social ridicule. When the grand duchess began actual childbirth, Peter was probably well in his cups, and he suddenly elected to show some sort of lingering pride or affection for his wife by charging into her rooms dressed in a Holstein uniform, brandishing a large sword, and shouting that it was in a crisis that one knew who one's real friends were. It would have been a crisis if the grand duke had not been persuaded to change into a Russian uniform before the empress arrived to supervise the delivery. The child was a girl and was named Anna for Peter's mother, Catherine having feebly but not unthinkingly requested that it be called Elizabeth. Peter ordered fireworks in celebration of the birth at both Oranienbaum and Kiel. Anna was dead within a year.

These marital and extramarital developments took place at a time of great tension in the Russian court: War was being waged with Prussia, and the health of the empress was failing. Peter was persistently tactless in his expressions of devotion to the Prussian king, and a movement arose to bypass him as heir to the throne. Although at this point Catherine was accepting gifts, some said bribes, from Prussia's ally, in the person of the British envoy, it was a problem more of her gambling debts than of her political inclinations. Whatever her original feelings about Prussia, Catherine had come to show herself ostentatiously Russian above all, her patriotism markedly distinguishing herself from her husband in the eyes of the empress and people who counted. Battles and retreats abroad and personality clashes and maneuvers at home culminated in the great crisis of 1758, when Bestuzhev was ousted as chancellor.

When a note from Poniatowski informed Catherine of the arrest of the chancellor, her jeweler, and others, she burned her papers and boldly took the offensive against vague accusations by her enemies. "I set myself to write a letter to the Empress in Russian, and I made it as pathetic as I could." To continue in Catherine's own words:

> I began by thanking her for all the favor and kindness she had shown me on my arrival in Russia, adding that, unhappily, events proved that

I had not deserved them, since I had drawn on myself the hatred of the Grand Duke and her Majesty's very obvious displeasure; that in view of my wretchedness and the fact that I was dying of boredom in my room, where I was deprived of even the most innocent of amusements, I begged her instantly to put an end to my miseries by dismissing me, in whatever fashion seemed best to her, and sending me back to my family; that as for my children, since I never saw them, even though I lived with them in the same house, it had become a matter of indifference to me whether I stayed under the same roof with them or several hundred leagues away; that I knew she took such care of them as surpassed that which my feeble abilities would permit me to give them; that I dared entreat her to continue in this, and that in this assurance I would spend the rest of my life among my own family, praying to God for her, for the Grand Duke, for my children and for all those who had been kind or unkind to me, but that the state of my health had been reduced through grief to such a condition that it was necessary for me to do what I could at least to save my life, and to this end I begged her to allow me to go to a spa, and from there to my family.

Inevitably, Elizabeth melted and granted an audience, typically, in the early hours of the morning. The grand duchess went on her knees and wept so persistently that the empress, always easily moved, was embarrassed, and she let Catherine play on her desire to avoid scandal and her obvious distaste for her nephew. Nonetheless, there were some telling remarks from Elizabeth, such as that Catherine imagined that "no one was more clever than herself" and that she "meddled" in Russian politics. Yet Catherine was relieved to note that "I perceived in her Majesty more anxiety than anger," and in the end the empress was persuaded that she was guilty of snubbing her nephew's wife. The renewed friendship of the two women was then shown by a private interview Elizabeth granted Catherine soon after. Peter had made wild accusations against his wife, only to find her more secure at court than ever. In his pique, the grand duke promised Elizabeth Vorontsova that he would marry her if he could get rid of Catherine, so the latter said.

One victim of the crisis was Poniatowski, who was sent out of Russia, accused of diplomatic indiscretions. Catherine, however, was not long in finding herself a new lover in the person of Gregory Orlov, all the while writing affectionate letters to her Polish admirer. Five years Catherine's junior, Orlov was like his predecessor, the more in love of the two. Moreover, the dashing but lowborn Guards officer was indulging political ambitions as well as sensual passions when he sought out the grand duchess and had clandestine meetings with her in a little house on Vasilevsky Island. Meanwhile, the cuckolded husband had openly installed Elizabeth Vorontsova in his apartments.

The final months of Elizabeth's reign passed in a frenzy of intrigue.

The Vorontsovs, with the head of the family now chancellor, expected great things of Peter and their prostituted daughter. Many other courtiers, however, notably the Shuvalovs and Razumovskys, had swung over to Catherine's side, and there was talk of her being proclaimed regent for her son. The ambassadors outdid themselves playing up to both husband and wife. Then Catherine became pregnant again, obviously by Orlov, and it was while she was carrying her third child and keeping in relative seclusion that Elizabeth died in early 1762.

4. Peter III

At the age of thirty-four Karl Peter Ulrich of Holstein, mostly German and Swedish but a true Romanov, became Peter III, autocrat of Russia. The accession ceremonies on the afternoon of January 5, 1762, went smoothly. The great officials, gathered in the palace, gravely heard the metropolitan's invitation to Peter to occupy the throne "the rightful possession of which all Europe and Asia acknowledge to be thine." After the allegiance oaths were sworn in the palace, Peter descended to the courtyard and rode out among the assembled Guards regiments and Corps of Cadets, looking poised and trim in the green uniform with red facings of the Preobrazhenskoe and wearing the wide blue ribbon of the Order of St. Andrew. The soldiers presented arms, dipped their standards, and cheered lustily. Beside himself with delight, the new emperor exclaimed to an ambassador: "I did not think they had so much love for me."

Peter showed himself willing to forgive and forget almost all. Catherine, now addressed as the empress, was treated not only with due ceremony but even with cordiality. Her debts were paid without question, and her estate was increased according to her station. The emperor's particular friends, such as Vorontsov and Trubetskoy, were confirmed in the highest posts, but Elizabeth's old favorites, including all the Shuvalovs, did well under the new ruler, too. Cyril Razumovsky stayed on as Hetman of the Ukraine, adding a field marshal's baton to his honors. Only Alexis Razumovsky had the sense of propriety to give over all his offices and dignities and to request retirement to a simple country house, settling in the end for self-imposed seclusion in the Anichkov Palace. Moreover, the exiles of Elizabeth's reign, including such bygone greats as field marshals Münnich and Biren, were generously recalled to court. The extent of Peter's goodwill and confidence was shown dramatically by the visit he paid to the ex-Emperor Ivan VI at Schlüsselburg Fortress in March: His cousin was found to be a disheveled, incoherent wreck of a man in his early twenties, and Peter took pity, ordered his treatment improved, and spoke vaguely of finding some employment for him.

Clearly not an imbecile, Peter sometimes gave people that impression. The emperor had fixed ideas and a natural obstinacy. He was also violent, febrile, and flighty in his interests, causing the Saxon minister, for example, to remark "the vivacity of his disordered noddle." The total effect was one of irrationality and unbalance. Essentially, the emperor was unfitted for his responsibilities, but he did not shirk them.

Peter prided himself on being enlightened and Western in his outlook. A promptly forthcoming decree forbade hat doffing to the ruler, a custom he regarded as outmoded and servile. The introduction of police patrols showed an appreciation of modern standards. Another enactment promised full religious freedom to all. For the lower orders Peter offered a boon in the form of a reduction of the detested salt tax. As usual it was the nobility which gained the greatest concessions: emancipation from state service and the right to travel abroad freely. The release of the aristocracy from civic or military duties without changing their economic privileges was a landmark in Russian social history, and, according to a contemporary writer, "this magnanimous act filled the whole nobility with indescribable joy."

Peter's failings of character were more those of a clown than of a bully. The emperor has been compared to a bad actor who had no choice but to pile one *gaffe* on another. In a state of perpetual agitation, Peter rushed rather than walked. Even at formal audiences with ambassadors, Peter was forever shifting his legs, waving his arms, making faces, and sticking out his tongue. He gabbled incessantly, his voice described as so strident that it rose above the loudest din and pierced the thickest walls. Probably, the emperor thought of himself as urbane, and his portraits are uniformly mocking and supercilious, all the while betraying a touch of madness, too.

"Discreet as a cannonball" was a famous phrase the wife applied to the husband. Without dignity himself, Peter took childish delight in jeering at others and compounding their embarrassment, but this was the limit of his meanness. However weak-headed, Peter III was essentially good-hearted, eager to be amiable, and forgiving. At times his temper got the better of him, and he would order a servant's instant execution, but no such sentences were carried out during his reign, and several devoted servants took to boasting of their survival of many such threats. Perhaps Peter was too cowardly to play with real violence. Catherine and other detractors would have Peter depicted as vicious, but truly he was victimized, if anything, by others. He made things easy for his enemies.

Peter's preferred routine was entirely different from Elizabeth's easy-going ways. Winter and summer the emperor was up by seven in the morning, and while he dressed, he was already discussing reports and issuing commands. After a formal meeting with his ministers, Peter would rush off to inspect the public offices, often finding them not yet fully functioning. This royal diligence and energy were less than admired by a bureaucracy which had long forgotten Peter the Great.

At eleven sharp Peter would be at the parade ground, the Field of Mars, to begin personally drilling the troops. This was his delight and his mania. No one was excused from his military duties, and Peter giggled at the discomfort of such old courtiers as Cyril Razumovsky and Prince Trubetskoy who could hardly keep on their horses, to say nothing of executing the new Prussian-inspired exercises. Besides changing the slovenly habits of Elizabeth's day, Peter introduced simpler and neater uniforms and curbed the use of the knout for punishments. All the well-meant changes inevitably produced mutterings among some of the military, which became increasingly serious in the face of Peter's more tactless actions. The emperor's Holstein Regiment was given preferment and the title of Body Guards of the Imperial Household. On several occasions Peter commented on the spoiled and probably seditious temper of the Preobrazhenskoe Guards, and it was soon reported that he intended to Prussianize them completely or even disband them.

The troops having been drilled, Peter always had dinner at one in the afternoon, taking the opportunity to consult with important people or to visit private houses, such as those of the rich English merchants. Following a nap, the restless ruler was off on his surprise inspection tours again—to a barracks, or a factory, or the mint, his favorite.

The evenings were given over to pleasure. In the capital or at Peterhof, Peter might preside fairly graciously at a banquet followed by card games. Frequently he ordered a concert and would play first violin himself, sometimes for hours on end.

The entertainments Peter arranged for himself at Oranienbaum included the company of foreign opera singers and actors, and a Russian observer described with horror the behavior of Peter's usual Holsteiner cronies after one of their supper and smoking parties:

> Presently they would all get up and shout and shriek and laugh and talk nonsense like so many urchins or creatures without reason. And sometimes they would proceed through the balcony to the sand-strewn court beyond and there play about like so many little children, hopping about on one leg, butting at their comrades, kicking their posteriors and bellowing "Come along, my brothers, see who will be down first." Imagine then our feelings to see the first men in the Empire, all bedizened with stars and ribands, butting at and trying to cross-buttock each other. And whenever anyone of them could keep his feet no longer but fell prone upon the floor, there would be laughter and uproar and shrieking

and clapping of hands 'til the grenadiers came in and carried the fallen in their arms.

Peter made a point of hating ceremony, and he somehow felt his masculinity enhanced by these boisterous evenings. To someone's expression of dismay at the emperor's using a pipe amid the general smoke-filled atmosphere, Peter was said to have burst out: "What is there to be surprised at, blockhead? Did you ever see a brave officer who did not smoke?"

Peter's enemies accused him of serious drunkenness, but his more intemperate outbursts could just as easily be attributed to a general state of excitement. There is evidence that strong drink did not agree with Peter from his youth, and that he confined himself largely to English ale or Burgundy and water, sometimes in large quantities. Drunkenness and horseplay were hallmarks of the entire reign of Peter the Great, so why should people resent them under his grandson? For one thing, the gaiety was too forced, and the ruler became too familiar. Worse, Peter III in his cups told state secrets.

The young emperor never passed out after one of his wild evenings. Often he would gather special friends with him in his quarters and discuss state affairs until two in the morning. He could not manage to sleep for more than a few hours at a time.

The empress' position became worse. Her seclusion was enforced during the first months of the reign by the fact she was carrying Orlov's child. Catherine's second son, christened Alexis, was born in April. Increasingly snubbed at court, Catherine found herself studiously ignored by the foreign representatives once so eager to gain her goodwill. She made herself pay daily visits to Peter, who still occasionally asked her advice, but she was unable to stomach the carryings-on at Oranienbaum, having put in an appearance one evening, for which Peter thanked her.

In the spring the imperial family moved into the newly finished Winter Palace—Peter, Catherine, the Grand Duke Paul (now heir), and Elizabeth Vorontsova. The empress and her children occupied a wing of the palace overlooking the Neva and the Admiralty, while Vorontsova was installed in a lavish suite directly under the emperor's. Peter's demanding favorite was named *Kammerfräulein,* giving her precedence over the other ladies, but so far the situation was more foolish than dangerous. One time at a banquet Peter ordered Catherine to pin the Order of St. Catherine on her rival's breast, but this affront backfired since the court was angered at seeing the mistress honored with a decoration intended only for anointed royalty. The cool-headed empress became sure enough of her position to go to receptions together with the gawky Vorontsova.

At another banquet Peter pointedly proposed a toast to the imperial family and sent an adjutant down the table to inquire of Catherine why she had not risen to drink. Upon her reply that she herself was part of the imperial family, Peter suddenly shouted, "Fool," and went on to say that his three Holstein uncles were those he meant to honor, in effect publicly declaring his hatred, if not repudiation, of her. Catherine averted completely breaking down only by getting a dinner companion to tell a humorous story. "It was then," Catherine was to write, "that I began to listen to the proposals which people had been making me ever since the death of the Empress" (in truth, since long before). Foolishly Peter antagonized Catherine without rendering her harmless.

Just as Peter's hysterical outbursts in the face of her dignity made friends for the empress, so, too, people were favorably influenced by her ostentatious piety in contrast with the emperor's religious unconventionality. At the very outset there was the matter of the funeral obsequies for Elizabeth, which included having her body rest in the cathedral for ten days. Peter never put in an appearance at his aunt's bier, whereas day after day thousands saw the heavily veiled Catherine there praying and weeping. A particularly obnoxious thing for the devout was Peter's behavior when he did attend a mass, the customary fidgeting and strutting about, loud talk and laughter, and even the sticking out of his tongue at the celebrant. Peter matched his thoughtless actions with lectures to Orthodox churchmen in which he aired his Lutheran principles and his prejudices against the veneration of icons and the traditional vestments of the priests. Already fully alarmed, the clergy were set aghast by the emperor's ukase of April transferring all church property to a new government college, putting the priests on salary, and projecting the complete secularization of the church lands. Granted that the church owned one-fifth of the serfs and that the nobility had much to gain from the reallotment, yet Peter's own ministers tried in vain to stop the unfortunate and hasty step that even Peter the Great had never seriously considered.

Peter's religious innovations were plainly motivated in part by a desire to appear a freethinker in the mode of Frederick the Great. Of all the emperor's follies his worship of everything Prussian was the most deeply pathological and the most completely disastrous for himself. Long before he came to the throne Peter made clear his strange feelings, confiding to Poniatowski, for instance:

> See, though, how unhappy I am. If only I had entered the service of the King of Prussia . . . now, I am sure, I should have had a regiment and the rank of major general and perhaps even of lieutenant general. But far from it, instead they brought me here and made me Grand Duke of this damnable country.

Instead of letting power change him, Peter indulged his idiosyncrasies further. He was known to refer to Frederick in public as the "king, my master" and kept a statue of his aunt's greatest enemy prominently displayed in his study. When the Russian emperor started appearing in the uniform of a Prussian colonel of the Guards and wearing only the long-sought Order of the Black Eagle, Russian patriotism could not have been more offended.

From the point of view of diplomacy, Peter III came to the throne with the unique opportunity of dictating peace to the defeated Prussians, indeed, to all Europe. Frederick the Great was already willing to cede Russia East Prussia and the British were quite prepared to leave their ally in the lurch. Instead, Peter abruptly recalled his army. Scarcely concealing his surprise beneath much flattery, the Prussian king addressed his deliverer as follows:

> . . . the first acts of your Majesty's reign have drawn down upon you the benedictions of your subjects and the blessings of the sanest part of Europe. . . . While all the rest of Europe is persecuting me, I found a friend in you. I find a friend who has a truly German heart. . . . In you I place all my trust and I vow to you a loyal and eternal friendship.

Instead of giving Peter perspective, Frederick's letter only elicited obsequiousness:

> Your Majesty surely laughs at me when you praise me so highly. In truth, you must be amazed at my nothingness while I am amazed at your Majesty's exploits. Your qualities are extraordinary. I recognize in your Majesty one of the greatest heroes the world has ever seen.

The Russian ruler suited his actions to his words, heaping favors on and spending much time with the first Prussian ambassador St. Petersburg had seen in a decade. Peter went even further and confided secret dispatches via him to Frederick, who, still not quite at a loss for words, replied: "You give an example of virtue to all Sovereigns which should draw to you the hearts of all honest folk." In the view of a contemporary, Peter III seemed to be born for the good fortune of Prussia.

One of the most preposterous about-faces in history came in May, when Peter signed a treaty of active alliance with Frederick just as it was submitted to him by the Prussian envoy, a treaty giving back all of Russia's gains of the past six years. Biren, or Münnich, or Osterman—the hated Germans—would never have dared flout Russia's interests and pride so insanely. The Winter Palace now became the scene of a great ceremonial banquet hailing the treaty, during which triple salvos from the citadel, the Admiralty, and a special battery in the square punctuated Peter's toasts, which were made not to any of Russia's own military heroes, but to the valiant officers and soldiers in the Prussian army.

The plan for the summer of 1762 was for a Russian army to join the ex-enemy King Frederick in delivering a *coup de grâce* to the former ally, Austria. In addition, 40,000 soldiers under Rumyantsev gathered in Prussian Pomerania and prepared to invade Denmark, Peter's hatred of that country for its hold on part of Holstein surpassing even his attachment to Prussia. Rumyantsev's force was ordered to move forward on July 6. Back in St. Petersburg the emperor busied himself putting his Holsteiners on a war footing and giving marching orders to the Guards regiments. Peter intended to join the army in Germany, and he put off his coronation accordingly. There was a last-minute round of social festivities. On one occasion Peter came over to Peterhof to be entertained by Catherine at an opera, during which the emperor joined the orchestra. Another day the empress repaid the visit, participating in a gay banquet and masquerade at Oranienbaum. The evening of July 8 the imperial couple were together at a sumptuous fete at Alexis Razumovsky's summer house. The following day Peter drilled his troops at Oranienbaum in the early morning and set off at ten o'clock to begin the celebration of his name day festivities with the empress at Peterhof. The party in six carriages was a merry one as they made the short trip without escort, arriving at noon. Catherine was gone. Weeks later in Germany, Rumyantsev's Russian army mysteriously began to retreat.

5. *The Coup*

By the summer of 1762 "the general discontent was no longer a timid whisper but an audacious clamor." The clergy were saying secret prayers against the ruler. The officer corps was aroused at the prospect of active service and against the wrong enemy at that. The emperor's beneficent measures were easily lost sight of.

Nothing seemed to rouse Peter's suspicions or to shake his goodwill. Warnings from several quarters were deliberately discounted or frivolously forgotten. Even Berlin was aware of potential trouble in St. Petersburg, but Frederick's letter of alarm sent in May merely gave his admirer a chance to show off his courage. Peter wrote:

> If the Russians had wanted to do me harm, they could have done it long ago, seeing that I take no particular precautions, always committing myself to God's keeping and going freely about the streets on foot. I assure your Majesty that when once one knows how to deal with the Russians one can be quite sure of them, . . . they who have always desired a man for their master instead of a woman, as I have heard the soldiers of my own regiment say twenty times over.

What Frederick was warning against was a rumored plot to dethrone Peter III and to restore Ivan VI, but the real danger, which Peter sensed but immediately dismissed to his satisfaction, was from "a woman." In any event, Peter was persuaded by Frederick and others to take the precaution of having the whole court accompany him to Germany, leaving a trusted uncle and a field marshal to govern Russia.

The obvious replacement for the emperor was his wife, both in terms of her demonstrated strengths of mind and character and in terms of her image, for since Peter's accession Catherine had taken every opportunity to disassociate herself from his follies and to show herself more Russian than the Russians, more Orthodox than the Orthodox. She made no mistakes and offended no prejudices. It is really impossible to say when Catherine became determined to rule. Whatever was going on in Catherine's mind, she easily rallied people to her cause. Bestuzhev was once her patron; and later Count Nikita Panin, tutor of the infant Grand Duke Paul, was a secret promoter of the project of bypassing the father altogether and of her ruling as regent for the son. Greater ambitions and greater energies, however, characterized the empress' newest partisans, the Orlov brothers in general and Gregory Orlov in particular. By 1762 the Orlovs and other groups of conspirators acting independently had thoroughly subverted several Guards units, in part with Catherine's knowledge and financial support.

The unexpected arrest of one of the conspirators on July 7 persuaded Gregory Orlov, after consulting Panin, to take action. At 6 A.M. on July 9 Alexis Orlov awakened Catherine in her room in the Mon Plaisir pavilion at Peterhof and breathlessly told her the news. She put on a simple black gown, forgoing her toilette, and slipped out the back door, accompanied by two trusted servants. They drove off in great haste, but all were in high spirits when five miles from the capital they met a second carriage with Gregory Orlov. With her lover at her side Catherine now drove to the barracks of the Izmailovskoe Guards. Drummers sounded the alarm upon the arrival of the conspirators, but then the soldiers came running out to kneel and kiss Catherine's feet, just as their fathers had done with Elizabeth twenty-one years before. After an appropriate speech on the current dangers to Russia and her love for same, Catherine took the oath as autocrat from the chaplain. Shortly afterward Cyril Razumovsky, the popular commander of the regiment, arrived on the scene and swore allegiance without hesitation. At the head of a now considerable force the empress proceeded to the Semenovskoe Guards' barracks, and the scenes of protestations of support were repeated. Just three hours after her awakening Catherine presented herself in the Kazan Cathedral, surrounded by a huge crowd, and the forewarned archbishop solemnly proclaimed her accession as bells pealed and cannons boomed. Then there was a grand military and religious procession to the Winter Palace, after which Catherine appeared on the balcony holding her sleepy son and proclaimed successor, the Grand Duke Paul. Later, units of the Preobrazhenskoe Guards appeared, half-dressed in their new Prussian-style uniforms, and, being behind events for once and overwhelmed by them, could only shout up: "Matyushka, forgive us for coming last of all." Another group of arrivals included Chancellor Vorontsov, Prince Trubetskoy, and Count Peter Shuvalov, who had just left the confounded emperor at Peterhof. To Vorontsov's reproaches of treason, the empress replied, pointing to the mob below: "Deliver your message to them, Sir. It is they who command here. I do but obey."

It was a classic type of palace revolution and was so far accompanied by no more violence than the roughing up of the emperor's uncle as he tried to escape. The populace at large were mollified by opening the wineshops. Catherine sent an admiral to secure Kronstadt, and messengers sped off to Germany to order both Russian armies to halt hostilities, even if it necessitated rejoining the Austrians against the Prussians. There was a real danger of civil war if Peter escaped Russia, rallied the armies abroad to his support, and returned with the backing of Frederick the Great. Accordingly, at 10 P.M. Catherine set off on horseback with her supporters to confront her husband. She wore a broad-brimmed hat, her hair was tied in a single ribbon, and she was all green and red in the uniform of the Preobrazhenskoe.

While Petersburg was in the deliriums of revolution, Emperor Peter III procrastinated, surveying the empty rooms and mocking fountains of Peterhof. Poking in and out of closets in hysteria, the emperor wailed: "Didn't I tell you she was capable of anything?" As news began to come in, Peter paced the gardens and ordered countermeasures, taking at the same time the belated precaution of exchanging his Prussian uniform for that of the Preobrazhenskoe. Vorontsov, Trubetskoy, and Shuvalov were sent off to reconnoiter but did not return. Field Marshal Münnich advised a show of force in the capital itself, but Peter demurred. "I can't do it. I don't trust the Empress. She might let them insult me." The Holstein Regiment came over from Oranienbaum, and that gave the emperor's dwindling group of supporters some heart. Orders to take flight to Narva were rescinded, and it was resolved to win over Kronstadt. At 11 P.M. the emperor and his suite embarked on a yacht, and two hours later, they approached the citadel of Kronstadt. When a midshipman yelled for them to keep off, Peter bared his Order of St. Andrew and shouted, "I am your Gosudar." The reply was: "Long live Catherine II. . . . She is now our Empress and we have her orders to admit nobody to these walls. Another step forward and we fire." Peter fainted into the arms of Elizabeth Vorontsova, and his party sailed off now to Oranienbaum, disconsolate but still unwilling to flee altogether.

At Oranienbaum Peter recovered long enough to see to the safe departure of the ladies, then fainted again on the sofa in the blue Atlas study (which his wife had designed), and later set about writing in French a letter to

Catherine combining apologies and an offer to share power. This was delivered to the empress at the Sergeievsky Monastery, halfway to Peterhof: She was obdurate. Peter found himself reduced to sending a second letter, this time offering to abdicate and to retire to Holstein, provided that Elizabeth Vorontsova could accompany him. The adjutant entrusted with this mission came back with a document for Peter to sign that heaped the gamut of sins on him, allowed no concessions, and ended with the words "I hereby renounce the sovereignty of Russia." Sitting under the portrait of his Aunt Elizabeth, Peter duly signed his rights away on July 10.

Peterhof was occupied by a detachment of hussars under Alexis Orlov early on July 11, and Catherine arrived later to acknowledge their cheers. The empress saw that she was occupied elsewhere when at noon the ex-emperor was brought over from Oranienbaum in a decrepit carriage, made to divest himself of his sword and medals and Preobrazhenskoe uniform, and finally locked in his old apartments clothed only in a dressing gown. Panin, sent to ask where Peter wished to be held until Schlüsselburg was ready for him, declared that the interview was the greatest misfortune of his life, his former sovereign being so pitiable.

Ropsha was Peter's chosen place of confinement, and there he arrived at 8 P.M. to find himself locked in a room with blinds drawn and forbidden to walk even on the terrace. Pathetically, he sent requests for his violin, his poodle, his Negro servant Narcisse, and his mistress. The last was refused by his wife "for fear of the scandal." His jailer was Alexis Orlov, who said he treated him kindly and played cards with him, even lending him money to pay his losses.

On July 18 Catherine was at a banquet when a courier brought her a message scribbled hastily, and probably drunkenly, by Alexis Orlov. It read:

> Matyushka, most merciful sovereign lady, how can I explain, describe what has happened? . . . Matyushka, he is no more. . . . [What] were we thinking of to raise our hands against our Gosudar? . . . He struggled behind the table with Prince Theodore, but we succeeded in separating them, and he is no more. I myself don't remember what we did, but the whole lot of us are guilty and worthy of punishment. Have mercy on me if only for my brother's sake. . . .

Some said the news of her husband's murder did not even dampen Catherine's partying. Others report her in tears, and one observer related that she fainted and awoke with the words "They will never believe me innocent."

How Peter met his end remains a mystery. Alexis Orlov's version is the only eyewitness account. Other reports varied, stating the emperor was poisoned, strangled, or suffocated under a mattress. Who the actual killer was is not clear, some heaping all the guilt on Alexis Orlov, others saying that he fled the scene in revulsion. The official manifesto regarding the death, following hard on the announcement of Catherine's accession, attributed it to a violent fit of colic, unexpected, but a clear indication of God's will. In a letter to Poniatowski, she declared disarmingly, "I had him opened but not the slightest trace of poison was found . . . inflammation of the bowels and a stroke of apoplexy carried him off." Orlov's letter, which Catherine kept locked in her desk for thirty-four years, seems to exonerate her of being an accomplice to murder, as well as to conspiracy. Alexis Orlov may simply have acted to remove the major obstacle to his brother Gregory's being able to marry his mistress and to make himself emperor. Yet it was also directly in Catherine's interest to have Peter dead, for Peter, either locked in Schlüsselburg like Ivan VI or in exile in Holstein close to Frederick the Great, was a permanent political menace.

The populace was invited to pray for the emperor's repose and to view the corpse. Peter's body lay dressed not in a Russian uniform, but in that of a Holstein officer. His darkened face was largely hidden by a large hat, his neck was wrapped in a more than adequate cravat, and his hands were concealed, contrary to custom. Catherine did not attend the funeral. The coffin was not placed in the Peter and Paul Cathedral at this time, but was put in a vault in the Alexander Nevsky Lavra next to the remains of Anna Leopoldovna.

So ended Peter III, occasionally too willful, often too weak, and consistently too well intentioned to save himself or to serve history. This was the first assassination of a Romanov emperor but by no means the last.

XII.
The Brilliant Empress: Catherine II

1. Lover of Men

CATHERINE'S outrageous sex life is the main basis of her legendary status and worldwide fame. Spice is added by the fact that she was a usurper. Neither Romanov nor even Russian, Sophia of Anhalt-Zerbst was to reign as Catherine II over the largest of empires for thirty-four years. Critics of her day and later, notably Tolstoy, saw her as unscrupulous and vicious in both her politics and her love life. Others have found wry or broad comedy in the same facts, two familiar cases in point being the archly vulgar woman played on the stage by Mae West (*Catherine Was Great*) and the only slightly more elegant empress portrayed on the screen by Tallulah Bankhead (*A Royal Scandal*).

Yet the same woman was regarded by her Romanov heirs as the savior of the dynasty and a genius. Her debaucheries were passed over, and the accolade of "the Great" was bestowed on the person considered second only to Peter as the organizer of the modern Russian state. This official view was also largely Catherine's view of herself, for no one worked harder at being, or at least appearing, brilliant, generous, and patriotic, as well as warmly human in her passions. Ambitious, oversexed, and able—Catherine was all these things.

In 1762 Catherine ascended the Russian throne over the dead body of her husband with the idea not so much of indulging herself as of ruling. Her true passion was government, and she was willing, unlike Elizabeth, to devote as many as twelve hours a day to state affairs, studying all the dispatches and petitions, conducting a tremendous correspondence, and acting, in effect, as her own minister in foreign affairs, economics, and everything else. The first moves were obvious: to rescind the most hated of Peter's acts, the war with Denmark and the confiscation of church wealth, while confirming the most popular act, the emancipation of the nobility. Rewarding her supporters was also clearly called for. From the Orlovs down to the common soldiers of the Guards there were handsome gifts of money, jewels, and estates, the total estimated to exceed half a million rubles. Panin was given important functions in the realm of diplomacy. Even old Bestuzhev was recalled from exile and loaded with honors, but though Catherine deferentially rose when her onetime mentor entered a room, she refrained from giving him any real power. The new empress was also generous with her enemies, keeping on Michael Vorontsov as chancellor and forgiving his daughter, Elizabeth, who was then married off to a senator and proved quite capable of bearing him the children denied to her lover, Peter III.

There was no mourning for the emperor, and Catherine's coronation—the date was set the day of the announcement of his death—speedily took place in Moscow in October, 1762. There were the traditional ceremonies at the Cathedral of the Assumption, but the magnificence of it all was unprecedented. Catherine was a born stage manager, and popular enthusiasm was at an unusually high pitch since the people were both relieved of a bad dream and excited by a new one. The coronation robes included an ermine coat made of 4,000 skins, and the new crown Catherine ordered contained four and a half pounds of gold and silver, 4,936 diamonds, several score huge pearls, with a surmounting 398-carat spinel ruby originally purchased by Tsar Alexis from a Manchu emperor. The day after the ceremony all four Orlov brothers were created counts and given appropriate jewels and medals.

Catherine's strength was in her ability to manage men, and her good fortune was that she was surrounded by many men, none of whom was strong enough to dominate her or to dispense with her. Soon after her accession the rumors of her impending marriage to Gregory Orlov provoked an officer named Khitrovo to plot the assassination of all the Orlovs. He was executed, even though he had been one of the staunchest movers of the empress' coup. This and other small mutinies among the power-conscious Guards regiments were treated unhysterically and usually secretly. Another crisis came when the frustrated Orlov boasted to Catherine before her coronation that he might dethrone her in "one or two months." This public outburst promptly drew the defiant reply of Cyril Razumovsky: "In that case we won't wait a month. We'll have you hanged in a fortnight." Yet but two years later, in 1764, it was Razumovsky's turn for comeuppance. As Hetman of the Ukraine, he sought to make his status hereditary and his domains semiautonomous, but Catherine had enough support to maneuver his resignation and eventual disgrace. Churchmen also discovered the limits to which they could assert themselves against the empress, whose accession they had helped so much. In 1764 Catherine boldly reversed herself and reinstated her husband's confiscation of church lands. The Archbishop of Rostov, who was so violent in his opposition as to call Catherine a heretic, found himself deposed and exiled for life under the name Andrew the Babbler.

Dynastic plots were also dealt with forcefully. An obscure officer tried in 1764 to seize Schlüsselburg Fortress in order to release and reenthrone Ivan VI, then a twenty-three-year-old wreck of a man mentally and physically. Ivan's guards followed standing orders in case of such an emergency and beat the hapless prisoner to death. His surviving brothers and sisters were kept in confinement until 1780, when Catherine allowed them to join relatives in Denmark.

Her own son was a rival to Catherine's power, especially after he had acquired years and knowledge of his history. In 1771 there was a plot to put the Grand Duke Paul on the throne. Again, there were men to rally to the empress' side, notably Orlov, who had discovered the conspiracy. Catherine got Paul's confession and forgave him. The empress had virtually no other relatives to distract her or to give her aid and comfort for that matter. Her mother had died of dropsy at the age of forty just before the accession of Peter III, after having lost Anhalt-Zerbst to Frederick of Prussia on the improbable grounds of her being a Russian agent and after having spent some fitfully grand years in Paris with a French noble for her lover. Catherine made efforts to pay her mother's huge debts, and she tried to secure the company of her brother, Frederick, a young officer in the Austrian army, who died soon afterward without her seeing him. From that time on, the empress forgot her German connections and assiduously fostered the image of being completely Russian.

In a very short period Catherine II revealed herself an astute manipulator of men in political affairs, but the fact remained that she desperately needed men in the physical and psychological sense. As she once wrote: "The trouble is my heart is loath to remain even one hour without love." Her craving for affection is explainable from her childhood, and her desire to be treated as a woman is entirely understandable in view of her first experiences with her husband. Beyond the loneliness and the femininity, however, was the factor of unusually strong physical appetites, a sensuality that made the three previous empresses pale by comparison. The nearest the professedly frank Catherine ever came to acknowledging her sheer animal desires was a story she told of herself as a girl, a story all the more revealing for its being told without regard to its implication: Many were the nights in her teens, the empress said, when she could not sleep but felt compelled to spend hours astride her pillow, galloping up and down the bed until she became exhausted.

Thirty-three at the time of her accession, Catherine faced few obstacles in satisfying her desires. She was not unattractive, although hardly the "dazzling" and "perfect" creature the ardent Poniatowski had worshipfully described a few years before. A detached view is offered by the empress' French secretary:

> One cannot say she is a beauty; her figure is tall and slender but not supple; she has a noble carriage, an affected and somewhat ungraceful walk, with a narrow chest, a long face, especially about the chin, an eternal smile on her lips, a deep-set mouth, a slightly aquiline nose, small eyes, an agreeable expression, and marked by smallpox. She is pretty rather than ugly but not so as to inspire violent feelings. Her height medium, rather thin.

The secretary mistakenly identified what were probably the aftereffects of chicken pox, for Catherine never had smallpox (although she is remembered for her courageous example in 1768 of being one of the first to submit to the novelty of vaccination during an epidemic). The eternal smile on Catherine's lips is a telling characterization, for she had long since been determined to make up in affability what she lacked in looks. Hers was a calculated effort to be pleasing, quite unlike the spontaneous warmth of the Empress Elizabeth.

In time Catherine was to enjoy the reputation of being the Messalina of the North, and her legend loomed only slightly larger than the reality. Her most famous paramour, Gregory Potemkin, once jealousy accused her of having fifteen lovers before himself, to which Catherine replied demurely that there were only five. As a girl barely in her teens, she had resisted the "passionate kisses," as well as the marriage proposal, of her young Uncle George, so that he did not count. "I took the first because I was compelled to," she explained, referring to her affair with Saltykov, a man she would never forgive for jilting her. As for the others, "God is my witness that it was not through wantonness for which I have no leanings." Catherine continued innocently, adding sanctimoniously that "had I been destined as a young woman to get a husband whom I could have loved, I would never have changed toward him." The empress' account did small justice to her second lover, Poniatowski, whose devotion never wavered. Knowing full well Poniatowski's ardor, Catherine was quick to write to him in Poland after her coup "not to hasten to come here." Yet she appreciated this cultivated aristocrat, and she casually kept up a correspondence with him. Then abruptly she came up with the project of having Poniatowski elected King of Poland, for her a politically promising move, not a romantic whim. This elicited a truly heartfelt response from the one completely unselfish man in Catherine's life: "Do not make me a king! Only call me back to you. . . . What is left to me? Emptiness and a frightful weariness of heart. Sophie, Sophie, you make me suffer terribly." Poniatowski, destined indeed to be king, not ingloriously but futilely, would have sacrificed any throne to marry Catherine, but she had her ambitions before her and Gregory Orlov at her side.

Easily pushing aside a nonentity who was number three, Catherine's fourth lover, Gregory Orlov, was the brave, brawny, brutish man who had saved her from collapsing in the hectic months of Elizabeth's dying and her husband's assuming rule. Fastidious aristocrats could only account Orlov's family background as preposterous in its nothingness. His first-known ancestor was that sergeant of the *streltsi,* Ivan Orel (Eagle), who escaped execution in 1798 by his show of bravado before Peter the Great. The ex-mutineer became an officer, and his son rose to the post of general and became governor of Novgorod, leaving a modest fortune to be rapidly squandered by his five sons—Ivan, Gregory, Alexis, Fedor, and Vladimir. The five were immensely clannish and fiercely loyal to one another, and they enjoyed a great reputation as reckless, and dissipated Guards officers, equally at home in taverns and salons, dance halls and boudoirs. The third brother, Alexis, was the most gifted, but he was less than handsome, being nicknamed Scarface, and he deferred to his brother Gregory where the Grand Duchess Catherine was concerned. The man most responsible for the murder of Peter III, Alexis lived on to amass one of the largest fortunes in Russia and served his empress well as the victorious admiral at the Battle of Chesme, Russia's greatest naval triumph to date (for this he earned the title Count Orlov-Cheminsky, but he left only a spinster daughter, who felt so guilty about her father's role in 1762 that she bequeathed all the money to a monastery).

Before becoming Catherine's lover, Gregory Orlov had made a name for himself as the best dancer in the army, as a heroic casualty at the Battle of Zorndorf, and as the man who seduced the mistress of his superior officer, Count Peter Shuvalov. Imposingly tall, Orlov was truly handsome. His portraits show superbly regular features and reveal his dreamy-eyed strength and smiling self-confidence. The devil-may-care officer became the brash and arrogant Count Orlov after his mistress' accession. Installed in apartments next to hers, he was often found in the early days of the reign sprawled on Catherine's sofa opening state documents and bawling orders to the servants to bring him refreshments.

Certainly Orlov hoped to marry the empress. One indication of how nearly this came to pass was the fact that Catherine tried to get Alexis Razumovsky to avow his secret marriage to the Empress Elizabeth and thus show a precedent. The opposition at court to such a marriage was too great, however, and so for ten years Orlov had only an unofficial status like that of a consort. "He lacks nothing but the title of Emperor," wrote the French chargé, "scorning etiquette he takes liberties with his sovereign in public which in polished society no self-respecting mistress permits her lover." Despite his equivocal position, the rewards were great—palaces, estates, countless decorations, and the privilege for him alone to wear the empress' portrait. There were three sons born to Orlov and Catherine. The first, who came in 1762 before her accession, was brought up in the palace quite openly acknowledged as their child; created Count Alexis Bobrinsky (after the name of one of his estates) by his half brother, the Emperor Paul, he left descendants, some of whom are living today. The two other children, born in 1763 and 1771, were suffered to lose themselves among the considerable number of royal protégés in the Corps of Cadets.

Orlov's intellect was too limited for him to play an important political role, although Catherine kept up the pretense of consulting him. He tried hard. Lomonosov was one beneficiary of Orlov's efforts to be a patron of learning. In 1765 Orlov organized a patriotic society, but some of its members became involved with projects to liberate the serfs, a situation which caused Catherine's displeasure, as did Orlov's attempts to correspond with Jean Jacques Rousseau. The count did show himself able to take charge courageously and intelligently in the Moscow smallpox epidemic of 1771.

The empress' break with Orlov came about because of his increasing unfaithfulness. His enemy Count Panin persuaded Catherine to break the increasingly complicated ties while Orlov was out of the country, committing blunder after blunder in peace negotiations with Turkey. A pretty young man named Alexander Vassilchikov was suddenly named aide-de-camp, given 100,000 rubles, and set up in Orlov's apartments. It did not take long for Orlov to come storming back to the capital, but he was kept virtually a prisoner at his Gatchina estate, ostensibly for reasons of quarantine which applied to all arrivals from the war zone. The empress went into a complete panic. All the locks on the palace doors were changed, armed guards were posted about, and she wailed to her courtiers that Orlov was capable of murder. Letters were sent telling Orlov to travel for his health and requesting her portrait back. He responded that he had never felt better and sent back only the jeweled casing of the portrait. Eventually, the count did present himself in the capital, but he was the picture of self-possession and indifference, joking about his fall from favor and even managing a condescending smile for Vassilchikov. Relieved, if not conscience-stricken, Catherine presented her ex-favorite with 6,000 serfs, a salary of 150,000 rubles, and a Sèvres dinner service valued at 250,000 rubles. To show that he was not mercenary, Orlov gave Catherine the celebrated 199-carat Orlov diamond, which cost him 460,000 rubles (it became the head of her golden scepter).

Thereafter, he did travel abroad restlessly and later married his second cousin, her ill health and early death adding to his woes. On his return to Russia, Orlov chose to play the man of moral virtue and the opponent of autocracy. Catherine continued to humor him. When the count died in

1783, Catherine wrote to the German philospher Frederick Melchior Grimm these strange words about her once-treasured brute: "a genius, extremely brave, strong, decisive, but as gentle as a lamb; he had the heart of a chicken." It is difficult to see how she rated the hero of war and coup as chickenhearted, unless, perhaps, she faulted Orlov for not completely dominating her, making her marry him, or at least taking her back forcibly.

Vassilchikov, who was number five among Catherine's lovers, turned out to be a sorry replacement for Orlov. Only his looks and his youth were in his favor. The empress, now in her forties, decided he was "an excellent but very boring citizen." A new favorite was already in the offing, however. It was to him that she had to confess the exact number of her affairs, as well as admitting her mistake with the foolish Vassilchikov. Sent on his travels for the usual reasons of health, Vassilchikov was to pout aloud that he was nothing more than a "kept woman," all the while counting his 100,000 rubles, 7,000 peasants, and a fortune in diamonds.

Gregory Potemkin was first known to Catherine as a twenty-three-year-old cavalry officer who played a role in the coup of 1762, legend having it that it was he who furnished the sword sash for her during the march on Peterhof. His name was duly noted in her letters, and at the coronation Potemkin was rewarded with 10,000 rubles and promotion, which went some way to compensate him for his previous life of dissipation and interrupted studies at Moscow University. As for family, Potemkin belonged to the lesser nobility of Smolensk Province, his first-known ancestor having served Tsar Alexis and his colonel father having had the distinction of being a bigamist. The youth who came to make a career in St. Petersburg was dark-haired, slim, a little too tall, not really handsome, but striking-looking. To Catherine he was a "veritable Alcibiades"—fiery, passionate, cultured, and supremely intelligent.

From the outset of her reign Catherine had dispensed with the elaborate entertainments of the Empress Elizabeth's day, pleading thrift, but actually the woman who could give away such huge sums so recklessly was bored by big parties. The new empress' preference was for intimate gatherings, informal but elegant, where the conversation was the glittering feature. At first, those invited were the friends of the Orlov brothers, and it was they who brought Potemkin into the circle. He had great wit and was so insolently bold as to imitate Catherine's German accent on their first encounter, provoking not displeasure, but her helpless laughter. It soon became obvious that Catherine was becoming strongly attracted to Potemkin's forceful personality, so obvious that the Orlov brothers turned against him, lured him to their house, and beat him half-dead. About this time Potemkin lost his right eye; some said it was a result of this brawl, although more likely it was because of a neglected abscess and a quack doctor.

Potemkin then left society and retired to a monastery for a year and a half, becoming so wrapped up in mysticism that he almost took orders. Timely inquiries from the empress persuaded him to return to the capital and assume important posts in the Holy Synod and at court. Then, in 1769, he impetuously volunteered for the Turkish War, and soon reports were coming from the south of what a brave, energetic, and able leader he was. It was at this point that Catherine sent him a letter that was virtually a proposal:

> You are so busy watching Silistria that you have no time to read letters. . . . I am sure that all you are doing is due to your devotion to myself and the beloved fatherland. But since I am most anxious to preserve zealous, courageous, intelligent, and skillful people, I beg you not to expose yourself to danger. . . . I am always your well wishing Catherine.

After Potemkin returned a hero to St. Petersburg, he became aide-de-camp in due course and much more, for Potemkin did not wish to be just a glorified playboy. Unlike Orlov, he was able to make himself genuinely powerful, and much of Catherine's greatness was really Potemkin's. When illness forced Panin to resign, Potemkin took over the direction of foreign affairs, bringing about territorial expansion in the south and supervising the founding of whole new cities. His final title was Prince of Taurida, in connection with the annexation of the Crimea. The Taurida Palace which Catherine had built for him became a major landmark in the area of St. Petersburg west of the Smolny Nunnery and was the seat of the state Duma after 1905. There were many great men in Catherine's time, but none enjoyed her confidence more than Potemkin.

The empress' love for Potemkin, ten years her senior, was based on a deep intellectual and psychological sympathy. By the time he became her lover, dissipation had wrecked Potemkin's looks, but he was still "the wittiest of men," in Catherine's words. Potemkin's jokes, like appearing in her dog's bedcover, made Catherine hysterical with laughter, and she relished his love poems, too. "She is crazy about him," wrote a senator. "They may well love each other for they are absolutely alike."

Catherine's and Potemkin's love letters numbered in the hundreds. They exchanged little notes all day long even if they were just a room or two apart. The list of nicknames she had for him was endless: Mr. Hero, My Golden Pheasant, Twin Soul, Daddy, Cossack, Lion in the Jungle, and, ironically, Your Serene Highness. There were numberless short notes like: "My pigeon, good morning. My dearest darling, I wish to know whether you slept well and whether you love me as much as I love you." Playfully, she might write: "General, do you love me? Me love General very much." She penned rambling effusions at seven in the morning, such as, "Oh, Mr. Potemkin, what a damned miracle you have performed in thus upsetting a head which heretofore was reputed in the world as one of the best in

Europe. It is time, high time, for me to become reasonable. What a shame! What a sin! Catherine II, to be a victim of this mad passion. . . ."

The empress' jottings revealed much about their relationship. For example, she pretended annoyance with Potemkin's sloppiness: "How much longer will you forget in my rooms things that belong to you! Please do not throw your handkerchiefs all over the place as is your Turkish fashion. Many thanks for your visit, and I love you a lot, a lot." There were complaints that Potemkin was indiscreet with the arrangements for taking baths together. Their illnesses were discussed casually, as in this instance: "My beloved soul, precious and unique, I can find no words to express my love for you. Do not be upset because of your diarrhoea—it will clean up the bowels well." Other notes were petulant and serious, as when Catherine waited for him in vain in the library or found Potemkin's door closed. Moodiness and melancholy were the lover's chief faults. Sometimes Catherine was imploring, as in: "Your Excellency has sulked yesterday all the evening, and I broken-hearted sought your caresses in vain and failed to get them." On occasion she could be acid, too: "If your silly ill temper has departed from you, kindly let me know. . . . [You] are a nasty Tatar." Hints of major lovers' quarrels are to be found also, as when once she wrote cajolingly: "No, my little Grishka, it is impossible for me to change as far as you are concerned. . . . Can anyone love anybody after having known you?" The theme of his jealousy is never long absent. What a scene must have preceded her writing the following: "Good morning, my heart. How are you? Darling, what a shame to have said what you said 'he who will take my place will not survive me.' What is the point of trying to keep a heart enslaved through fear? . . . Don't worry: some day I will probably bore you much more than you will ever bore me."

Late in 1774, a few months after their romance began, Catherine and Potemkin were probably married in secret. The wedding was said to have taken place in the St. Sampsonevsky Church in an unfashionable quarter of the capital, and the priest, the empress' maid, and two men were the only witnesses. A nephew of one of the men later asserted that the marriage certificates were buried in his uncle's coffin. Some confirmation of this is found in a strange dispatch sent by the French ambassador in 1787 noting Potemkin's lasting great influence: "The strange basis of his rights is a great mystery which is known only to four people in Russia: a happy chance has enabled me to discover it, and when I have fully ascertained it, I will inform the king by the first opportunity that presents itself." That this information was fit only for the ears of Louis XVI directly and not through his ministers is significant. Further confirmation is lent by Catherine's notes to Potemkin, for none of her subsequent lovers did she ever address as "dear husband" or sign as "your devoted wife." One revealing message read:

My master and tender spouse. . . . Why do you prefer to believe
your unhealthy imagination rather than the real facts, all of which confirm the words of your wife? Was she not attached to you two years
ago by holy ties? Have I since changed my attitude towards you? Have
confidence in my words, I love you and are bound to you by all possible
ties.

The Russian court was utterly astonished in 1776, when Catherine installed a new lover in Potemkin's place. Suprisingly, there were no scenes.
Most mystifying was that her little Grishka was not sent on his travels. Far
from being in disgrace, Potemkin not only continued on in his official work
but kept receiving every sign of deference and affection from the empress.
It became clear that only their sexual relationship had ended after two years;
Catherine's and his mutual adoration persisted. Why this happened was
ascribed to many things, all of which may have constituted the truth.
Potemkin was a confirmed debauchee, and he may have felt that his unfaithfulness combined with his temperamentality would eventually drive
Catherine from him and then deprive him of the political power he treasured above all else. The continual references in her letters to his jealousy
suggest that Catherine herself had a roving eye, and perhaps the gossips
were right to say that the forty-seven-year-old empress sought to satisfy
her ever-raging sensuality with younger men.

The most amazing part of the whole situation was not long to reveal
itself: Potemkin was playing pimp for his ex-mistress (or legal wife?). There
were to be fifteen more lovers for Catherine, as she entered her fifties and
sixties, and Potemkin was directly responsible for introducing her to all but
two. A story was spread around that the empress had a tester, as well as a
procurer. Rumor had it that her lady-in-waiting Countess Bruce not only
interviewed prospective favorites but also made them perform to her satisfaction, which presumably was that of her sovereign.

The succession of young men over the next twenty years went on efficiently and eventually, monotonously. They were mostly handsome speci-
mens in their twenties, a tribute to Catherine's taste, and all but one were
Russian, a mark of her patriotic wisdom, and they usually lasted less than
two years, a sign of her restlessness. Each in turn was installed in the continually refurbished apartments under hers in the Winter Palace, and each
was shown the winding staircase laid with green carpet (a decorative steal
from Louis XV and Madame Pompadour). To be dolls in constant attendance on the empress was all that was expected of these favorites; politics were for their betters. They had to be charming, ardent, but all the
while respectful, never showing Catherine any overfamiliarity in public
however obvious their positions were to everyone. When they were no
longer in favor, they were loaded with presents and sent abroad temporarily.
An amusing anecdote told of one new candidate meeting the old lover

descending the grand staircase. "What's new at court?" said the former, to which the other replied, "Nothing, except that you are going up and I am coming down."

Catherine aided the historian's task by writing letters to her European philosopher friends describing each favorite with fulsome pride. Any expressions of shock or disapproval were met with the disarming explanation that she was educating and polishing young men of potential to be useful civil servants. Indeed, Catherine was quite maternal with her protégés, as well as being infinitely patient and forbearing. Virtually all her gilded young men treated her meanly in one way or another.

Potemkin's chosen successor, Catherine's sixth lover, was a carefree Ukrainian named Peter Zavadovsky. This object of her unbridled passion lasted long enough to be portrayed with her on an icon specially painted for Mogilev Cathedral; his playing St. Michael to her St. Catherine is a prime exhibit in the Museum of Antireligious Propaganda in Leningrad today. After Zavadovsky came Zorich in 1777, a Yugoslav and middle-aged, and then Ivan Rimsky-Korsakov in 1778. By coincidence, this ancestor of the famous composer boasted a fine tenor voice, and Catherine even put up with that, but she could not tolerate his unfaithfulness.

Six lovers later, in 1780, Catherine took up with Alexander Lanskoy, a "house pet" who had been "educated" at the palace since early adolescence. Although rated the most ignorant of all by the court, this favorite seemed to stimulate all of the empress' motherly feelings, and, when he died tragically in 1783 from scarlet fever and angina pectoris, she wept for six months over the "child" she "hoped to be a support in my old age." To Grimm she wrote: "I drag myself about like a shadow. . . . I cannot set eyes on a human face without the tears choking my words."

There were to be two more lovers the year of Lanskoy's death. Ermolov, who was not a candidate of Potemkin's, was promptly driven out by the latter for trying to interfere in politics. In the public scene over this, Potemkin pointedly promised the empress to present her with better paramours. His selection was Alexis Dmitriev-Mamanov, whom he assigned to deliver to the empress a certain watercolor, causing her to write back to her pimp: "The outlines are good but the choice of colors is less felicitous." This meant that Mamanov's complexion needed attention. Unlike most of the empress' favorites, Mamanov had family pretensions: Genealogists disputed his family's Rurikovich claims but admitted their boyar status as early as the fifteenth century and an ancestor who secretly married the widow of Ivan V. Soon Catherine was writing that Mamanov was "beyond price." In return for Mamanov's makeup job, Catherine made changes, too, as revealed in this bemused commentary on their relationship: "We are clever as the very devil. . . . We adore music. We hide our fondness for poetry as though it were a crime." After six years and a countdom this aristocrat proved irresistible or unresistant to a girl his own age, and a furious, then sorrowful, Catherine made him marry her. Later, when Mamanov tried to renew his affair with the empress, she refused him.

2. Friend of the Philosophers

Catherine's favorites were an essential part of her life but were really not an important factor in her reign, other than the constructive uses to which she put ex-lovers like Potemkin. More telling than her love life was the fact that Catherine was the first educated Russian ruler. A recent historian has called her "the only articulate ideologist to rule Russia between Ivan IV and Lenin." Much of her schooling was self-education, and this she assiduously pursued throughout her life, continuing to read not as an epicure, but as a glutton and always annotating as she went. The weighty speculations of the ancients and of her contemporaries of the Enlightenment were her main fare. She was capable of plowing through the legal arguments of Blackstone's *Commentaries* and also the scientific data in Buffon's *Natural History*.

If not the genius her admirers saw, Catherine was intellectual, aware of the best culture of her day, and cleverly conscious of the value of this image. She was not merely a smiling patron of the arts and a fitful promoter of them, but a participant in them. The empress painted, sculpted, engraved, made cameos, and wrote fiction and history.

Her wish to bring Russia fully abreast with contemporary European standards was best symbolized in the architecture of her reign. Elizabeth's master builder Rastrelli was coldly dismissed, Catherine apparently agreeing with foreign estimates that his Baroque-*cum*-Russian palaces were slightly barbaric. Her favored architects, the Italian Quarenghi and the Scotsman Charles Cameron, were strictly Neo-classicists. A stately Hermitage was attached to the effusive Winter Palace, and a coldly symmetrical Institute for the Training of Daughters of the Nobility arose at Smolny next to the colorful nunnery. Tsarskoe Selo was endowed with numerous Greek-temple pavilions, while nearby at Pavlovsk vast new colonnaded structures were erected. The quantity, rather than the quality, of Catherine's building dominates St. Petersburg to this day: Immensely long government offices, palaces, and barracks arose everywhere. The ever-present white columns were usually set off by yellow walls, the only concession to Russian exuberance. While her predecessor's extravagance in architecture was largely for her personal pleasure, Catherine's ever greater outlays were a deliberate attempt to impress Europe. One project, never fulfilled, staggers the imagination: the Moscow Kremlin redone in Neoclassic style. The ancient cathedrals were to be kept but were to be lost in a geometric arrangement of colonnades, avenues, and circles. The whole south wall of the Kremlin with its towers, part of which was torn down in anticipation, was to emerge as a huge façade of columns more than 2,000 feet long. When Catherine no longer needed to show Europe that Russia was not suffering financially despite the war with Turkey, she blithely announced that the soil of the Kremlin hill would not support her grandiose project. In the end, there was erected only the triangular, columned Senate Building east and north of the flamboyant Saviour's Gate (today it houses the offices of the top Soviet leaders).

Literature too flourished under Catherine. In terms of just numbers of books published, the yearly rate was up from 36 titles in the last year of Peter's reign to 366 in hers. The poet Gabriel Derzhavin was just one of several who received Catherine's patronage and far outdistanced their predecessors in the previous reigns. The empress herself played a leading role in the founding of the first satirical journal, *All Kinds of Things,* and made contributions. Journalism in general, barely begun under Peter the Great and pioneered by Sumarakov under Elizabeth, developed rapidly, the leading light to emerge in this field being Nicholas Novikov, editor of *The Drone* and *The Painter* in the 1770's. Novikov's publishing activities, including translations of Voltaire, Diderot, and Rousseau, may be said to have formed the Russian reading public. Above all, playwriting was encouraged, for Catherine was not only an ardent theatergoer but also a dramatist on paper, as well as in life. In time, Novikov and the native writers he sponsored had to be curbed, for their satires bit too deep. For Catherine, novels and plays were meant to be instructive and enjoyable, but not upsetting.

What *did* the empress expect when she went to a play? Presumably, she made this clear in what she wrote herself.

O TEMPORA

ACT I, SCENE I. MR. SENSIBLE, MAVRA

Mavra. Believe me, I am telling you the truth. You cannot see her. She is praying now, and I dare not go into her room myself.

Sensible. Does she really pray all day long? No matter what time I come, I am told I cannot see her: she was this morning at matins, and now she is praying again.

Mavra. That is the way our time is passed.

Sensible. It is good to pray. But there are also duties in our life, which we are obliged to carry out. Do you mean to tell me that she prays day and night?

Mavra. No. Our exercises are often changed, yet all goes in a certain order. Sometimes we have simple services; at others they read the

Monthly Readings; at others again the reading is omitted, and our lady gives us a sermon on prayer, abstinence, and fasting.

Sensible. I have heard it said that your lady is very sanctimonious, but I have not heard much about her virtues.

Mavra. To tell the truth, I cannot say much about that either. She very often speaks to her servants on abstinence and fasting, especially when she distributes the monthly allowances. She never shows so much earnestness in praying as when creditors come and ask to be paid for goods taken on credit. She once hurled the prayer-book so violently at my head that she hurt me and I was compelled to lie in bed for nearly a week. And why? Because I came during vesper service to report that the merchant had come to ask for his money which he had loaned her at six per cent, and which she had loaned out again at sixteen. "Accursed one," she cried to me, "is this a time to disturb me? You have come, like Satan, to tempt me with worldly affairs at a time when all my thoughts are given to repentance and are removed from all cares of this world." . . .

Sensible. I am glad to find out about her habits. This knowledge will help me a great deal in the matter of Mr. Milksop's marriage. . . .

The sheer volume of her own writings is impressive. Her *Memoirs* are revealing history, despite all the white lies, unanswered questions, and exaggerations in the way of self-justification. Clearly Catherine wrote them to try to understand herself more than to impress others. Other writing projects were no less striking for their incompleteness. Interest in the early annals of Russia led the empress to attempt her own historical compendium, the main result of which was simply the useful concentration of source materials. Another wildly ambitious undertaking was a comparative dictionary of all the languages of the world. The occasion for this great amassing of notes was Catherine's genuine bereavement over the death of her "house pet" Lanskoy.

Catherine was notable for her correspondence. The letters poured out to Potemkin, to her diplomats, to her generals, and to the best minds in Europe. In twenty years there were 180 letters to Frederick the Great of Prussia, not solely in the way of diplomatic negotiation but teeming with observations on life in general. Even Gustavus III of Sweden, the empress' constant enemy in diplomacy and war, was the recipient of many thoughtful notes, while out of the other side of her mouth Catherine mercilessly lampooned him in her plays.

It was, however, Catherine's correspondence with the philosophers of the Enlightenment on which she staked her reputation, deliberately and by and large successfully. Again, it was made evident that she was not merely the patron of these celebrities, but one of them. A measure of her triumph in this role is that the German critic Grimm playfully revised the familiar religious formulas to "Our Mother, who art in Russia" and "I believe in one Catherine."

Although Grimm was the empress' most unflagging correspondent and twice a visitor to Petersburg, it was Voltaire whom she courted most earnestly, plying him with letters at once so respectful and so clever as to leave him no choice but to reply in kind. They developed into a kind of mutual admiration society of two. The empress wrote that "if I possess any knowledge I owe it to you alone," while Voltaire was capable of such effusions as "There is no God but Allah, and Catherine is the prophet of Allah," and on occasion he signed himself "the priest of your temple." Catherine heaped gifts on her friend, and he in turn built up her legend throughout Europe as the most liberal and just of rulers. Amid all the flattery there were lies and much that hardly could be taken seriously. Straight-faced, the empress reassured Voltaire that in Russia "every peasant has a turkey in his pot" and that people died not from hunger, but from overeating. The philosopher could blithely explain that the Russian rape of Poland and the assaults on Turkey were the victory of religious tolerance over fanaticism. To keep up her admirer's illusions, Catherine opposed his coming to Petersburg, as he suggested in 1778. "For God's sake advise the octogenarian to remain in Paris . . . ," she addressed Grimm. "He would die . . . of cold. Tell him that Cateau [Catherine] is best known from a distance." Catherine's grief at Voltaire's death was genuine, but she showed that she had missed the point when she referred to him as "the mirth and spirit" of "good humor" and "the god of pleasure."

Another of the empress' philosopher correspondents was the Encyclopedist Denis Diderot, who likewise was so enthralled by her attentions that he could unsmilingly describe her as a combination of Brutus and Cleopatra. Diderot paid her the supreme compliment of visiting St. Petersburg in 1773, causing Voltaire in jealous pique to send her his "last will" and a good-bye, soon retracted. The house at which Diderot stayed is still preserved. The personal encounter was a fiasco: Catherine was offended by the peppery Frenchman's tapping her on her knee and rasping "my good woman" as he expounded on the rights of man. There were later embarrassing questions about the real state of the people, and finally, Catherine was driven to derogate her critical admirer in a letter saying: "You work only on paper, which suffers all, while I, a poor Empress, I work in human skins, which are a great deal more irritable and ticklish." The bookman revenged himself with acid observations about Catherine's self-satisfaction.

Was Catherine's enlightenment just talk? In the final analysis there was fakery or at least gross self-deception in the autocratic woman who had once written: "Liberty, soul of things, without you all is dead." At the beginning of her reign, however, Catherine did seem to promise great things. For example, a worthy accomplishment was her aiding the foundation of a Free Economic Society in 1765, putting Russia abreast of Britain and France in this respect. Yet the first-prize essay of the society was banned from publication: It advocated the elimination of serfdom.

Seemingly the most revolutionary and certainly the most publicized of the new empress' undertakings was the calling of the Great Commission in 1766 to revise the law code dating from Alexis' time. Here was a shining opportunity for Catherine to display her liberalism. She spent a year and a half just drawing up her directions for the delegates, and the resulting *nakaz* was, indeed, celebrated, being considered so extreme by the French government that it was banned in that country. "Your genius conceived it, your pretty hand wrote it," purred Voltaire. The *nakaz* consisted mainly of formulas and aphorisms lifted directly from the writers of the Enlightenment, about half, for example, deriving from Montesquieu's *Spirit of the Laws* and one-sixth from Beccaria's *On Crimes and Punishments*. The *nakaz* was not all naïvely radical. For instance, the empress found it convenient to borrow from Montesquieu this prescription: "The extent of the empire dictates absolute power in the ruler." Nonetheless, Catherine's other observations on penal codes, on the inequities of serfdom, and on the need for universal education were startling enough to induce her advisers to modify or omit many of them. She insisted on keeping intact one pronouncement with subversive potential: that citizens (a radical word in itself for Russia) should be convinced of their "interest," as well as their "duty," to preserve the laws.

The Great Commission sat during the years from 1766 to 1768. Its 564 members were almost exclusively gentry, officials, and rich merchants, with the clergy largely excluded from representation, as well as the enserfed majority of the population. Out of the cumbersome procedures and ceremonious talk it soon became apparent that the delegates were concerned only for more rights and privileges for themselves. Catherine prodded them in vain with daily new instructions, and finally, she prompted one of her admirers to open a debate on serfdom, which proved noisily inconclusive. Later a small group of delegates began to advocate reorganization of the state on a constitutional basis as in Britain, and now it was the empress' turn to retreat. The Great Commission was prorogued in 1768, with subcommittees continuing to function for six more years. No new law code resulted, although Catherine did announce that she had gained valuable materials. The empress could well lay the blame on the apathy of the delegates, but her leadership had faltered, too. The whole thing was playacting on her part, in effect, if not in intent. Soon afterward a new portrait of Catherine as "Legislator" was executed by Dmitri Levitsky; she stood smirking with flowing classical robes hiding her no longer trim figure and her still delicate hand pointing to a pile of scrolls. The departing commission had already bestowed on her the title Catherine the Wise.

3. Bringer of Victory

The excuse for proroguing the Great Commission was the outbreak of war with Turkey, and this juxtaposition well illustrated the greatest paradox of Catherine's reign. "Peace is essential to this vast empire," wrote Catherine before her accession, and the later manifestos continued to give priority to internal reform. Yet there was continual war and tremendous aggrandizement under this empress; more than anything the military victories and annexations earned her the title the Great. Statistically, Catherine was responsible for fresh territorial gains amounting to a quarter of the area of Europe, and she thereby raised the number of her taxpaying subjects to 36,000,000, putting Russia well ahead of disunited Germany's 26,000,000 or aggressive France's 25,000,000. The Russian army and navy both were doubled.

The empress once said that her métier was administration, but more precisely Catherine's great talent was diplomacy. She was a master at it, having a great head for detail, an ability to manipulate men, and an instinct for showmanship which often enabled her to fool all Europe about the realities of Russia's position. In an era of shameless power politics, she never let womanly scruples get in her way, for she had by her own admission "a mind infinitely more masculine than feminine."

The difficult situation Catherine inherited was the Seven Years' War, in which Russia had intervened on the French-Austrian side under Elizabeth only to end up on the Prussian-British side under Peter III. The empress succeeded in disentangling her armies, playing both sides against each other, and ending up as all-powerful mediator when the conflict ended in 1763. Within the year Catherine was able to place her man on the throne of Courland, small but strategic, resurrecting the former duke, Biren, for this purpose.

Another throne became vacant in 1763, Poland's, and once again Catherine was able to have her way. In alliance with Frederick of Prussia, she declared her candidate to be her former lover Poniatowski, and forthwith Russian troops brought about his unanimous election. To calm Polish fears that the new king might marry the Russian empress, Poniatowski was made to promise that he would wed only a Catholic and preferably a Pole. In the end, the man who considered himself wretched in his love for Catherine never did marry, although he eventually, and apologetically, took himself a mistress, whom he installed in a modest cottage near the tasteful Belvedere Palace he built outside Warsaw (in the 1960's the site of periodic talks between the United States and Red China).

The complete destruction of Poland was in the offing, and Poniatowski was unable to do anything about it. Concerted national action was still paralyzed by feudal hangovers which Russian diplomacy supported in the name of traditional "Polish liberties." At length complicated diplomatic maneuvers led to the so-called First Partition of Poland in 1772, whereby huge chunks of the kingdom were simply appropriated by Poland's neighbors—Russia, Prussia, and Austria. A famous political cartoon of the period showed Catherine the Great, Frederick the Great, and Maria Theresa gleefully carving up the map. Actually, Maria Theresa was said to have wept over the sheer outrageousness of what they were doing, but, as Catherine observed, "she kept on taking."

Two more partitions of Poland followed in 1793 and 1795, until the entire country was gobbled up. Just before the end there had been a great patriotic movement led not by the king, but by General Thaddeus Kosciusko, veteran of the War of the American Revolution. In the final uprising his armies were no match for the huge Russian force fielded by the empress to punish the Poles for trying to be effectively independent. "Freedom shrieked when Kosciusko fell," wrote an English poet. The Partitions of Poland were the most flagrant crimes of the eighteenth century in the name of power politics, and Catherine was their prime mover. Now the Romanovs had a Polish problem to their last days.

Catherine's extravagant forward policy in the west was matched by the one in the south. In 1768 the presence of Russian armies in southern Poland alarmed the sultan into declaring hostilities, and the ensuing Russo-Turkish War lasted until 1774. The victories won by the empress' commanders were fantastic, both surprising and alarming a Europe that remembered Golitsyn's farcical campaigns against the Crimea only eighty years before and Peter's near disaster on the Pruth sixty years previously. The defeat of the Turks in the Crimea was child's play this time for Prince Dolgoruky, and in the Balkans, Russian armies reached well beyond the Pruth to the Danube itself (for the first time since Sviatoslav in the eleventh century, as Catherine the historian noted). Out of this campaign emerged some of the greatest Russian generals: Rumyantsev, the commander Elizabeth appointed too late in the Seven Years' War, covered himself with glory; Alexander Suvorov began the career that was to make him the greatest of national heroes; and General Gregory Potemkin deservedly received the empress' renewed attention. To the military exploits were added the naval efforts of Alexis Orlov, who brought a Russian fleet into the Mediterranean and presided over a victory against the Turks at Chesme that would have made the great Peter envious. The final peace treaty of Kuchuk Kainarji in 1774 was a huge triumph for Catherine and her diplomats, more than matching the work of her generals and admirals. Russia gained tremendous amounts of land all along the northern coasts of the Black Sea, giving her outlets on this waterway fully as significant as Peter's Baltic window on the West.

Russian foreign policy made itself felt throughout Europe. The clash between Austria and Prussia in 1778 known as the War of the Bavarian Succession ended after Catherine's gracious and successful mediation. Less to her real benefit was the empress' organization of the Armed Neutrality of the North in 1780, an effort to coerce England during the War of the American Revolution. Actually, the American Declaration of Independence of 1776 had greatly shocked the increasingly conservative Catherine, but she allied herself with the anti-British, avoiding actual hostilities, however.

In the 1780's Catherine promoted her incredibly bold Greek Project which called for nothing less than the complete destruction and partition of the Ottoman Empire. Her ambition was to have a Romanov prince ruling at Constantinople, and she struck medals to that effect and had her second grandson christened Constantine. This project necessitated the cooperation of Austria, and there was intense correspondence with Joseph II of the Holy Roman Empire, who also paid Catherine the signal compliment of making a state visit to St. Petersburg, the first ever by a major European ruler. Rivalries and jealousies prevailed between Russia and her needed allies, and the Greek Project was stillborn. In 1783, however, Potemkin annexed the whole Crimea, the local khan treacherously handing over this domain in return for Russian money and a title. The same year Russia declared a protectorate over the Christian state of Georgia in the Caucasus.

Catherine's famous grand tour of the new southern lands occurred in 1787. The impresario was Potemkin, and he was perhaps overzealous in trying to dazzle Catherine, the court, and the foreign ambassadors. Thousands of peasants were hastily transported hundreds of miles to provide local populations, and new villages proudly displayed in the distance turned out to be one-plane, movie-set constructions. Europe snickered, and "Potemkin village" became a Russian idiom for shame. Catherine's great minister got the undeserved reputation of being a charlatan, for the solid achievements were there or soon forthcoming—new roads and canals, whole new settled areas, and huge new cities, such as the great naval base at Sevastopol and later the teeming port of Odessa. The empress had much reason for self-satisfaction, when she visited or read about a whole new series of cities named for her—Ekaterinburg, Ekaterinoslav, Ekaterinodar, and so forth.

A second war with Turkey was fought from 1787 to 1792, during which Gustavus III of Sweden futilely tried to revenge himself on the successor of Peter the Great by carrying on hostilities in the north. Once again in the Balkans, Rumyantsev, Suvorov, and Potemkin presented Catherine with smart victories and handsome trophies. By the Peace of Jassy Russia acquired another large chunk of land on the Black Sea. This, followed by the final two Partitions of Poland, finished out the picture of Catherine as seemingly invincible, ever-victorious, and "Great."

All this aggrandizement looked good on paper. Some of the expansion was the natural seeking of sea outlets and the filling out of ethnic frontiers. But what was to do permanent damage to the orderly development of the Russian nation was that under Catherine the regime began to take on the problems of large alien populations, with different languages, religions, and social structures, just at a time when Russia's internal structure was being questioned in revolutionary ways. A celebrated historian once compared the Russian bear of this and later eras to a giant, staggering with one leg into new difficulties while the other leg sank deeper and deeper into the morass of old inequities. Perhaps the metaphor should be extended to place the bear's head in a hornet's nest as well, for, insofar as Russia came into closer geographic contact with the advanced West, it exposed itself to the most subversive ideologies—Rousseau in Catherine's day, Marx a century later.

4. Bringer of Order

Just when her generals were winning their first battles, Catherine found herself confronted with an unforeseen and desperate problem: Her husband, Peter III, was back—in a sense—and a great revolt was under way. The elements of mass discontent and mob hysteria were never far below the surface in Romanov Russia. The memories of Bolotnikov and Stenka Razin never died.

Russian tradition is rich in royal pretenders, and with a woman and a usurper on the throne it was inevitable that "lost princes" reappeared. In the first decade of Catherine's reign there were several bogus Ivan VI's and at least six Peter III's, some cropping up in various parts of Russia and some abroad, even as far away as Japan. Catherine's government rounded them up one by one, sentencing them to knouting or to the mines or occasionally pardoning them as harmless. One of the most melodramatic cases of a pretender was that of Princess Tarakova, who claimed to be the child of the Empress Elizabeth and Razumovsky. She advanced her pretensions from the safety of Ragusa (Dubrovnik) on the Adriatic, and it required not only a visit of a Russian naval squadron but Alexis Orlov's coming ashore and pretending to fall in love with her before the princess was lured away to Russia and prison.

The "Peter III" who appeared in May, 1773, soon lead an insurrection covering almost all of eastern and southeastern Russia. In actuality, the man was named Emilian Pugachev, he was a Don Cossack, and he had seen military service in both the Seven Years' War and the First Turkish War. While a fugitive from justice hiding at a monastery, he was persuaded by an Old Believer priest to declare himself the recently deposed tsar come back to life. The standard of revolt was raised among the Cossacks. It did not matter that Pugachev did not faintly resemble Peter III; he was stocky and solid, unlike the slim, narrow-shouldered tsar. "We can make a prince out of a turd," his followers were to boast. Later Pugachev did bring around old soldiers to attest to his authenticity, he carefully publicized his fatherly affection for the Grand Duke Paul, and he went to the trouble of setting up a court peopled with ministers named Panin, Orlov, and so forth. Pugachev saw the popular appeal of his royal pretense, and he was as good an actor as he was a liar. Moreover, he was fearless, energetic, and utterly compelling as a handler of crowds.

St. Petersburg shrugged off the first news of Pugachev in June, 1773, but alarm grew when the Cossack leader besieged Orenburg and captured Samara and other towns on the Volga. Prince Alexander Golitsyn twice defeated Pugachev's forces, but then the revolt shifted to the middle Volga and by the winter of 1773–74 a rebel army of 15,000 was threatening Moscow from only 100 miles away. What had started as a narrowly Cossack escapade had become a broad social rebellion. "Peter III" declared Catherine a usurper and the nobility "debasers of our power." Anti-landowner hatred became an orgy of burnings and rape, and the popular frenzy was so intense that Pugachev himself had to give up a noble widow he had attached to him and let her be hacked to pieces. Priests were also killed wholesale, not out of antireligious feelings, but in the name of the restoration of the old faith and such outward symbols as beards. The combination of a Cossack revolt and a serf insurrection amounted to an upheaval from beyond and from below, likened by one historian to a joint uprising of American Indians and Negro slaves. The insurrection boasted no great revolutionary army but involved widely scattered disturbances— a terrifying fact in itself.

None of the Russian gentry gave support to Pugachev, and this fact differentiated the situation from the Time of Troubles. The nobility in 1773–74 to a man opposed the "emancipator," but most of them did not fight him: They panicked and fled to the capitals. One of Catherine's generals, Bibikov, had nothing but contempt for these aristocrats who were not only cowardly but also so blind, incompetent, corrupt, greedy, and generally so wicked in their past actions as to arouse the universal hatred of the people.

The revolt had become so widespread that many in the court despaired, but not Catherine, who was dissuaded only with some difficulty from going to Moscow. As usual, she kept up a brave front for her European correspondents, even joking about "le Marquis de Pugachev" in a letter to Voltaire, all the while the "enlightened" empress was desperately writing her generals: "Hurry up and exterminate these criminals who disgrace us in the eyes of the world."

Pugachev's cause was hurt badly in 1774 by the coming of famine and by the release of the Russian army from the Turkish War. General Peter Panin, brother of the foreign minister, defeated the rebel forces in two pitched battles, after which Pugachev had to fall back on the Urals. It devolved on General Suvorov, commanding 300 mounted infantrymen and pushing them at the rate of 60 miles a day, to track down the heroic Cossack with the remnants of his followers and to bring him back to Moscow in a cage. The empress forbade torture before his trial. Subsequently, "Peter III" was quartered and executed in January, 1775, just a few months after his putative wife may have married Potemkin. Pugachev freely confessed to having committed a great "sin" against Russia and God and went to his death without any of the bravado that characterized the end of his nearest rival in the annals of great Russian rebels, Stenka Razin.

The ensuing repression was as ferocious as the revolt itself. Mass executions revenged the lynched landlords and priests. Catherine never showed that she really understood the underlying causes of the explosion, the nobility went back to their estates in undeserved triumph, and even such talk of reform as there had been before was now dropped. One change to come out of the Pugachev insurrection was of great and lasting importance. The Don Cossacks were given a special status in which they incurred military service in return for lands and other privileges. From being the plague of the Romanov tsars the Don Cossacks became the staunchest and ever-present upholders of the autocracy right down to the first street fighting in the capital in March, 1917.

Before she came to power, Catherine was capable of voicing the prediction that social catastrophe was unavoidable if nothing was done about serfdom. As empress she did not entirely blind herself to the terrible abuses the system generated, but she still turned out to be the autocrat whose actions extended the serf system to new peaks. Serfdom was introduced in huge areas where it did not exist before, notably in the Ukraine in 1764, affecting several million people and reducing the number of free peasants in Russia to insignificance. The confiscation of the church lands in 1764 meant giving more than 1,000,000 serfs to the nobility. Catherine was more than generous in handing out crown lands with their inhabitants to her favorites. Nor did the empress make any effort to mitigate the state burdens imposed on private serfs. How else but through tax money was Catherine able to send Diderot jeweled snuffboxes?

The kinds of abuses perpetrated on the masses multiplied during Catherine's reign as high society indulged itself and gambled the evenings away. The tastes of the absentee landowners required heavier exactions of money, produce, and labor from the serfs they never saw. The whims of the nobility also produced some bizarre requirements of their servants: Count Paul Skavronsky ordered all his butlers, footmen, and maids always to speak only in recitative; another lord trained a whole company of serf girls as ballet dancers and had them dance in the nude. In the end it counted little that a serf was a talented dancer, actor, architect, or scientist.

The people's only recourse was murder and arson, and these acts of violence were ordinary before and after major outbursts like Pugachev's. For every landlord killed for his economic impositions, there were ten done in for abuses with serf women, according to a social critic of the next century. The severest punishments were dealt out to the thousands of recalcitrants among the masses. Yet in all of Catherine's reign there were only twenty cases of landowners' being penalized for wicked actions. To make the system shockingly farcical, an edict appeared in 1767—a year of the Great Commission—providing that serfs who registered protests against mistreatment either individually or in concert were to be condemned to hard labor.

Originally placed on the throne by them, Catherine never went against the interests of the Russian nobility, even after she had acquired all the power and prestige of military success and longevity. Yet it could not be said that Catherine was a mere puppet: She was an autocrat. Just as jealously as a born Romanov, she guarded the inviolability of absolutism against the aspirations of some of the progressive nobility, like Panin and Prince Sheherbatov, to limit the sovereign through a constitution.

Although any thoughts of grand reform were abandoned and although the central governmental institutions remained unchanged under Catherine, the empress did set about making some partial improvements. The foundling hospitals in both capitals, the St. Petersburg public library, the Smolny Institute for the Training of Daughters of the Nobility, and the College of Medicine all were founded early in her reign. Perhaps her most notable legislation was the Charter of Nobility and the Charter of Towns granted in 1785. The former established a system of class self-government under elected marshals of the nobility at both the district and the provincial levels, meeting one of the main demands raised at the Great Commission. The Charter of Towns, based on the municipal traditions of the conquered Baltic cities, gave the Russian urban centers institutions of self-government, but cumbersome elective procedures, apathy, and the continuing wont of the central authorities to interfere meant that the new system was chaotic and often existed only on paper.

In 1779, about midway through her reign, Catherine already could boastfully list for Grimm's benefit:

Governments established according to the new pattern	29
Towns constructed	144
Treaties concluded	30
Victories	78
Memorable laws and edicts	88
Edicts for improving the life of the people	123
	492

"Governments" referred to the standardization of provincial administration. The new cities were genuine achievements, not merely Potemkin villages. As for "edicts to improve the lot of the people," Catherine was obviously thinking not of the serfs but of general economic measures to increase Russian prosperity. Great national prosperity there *was* in terms of output, trade statistics, and the size of the government's budget. A particular case of Catherine's farsightedness in economic affairs was the encouragement of immigration. So many Germans were invited in by their countrywoman that an extensive autonomous German region was created on the far banks of the lower Volga River.

In sum, Catherine had many reasons to be pleased with herself as an administrator. Pugachev was defeated and conveniently forgotten, by nice people at least. The nobility would long remember the empress as the bringer of stability, justice, and well-being, their own anyhow.

5. Grande Dame

In 1789 Catherine became sixty. That was also the year of the French Revolution, and she found that she had nothing but contempt and horror for the logical extension of the ideas of her once-beloved French philosophers. At the same time she was to take the last and most unsettling of her lovers. She was all-powerful but disillusioned. She was "great" but somewhat helpless in the hands of a young social climber. She was Olympian, compelling, and slightly comic—a *grande dame*.

There were countless portraits done of Catherine II, and to study them is to review an eventful life. The original was the portrait of her as Princess Sophia of Anhalt-Zerbst. A double portrait with her husband, the Grand Duke Peter, followed. A charming picture of her on horseback painted by Groot in 1745 shows a young huntress somewhat pinch-faced and fragile-looking but all the while pert and self-assured. A completely different Catherine came forth on canvas by an unknown in early 1762: She was in mourning for Elizabeth; she was pregnant with Orlov's child; and she had grave doubts about her future. After her coup later the same year she was painted on horseback again, this time looking triumphant in the uniform of the Preobrazhenskoe Guards. Still as of 1762, one of the finest portraits of her was executed by a Dutch painter for her coronation: It contained two images of her dressed in shimmering white and blue, the front face revealing the intelligent, inquiring, amiable woman of thirty-three while the profile is utterly regal and commanding. The pictures multiplied: a dramatically lighted Catherine poring over her books; Catherine walking her dog at Tsarskoe Selo and looking somewhat rustic; and the huge Levitsky effort depicting her as the self-satisfied legislator. A particularly striking representation of her was done on the occasion of her grand journey to the Ukraine in 1787: She is wearing a large black hat and a red, embroidered traveling tunic; the gaze is steady and confident. It is a perfect portrait of a crafty old grandmother. Paintings lie somewhat, of course. An observer of Catherine's last years noted that her "unclouded" and "tranquil" countenance was instantly "discomposed" when she opened her now-toothless mouth.

To the last Catherine was completely devoted to her métier. She combined a German methodicalness with a typically Russian habit of working in great bursts of energy, sometimes putting in as many as fifteen hours a day. Often she arose at five in the morning and lit her own fire, since she was kind and sensibly understanding in the treatment of her servants. The anecdote got around that once the old lady found her four footmen playing cards when she needed a document sent somewhere; forthwith the autocrat of Russia filled in as a fourth until the messenger returned. Walking in her gardens or in the Hermitage galleries (reserved for her and the mice) remained favorite pastimes, and she continued her reading and creative pursuits. Big entertainments still pleased her less than good conversation, although she was capable of staging the most magnificent spectacles if public relations required it. Like Peter the Great, she was a confirmed traveler (a trip to the Volga she once described as worth ten years of ideas), but unlike him, she never left Russia in fifty-two years.

Catherine was very much the overly concerned and interfering grandparent, having been less than a good mother, in part because she lacked the opportunity, as well as the inclination. The Grand Duke Paul, who reached the age of thirty-five in 1789, was afraid of his mother, and she was only too happy to keep this rival at a distance. She doted, however, on his first two sons, the Grand Duke Alexander and the Grand Duke

Constantine and virtually took them away from their parents, repeating just what Elizabeth had done to her.

When Catherine's twentieth lover, Mamanov, proved unfaithful to her in 1789, the court was hardly surprised that the old sensualist took up with her twenty-first. "I have come back to life like a frozen fly," wrote the empress in her delight with Platon Zubov, a twenty-two-year-old who was another of the "house pets" reared since early youth in the palace. A member of the court was less impressed with Zubov, describing him as a child with good manners and little brains and predicting wrongly that he would not last long—Zubov turned out to be an ambitious and unscrupulous political schemer, and alternating affection with unreasonableness, he acquired a hold over the aging Catherine out of all proportion to his limited talents. Among other things, Zubov interfered witlessly in Polish affairs, tried to gain a Persian domain for his brother, and maneuvered for himself the title Prince of the Holy Roman Empire.

Potemkin, for a change, had nothing to do with the choice of Zubov, and less than two years after the contemptible affair began he suddenly died. Catherine's grief was deeply felt, so much so that she ordered months of mourning and would not even see her grandchildren. "I have had a terrible blow," she wrote Grimm; "my pupil, my friend, almost my idol, died in Moldavia." She refrained only from calling him "husband."

Potemkin's death and Zubov's demandingness came at a time when the empress had to deal with the reality and specter that were the French Revolution. To one correspondent she announced: "I shall remain an aristocrat, that is my metier." She could find no sympathy for the constitutions and reforms any more than for the mob excesses. The members of the French National Assembly were described by her as Pugachevs or alternately "puppets of a few bandits who do not even deserve the title of illustrious criminals." With hurt and hauteur she now confronted the long-patient Grimm with the words: "I am awaiting the time when it will please you to exonerate in my mind those philosophers and others who have taken part in the revolution." To the paradox of forgotten liberalism she added the irony of great horror at the murder of an anointed king, when Louis XVI was executed in January, 1793.

The empress did not confine her new turn of thinking to her international correspondence. The measures of political reaction at home were swift and far-reaching, as were related moves in foreign policy. The journalist Novikov, whose publications had been already subjected to severe censorship during the 1780's, was arrested in 1791 and sentenced without trial to Schlüsselburg for fifteen years. Other suspected liberals were also arrested or exiled to their estates. With relentless zeal Catherine had Voltaire and others of the Enlightenment put on the index of forbidden books, and she even banned her own *nakaz*. The most spectacular single event of this reaction was the empress' persecution of the writer Alexander Radishchev, who had the great gifts and the great nerve to publish in 1790 a volume called *A Journey from Petersburg to Moscow*. A classic achievement in Russian literature, Radishchev's work described in persuasive detail and with great conviction what a horrible evil serfdom was. "Worse than Pugachev" was the empress' personal review of the book, which was ordered banned. Its author was sentenced to exile in Siberia after the original death sentence was withdrawn. Still another general feature of the complete turn against liberalism was the renewal of religious persecution in the 1790's; once again dissenters were charged with heresy and treason. The Freemasons suffered most, for the empress not only considered them radicals but specifically feared their hold on the Grand Duke Paul.

Lily-white in his legitimacy but without decisiveness, France's Louis XVI in his last plight had received financial aid from Russia's Catherine, the strong-willed upstart. After the Terror, the empress welcomed the *émigrés* to her domains, not without careful screening of them, and their presence fortified the backward-looking thinking of the court. It was a French aristocrat, the Duke of Richelieu, who brought about the founding of Odessa in 1795. Catherine's forceful diplomacy was decisive in organizing the First Coalition against revolutionary France in 1792–93, but at first she was content to let her allies—Prussia, Austria, and Britain —do the fighting. Cynics saw her policy as a means of diverting the rest of Europe while Russia gobbled up the remnants of independent Poland in 1793 and 1795. Catherine rationalized that the Poles were the "Jacobins of the East." It became apparent in time, however, that the common cause against revolution had suffered from Russia's nonparticipation. When French armies, already over the Rhine and over the Alps, threatened to strike far into central Europe, Catherine contemplated drastic action and Suvorov was ordered to march with an army of 60,000 to northern Italy.

Catherine's death in November, 1796, was by and large unexpected. Although sixty-seven, she still appeared healthy and energetic. A minor stroke early in the year had followed the affront of Sweden's Gustavus IV contriving religious reasons for not marrying Catherine's granddaughter Alexandra Pavlovna. The second stroke was sudden and severe, coming upon her in the lavatory and leaving her unconscious for more than a day. She did not live long enough to make any unsettling last wishes. Mourning was universally respectful, affectionate on the part of the few old friends left and her servants, and pointedly arranged on the part of her son and successor.

It was said of Catherine II that she first gave Russia style. The brilliance of her court (alternatively termed "the splendor of her vices") tended to obscure her tremendous successes in war and diplomacy. With these two things in mind and also her achievements in administration, Catherine saw herself as the worthiest successor to Peter the Great. It was no accident that she had a statue to her giant of a predecessor erected in Senate Square, "The Bronze Horseman" sculpture celebrated in the Pushkin poem. Beneath the rearing stallion and noble figure cleverly executed by Falconet (his talented daughter did the magnificently commanding head), the empress had inscribed PETRUS PRIMUS, CATERINA SECUNDA, making sure that no one would associate the tribute with Peter's own Catherine.

Many were Catherine's detractors. The glories of her reign were attributed to her commanders and even to luck. Her self-satisfaction, as well as all the calculating ambition that paid off, has been faulted. Her liberal hypocrisy, her showmanship, and her debauchery all have been exposed. In the end it comes down to just what is virtue in a ruler. Catherine herself avowedly preferred virtu à la Renaissance: willfulness, optimism, and accomplishment.

XIII.
A Father Undone by His Son: Paul I

1. Plots Past, Present, and Future

THE master of Mikhailovsky Castle was subject to nightmares, and his daytime fantasies were scarcely more pleasant. He thought of wives murdering husbands, of mothers disinheriting sons, and of sons deposing fathers. The cast of characters never varied, and the scenes had the freshness of recent memory.

Mikhailovsky Castle was finished in February, 1801, in the fourth year of the Emperor Paul's reign. It was destined to be occupied less than a month. The stronghold was built on the site of the Empress Elizabeth's Summer Palace, Rastrelli's extravagant creation having been torn down after Paul declared that he had had a vision of the Archangel Michael doing sentry duty in the courtyard. A result of the mysticism of the emperor, the castle was also a reflection of his unbalanced, largely unappealing character. The massive eight red granite columns in the front façade were grandiose to an extreme, while the rough masonry of the upper stories indicated hastiness and lack of patience in the planning. There were obelisks on top with pretentious royal monograms, gilded spires alongside plain roofs, and miserably sized statues and urns flung about—the whole effect one of disharmony to the point of sheer ugliness. The inner court of the rectangular structure was a huge parade ground fit for a martinet. The interior rooms were costly and tasteful. The family rooms were pleasantly intimate in feeling. What gave the whole building an ominous air, however, was the fact that it was entirely surrounded by a moat and approached only over five drawbridges—this in the day of Napoleon and Jefferson.

Bad memories were a reason for Paul to raze the palace where he had been born in October, 1754. There was the terrible question of just who his father was. His mother, Catherine, had mockingly insinuated in her *Memoirs* that it was Sergius Saltykov, not Peter Romanov, but she had her reasons for disparaging both husband and son. In looks and build Paul grew up to resemble Saltykov not in the least, while to a degree he recalled Peter III, if common ugliness and ungainliness could be weighted more than differences in eyes and shape of face. Politically accepted as the grand duke's son and heir, the infant Paul knew neither of his parents, since he was immediately spirited away to the suite of the Empress Elizabeth. Since the baby was almost smothered in black fox furs in his crib and sweated profusely as a result, it was no surprise that Paul grew up prone to sickness. Foreign governesses being in disrepute, ignorant, superstitious Russian *babushkas* nursed the little grand duke, and perhaps their fairy tales made him into a child as nervous as he was difficult. After this regimen of women, Paul hid under a table and cried when at six he was confronted with his newly appointed tutor, Panin.

Then came that startling night in 1762 for the eight-year-old when he was hustled through the streets of Petersburg in his nightshirt and held up to roaring crowds by the mother he had seen at best a few hundred short times in his life. The news of the disappearance of his father this same year affected him less than the fact that he received such marked attentions from his mother, the new empress choosing to come play with him daily and to interest herself closely in his schooling, as well as to nurse him through a nearly fatal illness. He became lovingly protective of her and also helplessly jealous to find Orlov lolling around his mother's apartments, but there was the small satisfaction that Orlov showed *him* respect.

Paul's original tutor, Panin, stayed. This outstanding Russian of his day first came to notice as a possible lover for the Empress Elizabeth; having been slipped into her bedroom, he fell asleep during the half hour's wait required by politesse. Panin did better as a diplomat abroad, and he returned to St. Petersburg a herald of the cultural rages of the West. Would-be critics of the grand duke's education said Panin confused his young charge with too much Leibnitz and D'Alembert. Probably more to the point was the fact that the tutor was too preoccupied with his duties as virtual foreign minister, his gourmet tastes, and his young women. Paul had many other instructors, however, ranging from professors of astronomy to contemporary authors. There is proof that he annotated the hundred great books of his day. His appreciation of all the nuances of the French language was attested to throughout his life. In sum, a French observer was to find Paul's education completely neglected, while an English envoy confounded historians by saying it left nothing to be desired.

Certainly some of Paul's tutors found him headstrong, undisciplined,

The Old Dynasty Ends in a Time of Troubles

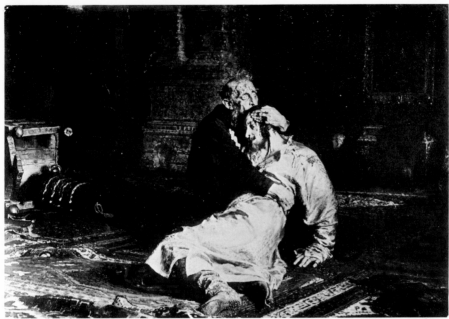

The Bettmann Archive

Ivan IV (1533—84) of the Rurik dynasty married Anastasia Romanov, and her death under suspicious circumstances drove him to the excesses which earned him the name Ivan the Terrible. Late in his reign Ivan struck down their son Ivan in a fit of rage. The hideous-faced father's remorse is depicted in this painting by the nineteenth-century artist Ilya Repin.

The Bettmann Archive
Another son of Ivan—and the first tsar with Romanov blood—was the weak-headed Fedor I (1584—98), whose death produced a fifteen-year contest for the throne.

Sovfoto
Dmitri the Pretender (1605—6) claimed to be a murdered son of Ivan the Terrible. He brought about the downfall of Tsar Boris Godunov and then was himself killed in a palace revolution in the Kremlin.

The Romanovs Come to Power in 1613

The crown of Vladimir Monomakh was the prize won by the Romanov family after young Michael Romanov (1613–45) was elected tsar by a national assembly. He was a nephew by marriage of Ivan IV. The fur-trimmed cap, surrounded here by the golden coronation chains, is today on exhibit in the Kremlin.

Alexis Michaelovich (1645—76), the second Romanov tsar, ruled Russia splendidly and autocratically. He consulted his council of boyars daily.

Their First Stronghold Is Moscow's Kremlin

The citadel of Moscow was the brick-walled Kremlin built by Ivan III in the late fifteenth century. This scene of the south and east walls shows on the summit of the hill from left to right the royal palaces, the three cathedrals, and the monastery buildings.

Looking south along the east wall of the Kremlin, one sees the Saviour's Gate tower with its high spire and fanciful upper works such as were added to all the bastions by the Romanov tsars in the seventeenth century. In the foreground is Red Square with its shopping stalls. At its foot is the famous Cathedral of St. Basil's, built by Ivan the Terrible.

Social Unrest and Family Feuds Threaten the New Dynasty

Stenka Razin, a Don Cossack, led a giant serf revolt against Tsar Alexis and the Russian nobility in the 1660's. This 1907 painting by Basil Surikov shows Razin as lord of the whole Volga region, before he was caught and executed.

The Tsarevna Sophia was a strong-willed woman who dominated events during the struggle for power between the two families of Alexis after his death. Regent of Russia (1682–89), she was overthrown by her famous half brother Peter. Her rage at being confined to a nunnery is depicted in this painting by Ilya Repin.

Peter the Great Builds an Empire and a New Capital

The Bettmann Archive

Peter I (1689–1725) became known as Peter the Great for the victories against the Turks and Swedes which made Russia a European power. Peter was painted by the French artist Jean Marc Nattier.

The Bettmann Archive

Peter's efforts to modernize his country were symbolized by his cutting off the beards of the boyars and making them wear Western-style clothes. This woodcut shows the royal barber at work.

Sovfoto

Two notable traits of Peter the Great were his huge stature and his tremendous energy, both of which are captured by the painter V. A. Serov in this scene of the tsar inspecting the levees of St. Petersburg, the new capital he built on the Baltic Sea beginning in 1703.

Peter Leaves the Succession in Chaos

The reforming tsar looks sternly at his unpromising heir by his first wife, the Tsarevich Alexis, in this painting by Nicholas Ce. Suspected of desiring to revert to the ways of old Muscovy, Alexis fled the country and then was lured back to meet torture and death in 1718.

Although Catherine I (1725–27), Peter's second wife, was a former servant girl and prisoner of war, she was put on the throne by the new St. Petersburg nobility.

The accession of Peter II (1727–30), son of the executed Alexis, represented the momentary triumph of the old nobility, and briefly the capital was returned to Moscow.

Peter's Daughter Makes St. Petersburg Dazzling

The Empress Elizabeth (1741–62) ended the period of short reigns and contending factions of the nobility. The new capital was transformed into a city of grandiose palaces and ornate churches. In the city environs were more fairyland palaces, such as Peterhof, from which the empress is seen emerging in this picture.

The view Elizabeth would see from Peterhof is this grand array of fountains and statues extending along a canal to the Gulf of Finland. Destroyed by the Nazis, Peterhof and the other Romanov palaces have been restored by the Soviets.

A Husband Is Overthrown by His Wife

Sovfoto

Peter III (1762), Elizabeth's nephew, alienated the nobility by his capricious domestic and foreign policies, and he was easily overthrown by his ambitious German wife.

Sovfoto

Although Peter III was murdered after his deposition, pretenders to his name and title turned up for years. The most brazen and famous, Emilian Pugachev, led another giant serf revolt in the 1770's.

The Bettmann Archive

Princess Sophia of Anhalt-Zerbst succeeded her husband as Catherine II (1762—96). This painting by Groot shows her in 1748 soon after her marriage to Peter.

Tass from Sovfoto

Catherine the Great is how Sophia comes down in history, great for her victories, notorious for her love life, and also celebrated as one of the enlightened despots of her age.

A Father Is Undone by His Son

Paul I (1796–1801) was Catherine's son, but Peter III was not necessarily his father. He resembled his unbalanced predecessor, however, particularly in his being a royal drillmaster, as shown in the above picture. A palace revolution soon brought about his murder.

Known as the enigmatic tsar, Alexander I (1801–25) connived in the death of his father, vacillated between reform and reaction at home, and made peace and war alternately with Napoleon.

Nicholas I (1825–55) succeeded his brother Alexander after a tragicomic dynastic crisis with another brother. As the "Iron Tsar," he was the Stalin of his day for both Russia and Europe.

Imperial Grandeur Rested on Oppression of the Serfs

The Winter Palace in the heart of St. Petersburg was the Romanov seat in the nineteenth century. Damaged by fire in the 1830's, the interiors were reconstructed lavishly to provide a backdrop for glittering ceremonies.

Romanov glory depended on the support of the Russian nobility, who in turn depended on the exploitation of millions of serfs. The least of the serfs' woes was having to prostrate themselves before their masters, as this wedding couple does in the picture.

Alexander II Becomes Liberator and Martyr

The years took their toll of Alexander II. His reforms pleased neither reactionaries nor revolutionaries, the latter bringing about his assassination in 1881.

Alexander II (1855—81) had the usual military education and conservative prejudices of his predecessors. Russia's defeat in the Crimean War forced him into the emancipation of the serfs.

This family portrait ten years before the tragedy of 1881 shows the influential uncles of the last tsar. Seated left to right are Tsar Alexander II, Tsarina Maria with the future Nicholas II, Tsarina Maria (Dagmar of Denmark). Standing left to right: Grand Duke Paul, Grand Duke Serge, Grand Duchess Maria (later Duchess of Edinburgh), Grand Duke Alexis, the future Alexander III, and Grand Duke Vladimir.

The Bull Is the Last Strong Tsar

The Bettmann Archive

Reacting against the liberalism of his father, giant Alexander III (1881—94) was the last real autocrat of Russia. In this family grouping he is surrounded by his petite wife Marie (upper left), his heir Nicholas (mustache), Olga, George, Xenia (between his knees), and Michael.

Nicholas and Alexandra Are a Love Match

The Bettmann Archive

One of the few times Nicholas II (1894–1917) showed decisiveness was in his insistence on marrying Princess Alexandra of Hesse, a granddaughter of Queen Victoria. They doted on each other ever after.

Brown Brothers

The close links and some close resemblances between Russian and British royalty are chronicled in this group photograph taken before 1910. From left are the future Duke of Windsor, Queen Alexandra, the future Queen Mary, Tsar Nicholas II, Princess Mary and Princess Victoria (standing behind him), the Tsarevich Alexis (on the ground), King Edward VII, Grand Duchesses Olga and Anastasia (on the ground), Tsarina Alexandra, Grand Duchess Tatiana, the future George V, and Grand Duchess Maria.

Politics and Hemophilia Overwhelm the Family

Nicholas tried to play autocrat, but the Revolution of 1905 forced him to grant a constitution. Here the glittering imperial family try to overawe the somber and hostile members of the Duma, Russia's first legislature.

Rasputin became the evil force in Russian state affairs because of his success at stopping the crippling attacks of bleeding suffered by Nicholas' son, Alexis. Rasputin came to make and unmake Russian ministers, until his assassination.

This photo of Nicholas II and the tsarevich was taken before the well-intentioned tsar went off on a daylong hike to test the new gear of the Russian infantryman. The pathetically crippled Alexis often had to be carried.

War and Revolution Bring Tragedy

Family tranquillity is indicated in this group portrait of Nicholas, Alexandra, and their strikingly handsome children. The First World War interrupted the idyll: The girls donned nurses' uniforms; Alexis joined his father at the front.

War disasters and misery on the home front led to Nicholas' abdication in the First Revolution of March, 1917. His children were reduced to rough clothing when the family were prisoners of Kerensky. Then, Lenin's Second Revolution led to the murder of all of them in Siberia in 1918.

Romanov Survivors Feud On

Brown Brothers

Grand Duke Michael, brother of Nicholas, was tsar for a day in 1917, declined the honor unless elected, and nonetheless suffered execution by the Bolsheviks.

The Bettmann Archive

Grand Duke Cyril, oldest first cousin of the last tsar, survived the Revolution. From France he proclaimed himself Russian emperor in 1924 and set up court modeled on Mussolini's Italy.

The Bettmann Archive

Grand Duke Nicholas Nicholaevich, Russia's commander in chief in the war, refused to recognize Cyril's pretensions and was supported by the majority of the émigrés.

Brown Brothers

Grand Duchess Anastasia was presumably murdered with the rest of her family. In the 1920's various pretenders appeared, notably Anna Anderson in Germany. The above photo is of her.

and less than a prodigy. More of a problem was that the adolescent became aware of the circumstances of his father's death. It has never been made known whether Catherine ever tried to talk him out of believing himself Hamlet to her Gertrude. In any case, there was the triumphant lover and all-but-actual murderer about in the person of "that lout Orlov," as Paul took to calling him. That idle rumors were sufficient to set him brooding is evident from his refusal to attend his mother's accession anniversary celebration when he was twelve. Then there was the all-too-undisguised plot of 1771 to put him on his deserved throne, and the next year Paul could ponder the phenomenon of an obviously fraudulent Pugachev leading a mass insurrection in the name of the grand duke's rights. Paul's response to this was to become proud and domineering, all the while being mistrustful and defensive. Now cold to Catherine, he was outwardly submissive, inwardly rebellious. He began his lifelong fixation on the fate of deposed princes, and he came to idolize and imitate his father, in particular taking up that parent's militaristic excesses.

The empress met chilliness with chilliness. Catherine withdrew her promise of twice-weekly initiations into dispatches and state affairs. She was later accused of ordering a tutor to bore Paul to death with unimportant documents. In any case, he was not given entrée even to the Senate, and his title of Admiral in Chief was strictly honorific.

An obvious but often unfortunate solution for problem sons is to marry them off, and this Catherine tried with seeming success. Paul was by no means a backward boy, having at eleven titillated the court by his passion for Vera Choglokov (daughter of Catherine's "dragon"). Moreover, the empress was so intent on making sure her son could function sexually, even at the age of fourteen, that she put in his way, inevitably via Countess Bruce, a voluptuous young widow, and a son, named Ivan Veliki, was the happy result. (This Romanov bastard received a careful education, entered the navy, and died as an observer on a British frigate in the West Indies in 1794.) The proposed proper marriage pleased Paul so much that there was a reconciliation with his mother. About the same time Paul could avow to his newly acquired best friend, the young Count Alexis Razumovsky: "You have already effected a miracle of good will in me, since I have begun to renounce my old defiances. . . ."

This particular Hamlet's Ophelia was Princess Wilhelmina of Hesse-Darmstadt. It mattered less that she was Frederick the Great's candidate than that Catherine found her charming and sweet and was assured that Paul was passionately in love with her. The marriage was solemnized in August, 1773, the princess being rebaptized as Natalia Alexievna. Paul was indeed madly in love, even if others found his wife extravagant, self-centered, and so frivolous as to not bother to learn to speak Russian. Then, in April, 1776, the wife died, after giving birth to a stillborn child.

Paul broke down completely, despairing of life, as well as of love. His mother chanced upon a cruel stratagem. Compromising letters were found in the departed wife's cabinet and were duly shown the bereaved grand duke: They were from his friend, Alexis Razumovsky.

The empress further tantalized him out of his grief with the potential charms of a newly selected mate, and indeed, Paul's second wife turned out to be all that anyone could desire. Tall, well proportioned, dazzlingly blond, delicately complexioned, cultivated, completely amiable, such a model princess was Sophia Dorothea of Württemberg, who became known as Maria Fedorovna after her wedding to Paul in December, 1776. The empress was emphatically taken with her choice. The husband was more reserved, but in newfound good spirits and pride he wrote: "Everywhere my wife goes she has the gift to spread gaiety and ease, and she has had the art not only of chasing away all my blues but even to return to me that good humor I had entirely lost through these unfortunate years." As for Maria Fedorovna, she made a next-morning promise to her less than handsome and tractable husband that she was never to go back on: "I swear, by this paper, to love you, to adore you all my life and always to be attached to you, and nothing in the world will make me change with regard to you." The loyal bride thereafter saw things only through her husband's eyes, perhaps too much so. Raised in idyllic circumstances, she found herself shocked at the goings-on in her mother-in-law's court.

The birth of robust sons to the grand ducal couple, Alexander in 1777 and Constantine in 1779, was a source of joy and also of much frustration, for the children were completely appropriated by the empress. As something of a consolation, Paul and Maria were sent off on a trip to Europe.

The grand tour of the Count and Countess of the North, transparent incognitos, began in September, 1781, and lasted for eighteen months. Militaristic Berlin was declared off limits. The first major stop was Vienna, where Paul met the Emperor Joseph II, his vis-à-vis in many respects. The Hapsburg ruler announced that the young Romanov had uncommon talents and a quite extensive knowledge. Paul visited Naples, too—as a tourist, not as a refugee like the tsarevich of sixty-odd years before. The greatest experience was the reception in Paris in May, 1782. The populace, which was to be erecting guillotines in scarcely ten years, was seemingly delirious over the visiting foreign royalty. Louis XVI and the aristocracy treated Paul to a fantastic series of balls, fetes, operas, readings, and even a pilgrimage to the tomb of Rousseau. Paul showed himself graciously interested and knowledgeable at the gardens and learned institutions. Marie Antoinette found him ardent and impetuous. The visit was slightly marred by his outburst in court after he discovered that the Empress Catherine's police were intercepting his mail and had arrested some of his friends. To the astonished Louis the grand duke exclaimed that if there were even a "poodle" with him "loyal to my person," his "mother would have had him thrown in the water before we left Paris."

Paul returned from being lionized abroad to find himself relegated to the background in Russia, if anything more so than before. "I am reaching age thirty without anything to do," he complained. The empress found a solution when she presented him with a new estate, in addition to his palace at Pavlovsk. Called Gatchina, it was located so considerably away from the capital (and her) that guests to Paul's twice-weekly soirees had to stay overnight. Gatchina was not just a country place; it was a huge domain with 5,000 inhabitants. Ironically, the original palace was built by Gregory Orlov, who offered it as a lure to J. J. Rousseau, writing the old iconoclast that it offered healthy air for walking, priests who could not dispute or even preach, and a populace that believed all it was told. The grand ducal couple set up their "little court" at Gatchina, Maria adding her own paintings to the Carrara marble galleries of the great semicircular mansion and seeing to the provision of a theater and a library. At first Paul's interests seemed to be such things as a new hospital, a school, a textile factory, and a chapel where Protestant and Catholic servants could worship. Then, however, Gatchina was gradually turned into a mad military establishment.

Gatchina was created by Paul, half-deliberately, as a model for all Russia when he finally attained power. Everything revolved around the military companies he organized, eventually reaching the number of 2,000 men, and Paul's soldiers were in every way the antithesis of the regular Russian military establishment. Peter the Great did the same sort of thing at Preobrazhenskoe in the 1680's, in the name of modernity, but Paul's play army was like a throwback to the Oranienbaum company of Peter III or like a caricature of Potsdam, not even that of the Potsdam of Frederick the Great but that of the martinet Frederick William I. The soldiers' uniforms were early eighteenth century with tricorns, powdered wigs, tight coats, gaiters, and buckled shoes. As for the officers, Paul had no trouble attracting men, some just spit-and-polish fanatics, others malingerers. "The most honest" of the Gatchina men "deserved to be broken on the wheel without being tried," this according to a friend of Paul's. There were many German names about at first, but the man who quickly raised himself from a twenty-four-year-old recruit to commander of everything was a Russian named Alexis Arakcheev, who was first called derisively a monkey in uniform but more fearfully in later decades the corporal of Gatchina. Arakcheev and the others fell in with Peter's ideas that the manual of arms and tight-order drill were everything, and they believed that the cruelest punishments were another necessity. (Arakcheev is accused of having once bitten off the ear of a soldier.) The grand duke happily supervised his bizarre troops for hours on end, tapping the ground with his cane that had a watch mounted in its head (preserved in Leningrad). Visitors felt as though they were in a foreign country set in the Russian forests when they arrived at Gatchina. Even a German relative was astonished to see the officers with "the air of coming out of an old album." It once occurred to the empress in St. Petersburg to cut short these infantilisms and treasons, but she did not, calculating that Gatchina served to make her rival laughable and unpopular. Catherine was confident that Paul was basically too unsure of himself to march his 2,000 against the one company of Grenadiers guarding her palace.

The longer he waited for real power, the more frustrated the Grand Duke Paul became. The empress, so lavish with money to others, was stingy with her son. When he tried to see real military service in the Turkish War of 1787, he was denied permission (the heir did participate in the mild Swedish campaign of 1789 and was actually fired at, only to have Swedish officers specially cross the lines to apologize). Political memorandums he submitted to the court were treated contemptuously. On the one hand, he opposed Russian policy in Poland, and on the other, he championed immediate intervention against the French Revolution. (Catherine told him sententiously: "You are a ferocious beast. Don't you understand that one cannot fight ideas with cannon.") Paul had disliked Potemkin, but he loathed Catherine's last lover, Zubov, who reciprocated his feeling. (Once at dinner Paul ventured to agree with some project of Zubov's, at which point the favorite turned to the company to remark: "Have I said something stupid?")

Already the diplomats were making dire predictions. From the French chargé: "He will be the most unhappy of tyrants." The friendly Prussian ambassador had to report: "He must change from top to bottom or his reign will not be happy or long." Under the influence of Zubov and others, the empress decided in 1794 that Paul should not rule at all. The proposal to set him aside was discussed at length in the Privy Council, but it was shelved. The grand duke found out and began to expect the worst. "We are lost," he exclaimed to his wife when a special messenger rode into Gatchina late in 1796. The news, however, was not of his arrest but of Catherine's second stroke.

2. Revenges and Reforms

What could be expected of the lord of Gatchina who had waited forty-two years to rule the Russian Empire? Even his closest associates and well-wishers were puzzled by Paul. One of his officers described him as "the most singular combination of the most violent being and the most amiable being." Was he really mad or just unbalanced like his supposed father? Would he go to pieces like Peter III once he had tasted power? Or would he use his education and experience to right the wrongs of his mother's regime? The new emperor himself thought he knew something of what he would be, having once written that he preferred to be hated doing good than to be loved doing evil.

Paul showed no emotion as he attended his mother's last moments, and he sought out her private cabinet with alacrity. If he found an act for his disinheritance, it was destroyed. Probably he read Alexis Orlov's scribbled note regarding the demise of Peter III and, having satisfied himself of his mother's innocence, had it burned (but not before an aide copied it). After receiving the usual oaths of allegiance from the dignitaries in the palace, he later rode out on his white horse, Pompom, to greet the arrival of his Gatchina soldiers, to whom he promptly assigned the honors and part of the quarters of the Guards.

The funeral arrangements were as macabre as they were vindictive. The public was invited to the Winter Palace to pass by Catherine's body lying in state, only to find next to the empress and slightly more in a place of honor the coffin of Peter III, the emperor having had his father's remains disinterred from the Alexander Nevsky Lavra. At the funeral procession to the Peter and Paul Cathedral, the three surviving leaders of the crime of 1762 led the cortege, Alexis Orlov in front, somehow imperturbable, carrying the crown on a gold cloth. The imperial family followed on foot, the emperor surrounded by his strange-looking Gatchina men and the highest officers of Russia, many of whom would participate in another murder four years later.

Having had his drama, the tsar confined himself to ending the government careers of Orlov and the others and to banishing them to their not inconsiderable estates. Paul's treatment of Catherine's surviving favorites was somewhat baffling in its gentleness. Zubov, of all people expecting the worst, was allowed to remain as inspector general of artillery and found himself moved from his Winter Palace to a handsome mansion, where he was even visited by the imperial couple, Paul requesting Maria Fedorovna to pour the tea "since there is no longer any mistress of the house." Dmitriev-Mamanov and Zavadovsky, both of whom had been unfaithful to their mistress, were designated counts by Paul, unaccountably unless Paul reasoned that sheer contact with royal flesh is sacrosanct. Another new title was that of Count Bobrinsky: Having satisfied himself that his bastard half brother had been genuinely neglected by his mother, Paul was lavish with honors for him.

The advancement of Paul's intimates was for the most part taken without comment. The unimpeachably aristocratic Kurakin brothers, friends of Paul since boyhood, assumed the highest posts in internal and external affairs. Less appreciated was the rapid promotion of Paul's valet, Koutaissov, a former Circassian slave and war captive, who, having pushed his way up to the highest posts in the imperial household, demanded and eventually won a countdom. The "corporal of Gatchina," Arakcheev, was promptly made governor of St. Petersburg, assigned Zubov's vacated apartments, and given estates. Paul filled the Winter Palace with military men, to the extent that one observer described it as looking like a fortress taken by storm. A frenetic barrackslike atmosphere replaced the languid majesty of the former reign.

Friends honored, enemies put in their place, the emperor did not forget past *causes célèbres*. The editor Novikov was released from prison, and the writer Radishchev recalled from exile. Ten thousand Polish prisoners were set free, and Paul himself was moved to visit their leader, Kosciusko, to tell the great patriot: "I know that you have suffered much. . . . I have always been against the Partition of Poland: it was an act as unjust as it was impolitic, but it is consummated." In his righting of wrongs, Paul rather spitefully dismissed the architect Cameron, and he brought out of storage a statue of Peter the Great by the elder Rastrelli to be erected in front of the Mikhailovsky Castle as a reply to Catherine's "Bronze Horseman." The pedestal was pointedly inscribed: TO A GREAT-GRANDFATHER FROM A GREAT-GRANDSON.

Ecstatic with power, Paul set about legislating his disagreements with Catherine's work. The emperor was at his desk at six in the morning; he gave political orders, all the while drilling his troops before noon; and he took up affairs assiduously in the afternoon and even at night. Decrees on a variety of topics issued forth relentlessly, Paul acting as if he could order the disparate Russian Empire as completely and easily as he could the never-never land that was Gatchina. Brilliant ideas alternated with brutalities, considered reforms with caprices. Too late the emperor found out that he had no people wise and bold enough to contradict him and few competent enough to assist him.

The measures of royal grace ranged from statutes restoring autonomous institutions to the conquered provinces in the west to the provision of grain stores for famine years. Paper-money inflation was curbed, tariffs were liberalized, and industries were subsidized. In his zeal Paul even established a mail drop for complaints and proposals. This suggestion box was given up in the face of the volume of idle witticisms and untraceable threats. Some of the royal enthusiasms seemed reactionary, at least to the privileged classes; the withdrawal of the charters of Nobility and Towns, in the name of efficiency, was a case in point.

Both the emperor's good intentions and his limitations were evident when he faced the serf question. If his remission of tax arrears was generous, the decree prohibiting the sale of serfs off the land was positively daring. On the occasion of his coronation Paul went even more to the heart of the abuses by requesting but not ordering that forced labor on the nobles' land be restricted to three days a week and banned on Sundays. Incongruously, Paul gave away to favorites even more crown serfs than had Catherine, apparently operating under the naïve conviction that they would be better off. In the end, the emperor's ill-formed hopes met with complete apathy, and he resigned himself to the old methods of public order: 278 peasant insurrections, 278 army repressions.

With regard to the French Revolution, Paul made no effort to break with Catherine's policies but rather intensified the reactionary trends of her last years. Ten thousand French *émigrés* were put on subsidy by the emperor, and he set up Louis XVIII in Biren's palace at Mitau. Then, with ludicrous fanaticism, Paul set about extirpating the subversive influences suggested by Paris-style dress, banning round hats, high collars, long pants, and top boots. One day his police accosted offending people in the streets, attacked their hats and clothes with shears, and sent some of the best people in the capital home in tatters. New offices of censorship were instituted to keep out foreign books and music, and Russian writers were punished for using such unsettling words as "society" and "citizen." Young aristocrats were forbidden to study abroad. Gratuitously vexing the nobility in their intellectual freedoms, in their fashions, and later, worst of all, in their military privileges, Paul seemingly "invented ways to make people hate and detest him," as one of his intimates admitted.

Paul's hyperkeen sense of his autocratic power was laughable when not enraging. Gossips said that he wore his crown to intimate family suppers, as well as to state banquets. On more than one occasion he beat his chest and intoned, "Here is your law." The Swedish envoy duly reported this observation by the emperor: "Know that no one in Russia is important except the person who is speaking to me and that only while he is speaking." Of all of Paul's bizarre violences to society, however, the one longest remembered was that he insisted that ladies curtsy to him on the street, meaning that richly dressed women would have to descend from their carriages and half kneel in the slush. (Once Paul shouted, "Sit," to a lady in the process of curtsying, and she collapsed into a puddle, when perhaps all he intended was that she return to her carriage.)

The portraits of Paul seem nearly comical, often suggesting a bad actor not quite at ease in his rich costuming. His genuine charm, breeding, and intelligence never quite show past the thrust-out chin and mocking expression, an expression intensified by abnormally sloping eyes and a wry mouth.

3. Family Complications

Paul was the only surviving Romanov in the years right after the unnatural deaths of Peter III in 1762 and Ivan VI in 1764. Father of nine healthy children, the emperor was the reestablisher of the dynasty, and he played the role of patriarch wisely and well at first. Then appeared an unworthy mistress, and worse still, Paul's suspiciousness extended to his own family—in time with some cause.

On the day of his coronation in 1797 Paul enacted a Succession Law, so needed and so just it was never changed. Few heirs to the throne had suffered as much as he from uncertainty because of Peter's arbitrary law of 1722, leaving the choice of successor up to the will or whim of the reigning sovereign. By the new law the succession was strictly defined in terms of hereditary primogeniture in the male line. Two years later Paul set up a Department of Appanages to manage certain crown lands set aside for the use of all future grand dukes and grand duchesses, and this, too, was so well conceived that right down to 1917 Russia was the only monarchy not requiring a civil list. A less fortunate tradition dating from Paul was that a dowager empress would take precedence over a reigning consort.

Paul's second wife, Maria Fedorovna, had won his love completely. Her many portraits show a square-faced, pink-complexioned, kindly, tolerant woman, who perhaps cried frequently. The empress was not politically minded, or at least she was too sentimental and prosaic in her thinking to exercise real influence on her husband. She did worry about her husband, but helplessly. Even before Paul's accession she had written a friend prophetically: "I tremble for him; I tremble because he does not know how to make friends, and he will perish one day if he does not have around him faithful and devoted beings." Maria Fedorovna's loyal concern intensified as the reign unfolded. "Our way of life is not gay," she wrote, "for our dear master is out of sorts. He bears in his spirit a profound sadness which undermines him . . . I stare at him often, and my heart breaks to see him in such a state." But she apparently could do no more than be a good wife and mother.

The imperial couple's fourth son and ninth child, Michael, was born in 1798. With the thoughtlessness of the despot, Paul had all the foreign ambassadors awakened in the dead of night with the news. Because this had been a difficult delivery, the doctors insisted, over the empress' strong protests, that she cease sleeping with her husband. Paul's continence was not strong apparently, for shortly thereafter he impregnated one of the chambermaids. More fatefully, Koutaissov, the ex-valet who was now master of Paul's household, seized the opportunity to promote a liaison between the emperor and a sixteen-year-old beauty of good family, Anna

Lopukhin, a coquette who proved willing to play a long game. Even after her father was installed in the highest offices of the empire, the daughter rejected Paul's ardent attentions and pleaded that she was in love with a young officer fighting abroad, Prince Gagarin. With seeming magnanimity, Paul had Gagarin ordered back to Russia, and he presided at the couple's wedding in 1800. All this turned out to be just a screen. The husband returned to the army, and the father retired to Moscow, leaving Anna his handsome mansion on the Neva. Here she established herself as Paul's mistress. Unimportant but strange was the fact that Koutaissov married Anna's sister, and stranger still, he took as his mistress the noted French actress Madame Chevalier, whose town house adjoined Anna's. It came about that the emperor and his ex-valet walked together each afternoon to their neighboring trysts, the cadets on parade receiving orders to avert their eyes at the sight. Later Paul had Anna installed in apartments over his in the palace. Her wiles had him so captivated that the court witnessed many new departures untypical of the increasingly conservative ruler: permission to dance the waltz; French-inspired styles; and crimson uniforms for the officers. While Anna Lopukhin was too frivolous to play a political role, her ascendancy over the tsar meant the disappearance from his daily routine of such humane and enlightened influences as that of the broken-hearted empress.

In time Paul came to feel that his wife and most of his children were plotting against him and surrounding him with spies. ("See that young hairdresser, perhaps, he too is charged with keeping me under surveillance.") Earlier his family's home life had been loving. The children sat for portraits at every possible age, their educations were the best, and all were destined to achieve greater or lesser prominence. The eldest son and heir, Alexander, and his brother, Constantine, had been born in Petersburg and reared by Catherine. First of the children born at Gatchina, Helen was to be Grand Duchess of Mecklenburg; Marie became Grand Duchess of Weimar; and Anna, almost married to Napoleon, was to become Queen of the Netherlands and thus a Romanov ancestor of all subsequent Dutch royalty. Catherine married first the Duke of Oldenburg and then the Duke of Württemberg. The last son but for Michael, the Grand Duke Nicholas, was born in Gatchina in 1796 and would rule Russia thirty years later.

As Paul well knew, royal sons are inevitably, even if unintentionally, rivals to their parents, and his eldest was no exception in both respects. From the day of his birth in 1777 Alexander had been taken by Catherine to be reared as the ideal kind of ruler his father showed little promise of being. This was Catherine's one real chance to be a mother and to show the world that she had read *Émile*. The infant she called Monsieur Alexandre received her energetic and detailed attention. The Academy of Sciences was ordered to print her *Elementary Instructions for the Upbringing of Children.* Alexander's every step and word were dotingly reported and exaggerated for the benefit of her soon-bored philosopher correspondents. Physically, he was to be made a "little Spartan," and so no cradling under too many furs for Alexander but sleeping in the fresh air under light covering on a leather and canvas cot, a habit he continued ever after. Putting him in the room nearest the ceremonial guns, in order to make him brave, resulted in making him deaf in one ear.

Failing to get the Encyclopedist D'Alembert himself as Alexander's educator, Catherine settled for the best religious, literary, and military minds she could find in Russia, all under the direction of a Swiss scholar of the humanities named Frédéric César de la Harpe. As a man who continued to influence the grand duke all his life, La Harpe must be accounted one of the major figures of the day. For all his open sympathy with the ideals of the French Revolution, earning him Catherine's playful title Monsieur le Jacobin, La Harpe was scrupulously honest intellectually. Through his tutor Alexander was exposed to the best writers of all time, and the highest aspirations were held before him. A tractable and gifted student, the grand duke had his formal schooling abruptly brought to a close when he was sixteen, for Catherine, pushing her political plans for him too fast, wanted him married. Critics of Alexander's education could point out that he was being left with many lofty ideals but nothing solid in the way of knowledge and experience. He had been taught how to feel but not how to think, having never been given work to do or examinations.

"The dear children looked happy as angels," purred Catherine after she had betrothed her sixteen-year-old dandy of a grandson to fifteen-year-old Elizabeth of Baden in 1793. Not mistakenly, the empress told her hearers that the bride was delightful and that the two were much in love. Deliberately Alexander had been saved from some of the less savory aspects of Catherine's court, but her other plans for him were to misfire. A portrait of Alexander about the time of his marriage shows a blond, curly-haired, handsome young man peering serenely over the high red collar and large epaulets of his trim green uniform.

It was deemed natural for the adolescent Alexander to visit his parents, now established in Paul's Germanized dreamland at Gatchina. Every Friday the young grand duke journeyed to Gatchina, where the next morning he would be required to drill a company of troops in the Prussian manner under the critical eye of his father. Such disparate atmospheres as Gatchina and St. Petersburg might have produced a psychological breakdown in a prince different from Alexander, who coolly adapted to both. "Two sets of company manners" is one description of Alexander's behavior under trying circumstances, and qualities of dissimulation were to be his all his life. In 1794 Catherine felt confident enough to propose to Alexander that he supersede his father as her successor, and to her consternation he refused.

Loyalty to his father was a factor, but the real truth was that Catherine's Émile-called-Alexander was disgusted with the falseness and corruption of the "grand court" as much as he genuinely admired the military orderliness of the "little court" of his father.

The Grand Duke Alexander was far too complex, however, to be put down as a complacent seconder of his father. To his friends he often spoke with critical appreciation of the French Revolution, and he fantasized about the future reign of law and justice in Russia and also about the dispensability of hereditary monarchy. His often-declared intention was to retire with Elizabeth to a chalet on the Rhine, but friends were able to dissuade him from premature renunciation of the throne at least until he had had a chance to give Russia "freedom."

It was a tribute to the Emperor Paul that his son expected the new reign to be a triumph of respectability and reform. The father returned his trust, and Paul rapidly designated Alexander a senator, inspector general of cavalry, and president of the War College. Independent authority, in the sense of really being able to give orders, was denied Alexander, however, and he found that in his duties, say, as commander of the Second Regiment of the Semenovskoe Guards, he was still likely to have a messenger from his father arrive and to hear himself called an imbecile for some error of spacing as his soldiers paraded that day. The heir was expected to spend much of his time with the father, causing his frequent separation from his wife and friends.

His disenchantment soon took a political turn. The kinds of thoughts that plagued the heir's mind were well illustrated in a long letter that he wrote to La Harpe in September, 1797:

> My father, mounting the throne, wanted to reform everything. His beginning, it is true, was brilliant enough, but what followed has not corresponded to it. Everything has been ordered changed at the same time, adding to the confusion. The military wastes almost all its time in parades. . . . What is ordered today is countermanded a month later. . . . It would be impossible to enumerate to you all the follies which have been committed; join to that a severity stripped of all justice, much partiality, and the greatest inexperience. . . . My poor country is in an indefinable state: farming confounded, commerce restricted, freedom and personal well-being abolished. . . . Judge what my heart must suffer.

Then Alexander went on to confide to his tutor that he had given up on his old plan of "expatriating myself," and instead, he hoped in the future to give Russia a constitution, representation of the people, and, above all, legality.

The grand duke's feelings were intensified by those of his wife. Elizabeth avoided Paul's court because "one could only await some gross indiscretion." As for Alexander's younger brother Constantine, he once observed that Paul had declared war on common sense with the firm resolve never to conclude a truce.

4. Madness in Diplomacy

The new tsar was quick to proclaim his attachment to peace in several manifestos, and he initiated projects to cut back Catherine's swollen army. Within two years, however, Paul was involved in war, plunging into the most contradictory foreign policy since the days of his unbalanced father.

It had long been apparent that Paul was a military pedant. So, unfortunately, were to be all his Romanov successors, in varying degrees but without exception. Unlike them, however, Paul did not just identify himself with the army; he set himself above it. The emperor's interference with their traditional military habits and prerogatives did more than anything else to set the nobility against him. With too-zealous logic, for example, Paul insisted that young nobles actually rise through the ranks instead of being inscribed on a regiment's rolls at age one and finding themselves an ensign when they were sixteen. Hundreds of officers were weeded out. All units were put into the new Gatchina type of uniform.

The emperor's daily passion was the precision of Prussian drill, and because he prided himself on his ability to withstand sub-zero weather without an overcoat, venerable generals were sorely tried to do likewise. As for the subofficers, day after day they faced reprimand, demotion, whipping, or banishment, depending how Paul happened to feel about an unpowdered wig, an askew buckle, or an improper cadence. Officers of the day often stayed up half the night dressing themselves, taking care to say good-bye to their loved ones and to provide themselves with traveling needs. However, the common soldiers were mistreated no more than before, perhaps less, and they probably often enjoyed seeing their superiors pestered and punished.

Few dared protest openly. Once when a field marshal murmured against some royal brutality, Paul snapped: "Do you see that body of guardsmen? There are four hundred of them. One word from me, and they will all be marshals." The great Suvorov constantly and wittily spoke his mind. After observing that all the new hair powder made him faint, he declared: "Russians have always fought Prussians. Why copy them?" Another rejoinder was: "Sire, buckles are not cannon." More seriously, when told that the marching cadence was being reduced from 100 to 75 steps a minute, Suvorov said acidly: "My pace is reduced to three-quarters; then when I go to attack the enemy, it will no longer be thirty but forty versts which separate us." Suvorov presently found himself dismissed to his

estates, Paul's excuse being that there was no employment for him in peacetime.

The War of the First Coalition against revolutionary France petered out
in 1797 without Russian troops ever having taken part. Napoleon won his
first smashing victories in Italy, and Austria sued for peace. The next year
the French Directory became increasingly aggressive, invading Switzerland
and threatening the domains of the Pope. In May Napoleon set off for
Egypt to menace the British Empire in India. These events, coupled with
French propaganda concerning the liberation of Poland, persuaded Paul
that the "Jacobins" he had always hated were now seeking no less than
"world domination" (a phrase used in a manifesto by Paul that has remained in vogue ever since). Accordingly, Russia took the lead in organizing the Second Coalition, allying itself with the ever-fighting British in
December, 1798, and even taking the unprecedented step of signing a
mutual territorial guarantee with Turkey. The emperor, rebuffed several
times, virtually had to beg Suvorov to assume command. "I accord you all
my confidence," he was able to write at last. "Go save the kings." In a
sense, an ultimate result of the declaration of war was the occupation of
the Kremlin by French troops fourteen years later.

Paul's about-face on peace and war was in large part motivated by a
caprice connected with his being designated grand master of the Knights
of Malta in 1798 and given the sword of Jean Paresot de Valette, the sixteenth-century hero of this island outpost against the Turks. Pious to the
point of mysticism and always preoccupied with the chivalry of old, the
emperor sought a dramatic new role and hastened to have himself painted
in the robes of grand master. It did not occur to him that the Pope was
logically his superior. What enraged the emperor to the point of war fever
was the fact that Napoleon had seized Malta on his way to Egypt.

The year 1799 saw great victories and then debacles. The Russian navy
in the Mediterranean wrested the Ionian Islands from the French. Marshal
Suvorov, leading a combined Russian-Austrian army into northern Italy,
scored a magnificent series of victories that brought Cossacks clattering
over the streets of Milan and Turin. The emperor ordered no less than an
invasion of southern France in the rather unrealistic expectation of a great
royalist uprising there. Suvorov eventually turned north to join the main
Austrian forces. A huge inscription in Russian carved on a mountainside
near the Lake of Lucerne still commemorates Russia's greatest general
successfully bringing his hard-pressed army across the Alps, in the manner
of Hannibal. Briefly the Russians held Zurich, only to be forced into a
gallantly executed retreat through other Alpine passes northeastward because of lack of Austrian support. The emperor, already dismayed that
Suvorov's troops had dispensed with their wigs and garters, was infuriated
at the treachery of the Austrians. Suvorov was recalled. Paul promised a

triumphant reception "worthy of the heroes of all centuries." Then in St. Petersburg there was a nasty scene between Suvorov and Koutaissov, the less than military or noble person sent by Paul to greet him, and the victory celebration was willfully called off. Within a short while Suvorov was dead, his funeral services, which Paul did not attend, being a massive drama of popular tribute and discontent.

Paul's foreign discomfiture was complete when, also in the fall of 1799, a British-commanded force that included many Russian troops capitulated in Holland. Meanwhile, Napoleon, having slipped back to France without letting on to the French about the disaster that had befallen him in Egypt, took over the government by coup, proclaimed himself first consul, and prepared to repeat his victories against Austria.

At this point Emperor Paul not only took Russia out of the war but did a complete switch and proclaimed his friendship with Napoleon. From being a revolutionary, Napoleon was now recognized as the restorer of law and order in Western Europe, the role Paul intended to match in the East. Louis XVIII and the French royalists were unceremoniously ousted from Mitau as troublemakers. The Russian ruler did not see his foreign policy as contradictory but explained that he was seeking justice where he found it. Not unworthy in any era was the following message addressed to Napoleon:

> The duty of all those whom God has given the power to govern the peoples is to think and occupy themselves with their well-being. I do not speak or wish to discuss the rights or principles of different governments which each country has adopted. Let us seek to give the world the repose and calm it needs so much. . . .

A not unrelated move of this time, which Paul at least found madly funny, was having the German journalist August von Kotzebue publish a paragraph to the effect that the Emperor of Russia, despairing of peace, was going to invite all the monarchs of Europe to a place where they could settle their quarrels in hand-to-hand combat

Napoleon now offered Malta to its grand master, but in September, 1800, the British navy got there first, before a Russian squadron. Berserkly, Paul now prepared to war on his British ally of the year before, the same sort of complete military reversal that had helped bring his father to grief. The simple fact was that the British fleet could ultimately mobilize 205 ships of the line to Russia's 47. The emperor sought additional strength by renewing Catherine's Armed Neutrality of the North, but Prussia, Sweden, and Denmark were less than enthusiastic. Nonetheless, Paul blithely proclaimed an embargo on all English shipping, meaning no more luxury goods for Petersburg society and, more important, no trade outlet for Russia's exports of wheat, flax, and naval materials. This was the last straw for many of the nobility: Insecurity in their military careers was one thing; financial ruin another.

If a final touch of madness was needed, Paul provided it in the form of ordering General Orlov and 22,500 Cossacks to invade India. The expedition marched off in January, 1801, the emperor confident that they would reach the Russian jumping-off point at Orenburg in one month and, passing through Khiva and Bokhara, gain the plains of the Indus in three more months. (In one letter Paul had to apologize for having no suitable maps beyond Khiva.) The fourteen cannons they took were considered a decisive advantage. Actually, the plan was not beyond all reason, in view of two facts: The British had only 2,000 troops in India, and no less a strategist than Napoleon was at the same moment hoping to have the still-unsurrendered French army in Egypt march to join his new Russian allies. Logistically, however, Paul's India expedition proved unfeasible, and Orlov, with a crippled army, traveled no farther than Orenburg before dramatic news from the capital saved him from complete disaster.

5. Murder

The imperial family moved into the Mikhailovsky Castle in February, 1801, Paul being so enthralled with his creation that he could scarcely wait for the lime and the varnish to dry. Shortly afterward invitations went out to 3,000 people to party amid the new splendors, but at the ball the social atmosphere proved to be as oppressive as the strange mist created by thousands of badly burning candles. Thereafter the castle took on the air of a fortress, deserted of virtually all except its guards, for Paul's suspicion of plots was becoming increasingly acute. Once the emperor came down to the Grand Duke Alexander's apartments on the first floor to find a copy of Voltaire's *Brutus* on the table; it was pointedly ordered that it be replaced by a history dealing with Peter the Great and Alexis. St. Petersburg was put under martial law, only officers and medical personnel were allowed to go about the streets at night, and barricades were erected at the gates and major crossroads.

The emperor placed all his confidence in the new governor general of the capital, Count Peter Ludwig von Pahlen, a fifty-six-year-old Courlander who had served Russia with distinction in three wars. Once suddenly demoted by Paul for "servile cowardice" because he had entertained a person out of favor, Pahlen had just as abruptly been forgiven and promoted to lieutenant general. ("I am like one of those dolls that rebound if you push them back," said Pahlen, laughing off the earlier insult.) Coolly, when his own son was arrested, Pahlen waited for Paul to raise the question of loyalty and then replied: "Sire, you have performed an act of justice which will be salutary to the young man." The general entirely endeared himself to Paul when, in response to an order to give a refractory countess a "soaping down" (a French idiom for reprimand), Pahlen actually marched into her room, pushed the hairdresser aside, and personally administered a shampoo to the furious lady. The empress, who was completely disgusted with the rest of Paul's rapid succession of new friends, said of Pahlen: "It is impossible to know this excellent man without liking him." Made a count, Pahlen amassed many controls in his hands—the Guards regiments, the foreign office, the police, the post, and the ports. His wife was insinuated into the Grand Duchess Elizabeth's household as its head, giving Pahlen means of surveillance of the heir to the throne.

For all the precautions, the emperor was still worried about conspiracies and once gloomily expressed his doubts to Pahlen. The count's confident response was: "Sire, I hold all the threads in my hands and nothing has escaped my knowledge. Be calm, a conspiracy is impossible without me. I stake my head on it." Fearful all the same, Paul sent for the corporal of Gatchina, Arakcheev having been exiled to his estates for denouncing a loyal officer and causing his suicide, all to protect his own guilty brother. The loyal of the loyal to Paul, Arakcheev set off posthaste for the capital but arrived to find the barricades manned by hostile soldiers and the capital in an uproar.

On the evening of March 10, at a concert, Paul had been in one of his blackest humors, going so far as to sneer at and then to snub his wife and sons. All was forgotten the next morning until somebody's error on the parade ground produced a new rage, followed by Pahlen's assembling all the officers for the worst dressing down ever. At supper on the eleventh the emperor was in good spirits again and, after fondling a new set of porcelain, declared that "this is one of the happiest days of my life." He joked with his dinner guests, who included General Michael Kutuzov, the Grand Chamberlain Stroganov, Grand Marshal Naryshkin, Count Sheremetev, and Prince Yusupov. Affably, Paul told his son, who seemed unusually taciturn, to go consult a doctor. On the way out of dinner through the anterooms, however, Paul found occasion to shout at an officer of the guard: "You are all Jacobins." Then, calmly he made his way to the apartments of Anna Gagarina, where for a few hours he transacted some state business, including drafting an ultimatum to the court of Berlin. He retired about midnight.

The same evening there was an unusual concourse of officers in the city streets. After lavish dinner parties and much drinking at the Zubovs' and other mansions, officers from all the regiments made their way to the barracks of the Preobrazhenskoe Guards, where they assembled for more drinking in the sumptuous quarters of a general. All wore dress uniforms, and they did not check their sidearms, thus alarming the servants. There was much heated discussion of the evils of despotism and of counteractions, when suddenly the doors opened and there stood General Levin Augest von Bennigsen and Count Pahlen, the latter looming tall and smiling sardonically. He said: "We are among friends, gentlemen, and we understand each other. Are you ready? Let us drink a toast of champagne to the health of the new sovereign. The reign of Paul I is ended."

Pahlen's motives for betraying his master were a mixture of patriotism and the knowledge that in the present regime his position was held only by a string. A serious plot against Paul had been conceived as early as 1799 by Nikita Panin, the nephew of Catherine's chancellor and a man with career grievances. Panin, Pahlen, a high admiral, and others began to hold secret political meetings at the house of Olga Jerebtsev, sister of Zubov and mistress of the British ambassador. French sources later had their own reasons to say that British money was behind the plotters (Paul's removal was, indeed, in the British interest), but actually the diplomat in question was innocent, and many of the people involved were themselves so rich as to be unimpeachable. The original group fell apart through various mischances, but Pahlen readily found others. For instance, the Zubovs—Catherine's last favorite, Platon, and his two brothers—had all the money in the world but not their former glory at court. With diabolical cleverness, Platon Zubov had requested permission to marry Koutaissov's daughter, and it was the emperor's flattered valet turned count who secured the Zubovs' reentry into army circles. The popular Hanoverian General Bennigsen joined the plot, having no romantic illusions about Russian emperors. As for rank and file, Pahlen had no trouble finding revengeful young officers who might have been struck by Paul's cane or jailed for ogling his mistress.

The plan was to force Paul's abdication in favor of Alexander, and obviously the grand duke's complicity in the plot was needed. Even assured that his father would not be killed, Alexander demurred. The heir did not tattle either, and eventually he was brought to an attitude of acquiescence. Alexander learned that the police chief had blanket authority to imprison any member of the imperial family caught in the act of extramarital intercourse, and indeed, the grand duke had his secrets in that area. Pahlen himself relayed to Alexander his father's alleged words: "In a short time I will see myself forced to make fall some heads once dear to me." In the end, it was Alexander who suggested that the night of action, originally set dramatically for the ides of March, be advanced to March 12 when the Third Battalion of his own Semenovskoe Regiment was doing guard duty at the castle.

By way of the Field of Mars and the Nevsky Prospekt two columns converged on the Mikhailovsky Castle. When Pahlen's group proved late, the detachment led by the Zubovs and Bennigsen gave secret passwords at one of the drawbridges and entered the palace through a service entry, easily gaining the second floor. There were only two hussars to deal with at the door of the emperor's library, Pahlen having advised Paul to dismiss the usual sentries. Paul's adjoining bedroom turned out to be empty, seemingly, and the only other door, which led to the empress' quarters, locked. The bedroom was furnished with Gobelin tapestries, once given Paul by the lately deceased French royal couple, and a Spanish folding screen, under which two bare feet were discovered. Coming out from hiding, Paul listened to Platon Zubov's demand for his abdication and Bennigsen's pledge to protect his life. Courageously, he replied: "No, no, I will not at all agree to that." Platon Zubov rushed out, followed by Bennigsen. The junior officers, momentarily cowed, then began to become menacing toward the emperor, especially since the noises outside suggested enemies on the way. Nicholas Zubov threw a gold snuffbox, staggering Paul, and then all fell on the emperor until there was just a disfigured corpse in a white nightshirt on the floor.

The whole palace had been aroused by the boot steps and cries. A group of ex-Gatchina soldiers were faced down at the head of the grand staircase by Count Pahlen, who had just arrived at the scene. It is not improbable that Pahlen was prepared to play the emperor's man and to arrest the grand duke if things had gone wrong. The news of the tragedy made the empress, recently so ill used, insane with grief, her first reaction being to scream, "Paulchen, Paulchen," although subsequently she got it into her head that she was expected to play another Catherine the Great. Pahlen led the way into the ground-floor apartments where the Grand Duke Alexander, fully dressed, sat sobbing in the arms of his wife. The first harsh words were: "That's enough of playing the child. Come, reign!"

The nightmare of Paul was over, and people danced in the streets in the once-forbidden Paris coiffures and clothes. If Paul had been less of a visionary and a perfectionist, perhaps the caprices and brutalities of this Romanov would have been forgiven. As it was, the plot against him was virtually universal. "The common misfortune had united all hearts," wrote a Russian. There was not even a single loyal flunky to denounce the conspirators, and scarcely a person raised an arm in Paul's defense. Few rulers have lived as unhappily as Paul or died as miserably.

XIV.
The Enigmatic Tsar: Alexander I

1. A Guilty and Gregarious Young Man

THE quarter century reign of Alexander I (1801–25) was full of great shocks, convulsions, and zigzags. Major projects of internal reform alternated with huge defeats and heady triumphs in the struggle with revolutionary France under Napoleon. When it was all over, Europe was still in chains and Russia still in chains, and one might wonder, or worry as Alexander did, whether it was worth the costs and sacrifices, first of which had been the murder of his father.

Personally, the Emperor Alexander was far more consequentially enigmatic than the tragic Paul I. The new ruler had been both a pupil of La Harpe and a product of Gatchina. The contradictions in his makeup are multiplied endlessly—humility mixing with pompousness, studiousness with frivolity, candor with secretiveness, companionability with withdrawal, determination with vacillation, kindness with harshness, humanitarianism with militarism, and liberalism with conservatism.

His suite nicknamed him Alexander the Charmer, for the emperor did have an extraordinary ability to approach people, to say what his listeners wished to hear, and to cajole people into doing what he wanted. A "consummate actor" is another description of the man who had received unusual training as grand duke in the arts of dissimulation and self-control. Napoleon was to call his great opponent the Northern Talma or the Northern Sphinx. "Hypocritical" is not too strong a word for the tsar.

A great part of Alexander's ability to charm was his fine appearance, which he was quite vain about. His tall stature and majestic bearing were inherited from his Württemberg mother (they were to distinguish all her progeny and their successors, except the last). His body, only hinting at corpulence, was like those of ancient statues, and his head was so classical in profile as to seem to demand a laurel wreath. A high forehead, thinning hair, and an open face gave him an unforgettable look of serenity and benevolence. Among his fine features were his straight nose and cherubic mouth, but above all, the captivating thing was his large, intensely blue eyes. The French were to call him a master of the smile of the eyes.

The accession of the noble-looking twenty-four-year-old was an answer to the prayers of the people who had suffered the brutalities of Paul. "I breathe peacefully together with all Russia," wrote the new empress. The grim Mikhailovsky Castle was abandoned, and the imperial couple took up residence in the Winter Palace of the beloved Elizabeth. Alexander's first manifesto gave his promise "to rule over his people on the throne conferred on him by God in accord with the laws and heart of the Great Catherine." After invoking the memory of his grandmother, the emperor took the necessary restorative steps: the recall of 15,000 exiles; the elimination of the censorship; the end of the ban on travel abroad; the regranting of the charters of Nobility and Towns; the de-emphasis of the military; and the proclamation of peace with everyone. Even the personal mode of the emperor was a marked change: Alexander rode about his capital unattended, wearing his green Semenovskoe uniform without any decorations. His first appearance thus in Moscow produced an extraordinary popular outburst, the citizens of the old capital crowding around, murmuring endearments, and kissing anything they could touch—his clothes, his boots, and his horse.

An immediate decision facing Alexander concerned the fate of the conspirators of 1801, the men who had gained him the throne but had overreached themselves in the slaying of his father. The guilt-ridden son temporized. Then came sharp letters from La Harpe telling him to let the law follow its course or at least to exile the murderers to their estates. Alexander chose the latter course but acted in a devious manner. Count Pahlen, still in his commanding position, had become alarmed over certain memorials that Old Believers were sending the dowager empress. The religious dissidents believed the late emperor to be their particular protector and picked out such ominous passages from the Second Book of Kings as "Had Zimri peace, who slew his master?" In time the dowager resented Pahlen's effort to associate her with treason, and this was the excuse Alexander needed to have Pahlen's carriage halted at the parade ground and ordered out of the capital all the way to Courland. Forthwith, Nicholas Zubov was likewise banished to the country. Others of the conspirators escaped even this mild punishment, the emperor feeling that he needed Panin, for example, as head of foreign affairs and Bennigsen as a leading army commander. The psychological scars of 1801, however, were not to be so lightly dealt with by Alexander.

Alexander's first reaction on becoming emperor was reportedly the words: "I cannot go on with it. I have no strength to reign." His wife, among others, rekindled in his mind the thought that he could greatly serve Russia. La Harpe returned to Petersburg and acted as a reminder of past idealism.

Alexander came to surround himself with a private committee, a group of liberal young men, who unofficially constituted Russia's Committee of Public Safety, Alexander himself adopting this French Revolutionary term. The four men who came daily to private soirees with the emperor were Count Victor Kochubey, Count Paul Stroganov, Prince Adam Czartorysky, and Nicholas Novosiltsev, aristocrats all but men as liberally educated as Alexander himself (Stroganov had been tutored by the French Jacobin who authored the famous revolutionary calendar; Kochubey and Novosiltsev had been given prolonged exposures to English parliamentary politics). To jealous outsiders Alexander's four friends were Jacobins, who could calmly discuss such things as serfdom. They planned first to investigate, then to reform the administration, and ultimately to come up with that bugbear called a constitution.

Matching the emperor's secret consultations was a marked increase in public discussion of affairs. The government itself directly stimulated this when the Ministry of the Interior undertook to publish *The Review of St. Petersburg,* which included not only final decrees but projects for decrees and even critiques of them. Publishing in general resumed its former volume, and Russians were again exposed to foreign books, including such recent thought-provoking works as those of the Englishmen Adam Smith and Jeremy Bentham. Aspiring Russian authors sometimes sent their manuscripts directly to the emperor, in the hope of subsidies or at least free publication, which Alexander granted frequently. The talented writer Nicholas Karamzin, for example, was named official historiographer, given a pension of 2,000 rubles, and underwritten in the cost of producing a monumental history of Russia, a particularly useful project since many of Karamzin's source materials were subsequently destroyed by fire.

The practical results of the first phase of reform under Alexander were limited but not negligible. A lasting change in the central government was the creation of government ministries in 1802, replacing the cumbersome colleges of Peter the Great. In time, Alexander's friends on the Committee assumed some of these ministerial posts: Czartorysky in Foreign Affairs; Kochubey in the Interior, and Stroganov in Education.

The reformers were willing to raise the serf question, in part as a lever to curb any oligarchic pretensions of the nobility. In 1803 the Free Agriculturalists Act was Alexander's response to Count Nicholas Rumyantsev's proposal to give freedom to all his serfs: The decree regularized manumissions, but the number of peasants thus freed numbered only in the several thousands. In the end, even La Harpe advised Alexander to proceed slowly on serfdom in the face of inadequate data and the opposition of vested interests. The greatest thing Alexander could boast was that he kept his vow never to give away crown serfs in the manner of his recent predecessors.

The continuing stumbling block to the reformers' efforts was the lack of educated response and the absence of local leadership. Accordingly, Alexander's friends came to lay the greatest stress on the school system, increasing the appropriations for education until in 1804 they reached 740,000,000 rubles, or four times the outlay under Catherine. Forty-seven new Gymnasiums were opened, and in the course of Alexander's whole reign the number of universities reached six. Quantity was accompanied by quality in the form of the University Statute of 1804 giving the institutions autonomy under faculty councils. In a short time, war needs appropriated much of the educational budget, but of all the starts made by Alexander, this was to prove the real groundwork for revolutionary changes in later reigns.

Two years after his accession Alexander was still optimistic about bringing the fruits of enlightenment to Russia, all the while disdaining power for its own sake. His old dream of self-imposed abdication was repeated in a letter to La Harpe. It was not long, however, before the liberal phase led to disillusion. Like the unfinished schoolboy he had been, Alexander originally approached his governing tasks almost lightheartedly, and his subsequent discouragement in the face of the apathy of the ruling classes was sharp and overwhelming. "I do not trust anyone: all men are scoundrels" was to be one royal outburst. As for his Private Committee, they eventually quit their jobs and drifted back to their estates or England. More than anything else, however, Alexander's satisfactions in war and diplomacy ended his first efforts to transform Russia internally. The restoration of the secret police in 1805 in the face of rumored plots, foreign and domestic, was an indication to many, some relieved and some outraged, that Alexander's liberalism was past.

The emperor was too complex and deviously calculating ever to drop a role altogether. In 1806 he was still posing as a liberal for the benefit of U.S. President Thomas Jefferson, exchanging correspondence with him on the subject of the constitutional structure of the United States. Tsar and President might have more profitably shared their experiences in reconciling theory with practice, for both were to go down in history as frustrated, if not hypocritical, in following their own precepts.

As late as 1809, in the face of bitter hostility to the vagueness of his foreign policy, Alexander again turned to internal reorganization, by way of both threat and promise. The man entrusted with Alexander's second phase of reforming zeal was Michael Speransky, son of a priest, teacher of mathematics in his own seminary at the age of eighteen, and student of such brilliant promise as to be given special dispensation to escape holy orders. As a minor civil servant, Speransky came to Alexander's attention accidentally—as the result of the sickness of his superior, Kochubey—and a prolonged and informal conversation between the two men was followed by Speransky's designation as "attached to the person of his Imperial Majesty for special affairs." The special affairs the emperor had in mind were nothing less than the completion of a new law code and the formulation of a constitution. In time the priest's son gathered all offices of state in his hands, so that about 1810 an Italian diplomat was to describe him as "the great and almighty Speransky, secretary general of the empire and in fact Prime Minister, if not *the* minister."

Speransky's major memorandum to Alexander was as bold as it was pseudosophisticated about Russian history under the Romanovs. Tsar Alexis' time was cited as one when there were beginnings to the limitation of the autocracy. Although Peter the Great reversed this trend, it was noted that he set the stage economically and educationally for political changes. Even the abortive effort of the nobility to impose controls on the Empress Anna was considered favorably. From these precedents Speransky reached such conclusions as: "The despotic form of government can be permissible only during the infancy of a society"; "a government should have no other authority than that entrusted to it by the nation"; and "all public officers should be subject to election." The completed Speransky constitutional project was published in November, 1809, and it showed clear signs of borrowings from the French Constitution of 1799 and the Code Napoléon. It envisaged a highly centralized government based on four great institutions: the emperor, the Senate as a supreme court; a Council of State to initiate legislation; and a hierarchy of elected Dumas, including a national Duma, to provide popular consent. A scheme of government such as would have made Catherine choke, the Speransky constitution was almost exactly a century too advanced for the Romanov dynasty. Alexander recoiled and finally contented himself with formally instituting only the Council of State in 1810. A lasting innovation, this appointive advisory body was important at least as a training ground for grand dukes, who constituted much of its membership.

Speransky at the height of his influence was feared as a Jacobin by people such as the dowager empress, the Grand Duke Constantine, and an important man of unpopular memory, Arakcheev. The last, Paul's chief henchman, oddly enough also enjoyed the good graces of Alexander, who employed him in military administration, for which he had considerable talents. In 1810 Arakcheev emerged as a reactionary counterbalance to progressives in the emperor's suite, after Alexander was subjected to eerie experiences on the occasion of his first visit to Arakcheev's estate at

Gruzino. The emperor was led into the local church only to behold a huge bas-relief of the Emperor Paul, commissioned by Arakcheev, who had also dared put up an inscription in gold: MY HEART IS PURE AND MY SPIRIT JUST BEFORE YOU. Arakcheev further played on Alexander's guilt by exposing the miniature of the murdered master which he carried on his breast, and this charlatan mesmerized his sovereign even more by showing him a study in the Gruzino mansion that re-created Alexander's own study in Petersburg down to the last candlestick and inkwell. After this visit the emperor was to exchange over the years hundreds of letters with his "faithful friend," whose detestation of reform was almost pathological.

Another push away from liberalism given the emperor occurred during a visit in 1811 to the estate of his sister Catherine, at Tver. Here he was shown the latest work of Karamzin, the widely traveled historian whom Alexander originally sponsored. Karamzin's *Memoir on Ancient and Modern Russia* set out deliberately to refute Speransky's version of constitutional trends in the country's history. Alexander was brought short by the words:

> The autocracy founded Russia; any modification of its structure would be disastrous. . . . Our political principles are not inspired by the Encyclopaedia edited in Paris, but by another Encyclopaedia infinitely more ancient, the Bible. Our tsars are not representatives of the People . . . they are the representatives of Him who rules over all empires. . . . The Emperor is our living law.

In March, 1812, soon after Arakcheev and Karamzin got Alexander's ear, the reformer Speransky—a man too trustful to intrigue in his own defense and a scapegoat in the interests of national unity on the eve of the French invasion—was dismissed. That Alexander was still of two minds, liberal and conservative, was attested to by his plaint to a courtier: "Last night they made me part with Speransky and he was my right hand." Loyally but realistically, Speransky concluded about his master that he was too weak to rule and too strong to be ruled.

2. *Opportunist in Diplomacy*

At the outset of his reign Alexander readily subscribed to enlightened and pacifist sentiments about the futility of further conquests and the need for victories against internal problems. Catherine, before becoming the Great, would have endorsed such views. Yet like his grandmother, Alexander soon found himself drawn into an active policy of war and conquest, in part because external affairs were less boring and frustrating than internal reforms and in part because the emperor discovered himself to be every bit as much a born diplomat as the illustrious empress.

Alexander's peculiarly female traits underlay this success. A French ambassador declared bluntly: "If Alexander were to be dressed in woman's clothes he would have made a shrewd woman." In the view of Metternich, "Alexander's character represents a strange blending of the qualities of a man and the weaknesses of a woman." Yet the female weaknesses were precisely what made Alexander a supreme negotiator—deviousness, dissimulation, tenaciousness, and stubbornness, among others. The person Napoleon called the Northern Talma emerged as great a diplomat as the Frenchman was a general. Indeed, in the Age of Napoleon Alexander was the other great historical figure. The sometime allies, sometime enemies had many things in common: Both were educated in the shadow of the French Revolution; both were usurpers in a sense; both had to expiate their sins; and both were to accomplish in myth what they failed to realize in life.

In the manner of Catherine II following Peter III, Alexander's first tasks in foreign policy were to disentangle Russia from the follies of his predecessor. The India expedition was recalled, and the embargo on British shipping lifted. Napoleon's offers of alliance were rebuffed, but then the French leader's need for Russian friendship ended. In March, 1802, France and Britain signed the Treaty of Amiens, and peace came to all Europe for the first time in a decade.

The lull was a short one. The French and the British resumed hostilities in 1803. Other events led to the formation of a Third Coalition against France, Alexander emerging in the lead. High-handed actions by Napoleon in Italy and Germany aroused alarm, while his proclaiming himself emperor in May, 1804, excited contempt, if not envy, among born rulers. A great *cause célèbre* was Napoleon's execution of the Duc d'Enghien, darling of the French royalists. True to his class, Alexander sent vehement protests to Paris, to which Napoleon replied with calculated tactlessness by reminding the Russian emperor of his own part in the murder of royalty, as well as accusing him of taking British money in the process. The French ambassador was peremptorily dismissed in May, 1804, and by the spring of 1805 Russia had military alliances with Austria, Sweden, and Britain. Prussia decided to avoid this coalition, since it was unprepared for war and felt no real national interests were involved, factors that also applied to Russia. But Alexander's crusade was not to be stopped. The prospects of needed reform at home ended.

The emperor left for the war in September, 1805, reaching Austria after one of his ally's armies had already surrendered to Napoleon. Simultaneously, in October, 1805, Admiral Horatio Nelson smashed the French navy at the Battle of Trafalgar, Napoleon having already abandoned his project to invade Britain in favor of lightning moves against his enemies on the Continent. The remaining forces of Emperor Francis I of Austria and the fresh Russian army joined under the command of the Russian General Michael Kutuzov. This veteran's cautiousness and desire to negotiate were undercut by fire-eating younger officers, who persuaded Alexander to interfere actively in the military decisions. This interplay is dramatized, incidentally, in the opening part of Tolstoy's *War and Peace*. The Soviet movie version of this classic contains a striking scene of a perfectly re-created Alexander and his brother, the Grand Duke Constantine —both of them all glitter, handsomeness, and insouciance—reviewing the army before the famous Battle of Austerlitz, the clash itself being treated in the movie as an unforgettable aerial panorama.

Napoleon had tried negotiations previous to Austerlitz, asking Alexander's envoy, Prince Peter Dolgoruky: "How long do we have to fight? What do you want from me? What does Emperor Alexander desire? If he wants to enlarge his states let him do so at the expense of his neighbors, Turkey especially, and then he will have no disputes with France." The young Russian's supercilious reply and unmannerly departure caused the French emperor to report him in dispatches as "an insolent nincompoop, that mischievous Dolgoruky." The insult was redeemed by the greatest military victory of Napoleon's career. After advancing through a fog only to find the French where they were not supposed to be, the Russian army was cut to pieces and driven to helpless flight, all before the noon hour was out. After the disastrous battle, when he at last reached safety, Alexander threw himself on the ground and wept convulsively. The Russian emperor had to spend the night in a peasant hut, being refused even a glass of wine by the Austrian marshal of court, who declined to disturb the Emperor Francis, asleep in a palace, to get the requisite permission. This example of Austrian cooperation was used by the Russians to explain the general debacle at Austerlitz.

Austria promptly made peace with Napoleon, allowing the millennium-old Holy Roman Empire to lapse and southern Germany to be reorganized as a French satellite called the Confederation of the Rhine. Sobered, resentful, but more determined than ever, Alexander returned to cheering crowds in St. Petersburg and vowed to fight on. Six hundred thousand militiamen were called up, while the Holy Synod composed a manifesto to be read in every parish describing Napoleon as "the chief enemy of mankind, who worships idols and whores." A two-front war was now forced on Russia, since French intrigues brought about hostilities with Turkey in August, 1806. Hopes rose when Prussia belatedly joined against France, but in October the world was astonished to see the great Prussian war machine, the pride of Frederick the Great, in complete ruin after Napoleon's triumph at Jena and Frederick's son a fugitive. Napoleon occupied the Prussian capital, and it was there that he issued his Berlin Decree of November, proclaiming the Continental System—the French Emperor's grandiose effort to reduce Britain to submission by closing all European ports to British trade.

In 1807 French and Russian armies clashed in northern Germany. The drawn Battle of Eylau in February was a bloody mess, costing Bennigsen 26,000 casualties. The Battle of Friedland in June was definitely a Russian defeat, and the French were able to occupy all East Prussia. In his disgust at the losses, Grand Duke Constantine suggested that the emperor order each soldier to load his rifle and shoot himself. Russian opinion still clamored for victories, not for peace. Peace is what it got, however, when Alexander, in one of the great about-faces in history, allied himself with Napoleon after a dramatic meeting with him at Tilsit in July, 1807.

The negotiations had been initiated by Alexander. The personal encounter could not have been more theatrically arranged. It took place on a raft in the middle of the Niemen, where a white linen pavilion with *N* and *A* on each side seemed to proclaim that the two emperors would decide the fate of the world between them. Alexander at once showed his ability to say what his rival wanted to hear by beginning with: "I hate the English no less than you do and I am ready to assist you in any undertaking against them." Napoleon could only reply: "If such be the case then everything can be settled between us." After two hours on the raft, the discussions were transferred to the town for the next several days, the two emperors riding about together and exchanging complimentary passwords, such as "Alexander, Russia, Greatness" and "Napoleon, France, Bravery." After dinner they would escape their own diplomatic staffs for more informal direct discussions into the night. Napoleon said with conspiratorial friendliness, "I shall be your secretary and you shall be mine."

What the two men actually felt behind their masks of affability was revealed in correspondence. Napoleon wrote to Josephine: "I have just seen Emperor Alexander. I am very pleased with him; he is a very handsome, good, and youthful emperor and he is cleverer than he is usually thought to be." In a letter to his sister, Alexander revealed relief, mingled with snobbery: "God has saved us: instead of sacrifices we have come out of the fight almost gloriously. But what will you say to all these events? *I! to spend my days with Bonaparte,* to be whole hours engaged in conversation with him! I ask you does not all this seem like a nightmare?"

The Tilsit agreements consisted of twenty-nine articles, seven secret articles, and a treaty of friendship and alliance between the two countries that Napoleon called a "great and beautiful idea." Seemingly France got a free hand in the West, while Russia could expand in the East, but the treaty was never so explicit, and complications arose almost immediately. Alexander made two tremendous sacrifices: allowing Napoleon to create a satellite grand duchy of Warsaw out of the former Prussian parts of Poland and placing Russia under all the restrictions of the Continental

System against Britain. In return, Napoleon agreed to any future Russian annexation of Finland, grandly saying, "St. Petersburg is too close to the Finnish borders: the belles of St. Petersburg in their palace should not be forced to listen any more to the roar of Swedish guns." Russian gains against Turkey were also countenanced but did not include the capital since Napoleon believed that "the possession of Constantinople assures the control of the whole world." The agreements ratified, Napoleon received the Order of St. Andrew and Alexander the Grand Cross of the Legion of Honor; they embraced and went off, each thoroughly convinced of having captured the other.

Alexander returned from Tilsit to no cheers. To make not only peace but alliance with Napoleon, the man previously denounced as the Anti-Christ, was as incomprehensible and hateful for Orthodox Russians in 1807 as the signing of the Hitler-Stalin Pact was to be for orthodox Communists 132 years later. High society expressed its opposition by closing their doors to the newly appointed French ambassador, the Grand Duke Constantine for one declaring that he would sooner seat a convict at his table. The marked friendship for the Marquis de Caulaincourt that the emperor alone displayed had in the end the useful effect of making the French ambassador more Alexander's agent than Napoleon's. Only a few people appreciated the difficulty of Alexander's position, one, for example, writing: "What could he do when he saw the innumerable armies of the enemy facing his own defeated troops? . . . I come to the conclusion that nations can be as villainous as individuals." No one at all really knew what was going on in the enigmatic ruler's mind; in retrospect, it appears that Alexander was much less blinded by Tilsit and much more farsighted in his intentions than Stalin was in a similar situation.

Napoleon's downfall began with events in a country remote from Russia —the national uprising in Spain following his putting his brother Joseph on the throne of Madrid in May, 1808. The Spanish were to invent guerrilla tactics and tie down large French armies for the next six years. Now more confident of his diplomatic position, Alexander braved his growing unpopularity and went off to another meeting with Napoleon at Erfurt in the fall of 1808. The harassed Napoleon soothed his ally, although he allowed himself a private outburst that Alexander made himself "deaf to what he does not want to hear."

What Napoleon sought at Erfurt was Alexander's active participation in the preventive war the French ruler felt he had to wage against a revitalized Austria. Alexander temporized with tremendous finesse, reassuring both sides and thereby driving Napoleon into a frenzy. It was only after a French army had captured Vienna in May, 1809, that Alexander made a token invasion of Austria with 32,000 men. During the action the salons of St. Petersburg were openly drinking toasts to the enemy. Even the simultaneous war that saw Russian forces wrest Finland from the traditional foe, Sweden, was highly unpopular.

After his victory in 1809, Napoleon enjoyed an alliance with Austria, as well as with Russia, all the while distrusting each. A marriage tie offered a firmer mutual commitment, and accordingly, Napoleon ordered Caulaincourt to get an answer within forty-eight hours to his proposal to marry the Grand Duchess Anna Pavlovna. Alexander gagged and left the decision to his mother. The childless Napoleon was ready to abandon his wife, Josephine. Just as incredibly, the Romanov family finally agreed to marry the fifteen-year-old tsarevna to the forty-year-old usurper from Corsica, provided only that there be a two-year wait. The Russian courier with this message was on his way when, in April, 1810, Napoleon announced his betrothal to the Archduchess Marie Louise of Austria, the sacrificial lamb of the Hapsburgs.

The falling through of the marriage alliance was just one of several events that ended any illusions Alexander may have had about a permanent accommodation with Napoleon. French appropriation of his brother-in-law's domains in Oldenburg was rankling the tsar, but more alarming were reports of French agents promising the liberation of Russian Poland. The greatest strain on Russia and the major source of the emperor's unpopularity was the embargo on British shipping required by the Continental System. Since even a few months' embargo had helped overthrow Paul, Alexander was aware of the ruin implicit in a long one, and late in 1810 the ports were reopened. This step completed the break with Napoleon, who, confident in his Hapsburg marriage, was talking of the reappearance of Charlemagne's European empire. In 1811 Napoleon predicted to a French abbé that "in five years I will be ruler of the world." That same year hostilities may be said to have broken out if one counts a duel fought in Naples between the French ambassador and his Russian counterpart, the ever hotheaded Prince Peter Dolgoruky.

In the spring of 1812 Alexander did by far the best in the diplomatic maneuvering prior to all-out war. The Russian-Swedish hostilities were ended by treaty in April. The Russo-Turkish War was also concluded, freeing Kutuzov's recently victorious armies for action elsewhere. In internal policy, Alexander chose this time to dismiss the reformer Speransky, thus ridding himself of an obstacle to complete harmony with the ruling classes.

Hostile French and Russian armies were in position by February, 1812. After perfunctory negotiations, Napoleon crossed the frontier on June 22. That day Alexander was at a ball at the estate of General Bennigsen outside Vilna and stayed as in control of himself as he had been in the different circumstances of Tilsit five years before. A witness later recorded:

He did not sit down at table but moved from table to table with the appearance of perfect enjoyment. I say "appearance" because he played his role marvelously, having already been notified that at this very moment, while the ball was going on at Zakort, a scene much more magnificent and solemn was being enacted twenty miles from there. Napoleon crossed the Niemen with 600,000 soldiers. . . .

Shortly after, the emperor issued a manifesto containing the ringing defiance: "I will not lay down arms so long as a single enemy soldier remains in my empire."

The French army entered Vilna within six days. A final Russian envoy of peace was rebuffed and even twitted with a question about the best road leading to Moscow. The envoy's brave rejoinder was: "In Russia we think all roads lead to Moscow—including the one of Poltava taken by Charles XII." Fine words, however, did not halt the French invasion, which swept past the central fortress city of Smolensk in August, its momentum barely contested.

Napoleon's original strategy for the Russian campaign was to seize Vilna, Minsk, and Smolensk and to entrench himself. By the fall of 1812, however, the French leader came to feel that his popularity required another grand coup, and thus he pushed on in search of the enemy army. Alexander said of his counterplan: "I am ready to suffer some defeats at the beginning but they will not discourage me. In beating a retreat I shall place a desert between our armies. I shall evacuate everyone and everything." This scorched earth strategy was modified as a necessary concession to the popular clamor for making a stand. Originally, Alexander had stayed with the army, but this caused criticism, including a blunt message from his sister Catherine: "For God's sake do not decide to assume command yourself. There is no time to lose to give the armies a chief in whom the men would have confidence." Alexander reluctantly appointed Kutuzov supreme commander a few days after the fall of Smolensk, remarking: "The public wants his nomination. I have named him. As for myself I wash my hands of it." Known as the Old Fox of the North, Kutuzov at sixty-seven had been the loser at Austerlitz, as well as a hero of Suvorov's old campaigns and of the recent Turkish War. Fat, licentious, lazy, blind in one eye, typically lying panting on a divan, the general was also sharp-witted, cautious, tenacious, fertile in stratagems, imperturbable in battle, and beloved by his men.

Kutuzov ended the retreat and took up a strong position 60 miles west of Moscow, bringing about the Battle of Borodino in September, 1812. For fifteen hours the finest units of the French army attacked and attacked, but still the Russians held. That night Kutuzov and a council of war decided that their appalling losses required retreat again. A week later the

French occupied Moscow, and within a day the city was in flames, the cause of the fire remaining a mystery. Alexander in St. Petersburg remained defiant: "This will not decide the struggle. When I shall have used all the means in my power, I shall let my beard grow and live like the poorest peasant, eating potatoes, but I will not sign the dishonour of my country and of my dear subjects, whose sacrifices I do appreciate." The tsar on other occasions spoke of fighting on the shores of the Volga. Yet the five weeks Napoleon stayed in Moscow were the most trying Alexander had spent since 1801. His popularity was at its lowest; his throne itself was in jeopardy. At Alexander's coronation anniversary celebration there was not a single cheer.

As the world soon learned, it was Napoleon who was really in desperate trouble. With little sense of history, he had expected the boyars to greet him outside Moscow, and he completely failed to exploit the real possibility of social revolution in Russia. He wanted Alexander to sue for peace and later found his own appeals unanswered. Without supplies, the French army began its retreat in October, being forced to take the devastated route by which it had come, for Kutuzov's armies now hotly contested French forays in other directions. The Russian people began to wage a guerrilla struggle with ruthlessness and fanatic religious overtones. Napoleon abandoned his army at length, leaving his heroic marshals to accomplish such frozen and bloody miracles as the crossing of the Berezina in late November. In Paris in December the French emperor assured his stupefied subjects that his health was never better. At the same time a fraction of his "Grand Army" was recrossing the Niemen River.

Never before Napoleon's invasion and never afterward was the feeling of identification to be so strong between the Romanov dynasty and all classes of the Russian people. Tchaikovsky's *1812 Overture* is just one of many recurring manifestations of national catharsis over this event. Personally, Alexander reached the apogee of his popularity, even the fickle salons according him every praise. The patriotic response had been overwhelming. The nobility freely contributed 200,000,000 rubles to the state, the equivalent of more than half the annual budget. Individual aristocrats like Mathias Dmitriev-Mamanov, son of Catherine's lover, equipped whole regiments at their private expense. The sacrifice of the peasants was proportionately greater as they relentlessly burned crops and homes to deny them to the invader. A good indication of the fervor aroused is the report that for months after the French retreat peasants kept turning up from the remotest parts of Siberia to defend holy Moscow against the foreign heretics. The completeness of the victory should not obscure the staggering costs, casualties in the hundreds of thousands and an estimated net loss of population nearing 3,000,000. Among other things, the financial exertions of the nobility in 1812 put many of them so badly in debt that a radical solution to the serf question became necessary within half a century.

3. Hero of Russia and Europe

New Year's Day, 1813, the emperor led the Russian army across the Niemen River, his destination Paris, his new role that of the Agamemnon of Europe. The momentousness of this decision cannot be overestimated.

A considerable segment of Russian opinion opposed crossing the frontiers, most notably Kutuzov, newly a recipient of the Grand Cross of the Order of St. George, a field marshal, and Prince of Smolensk. As Alexander advanced farther and farther into Germany, Kutuzov was to grumble: "Nothing is easier at present than to go beyond the Elbe. But how shall we return? With a bloody nose." The emperor fretted at the strictures of the war hero and was relieved that Kutuzov died in April, 1813. Accused of glory seeking for himself, Alexander drove his forces westward, offering, as always, riddles. What of the erstwhile reformer at home? What of the peacemaker at Tilsit?

The Prussian king joined Alexander's war of liberation in March, 1813, and Austria followed in August. The British, who had been fighting France almost uninterruptedly for twenty years, now were willing to pay out 2,500,-000 pounds yearly to keep the allied armies in the field. The Fourth Coalition against revolutionary France was under way, and it was the final one (Catherine having distracted the first of 1793; Paul having deserted the second of 1798; and Alexander having bungled the third of 1804).

The forces in the final struggle were not unevenly matched, with roughly 500,000 soldiers and 1,200 cannons on the French side and slightly more on the Russian-Prussian-Austrian side. Although the British supplied mainly money, the British-Spanish army was the first to invade France, from the south, in late 1813.

The allies were divided, and they did not have a Napoleon. They were driven out of Saxony again in the summer of 1813. However, Alexander did distinguish himself as something of a general during the retreat on Bohemia, inflicting a spectacular defeat on a French diversionary corps. In the fall the allies again struck at Napoleon, and at Leipzig in October won a huge victory in the three-day Battle of the Nations. Again, Alexander's generalship was an important factor, not only in setting a general line of strategy, but also in tactically committing the Russian artillery in the first decisive day of the battle. After Leipzig the allies were able to cross the Rhine on New Year's Day, 1814.

Following the first battles on the soil of France in long memory, the allied armies entered Paris on March 31, 1814. Alexander led the triumphal march down the Champs Élysées, having told the Parisians he "entered their walls not as an enemy but as a friend." Cossacks thereupon bivouacked on the heights of Montmartre, leaving a memorial to this day in the form of the first bistro, named Mother Catherine. The last to consider peace negotiations previously, Alexander was the first to treat France leniently. The enigmatic tsar insisted that full honors be paid the abdicated Napoleon. In response to a proposal to raze Paris' Austerlitz Bridge, Alexander replied grandly: "It will be sufficient for future generations to know that Emperor Alexander crossed the Austerlitz Bridge with his army." The future of the French body politic was a more ticklish problem. Perhaps Alexander let himself be taken in by Talleyrand, who assured him that his mansion was the only place in Paris not mined with explosives and then proceeded to ply his guest with arguments in favor of bringing back the Bourbon dynasty. The Russian autocrat briefly toyed with the idea of allowing France to be a democratic republic. When Louis XVIII was, nonetheless, installed in the Tuileries, there was an embarrassing scene. At a banquet the servants not unnaturally gave first attention to the all-powerful Emperor of Russia, driving the sensitive old king to squeak in protest. "You would have thought *he* had restored the throne to me," wrote Alexander. In the end, Alexander and his British allies were obdurate in forcing Louis XVIII to grant his subjects a constitution, all the while offering him, by the First Treaty of Paris in May, 1814, peace terms lenient enough to make his regime politically viable.

After his tour de force in Paris, Alexander journeyed to London, where he was banqueted by the regent and mobbed by the citizenry. He was treated not as the barbaric curiosity Peter the Great had been but as the most civilized liberator of Europe. Later the emperor went to Baden to share his wife's childhood memories and to meet more royalty. Seemingly, the emperor had forgotten Russia, but not Russia him, for a delegation of Russian dignitaries arrived in Baden to beg to confer on the arbiter of the Continent the title Alexander the Blessed.

In September, 1814, Alexander was lavishly established in the Hofburg Palace as a central participant in the Congress of Vienna, called to redraw the map of Europe after a quarter century of unprecedented convulsions. Alexander realized that Russia's was not the only decisive voice: Austria's joining the Fourth Coalition at the critical moment in 1813 won Metternich's country the seat of the Congress; Britain had fought France since 1793 and literally ruled the seas; France, particularly as represented by the wily Prince Talleyrand, was still a leading nation; and Prussia, the least of the victors, had revived spiritedly from defeat and had aroused an all-German nationalism. The Congress of Vienna also included several lesser European kings and apprehensive German princes numbering in the hundreds, but the big five powers made the real decisions. The concourse of royalty included a number of Romanovs besides Alexander and his empress: specifically, the Grand Duchess Anna (still unmarried), the Grand Duchess Catherine (newly engaged to the Prince of Württemberg), and the Grand Duke Constantine (easily bored and eager to get back to Warsaw and the Polish lady who was to become his morganatic wife). The sacrifices of war did not crimp the family style. A great banquet Alexander threw on his name day at the palace of the Russian ambassador cost hundreds of thousands of rubles. The menu included items from the far reaches: oranges from Sicily, oysters from Belgium, pâté from Périgord, sterlets from the lower Volga, cucumbers from the royal hothouses of Moscow, and cherries from the same in St. Petersburg (reported to have cost Alexander fifty kopecks apiece).

During the serious negotiations at Vienna, the Russian-Prussian territorial ambitions in the east of Europe provoked Britain and Austria to join in a counteralliance with their ex-enemy France in January, 1815. The possibility of a new war was real for a brief time, but it was already bygone in March, when Napoleon escaped from the island of Elba and returned to France to regalvanize the empire during the celebrated Hundred Days. Alexander was not deterred when his ex-ally of Tilsit sent him the secret Austrian-British-French treaty; the tsar summoned Prince Metternich and, handing him the document, said evenly: "This should never come between us . . . our very law commands us to pardon offenses." But privately the emperor, who mistakenly believed himself to be the savior of civilization, whined that "human gratitude is as rare as a white raven."

The coalition of Napoleon's enemies closed ranks against him. La Harpe tried in two letters to suggest to Alexander that Napoleon *was* France and should be left in peace, but the emperor was now obsessive in his opposition. His reply to his ex-tutor read: "To submit oneself to the genius of evil means to enforce his power, to place in his hands a tool for the erection of a tyranny much worse than the previous one. It is necessary to have the bravery to fight him. . . ."

The recalled Russian armies had time only to reach the Rhine before the British Duke of Wellington and the Prussian Gebhard Leberecht von Blücher dealt Napoleon his Waterloo in June, 1815. The battle was followed by the French Emperor's second abdication and definitive exile to St. Helena. Alexander entered Paris again but left without uttering any noble sentiments to the French. The Second Treaty of Paris was harsh economically and territorially on France, even after Louis XVIII was allowed to return to his capital.

Even before Napoleon's final downfall, the powers had agreed to the comprehensive Act of the Congress of Vienna in early June, 1815. Historians have put much of the responsibility for the territorial settlements on the Austrian Chancellor Metternich. A guiding principle was legitimacy, or the restoration of pre-1789 rulers. All the changes made by the French Revolution and Napoleon could not be ignored, however, so that, for example, an area like Germany emerged as thirty-nine states instead of the ten times that number that existed two decades previously. The principle of compensation was also applied, meaning that the winners against France were rewarded territorially for their trouble and the losers, Napoleon's allies, were penalized. Critics of the Vienna settlement, then and later, complained that nationalism was ignored, citing in particular the fact that the German and Italian peoples remained divided up among petty principalities. However, it was not German and Italian nationalists who defeated Napoleon but the professional armies of the emperors and kings. Moreover, Metternich's arrangements prevented major wars for forty years. The Emperor Alexander did not oppose any of the main decisions at Vienna, although he was frustrated in his efforts to extend discussion to the Balkans and Ottoman Empire. By the treaty Russia duly received more of Poland, and her conquests of Finland from Sweden in 1809 and Bessarabia from Turkey in 1812 were recognized.

The particularly cherished project of Alexander in 1815 was the Holy Alliance. Its signing in September followed a great demonstration of Russian armed might at Châlons in France, where 107,000 Guards and Cossack units were paraded before the assembled greats of Europe. Even the Duke of Wellington was awed: "I could never have imagined that it was possible to bring an army to such an extraordinary state of perfection." The elaborate religious services for each of Alexander's seven army corps impressed the non-Russians as much or more than the military display. It was, indeed, religious mysticism which underlay the Holy Alliance, Alexander explaining that "the fires of Moscow have lit my soul." The alliance, signed by virtually every country, simply pledged rulers to govern in accordance with justice, benevolence, and Christian principles. "An empty noise" was Metternich's evaluation, while the British foreign secretary called it "sublime mysticism and nonsense" and speculated whether the tsar was quite right in the head. In due course the Holy Alliance would be denounced as a diabolical conspiracy of blind reactionaries to maintain the status quo everywhere, but at its inception the document symbolized new hopes and caused Alexander to be approached with subprojects by the celebrated British Utilitarian philosopher Jeremy Bentham and the Utopian Socialists Robert Owen and Charles Fourier. In 1815 the best minds in Europe could still believe that Russia's autocrat came to them as a liberator, not as an oppressor.

Poland seemed the key test of the emperor's intentions. Polish patriots, such as Kosciusko, had come to Paris to plead the restoration of the kingdom of 1772, knowing that Alexander, like his father before him, had expressed his antipathy to the partitions perpetrated by Catherine. The tsar's plans for the Poles appeared enlightened enough: "My intention is to return to them all that I can get of their country and to give them a constitution, the elaboration of which I reserve to myself." Although politically unable to give up the large Russian parts of Poland, the emperor did gain a special status for the Prussian parts that Napoleon had briefly constituted as the grand duchy of Warsaw. Called Congress Poland, after Vienna, this area centering on Warsaw duly received a constitution and Alexander as king. When the elected Polish Diet first met in 1818, advanced public opinion abroad and in Russia was pleased, if not astonished, to read Alexander's speech of welcome. The Russian autocrat declared that "free institutions" are "not a dangerous dream" but "confirm the well-being of nations," and then he added momentously that he hoped to extend them to "all countries entrusted to my care" and was "glad of the opportunity to demonstrate to my country that which I have been preparing for it since long." The Polish Diet proceeded to pass most of the laws Alexander submitted to it, but it rejected one measure, and the constitutional King of Poland congratulated the Diet on the independence of its opinions.

Three years after the defeat of France the emperor was still enjoying a reputation abroad as a liberal autocrat. In 1818 he journeyed to the Congress of Aix-la-Chapelle and, countering Metternich's lingering bitterness, insisted on the evacuation of France by the forces of the allies. Shortly afterward, however, Alexander's pretense of liberalism in European affairs ceased: He became the henchman of Metternich's reactionary policies, and his Holy Alliance emerged as truly a symbol of benighted opposition to all change.

In 1820 a revolution in Spain forced the king to regrant the constitution of the heroic days of 1812, and this was followed by similar radical coups engineered by army officers in Naples and Piedmont. At the hastily called congresses of Troppau and Laibach, Alexander endorsed Metternich's position that such illegal changes should be stopped by force and rulers restored to their absolute rights. The British at these meetings considered such policies wrongheaded and began to disassociate themselves from the others. Austrian troops suppressed the revolutions in the Italian states in 1821, and the French royal army crushed the progressive forces of Spain in 1823. In each case Alexander offered Russian intervention if necessary. Closer to home, the emperor faced a crisis in the kingdom of Poland, when the Diet in September, 1820, rejected all proposed bills as a protest against the high-handed actions and rampant militarism of the governor, the Grand Duke Constantine. Alexander's response was to send the elected representatives home for five years, and when the Diet did meet again in February,

1825, the members were soundly lectured and were told they represented nothing more than an experiment.

There were two special cases when the new zigzag from liberation to oppression in Alexander's diplomacy ran into impossible difficulties. One is associated with the historic Monroe Doctrine of December, 1823. Alexander and all the armies of Europe could not hope to restore the revolted colonies of South and Central America to the Spanish king, less because of American defiance than because the British navy stood in their way. The Monroe Doctrine was also directed specifically against Russian encroachments in North America. The Russian-American Company had sold out its California settlements but remained firmly entrenched in Alaska, and in 1821 Alexander decreed that its jurisdiction there extended southward to the fifty-first parallel. American protests led Russia to back down, and the line was set at 54° 40'. The other special case where Alexander's reactionary policy floundered was the matter of the Greek revolt in 1821 and the eight-year struggle for Greek independence from the Ottoman Empire. Here the emperor was caught in the dilemma of opposing any revolution or of following the traditional Russian diplomacy of enmity to Turkey and protectorship over the local Orthodox population of the Balkans. Alexander ended up doing nothing in the crisis.

The tangible results of all the shifts in the foreign policy of Alexander were negligible. Napoleon had been defeated, but the stability of Europe had hardly been assured. Russia could not disarm, and after 1815 Alexander felt compelled to maintain a costly standing army of 450,000, specifically equal to the combined forces of Prussia and Austria. Like Catherine, Alexander found himself annexing many new areas—Finland, Congress Poland, Bessarabia, Georgia, and huge areas of central Asia—and thus adding new commitments to an already chaotic, rotten state. Schizophrenia in foreign policy, as in domestic policy, served Alexander and Russia ill.

4. Spiritualist

When Alexander I returned to St. Petersburg in 1815, he was hailed as the "victor of the invincible." In reply he had medals struck "Not unto us, O Lord, not unto us," adding that it was all really the work of God before whom "humility will better our morals, will efface our sins, will bring us honor, and real glory." The strong religious note in the message revealed a new spiritual side to Alexander.

The internal state of Russia after the strains of the French invasion was even worse than before objectively, while subjectively it was all the more shocking to those officers and diplomats who had been exposed to the advanced societies of the West. There were a thousand problems awaiting

decision, and it was the autocrat's duty to dispose of them or establish a
system of government whereby others could do so. Alexander remained a
bundle of contradictions in his approach to the needed reforms.

In the matter of the broad structure of the Russian state, Alexander in
1816 could still present himself as a convinced, if sometimes frustrated,
constitutionalist. He had made Louis XVIII grant his charter, and he had
written the constitution for Congress Poland, avowing publicly that it was
a promise of things to come in Russia. To the Private Committee projects
of 1802 and the Speransky plan of 1809 was now added a report drawn
up by Novosiltsev calling for a federal constitution for Russia (based in
part on the American model). Simultaneously, Speransky was recalled and
set to work again on the law code. After nine years nothing happened; the
grand manner reforms were neither pushed to conclusion nor abandoned.

As for improvements of conditions and attacks on specific abuses, hesitation reigned again. The crippling national debt of a billion rubles was attacked only fitfully. A proposal to buy up all the private serfs in Russia at
the rate of 5,000,000 rubles a year was initiated by Alexander and then
dropped. A law to restrain landowner abuses enacted in 1811 was eliminated from the books in 1822.

The most extensive of the emperor's reform projects in the post-1815
era, the military colonies, proved to be less than progressive and was intensely unpopular among the supposed beneficiaries. The emperor's passion
for symmetry was remarked in many things, such as the Classical architecture which reached a peak in his reign, the fastidiously exact arrangement of the objects on his desk, and his demand that all the documents he
signed be the same size. What could be more symmetrical and orderly than
to introduce military discipline into the lives of the crown peasants? The
main promoter of the scheme was none other than Arakcheev, who had
militarized his own serfs at Gruzino as early as 1810. The military colonies
were begun in the whole district around Gruzino in 1816, and in a few
years they embraced such large areas that they supported one-third of the
peacetime army. Considerations of the military budget were a major factor
for forcing tens of thousands of men to support themselves as farmers while
serving as soldiers. The state provided capital equipment, but the required
look-alike houses, prescribed meals, uniforms day and night, and arranged
marriages were detested. In 1820 a mutiny involving more than 1,000 persons was brutally suppressed by Arakcheev. In his report the drillmaster
told Alexander: "I will not hide from you that some of the criminals, the
most wicked ones, have died after receiving the punishment prescribed by
law, and I am beginning to be tired of all this. . . ." To this, Alexander
could respond: "I was able to understand fully what your tender heart had
to suffer under the circumstances described." Either the emperor's reply

was incredibly naïve, or else he and Arakcheev were operating under a code of behavior not readily understandable outside spiritualist circles.

Good intentions lay behind the military colonies, however mistaken, and Alexander could still be stung by criticisms of his internal policies, as was evident in the following outburst: "The army, the civil administration, everything, is not as I would have it—but what can you do? You cannot do everything at once; there are no assistants." Nonetheless, the paradox does exist that the sometime reforming emperor at all times surrounded himself with narrow-minded militarists, of whom Arakcheev was simply the worst, and dreamy but largely idle aristocrats, of whom most of the great names of Russia furnish examples. In contrast with Alexander, his great-great-grandfather, Peter the Great, achieved results in part by finding doers among the aristocracy, the merchant class, the utter nobodies, and the foreigners. Soviet historians today devote themselves to discovering progressive elements among the population of a given era, and to the extent that Alexander and the Romanovs generally ignored such potential state servants, all the pleas of "I have no assistants" ring false.

The progress of the arts and sciences—a bare beginning under Peter, still a novelty under Elizabeth, and something of a triumph under Catherine—continued solidly, if not dramatically, under Alexander I. If the German technician had been the idol of the first era, to be superseded by the French dandy and still later the French philosopher, the model of the late Alexandrine era was the Britisher in all his varied aspects. The styles of Beau Brummel were the rage of the chic set. For the serious, the most popular translations were the legal and economic works of Bentham, Smith, and Malthus, and the procedures of the still-unreformed House of Commons were almost as well known in certain Russian salons as in the clubs of London. Byron, of all the romantic poets, appealed most to young men of letters, such as Alexander Pushkin, who at twenty produced a bleak poem called "The Village," in its feelings not unlike his ideal's concern for the English weavers. Personally appreciating Pushkin's effort, the enigmatic tsar let his censors ban it. The next year, when Pushkin published a Byronesque "Ode to Liberty," he was summarily exiled to his estates.

Neither the smart ideas current nor the sheer problems to be solved proved sufficient to stimulate the emperor to meaningful action. Metternich went so far as to write of the postwar era that "it was from this time Alexander became visibly tired of living." Bored with the capital, the emperor took refuge in travel, in the nine years after 1815 making fourteen extensive tours of Russia and four trips to European congresses. About two-thirds of his total time was spent away from St. Petersburg, and most of the remainder he was in the seclusion of Tsarskoe Selo. Military parades seemed the emperor's greatest delight wherever he was.

One of Alexander's generals most clearly perceived his sovereign's new mood under his old manners. A diary entry dated 1816 reads:

> I was able to observe him constantly and I found little sincerity in all his actions. . . . As usual he was gay and talkative. He danced much and wanted through his simplicity to have people forget his rank. Notwithstanding his inimitable amiability and the charm of his behavior, I could observe him from time to time casting glances which indicated that his soul was troubled and that his innermost thoughts were directed to objects far removed from the ball. . . .

"Troubled soul" was, if anything, too mild a term for a man who had become a confirmed religious mystic.

Alexander's mysticism began in those worst days of 1812. His old friend Prince Alexander N. Golitsyn advised him to turn to God, God as revealed in Scripture. Ironically, Catherine's vaunted library did not include the Holy Book, and Alexander had first to read the Vulgate belonging to his empress. In his own words: "I simply devoured the Bible, finding that its words poured an unknown peace into my heart and quenched the thirst of my soul. Our Lord, in his infinite kindness, inspired me in order to permit me to understand what I was reading."

The flush of victory over the Anti-Christ Napoleon saw Alexander yet more persistent in his quest for salvation. While being lionized in London in 1814, the emperor found time to receive two prominent Quakers. The interview was described by them with quaint pride:

> . . . he inquired into several of our religious testimonies, principles, and practices to which dear William Allen answered in English, which language the emperor speaks well . . . the emperor said several times, "These are my own sentiments also." We entered fully into the subject of our testimony against war, to which he fully assented. . . . With tears he took hold of my hand, which he held silently for a while and then said: "These, your words, are a sweet cordial to my soul; they will long remain engraven on my heart."

A greater impetus to exalted spirituality than the relatively plainspoken and definitely peace-loving Quakers was Alexander's association with the Baroness Barbara Juliana von Krüdener, which began while he was at military headquarters in Germany about the time of the Battle of Waterloo in 1815. Later the emperor was to claim that he was sitting in his office examining his soul and found himself wishing to meet the celebrated lady mystic. Prince Peter Volkonsky knocked on his door to announce that an insistent woman was outside, and it was none other than Krüdener, of course. For several months the exotic baroness was Alexander's companion at military reviews and victory celebrations, but she did not return to Russia with her convert, having overplayed her hand. A jealous sense of his position won out in Alexander's mind when Krüdener began to boast of her great hold on the emperor, claiming even authorship of the Holy Alliance. The emperor and the baroness maintained an eerie correspondence, but in 1821, when Krüdener did arrive in Russia to plead the cause of Greek independence, Alexander the politician had her sent away without ceremony.

The emperor's religious enthusiasm was such as to humble him before all men of God without discrimination. Spiritual experiences on his travels alternated with the routine of military reviews and diplomatic congresses. On a visit to Kiev in 1816 he spent four hours with the blind monk Vassian and refused to let the venerable hermit bow to him. Thereafter, the Holy Synod was ordered to instruct priests to glorify the tsar less and the heavenly king more. A second visit by Alexander to Kiev's Monastery of the Caves in 1817 was the occasion of his announcing that rulers should retire when their health requires it (when "no longer able to mount a horse") but that he was still able to continue for ten or fifteen years.

One of Alexander's most truly bold acts of religiosity was to assist at a Dukhobor service in the Crimea in 1818, after which he declared himself the protector of this hallucination-practicing offshoot of the Old Believers. That same year his British Quaker friends were cordially welcomed in St. Petersburg, and Alexander promised them to fight hard against the international black slave trade at the forthcoming Congress of Aix-la-Chapelle. During his journey to the Congress of Verona in 1822, the meeting devoted to suppressing revolutions, the emperor spent hours with a Roman Catholic abbot in Vienna, after promising the dowager empress that he would not pay a visit to the Pope. Great were the fears of the possible directions of Alexander's soul-searching.

Prince Golitsyn devoted the postwar years to espousing Bible societies throughout Russia. His activities became politically and intellectually consequential after he persuaded the emperor to combine the ministries of Religion and Education with himself as head. The ensuing reaction against free thinking in the schools was so intense that the expulsion of all foreign professors and the complete closing of Kazan University were demanded. Although Alexander could not bring himself to destroy this early achievement of his, he did permit the reorganization of studies at Kazan so that everything was centered on the Bible (the Trinity, for example, being the starting point for a kind of new mathematics).

Even Golitsyn proved to be too old-fashionedly enlightened for the political-religious fanatics who began to see all Russia's troubles as stemming from the foreign and rationalist ideas that had been in vogue since Catherine. The prince encompassed his own downfall in church and educational affairs by introducing Alexander in 1822 to the Archimandrite Foty, a weird man of God so persuasive in working on people's guilt feelings that it was he who convinced the spinster Countess Anna Orlov-Chesminsky to give all her family millions to a monastery. Foty had made a reputation for himself by wearing chains that caused sores and a hairshirt that kept the sores from healing. His greatest spiritual crisis had been resisting the devil's temptation that he walk across the waters of the Neva opposite the Winter Palace. The recipient of a diamond cross and valuable properties from the imperial couple, Foty was a major force in cutting Alexander off from all progressive, realistic intellectual currents. Actually Foty was in league with Arakcheev, a rival at court to Prince Golitsyn. When Foty suddenly pronounced Golitsyn anathema, Alexander felt that he had no choice but to dismiss his life-long associate from his ministries. "Rejoice," wrote Foty, "the evil is destroyed, the devil's army is no more, all these atheistic societies are suppressed," meaning Golitsyn's Bible societies, which apparently were not backward-looking enough.

Foty's triumph was a triumph for Arakcheev, but the latter's ascendancy was short-lived. The sudden downfall of Arakcheev was no victory by the forces of liberalism but the result of a scandalous accident. In late 1824 the household serfs of Gruzino slit the throat of Arakcheev's mistress, a drunken, foulmouthed ex-serf with whom the emperor's faithful friend had been conducting a liaison for decades. The brutal old count's grief was unquestionably real. He resigned all his posts after making a few political arrangements that actually were the emperor's sole prerogative. Disregarding this high-handedness, Alexander wrote graciously, begging Arakcheev not to desert him. The emperor's complete disillusionment was at hand.

The 1820 mutiny of his old Semenovskoe Guards over purely disciplinary matters was deeply disturbing for Alexander, who usually identified his soldiers with the nation. This incident was played upon by Metternich. In 1824 a widespread and radical political plot was discovered among Russian army officers, but his new conservatism and mysticism did not suffice to blind Alexander completely to the contradictions of his position. Realistically, even nobly, the enigmatic tsar declared: "I have joined in and encouraged these illusions. It is not for me to punish."

5. Mystery Even in Death

Abdication was an obsession of Alexander's throughout his life. The responsibilities of power so frightened him that as a young man he had proposed to retire to the Rhine. In 1801 a tearful son had to be begged to mount the throne over the battered corpse of his parent. During his later years religious mysticism was combined with diffidence and world-weariness to reintensify Alexander's thoughts on the subject.

Family problems were to be the least of Alexander's troubles in his lifetime. His marriage to Elizabeth of Baden in 1793 was followed by a decade of extreme happiness for the couple, who were to lean on each other through many political crises. Once called a siren by Catherine, Elizabeth was distinguished by an angelic face and a soft, melodious voice. She bore Alexander two daughters, who died in infancy.

The grandson of Catherine the Great had his sexual flings, but not until 1803 did he flaunt an official mistress. He first met the Princess Maria Czervertinska at a soiree ten years before and was immediately taken with the big black eyes and raven hair of the Polish beauty, daughter of a pro-Russian Polish aristocrat who had been hanged for his politics. From being a refugee lady-in-waiting to being wife of Prince Dmitri Naryshkin was Maria's next success, and then came her installation as favorite of the emperor, with the tacit consent of her husband and the sorrowful acquiescence of the empress. It is a coincidence that both Alexander and Napoleon chose Polish mistresses.

A stupid, cunning courtesan to her enemies, Maria pleased Alexander for many years. She once had the effrontery to reply to the empress' polite inquiry about her health with the words "I think I am pregnant." There were three royal bastards. The eldest daughter, Zinaida, died as a child in 1810. The second daughter, Sophia, a real beauty, was a favorite of the emperor, but she too died at seventeen on the eve of her marriage to Count Andrew Shuvalov. A son, named Emmanuel, not only survived but, several generations of Romanov rulers later, was around as chief master of the household of Nicholas II.

Alexander treated his wife badly—indifferently, rather than cruelly, and all the while ceremoniously. Elizabeth was too soft and placid to hold a man as restless and soul-tortured as Alexander. Toward the end there was a marked reconciliation between the emperor and the empress, who had never ceased to call him her whole life.

Alexander was much beloved by his family at large, who dubbed him the Angel, and he responded to them with light-handed paternalism. He was worshiped by his three brothers, Constantine, Nicholas, and Michael—all such one-sided militarists as to be in awe of the eldest's other facets. His sisters eventually married into the great courts of Europe but remained his faithful correspondents. The Grand Duchess Catherine was Alexander's special delight and one of his few real confidants. His letters to her were playfully warm, human, and often frivolous. Her sudden death in January, 1819, was a shock and a sorrow to Alexander and accelerated his thoughts about his own retirement.

Twice in 1819 Alexander was to mention abdication to members of his family. At dinner after a review of a Guards unit commanded by his brother Nicholas, the emperor told the grand duke and his wife: "I have decided to free myself from my present obligations and to retire from this sort of life. Never before has Europe stood in need of young sovereigns in the plenitude of their strength. . . . I am no longer the man I was, and I think it will be my duty to retire." A few months later the emperor confided in his brother Constantine during a visit to Warsaw: "I want to abdicate; I cannot bear my burdens any longer." Constantine's reply revealed much about the family relationships: "Then I will become one of your valets and polish your boots."

After these ominous conversations several years elapsed before Alexander again became preoccupied with thoughts of the future. One cause was a serious illness lasting two months in 1824, an illness involving a leg injury resulting from a horse's kick. That year the death of his illegitimate daughter Sophia was a cruel disappointment. Finally, the most serious floods in the records of St. Petersburg, bringing the destruction of thousands of houses, were duly interpreted by the occult associates of the emperor as a sign of the wrath of God.

Early in 1825 Alexander again confided his intention to retire, this time to his brother-in-law the Prince of Orange. The year wore on without anything noteworthy happening until it was announced that the emperor and empress were going to Taganrog on the Black Sea. Elizabeth Alexievna's lung condition and nervous indispositions were so acute that her doctors advised her to take a rest cure in a temperate climate. The choice of Taganrog was a puzzling one: The windswept naval base offered no comfortable palace and seemed far less salubrious than more southerly Crimean locations. The emperor showed unusual energy in making the arrangements for the journey, leaving in early September in order to prepare the way for his wife, whose departure came about a week later. The imperial couple were established in a modest house in Taganrog by October 5, and their doctor wrote: "The household took heart to see them so happy together."

Using Taganrog as a base, Alexander soon set off on his restless tours, ranging over the Don Cossack area and the whole Crimea. Royal farms, Mennonite colonies, monasteries, mosques, hospitals, arsenals, and army camps were among the diverse places visited. While inspecting a new royal estate in the Crimea, Alexander bluffly told Prince Volkonsky: "I think that I would like to live there—as a private individual. . . . I shall soon have done my twenty-five years of service when any soldier is free to claim his release." On November 17 the emperor returned to Taganrog a sick man, a cold contracted on a solitary visit to a monastery having become a lingering and deep fever.

The emperor's serious illness was chronicled by three witnesses, Prince Volkonsky, Dr. Dmitri Tarasov, and the empress. Their accounts of the two weeks of late November differ strangely: On a given day, one writer has Alexander "prostrated," while another reports him better to the point of being "animated." On November 26 the emperor and empress spent a long time together in private, after which she wrote her mother a letter full of foreboding: "Where can one find a refuge in this life," she moaned, adding that "a new and unexpected trial" had arisen to upset well-laid plans. What Alexander told her about his intentions for the future remains unknown from this. Less than a week later at 10:30 A.M. on December 1 the local populace learned that the emperor was dead, the news taking eight days to reach St. Petersburg.

Alexander's funeral progression was delayed until January 10, 1826, because of a crisis over the confused succession to the throne. The coffin, opened to the populace in Taganrog, was closed on all the stopovers, including Moscow, until it reached St. Petersburg, where the body was viewed by the royal family at Tsarskoe Selo before lying in state at Kazan Cathedral. On March 26, 1826, the dead tsar was placed in his tomb beside those of his predecessors in the Peter and Paul Cathedral. About two months afterward, during her return journey to the capital, the new Dowager Empress Elizabeth died at Kaluga, just a few hours before she was to meet the old dowager empress, who was hurrying south to greet her. Three days after her husband's death Elizabeth had written her mother: "Do not worry too much about me, but if I dared, I would like to follow the one who has been my very life." Was this a death wish, or was Alexander somewhere other than in his supposed coffin?

It is ironic that Alexander I, who had been so enigmatic in life, should also be a riddle in death. There is really no question about his frequent wish to abdicate. The never-long-absent guilt about his father's death, the failure of his early projects of reform, the contradictions of his relations with Napoleon, the frustrations of the Holy Alliance, and the awareness of growing internal dissensions were more than enough to drive a crowned Hamlet into retirement. The question arises whether or not the religious mysticism that increasingly dominated Alexander's middle age was of such a nature as to lead him to contemplate some step other than formal abdication, a step such as becoming a hermit. The Russian populace was more than prepared to believe this of a popular ruler.

One theory of 1825 advanced by many writers, foreign and Russian, remote and recent, combines circumstantial evidence and conjecture to prove that the emperor faked his death and was to turn up as a holy man in Siberia, who lived until 1864. The whole trip to Taganrog can be interpreted as strange, and the discrepancies in his intimates' reports on the emperor's health can be seen as the failure of accomplices in a secret to coordinate their false evidence. When Alexander's condition was supposedly most critical, his friend Volkonsky occupied the room next to him, actually taking it away from an English doctor on hand. An imperial courier of appropriate physical build was killed in a road accident that November, and the story goes that it was his body, brought into the Taganrog house in a bathtub, that was exposed in December as the corpse of Alexander I. It still remains difficult, however, to explain what the servants were doing during this crisis.

A genuine mystery concerns the presence of the yacht of the English Lord William Schaw Cathcart in Taganrog Harbor long after other shipping had departed the wintry weather. The conjecture is that this ship took a mysterious stranger on a pilgrimage to the Holy Land, the absence of log entries for December being considered noteworthy. An intriguing fact is that the Cathcart family have refused access to their papers to all historians, including Alexander's great-nephew, the Grand Duke Nicholas Michaelovich, before the Revolution and Prince Vladimir Bariatinsky in 1925, the latter expecting the hundredth anniversary of the official death to be an appropriate occasion for any revelations.

The legend of a live Alexander suffers a gap until 1836, when a man looking as though he should not have such a good horse was arrested in Siberia, whipped by the authorities, and deported with a group of convicts eastward. (Alexander's brother, the Grand Duke Michael, later passed through the area and was reported to be furious at what had been done.) The deportee emerged in 1842 as an unfrocked holy man calling himself Fedor Kuzmich. A rich peasant allowed Kuzmich to live in a hut as a bearded hermit who kept bees, fasted rigorously, and slept on a thin mattress, all the while being very neat and orderly. Visitors to the not unfriendly recluse reported that he liked to reminisce about the court in the days of Catherine but not about the era of Paul and Alexander. There is unconfirmed testimony that a holy girl protégée of Kuzmich's held mysterious conversations with the new tsar, Nicholas I, and that his heir, the Grand Duke Alexander Nicholaevich, and his bride visited Kuzmich at his hut and left their marriage certificate with him. Twice old soldiers were said to have recognized Kuzmich as Alexander, causing him anger once, benevolent confidences the other time.

Later Kuzmich lived in the city of Tomsk, again as a recluse with a rich patron. He died on February 1, 1864, revered locally as a man of God. A simple wooden cross was put on his grave with the inscription HERE LIES THE GREAT AND BLESSED FATHER FEDOR KUZMICH. This was replaced by a marble slab enclosed in a chapel after Nicholas II visited the site.

The son of the then governor general of Siberia said that his father had Kuzmich's effects gathered up and sent to Tsar Alexander II and that expensive icons and monogrammed items with *A I* were among them. On the other hand, the morganatic widow of Alexander II was asked in her old age about Kuzmich directly, and she replied that he was only an old man with an extraordinary resemblance to Alexander I. The nephew of Dr. Tarasov (on hand in 1825) claimed that his uncle never attended the requiem masses for Alexander I until after Kuzmich's death in 1864. Similarly, Count Dmitri von der Osten-Sacken testified that his grandfather that same year put on his full-dress uniform and ordered the first special mass for his onetime master. Another handed-down story was that Alexander I on his way to Taganrog stayed with a family whose newborn baby was about to be christened Fedor Kuzmich.

In 1926, when there was a spate of newspaper speculation about Alexander I, the Soviet government had his tomb broken into, and it was found empty. This is not surprising if one believes a report that Alexander II had the coffin opened in 1866 under secret circumstances and the remains buried elsewhere.

The most exhaustive biographical study of Alexander I was written by the talented cousin of the last tsar, the Grand Duke Nicholas Michaelovich, at the turn of the century. Regarding the legend, he wrote:

> I confess that the story attracted me for several years. . . . I decided not to spare any efforts to unveil the mystery surrounding the name of Fyodor Kuzmich. I learned everything about his life in Siberia . . . One thing alone is clear: the hermit was not and he could not be Alexander I.

The real identity of Kuzmich was unsolvable, according to the grand duke. Less convincing is the argument of this Romanov that his ancestor would never have submitted to a police beating. History affords many examples of mystics who put up with far more. Regarding Nicholas Michaelovich's research on Alexander, Felix Yusupov, assassin of Rasputin, wrote that the grand duke's conclusion about the legend was imposed on him officially and that privately he said otherwise. With equal conviction, a recent biographer of the tsar, E. M. Almedingen, who is also a Russian *émigrée,* declares that the grand duke in her presence specifically denied that he ever denied his conclusion.

The possibility of a tsar turned hermit, which is anything but inconsistent with Alexander's character, must be considered in the light of the persistent Russian tradition of lost princes and princesses, the current examples of which are two Anastasias and a tsarevich. England had a couple of putative Edward V's and France a few Louis XVII's, but Russian history boasts several each of Dmitri Ivanovich's, Peter II's, Ivan VI's, and Peter III's (notably the patent fake, Pugachev), to mention only the names of greatest interest. A great many people believed in an Emperor Alexander-Kuzmich, and many also accepted an Empress Elizabeth-"Vera the Hermit" as living after the wife's recorded death in 1826.

Fedor Kuzmich was further identified by some as a Romanov other than Alexander, a cousin, for example, who was a forgotten great-grandson of Peter the Great (explaining, of course, any special attention from the Romanov family). One theory is that Kuzmich was the son of Princess

Tarakova, herself a lost daughter of the Empress Elizabeth, born in an appropriate year after a liaison with Prince Radziwill.

The great old Polish aristocratic name of Radziwill turns one's mind to the great new Irish-American name of Kennedy. Many Americans have refused to accept the officially designated assassins of their presidents as fervently as many Russians have questioned the legal death certificates of their tsars. For every Texan who saw Lee Harvey Oswald where he was not supposed to be, there is a Russian aristocrat whose grandfather had special knowledge of the death of Alexander I. Such things fascinate historians, confound them, and humble them.

XV.

The Iron Tsar: Nicholas I

1. Counterrevolutionary

FOR a few weeks in December, 1825, Russia had two tsars simultaneously—three, if one believes that Alexander I was still alive. This situation, which was the result of a series of Romanov family misunderstandings, then provided the opportunity for a bloody army revolt.

Such was the state of Russian roads in 1825 that couriers from the Black Sea shore needed a full week to reach Warsaw with the official announcement of Alexander's demise. The governor general of the kingdom of Poland was the late tsar's oldest brother, the Grand Duke Constantine, who in 1817 had married the wrong sort of Polish woman and had secretly renounced his claims to the Russian throne at that time. In Warsaw on December 7 Constantine had allegiance sworn to the next brother, Nicholas, and the following day sent off the youngest brother, the Grand Duke Michael, to inform "Tsar Nicholas" of their loyalty. Meanwhile, the couriers from the south reached St. Petersburg on December 9. Their arrival interrupted Nicholas' participation in a *Te Deum* being sung at the cathedral for Alexander's recovery. Nicholas promptly had the assembled dignitaries swear allegiance to "Tsar Constantine." The Grand Duke Michael turned up on December 15 with the news from Warsaw, and so was revealed the undignified spectacle of Constantine and Nicholas each hailing the other as ruler. The two brothers then initiated a time-consuming and increasingly angry correspondence between Petersburg and Warsaw. The French ambassador cagily provided himself with three sets of credentials so that he could be the first officially to congratulate Constantine, Nicholas, or even Michael, when the dynastic contretemps was resolved.

The confusion in 1825 was primarily the fault of Alexander I and his secretiveness. The late tsar had drawn up a manifesto in 1822 revealing Constantine's renunciation and naming Nicholas as successor. Copies of this were deposited in Moscow's Uspensky Cathedral and in two other institutions with instructions that the manifesto be read immediately upon Alexander's death, but neither of the younger brothers was informed of the precise contents of the document or even of the procedure to be followed. Several factors lay behind the tsar's reluctance to make public his intentions during his lifetime. Alexander still played mentally with Novosiltsev's project of a constitutional reorganization of the state, and he was also toying with the idea of abdication. To leave the 1822 manifesto unpublished left him freedom to change his mind.

A dominant factor in the situation was the Grand Duke Nicholas' unpopularity, especially in army circles. Even after Alexander's clear and precise testament was read by the imperial family in Petersburg, Nicholas was dissuaded from proclaiming himself tsar by officials aware of how generally he was hated. Nicholas also realized that the document smacked of family arrangements and seemed inconsistent with the Emperor Paul's Succession Law of 1797, which was intended to eliminate willful choices by dying rulers. Hence, Nicholas had all the troops he controlled take oaths to Constantine, but the grand duke in Warsaw remained unmovable and unwavering in his refusal to ascend the throne.

The family farce was too dangerous to continue much longer, and finally, on December 26, after an all-night session of the Council of State, Nicholas was persuaded to proclaim himself ruler. The officials swore allegiance in the Winter Palace that morning, and the troops were prudently ordered to take the new oath in their quarters, rather than at any sort of traditional grand review.

The faltering of the Romanov family in 1825 was an invitation to revolution in an era when there were for the first time organized revolutionists in Russia. Within hours after Nicholas' proclamation of himself, the Senate Square of St. Petersburg was filled with a disloyal mob. The first troops to mutiny were the Moscow Guards regiment, and after their noisy march to the center of the city they were joined by other Guards companies, marines, and a company of artillery, until the number of rebels was about 3,000. Their officer leaders, members of secret groups, got the men chanting the cry "Constantine and Constitution." The conspirators were proceeding on the assumption, actually mistaken, that the older grand duke was more liberal than the martinet Nicholas. The rank and file—according to the most familiar joke in Russian history—happily shouted away in the belief that Constitution (*Konstitutsia*) was Constantine's wife. The situation grew more ominous as crowds of civilians gathered and began to express open sympathy with the rebels.

In the Winter Palace, only a few hundred yards away from the tumult in Senate Square, the dowager empress began to wail hysterically, "What will Europe say?" While his mother worried about the family reputation, Nicholas feared for his throne and life, but his initial panic gave way to coolness and courage. After hours of searching, sufficient loyal troops were found to protect the palace and then to seal off the mutineers in the square. Somewhat ironically, Prince Alexis Fedorovich Orlov was responsible for bringing the first loyal regiment onto the scene, and he ever after was one of the tsar's chief aides. The opposing bodies of troops faced each other throughout the late afternoon. Nicholas was anxious to avoid bloodshed and sent several mediators to the rebels, including the governor general of the city, the archbishop, and Grand Duke Michael. Only after another go-between was shot in the back did the tsar order the rebels dispersed by cavalry and artillery. About dusk the government's guns encircling the square fired, first a blank volley and then grapeshot, continuing to strafe the mutineers and civilians as they fled over the Neva bridge in helpless disorder.

Such was the main action of the Decembrist Revolt. A related mutiny of troops near Kiev in January, 1826, was even more easily suppressed. However discouraged and uncoordinated the revolt proved to be, it revealed the existence of widespread subversion in the army and ideological strivings that were to be fulfilled only in 1917. Investigation of the Decembrists indicated that hundreds of Russian officers had been intellectually seduced during their service in Western Europe against Napoleon. Their newfound ideals were both stimulated and frustrated by the hot and cold liberalism of Alexander I. A political constitution was the chief aim of the revolutionists, but they were also inflamed by nationalist causes such as the hatred of Russian subservience to Metternich's policies and the desire to liberate the Greeks. There were several secret societies in existence in the decade after 1815, some frankly political, others disguised as lovers of literature or nature. The leaders, who often moved about with their army units, ranged from the moderate Nicholas Muraviev to the fiery radical Paul Pestel.

The Decembrist Revolt was in one sense the last attempt of Guards officers to dictate the fate of the dynasty, the last of a series that included 1801, 1762, 1741, 1730, and 1725. In another sense, the Decembrist Revolt has been called the First Russian Revolution because of its far-reaching aims, but this interpretation ignores the from-the-bottom upheavals threatened by Pugachev in the 1770's and Razin in the 1670's. Indeed, the lack of any contacts with the masses of Russians was the chief mistake of the Decembrist army officers. Another cause of failure was disagreement on specific programs and courses of action. But the tsar's police would have done well to study more carefully the Decembrists' inconclusive debates, for the questions they raised became a lexicon of the revolutionary ferment that overthrew the Romanovs, questions such as to assassinate or not, to centralize or decentralize, to have a republic or a monarchy, to be dictators or to heed the popular will, and to expropriate or to pay off the landowners.

Several hundred Russians were arrested for connections with the Decembrist Revolt, and the first six months of the new reign were given over to exhaustive investigations and then farcical trials, which were personally directed by Nicholas, who came to exaggerate greatly the extent of disloyalty in Russian society. Intellectually, the tsar was capable of differentiating between the aims of Pestel, whom he termed a "hell-born fiend," and the motives of some of the moderates, which he saw as pure and lofty, but perversely, he allowed all five chief leaders to be condemned to hang, commuting the sentence of quartering but ending the Alexandrine tradition of no capital punishments for the officer class. Thirty-one Decembrists were given hard labor for life, and hundreds were sent to Siberia or reduced to the ranks. One Decembrist, who shortly afterward died in prison, became a raving lunatic upon confessing in person to Nicholas that he had spent all the crucial day in the Winter Palace near the tsar with a brace of pistols and a dagger waiting for the right opportunity to kill his ruler.

The roster of convicted Decembrists reads like the Russian *Social Register*. Among the Rurikovich names were those of Bariatinsky, Obolensky, Odoievsky, and Trubetskoy. Also to be found were a Golitsyn, a Bestushev, an Orlov, and a Tolstoy. Suspicion of the nobility as a class became a hallmark of Nicholas' regime, which was to be dominated not by gentry, but by policemen and bureaucrats.

Nicholas was to admit that investigating the Decembrists not only showed the general need for reform, but also put in mind practical projects. By his lights, however, reform should be dictated, not discussed. As stated in Nicholas' Coronation Manifesto: "Not by impertinent, destructive dreams but from above are gradually perfected the statutes of the land, are corrected the faults, are rectified the abuses. . . ." However, repression, not reform, was the main result of Nicholas' obsession with the Decembrists. The government did worse than mark time; it tried to go backward in a period when Russian society was seething with new creative forces. Russia lost thirty years under Nicholas, which it probably never regained. Nicholas I, the iron tsar, was to be the Romanov Stalin, a man of sickly suspicion and cruel action.

What of the almost-tsar, Constantine, the liberal candidate of the Decembrists? To his sister-in-law he was simply a "sot and a bully" who had cast off his first wife, Princess Juliana Coburg, in order to marry his Polish paramour. After 1825 the grand duke stayed on as governor of Poland, making rare and brief visits to St. Petersburg, during which he revealed himself to be even more vindictive against dissent and more antireform than his younger brother. In a dynasty notable for martinets, Constantine was outstanding as a parade-ground militarist, so reactionary in his thinking as to ban soldiers' shouting huzzahs because it meant they showed too much independence of judgment. He once declared: "I do not like war: it spoils soldiers, soils their uniforms, and destroys discipline." A contemporary said of Constantine: "His greatest merit was his renunciation of the throne, which testifies to his good sense. God knows where he would have dragged Russia."

2. The Man of Duty

Probably Nicholas was sincerely reluctant to take power in 1825. He came to adopt the psychological crutch that as the third son he was an outsider ill prepared to rule but forced nonetheless to assume the Romanov burden.

Born in July, 1796, Nicholas scarcely remembered his murdered father, Tsar Paul. His mother, who lived on as dowager empress to 1828, gave much attention to her third son but yet was essentially cold and over-demanding. The older brothers, Alexander and Constantine, who were nearly two decades older than Nicholas, grandly ignored him. A younger brother, Michael, was Nicholas' favorite playmate, and inevitably in this family, toy soldiers were their chief diversion. The little grand dukes' games were seldom peaceful, and Nicholas was the worse offender when it came to smashing things or hitting someone. As a child Nicholas appeared self-willed and obstinate, raging at criticism one time and withdrawing into himself the next.

Nicholas learned his alphabet from a Scots nurse who was assigned him by Catherine the Great. From the time he was six, however, he was taught by male tutors, notably a General Mathew Lamsdorff, a Baltic nobleman whose chief distinction was his war record and whose main idea of education was to break the will of his charge. Lamsdorff's disciplinary measures included corporal punishment, but Nicholas was to show no resentment of this and, in fact, was later responsible for introducing Lamsdorff's methods in all Russian schools. Another tutor was an *émigré* from France, but this man's prejudices were balanced by studies under many leading Russian scholars. The range of subjects covered by the grand duke was unlimited —history, geography, philosophy, law, arithmetic, physics, drawing (his favorite), dancing, French, Latin, Greek, and English. Later Nicholas' detractors were to say that his education was neglected, but there is written evidence to the contrary in the form of all sorts of complex study tables that were compiled, desperately it appears, by the dowager and his tutors. The simple fact was that Nicholas was a bad student. He was inattentive, lacking in curiosity, and stubbornly self-satisfied.

After the French invasion of 1812 Nicholas' fascination with the military excluded all other subjects, but he and Michael were not allowed by Alexander to join the army until 1814. They saw no action that year or during the thrilling Hundred Days of 1815, but twice there were opportunities for sight-seeing in Paris.

Nicholas made a tour of the Russian provinces between May and September, 1816, but it was the usual superficial round of shrines and parades. The journal he was ordered to keep revealed little of interest except a prejudice against Poles and Jews. In 1816 and 1817 Nicholas spent four months in England, after having been carefully briefed by the Foreign Ministry to the effect that British political institutions were unique and not applicable to Russia. This warning was the dowager's doing, but it was not necessary in view of Nicholas' blandly unfavorable reaction to the parliamentary system. His favorite Englishman proved to be that Tory of Tories, the Duke of Wellington.

During a visit by the Russian imperial family to Berlin in late 1815 Nicholas' engagement to Princess Charlotte of Prussia was announced. The princess was duly renamed Alexandra Fedorovna, and the marriage took place in July, 1817. Politically the match had the effect of tying Nicholas closely to the Prussian court and army for the rest of his life. He developed tremendous respect for his father-in-law, Frederick William III, calling himself his subordinate, and he continually visited him and his new brothers-in-law, the future Prussian kings Frederick William IV and William I.

Personally, the marriage proved to be an exceedingly happy one. As grand duke and as tsar, Nicholas was a model family man, loving the simplicity and quiet of his private life. And although not an independent political factor, Alexandra Fedorovna was always confided in and consulted by her husband. No more revealing or touching evidence of the completeness of his attachment to her is afforded than by the following letter Nicholas wrote Alexandra about twenty years after their wedding:

> God has given you such a happy character that it is no merit to love you. I exist for you, yes, you are I—I do not know how to say it differently, but I am not your salvation, as you say. Our salvation is over there yonder where we shall all be admitted to rest from the tribulations of life. I mean, if we earn it down here by the fulfillment of our duties. Hard as they may be, one performs them with joy when one has a beloved being at home near whom one can breathe again and gain new strength. If I was now and then demanding, this happened because I look for everything in you. If I do not find it, I am distressed. I say to myself, no, she does not understand me, and these are unique, rare, but difficult moments. For the rest, happiness, joy, calm—that is what I seek and find in my old Mouffy. I wished, as much as this was in my power, to make you a hundred times happier, if I could have divined how this end could have been obtained.

Nicholas could have lived contentedly forever with his two passions, his family and his military duties. If the incipent militarist was not necessarily foreordained in the games of the child, he showed himself alarmingly in the fact that as a fourteen-year-old Nicholas persisted in a flat refusal to produce an essay on careers other than soldiering open to aristocrats. In the last decade of his brother's reign Nicholas enjoyed the position of inspector general of engineers, giving him a huge establishment to drill and supervise. His first order to his men declared that "the slightest negligence . . . will never and under no circumstances be pardoned." Like his grandfather, Peter III, and his father, Paul I, Nicholas was a parade-ground soldier, the minutiae of army regulations being his "one true delight," in the words of an associate. The details of uniforms enthralled him, and he rushed to appear in new outfits occasioned by honorary appointments to, say, Prussian or Austrian regiments. Huge reviews literally reduced him to tears, as on the occasion, when he was tsar, he blubbered: "God, I thank Thee for making me so mighty, and I beg Thee to give me the strength never to abuse this power."

Soldiering pervaded Nicholas' thinking. He built his political philosophy about the army, of which he one time wrote:

> Here there is order, there is strict unconditional legality, no impertinent claims to know all the answers, no contradiction, all things flow logically one from the other; no one commands before he has himself learned to obey; no one steps in front of anybody else without lawful reason; everything is subordinated to one definite goal, everything has its purpose. That is why I feel so well among these people, and why I shall always hold in honor the calling of a soldier.

It was Nicholas' exaggerated spit and polish that made him so unpopular as grand duke. One of his favorite subordinates was known to order floggings that nearly caused deaths for soldiers appearing out of uniform or making mistakes in drill.

Nicholas had been given only hints that he would succeed Alexander. He was not even initiated into the affairs of the Council of State. His sense of duty was such, however, that he would loiter in the palace anterooms in an effort to stay abreast of what was going on. Then came 1825, and thereafter he never hesitated in his assertion of control.

"The native beauty of this classic head" was one description of Nicholas. The writer was the Marquis de Custine, the French traveler to Russia in the 1830's who was responsible for the most devastating critique of Nicholas' police state. Yet Custine could not deny his admiration for the man with "a tone of voice one cannot forget—so much authority it has, so grave and firm it is . . . that of a man born to command."

A British critic was fulsome in his awe:

> Nicholas I was a most imposing personage and was generally considered the most perfect specimen of a human being, physically-speaking, in all Europe. . . . Colossal in stature; with a face such as one finds on a Greek coin, but overcast with a shadow of Muscovite melancholy; with a bearing dignified but with a manner not unkind, he bore himself like a god . . . whenever I saw him . . . there was forced to my lips the thought: "You are the most majestic being ever created."

Thus, the man who did not expect to be tsar struck people as autocracy personified. Nicholas had genuine beauty in his features—the family's blue eyes, a slightly aquiline nose, a firm, well-formed mouth set off by a light mustache and a solid chin. More than six feet tall, he held himself perfectly. With all the stunning nobility of looks of his brother Tsar Alexander but without his gentleness, Nicholas appeared forceful, monumental, and somewhat inhuman.

While the late tsar had been a fascinating enigma, Nicholas' character was simple and straightforward. He was unintellectual, blunt, and honest. Complete humorlessness was another dominant trait. Nicholas managed the rudiments of charm, but his was the "smile of civility" while "his heart is closed," wrote a contemporary.

To be lofty and efficient was Nicholas' approach. "He poses incessantly," commented Custine. Outwardly always detached and calm, the emperor stressed orderliness, regularity, and precision in his daily routine. When much of the Winter Palace was destroyed by fire in 1837, no state documents were lost, for Nicholas always cleared his desk and sent papers on to the appropriate offices. There were occasions that suggested Nicholas really was a bundle of nerves, a man seething with rages, fears, and frustrations beneath the appearance of competence and determination and a person so insecure as to overcompensate with regimentation. Custine best summed up the interplay of majesty and tension in Nicholas when he wrote that "the Czar of Russia is a military chief and each of his days is a day of battle."

There was an element of self-pity in the ruler who became one of the greatest tyrants of modern history. Nicholas once philosophized:

> How remarkable really is my fate. I am told that I am one of the mightiest rulers of the world, and . . . that, within the limits of discretion I should be able to do what I please and where. But in fact just the opposite is the case as far as I am concerned. And if one asks about the basic cause of this anomaly, there is only one word: Duty.

After expounding on the sacredness of the word "duty," Nicholas concluded that "I have been born to suffer."

The most hardworking of rulers, Nicholas was the sort who felt that he had to attend to everything himself. "Everything must proceed from here," he once declared, thumping his chest. His few personal friends played little role in politics. Except for his mother who died in 1828, the Grand Duke Constantine who died in 1831, and his wife, everyone was treated as a servant by Nicholas, never as an associate. Some of his ministers were competent, and Nicholas was loyal to them, but he was capable of dismissing them airily, simply saying on one occasion, "I shall myself be Minister of Finance." Many of his bureaucrats were utterly characterless, an extreme case being the minister of education who declared to his assistant, "You should know I have neither a mind nor a will of my own—I am merely a blind tool of the emperor's will." Nicholas often complained that he lacked gifted officials, but the situation was his own doing. Oddly, he rewarded his subordinates generously, creating no fewer than sixteen princes, almost more than all his predecessors together had done. This was perhaps a blow struck at the old nobility.

Nicholas saw to everything, from the style of new uniforms to the design of new churches in the far reaches of the country. In his passion for detail he studied and annotated thousands of documents. When the church once annulled a particular marriage, Nicholas with utter humorlessness ordered a proclamation to the effect that "this young lady shall be considered a virgin."

The emperor did not feel he should be tied to his desk. He would show up to direct the Petersburg firemen, if need be. In the summer of 1831 he showed great bravery in calming a mob that had stormed hospitals and killed doctors during a cholera epidemic. On this occasion he drove virtually unattended to Haymarket Square and brought several thousand people to their knees with a grandiloquent lecture, in which, however, he neglected to dispel their misinformation about the doctors and about the disease.

The tsar was a tireless traveler, who enjoyed arriving unexpectedly in this provincial town or that. Near the end of the reign the minister of war added up the statistics, writing obsequiously: "In ceaseless activity, Your Imperial Majesty, during twenty-five years, deigned to traverse in the course of august journeys: 124,486 versts by land and 12,850 by sea; out of this total, 114,640 versts within the empire and 22,696 abroad [a verst equals two-thirds of a mile]." One of the flying inspections might involve diverse activities such as these described in Nicholas' own words:

> We reached Bobruisk late at night. On the morning of the twelfth of August I inspected the Fifth Infantry Division and the fortress works. Both here and in Duenaburg I look at them with particular joy; everything I planted has already grown into enormous trees, especially Italian poplars. The hospital enraged me. Imagine, the functionaries have taken for their own needs the best part of the building. . . . For that I put

the commandant in the guardhouse, dismissed the supervisor and taught everybody a lesson in my own manner. . . .

Other people often saw the imperial visitations as superficial and arbitrary. A young student diarist wrote:

> Today Nicholas visited our First High School and expressed dissatisfaction. . . . He entered the fifth class where teacher Turchaninov was teaching history. During the lesson one of the pupils, the best by the way, both in conduct and achievement, listened attentively to the teacher, but only leaning on his elbow. This was taken as a breach of discipline . . . the curator was ordered to fire teacher Turchaninov.

3. The Stick

Nicholas' maddening interference in everything might have been forgiven and forgotten, if he had not also set out to reorder the state and society backward. Actually, the first five years of the reign were only mildly conservative, with the tsar learning his job and with talk of enlightened reform still being heard. But after the 1830 revolutions in France, Belgium, and Poland the regime in Russia became openly reactionary and dedicated to the suppression of all new ideas. The intelligentsia, who were emerging powerfully at this time only to be beaten down by a greater force, woefully called Nicholas I the stick.

As in the case of many police states, Nicholas' regime came up with a formula. The new minister of education, Sergius Uvarov, first circulated among the schools in 1833 the slogan: "Orthodoxy, autocracy, and nationality." It did Uvarov's detractors little good to point out that he personally tended toward atheism, that he once held constitutional views, or that he used French or German more than Russian. Uvarov was eventually even granted a family motto: "Faith, tsar, and fatherland."

Religion was the first concept of Uvarov's triad and the one used to justify the others. Orthodoxy covered the new policies of pressuring everyone in the Russian Empire to practice the same religion. Nicholas personally took his faith seriously, believing "in the manner of a peasant," to use his own words, and indulging in no soul wrestling and sect shopping like his predecessor. It was said of Nicholas that he felt himself a subordinate officer of God awaiting the grand review in heaven. That the tsar believed he was God's agent is suggested alarmingly in a message he wrote after suppressing a revolt of military colonists and supervising the floggings that caused 129 deaths. He wrote: "God rewarded me for my journey to Novgorod, for, several hours after my return, He granted my wife to be delivered successfully of a son, Nicholas." Fatalism about God and duty are apparent in Nicholas' indifference to assassination plots.

Religious affairs during most of Nicholas' reign were directed by a procurator of the Holy Synod whose training was that he was a despotic cavalry officer, military men recommending themselves to Nicholas in almost all departments. The procurator's chief activity was the persecution of dissenters, and to make this possible, the government conducted the first systematic investigation of those who did not adhere to Orthodoxy, estimating their number at 1,000,000, although independent scholars later figured 8,000,000. The schismatics and heretics were officially classified as "most pernicious," "pernicious," and "less pernicious" in terms of their willingness to swear allegiance to the tsar, pay taxes, bear arms, and meet certain norms of religious and family life. Those in the first category had their churches closed, their leaders transported, their children banned from the schools, and their young men forced into the army. Thus, beginning with Nicholas, the Romanov tsars deliberately widened the gulf separating them from a huge number of their subjects who were often highly creative, intellectually and economically. The pursuit of Orthodox uniformity also saw the persecution of Polish Catholics and the Jews.

Autocracy, the second element in Uvarov's formula, was a watchword in Russia predating the Romanovs. It was Nicholas, however, who had it dinned in the ears of Russians that "God himself commands us to obey the Tsar's supreme authority, not from fear alone but as a point of conscience." Procedurally, Nicholas made the autocracy even more unlimited by cutting down or ignoring the pathetic amounts of independence that had been won by such institutions as the Senate, the Council of Ministers, and the Council of State. Significantly, for example, the phrase "having listened to the Council of State" was dropped from imperial manifestos after 1842.

The various projects for constitutional reform of Alexander I were dropped completely by Nicholas. When Novosiltsev's federal plan was spitefully published by the rebellious Poles, the tsar found it "most annoying," explaining that he was worried "above everything else" that "out of a hundred of our young officers ninety will read it, will fail to understand it, or will scorn it, but ten will retain it in their memory, will discuss it, and, the most important point, will not forget it." Nicholas did appoint a reconstructed Speransky to undertake a codification of the laws, something directly suggested to the tsar by the Decembrists' grievances, with the specific instruction to exclude the *Punkti* of 1730, briefly forced on Empress Anna by the nobility. The law code of 1832 was a genuine legal achievement, one of which no other Russian ruler after 1649 could have boasted, but it was, in effect, just the reentrenchment of autocracy and serfdom.

Nicholas' Russia was above all bureaucratic Russia. From his time Russian life seemed pervaded by an all-powerful, usually incompetent, officialdom, in the provincial towns, as well as in the capital. From the emperor down to the lowest police officer, all were exempt from public criticism. The emperor once even said that neither blame nor praise was compatible with the dignity of the government.

In addition, Nicholas frequently governed outside the normal or legal channels of administration, something that also suggests that the tsar did not trust his own bureaucrats. The emperor had a penchant for special commissions and envoys extraordinary. More important, Nicholas made his Personal Chancery a new and overriding arm of the government. A Second Section of the chancery was given charge of the law code, and the infamous Third Section became a political police force in addition to, and often in competition with, the regular police. Nothing is more typical of the reign than that this Third Section not only bypassed normal procedures but also created a new level of organized and oppressive investigation into people's private lives.

Although one of Nicholas' great fears was that the nobility would wrest a constitution from him, even greater was his apprehension that the serfs would stage an upheaval from below. Potential Decembrists could be and were dealt with by the Third Section, but to avoid another Pugachev rebellion, Nicholas felt that drastic reform was necessary, and he created no less than six secret commissions to investigate the serf problem. In the end, the tsar's own great bureaucratic machine, still gentry-recruited, blocked effective action. Only the state serfs in Russia received some amelioration of their lot. A ukase permitting private serfs to buy their freedom was so violently opposed that Nicholas let it drop, finally deciding that although "serfdom . . . is an evil, palpable and obvious to all," to "touch it would be a still more disastrous evil," in view of past experiences with the "popular rage." In the course of the reign there were more than 700 major peasant uprisings.

Nicholas futilely, if not hypocritically, hoped that the Russian landowners would come voluntarily to improve the condition of the serfs. In the same vein, he made an unprecedented address to the Moscow manufacturers in 1835 exhorting them to care for their workers—paternalistically, as in the army. About this time the British Parliament was passing factory laws with teeth in them, but of course, Russia did not yet have more than a fraction of the industrial proletariat Britain had, although the number of workers doubled in Nicholas' reign, reaching 500,000. Yet the beginnings of a drastic economic transformation were already apparent, spurred on by the coming of the railroad age.

The first Russian railroad line was opened in 1835, running for the imperial convenience from Tsarskoe Selo to Petersburg. Nicholas chose to override his minister of finance, who declared that a railroad network was unnecessary, costly, and dangerous to public morals. The great St. Petersburg-Moscow line was begun in 1842. Legend has it that the wranglings over alternative routes for this line were ended when the emperor took a ruler and drew one long stroke (the railroad today looks oddly straight on the map). An American engineer was largely responsible for finishing this main line and also for standardizing the wide Russian gauge—George Washington Whistler, the father of the painter.

In Uvarov's formula "Orthodoxy, autocracy, and nationality" the third concept was hardest to define. Nationality implied, in part, an official Russian point of view in education, in the arts, and in literature. More immediately, it meant the same sort of crackdown on non-Russian nationalities in the empire as on the non-Orthodox.

The most significant non-Russian group among Nicholas' subjects were the Poles. At the beginning of his reign the tsar found himself bound to rule as constitutional King of Poland, an incongruous role but one Nicholas fulfilled even more scrupulously than his predecessor. Then the Polish Diet of 1830 threw out a government bill restricting civil divorce, there was popular excitement and something of a palace revolution in Warsaw, and the Grand Duke Constantine foolishly withdrew all Russian troops from the Polish capital. It took from November, 1830, to September, 1831, for large Russian forces to defeat organized Polish resistance and to retake Warsaw. There were great casualties, particularly from cholera, of which the grand duke himself died.

Field Marshal, later Prince Ivan Paskevich, who was the Poles' reconqueror and then governor general, was commissioned to Russify his area. A letter of the tsar ended with the specific order "to withdraw little by little everything that has historic national value and deliver it here," meaning that the Poles would have to forget about Kosciusko's sword, their old army standards, and the university library. The 1815 constitution was rescinded, and although Poland kept its administrative autonomy, it really fell under the rule of Russian bureaucrats. Russian was the official language of administration and in the high schools. The severest censorship was imposed. In a letter to his Prussian brother-in-law Nicholas acknowledged his mission to make the Poles "happy in spite of themselves," but a more accurate observation by a historian was that "it was as if Russia could hold Poland only by uncivilizing it."

Another national group that faced Russification were the Ukrainians. A secret society of Ukrainian nationalists was harshly persecuted. Official nationality policies were not extended against the Baltic Germans, however, for too many Baltic Germans were high in Nicholas' government and army.

Public education was necessarily a subject of great concern to Nicholas. Quantitatively, his policies produced minor triumphs; qualitatively, disasters. The tsar's admirers could say pridefully, although many saw no good in it, that between 1800 and mid-century the number of university students climbed from 350 to 3,500 and the number of Gymnasiums from

48 to 74. The regime especially stressed technical institutions as politically harmless, founding the Pulkovo Observatory, the St. Petersburg Institute of Technology, and a school of architecture.

Although the ordinary schools were sometimes seen to offer opportunities for indoctrination of "Orthodoxy, autocracy, and nationality," they were more often treated as suspect and subversive. The best justification of his service Minister of Education Uvarov could offer was to make the schools "mental dikes for the struggle with destructive notions." The first restrictive laws came early in the reign and grew worse. An 1828 statute curtailed foreign teachers in the lower schools and restricted their curricula to technology. A particular prejudice of the tsar was that "children belonging to different social groups must not be educated together," for, as he firmly believed, nobody ought to aim at rising above his allotted position. The turn of the universities for being pushed backward came in 1835, when a statute severely restricted their autonomy. The year before, the government introduced full-time inspectors to meddle in the extracurricular life of the university students, who were rendered more identifiable by putting them in special uniforms. Uniforms for everybody was, indeed, a long-lived contribution of Nicholas to imperial Russia.

New censorship laws decreed in the late 1820's were intended, in their sponsor's words, "to make printing harmless." The censors' hands were more than full blue-penciling an incredible literary outpouring. Nicholas was ultimate censor, and he tried to keep up with all Russian publication, which grew tremendously during his reign. Personally, the tsar's tastes were toward the sentimental and second-rate, and he judged books too much on moral and political grounds. More important, the general effect of his police state was to terrorize the best of the intelligentsia into silence or exile, self-imposed or otherwise.

The very word "intelligentsia" is not only Russian but belongs to Nicholas' reign. It designated a stratum of educated, usually socially concerned people not necessarily of the nobility—people like sons of priests, middle-class professionals, and even peasants with higher school training. The emergence of this group was a matter of delight to Russian cultural historians but hardly to the iron tsar.

Another factor in the cultural upsurge was the influx of German professors to Russia and the even greater outflow of Russian students to the universities at Bonn, Jena, and Berlin. Although the government seemingly might have been pleased to see its young men studying in the land of Metternich's reactionary influence, it realized that the real vogue was not Metternich but philosophers whose views could be interpreted radically in political terms.

With a new large class of Russians capable of arguing Hegel versus Feuerbach, the 1830's saw a signal debate in general terms about the destiny of Russia. An opening gun in this healthy controversy was the "Philosophical Letter" of Peter Chaadayev published in September, 1836, in the *Telescope*, one of a considerable number of Russian journals. (There were 140 in 1851.) Chaadayev seriously questioned Russia's past and future because of its Byzantine ways, proposed a relook at Western Catholicism, and took a few swipes at autocracy and serfdom. The tsar's reaction was forceful: Chaadayev was declared insane and put under medical observation, a practice toward intellectuals revived in the 1960's by Nikita Khrushchev's successors.

Following Chaadayev, the Russian intelligentsia began to split into two loosely defined camps, the Westernizers and the Slavophiles. The Westernizers made Peter the Great their hero, tended to be rationalistic, slightly anticlerical, pro-Europe, and proconstitution, and even dabbled with Socialism of an intellectual sort. Their philosophic opponents, the Slavophiles, usually stressed the historic mission of the Orthodox Slavic peoples, often exaggerated the good old days before Peter, and sometimes propounded an anarchism based on the idealization of traditional Russian peasant institutions. The government found both schools extreme and distasteful and persecuted them equally. For example, regarding a drama about Peter I by Michael Pogodin—Peter being the philosophic touchstone really and the drama in question a gushy panegyric—Nicholas intoned in writing: "The person of Emperor Peter the Great must be for every Russian an object of veneration and of love; to bring it onto the stage would be almost sacrilege and therefore entirely improper. Prohibit the publication." Historical and philosophic controversies were so abhorrent to Uvarov that he declared that he would die happy if he succeeded through the schools in keeping Russia back fifty years from what the theorists dreamed of.

Russian poetry had its golden age in the 1820's and 1830's. In an era of searching Romanticism in Western Europe, Russian poets, now no longer imitators, were classical in their pursuit of form, directness of language, and moderation of sensibility. Three of the greatest were Alexander Pushkin, tragically killed in a duel; Michael Lermontov, likewise killed prematurely; and Basil Zhukovsky, who also enjoyed celebrity as tutor to the heir to the throne.

Pushkin figures so large in Russian literature that the circumstances of his life and death may be taken as a major commentary on the reign of his sovereign and acquaintance, Nicholas I. Descended from a boyar family as old as the Romanovs on his father's side and from the Negro favorite of Peter I on his mother's, Alexander Pushkin was born at the turn of the nineteenth century, underwent schooling at the *lycée* at Tsarskoe Selo, and at the age of twenty-one was exiled from the capital for writing his "Ode to Liberty." He was permitted to return under Nicholas, even given a job in the Ministry of Foreign Affairs, and produced in a brief span of years such poetic and prose masterpieces as *Boris Godunov, Eugene Onegin, The Queen of Spades* and the short panegyric to Peter the Great, "The Bronze Horseman." His contribution was essentially originality and realism, not political radicalism. Nicholas did once say that he would have preferred a more innocuous *Boris,* one "in the style of Sir Walter Scott," while Pushkin, for his part, had the boldness to tell the tsar that he would have been among the Decembrists if he had been in the capital.

Pushkin's wife was a silly flirt, and there was gossip about her and Pushkin's new brother-in-law, a lout named George Heckeren d'Anthès, who was the ward of the Dutch ambassador. After complicated exchanges and maneuvers that most of the capital knew about, a duel took place in early 1837, and Alexander Pushkin—a man whom many contemporaries recognized as a "divine star," "incomparable," and "the national pride"—was killed. Russia had "exhausted herself" in producing Pushkin, wrote one. Considerable controversy arose over the tacit and direct responsibility of Nicholas I in the tragedy. There is evidence that the tsar made an effort to get Pushkin's promise not to duel, and Zhukovsky reported his friend's last words as "a pity I must die. I would have lived for him" (meaning Nicholas). Others said that these words were fabricated only to mollify Nicholas and that the tsar was guilty of encouraging the hostility to Pushkin of the chief of police (who saw Decembrists everywhere) and others. Pushkin, needlessly lost, was essentially the victim of Russian high society.

Prose and journalism came to predominate over poetry in Russian literature after Pushkin. Russia's first great novelist Nicholas Gogol received both encouragement and difficulty from Nicholas I and the censors. His celebrated play *The Inspector General* aroused the wrath of bureaucrats for its devastating satire of their stupidity and venality, but the tsar saw it as both amusing and salutary. Gogol had much more trouble publishing his novel *Dead Souls*, which probed the serf system through the device of an adventurer traveling about Russia purchasing serfs who were deceased but still on the tax rolls so that he could own enough to attain a rank of nobility.

Gogol's best literary successors experienced increasing persecution at the hands of the government—exile as in the case of the young Turgenev, near death on the scaffold for Dostoievsky. The 1840's and 1850's did not fulfill their great promise, largely because of repression and fear. As for journalism, it gradually became insipidly innocuous. Alexander Herzen, Russia's first great social analyst, suffered Siberian exile in 1835 for student activities and later found that the only way he could theorize on the larger issues, to say nothing of criticizing specific abuses of the regime, was to publish in London. His informative and scathing *The Bell* was smuggled into Russia for years, and a copy was always to be found on the desk of the police chief.

A first in Russian music was the performance of Michael Glinka's entirely original and national opera *Ivan Susanin* in 1836. Violent opposition in aristocratic circles greeted this glorification of a simple peasant's heroism in saving Michael Romanov in 1613. Nicholas attended, applauded, but ordered the title changed to *A Life for the Tsar*. Music was one area where politics did not often intrude, and Nicholas was kindly remembered for his horn playing in a palace quartet and his sponsorship of concerts by Lizst.

The tsar considered himself a specialist in the arts and architecture. To his credit was the construction of a building for the Hermitage collection of paintings, which was opened to the public. Nicholas' interference in architectural matters was typical in its intensity and questionable in its taste. Primarily, he showed interest in perpetuating, indeed standardizing, a monumental and severe Classical style in public buildings and private dwellings. At the same time he sponsored the Byzantine-Russian revivalism of the architect Constantine Thon, which critics said produced lifeless imitations of a bygone era and, in the case of the huge Grand Kremlin Palace, erected in the 1840's, meant atrocity replacing simple neglect in the national historic shrine. This pseudomedieval Grand Kremlin Palace may be the most apt symbol of a regime that was trying to go backward all the while it was going forward.

4. Gendarme of Europe

Events elsewhere than Russia were greatly responsible for making Nicholas' internal policies more reactionary after 1830, and the European revolutions of 1848 made the last seven years of the iron tsar's reign a peak of hysterical, brutal, and total oppression. A popular witticism about this interaction ran: "If they play tricks in Europe, the Russian gets hit on the back." Nicholas' foreign policy, almost consistently directed against change in the status quo anywhere, and his million-strong army, to back up his words, made him the most hated ruler in the world. In the end, selfishness, pigheadedness, and muddle in both diplomacy and war were Nicholas' undoing.

More narrowly Russian and less cosmopolitan than his brother, Nicholas nonetheless maintained the policies he inherited from Alexander I—closeness to Prussia; dedication to the Holy Alliance and the Metternich system; and, above all, support of legitimate rulers. The tsar was very much his own foreign minister; the actual holder of that title for the whole reign, Count Karl Robert Nesselrode, considered himself merely Nicholas' tool and is more remembered for pie than for policy.

A legacy of the last reign was the problem of the Greek struggle for independence against the Ottoman Empire. Here Nicholas abandoned his predecessor's hands-off policy by going to war with Turkey in April, 1828. Actually, complicated diplomatic tensions were the cause of the war, for Nicholas was no Hellenophile, like Byron, a casualty in Greece, or like his admirer Pushkin. The tsar made this perfectly clear, writing: "I abhor the Greeks. I consider them as revolted subjects and I do not desire their independence. My grievance is against the Turks' conduct to Russia." The Russian army, easily crossing the Danube in 1828, for the first time traversed the Balkan mountains and captured Adrianople in the campaign of 1829. Catherine's dream of taking Constantinople seemed at hand except for the exhaustion of the Russian troops and Nicholas' desire to maintain the Ottoman Empire as an essential part of the balance of power. The relatively moderate Treaty of Adrianople signed in September, 1829, gave Russia territory in the Danube Delta and the Caucasus, an indemnity, and the right of passage for merchant ships through the Dardanelles and Bosporus straits. Autonomy was granted Moldavia and Walachia, and somewhat incidentally, a small Greek state secured its independence.

Nicholas showed courage by personally joining the 1828 campaign. He also demonstrated for all time his utter humorlessness when he ordered that if recaptured, the Russian frigate *Raphael* was to be burned, as if it had been the ship itself that had struck its flag to the enemy.

The 1830 Revolution in France, which overthrew Bourbon Charles X in favor of Orléans Louis Philippe, enraged Nicholas. Ironically, after a meeting with Louis Philippe in 1815 Nicholas had become a great admirer of his family life and imitated it, but now the Frenchman was merely a usurper and a "traitor to the King and Dynasty." The tsar eventually recognized the new French regime only because all the other powers did. Persistently refusing to address Louis Philippe with the customary "brother," Nicholas further vented his spite by banning French styles in Russia and excluding Frenchmen from the foreign engineers invited in as railroad consultants.

The Belgian Revolution of 1830, which gave that country its independence from the King of the Netherlands, was also vehemently opposed by the tsar. King Leopold of the Belgians, who was Queen Victoria's well-known uncle, had to wait until 1852 before relations with Russia were established. Other revolutions in Germany and Italy in the 1830's were suppressed by Austrian troops with Nicholas' earnest encouragement. The tsar himself concentrated excessive numbers of troops in Poland and possibly would have moved them west against the French and Belgians except for the great Polish Revolt of 1830–31.

The 1830's also saw two crises in the Near East, each involving armed struggles between the sultan at Constantinople and his nominal vassal, the Khedive of Egypt. Nicholas treated the Egyptian as another insurrectionist. In 1833 the seemingly impossible occurred when a Russian fleet and an army of 10,000 were invited in to protect Constantinople, and the ensuing Treaty of Unkiar-Skelessi appeared to make the Ottoman Empire a protectorate of Russia. London and Paris feared Russian aggrandizement, but Nicholas justified his moves as designed to preserve, not change, the status quo. In 1841 Russia readily signed the London Treaty internationalizing the straits and banning all foreign warships from it. This retreat, or shift at least, Nicholas explained as the same basic search for stability.

Nicholas I tried to stick to his antirevolutionary principles at a time when many Russians, conservatives and radicals alike, looked to the overthrow of the sultan and the liberation of the Slavs and Orthodox in the Balkans. Such Pan-Slavism seemed the logical extension of the policies of the Great Peter and the Great Catherine. Yet Nicholas instructed his agents in the Balkans to discourage local revolts, and he even advanced the fantastic suggestion that the whole problem would disappear if the sultan became Orthodox.

The Near Eastern situation weighed heavily on Nicholas' mind when he made an extensive state visit to Britain in 1844. The young Queen Victoria was impressed with how handsome and magnetic her guest was, also writing accurately about him: "He is stern and severe, with fixed principles of *duty* which *nothing* on earth will make him change." At this time Nicholas had fateful conversations with the British foreign secretary during which he advanced the thesis that the Ottoman Empire was the "Sick Man of Europe," which could be bolstered but which eventually would disintegrate. The tsar thought it essential for the great powers to agree on a partition plan beforehand. Nicholas' not unrealistic reasoning was generally construed as typical Russian aggressiveness by his hosts, but he was allowed to leave Britain thinking a binding understanding had been achieved.

In 1848 major revolutions occurred all over Europe; it was a world gone mad in the eyes of conservatives. Louis Philippe was overthrown; France once again had a republic; and there was even the possibility of a workers' regime in Paris. Mobs took over Berlin, humiliated King Frederick William IV, and forced Nicholas' brother-in-law to grant a constitution. A congress met in Frankfurt to bring about the reunification of all the German states on a liberal basis. Metternich had to flee Vienna, and the armies of the Hapsburg emperor were driven out by revolutionists from Vienna, Prague, Budapest, Venice, and Milan. Princes up and down Italy were compelled to grant constitutions, and a republic was proclaimed in a Pope-less Rome.

At a reception surrounded by his courtiers and colonels, Nicholas was supposed first to have exclaimed, "Saddle your horses, gentlemen!" when he was told of the February Revolution in Paris. The tsar later had second thoughts about the fate of Louis Philippe and was able to sneer, "Here the comedy is played out and finished, and the scoundrel is down," adding, "by the same door by which he came in." Nonetheless, in the western provinces Nicholas once again began assembling an army numbering upward of 300,000 in preparation for a march to the Rhine.

In March, 1848, when the full extent of the insurrections in European capitals was known, Nicholas issued a violent manifesto, a document completely composed by himself, while tears of anger and exaltation rolled down his cheeks. The tsar declared, "Insolence, recognizing no longer any limits, is in its madness threatening even our Russia entrusted to us by God. We are ready to meet our enemies." He added, "Our ancient battle cry: 'for faith, tsar, and fatherland' will now once more show us the way to victory." The main incongruity in this almost hysterical outburst was that no armies were marching against Russia; the opposite was true.

In July, 1848, Nicholas was asked by the sultan to send troops to restore order in Moldavia and Walachia. Throughout the year he chafed for such an invitation from the King of Prussia, and he was greatly relieved when the Prussian army gained the upper hand over the constitutionalists. The tsar was also persistent in his attempts to dissuade Frederick William from accepting the crown of a united Germany from the Frankfurt Congress, and indeed, that whole unification movement eventually collapsed.

The most memorable of Russian actions at this time was armed intervention in Hungary. By 1849 the Hapsburg house was in order in Vienna, Milan, and Prague, but Budapest was ruled by Louis Kossuth in the name of a Hungarian republic. That summer 200,000 Russian soldiers joined the Austrian armies in the successful suppression of the Hungarian rebels. This costly effort to aid the Hapsburgs without any direct gain for Russia was unpopular in St. Petersburg, seeming merely quixotic on the tsar's part. As for the Hapsburgs, a Vienna statesman declared with surprising and prophetic candor: "Austria will surprise the world with her ingratitude."

It is puzzling how there could be so much revolutionary action in so many places in 1848 and 1849 and so little result. If history failed to turn at this seeming turning point, it was in great part because Tsar Nicholas acted determinedly and so powerfully against changes. His success at encouraging counterrevolution appeared to make him virtual dictator of the European continent, and he emerged from his triumphs even more singleminded and uncompromising than before. However, Nicholas did not stand unsupported in his principles. Influential Russian writers, some of whom were Slavophiles, interpreted 1848 as the signal that Europe was dying and that Russia was the new holy ark of political truth.

In Russia the years beginning in 1848 became a nightmare. All foreign travel was banned. Further harassment of the schools incredibly swept out even Uvarov as too liberal. Nicholas' advisers talked of closing down the universities altogether, but the government confined itself to restricting the number of students drastically and to reordering the curricula so that philosophy and logic could be taught only by professors of theology.

The censorship reached absurd levels, with no less than twelve departments responsible for it in some way, including a secret committee that amounted to a censorship over the censors. Fanatic bureaucrats looked for conspiratorial ciphers in sheet music and eliminated the phrase "forces of nature" from a physics text as suggestive of revolution. It was no longer possible to write of the Russian Dumas of old, and Roman emperors were no longer "killed" but "perished." There is the amusing case of a censor who moralistically upbraided the writer of a third-rate love story for having his hero say that his love's "one tender look" was worth more than the "attention of the entire universe," it being pointed out that the universe "includes tsars and other lawful authorities."

If Nicholas smelled the smoke of subversion everywhere, there was precious little fire to be found in Russia—one tiny flame of note, perhaps. A Russian gentleman intellectual named Michael Petrashevsky had become such an admirer of the French Utopian Socialist Fourier that he even tried to set up a model phalanstery on his estate (his ungrateful serfs promptly burned it down). In St. Petersburg, Petrashevsky gathered around himself a circle of fellow spirits who met every Friday for several years to discuss civil rights, emancipation, and, rarely, revolutionary action. In 1849 the police moved in and arrested fifty-two men. Forthwith, Petrashevsky, fiery young Fedor Dostoievsky, and thirteen others were sentenced to hanging, to serve as a lesson to all young Russians. The condemned actually were on the scaffold with nooses in place before a messenger arrived with an announcement of imperial reprieve and a new sentence of exile. One of the conspirators went insane on the spot, while Dostoievsky was eventually to return from Siberia a drastically disturbed man psychologically.

Dostoievsky was not the only writer silenced in the post-1848 era. Many others were sent into exile or simply shut up, and one celebrated philosopher closely connected with the court committed suicide in politically motivated despair. The tsar could boast that Russia was quiet, but, as a sometime admirer of his wrote secretly, it was "the quiet of the graveyard, rotting and stinking, both physically and morally."

Around 1849 it was increasingly brought to Nicholas' attention that his brother the Grand Duke Michael was provoking tremendous hostility in the army and populace by the intensification of his already brutal drillmastering of the troops. The tsar wrote of Michael's ill humor, "This is deplorable, and what can I do? He is sick. . . . It is not at the age of fifty that one corrects such a nervous condition." The grand duke died of a stroke in 1849 during a review. Unfortunately, Nicholas was not such a good diagnostician of himself at this time. Tensions and his frenzied work habits had affected not only his nerves but his general health. He looked worn out long before he entered his mid-fifties.

Another great change in Nicholas' later life was that he took a mistress. Sensual by nature and always gallant with women, the tsar, nonetheless, had been a model of fidelity to the Empress Alexandra, until the 1840's, when he started a liaison with a Mademoiselle Valerie Nelidov. After some years' hesitation he subjected his wife to the distress of having Nelidov recognized as official and permanent favorite by installing her in the empress' own entourage. The intermediary in all this was an ex-aide of Arakcheev, Count Peter Kleinmichel, who conveniently adopted all the imperial bastards. Later there was another mistress, Mademoiselle Kutuzov. Politically, these women counted for nothing.

The final act of Nicholas' reign began in 1850, when a dispute broke out whether the French Catholics or the Russian Orthodox priests should control the Holy Places in Turkish Jerusalem, the latter losing out. Three years later, after a special Russian emissary had delivered an ultimatum to Constantinople and had been rebuffed, Nicholas ordered his army to occupy Moldavia and Walachia as material guarantees until the Turks came around. Instead, the Ottoman Empire declared war in October, 1853, and shortly thereafter a Russian squadron smartly smashed the Turkish navy at Sinope. In March, 1854, France and Britain declared war on Russia, and thus began the Crimean War, the first great power conflict since 1815.

The responsibility for causing the Crimean War is a hugely complex question, in which Nicholas' role is just one subproblem. At times the tsar acted rashly and with typical arbitrariness, as when, for example, he dispatched two army corps to the border without telling his foreign and war ministers or even the Third Section. At other times Nicholas seemed to lead the search for peace, and he probably believed he had a genuine understanding with Britain about carving up the Ottoman Empire to the satisfaction of all concerned except the Turks. Western newspapers could and did howl hysterically about Russian aggressiveness and Nicholas' truculence, all the while ignoring the local political reasons that made Britain and France gleefully rush to war.

Once the war was on, Nicholas deceived few, except perhaps himself, when he expressed surprise that Christian Britain and France could ally with the infidel. To his Prussian brother-in-law he wrote that "now nothing is left to me, but to fight, to win, or to perish with honor, as a martyr of our holy faith, and when I say this, I declare it in the name of all Russia." Nicholas and "all Russia" fought the war very badly.

The allies' strategy was to teach Nicholas a lesson and to gain bargaining power at the peace table by seizing the great Russian naval base at Sevastopol near the bottom of the Crimean peninsula. British-French naval supremacy led to the Black Sea's being swept clear of the enemy. The

Russian warships were sunk at the entrance of Sevastopol Harbor. This was the true dawn of modern naval warfare (not the *Monitor-Merrimack* duel of nearly a decade later), for the allies used steamships with iron armor and shell-firing guns. They were able to land armies north of Sevastopol and, after defeating a Russian force, moved south to half-encircle the fortress city and to begin bombardment of it. The siege was to last 359 days, the first warfare reported by telegraph, camera, and newspaper correspondents.

The Russian commander, Prince Alexander Menshikov (great-great-grandson of Peter's lieutenant) had a force of 35,000 defending the city and outside it, in the Crimean uplands, a somewhat smaller field army. In two hotly contested battles at Balaklava and at Inkerman in the fall the Russians failed in their efforts to drive the allies into the sea (a completely incidental and unnecessary action after the former battle was the celebrated charge of the British Light Brigade). As the winter of 1854–55 took hold, the losses for the opposing armies from disease and exposure were appalling. Emperor Nicholas declared that he expected "Generals January and February" to win for him, but the bald fact was that 70,000 Allied troops in the Crimea could not be dislodged by the Russian army, which boasted an overall total of 1,000,000 (most of which were needed to guard other frontiers). Such was the state of Russian military incompetence, corruption, and disorganization that it took longer for supplies to reach the Crimea by land from Moscow than by sea from Paris and London.

The Crimean War was still raging when Nicholas I died. The tsar had caught an ordinary cold at a court wedding reception in February, 1855; he neglected his condition, some say suicidally; and on March 1 his doctors diagnosed his lungs as paralyzed and his remaining hours as few. At the end the iron tsar retained his usual calm dignity and his sense of duty. After prayers, he bade considered farewells to his family, to his few personal friends, to his servants, and to picked soldiers who were to relay his last wishes to the defenders of Sevastopol.

In typical military terminology, Nicholas apologized to his son Alexander that he was "not handing over the command to you in good order." At the last, he held his wife's and his son's hands in his own, and his dying words were reported to be:

> I wanted to take everything difficult, everything heavy upon myself and leave you [Alexander] a peaceful, orderly, and happy realm. Providence determined otherwise. Now I shall ascend to pray for Russia and you [imperial family]. After Russia, I loved you above everything else in the world. Serve Russia.

For Russia, Nicholas' death ended what was at best a short nightmare of reaction, at worst thirty lost years. For Europe, it meant that Russia would cease for a while to play the forward role begun by Peter, extended by Catherine and Alexander, and pushed beyond all reason by Nicholas. Perhaps, this contemporary Russian evaluation of Nicholas is not unfair: "The chief fault of the reign of Nicholas I consisted in the fact that it was all a mistake."

XVI.
The Reforming Tsar: Alexander II

1. Willful Young Conservative

IN a double paradox, Alexander II was a great reformer in spite of himself and a political martyr in spite of his great accomplishments. He was the last Romanov with any claim to the plaudits of his people or of his historians.

The first of seven children, Alexander Nicholaevich was born in Moscow in April, 1818, to the then Grand Duke Nicholas and the Grand Duchess Alexandra Fedorovna, formerly Princess Charlotte of Prussia. Few princes could look back to parents more devoted to each other and to their family.

It was no surprise that the son of the royal drillmaster should have his nursery walls covered with pictures of soldiers. Alexander started his military training at the age of six. He was a plucky boy of seven when in the Winter Palace he heard the cannon of his newly proclaimed father shatter the ranks of the Decembrists. At nine, when he made his first visit to his Hohenzollern relatives, he was thrilled to be able to parade before Frederick William III and even more delighted to be appointed colonel in chief of the Third Prussian Uhlan Regiment, with an appropriately exotic new uniform. In 1829 he entered the Corps of Cadets, serving first as a soldier, then as an officer, under the watchful eye of his father, and seven years later he was commanding the First Battalion of the Preobrazhenskoe.

Tsar Nicholas wisely acquiesced in his wife's wish that their son's chief tutor be a civilian. An avid reader of the German Romantics Goethe and Schiller, the empress chose Basil Zhukovsky, a poet who already was beginning to enjoy the reputation of being the leading light of a Russian Romanticism. Son of a Russian noble and a Turkish captive, Zhukovsky was a humanist who had freed his family's serfs, and he was a close friend of Pushkin, although less outspokenly liberal. The patient, idealistic, often frustrated tutelage of Zhukovsky, which lasted many years, has been credited with giving the tsarevich a "predilection for the good" in the face of the pupil's basic nonintellectuality and interests in the military and in the outdoors. His good memory enabled Alexander to gain a command of five languages, but it was sadly noted by his tutor that the tsarevich was prone to back off from the hard problems of learning and to become apathetic.

Alexander also had a military tutor, Captain Moerder, who was enlightened and frank enough to warn the tsar of some of his son's psychological difficulties. While basically amiable, Alexander could be troublesome and arrogant. Moreover, his overconcern for the bagatelles of military life was matched by an indifference to real military science. Moerder suffered from heart attacks in direct proportion to his charge's displays of truculence, leading eventually to his going abroad for his health and to his death, when Alexander was sixteen. Alexander cried mightily at this news in a public display of emotion, which became typical of him.

When Alexander was nineteen, his formal education ended. Essentially he had resisted the earnest efforts of Zhukovsky and Moerder, and he appeared to have gained little from the special lectures of the greatest diplomats, financiers, and jurists of Russia, including Speransky. The conclusion of the leading Russian historian of the era is simply that "the parade ground ideals triumphed in Alexander's education."

The heir's tour of the empire in 1837 was impressive, at least statistically. Thirty provinces were visited over seven months, and 16,000 petitions were received by the traveler, who was the first Romanov to cross the Urals into Siberia. Zhukovsky saw to it that Alexander was exposed to something more than the usual round of military and religious ceremonies. On his own initiative and despite official obstacles, Alexander made contact with some of the political exiles, including former Decembrists and Alexander Herzen, then a radical student only slightly older than his visitor and destined to be his most telling critic. When the tsarevich was moved to write his father asking for mitigation of the exiles' sentences, Zhukovsky said that it was "one of the happiest moments of my life." Generally, however, the tour raised few doubts or questions in Alexander's mind, and he could write a teacher pleasantly enough: "I have seen our mother Russia, and I have learned to love and respect her even more."

Next came the grand tour of Europe, which took Alexander as far north as Stockholm and as far south as Rome, where he was received by the Pope. In the Netherlands he had a reunion with the queen, his aunt Anna Pavlovna, and in England he met the new young sovereign, Queen Victoria. Once again Zhukovsky was on hand to try to broaden Alexander's horizons.

At the resort of Ems the tsarevich happened to encounter the Marquis de Custine, Tsar Nicholas' most publicized detractor, and the Frenchman duly left this full description of the heir at twenty:

> He is tall but seemed a little heavy for such a young man. His features would be handsome if it were not for the puffiness of his face which blurs his expression. His round face is more German than Russian. . . . The expression of the eyes of the young prince is benevolent: his bearing is pleasant, easy, and aristocratic—truly that of a prince. He had an air of modesty without timidity . . . if he ever reigns . . . he will make himself obeyed and not through terror.

Custine also perceived "some inner suffering" in the face of Alexander. This was a matter of the moment, not a characteristic, for the fact was simply that the successor to the throne of St. Petersburg was lovelorn.

A major purpose of Alexander's travels, if not the main one, was to meet suitable princesses. Already Alexander had had an affair with a lady-in-waiting, and in fact, he had announced his desire to marry the young Polish noblewoman. Bitterly opposed to this, his mother wrote sadly and somewhat prophetically: "What will become of Russia one day in the hands of a man who does not know how to conquer himself?" The tsarevich, who now had been provided with a list of preferred German brides, once again confounded his parents by showing up in Darmstadt, where he was not supposed to go, and by courting the fifteen-year-old Princess Maria of Hesse, a Cinderella he was not supposed to meet. "We don't have to go farther," he told his companion Prince Alexis Orlov, the next morning. "I have made my choice."

Abruptly recalled to St. Petersburg, Alexander was apprised of the particular unsuitability of his romantic dreammate. Princess Maria's supposed father, the Grand Duke Louis II of Hesse, had chosen to live apart from his wife once an heir had been born in the first year of their marriage. The grand duchess, who became notoriously adulterous thereafter, suddenly became pregnant after thirteen years, duly gave birth to a son and the next year repeated her indiscretion by producing a daughter, both of whom were apparently sired by one of the least prepossessing of her servants. Louis II amiably assumed paternity of these bastards, the son in due time becoming the ancestor of the British Mountbattens and the daughter, Princess Maria, becoming Empress of Russia, for Alexander would have none but her. It did iron-willed Nicholas no good to threaten his heir with the example of Peter the Great and the Tsarevich Alexis. Alexander was blithely willing to renounce the throne, and his stubbornness in this affair was to prove a portent of later political actions. Public opinion was against the match, and perversely, the tsar then came around to sanctioning it. The couple were betrothed in the spring of 1840, Maria was subsequently received into the Orthodox Church as Maria Alexandrovna, and within a year Alexander and Maria were united as man and wife in a magnificent ceremony that saw Tsar Nicholas escorting on horseback the bride's golden carriage. The occasion was used for a widespread amnesty of political prisoners.

The tsarevich's bride soon won over the whole court with her good looks and perfect manners, and she touched wider circles of society with her sincere conversion to Orthodoxy and devotion to good works. The heir seemed to have found the happy family life which he once declared was more important to him than the throne. After losing their firstborn daughter in infancy, the couple were blessed with four sons and a daughter, thus enlarging the dynasty once again as much as Alexander's grandfather and father had each already done.

Alexander's defiance of Nicholas in the matter of his marriage proved to be a brief sour note in a father-son relationship that was unusually close and respectful. The heir was unhesitantly initiated into governmental and military responsibilities and was allowed to attend sessions of the Council of State. During one of the tsar's absences abroad, Alexander was given full powers as regent, a striking thing in view of the Romanov history of parent-son antagonisms. Credit should go to Nicholas for making Alexander probably the most fully trained successor to the throne in terms of practical administrative experience.

As for his politics, Alexander was by no means a liberal, although this was reported on the basis more of hope than any fact. The tsarevich was not even an enigma like his namesake uncle. Rather, Alexander, especially in the period after 1848, completely and consistently seconded his father's repressive regime in such matters as the censorship and the deportations. He went even further than his father in his efforts to oppose any change in the serf system. Appointed chairman of one of the secret committees on the serf problem, he distinguished himself by blocking or vitiating even mild proposals for redress. That Alexander essentially admired Nicholas' harsh rule was indicated by his expressed wish not to outlive his parent. Awe and diffidence combined in this attitude.

The successor to the throne in 1855 appeared to be more a pupil of Nicholas I than of Zhukovsky. The autocracy and militarism were his basic convictions, and no bigger ideas than these troubled his intellectual horizons. Yet somehow Alexander seemed more open to suggestion than his predecessor. For one thing, he allowed himself more human failings, more breaches of discipline. Alexander could display fits of stubbornness, but he was known to give way to hesitation and to taking the easy way out. His ordinary amiability was varied by outbursts of anger or even of tears. In character and training Alexander Nicholaevich was something of Alexis Michaelovich, and like that tsar of the good old days, he turned out to be an innovator in spite of himself, a man who let himself be carried along by irresistible forces of change.

2. *Liberator*

Alexander began his reign in March, 1855, at a time when his country's fortunes in the Crimean War were deteriorating rapidly. The preliminary peace negotiations begun at Vienna under Nicholas I were continued under his successor, but the new tsar felt compelled to maintain a front of defiance and to hope for a miracle. Disaster came, instead, when the defenders of Sevastopol finally evacuated the city in September, 1855, courageous to the end, but helpless in the face of the overwhelming allied bombardment. Then Austria duly showed "her ingratitude" for 1849 and threatened to join Russia's enemies. While a peace party in St. Petersburg wrung their hands over the casualties and over the bankrupt treasury, a war-minded group led by the tsar's brother the Grand Duke Constantine clamored for fighting on in the depths of Russia. In his first major decision, Alexander at length chose to accept the peace terms offered.

The Crimean War was formally settled at the Congress of Paris in February and March, 1856. Russia had to cede part of Bessarabia to the principalities of Moldavia and Walachia which became the newly autonomous state of Rumania. The fortress of Kars in the Caucasus, which once again the Russians had heroically stormed, was once again returned to the Turks. By the Black Sea clauses Russia was denied the right to have either warships or fortifications in the area of the Black Sea. Since it might have been worse, the treaty was greeted as something of a success in St. Petersburg. There was no indemnity to be paid, for example, and the hopes of Napoleon III to detach Poland from Russia had been thwarted.

The tsar's manifesto declaring the peace terms ended with these significant words, which could not fail to stir the public:

> With the aid of the Divine Providence, forever gracious to Russia, may her internal welfare be established and perfected; may truth and kindness reign in her courts; may the aspiration for enlightenment and for all useful activities develop all over with new force, and may everyone peacefully enjoy the results of honest labour under the shelter of laws equally just for all, equally protecting all. . . .

What the Crimean War had made painfully inevitable was to come to pass immediately: With the Crimean War concluded, the country was to turn inevitably to its internal problems, to reform. Already, in the first months of his reign, Alexander had casually bowed to public opinion and put an end to the harsher features of his father's regime. This thaw, analogous to what happened in Soviet Russia after the death of Stalin, saw the lifting of restrictions on foreign travel, on students, and on publications. Further concessions were announced in connection with Alexander's coronation in Moscow in September, 1856: the cancellation of tax arrears for the poor; a temporary halting of recruiting; and a widespread amnesty, including all surviving Decembrists. Dostoievsky, who returned from Siberia, wrote of "our Angel Tsar."

Rumors began to fly about the tsar's ultimate intentions, particularly on serfdom, a problem the press was still forbidden to discuss. Alexander felt obliged to speak out, and in the spring of 1856 he assured an assemblage of Moscow nobility that the autocrat would not abolish serfdom with a stroke of the pen, adding, however, that "it would be better to abolish serfdom from above than wait till it will begin to liberate itself from below." He then requested the gentry to "deliberate on the way by which this can be accomplished."

The tsar's essentially private appeal to the nobility got no response at all. The liberal Minister of Interior Sergius Lanskoy, in his youth a Decembrist sympathizer, waited around in vain for emancipation projects to be submitted to him. The tsar's extremely enlightened aunt, the Grand Duchess Helen, was almost alone in offering suggestions. Hope in progressive circles faded in the face of reports of Alexander's basic apathy and indolence. A British envoy informed Queen Victoria that the tsar was "well-intentioned but weak as water," without strength of "either intelligence or character." Alexander, still largely surrounded by aristocrats of the previous era, seemed more interested in bear hunting than anything else. Then, in early 1857, the tsar turned away from his wife, considered a progressive influence on him, and took up with one of her ladies-in-waiting, Princess Alexandra Dolgoruky, a laughing, spontaneous creature described as a "young tigress." The tsar had thrown away his initial popularity.

A secret committee on the serf question sat on and off in 1857 under the chairmanship of the tsar, while Prince Orlov, one of the greatest serf owners in the country, and most of the other members tried to make sure that as little as possible was done. That summer the tsar lamely assured a listener that "I am more than ever determined but have no one to help me." Assistance was forthcoming. The ardently reformist Grand Duke Constantine, the tsar's brother, got on the committee. The foreign minister, old Prince Alexander Gorchakov, made strong representations of the need for measures to impress European opinion. Oddly, there developed an alliance in favor of reform between Alexander's mistress and the empress, who successfully changed her tactics from hurt chilliness to cajolery.

The turning point came with an unexpected proposal, induced by fright, from the Lithuanian provinces that the nobles there be allowed to free their serfs without giving any land to them. Alexander vetoed this as patently unjust and instructed Lanskoy to proceed with emancipation-with-land projects. In the face of growing confusion the tsar told the nobility of St. Petersburg at a ball in December, 1857, "It is necessary to get on with the business without delay. That is my categorical will." Herzen wrote ecstatically in his London journal *The Bell,* "Thou hast conquered, O Galilean."

In 1858 the secret committee gave way to the official Main Committee on emancipation. Once again the bureaucrats, reflecting the hostility of the nobility to reform, did their best to have things bog down. Grand Duke Constantine in a rage on one occasion told Prince Orlov that he "greatly doubted the sincerity of these gentlemen" who made obstacles instead of removing them. When Orlov remonstrated about his personal honor, the grand duke reportedly said that the Russian nobility were not worth his spitting on. The tsar sent his brother off on a naval voyage.

A new problem arose in 1859, when deputies from the provinces arrived in the capital to present local proposals. These men began to question the whole government program and even talked of setting themselves up as some sort of national assembly. "No Notables. I want no 1789," Alexander exclaimed to the Prussian ambassador, Otto von Bismarck, referring to the beginning of the French Revolution. The deputies were reprimanded.

Yet the tsar persisted in drawing up final proposals for emancipation, the work now being done in a smaller Editing Commission. The obstructionists led by Prince Paskevich told Alexander that the government might have to use force. "Yes, if the nobility continue to be obstinate" was the reply.

One of the tsar's chief supporters was venerable Prince Jacob Rostovtsev, who had come around from coolness to enthusiasm for reform. In early 1860 Rostovtsev died from overwork and strain, actually collapsing in Alexander's arms. His last words were "Sire, don't be intimidated." Liberals were even more disheartened when Rostovtsev's successor was named— Count Victor Panin, owner of estates with 21,000 serfs yielding him an income of 136,000 rubles a year. Alexander quickly checked the dismay: "You do not know Panin; his only conviction is the exact fulfillment of my orders."

Panin did secure some concessions for the conservatives, but the Editing Commission met its deadline to approve an emancipation draft in October. A similar interplay of pressure and concession got the draft through the Main Committee. Forthwith Alexander set February 27, 1861, as the deadline for the Council of State, showing the virtues of autocracy in these ringing words: "This I desire, I demand, I command." Delay after four years would be playing with the popular passions, and the tsar wanted to anticipate the planting season. The Council of State ended by voting against many items in the draft, but in each case Alexander decided in favor of the positions of the Editing Commission, on occasion upholding a minority of 8 votes to 35 opposed.

The emancipation was signed on March 3 (February 19, Old Style) on the sixth anniversary of Alexander's accession. (An interesting coincidence of dates is that Lincoln's first inauguration occurred the next day.) All over Russia from pulpits and from porches of manor houses the ex-serfs heard the new dispensation. The young writer Tolstoy happily informed his peasants of their rights and later at a party drank a toast to Alexander, saying no other toasts were necessary "for in reality we owe the Emancipation to the Emperor alone." In actuality, the reform had been accomplished not by a liberal tsar and liberal assistants, but by unidealistic men motivated by fear of revolution, awareness of economic needs, and pride of nation based on a dim consciousness of what the world expected of a civilized country.

The series of agrarian laws after 1861 dealt in intricate detail with various categories of peasants, according to political expediency. Polish serfs were rewarded for being more loyal than Polish gentry; Caucasian peasants were penalized for rebelliousness. Imperial family serfs received better treatment than the 25,000,000 state peasants, who in turn fared better than the 21,000,000 privately owned serfs. A million and a half household serfs were simply declared free without any property, whereas the main class of private serfs received personal liberty, plus land. Actually, the conservative nobility had seen to it that the private serfs received substantially less land than they had been using for feeding themselves under the old system; moreover, to redeem this land and their lost labor services, they were obliged to make sizable money payments to the nobility via the government over a period of forty-nine years. All the peasants remained less than first-class citizens, having special courts and special liability to corporal punishment. Yet the chief significance of the emancipation was in the realm of human rights: ended for the peasants was "the unlimited interference in their life which the landowners had exercised, even to the extent of arranging marriages for them."

The emancipation pleased neither landowners nor serfs, without driving either class to organized resistance. The passing of the old order was wistfully regretted by many of the nobility and strongly resented insofar as it meant that they had to become business-minded farmers of their remaining holdings. In the pithy observation of one: "Formerly we kept no accounts and drank champagne; now we keep accounts and content ourselves with kvass." The peasants were generally disappointed and sometimes defiant, convinced that the landowners were giving them a "forged freedom" instead of the "real freedom" the tsar intended. In one locality the audience of ex-serfs actually burst out laughing when told of the forty-nine-year burdens placed on them. Amid growing unrest, the tsar was driven to lecture a peasant delegation in the following words: "There will be no emancipation except the one I have given you. . . . Work and toil! Obey the authorities and the noble landowners!" After a lull of several years, there were about 500 major rural disturbances in the months of 1861 after the manifesto.

Progressive circles were alarmed when the tsar let the aging Lanskoy resign and then appointed an extreme conservative, Peter Valuiev, in his place as minister of interior. Valuiev did indeed pledge himself to execute the emancipation provisions in a conciliatory way, meaning for the benefit of the nobility, but he could go only so far.

The tsar contrarily saw fit to appoint progressives to the other key ministries—War, Education, Finance, and Justice. Reform did not stop. It could not stop. Once serfdom was out, many other Russian institutions had to be drastically overhauled. As Foreign Minister Gorchakov assured the courts of Europe, "Our motto is neither weakness nor reaction."

Some sort of local self-government was inevitable in view of the end of the landowners' arbitrary powers over their former human chattels, to say nothing of the humanitarian standards of the day in the way of health, education, and welfare. One of the greatest of the Alexandrine reforms was the institution of the Zemstvos in early 1864. The Zemstvos were elected bodies at both the district and provincial levels with competence in areas hitherto neglected by the governors and lesser officials. The tsar eventually agreed to the conservative position that the local marshals of nobility should control the Zemstvo chairmanships and that the richest landowners have a predominance on the Zemstvo boards. The bureaucracy also dissuaded Alexander from granting the Zemstvos genuine taxing powers. The tsar rejected efforts to exclude areas like education and sanitation from Zemstvo concern, however. The Zemstvos were to prove needful in what had been a vacuum; the measure of their success is contained in the statistics of thousands of new schools, hospitals, and agricultural aids.

Penal reforms came in 1863 with the abolition of the more barbarous forms of punishment for both civilian and military offenders, the conservative spokesman Panin and the metropolitan holding out in vain in favor of floggings and brandings. General judicial reforms of the most radical nature were decreed the next year. These had really been Alexander's first promise in 1856, and his instruction to the drafting commission to apply "science and the experience of Europe" was a symbolic break with the know-nothing pride of the previous reign. "At the thought of the old courts . . . my blood goes chill," a leading Russian writer once said. The new dispensation of Tsar Alexander was for "fast, just, and merciful" courts. Higher judges were given security from arbitrary dismissal. Local justices of the peace were to be elected through the Zemstvos. A great innovation for Russia was the institution of trial by jury. In the words of a historian, these were "the most radical and in principle the most consistent of the great reforms of the Sixties."

The new laws on education were less innovations than returns to precedents of happier days. The minister of education, Alexander Golovnin, was authorized to promote schools, public and private, without undue restrictions on their curricula and with all classes of society given equal entry. The tsar rejected the pleas of churchmen to give them a predominant voice in teaching. A University Statute of 1863 provided for their autonomy under elected rectors, elected councils of professors, and elected disciplinary tribunals. The approval of central authorities was limited to a few administrative matters. The result was two decades of unparalleled growth for Russia's highest schools.

The Temporary Press Rules approved by the tsar in 1865 established norms of censorship for the next forty years. The system as a whole, however, remained complicated and exasperating, a redress, not a full release for the press, for although Alexander opposed "oppression" of editors, he was also against "evil tendencies."

Military reforms under the brilliant minister of war, Dmitri Miliutin, responded to technical needs and to humanitarianism. The military courts were modernized. The Crimean War had taught the tsar and his advisers many lessons regarding such needs as a general staff, an effective commissariat, and medical services. Not until 1874, however, did the regime dare put into operation the long-suggested plan for universal military service. The effectiveness of the Prussian army in the Franco-Prussian War finally outweighed in Alexander's mind the plea of the rich for class exemptions and privileges. All Russians by lot became eligible for six years' service and reserve status for eight years more. The old standing army of 1,000,000 men was given up. Of all of Alexander's reforms, the military ones were the most potentially revolutionary: Universal service meant giving millions of recruits some education and, with it usually, some political consciousness.

The reforms of the 1860's, the most far-reaching since Peter the Great, created an ineradicable dividing line in Russian history. Reaction, when it came, could only hamper and distort progress, not turn things back. Wise enough to see what changes were unavoidable and strong enough to push them through, Alexander II deserved great personal credit for the reforms, the more so because he was by nature disinclined to innovation. The tsar's later critics, however, were to say that his vision was insufficiently lofty and that his firmness was all too erratic. Because the tsar had no real plan, the old and the new were compelled to exist uncomfortably side by side in Russia, just as liberal and reactionary ministers in office at the same time worked at cross-purposes under Alexander. Both conservatives and radicals were unhappy with the new regime, and Alexander rarely enjoyed much personal popularity. Yet to have enemies on both the right and the left was perhaps Alexander's greatest virtue—and one unique in modern Romanovs.

3. Despot in Spite of Himself

The relaxation of controls on education and publication, begun even before the emancipation, produced a fantastic outburst of creativeness in Russian arts and letters in the 1860's and 1870's and at the same time furthered a new revolutionary movement in politics that was to develop relentlessly down to 1917. Alexander II scarcely appreciated the first phenomenon and found himself barely able to cope with the second.

The first ten years of the reign saw the annual number of book titles double, while the number of newspapers went from six to sixty-six. These statistics, which give an indication of the size and influence of the intelligentsia, say nothing of the quality of the cultural renaissance, which, put simply, was the highest attained in Russia before or after. In many fields Russia led the world.

Leo Tolstoy, of a substantial aristocratic family living near Moscow, became the greatest of Russian novelists, by fairly general agreement. A veteran of the Crimean War, he first attracted attention with his Sevastopol sketches, but his great fame lay with his epic, realistic, philosophical account of 1812, *War and Peace,* published serially after 1866, and with his thoroughly contemporary novel *Anna Karenina* (1877). Tolstoy's liberal politics gave little trouble to the authorities, until his conversion around 1881 to a kind of Christian Socialism which was based on nothing less than a sweeping condemnation of the whole social system.

Slightly greater or lesser than Tolstoy, according to a person's taste, was the novelist Fedor Dostoievsky, whose background as the son of a minor army doctor qualified him eminently as a symbol of the new, non-aristocratic intelligentsia. Dostoievsky's youthful radicalism found expression in his early novel entitled *Poor Folk* and in his association with the Petrashevsky circle of 1849, which nearly brought about his execution and did result in Siberian exile. Returned to Petersburg under Alexander's amnesty and deeply changed, Dostoievsky was to write of his experiences as political prisoner in *The House of the Damned* (1861) and again dissected revolutionary types in *The Possessed* (1871). His tremendous reputation was made by the works *Crime and Punishment* (1866) and *The Brothers Karamazov* (1880), both of which were acceptably conservative in outlook except for the author's disturbingly religious soul-searching, his unprecedented psychological probing, and his depiction of the down-and-out. Before his death in 1881 Dostoievsky was reported to have told a friend that in the sequel to *The Brothers Karamazov* he could see no other conclusion than to have Alyosha assassinate the tsar.

Another Russian novelist of first rank was Ivan Turgenev, born into the lesser gentry and destined to be more Western-minded and more politically topical than Dostoievsky or Tolstoy. Turgenev also suffered exile under Nicholas I, but his *A Sportsman's Sketches* of 1852 was credited by Nicholas' successor with opening his eyes to peasant misery. The author's *Fathers and Sons*, published in 1862, treated the conflict of the old and new generations at the time of the emancipation and popularized the word "nihilist" as a designation for a younger generation who wanted to destroy all authorities except science. Himself a moderate, Turgenev did much to stimulate political ferment.

Tolstoy, Dostoievsky, and Turgenev were only the most celebrated names in a huge outpouring of literary talent, the lesser names being household words in Russia ever since. For example, Ivan Goncharov was the literary sensation of 1858 with his novel *Oblomov*, a story of an aristocrat full of social conscience but too disorganized to get out of bed. Michael Saltykov-Shchedrin's *The Golovyev Family* (1881) anticipated Chekhov's chronicles of family decay. Alexander Ostrovsky made himself the classic Russian dramatist, producing a whole repertoire of plays which are still performed, dealing often with sensitive social issues.

Somewhat apart from the literary intelligentsia were the radical intelligentsia of the 1860's, writers directly concerned with political problems and reform. Herzen's illegal *The Bell,* published abroad, stimulated Socialist-minded critics like Nicholas Chernishevsky and Dmitri Pisarev, both of whom faced police persecution. Chernishevsky's novelistic *What Is to Be Done?* (1863) was written in prison and became a handbook for revolutionaries. Pisarev fully accepted the leadership of the nihilist movement, expounding his views in *The Destruction of Aesthetics* (1865). "Smash right and left," he wrote, "no harm may come of this."

The most famous Russian painter, Ilya Repin, made his reputation as leader of a group of artists called the Wanderers, who in 1862 noisily broke with the stuffy and stylized studio work expected by the St. Petersburg Academy. A populist in art at the same time young political radicals were going out among the people, Repin is best known, perhaps, for his huge canvas called "Haulers of the Volga" (1870–73) depicting all the misery of this class of boatmen and at the same time suggesting deliverance in the uplifted face of the youngest of them.

The Russian school in music also dates from the era of Alexander II. Like the Wanderer artists, "the mighty handful" of St. Petersburg composers represented a revolt against the academic establishment. They were oddly amateurs in music at first, men like the chemist Alexander Borodin and the naval officer Nicholas Rimsky-Korsakov. Most influential musicologically was Modest Moussorgsky. The first performance of his opera *Boris Godunov* in February, 1874, was a sensation with great political implications. Moussorgsky considered himself a populist and declared himself more interested in the common people than the tsars. His genius added the famous revolutionary scene to Pushkin's *Boris*. Later his friend Rimsky-Korsakov was to rewrite the opera in such a way as to overemphasize the tsar, sweetening the music as well.

Although Alexander II could choose to go hunting rather than attend concerts or literary discussions, he could not ignore the revolutionary actions of part of the intelligentsia, especially insofar as they were establishing contact with the masses. Within a year of the emancipation the government faced major riots in the universities, the students demonstrating in sympathy with the peasants of Bezdna whose open protest against the emancipation terms cost them 50 dead and 300 wounded. Some universities were closed and the students sent home, provoking Herzen to make his famous exhortation "To the people" (in Russian, *V Narod,* and hence the basis for the later Narodnik movement).

By coincidence, in the same year, 1862, events occurred that were to prefigure the three main currents of the Russian opposition movement over the next fifty years. Someone translated Karl Marx's *Communist Manifesto* into Russian for the first time, an omen of the worker-oriented movement which developed much later in Russia and begat, of course, the Social Democrats and Lenin's Bolsheviks. A pamphlet called *Young Russia* was circulated in St. Petersburg. Its call for expropriation of all the land and bloody violence against the tsar and ruling classes became in time the main concerns of the peasant-oriented movement that culminated in the Socialist Revolutionary Party. Finally, the liberal or constitutionalist tradition of protest, which went back to the Decembrists, found a new expression in the Tver Address of February, 1862, whereby thirteen nobles of that province publicly petitioned the tsar to the effect that "the summons of men elected by all Russia is the only means for a satisfactory solution of the problems aroused, but not solved by the act of February 19."

If worker or peasant Socialisms were probably beyond Alexander's comprehension, he readily recognized the implications of the Tver Address. Its signers were made an example for all persons thinking of limiting the autocracy: They were imprisoned in Peter and Paul Fortress, put on trial, placed in a lunatic asylum for a while, and then released with temporary loss of civil rights. The previous year Alexander had occasion to expound his views on constitutions to Ambassador Bismarck, saying that the Russian people's respect for "their paternal and God-appointed ruler" would diminish if he shared his power. Later, in a friendly conversation with an avowed constitutionalist, he declared that "he would be ready to sign a constitution on the spot this day" if he did not think that Russia would "fall to pieces tomorrow." The liberals were thus effectively squelched for another decade, making it that much more appealing for a man of conscience to join the truly revolutionary groups.

A sudden turn of events in a new quarter aggravated the political situation. Poland rose up in the greatest revolt since 1830–31. In the first years of Alexander's reign a succession of Russian governors in Warsaw alternated conciliation and repression in vain. Even the radical Grand Duke Constantine was nearly assassinated there. Then an attempt to round up Polish revolutionists by putting them in the army precipitated a prearranged insurrection in fifteen garrison towns in early 1863. It took 80,000 regulars more than a year to destroy about 10,000 Polish guerrillas. "How unlucky I am," exclaimed the tsar, "I am forced to spill blood without glory."

Ever after resenting Polish ingratitude, the tsar returned to the policy of rigorious Russification, even eliminating the name Poland in favor of the Ten Provinces of the Vistula. One by-product of the Polish Revolt was a tremendous upsurge of Russian patriotism. Herzen's pro-Polish *The Bell* and other radical journals were discredited, and the new intellectual touchstone became Michael Katkov's Moscow *Gazette,* which was ultranationalist and conservative.

Finland in these same years was able to win greater autonomy within the Russian Empire, suggesting that it was Polish intransigence, not unreasonableness on Alexander's part, that was at the root of Poland's new misery. Even while the fighting proceeded around Warsaw, the tsar courageously permitted the meeting of the Finnish Diet, the first such in many years. In the opening ceremony the tsar went so far as to declare: "In the hands of a discreet people . . . liberal institutions so far from being a danger become a guarantee of order and prosperity." His confidence was rewarded, the Finns in turn honoring to this day Alexander's statue in Helsinki's Parliament Square.

The first attempt to assassinate Alexander II occurred in April, 1866, as he was getting into his carriage after taking his daily stroll in St. Petersburg's lovely Summer Garden. A bystander deflected the assassin's revolver; for this act the man, an illiterate living in one room with his family of eight, was made a noble and was invited to the tables of high society. The assassin, named Dmitri Karakozov, had recently been expelled from the University of Kazan and was the agent of a conspiratorial group, as well as a firm believer that the peasants had been cheated by the emancipation. He was hanged, but currently in Leningrad it is Karakozov, not the tsar, who is memorialized with a bronze plaque on the iron fence near where the attack took place. The following year a Pole tried to gun Alexander down in Paris when he was riding with Napoleon III.

The response of the government was severe repression of Russian students. Some historians even see the year 1866 as a general dividing line between the liberal and reactionary phases of Alexander's reign, although others detect both tendencies all along. The new minister of education, Dmitri A. Tolstoy, a very distant relative of the novelist, became the symbol of the increasingly restrictive policies of the regime; he was one of the few outspoken opponents of all the reforms of the sixties. Denouncing the senseless pretensions of the students, Tolstoy decided that their restlessness and nihilism were caused by natural science courses, and forthwith all science was eliminated from the curricula of the lower schools and a disproportionate emphasis put on the classical languages as good for discipline. The minister himself felt obliged to learn Greek secretly, while observers chuckled about the tsar's complete ignorance of the ancients.

The chief of the Third Section resigned in tears after the assassination attempt on the tsar, and in the ensuing police shake-up rather extraordinary political intrigues took place. Peter Shuvalov, appointed the new chief, was as unscrupulous as he was able. General Fedor Trepov was Shuvalov's candidate for chief of the St. Petersburg police, but Trepov refused to be subordinate to the liberal governor general of the city, Suvorov. When Alexander demanded that Trepov take the post anyhow, the man sullenly replied: "At your Majesty's command . . . but I must warn your Majesty that I cannot accept the responsibility for the safety of St. Petersburg." Observers recalled that Nicholas I would have arrested a man for such insolence. The increasing acts of insubordination within the regime revealed that Alexander was an autocrat who often would not play the role.

Many observers detected a physical and psychological transformation in Alexander beginning after the Karakozov attempt. For example, a French visitor reported: "Russians agree that a great and regrettable change has taken hold of His Majesty, whose humor is less even and often turns to melancholy. His features are drawn and emaciated, and his expression is severe and preoccupied." The tsar was becoming resigned, resigned to the new regime where more stress was put on police activities than on reform.

St. Petersburg society was shocked to hear a high police officer's indiscreet remarks to the effect that the Third Section spied on the imperial family, including the tsar. In fact, it was boasted that "the Emperor is the most closely watched person in Russia." The safety of Alexander was indeed a special police concern; one major reason was a new romantic passion.

After Alexander's wife had borne him seven children, he became tired of her, to the point of estrangement. Like so many German princesses who came to Russia, Maria Alexandrovna became too fanatically religious, and her political views became decidedly unliberal. The empress was now described as "vaporous," living in the dreamworld of a medieval princess.

The fresh, sensuous young girl who became the emperor's second mistress, Catherine Dolgoruky, was a distant relation of the first, Alexandra Dolgoruky, who had left him abruptly. Gossips with an eye to genealogy were quick to note that Romanov involvements with Dolgoruky ladies always had tragic denouements, cases in point being Tsar Michael's poisoned bride and Peter II's deathbed partner. Alexander II, however, was simply too much in love to listen, having first noticed Catherine when she was a ten-year-old ward of the court and having arranged for her to be sent to the Smolny Institute until she was seventeen. The official beginning of what was to be her only affair took place in July, 1866. The police were not only witnesses but assistants to her coming several times a week to a secluded apartment in the Winter Palace, which she entered after unlocking a low door giving onto a garden. Soon Alexander was so infatuated that he declared Catherine his "wife before God." Alexander's general new mood was revealed in a love letter in which he said: "Don't forget that all of my life is in you, Angel of my soul, and the sole aim of this life is to see you happy as much as one can be happy in this world." Among other souvenirs of this royal romance are drawings the tsar did of Catherine in the nude.

The times were literally the height of the Victorian era: Rulers did not dispose of their wives; they even had scruples about openly displaying their mistresses. Catherine's family was anything but honored when news of the affair reached society. The girl was whisked off to Naples, but she and Alexander contrived—through the Third Section—to write each other daily. Sure of herself, Catherine returned to St. Petersburg and was installed in a sumptuous mansion on the north side of the river.

Having to maintain what was a second home for him in secret taxed the emperor and made him increasingly a victim of his own police. The tsar did rouse himself to fire Shuvalov, after the all-powerful police chief made some indiscretions about Catherine. A son was born to the couple in 1872, followed by two daughters, and they were secretly authorized to use the imperial title and the patronymic.

As the 1860's passed into the 1870's, Alexander's government continued to serve up a combination of reform and repression that pleased no one. For example, a Municipal Statute of 1870 gave the cities new institutions of self-government albeit with the same restrictions and class weighing of votes that hampered the Zemstvos. A measure of the need for this release of local energies was the fact that St. Petersburg's schools expanded almost sixfold in one decade.

Severe famine in Smolensk Province in the late 1860's produced peasant disorders and demonstrations of sympathy from students. The police were also kept busy on a new front after St. Petersburg's first industrial strike in 1870. The government's repressive actions occasionally backfired, as when they ordered home all the Russian students in Switzerland, many of whom were under the influence of revolutionary *émigrés* such as the anarchist Michael Bakunin and the radical Socialist Peter Lavrov. Hundreds of students did return to join the ranks of those already yearning for action. In the summer of 1874 action came in the form of the historically unique Narodnik movement, the spontaneous, planless going to the countryside of thousands of the young intelligentsia, to learn, to work, and to propagandize among the peasants. The locals turned in to the authorities many of the strange-looking, strange-talking city people. After the eventual arrests of about 1,000, the police treated Russia to the spectacle of mass political trials, such as those of the 1930's, although the crimes of the defendants were never clearly defined. Russia's new courts treated the Narodniks so lightly that Alexander became infuriated and on his own ordered hardship penalties.

The severe treatment of the peaceful Narodniks drove others of the intelligentsia to secret organization and a definition of revolutionary goals. The first important nationwide conspiratorial group, calling itself Land and Freedom, eventually was bold enough to stage, in December, 1876, a demonstration in front of St. Petersburg's Kazan Cathedral, just a few miles from the mansion where Alexander II was enjoying the company of his mistress and second family. The police laid out a garden in front of the cathedral to prevent such riotous gatherings in the future, but gardens, no more than jails, could stop the tide of protest.

The following year, war with Turkey was added to Alexander's troubles. The war, forced on him by Pan-Slavism, began the final act of his often frustrated, increasingly tragic reign.

4. Helpless Expansionist

The outcome of the Crimean War had revealed Russia's weakness and subsequently the Black Sea clauses, the disarmament required by the peace treaty, made it strategically impossible for Russia to pursue any longer a forward policy in southern and western Europe. The country's diplomats and soldiers looked to other areas for action, and Alexander II found himself as often the victim as much the leader of heedless, needless, and sometimes dangerous expansionist drives in the Far East and in central Asia. Eventually, Russia turned back on Europe and undertook a war in the Balkans to the detriment of most concerned and of the tsar in particular.

Realizing Russia's need for peace after 1856, Alexander stood almost idly by during the decade and a half which saw Italy and Germany each united as nations, the greatest changes in the map of Europe since the downfall of Napoleon. Austria's treachery during the Crimean War was an added reason for Russia's doing virtually nothing during the French-Sardinian War with Austria in 1859, and Alexander's belated thought to send a Russian fleet did not stop Garibaldi's advance through Sicily and Naples in 1860, which culminated in the proclamation of the kingdom of Italy in March, 1861, the month of Russia's emancipation. Whereas Nicholas I had twice vetoed German unification under Prussia, in 1848 and in 1851, Alexander II chose only to look on benevolently while Bismarck smashed together a German Empire by means of Prussian wars with Denmark (1864), Austria (1866), and France (1870–71).

Alexander essentially sought rapprochement with all the European powers in these years. He even wrote the ex-enemy Napoleon III about a "sincere entente," but he soon encountered difficulties. During the Polish Revolt of 1863 France led Britain and Austria in endeavoring to mediate and to secure an international conference on what Alexander considered his private problem. The humiliating notes and protests received from these powers in 1863 were only counterbalanced by demonstrations of support from Prussia and, surprisingly, from the United States. Prussia had its own Polish subjects to worry about, and Bismarck was, perhaps, farsighted enough to see that he needed Russian friendship in the fateful decade ahead for Germany. As for the United States, the threat of European intervention at this time also hung over the North at the height of the Civil War. The strange identity of diplomatic interests between American democracy and Russian autocracy received sensational expression in 1863 when Russian fleets anchored in San Francisco and New York. Tsar Alexander's naval move represented no real show of sympathy to President Lincoln but the practical desire to have Russia's warships, too few to resist a possible British-French attack, in a position to be commerce raiders.

The 1863 crisis produced merely a flurry of Russian attention to European affairs because its main energies were being directed to other fronts. Right after Alexander's accession, Russia embarked on its first great thrusts into the Far East. Relations were established with Japan in 1855, a Russian squadron overawing Nagaski just two years after Commodore Matthew Perry's pioneer visit. However, the greatest gains were achieved on the Chinese mainland of Asia. The Russian proconsul in eastern Siberia, Nicholas Muraviev, began to establish forts on the Amur River in the 1850's, largely on his own authority and in defiance of existing treaties with the Chinese Empire. The tsar later personally endorsed Muraviev's moves, and in 1857 all the lands north of the Amur were declared a Russian province. Three years later, when China was at its weakest in a war with the Western powers, a Russian diplomat secured the Treaty of Peking, whereby the tongue of land between the Amur and the Pacific was ceded. The future stronghold of Vladivostok ("Ruler of the East") was founded by Muraviev in July, 1860, at the southern tip of this new maritime province. It is ironic that today these territorial gains of Tsar Alexander II are an essential part of Communist China's grievances against Soviet Russia.

Late in the 1850's Russian armies completed the annexation of the Caucasus region. The Caucasian mountaineers fought doggedly for several years under their fabled leader Shamil until he was captured by Prince Alexander Bariatinsky in 1859. In an amusing personal sequel, Prince Bariatinsky received Alexander's permission to have Shamil retire with him to his estate so that the two old men could daily refight their campaigns over the dinner table.

Across the Caspian Sea from the Transcaucasus lay arid wastelands, but beyond them were the storied kingdoms of central Asia. Here Russian expansionism assumed irresponsible proportions often without St. Petersburg's authorization. The possibility of a confrontation with Britain was the great hazard. The most outrageously bold of the Russian moves was Colonel Michael Chernaiev's seizure of Tashkent in 1865, and then followed in the next years the relentless subjugation by force or by guile of the cities of Kokand, Bokhara, Samarkand, and Khiva, some of the feudal Moslem rulers of these areas saving their thrones by becoming tributaries of the Orthodox tsar.

Commercial interests with government connections were a factor in the conquest of these huge new areas, which in time provided markets and raw materials, as well as new ethnic-religious problems. The main movers, however, were ambitious and underemployed soldiers like Chernaiev. Even the British ambassador saw Alexander's dilemma:

> The Tsar is very powerless in this question. Fresh conquests of territory are laid at his feet, gained by the prowess and blood of his troops. He cannot refuse them without offending his army; and troops so far distant as Central Asia is from the control of the central power, are difficult to restrain. . . .

As another observer noted, it was a matter where a successful territorial raid could make a lieutenant a general almost overnight. Time after time Alexander's government was forced to accept local *faits accomplis* by promotion-minded officers.

Alexander II revealed all his weak and hesitant tendencies in this area of foreign policy. None of the overzealous military men were removed or reprimanded. The ardently expansionist Grand Duke Michael was made governor general of the Transcaspian region in the 1870's, and he, for example, soon learned to pay little heed to imperial orders, which were usually ambiguous anyhow.

The Franco-Prussian War diverted all Europe in 1870 and 1871 and gave Alexander a chance unilaterally to denounce the Black Sea clauses and to rearm his military and naval forces in that area. A few years later Alexander helped bring about the Three Emperors' League, whereby Russia, Prussia, and Austria gave one another mutual guarantees, pledged to fight revolution together, and agreed to prior discussion of any Balkan problems. The tsar seemed to have gained Russia a strong, secure stance in the West, only to become victim of a new surge of expansionism in the name of Pan-Slavism.

Like his father, Alexander II originally set himself against the Pan-Slavists whom he regarded as troublemakers and Utopians. Once he pointedly declared to the Austrian ambassador: "I am a Russian before I am a Slav." The tsar was to find, however, that these convictions were not shared in influential circles and even in the imperial family. Moreover, general public opinion for the first time seemed to lead a Romanov tsar by the nose.

In 1875 Bosnia-Herzegovina rose in revolt against the Ottoman Empire, and the next year Bulgaria also took arms against Turkish misrule. Alexander's official pronouncements always had discouraged such local insurrection, but Russian agents on the spot, often Pan-Slavists, gave money and advice. In the summer of 1876 semi-independent Serbia declared war on Turkey in the name of aiding its fellow Slavs, but here again Alexander declared that Serbia could not expect Russian support. The tsar returned from giving diplomatic reassurances in Vienna and Berlin to find Pan-Slavist hysteria in Russia virtually out of control. No less a military hero than General Chernaiev had gone off to put himself at the head of Serbia's forces. The tsar was angry that this was done without his permission, but he did not dare disavow Chernaiev. Soon recruiting offices were openly operating in St. Petersburg, and eventually nearly 1,000 officers had resigned their commissions to go off to fight for the Serbs. These unheard-of activities of the officer corps, described, incidentally, in the last part of Tolstoy's *Anna Karenina,* found wide backing elsewhere. Their arms were blessed in special services by the Metropolitan of Moscow, and Katkov's newspapers thundered Pan-Slavist slogans. Even the empress played an unusual political role as protectress of the barely disguised war activities of Red Cross committees and Slavonic friendship societies. She is credited with dissuading Alexander from a general curb on such organizations, and local authorities showed no heart for stopping aristocratic ladies from soliciting for the cause in public places.

The crushing of the Serbians in September, 1876, disheartened the Pan-Slavists, and regular diplomacy reasserted itself. Later in the fall Alexander met at Livadiya in the Crimea with his closest advisers, with the empress, the tsarevich, and two grand dukes also present. Although far from public hysteria, this conference saw the tsar seduced by the war party. Forthwith, an ultimatum was sent off to Constantinople, partial mobilization was ordered, and the grand dukes Nicholas and Michael took up their posts as commanders of the Balkan and Caucasus fronts.

Even at this stage, Alexander was "tormentingly anxious to preserve peace," according to a British leader. Russia joined the international conference which tried to obtain reforms from the Ottoman Empire. The new sultan proved utterly intransigent, however, and in April, 1877, Alexander's manifesto announced Russia's declaration of war without consultation of other powers. Typically caught up in emotion, the tsar, nearly sixty, announced his wish to serve as a male nurse.

"A war of the one-eyed with the blind" was the German Helmuth von Moltke's appraisal of the Russo-Turkish War of 1877–78. The Grand Duke Nicholas was incompetent in both strategy and tactics, and Miliutin's reforms of supply and hospitals produced little better results than in Crimean times. The Russian army of 300,000 found itself bogged down in the siege of Plevno beginning in June. The campaign has been described as the breakfast war for during that summer newspaper readers got daily reports of the bloody fighting in the trenches. "Would to God this odious war were over," Alexander wrote from the Danube area to the mistress he hated to be parted from. The tsar was there just as an observer. Plevna did not surrender until December, preventing the quick Russian triumph against Turkey which was expected and which would have raised the personal fame of Alexander II toward the levels of Peter the Great and Catherine the Great.

The Ottoman Empire appealed to the great powers in January, 1878. By February the British fleet was at Constantinople, and once again London was gripped with patriotic fervor against the expansionism of the Russian bear. The term "jingo" dates from the genuine war scare of this time when a music hall ditty ran: "We don't want to fight/But, by jingo if we do/We've got the arms, we've got the men/We've got the money too." It merely raised Russia's taste for what could have been when the supine Ottoman government signed the Treaty of San Stefano in March, surrendering much of its Balkan territory in the huge Bulgarian state that was to be under Russian protection. The British moved troops, and Austria called for an international conference. A new treaty was signed at the Congress of Berlin in July, 1878. Russia, its winnings severely pared, had to accept gains for Britain and Austria, who had never fought. Only a tiny Bulgarian state emerged in the settlement. (That country had the sense of fitness to erect a statue to Alexander II, which the present Communist regime has kept—but not the later one to Stalin.)

The public was severely disappointed in the tsar. He was criticized for neither controlling nor profiting by the patriotic upsurge. In a speech denouncing the peace terms, a leading Pan-Slavist went so far as to accuse the tsar of being surrounded by "flattery and falsehood"; he was banished.

More perceptive critics, however, wondered why such an oversized and underdeveloped empire, so backward and so in need of internal reorganization, bothered at all with the Balkans or bothered with the far reaches of Asia for that matter.

5. Martyr

Political disturbances continued unabated during the war and intensified during the postwar letdown. The police kept arresting Narodnik propagandists in the countryside. The first union of industrial workers appeared, only to be suppressed. Zemstvo liberals revived their agitation for greater self-government, such as that Alexander had just given the Bulgarians, but they encountered only persecution and once again realized that they were obliged to be just as conspiratorial as the extremists. The most important development of these years, however, was an unprecedented wave of assassinations.

In February, 1876, a young girl, Vera Zasulich, shot at and gravely wounded General Trepov, the St. Petersburg police chief. Her immediate grievance was the brutal flogging Trepov had ordered for a political prisoner. She did deny her crime during one of the first major trials under the new jury system. The jury promptly found her not guilty, and the cheering spectators subsequently prevented the police from rearresting her. Alexander's angry government promptly reinstated military courts for political cases.

The military courts were useless if the police could not catch the terrorists. A sword-wielding assassin killed the chief of the Third Section, General Nicholas Mezentsev, in August, 1876, on one of the main streets of the capital. The governor of Kharkov was assassinated in February, 1878, in reprisal for his harsh repression of student demonstrations, and the next month the new head of the Third Section was fired on. In each case the assassin got away. Public apathy was plain in these outcomes, and police incompetence was also obvious. Alexander found that his police could produce only one revolutionist when he asked for a roundup of the terrorist ringleaders in 1878. In April of that year a youth fired three shots at the tsar himself outside the Winter Palace. This time, for once, the assassin was captured and executed.

Land and Freedom, the most effective organization of revolutionists since 1876, split into two factions during a secret congress held in southern Russia in the summer of 1879. One group, the Black Partition, urged peaceful propaganda and social revolution as the means and goal. (Its chief spokesman, George Plekhanov, was to evolve from this position to Marxism.) The more important faction declared assassination and political revolution to be necessary before social revolution was possible, and to these ends they constituted themselves that summer as the People's Will. This Jacobin-like organization was sophisticated enough in its conspiratorial techniques to plant a man in the Third Section and to circulate thousands of copies of a revolutionary journal.

Alexander Romanov was formally condemned to death by the Central Executive Committee of the People's Will in September, 1879, and a regular manhunt was instituted. Two of the chief terrorist organizers were Andrew Zheliabov, a worker, and Sophia Perovskaya, the aristocratic daughter of a governor: the two were in love with each other, as well as with the cause. That fall they made three attempts on Alexander's life in the course of his return from the Crimea to St. Petersburg. At Odessa the revolutionists arrived after the tsar's train had left. At Alexandrovsk the mines laid under the railroad tracks failed to explode. At Moscow the imperial train was blown sky high, but it turned out to be the advance baggage section, and Alexander reached his capital safely on a second train.

By early 1880 the terrorists had pinned their hopes on a man insinuated into the Winter Palace itself. Stephen Khalturin might have remained a peaceful trade-union organizer but for the frustration of his efforts by the police, which caused him to join the People's Will. Khalturin's skill got him a job as an icon refurbisher in the palace, where his workroom was located two floors directly under the imperial dining room. On his days off he smuggled small quantities of dynamite into his quarters, keeping them under his pillow and getting headaches for his trouble. The palace guards eventually discovered some notes compromising Khalturin, but these and other warnings were ignored, in part because a chief guard was so admiring of Khalturin that he wanted him as a son-in-law. The grand explosion took place as planned one evening in February, but because the Prince of Bulgaria was a half hour late as guest of honor, Alexander had put off dinner. All the royal party were knocked flat just as they were coming downstairs, but the only fatal casualties were forty Finnish guards killed on the floor between the dining room and workroom. Khalturin escaped. Even this outrage produced little public concern. One of the tsar's chief ministers heard the explosion as he drove past the palace, but he continued on to dinner anyhow. The party at the French ambassador's was scarcely disturbed by the news. The German ambassador, who left the gaiety in disgust, arrived at the Winter Palace and found Alexander calmly playing whist. "God has saved me again," he said. His solicitous visitor later wrote: "One was tempted to regard as moribund a social body which fails to react to such a shock."

At the age of sixty Alexander was a spent man. He had returned from the prolonged peace negotiations near the point of a nervous breakdown. His unpopularity seemed to him undeserved. He was reminded daily of the bad state of affairs by the newly instituted Cossack escorts and the ever-present plainclothesmen. Only one thing sustained Alexander now—his second family—and he went through the motions of being an autocrat only in the expectation of happy evenings with Catherine Dolgoruky and their three children.

Actually, the tsar's relationship with Catherine had become still another factor in his unpopularity. Most of the imperial family affected to be appalled. Some grand dukes, however, took the tsar's behavior as carte blanche to carry on scandalously themselves. What could the head of the Romanovs say to them? High society chose to be hostile. The public at large knew of the secret, and murmurs were widespread about Alexander's ill-treatment of his dying wife, the empress' charitable and Pan-Slavist activities being appropriately exaggerated. The coincidence of the Dolgoruky affair and the terrorist movement was seen as some sort of divine retribution.

The leader of the opposition to Catherine was none other than the Tsarevich Alexander, whose bitter behind-the-back criticisms of his father generally did little to bolster the prestige of the dynasty. When Catherine and family were installed in an apartment in the Winter Palace over the empress'—for police reasons—the tsarevich's outbursts knew no bounds. There was talk of a palace revolution to place Alexander III on the throne, but there was also talk of the tsarevich's being passed over in favor of his half brother. The tsarevich had to content himself with snubs. Asked to give a party at Peterhof for some visiting German princes and to invite Catherine, the junior Alexander complied with due formality, but the festivities were pointedly halted as soon as the tsar and his mistress had left.

The kind of scene that could take place in the imperial family at this juncture was described by a young cousin of the tsar who came up to St. Petersburg from the Caucasus with his father, the Grand Duke Michael, on the occasion of family rejoicing after the failure of the Winter Palace assassination attempt. The tsar now had his Catherine sitting next to him at dinner. Her youthful chic and Alexander's obvious rejuvenation in his attentions to her excited the grand dukes with admiration and sympathy, but the assembled grand duchesses, the wives and mothers, were not just disapproving but icy. The women rejected all of Catherine's efforts to begin conversations, and they shuddered the best Victorian shudders when she, forgetful in her nervousness, addressed the tsar with the familiar Sasha. The hitherto unseen children were trotted out for the occasion, too. "Gogo," Alexander said bemusedly to ten-year-old George, "would you care to be a Grand Duke?" The child's unconcerned reply was lost in the sound of the tsarevich's choking.

The empress died in the summer of 1880, and Alexander waited only the minimum forty days required by church law to marry his Catherine. "It is the happiest day of my life," he wrote. The marriage was morganatic, meaning that Gogo and the others had no rights of succession, but they were legitimized. Alexander's barely precedented step was now seen as a huge blow to dynastic discipline and solidarity. It was the first time a Romanov ruler had married a Russian since Peter the Great. The tsar gave his second wife the title Princess Yurievskaya, which was high-sounding to her detractors because it reminded them that she was a Rurikovich, in a sense more royal than the Romanovs themselves. A direct descendant of St. Vladimir, Catherine was reportedly determined to be crowned empress, a possibility that led to violent scenes between tsar and tsarevich, who had been informed of the marriage only several weeks later.

Catherine Dolgoruky, now Princess Yurievskaya, was undoubtedly a political influence on Alexander, something unknown in royal mistresses of recent memory and particularly resented in troubled times. That some of her intimates were successful business entrepreneurs or shady speculators with inside connections was put to her discredit in idle aristocratic circles, as well as among the hardworking. Her conniving was generally overestimated by her enemies. Actually, as one astute observer realized, Catherine would probably have happily abandoned all titles and even seen Russia declared a republic if she could have had her Sasha entirely to herself. Her second-best choice was to influence the tsar toward liberalism, in the hope of somehow conciliating the terrorists who seemingly were always lurking out there beyond the palace fences.

The vague urgings of his wife and her entourage were seconded from other quarters, notably the Grand Duke Constantine and the ex-Minister of Interior Valuiev, who reminded Alexander of the constitutional hopes of the 1860's. This line of thinking was hotly opposed by the tsarevich, who demanded instead that a dictator, like Shuvalov, be put over all government departments. Alexander recoiled from delegating any of his authority either to an advisory assembly or to a strong man. Then, in a fit of inspiration, he combined both proposals and instituted a dictatorship of the heart in the person of an Armenian nobleman named Michael Loris-Melikov, a war hero and a man who had shown himself both firm and flexible in his dealings with revolutionists while governor of Kharkov. A devoted friend to Catherine and the tsar, Loris, as it were, set about creating a regime that would prolong their newfound happiness.

Loris demanded and received almost absolute powers in February, 1880, including choice of his colleagues and the centralization of all police activities under a man named Vyacheslav Plehve. D. A. Tolstoy was replaced as minister of education by a liberal. One of Catherine's circle became Minister of Finance. Conservatives were also included in the Council of Ministers, and the tsarevich's ex-tutor, the ultrareactionary Constantine Pobedenostsev, became procurator of the Holy Synod. The main aim of Loris, however, was to reverse the repressive tendency increasingly apparent since the assassination attempt by Karakozov in 1866. The censorship was greatly relaxed. Political prisoners were granted amnesty in the wholesale fashion characteristic of the beginning of the reign. The Zemstvo and judicial institutions were told to function in the full freedom of their original conception. After ten weeks the absence of political disturbances persuaded Loris that his policies had succeeded, and he relinquished extraordinary civil and military powers in favor of functioning simply as minister of the interior.

Loris held an unprecedented press conference in the fall of 1880, and his popularity was such that he obtained the editor's pledge not to discuss openly constitutional reform. Indeed, the word "constitution" was once again in the air and for good reason. Select people were quietly being asked to discuss and advise regarding Senate investigations of provincial abuses and Zemstvo researches into the peasant question. Eventually, Loris came up with a concrete project: Two commissions composed of officials, Zemstvo representatives, professors, and publicists were to prepare laws on administrative and financial matters; their drafts would be submitted to a general commission of members of both, plus elected experts from each Zemstvo and major city. The proposed institution of what would be a near approach to a constitutional monarchy was represented to Catherine as a palliative to the public before or coincident with the announcement of her coronation. When the tsar made clear that Loris' plan had become his dearest wish, even the tsarevich demurred in his opposition to concessions.

The progressive tone of the new administration, combined with astute police work, made the revolutionists desperate. A captured conspirator was tricked into revelations that soon reduced the membership at large of the People's Will to a handful. Zheliabov, Sophia Perovskaya, and others decided on a final assassination try, relying on expert knowledge of the tsar's customary movements in St. Petersburg and the once-rejected tactic of operating bogus businesses so as to be able to plant dynamite under the streets. One of these fronts, a cheese shop, was so uneconomically run by them, all the while they were digging, that customers became suspicious, as well as grateful.

Loris, himself a target for an assassin in February, 1881, realized that "there need only be another unfortunate shot and I am lost and with me my entire system." In March his police arrested Zheliabov, who was provoked to hint darkly, without confessing, that a major plot was afoot. The tsar was informed of this the next day, March 12. That night Alexander was heard to say as he led Princess Yurievskaya into dinner: "I am so happy at present that this happiness frightens me." The following morning, Sunday, Alexander, pleased with himself, signed Loris' constitutional project.

Sundays were parade days for the tsar and military society. Elsewhere in St. Petersburg the artistic avant-garde attended a gallery opening to view admiringly the Wanderer painter Basil Surikov's eerie historical canvas "The Morning of the Execution of the Streltsi." For several weeks previously Catherine had dissuaded the tsar from attending the military review, but the newly apparent serenity of Alexander and Loris convinced her that worry was unnecessary. The parade went off uneventfully, and Alexander then paid a call on his cousin, a grand duchess, to whom he confided his new political plan. On his return to the Winter Palace, the tsar chose to avoid the streets mined by the revolutionists—Catherine having had a premonition that they were dangerous. He now took an unannounced route via Catherine Street. His police had supposedly checked it out, but actually it now harbored no less than four bomb-carrying members of the People's Will, with Sophia Perovskaya at the corner to wave a white handkerchief if he was to pass that way.

The tsar was allowed to drive past the first assassin, in case he turned back. The second bomb thrower missed his target and blew up several of the Cossack escort. Against the advice of his driver, Alexander ordered his carriage stopped and got out to attend the wounded. Then, the third bomb thrower rushed up to explode the contraption that killed him and maimed the tsar fatally. His legs just about separated from his body, Alexander could only mutter to the Grand Duke Michael that he wished to die in the palace.

At the Winter Palace, Princess Yurievskaya, dressed in anticipation of a walk with her husband in the Summer Garden, was now confronted with a bloody, dying Alexander. She came in time to bemoan the fact that if only Alexander had lived, however shattered in body and of necessity abdicated, she would for the first time have had him all to herself. An equally touching expression of love occurred in an unpalatial quarter of St. Petersburg where Sophia Perovskaya, after wandering the streets distractedly, gave herself up to the police because she could not bear to live on in separation from her imprisoned lover, Zheliabov.

Alexander's son was to have a cathedral erected on the spot of the assassination. This bad imitation of Moscow's St. Basil's was a formal expression of grief in the absence of real public sorrow. True, a mob had rushed to soak up in handkerchiefs the tsar's blood on the street, but apathy was the rule.

Good intentions did not save Alexander from the assassin's bomb, nor did they earn him that much general popularity. A realist, even if a conservative, the emperor encouraged the greatest changes in Russian life since Peter the Great, changes much more humanitarian in motivation than those of his great-great-great-great-uncle. For this he was hated both for doing too much and for doing too little. A militaristic-pacifistic puzzle, Alexander made territorial gains for his bloated empire that failed to satisfy the extreme Pan-Slavists. Essentially a decent man, the tsar tried to legitimize his irregular romantic life. Reactionaries, revolutionists, reckless expansionists, and rigid prudes in effect conspired to create an atmosphere in which the tsar's murder can be described only as a martyrdom.

XVII.
The Last Autocrat: Alexander III

1. The Bull

THERE were three Romanov tsars named Alexander. The first, Napoleon's contemporary and nemesis, was a fascinating riddle, his refinement counterbalanced by mysticism, his chivalry matched with cunning. The second Alexander, the liberator, was more crudely drawn, but still there were elements of paradox—soldierly conservatism alternating with fuzzy liberalism, softheartedness giving way to petulance. Gruff Alexander III was seemingly all of a piece in character and politics and thus was altogether unlike either of his namesakes, who were his great-uncle and his father.

When the doctor announced that Alexander II was dead, the crowd of dignitaries in the imperial study of the Winter Palace looked over to the giant man standing at the window. The tsarevich, now automatically the Emperor Alexander III, had been watching the Guards regiments hurriedly taking up a protective triple line outside the palace fences. The new emperor had been struggling to control his grief, but he faced the assemblage with no trace of indecision on his face—no hint of self-doubt or bewilderment or even awe. Certain grand dukes hastened to suggest that this or that be done, but Alexander broke in and began to issue orders rapidly and bluntly. The police had lost control of the capital, he said, and the army must take command of the situation. After impatiently acknowledging the traditional oath taking by those present, the tsar swept up his tiny wife and eldest son and charged out of the room. Downstairs the imperial party entered a carriage, which then drove briskly out the gate as scores of Cossack escorts ranged themselves about on all sides. As a French observer put it, Alexander had mounted the throne as a soldier mounts the breach.

Thirty-six when he ascended the throne, Alexander Alexandrovich was a second son and had been groomed as tsarevich only after his adolescence. His elder brother, Nicholas, was considered one of the most gifted princes of his time: He was quick-minded, overwhelmingly charming, and handsomer than any of his predecessors. This most promising of Romanov heirs tragically died near Nice* in April, 1865, after a fall from his horse had brought on complications in an underlying physical debility variously described as consumption or cerebrospinal tuberculosis. The two brothers had been very close, and Nicholas passed on to Alexander not only his title but also his fiancée, Dagmar of Denmark.

Alexander apparently surpassed his brilliant brother in only one respect —height. About six feet six, Sasha, as his family called him, was the tallest Romanov since Peter the Great. When he was young, Sasha was dubbed the bullock by his father, who was amused by the way his second son drew his head forward and back into his huge shoulders, even as he sensed that Alexander was the family blockhead. The bullock grew up to become the bull, so called behind his back in some circles. Others, especially foreigners, delighted in the resemblance they chose to see between the awkward, shambling, giant grand duke and the standard Russian bear of the cartoonists.

Among all six of the brothers, Alexander appeared the least educable. He shared with Nicholas an enlightened lieutenant general as major tutor and was the beneficiary of lectures from Russia's first illustrious historian, Sergius Soloviev. A lasting influence on him was Constantine Pobedenostsev, a would-be priest turned jurist and a man destined to be the evil genius of the Russian court for five decades. The slight, ascetic Pobedenostsev, peering mockingly at the hulking young grand duke through his gold-rimmed glasses, must often have despaired of Alexander's inability for prolonged mental effort. But the second son was basically diligent, as well as plodding and stubborn, and he was receptive to formulas. Such a watchword as "Orthodoxy, autocracy, and nationality" suited his mind perfectly, and Pobedenostsev realized that he had no need to display his more sophisticated rationales for conservatism. The court doctor later summed up Alexander's education as little besides an "unshakeable belief in the omnipotence of the tsars of Russia."

To the relief of his teachers and especially of himself, Alexander soon went off to the elite military establishments to become a professional soldier. So in time did all five of his younger brothers, except Alexis, who went into the navy. The senior grand duke's huge physique and firm manner com-

---

* In memory of the Tsarevich Nicholas a large church was erected in Nice, and the visitor today, initially startled to see such a display of Russian onion domes on the Côte d'Azur, is further bemused to find fresh flowers on the monument to the last tsar, the church's sponsor.

manded respect in military circles. Alexander was an indifferent horseman, however, and parades and drills never captured his interest to the fanatic degree they held for every generation of Romanovs after Peter III. As a military commander, Alexander was neither brilliant nor dashing, merely conscientious, nor did the off-duty escapades expected of a grand duke appeal much to this stolid, lethargic man, whose name was never connected with any scandal.

A junior officer describing Alexander said that "he glowered rather than looked and had a habit of thrusting his head forward in the most menacing way, when anything displeased him." For all his formidable manner and gruff ways, "the bull" was actually even-tempered and generous. Unsociable in public, Alexander was treasured within his family, especially by his mother and older brother, and his personal friends deeply appreciated his constancy.

The heavy build, the complete lack of grace, the indifference to appearance, and the abruptness and directness of manner seemed incongruously peasantlike qualities in this Romanov heir, who indeed was to be known as the muzhik tsar. Alexander came to rejoice in being as rough-hewn as the least of Russians, in a kind of inverted snobbery. His straightforwardness and honesty were painful at times, as many anecdotes attest. Typical was the time he reportedly responded to the formal thank-you of his dancing partner, a German princess, with these words: "Why can't you be honest? It was just a duty neither of us could have relished. I have ruined your slippers and you have made me nearly sick with the scent you use."

When the Tsarevich Nicholas died in 1865, there were rumors that the tsar would pass over Alexander as successor to the throne in favor of the third son, the intellectually gifted and politically ambitious Vladimir. Such a possibility was actually ridiculous. The tsar had no cause to doubt Alexander's essential goodwill and good sense. The Romanovs as a dynasty had learned the consequences of arbitrary succession from the family turmoil of the eighteenth century and from the near disaster as late as 1825, when a younger son superseded an elder. Alexander II dispelled all doubts when he sternly introduced his namesake to a Polish delegation as his heir and gave him appropriate official duties as tsarevich.

Marriage in November, 1866, also meant changes in Alexander's hitherto unpretentious career. Dagmar of Denmark, who was rechristened Maria Fedorovna, was bright and cultivated, and she aspired to be tutor and hostess for her bearish husband, who repaid her concern with utter faithfulness. Under Maria's, or preferably Marie's, guidance, the new tsarevich returned to his books and was provoked to make notes and begin discussions. Their residence, the Anichkov Palace, became the site of a salon as brilliant as Marie could make it in the face of her husband's inborn disdain of high society.

Inevitably, the tsarevich's court was rival to the tsar's, if only that its members were younger and interested in new things. Such a wide assortment of political types came and went from the Anichkov that some people labeled the heir a liberal. In the course of the Franco-Prussian War of 1870 and 1871 Alexander's outspoken anti-German feelings, eagerly seconded by his wife, put him at odds with his father and his mother, who was German-born, like virtually all Romanov consorts since Peter—except Dagmar. During the Russo-Turkish War of 1877 and 1878 the tsarevich became the darling and unofficial leader of the Pan-Slavists, but Alexander, for his part, came to view with alarm the excesses of an aroused public opinion. During the fighting Alexander went off to command a sector of the front, a safe sector, and if he did not return a war hero, he did come back untainted by the charges of corruption and incompetence leveled at many of his relatives.

The tsarevich emerged from his associations with parlor liberals and powder-eating Pan-Slavists as anything but a radical. In his administrative capacities Alexander set himself against any reforms, ironically just as his father had done as tsarevich in the days of Nicholas I. Alexander favored a dictatorship in 1880 but was displeased when the dictator, Loris-Melikov, made concessions. Devoted to his mother and a model family man, Alexander indulged in frequent outbursts against his father's infatuation with Princess Dolgoruky, this woman, in fact, rather than the tsarevich, being the catalyst for the progressive party of the day.

Upon ascending the throne in March, 1881, Alexander III immediately faced two decisions: what was to be done with his father's assassins and what was to be done with the constitutional project which bore his predecessor's signature. The decisions were related and were vital for setting the tone of the reign.

The revolutionists anticipated the new emperor's dilemmas. Nine days after the assassination Alexander found on his desk a letter from the Central Executive Committee of the People's Will in which they addressed him "as a citizen and as an honest man." Putting aside "the feeling of natural delicacy" in this time of bereavement, the People's Will declared that the Catherine Street tragedy was "absolutely inevitable." If Alexander had lost a father, so had the revolutionists lost fathers, wives, children, and friends. A long recital of the wrongs and abuses of the police type of regime was concluded with: "These are the reasons why Russia brings forth so many revolutionists. These are the reasons why even such a deed as Tsarecide excites in the minds of a majority of the people only gladness and sympathy." Then his hidden enemies dared to offer the august tsar two choices: revolutionary violence or constitutional reform. They demanded "a general amnesty to cover all past political crimes for the reason they were not crimes but fulfillments of civic duty" and "the summoning of representatives of the whole Russian people to examine the existing framework of social and governmental life and to model it in accordance with the people's wishes."

Although the People's Will may have overestimated its immediate power and degree of popular support, the depth and sincerity of its convictions should not have escaped the notice of the tsar and his police. Simply bomb-happy, power-grabbing men would not have bothered to publish regrets when U.S. President James A. Garfield was assassinated by a disappointed office seeker just a few months after the St. Petersburg murder. The Central Executive Committee declared in all honesty:

> . . . In a country in which freedom of the person guarantees full possibility of an honest struggle of ideas, where a free people's will not only makes the law but also elects the rulers—in such a country political murder as an instrument of political conflict is an expression of that very spirit of despotism from which it is our aim to extricate Russia . . . violence can be justified only if it is directed against violence.

Alexander III authorized the execution of the assassins in April, 1881; the lovers Zheliabov and Perovskaya were hanged with the others. One strong appeal for clemency had been made by Vladimir Soloviev, the son of the tsar's tutor and a young intellectual on the threshold of becoming one of Russia's greatest philosophers. He asked not for sympathy for the revolutionists but for a demonstration of the perfection of the Orthodox religion and the greatness of forgiveness. Soloviev was severely penalized for his outspokenness by a tsar who was to authorize cheap reproductions of a painting showing a seated Christ blessing a standing Alexander, a kneeling Marie, and their cherubic children (a prime exhibit today in the Museum of Antireligious Propaganda in Leningrad). Likewise, the great Tolstoy appealed against more bloodshed, advising that "as wax before the fire, every revolutionary struggle will melt before the man tsar who fulfills the law of Christ." Pobedonostsev had this letter withheld, and the grand inquisitor later acknowledged chillingly but accurately to the newly gentled novelist that "our Christ is not your Christ."

There still remained the problem of what to do about the constitutional manifesto which lay locked in the late tsar's private desk. Gossips later invented stories about struggles for possession of the document between Princess Yurievskaya and various grand dukes in the manner of family and stepfamily fighting over wills. The existence of the constitution was widely known enough to prompt Alexander's uncle, Kaiser William I, to sign vehement letters written by Bismarck advising against its enactment. Filial piety, however, if not a sense of legality, seemed to dictate that the new tsar put into being his father's intention. In the course of two councils, Loris-Melikov argued warmly for the speedy implementation of his project, which he delicately refused even to call a constitution, but he made the mistake of also asking for the institution of a board of ministers, responsible to each other and not individually to the tsar, which he delicately refused to call a cabinet. Pobedenostsev was the decisive voice in setting Alexander against any diminution of the tsar's power, arguing that the West had been corrupted by parliamentarianism, whereas "Russia has become powerful by virtue of the autocracy . . . by virtue of the close bonds by which the people are attached to their tsar." Katkov's newspapers also screamed conservatism, and Alexander finally decided that public opinion would support abandonment of the reform project.

The inaugural manifesto of the reign in May, 1881, essentially dictated by Pobedenostsev, declared Alexander's intent to defend, consolidate, and strengthen the "power and truth of the autocracy." Unconsulted in this declaration of the infallibility of the old ways, the liberals resigned their posts, Loris as minister of the interior, Dmitri Miliutin as minister of war, and Alexander Abaza as minister of finance. Alexander III had demonstrated his belief that too much freedom, not too much repression, was the villain. Increasingly in the following decade, the tsar acted as if it were his divine mission to stamp out subversion with no thought to its deeper roots. The formal coronation of Alexander and Marie took place in Moscow in May, 1883, in the apparent conviction that medieval pageantry corresponded adequately with contemporary reality.

Although Alexander III was fully determined to be his own man, Constantine Pobedenostsev was allowed to emerge as the most powerful voice behind the throne. Ironically, Pobedenostsev had had a hand in the reforms of the 1860's, but now he disowned them and sneered at his former liberal associates. Another irony was that the man whose field was constitutional law should coin the famous phrase that parliamentary institutions were "the great lie of our age." Education, according to Pobedenostsev, was useful only for an elite. "Mystery and authority" were sufficient for the "manipulation of the masses," the latter term his own invention. Pobedenostsev's succinct advice to Alexander after his accession was "to end at once, now, all the talk about freedom of the press, about high-minded meetings, about a representative assembly."

As part of the general reaction, the new minister of the interior, Nicholas Ignatiev, was quick to promulgate a law stating that local authorities could designate a whole district as under martial law. Right down to 1917 this was reenacted every three years and enabled the police to pursue such courses as surveillance of suspicious persons, closing down of newspapers and social organizations, and arrest and banishment of the politically suspect. Ignatiev at first seemed a safe man to Pobedenostsev, but the minister's ambition and Slavophile ideas got the better of him. Early in 1882 he had drawn up an elaborate proposal for the revival of the medieval Zemsky Sobor as a kind of consultive national assembly. Even though the plan in practice would have meant scarcely more than convening the 3,000 most loyal subjects of the tsar, it was too extreme for Pobedenostsev, and Ignatiev was ousted after just one year in office. His replacement as minister of the interior was none other than D. A. Tolstoy, the benighted former minister of education whose name was already anathema to the intelligentsia.

One of Tolstoy's first acts was to issue some supplements to the Temporary Press Rules of 1865, and the new heavy-handed censorship regulations lasted until 1906. One by one the great liberal journals were closed by bureaucratic harassment: To show a "prejudicial tendency" was the warning formula, while an "unquestionably pernicious tendency" meant the presses were stilled forever. Even the editor of the semiofficial *Police Gazette* was thrown in jail for allowing a typographical error in an edition that read a "requiem for Alexander III" (II was intended). Censorship of books was maddeningly arbitrary and occasionally amusing in retrospect. John Stuart Mill, Ernest Renan, Herbert Spencer, and Adam Smith were among the modern writers banned. Just after rejecting the *Wealth of Nations,* the censor allowed through Marx's *Das Kapital,* dismissing it simply as too heavy going.

Russia's hard-won educational institutions were a natural target for Pobedenostsev. If he could not stop education, the procurator could at least transfer many primary schools to the control of his Holy Synod. The secondary schools were too solidly accepted by the public to be touched, but their students were subjected to new harassments. Officials were directed to snoop into students' homes, and tuition fees were raised, to exclude "children of coachmen, servants, laundresses, and small shopkeepers and the like," in the words of the minister of education. Such official sanction of social immobility was a reversion to the days of Nicholas I. So, too, was the breaking of university autonomy by a statute of 1884 which gave the Minister of Education control of the faculties. At the same time university students were forbidden to belong to clubs, the penalty for even the most innocent associations being immediate conscription into the army. These measures to silence the intelligentsia were warmly applauded by the increasingly subversion-haunted Katkov, who crowed editorially about the new regime: "Rise, gentlemen, the government is coming, the government is coming."

Intensified Russification was another recourse of Alexander's regime, the tsar himself being dominated by an intense fear and hatred of foreigners. His personal chauvinism was soon reflected in high society, which came to disdain speaking French or German and even affected medieval Russian styles of clothing. Alexander's antipathy to the German influences in his father's court was eventually translated into such caprices as banning the purchase of the pastries of St. Petersburg's predominantly German bakers. The rolls of regiments were culled for German names, even to the point of raising lowborn Russian ensigns to commanding positions. And now for the first time the German gentry of the Baltic provinces were added to the list of nationalities subjected to Russifying persecution in their schools, local institutions, and churches.

Although only one Jewish girl was at all connected with the assassination of Alexander II, the signal was given for wholesale attacks on Russian Jews. Within the year 215 pogroms had taken place in various cities and towns. Alexander personally hated Jews, as his marginal notes on many state documents attest. Pobedenostsev divided the Jewish population into three parts: one-third, it was hoped, to be converted, one-third to emigrate, and one-third to disappear somehow. In 1882 the government made an unprecedented invitation in the form of the announcement: "The Western Border is open to the Jews." The ensuing wave of emigration included nearly 1,000,000 people.

Harassment of editors and students and non-Russians and Jews was designed to supplement a direct police crackdown on the revolutionists, which the tsar saw to it was total and successful. The public was largely cooperative. Crippled by arrests, the terrorist People's Will still managed to keep some of its underground presses and bomb factories going at home and abroad, and as late as 1883 they assassinated the chief of the Third Section. The next year more than 400 People's Will members were rounded up, and the national organization of revolutionists was no more. Thanks to Alexander's police, revolution became once more a "cottage industry," in the rueful words of a surviving Socialist.

Throughout his reign Alexander III left no doubt about his determination to maintain the old order. His giant physique was matched by a spiritual strength, however misdirected. There were no disturbing changes of mind and purposes. As an absolutist should be, Alexander was his own prime minister, picking subordinates qualified for specific functions and programs. He repaid his ministers' services with consistent support. The self-disciplinarian was capable of storms of anger over what he considered derelictions of duty, but once an incident was closed, he harbored no ill feelings. "The bull" appeared to be the perfect autocrat, just as his grandfather had once seemed so.

As with Nicholas I, the flawless majesty of Alexander III may have been just a successful pose. A hostile German witness wrote that the Emperor of Russia was actually "crushed by his position and compelled to the constant repression of his true nature." For all of Alexander's commanding presence, the writer continued:

> Still the inner discord betrays itself to the attentive observer everywhere—in the salon, on parade, and even in the midst of festivities. . . .
> This explains how he, who as a prince was merely unsociable, has ar-

rived at a degree of isolation within the last few years which surpasses anything ever shown by his predecessors.

The isolation of Alexander III was indeed a fact, in part explained by a certain misanthropy on his part but basically necessitated for police security reasons. However many subversives were jailed and however many suspects packed off to Siberia, the tsar himself remained a "prisoner of the revolution," in Marx's perceptive phrase. In 1881 at the time of his accession Alexander did not leave the Anichkov Palace to take up residence in the Winter Palace; instead, the imperial family moved to Gatchina Palace outside the capital to the southwest. Personally courageous as he might be, the tsar was persuaded that his safety required his ruling his vast empire from a small estate entirely surrounded by a high wall, which in turn was patrolled every few yards by Cossacks. Thus, circumstances, rather than neuroses, compelled Alexander to live somewhat in the manner of the Emperor Paul. It was a case of a corral to protect the bull, not the onlookers.

2. Firm Patriarch

Alexander III once told relatives he was visiting abroad that for him returning to Russia was like returning to prison. The atmosphere of siege around Gatchina was indeed galling to a proud man. Yet the enforced isolation of the tsar had its advantages, in that he could enjoy his family and pursue his homely pleasures. Moreover, Alexander was freed of visits by bothersome relatives—uncles, brothers, and cousins—although he discharged his responsibilities as head of the Romanovs conscientiously and well.

Russia's ruler, so august and dignified to the popular eye, was at heart a simple man. No lover of ceremony, no devotee of uniforms and medals, he might frequently be found dressed in a cotton blouse hanging out below his belt to the fingertips, the age-old costume of the peasants. Usually the accompanying striped linen pants he wore were bagging at the knees, if not actually patched and soiled. So dressed, Alexander liked to step into the palace kitchens and demand a share of the servants' fare of cabbage soup, millet gruel, or pickled cucumbers. Foreign extravagances at the imperial table were not at all favored by the tsar, whose austerity and parsimony about entertaining led the experienced to warn dinner guests to fortify themselves beforehand.

One of Alexander's greatest delights was his elaborate carpenter's bench at Gatchina, where he could turn his huge hands to carving and cabinet-work. He loved to show off his strength to guests. If he had forgotten to buckle a silver plate at dinner, he usually remembered sometime later in the evening to rip a pack of cards in two or to make a fire poker into a pretzel. Alternatively he would pick up his tiny wife and her sister, the Princess of Wales, holding them up to his eye level at arm's length.

The robust tsar loved the outdoors and was a devoted hunter and fisherman. When he went striding off into the woods, his knapsack usually contained a hunk of black bread and common sausage.

Music was a passion of Alexander's, the passion of a participant, as well as a listener. As a young grand duke he evaded the social amenities at entertainments by taking the place of one of the band members and sometimes ended up performing on almost every instrument in the course of an evening. As tsar, Alexander confined himself to playing the double bass exuberantly in an impromptu palace orchestra. At the bass drum in this group, incidentally, was a General Genghis Khan, an authentic descendant of the Mongol conqueror and his image as well.

The bearded Hercules had the most petite and cultivated of princesses for a wife. Marie Fedorovna complemented her husband, softening his rough edges and sweetening his gruff effect on people. As Dagmar of Denmark she had been brought up in circumstances modest to the point of seediness when her father was merely Prince Christian of Schleswig-Holstein-Glücksberg. He and her mother, Louise of Hesse, had to manage on a soldier's salary. Then Christian was named heir to the childless Frederick VII and in 1863 assumed the Danish throne as Christian IX. This kindly, unpretentious man was destined to be one of the greatest royal patriarchs in modern history, his children and grandchildren occupying thrones all over Europe. The reign began with great tragedy and humiliation, however, for Prussia goaded Austria into a joint invasion of Denmark's southern provinces. The memory helped make Princess Dagmar anti-German for the rest of her life.

Dagmar's older sister, Alexandra, won the heart of Albert Edward, the Prince of Wales. In the course of the wedding festivities in 1863, Dagmar met Queen Victoria and saw imperial style on a scale she had never known or even imagined in Copenhagen. To the younger princess fell more than a consolation prize: She became betrothed in 1865 to the Tsarevich Nicholas Alexandrovich of Russia, at once the personally favored and promising heir to a huge and mysterious empire. Nicholas and Dagmar were a love match, but the fact that the tsarevich was marrying into non-German royalty was not without political implications. Actually, both the royal mothers had been reared in Germany at the court of Hesse, and Nicholas and Dagmar were introduced there amid festivities and gossipmongering that barely concealed that this was a royal marriage mart.

The tragedy of the tsarevich's demise at Nice was ameliorated only by the dramatic, touching deathbed scene when Nicholas put his fiancée's hands into those of his brother Alexander and pledged them to marry. Their wedding in November, 1866, in the chapel of the Winter Palace thus came about through an enforced promise, but Alexander and the now Marie Fedorovna were to be blessed with an unusual compatibility, based perhaps on the fascination of opposites for each other as much as on personal high moral standards. Both were twenty-one at the time of the marriage.

For the rest of her life Marie remained very close to her sister Alexandra, and accordingly, she brought Alexander into frequent contact with Britain's comfortably disreputable and wise Prince of Wales. At a time when memories of past clashes and new suspicions made Queen Victoria fume against Russia and Russian society reciprocated by calling her a she-devil, it was salutary for peace that the two imperial heirs were brothers-in-law. "Sasha" and "Bertie" saw each other often at Fredensborg, the summer residence of King Christian IX, which yearly became a pleasant sparring and mating ground for half a dozen related royal houses. "We are an immense family gathering—quite a Babel, seven different languages spoken, never sitting down to dinner less than fifty or sixty," wrote Albert Edward to a friend. After the Prince of Wales had made the unprecedented trip to attend their St. Petersburg wedding, Alexander and Marie visited London, the tsarevich reviving memories of the Romanov tours in England going back to Peter the Great. Marie and Alexandra particularly surprised and delighted the crowds by their unflagging pursuit of concerts, parties, and parades at which they would appear in dazzlingly high fashions but always dressed exactly alike.

Maria Fedorovna was immediately and permanently a great personal success in her adopted country. When still just wife of the tsarevich, she had the opportunity to take over all the charitable functions of her ailing mother-in-law, and as Lady Bountiful she proved able and popular. With equal ease, she could glide through the intricacies of the stiff court etiquette of the day. Moreover, people were amazed that Marie always seemed to be pleasantly informed about their personal and family affairs. She always had a kind word, and she discreetly made her way through the inevitable court intrigues without arousing enmity.

Count Vassili, pseudonym of a court figure who wrote a secret memoir on St. Petersburg of these and later days, was fulsome in her admiration of Maria Fedorovna:

> She was a charmer in the widest sense of the word. Her charm was quite indescribable. It exercised a fascination to which it was impossible not to succumb. Her lovely smile, the gentle look in her eyes—those great luminous dark eyes that seemed to read into one's soul—brought more friends to her husband than millions spent on years of effort would have done.

Besides being endlessly good-humored and unaffectedly radiant, Marie was poise and stateliness to perfection. Majesty in a small woman is not easy, but Alexander's wife possessed it in as full measure as Queen Victoria.

The empress sought and won no more and no less than the position as the most loved and admired figure of the highest society. She was a woman of the world, far better educated than her husband, but she eschewed politics, except perhaps in promoting Russian friendship with France. After all, Paris dresses were the particular love of a woman fond of clothes and jewels and parties. In the words of a German reporter: "Because the Emperor is unsociable, he is glad that his wife finds inexhaustible joy in dancing and amusements, even though she runs up bills to the goddess of fashion, which are not seldom as long as those of Josephine, the first wife of Napoleon, who spent half her life in the dressing room."

Along with the Paris gowns came another French indulgence for which Marie made the Russian court famous—Fabergé jewelry and knickknacks, if the latter is the right word for the series of fifty-six Easter eggs given to the empress beginning in 1884. One of these incredibly costly eggs, for example, contained a tiny cockerel that crowed on the hour.

As an entertainer the consort Marie recalled the empresses in their own right, Elizabeth and Catherine. The festivities of the court and of the aristocratic houses under the aegis of this Danish princess were never again to be so glittering. Whole trainloads of people were brought out to Gatchina for her more informal parties. The Anichkov Palace, when the police would allow it, provided the setting for more elaborate dinners and balls. Several times a year traditional state occasions required that the full facilities of the Winter Palace be used, and foreign visitors would be treated to the spectacle of the entire imperial family leading an hourlong procession through endless galleries manned by lavishly dressed guards and salons crowded with the important and the beautiful. After the emperor and empress began proceedings with a sedate waltz, the grand dukes led the rest of high society in a lively pageant of mazurkas and contemporary rhythms.

One of the most treasured memories of these dazzling splendors was the empress' *bal noir*. She had planned a grand affair, only to be forced to cancel it because the death of a little-known Austrian archduke required that the Russian court go into mourning. Petulant but only momentarily thwarted, Marie recalled a remissness of the Hapsburg court in the same sort of circumstance and promptly sent out a second set of invitations, offering a new form of politeness between courts in the requirement that the partygoers were to wear nothing but black—and their jewels, of course. The empress never looked more ravishing, the pearls and diamonds of all the ladies never better displayed. Alexander III contentedly authorized all his wife's extravagances and caprices, but unless ceremony required it, he often absented himself from the parties altogether. On some occasions he resorted to the amusing expedient of secretly ordering the dance orchestra to leave one player at a time, so that Marie's guests might suddenly become aware that they were being entertained by a trio or even a lone violinist.

Children were more to Alexander's liking and skills than cotillions. Marie bore him four sons and two daughters. The tsar appeared at his happiest when he was playing host to his own children and their Romanov cousins at Gatchina or Fredensborg. An annual ceremony in Russia, quite unknown to the tsar's awed subjects, was his testing the ice on the palace pond. Each time Alexander would solemnly creep out on the newly frozen surface, heave his bulk, and then join in the peals of children's laughter when he found himself in water up to his baggy knees.

The royal couple's first son, Nicholas, was born in 1868. A second child, with exactly the same names as his father, came along the next year but died of pneumonia while still an infant. Later it was alleged that this singularly promising child—shades of other Romanov eldests—was really the senior and that the demise of the dynasty could thus be blamed on an ignorant nurse and incompetent doctor. The dates on the sarcophagus in Peter and Paul prove otherwise—Alexander Alexandrovich, Tsarskoe Selo, May 26, 1869–St. Petersburg, April 20, 1870. As for the true heir, Nicholas, some people noted that he was small by comparison with other recent Romanov babies, but the child grew up normally endowed both physically and mentally. A wistful personality, Nicholas was his mother's child and never won his father's appreciation. Yet as a young man Nicholas came to admire Alexander uncritically, possibly out of guilt, and this may have been the ultimate tragedy of the dynasty. The tsarevich's decision to marry Alexandra of Hesse in 1894, over the objections of both his parents, was a strain on a family that prided themselves on being close to one another and by all observations were indeed well knit.

George Alexandrovich, born in 1871, struck some observers as much more favored in mind and character than his older brother, but this clever, high-spirited, and handsome grand duke was early struck with a respiratory ailment so severe that his life was despaired of. A fourth son, Michael, four years younger, grew up to be the family dolt; he was utterly good-natured, vacant-minded, and so credulous that his bemused father once said that a person could tell Michael anything.

Two daughters spanned Michael in ages. Xenia, born in 1875, was the particular delight of her father, and she grew up to be a delicious image of her mother. Marie Fedorovna took personal charge of her lessons long beyond the age when polite society said the grand duchess should have had a governess. With a rare delicacy of looks and manner, Xenia in her teens was a prize princess in the calculations of many European capitals, but her hand went to a cousin, the Grand Duke Alexander, thus breaking the tradition that Romanovs married foreigners. The wedding took place in 1894, only after the whole imperial family plotted and pleaded with the

Empress Marie, who could not face the loss of her favorite. The Grand Duchess Olga, born the year after Alexander's accession, was plainer and quieter than her sister.

The tsar's five surviving children joined the now several score of persons of Romanov blood populating grandiose mansions in St. Petersburg or presiding over foreign capitals or resorts. Alexander III was expected to play head of the family and did so. His relations included such curiosities of bygone eras as the Grand Duchess Catherine Michaelovna, this daughter of the younger brother of Alexander I living from 1827 to 1894 and dying without ever having caused a fuss, good or bad.

Princess Yurievskaya, the stepmother Alexander detested, was still alive, and she and her children enjoyed the ultimate title Serene Highness, although she could not claim to be dowager empress. A witness recalled the pathetic scene at the funeral of Alexander II when the Yurievsky family uncomfortably stood apart in an entryway, receiving no place in the procession of the imperial family and even having to attend a separate mass for the murdered tsar. The Empress Marie did unbend from etiquette long enough to embrace the bereaved wife, and the emperor made an honorable financial settlement on his mother's rival. The stately and elegant princess bought houses in Paris, Nice, and Biarritz, where she indulged herself as the most lavish hostess. Essentially an exile, occasionally she returned on her private railway car to St. Petersburg, where her salon caused brief flurries of excitement. By 1890 the children George, Olga, and Catherine all were in their teens, princely bastards.

The tsar had three uncles living at the time of his accession, the Grand Dukes Constantine, Nicholas, and Michael, but these once-formidable men were from the start allowed little or no influence in state affairs. The oldest grand duke, Constantine Nicholaevich, had been an outspoken leader of the radicals of the 1860's and had used his position as head of the navy and as president of the Geographical Society to create lasting strongholds for reform-minded people. The tall, gaunt, hawklike man was considered by many unpredictable, if not sinister and dangerous. Rumor had it that the police of Alexander III had the grand duke under constant surveillance because of his supposed nihilist connections, and it was even said that an ambitious Constantine had supplied the funds for the assassination. The tsar and Constantine's wife, née the Princess of Saxe-Altenburg, suffered the old man to retire to his estates in the Crimea with his ballerina mistress, and he died there in 1892 at the age of sixty-five.

There were five children of the grand duke, first cousins of the tsar—Nicholas, Constantine, Dmitri, Vlacheslav, and Olga. The eldest, Nicholas Constantinovich, lived out his mature life somewhat mysteriously in Tashkent; the chief rumor was that he had once stolen his mother's jewels and was suffering from incurable mental illness. By the time he was thirty,

Constantine Constantinovich, born in 1858, had achieved renown as a poet and was credited with the best translation of *Hamlet* into Russian (at least until Boris Pasternak's). His house, where the highly cultivated grand duke assisted at musicales and amateur plays, was an intellectual focus of the capital. The next brother, Dmitri Constantinovich, born in 1860, was also tremendously well educated. Destined by his father to keep up the family naval tradition, Dmitri found that even icons did not work against his congenital seasickness, and he was eventually allowed to join the Horse Guards, later becoming commander of the Grenadier Guards. The youngest son, Vlacheslav Constantinovich, died before reaching manhood. The Grand Duchess Olga Constantinovich, born in 1851, became Queen of Greece, after King George I, visiting St. Petersburg in search of a bride, saw the fifteen-year-old beauty peeking at him over a banister and declared he would have no other. The once Prince George of Denmark was the younger brother of the Empress Marie and of the Princess of Wales, and he had been selected by Europe's diplomats in 1863, when he was eighteen, to go off and rule turbulent Athens and to found a new dynasty. The children of this king and his Grand Duchess Olga were the ancestors of not only the present Greek ruler but also of the Duchess of Kent and the Duke of Edinburgh.

The tsar's second uncle, Nicholas Nicholaevich, was in semiofficial disgrace ever since the campaign of 1877, when, as commander in chief, he was accused of mismanagement and venality. Still popular in some military circles, this grand duke became an amiable, picturesque man who enjoyed attending every fire in St. Petersburg day or night. His love affairs were the talk of the town but only partly explained his wife's leaving him. Herself a Romanov by descent from a daughter of Paul and the Prince of Oldenburg, the Grand Duchess Alexandra as a convert to Orthodoxy eventually plunged into the extremes of mysticism and surrounded herself with fanatic monks, who persuaded her at length to take the veil. Her husband died in 1891, leaving two sons, Nicholas and Peter. The junior Nicholas Nicholaevich, born in 1856, passed through various military commands to emerge in the next reign as the first soldier of Russia and a man destined to play a signal political role among the Romanovs even into the 1920's. This hulking, excitable man, who was whispered to suffer from the "hereditary hysteria of the Oldenburgs," created a sensational scandal when he took away and married the Prince of Leuchtenberg's wife, Princess Anastasia of Montenegro. His intelligent but overshadowed brother, Peter, eight years younger, suffered from consumption and, after an undistinguished military career, went into retirement, living for several years in Egypt, among other places, with his wife, Militza of Montenegro, sister of his sister-in-law.

To the collateral Romanov clans known as the Constantinovichi and the Nicholaevichi were added the even more numerous Michaelovichi. The fourth son of Nicholas I and youngest uncle of Alexander III, the Grand Duke Michael had made his reputation in the 1870's as viceroy of the Caucasus, where he often grandly undertook expansionist moves in Asia as if the tsar's orders did not count. Despite being compromised in the scandals of 1877, Michael Nicholaevich was named to preside over the Council of State after 1882 at the age of fifty. Although he was not particularly gifted intellectually, the gray-bearded patriarch was serious-minded and was well thought of for his equanimity of character and his unfailing courtesy. He came to be the peacemaker in the family, having been almost alone in befriending Princess Yurievskaya, for example, and he was venerated for all his tactful interventions in favor of errant grand dukes. After the death of his wife, Princess Cecilia of Baden, in 1891, the old grand duke preferred his villa, Wenden, at Cannes to his palaces in St. Petersburg or even to the beautiful Crimean estate Ai-Todor, where the exquisite gardens had been the grand duchess' great joy.

The "wild Caucasians" was the affectionate epithet of Tsar Alexander II for the seven Michaelovich children when this tanned, rugged, unpolished brood first encountered St. Petersburg society after spending their youths in frontier areas some thousands of miles from the capital. The oldest son, Nicholas, born in 1859, started off on a military career in the Chevalier Guards but quit his regiment to pursue historical studies, eventually becoming president of the Russian Historical Society. While in service, he had made himself unpopular for his advanced political views, earning the title Philippe Égalité from his fellow officers. The handsome, talented, and intelligent Nicholas Michaelovich became a natural rival within the dynasty to his cousin and contemporary Nicholas Nicholaevich (the soldierly "Nicholasha"). Frustrated in his efforts to play a role in state affairs, "Nick-Mish" also found church and emperor blocking his marriage to his first cousin Princess Victoria of Baden (who became instead the wife of Gustavus V of Sweden), and he reigned as a bachelor thereafter in a grand Petersburg palace.

Frustration also attended the grand ducal path of the second son, Michael Michaelovich. After making a great splash in a Guards regiment solely for his looks, generosity, and dancing ability, he set about in 1881, when he was twenty and had come into his money, building a fine new palace in the capital and seeking an appropriate bride. Michael's search for love throughout Europe was both comic and embarrassing to the family, ending with his decision to marry the lovely daughter of the Duke of Nassau. Unfortunately she was considered a commoner as the product of a morganatic marriage, even though she could boast Pushkin as her grandfather. The grand duke's persistence resulted in his own morganatic marriage hitherto very rare in the Romanov family, and his exile to London with his lady, created Countess Torby. The new Russian palace was never to be enjoyed, but Michael bought Kenwood, that finest of Adam creations on Hempstead Heath, and cantankerously set about becoming more English than the English.

George Michaelovich, the third son of the Caucasian clan, born in 1863, showed talent as a painter when he was a child, leading his martinet father to deprive him of desserts on occasion. Sent to St. Petersburg to join the Horse Artillery, he eventually comfortably adapted to the hell-for-leather, spit-and-polish life. He married his cousin Princess Marie of Greece, daughter of King George and the former Grand Duchess Olga.

The fourth of the Michaelovichi, Alexander, became the most well known by virtue of his becoming brother-in-law of a tsar and also because of the fascinating memoirs he left in the 1920's. His birth in Tiflis in 1866, he wrote, was greeted with a 101-gun salute, and within twenty-four hours he had several military titles. Youth for him meant hard beds, scant breakfasts, barracks discipline, and play with a mountain gun. It took the direct intervention of the tsar against his father to allow Alexander to fulfill his wish to join the navy, where he found that as an ensign-grand duke he had to dine with the admiral and be accompanied by a tutor when on shore leave. At the age of twenty, in 1886, his 50-rubles-a-month allowance from his Spartan-minded parents was replaced with an annual income of 210,000 rubles from the dynastic funds. A voyage on a steam-sail warship took him to Brazil, Singapore, and Japan, where this first Russian royal visitor shocked the empress when he tried out on her his Japanese phrases—recently learned in a whorehouse. Soon he had high naval command positions and was selected to take the cruiser *Dmitri Donskoy* to New York in 1893 to thank Americans for their famine relief efforts. By his own story, being prudently scared of the wiles of American debutantes, he had beforehand asked Alexander III for the hand of his daughter Xenia, and the two Romanov cousins were married in July, 1894.

Sergius Michaelovich gladdened his father's heart by becoming an enthusiastic artillery officer. He never married but had his faithful ballerina. The baby boy of the Michaelovich clan, Alexis, was beloved for his brilliance and good heart, but he died of consumption in San Remo in 1895, not yet twenty years old. His sister and the one daughter in the family, the Grand Duchess Anastasia, was a high-spirited, extremely pretty girl, and the future Kaiser William II was among her many suitors. She eventually married the Grand Duke Frederick of Mecklenburg-Schwerin and went to live in Germany, where she angered her royal former admirer by her outspoken Russian sympathies.

Somewhat more troublesome for Alexander III than his uncles and cousins were his four brothers, Vladimir, Alexis, Sergius, and Paul, and his one sister, Maria. Vladimir, two years the tsar's junior, was considered the intellectual of the family of Alexander II as a youth, and some even fantasized that he would be named successor. Alexander III, as tsarevich, far from showing jealousy, always respected Vladimir's political advice, and even after his accession this grand duke was the only person who could make his way unannounced into the imperial study. Raised to undertake military commands, which he did, Vladimir made his real mark in St. Petersburg as president of the Academy of Art and as a patron of ballet. A booming-voiced man, he would cut down unmercifully younger grand dukes or members of his several clubs if they could not discuss either art or cuisine, for Vladimir was also a dedicated gourmet who kept an immense collection of signed and annotated menus.

Vladimir's wife was as formidable as he was—tall, commanding, intellectual, and energetic. Born Princess Maria of Mecklenburg-Schwerin and thus sister-in-law of Anastasia Michaelovna, she was known after her marriage as the Grand Duchess Maria Pavlovna (or sometimes simply as the Grand Duchess Vladimir). It was said that as a young girl in Germany she caught sight of the eligible Russian prince and never stopped pleading and intriguing until Alexander III forced his brother to end his carefree pleasures and marry her. Her unprecedented refusal to convert to Orthodoxy then greatly angered the tsar, who also found her overbearing intellectually and socially. When Maria Pavlovna was discovered to be in correspondence with Bismarck, there was a summons to Gatchina and an outburst from the tsar that was among his most memorable, even though the incriminating letters were just smart talk, not espionage. Ambitious for her husband and herself, Vladimir's wife resigned herself to being third lady of the land and waited her chance. The grand ducal couple had four children between 1876 and 1882, Cyril, Boris, Andrew, and Helen—the first destined to call himself emperor.

The tsar's second brother, Alexis, entered a career in the navy and eventually became grand admiral to Russia's misfortune. His status as grand duke made his professional career, for he remained woefully ignorant of naval technology, all the while opposing any innovations to improve the morale of the service he had inherited from his radical Uncle Constantine. He enjoyed entertaining his fellow admirals at his palace, never failing to remind them of his experiences when he had actually served on the sail frigate *Alexander Nevsky*. Tall and a little on the heavy side, Alexis was admitted to be the best-looking man in the imperial family, according to his cousin the Grand Duke Alexander, who went on to describe him as follows: "A man of the world to his fingertips, a Beau Brummel, and a bon vivant hopelessly spoiled by women, particularly by those of Washington, D.C. he travelled a great deal. The necessity of spending a year away from Paris would have caused him to resign his post." Another acquaintance of the grand duke noted that so fine was his figure and bearing that even the most blasé Paris *boulevardiers* turned around to admire him. As for the Washington, D.C., women mentioned, Alexis achieved a great success in the United States when he visited this country and among other things went hunting in the West with Buffalo Bill, to the iconoclastic delight of American cartoonists. Woman chaser that he was—in the critical eye of his brother—Alexis never married. His affair with the incomparable Zia, wife of the half Romanov Duke of Leuchtenberg, was a badly kept secret that rocked the capital with stories of a *ménage à trois.*

Junior to the tsar and the grand dukes Vladimir and Alexis was Sergius Alexandrovich, who grew up to be the most arrogant and unpopular Romanov in Russia. The only people who liked him were the officers of his Preobrazhenskoe Regiment, of which he became commander, since he appeared smart and elegant in their eyes and was envied for his aggressiveness with the ladies. Most people he came into contact with, however, found him stupid, stubborn, supercilious, and insufferable, with a reputation for tyranny and disagreeableness. His notoriety for being the grand duke who caroused most often and most earnestly was put down to depravity. "I cannot find a single redeeming feature in his character," wrote the Grand Duke Alexander, who recalled his cousin in the 1870's as a snobbish, bored-looking officer with a bristling mustache and a close-cropped head that seemed to emphasize the grand duke's small-mindedness. Nonetheless, in 1891 Alexander III appointed this brother, at the age of thirty-four, to be the governor general of Moscow, a post in which he showed a greater ability at peculation than administration.

Sergius' treatment of his wife added to his repugnance. Christened Elizabeth Fedorovna in the Russian Church, the grand duchess had been born Princess of Hesse, and this granddaughter of Queen Victoria was related to a remarkable group of royalty—her brother in time reigned as Grand Duke of Hesse; one sister married into the German-English Battenbergs; another sister as Princess Henry of Prussia was wife of the brother of the kaiser; and finally a third sister, Alexandra, became the fiancée of Nicholas, heir to the Russian throne. Elizabeth matched the virtue of her royal connections in the sheer ravishing beauty of her classic features, her luminous gray eyes, and her slender tallness, as well as in giving many signs of exceptional intelligence. This paragon was warned against the grand duke, who proceeded to be an utterly faithless husband. His brutality excited much sympathy for Elizabeth, but she was as proud as he and put up a front of cool serenity. Her interests dwindled to acquiring smart clothes and giving brittlely elegant parties in the palace on the Neva. The couple remained childless.

The Grand Duke Paul Alexandrovich was fifteen years younger than the tsar. He had been brought up with Sergius and shared that brother's haughtiness and licentiousness but to a less exaggerated degree. He was basically kind and considered more open-minded. A brilliant army officer, the carefree grand duke prided himself most on his abilities as a dancer. After having his fun, he submitted to family pressure and unenthusiastically married his cousin, Princess Alexandra of Greece. In the early 1890's she bore him two Pavlovich children, Dmitri and Maria.

Maria Alexandrovna was the only surviving daughter of the generation of Romanovs sired by Alexander II. Carefully educated by her mother in traditional ways, the grand duchess early showed independence of spirit and a consciousness of her extreme eligibility and her physical attractiveness. For a husband she won no less than Alfred, Duke of Edinburgh, Queen Victoria's second son. This deepening of English-Russian royal ties was resented in certain quarters of both countries, but Empress-to-be Marie and the Princess of Wales persisted, and "Bertie" was enthusiastically on hand at the wedding in the Winter Palace in 1874. The twenty-one-year-old bride went off to England and was soon sending back letters of alarming frankness to the effect that her mother-in-law was a "silly, obstinate old fool." There had been a clash because Victoria thought Maria's tiara too costly for a young girl (her own daughter's jewels looked commonplace by comparison). On another occasion, the English matriarch found her daughter-in-law too Russian in her love of a warm apartment; she ordered Maria's fire put out when not attended. The marriage, however, was happy and fecund as well, there being five children born between 1874 and 1884: Alfred, Marie, Victoria, Alexandra, and Beatrice.

As the number of Romanovs grew, so did the pressure on the family treasury, which consisted of lands, or appanages, set aside by Paul and other rulers specifically for the support of the lesser members of the dynasty. Alexander III decided on a drastic reform, and such was his patriarchal strength, as well as legal authority, that there were no protests in his lifetime. A Statute on the Imperial Family provided that only sons and grandsons of tsars were to be entitled to the dignity of grand duke and an annual allowance of roughly 280,000 rubles. Great-grandsons herewith were to be titled princes, and a lump sum of 1,000,000 rubles was to take care of them and their descendants forever. The tsar's wise economy in the face of a too-big family made the Romanovs the only major royal house that never had to go begging for a civil list from a legislature. Because of this statute, with an assist from the Bolsheviks, there are no grand dukes or grand duchesses living today. Romanov princes and Rurikovich princes still abound, of course.

Alexander's new law hardly reduced the Russian grand dukes to being penny-pinchers. Paris headwaiters went wild with joy at the mere sight of one of the tsar's brothers or cousins, and no royalty seemed to travel about with as many servants. The openhandedness of Catherine the Great was more a family tradition than the frugality of Peter the Great. One striking tale of Romanov entravagance concerns the grand duke sojourning at Cannes who developed a longing for the snows of Russia: He received permission from the mayor to have the entire Boulevard des Anglaises covered with rock salt and then drove a troika down it.

Open criticism of the imperial family was still unheard of, but many were the private whispers about the love lives of the grand dukes and their role in the state, especially concerning their monopoly of high office in the military. Essentially a general social-political judgment is intended by a writer who once described a relative of the tsar as "one of those self-satisfied, stalwart Guardsmen who watched the world go by through the short end of their opera glasses fixed on the limbs of a twirling ballerina." The political abilities and cultural interests of the grand dukes concerned Alexander III less than the image of the dynasty. The wilder extravagances infuriated the tsar. One of his greatest fits of temper was reserved for a young Romanov who gambled away an impossible amount of money. Romantic gossip about grand dukes did not bother Alexander—in fact, he enjoyed it—but scandals in public drove him to frenzy, as when a party of Romanovs became involved in a brawl in a racy Petersburg café. A grand duchess had lightheartedly dared an entertainer to show her what he had done to make the people in the next room laugh so much, and the man, after demurring, finally bent over and kissed the royal cheek. Fists were soon flying between enraged Romanov men and the entertainers, while the bejeweled ladies engaged in a losing match of hair pulling and scratching with the gypsy girls. Such incidents were rare in an otherwise dazzling, extravagant era, for the adult Romanovs feared the wrath of the patriarch in Gatchina who loved to play with children and was faithful to his wife.

3. Blind Reactionary

As the 1880's passed, Russia seemed to stand still. What was officially boasted of as public calm was in actuality shocked silence on the part of the intelligentsia. Emboldened by the seeming acceptance of his antiliberal regime, the tsar even attempted to set the clock back in certain of his policies by reversing the reforms of his predecessor. Yet Alexander was unknowingly responsible for some new departures in Russian economy and foreign policy which were to make the forward movement of revolution irresistible.

Alexander had mastered the routine of ruling but was too parochial of mind to grasp the larger issues. According to one observer, the tsar deliberately shunned everything but administrative details.

[He] prefers to transact business with his ministers and generals rather by writing than by word of mouth, as he wishes to avoid the discussion of subjects with which he is unfamiliar. As a matter of duty he receives hundreds of his subjects from all parts of his enormous Empire; but he never allows them to discuss minute points, because he fears explanations which may lead to difficulties. He avoids as far as possible direct and lengthy transactions with foreign diplomatists because he has no confidence in his power of estimating them at their proper value, and because he has less facility in expressing himself in French than he would like to avow. Conscientious and industrious, he has gradually learnt to master the little round of his official duties: what lies outside this is carefully avoided, and for this reason meetings and intercourse with foreign monarchs are limited to the utmost (his friendly and unpretentious father-in-law naturally excepted).

This unfriendly evaluation of the tsar was basically a true picture of a man of limited mind with unlimited responsibilities.

The Russian intellectual community was aghast in 1885 at an imperial manifesto extolling a kind of modern feudalism. On the occasion of the hundredth anniversary of Catherine's Charter of Nobility, the tsar proclaimed that "Russian nobles preserve the preponderance in the command of the army, in local administration and in the courts, and in the propagation by their example of the precepts of faith and loyalty and sound principles of popular education." This anachronistic appeal was backed up in practice by revitalizing the Nobles Land Bank to provide them easy credit as a "means of preserving for their posterity the estates in their possession." In twenty years one-third of all the estates of the nobility were mortgaged to the state, a commentary on the business abilities at least of the most privileged class.

Another backward-looking step came in 1889, when the Zemsky chiefs were instituted. These officials, to be hated and notorious in time, were elected by the local nobility, confirmed by the minister of the interior, and then set over the self-governing organizations of the peasants. In a related move the following year, the regime remodeled the Zemstvos in a retrogressive manner. A new City Statute in 1892 increased the property qualifications for participation in municipal self-government, so that in the case of St. Petersburg the number of voters decreased from 21,000 to 8,000, out of a population of 1,000,000.

Alexander's official acts to reverse political progress were matched by new efforts within the revolutionary movement. Marxist-oriented Russians led by Plekhanov had an effective propaganda group functioning abroad by 1882, and both they and remnants of the People's Will became affiliated with the powerful Second International of world Socialists, founded in

1889. The first open May Day demonstration took place in St. Petersburg in 1891. A decided upsurge in political ferment followed the great famine of 1891–92, a crop failure combined with a cholera epidemic that ravaged a score of provinces. What many people realized was that government disorganization was as much at fault as the disaster of nature: Food stocks and medicines were available, if only the ministries of the Interior and Finance could stop fighting subversives and each other long enough to do something. The Zemstvos proved to be the most effective relief organizations, and this success served to revive the aspirations of thousands of liberals. The cries of public outrage had been led by Leo Tolstoy, and the opposition to the autocracy, renewed after 1891, never died down again.

In 1887 the police had discovered a plot to assassinate the tsar by student perpetuators of the People's Will. Among the executed conspirators was Alexander Ulianov, older brother of the man to be known as Lenin, who was expelled from the University of Kazan that year for revolutionary activities. Another victim of the wave of arrests in 1887 was Joseph Pilsudski, actually an opponent of terrorist methods but a forceful young nationalist and Socialist, who was to return from Siberian exile to help found the Polish Socialist Party in 1894 and decades later was to become his country's dictator.

The destruction of Alexander III and his entire family nearly came about in 1888, when the imperial train was violently derailed in a gorge at Biorki. All the royal party were in the dining car, when it was suddenly lifted from the tracks and wrenched apart except for the roof, which came down on the tsar's back. The Herculean ruler actually found himself standing in the roadbed, and he doggedly shouldered the wreckage until his wife and children were pulled to safety. His brave act may have impaired his health ever after. The revolutionists were immediately blamed for the near tragedy, but the police found no evidence of a bomb plot by them, nor was there any ground for the ensuing newspaper hysteria about possible machinations by the Jewish railroad owners.

The Biorki disaster was finally explained to Alexander's satisfaction only after a bright young man in the railroad administration submitted a report that the imperial train was going too fast. The official's name was Sergius Witte, and this man was forthwith named minister of railroads and soon afterward minister of finance. In the latter post Witte was to preside over fantastically rapid changes in the Russian economy all through the decade of the 1890's and beyond. Witte has even been called the founder of Russian capitalism, a kind of state capitalism or superpaternalism. Alexander supported him in many economic innovations, the most dramatic of which was the Trans-Siberian Railroad, begun in 1891. The grandiose railroad helped spur industrialization generally, and the number of city workers increased drastically. Such was the kind of economic revolution the tsar sponsored, while at the same time treating Russia politically as if it were the patrimony of a medieval prince.

In foreign policy, too, Alexander III unwittingly inaugurated trends that could not fail eventually to shake dynasty and country. At the beginning of his reign the tsar made clear his paramount desire for peace in order to consolidate the regime internally. In 1881 he joined Austria and Germany in a revival of the Three Emperors' League, forgiving them the humiliations of 1878 in the interests of a common front against revolution. These official friendships did Alexander little good in the face of two major diplomatic crises. One was a new confrontation with Britain in 1885 after a Russian expedition occupied Merv and appeared to threaten Afghanistan. Unlike his predecessor, Alexander III was able to hold back the expansionists, squelching a general's project to invade India and instigate a social revolution there. The second crisis involved recently independent Bulgaria, where the ruling prince proved not to be the expected Russian puppet and was forced to abdicate in 1887. Then the new Hohenzollern prince given to the Bulgarians chose to ally his country not with Russia, but with Austria. During the complicated diplomatic maneuvers Serbia also turned to Russia's rival in the Balkans. In 1889 a disillusioned Alexander made a startling toast to the visiting Prince of Montenegro: "To Russia's only sincere and faithful friend."

The semisecret German-Austrian Alliance of 1879 was directed specifically at Russia. The diplomatic expedient advocated by Katkov and others was a counteralliance of Russia and France. Yet at first Alexander mastered his anti-German feelings and maintained the sentimental ties to Kaiser William I, his uncle and a fellow archconservative. Bismarck, whom the tsar distrusted but admired, cleverly lulled Russian suspicions by concluding a Reinsurance Treaty with Alexander in 1887, whereby Germany disassociated itself from any possible Austrian aggression. Then the old kaiser died in 1888, to be succeeded by the brash, sword-rattling William II. The Reinsurance Treaty was allowed to lapse, and Bismarck himself was dismissed from the chancellorship in 1890. The next year a French naval squadron paid a ceremonial visit to Kronstadt, and there the world was treated to the strange spectacle of the autocrat of Russia standing bareheaded on the deck of the flagship while the band played the "Marseillaise," a song otherwise banned in Russia as revolutionary.

Russian-French military agreements followed in 1892, and the Third Republic went wild with joy when Alexander's navy paid a return call at Toulon in 1893. A hard and fast alliance with France, directed against Germany, was signed in early 1894. One of the first actions of the new allies was a joint diplomatic intervention against Japan, since the Far East was an area in which Russia was becoming increasingly interested and increasingly belligerent. In these ways, the avowedly old-fashioned Russian, the would-be Alexis named Alexander III, launched Russia into the fateful toils of imperialist power politics.

Crudely chauvinistic reports of Russian foreign affairs were acceptable journalistic fare in the eyes of Alexander's censors, as were Siberian adventure tales, sex sensationalism, and other kinds of escapist literature. A genuine intellectual ferment was the last thing desired by the tsar, Pobedenostsev, and Katkov, and their repressive efforts were rewarded by a stunned silence in Russian cultural circles. The idealistic populism and exalted realism of the 1860's and 1870's gave way to depression, and the exciting—indeed, astonishing—achievements in literature and the arts were replaced by petty accomplishments. Death had claimed virtually all the greats by 1887—the writers Turgenev, Ostrovsky, and Dostoievsky and the musicians Borodin and Moussorgsky. (Dostoievsky's and Moussorgsky's graves are side by side in the cemetery of the Alexander Nevsky Lavra.)

Tolstoy remained, now less a literary celebrity than a thunderous voice advocating a Christian Socialism. Officially in complete disfavor, Tolstoy found the censor banning the sale of his dramatic masterpiece of 1889, *The Power of Darkness,* a searing and disturbing view of peasant degradation. The one major new talent was Anton Chekhov, a doctor who gave up his profession after the acclaim that greeted his first short stories in 1886. Chekhov's harsh tales of ordinary Russian people aptly conveyed the wider gloom of the reign.

Peter Tchaikovsky emerged as the master Russian musician in the 1880's. His famous ballets *Swan Lake* and *The Nutcracker* were to be described as "child-like interludes of graceful fancy for a harassed people." The harasser, Alexander III, was personally a great enthusiast of ballet and opera, and his special passion for Tchaikovsky's *Eugene Onegin* helped explain its popularity. Here was an entirely Russian-theme opera, lushly melancholy in its music and safely nonideological in its story of personal tragedy among the best people. Tchaikovsky died of cholera in 1893, just nine days after conducting his Sixth Symphony, called the *Pathétique* for its expressing a matchless intensity of personal frustration and grief in a frustrating age. Beautiful melancholy is likewise the dominant impression produced in the music of Sergius Rachmaninoff, whose 1893 opera, *Aleko,* was the start of his fame.

Russian science continued to make notable strides, often in spite of the regime. The chemist Dmitri Mendeleev, most noted for his periodic table, was just one of several internationally celebrated scientists who lost academic posts for being politically suspect. In 1883 a Russian inventor piloted a primitive airplane in a demonstration at the army camp of Krasnoe Selo. The tsar's generals ignored this feat as studiously as Soviet writers have since boasted of it.

The reign of Alexander III was over after just fourteen years. The health of the seemingly indestructible giant had deteriorated ever since the Biorki accident of 1888. In the summer of 1894 Alexander's condition was so bad that the imperial family left early for the healthful shores of the Black Sea, but once at Livadiya Palace Alexander was informed by his doctors that he had nephritis and would live but a few months. His death came in November.

To liberals, to the politicians who tried desperately to master the explosions of 1905 and 1917, the reign of Alexander III seemed all one dreadful provocation. To conservatives, to the old men who survived to haunt Paris cafés in the 1920's, the reign of the giant tsar represented the good old days. In their eyes the next to last tsar's sincerity, honesty, and devotion to duty counted only less than his sheer force of will. Everyone would agree that the autocracy died in 1894. Alexander III represented a last try, a swan song. His statue is left standing in Leningrad today, the Soviet regime affecting to see a satiric intent on the part of the sculptor, Prince Paul Trubetskoy. The huge equestrian monument is stern and immobile, a symbol, intentionally or not, of a frozen era.

XVIII.
Nicholas II: Unhappy Beginnings

1. The Little Colonel

THE giant tsar, Alexander III, was succeeded by his slight and unprepossessing son, Nicholas II. Their difference in physical stature was symbolic of profound and ultimately disastrous changes in the governing of Russia. Decisiveness was replaced by hesitancy. Force of will gave way to willfulness. The frank avowal of authority subsided in favor of deviousness and intrigue. Policy making eventually moved from the tsar's office to the tsarina's boudoir. The great officers of state in time counted for less than a debauched, self-styled man of God.

Nicholas was to enjoy a lifelong love affair with his wife and the greatest happiness in the company of his family, yet his actions brought about the murder of them all. The most conscientious of rulers and the most patriotic of Russians, Nicholas delivered his country over to unprecedented chaos and change, the loss of millions of lives, and an all-transforming social revolution. In the end, a few survivors of the Romanov dynasty, ruined and in exile, were left to ponder how Nicholas had failed them or, perhaps, how they had failed Nicholas.

Nicholas Alexandrovich was born in 1868 on May 6, according to the Old Style Russian calendar. In the eyes of the church, Nicholas' birthday fell on the Day of Job, a coincidence the tsar often mentioned to his ministers in later years. Whereas the infant who became Ivan the Terrible had to contend with merely the curse of a contemporary churchman, Nicholas could turn to the pages of divine Scripture itself and read Job's discourse of despair: "Let the day perish wherein I was born. . . . Let that day be darkness; let not God regard it from above, neither let the light shine upon it . . . let a cloud dwell upon it; let the blackness of the day terrify it."

Conscious of his birthright, Nicholas was to accept his trials fatalistically and unflinchingly. When responsibility was taken from him in the end, he seemed relieved, without remorse, and unaware of the possibility that his woe was self-made.

A healthy, normal child, Nicholas passed his early years without untoward incident. The heir of the heir to the throne soon had two convivial brothers, George and Michael, and two loving sisters, Xenia and Olga. The royal nursery encompassed five ornate rooms on the first floor of the Anichkov Palace. For the little grand dukes and grand duchesses of the 1870's life was mildly Spartan—things like camp beds and six o'clock risings, in accord with Victorian practice. There were no bathing facilities immediately at hand, however, so that it was not a case of cold showers but of giggling excursions to their mother's warm and luxurious bath on the third floor. There was the starchy but kindly governess, Scandinavian like her mistress. The governess' son became Nicholas' companion, and years later he was to write that his royal playmate was a lively and boisterous boy, although unassuming to the point of naïveté.

A charming vignette of Nicholas at the age of six is given by his cousin, contemporary, and lifelong confidant the Grand Duke Alexander Michaelovich. The scene was the bottom of the great marble staircase leading from Livadiya Palace to the rocky beach of the Black Sea. The two boys met and sized each other up for the first time. Nicholas wore a pink shirt, his eyes were instantly friendly, and he forthrightly extended his hand. "I guess you are my cousin Sandro. I didn't see you last summer in St. Petersburg. Your brothers said you were ill with scarlet fever. Don't you know me? I am your cousin Nicky, and this is my little sister Xenia."

The next recollection of "Nicky" by "Sandro" is of a darker day. It was in 1881. The place was St. Petersburg. Two explosions had heralded the assassination of Alexander II, and the horribly mangled body of Nicholas' grandfather was lying in the Winter Palace. He took in the whole scene "deathly pale in his blue sailor's suit," as he stood silently by his mother, who was still holding a pair of skates in her hands. At the age of thirteen Nicholas was confronted with the bitter truths of his heritage and his destiny.

The governess gave way to a tutor and numerous teachers. The tutor chosen by Alexander III for his tsarevich was a far call from the brilliant souls called on to mold the new tsar's namesakes and predecessors when they were young men. The first Alexander had the enlightened Jacobin, La Harpe; the second studied with the poet laureate of his day, Zhukovsky; Nicholas was placed in the care of General Gregory Danilovich, a man whose military exploits were obscure but whose conservative prejudices were all too apparent. Known as the Jesuit in court circles, General Danilovich was credited with developing in Nicholas great powers of self-discipline, a deep reserve, and an unquestioning faith in tsar and God. Nicholas' extraordinary ability to hide his inner feelings became the salient characteristic of the man, as well as of the youth.

Besides Danilovich, Nicholas was exposed to the tutelage of an eccentric Englishman, Charles Heath, who knew and cared nothing about the realities of his adopted country but who did implant in his charge a flawless command of spoken and written English. There was a succession of instructors of French, one of whom had to be dismissed after an erotic scandal, but another of whom had time to render an interesting report on his pupils, Nicholas and George, to their father. He wrote: "I am astonished at the docility, gentleness, and submissiveness of the grand dukes. . . . I have never caught a bit of boredom, lassitude, or impatience. . . . This evenness of humor, this spontaneous obedience is surprising."

When he was somewhat older, Nicholas was given special lessons by the venerable Constantine Pobedenostsev and lectures by Professor Basil Kliuchevsky, a fact that came as a surprise to many people since the censorship would not allow the publication of the writings of the man who was Russia's greatest historian. Pobedenostsev did no more than put the final seal on an already closed mind, while Kliuchevsky succeeded merely in inspiring in Nicholas a love of antiquity. Curious as it was to expose Nicholas to two great intellects of such opposite viewpoints, even more astonishing was the imperial etiquette that still restricted these men to lecturing their pupil without questioning him or giving him examinations. The identical method of instruction had obtained for the Tsarevich Alexis more than 200 years before.

Also, as with his remote Romanov predecessor, Nicholas was enjoined to keep a diary, which he maintained to his last days—frank, laconic, and untroubled by intellectual fancies or doubts.

Lack of inclination and tradition conspired to bring an end to Nicholas' formal education when he was eighteen. Now began his lifelong romance with the army. He started off as a squadron chief in the Hussars, the most elegantly uniformed and devil-may-care unit in the capital, and later he became commander of a battalion of the Preobrazhenskoe Guards, the preserve of the socially elite and politically ambitious. As in all things, Nicholas was a conscientious officer, whether conducting drills, making night checks of sentry boxes, or dealing with the personal problems of his men. The natural simplicity and generosity of the tsarevich, in contrast with the behavior of his relatives, made him popular with his fellow officers, and Nicholas rejoiced in their comradeship and in the complete lack of initiative expected of him. He also enjoyed the artificial but unceremonious life of barracks discussions, champagne parties, guitars, and group singing, with the outside world represented by nothing more alarming than the gypsy nightclubs. Nicholas' diary of these happy years honestly records his hangovers and the night he had to be carried home. Once he wrote: "It truly bothers me to go to bed so late all the time, but there isn't anything else to do."

The heir to the throne was too self-effacing to attract a smart young set about his person. His few close friends, like the young counts Sheremetev and the Count Vorontsov-Dashkov, were aristocrats with greater names than gifts. At court functions and at his mother's brilliant parties Nicholas was simply a docile attendant. In his father's presence he was completely awestruck, so overwhelmed by that authoritarian personality that he became diffident and secretive. It was a great relief for him that state affairs were a forbidden subject of discussion during the routine of royal family life. Describing Nicholas when he was twenty-one, an observer at the court declared that "he so much loses himself in the crowd that it is difficult to distinguish him from the mass. A little Hussar officer, not ill-favored, but commonplace, insignificant." Soon afterward people began to refer to the Romanov heir as the little colonel.

So far Nicholas' preparation for ruling after he turned eighteen was confined to attentive but silent attendance at meetings of the Council of State. A genuine opportunity for service came when Witte proposed that he be named president of a committee to facilitate the construction of the Trans-Siberian Railroad. Alexander III was astonished at the proposal. "But do you know the Grand Duke, my heir? Have you ever had a serious conversation with him? He is a child. His reasoning is childish. How could he preside over this committee?" Despite his father's disdain, Nicholas got the job and acquitted himself well.

His fellow officers and his uncles took less interest in Nicholas' politics than in his sex life. In time he was prodded into having an affair with an entertainer at a Petersburg restaurant, but this episode was cut short by the prefect of police, who provided the girl with a one-way ticket to Paris. Subsequently, Nicholas began a long involvement with a Polish ballet dancer, Matilda Kshessinska. The tsar himself had a hand in this affair by directing that Nicholas sit down at a table with Matilda following a recital at the dancing school. At the end of the evening, according to her memoirs, she and the tsarevich felt "irresistibly attracted to each other." She was very young, more vivacious than pretty, and genuinely talented as an artist.

The romance was interrupted in 1891, when Nicholas made a trip to the Far East. Although the tsarevich had already visited Denmark and Germany to see relatives, he broke with tradition by not going on the grand tour of the Western capitals. Instead, he journeyed to the Orient on a warship accompanied by his intelligent and perceptive brother George, but unfortunately sickness forced the grand duke to return to Russia halfway out. An assortment of carefree princes and a supremely ignorant general were Nicholas' other companions on what became strictly a luxury excursion: at Cairo, camel rides and the Pyramids; at Bombay, a tiger hunt on elephant back; at Saigon, temples and a tumultuous welcome from Russia's would-be French allies. In the face of so many official ceremonies, Nicholas himself wrote that he might as well have stayed home: "Palaces and generals are the same everywhere." The trip nearly ended in tragedy. Several days after his arrival in Japan, Nicholas was set upon by a fanatic wielding a samurai sword. The first slash across his temple scarred Nicholas for life, causing no brain damage but producing eventual headaches. A second, possibly fatal, blow was fended off by the action of Nicholas' cousin Prince George of Greece. Despite the most obsequious apologies from the Japanese imperial family, Alexander III ordered his son home forthwith. Before the long return trip overland, Nicholas laid the first stone for the Trans-Siberian Railroad.

On his return to St. Petersburg Nicholas did his duty by his parents and the next evening rushed off to the home of Kshessinska. Despite the gossip well under way and despite her family, Kshessinska boldly moved into a house of her own, a mansion originally built by the Grand Duke Constantine for *his* prima ballerina, the artistic title Kshessinska herself soon acquired. The idyll came to an end after two years when Nicholas announced, not altogether honestly, that he was departing for Europe to meet the princess who had been designated as his wife.

Nicholas' parents were not shocked about his little ballerina; it was simply a matter of continuing the Romanov line and of putting an end to much journalistic speculation and court intrigue. With the son of the Prince of Wales of England newly married, Nicholas was the most eligible royal bachelor in Europe. One of his visits to Germany gave the newspapers cause to link him to the Princess Margaret, youngest sister of Kaiser William II. The rumor caused immediate satisfaction in Berlin and little surprise in a St. Petersburg inured to German royal consorts for several generations. The match was vetoed, however, by Alexander III, whose anti-German feelings in general were fortified by the specific fact that Margaret's father had recently died of cancer of the throat, a disease the tsar thought might be carried on by "contaminated blood," an irony he would not live to realize. The Empress Marie was reported to be very favorable to a match with the French Bourbons in exile, but Nicholas had made his own choice and for one of the few times in his life persisted despite tremendous obstacles.

The princess destined to be the last Tsarina of Russia was Alix of Hesse-Darmstadt, daughter of the future Grand Duke Louis IV of that truly ancient German dynasty. Born in 1872, Alix could count among her ancestors Mary Queen of Scots and St. Elizabeth of Thuringia, the latter known in history for her surrender to the mystical blandishments of a cruel monk. Alix's mother, who was the fourth daughter of Queen Victoria, died when Alix was six, and the little German princess was brought up by her formidable but loving grandmother in the great English palaces of Windsor, Sandringham, and Balmoral. Indeed, Alix was to remain all her life a Victorian Englishwoman in the full sense of the term. The premature death of her mother followed shortly afterward by the loss of her older brother and her younger sister produced in Alix a deeply reflective and religious nature, an utter seriousness about life. Yet for all her sadness of expression and seeming unconcern with outward appearance, Alix in her teens developed into one of the most strikingly beautiful princesses of Europe— golden-haired, blue-eyed, tall, graceful, and stately.

Nicholas was sixteen and Alix twelve when they first met in St. Petersburg in 1884 during the wedding of her sister Elizabeth to his uncle Sergius. If a few observers at the time found amusement in detecting a flirtation between the young pair, Alix herself, writing to her husband during the First World War, could passionately avow that "thirty-two years ago my child's heart already went out to you in deep love." Their next encounter was in 1889 during a six weeks' visit by Alix to her sister, and on this occasion all St. Petersburg society took the trouble to appraise the princess. (Her beauty counted as a great plus; her shy aloofness a great minus.)

Nicholas again met Alix in the summer of 1894, this time during a grand concourse of royalty at Coburg for the marriage of the Grand Duke of Hesse. There is a well-known photograph of the occasion with Queen Victoria seated in the center, her grandson Kaiser William fawning at her side, Nicholas in a derby and Alix at her most ravishing standing side by side behind, and the others grouped around, including two empresses of Germany and the Russian grand duchesses Sergius and Vladimir. All these gave encouragement as Nicholas pressed for an engagement with Alix. The first formal interview had been very discouraging: "She looked particularly pretty but extremely sad. They left us alone, and then began between us that talk I so long wanted and so much feared. We talked to twelve but with no result; she still objects to changing her religion. Poor girl, she cried a lot. . . ." In a few days, however, Alix capitulated. To his mother, whose belated consent to a German union was a crucial factor, Nicholas wrote in triumph: "The whole world is changed for me: nature, mankind, everything, and all seem to be good and lovable and happy."

On his return to Russia, Nicholas broke with Kshessinska and soon was off to England on the yacht *Polar Star* to spend several weeks with "Granny" (Queen Victoria). There were boating parties and picnics on the Thames, and Granny even permitted chaperonless drives. At one point Nicholas told of his past liaisons, a confession that induced Alix to write: "I lack words to tell you of my love and admiration—that which is past is past. We all undergo temptations when we are young."

That summer in England was the nearest thing to a honeymoon that Nicholas and Alix ever had, for in the fall of 1894 came the unexpected death of Alexander III. Alix was hastily summoned to the Crimea in October to receive the dying tsar's blessing. Amid the last days of sorrow and confusion Alix saw fit to insert a note in her fiancé's diary, a note portending their whole future relationship:

> Sweet child, pray to God. . . . Your Sunny is praying for you and the beloved patient. . . . Be firm and make the doctors . . . come alone to you every day . . . so that you are the first always to know. Don't let others be put first and you left out. . . . Show your own mind and don't let others forget who you are.

Already Alix was well aware of her betrothed's self-effacing tendencies.

While still in the Crimea, Alix made her conversion to the Orthodox faith as Alexandra Fedorovna, there being no Alix in the church calendar. Fedorovna was a traditional patronymic of the Romanovs. During the endless funeral ceremonies, the betrothed of the new tsar was first presented to the Russian public, and she made a distinctly bad impression, for her face appeared saddest of all, a combination of her natural seriousness with her awareness of new sorrows and burdens.

Mourning was briefly put aside for the wedding in November, 1894. The ceremony in the chapel of the Winter Palace saw a harassed-looking Nicholas, resplendent in his red Hussar's uniform with a white cloak on one shoulder, and a set-lipped Alexandra, dazzling in white silk with silver flowers and a gold brocade mantle, her train carried by five chamberlains and her lovely head afire with the imperial diamonds. The crowds went wild after the *Te Deum* at Kazan Cathedral, and the Duke of York wrote off to Granny: "I never saw two people more in love with each other." Within the month Nicholas was to note in his diary that his was the "greatest bliss on this earth," to which Alexandra added: "I would never have believed that one could have so perfect a happiness in this world, such a sentiment of unity between two human beings."

2. Bumbler from the Start

Nicholas' first impulse was to renounce the throne. According to his diary, in the days following his father's death he spent "long hours on the beach of the Black Sea plunged in the most dismal thoughts." In the end, he was brought to a sense of his duty by the local military governor, and Nicholas thereafter bore his burden manfully for twenty-three years. Once he allowed himself the wistful observation to an ambassador that he would have preferred to be a sailor than to be tsar.

The first months of the reign were a nightmare, with the funeral arrangements, the hasty wedding, and policy setting all competing for attention. The dowager empress emerged strong and helpful from her grief, and it was to her Anichkov Palace that Nicholas and Alexandra moved following their marriage. That Nicholas turned so completely to his mother for advice and comfort was as natural as it was rankling to his bride. The young imperial couple, despite their great love, were together very seldom because of Nicholas' obligations of state.

Unlike many previous Romanovs who could hardly wait to fire their predecessor's advisers, Nicholas kept on his father's ministers, the two most influential being Pobedenostsev in the Holy Synod and Witte in Finance. The young tsar was not of a sort to assert himself against these prestigious older men, one his former teacher. An even worse situation was dealing with the several bristling uncles and cousins who proceeded to arrogate to themselves full authority over their chosen positions, whether the command of the army, or the direction of the navy, or the governorship of the city of Moscow. Ceremonious deference to their sovereign in public gave way in private to subjecting their nephew to shattering displays of argumentation, swearing, and fist pounding. Most to be feared by Nicholas was a private interview with the Grand Duke Sergius, his former regimental commander. A resentful but largely helpless witness to Nicholas' predicament was his wife, who wrote a childhood friend the following: "I feel that all who surround my husband are insincere . . . serving him for their career and personal advantage, and I worry myself and cry for days on end. . . ." "We" versus "they," with "they" rather all-inclusive, became an increasing obsession of Alexandra.

Practically the first of Nicholas' public statements was a major blunder. A delegation of liberals from Tver Province included in their congratulatory address the hope "that the voice of the people's need will always be heard from the height of the throne." Nicholas' initial reaction to this was sympathetic enough, but thereafter he was persuaded by Pobedenostsev that the phrase hid subversive notions. When the tsar confronted the delegation, he saw fit to score "the senseless dream of participation by Zemstvo representatives in internal government" and concluded with the declaration that "in devoting all my strength on behalf of the welfare of my people, I shall defend the principles of autocracy as unswervingly as my deceased father."

Nicholas' formal coronation took place in Moscow during May, 1896, and proceeded from minor mishaps to a major disaster. There were portents for those that sought them: While dressing the empress, a lady-in-waiting pricked her finger and got blood on the ermine; during the crowning, the Order of St. Andrew, one of the highest and oldest decorations of the empire, fell from the emperor's shoulders clattering on the floor (rumor eventually magnified this incident into the tsar's dropping his scepter).

People observed that the imperial couple seemed unusually pensive and grim-faced, and the popular response to the new empress was chilly in contrast with the cheers brought forth by the appearance of the Dowager Empress Marie. Otherwise, the ceremonies went off among the great cathedrals of the Kremlin in faithful accord with the traditions handed down since the fifteenth century. Visibly moved, Nicholas never allowed himself to forget that he had been anointed as the autocratic representative of God on earth.

Tragedy struck some miles away from the Kremlin on the field of Khodinka, where, also in accordance with tradition, several hundred thousand peasants and workers were assembled to receive the newly crowned tsar's bounty in the form of food and drink and commemorative tin cups or plates with the imperial eagle and monogram. There were not enough of the last-mentioned prizes; army exercises had cut up the fields with treacherous ditches; and, above all, police controls were inadequate and faulty. A sickening melee in the early morning caused no less than 2,000 casualties. The royal party reached the scene after passing the first carts taking away corpses, and hundreds of bodies were hastily put out of sight under the reviewing pavilion. When Nicholas became aware of the extent of the catastrophe, he proposed that he retire to pray at the nearest monastery, but once again, his generous first impulse was changed by his advisers, who argued that royal prestige required acting as if nothing had happened. In particular, the Grand Duke Sergius sought to minimize the incident, since, as governor general of Moscow, he was the most responsible. The very evening of the Khodinka deaths Nicholas not only appeared at a ball at the French Embassy but led the dancing with the empress.

Nicholas' reign had got off to a bad start, but the tsar soon settled into the routine of ruling, and the first ten years of his reign were only mildly eventful. People were able to consider their new sovereign leisurely and carefully. As Nicholas passed into his thirties, he revealed himself a complex individual. The tsar had dignity but was essentially shy, his great personal charm was counterbalanced by complete impassivity, he was intelligent without being wise, and his indecisiveness hid a basic willfulness.

Physically, in looks and in strength, Nicholas was endowed well beyond the average. However, like all the children of the Danish-born dowager empress, he lacked the huge stature of the previous generation of grand dukes. Of medium height, Nicholas was well proportioned and muscular, his facial features and hands suggesting refinement without the decadence observable in some of his generation of Romanovs. The tsar was to be singularly healthy throughout his life, a man devoted to swimming, rowing, tennis, and hunting. One time he wished to test out the new uniform, pack, and gear being issued the Russian infantry; he did so, without fanfare, by donning the full equipment and going off on a strenuous eight-hour hike.

When the tsar rode alone before great masses of troops or when he stood still to review the onrush and sudden halt of thousands of cavalry during the exercises in the Field of Mars, he was at ease and seemed the most commanding of men. Yet at small gatherings of people he betrayed nervousness and diffidence. His habit of twisting his mustache during receptions suggested discomfiture, and his soft voice and gentle movements, without a trace of his father's brusqueness, gave the impression of a lack of assurance.

Of fine bearing before a crowd, ill at ease with a group, Nicholas was altogether relaxed and relaxing in a private interview. He had "a charm that attracted all who came near him," wrote the British ambassador, George Buchanan, who had to remind himself he was talking to an emperor. One official referred to "his usual simplicity and friendliness"; another noted "a rare kindness of heart." Even Witte, something of a boor himself and a critic of the new tsar, could not refrain from saying, "I have never in my life met anyone who had nicer manners than our Emperor." Nicholas' beautiful blue eyes were particularly magnetic: They were sad rather than bright; they appealed for rather than commanded support.

The other side of Nicholas' anxiousness to be pleasing was his abhorrence of scenes. To avoid unpleasantness or to shield himself from it, Nicholas cultivated in himself an attitude of complete impassivity. This imperturbability, particularly his silence in the face of bad news, was taken by many as an indication of indifference or heartlessness, but actually it was the defense mechanism of a sensitive person who as a youth had to cope with the brutal manners of an Alexander III and a General Danilovich. Nicholas' outward serenity also reflected an inward calm, a basic acceptance of things. His religious convictions fortified his basic fatalism.

To his duties as ruler Nicholas brought goodwill, a willingness to work, and a natural intelligence that fell short of either intellectual brilliance or intuitive understanding. The testimony of all the Russian officials who served the tsar is that he was anything but stupid. Yet, while Nicholas' comprehension was rapid, it was superficial. A general expressed it aptly when he wrote: "Nicholas II was a miniaturist. The view of the whole escaped him. He was incapable of coordinating his very numerous impressions and of drawing concrete conclusions from them."

The ready charm and quickness of mind ill concealed Nicholas' basic lack of self-confidence. "His force of will does not correspond to the sincerity of his intentions," a friendly British ambassador concluded, while a German diplomat was eager to report that the tsar was "hesitant and dilatory in his decisions" and was known "most often to go along with the enterprise of whoever happened to speak with him last." This basic feebleness was "the source of all the misfortunes of Russia," according to Witte.

Whereas Alexander III was his own prime minister, Nicholas merely parceled out authority, hiring and firing ministers according to his impressions of the moment. The choice of officials was haphazard in the extreme, often incomprehensible to people who considered themselves politically astute. For example, Nicholas had to appoint a minister of the interior early in the reign. He was persuaded at the time by Pobedenostsev not to name Sipiagin—"an imbecile"—or Plehve—"a scoundrel." Nonetheless, four and seven years later respectively, each of these men was appointed to that job. A still later minister of the interior cynically admitted that he owed his position to his faculty for telling Nicholas funny stories. Eventually all officials found that Nicholas' confidence in them was shallow and short-lived. Often ministers interpreted Nicholas' refusal to come to the point as agreement with them, only to read in the newspapers of their dismissal. Others learned to read their fate in Nicholas' preoccupation with objects on his desk and the faraway looks directed at the window. Double-dealing became the chief characteristic of the new regime. A minister could never be sure what other people had Nicholas' ear and who most recently.

For all his impressionableness and hesitance, Nicholas had a few basic principles, perhaps better termed obsessions. One fixation was the overriding importance of the Russian army. Parades filled Nicholas with ecstasy, as they did virtually all his predecessors, and the last Romanov was completely blind to any alternatives to a militaristically dedicated society. Equally obsessive was Nicholas' regard for the autocracy, the sacredness of maintaining unimpaired absolutism being fortified in his mind by his oaths at the paternal deathbed and at the coronation. Nicholas rarely bothered to justify this principle. Once he told Prince Trubetskoy, combining mysteriousness and glibness, that he would be glad to share power with the people but that this would mean to them their "triumph over the tsar" and forthwith they would "efface the superior classes of society from the surface of the earth." It was later said, with good reason, that the forces of the occult that triumphed during the reign began with the tsar himself.

In a position to be obstinate and willful, Nicholas could not give firm and unambiguous direction to the state. In these respects, he closely resembled Louis XVI of France, who also was perfectly mannered, well intentioned, and brave. And like his French counterpart, Nicholas welcomed the fatal domination of an ambitious, ill-informed, foreign wife.

In the first years, when Nicholas was mastering the task of appearing to rule Russia, Alexandra gave him but minimal support, for the tsarina had severe difficulties of her own. Both in 1889 and in 1894 she had been received hostilely by society, and the estrangement became mutual and grew. What was truly appealing in Alexandra's character, her directness and truthfulness, was not allowed to show forth because of the rigors of

Russian court etiquette. If Alexandra could have been regally banal, super-ficial, and frivolous, she might have been accepted; she could not and was not.

In public the empress seldom smiled and never was first to smile. An ambassador declared that the tsarina gave the impression of wanting to get every interview over as soon as possible. With delegations she became nervous and virtually catatonic.

The members of the imperial family failed or refused to make things easier for Alexandra. The Dowager Empress Marie, whom Alexandra called Motherdear, scarcely concealed her reservations about her daughter-in-law, and the older woman's persisting vivaciousness, charm, and dignity seemed almost a deliberate challenge to the younger's hesitancy and chilli-ness. If the dowager was generous in giving support to her son during his initial trials, she was selfish or at best unthinking with his expatriated, lonely, and inexperienced bride. In the days before the coronation, Alex-andra was shocked to find that the dowager claimed precedence over her: Marie went into dinner on Nicholas' arm while Alexandra had to content herself with the senior grand duke. The dowager kept not only her vast private collection of jewels but also the tiaras, necklaces, brooches, and rings on loan from the state treasury. After a scene, some of the jewels were relinquished, but not so the charitable activities traditionally associated with the tsarina. In these, Alexandra had to take second place or to start out on her own.

During the first winter season Alexandra bore the humiliation of being a guest in her mother-in-law's house, living in a small suite in the Anichkov Palace. In the spring of 1895 the dowager was departed for the relative seclusion of Gatchina Palace while the young imperial couple took up residence in Tsarskoe Selo, the complex of palaces a few miles south of the capital that had been the favorite of Alexander II and Princess Yuriev-skaya and unused since their day. The young tsarina renovated the Alex-ander Palace there to her own taste, which ran to cumbersome mahogany furniture and cozy corners.

Without the gifts and without the determination to cut a figure in society, Alexandra's attempts to establish her court met with small success. Her painfully learned Russian, which was absolutely essential with the servants, brought derisive smiles from the younger, nationalistic generation, while her halting French failed to satisfy the older. Her native German pleased no one, and few understood English, which was the language she and Nicholas used in both conversation and writing.

Her Victorian ways of thinking also set society against her. Simple prudishness on Alexandra's part led her to pare the invitation lists for her first official ball at the Winter Palace, eliminating those touched by divorce or other scandal. The result was that almost nobody came, to Nicholas' puzzlement and his mother's amusement. On another occasion, Alexandra's obvious disapproval cast a pall on the production of an unexpurgated *Hamlet* arranged for the court by the talented Grand Duke Constantine. The tsarina's frank expressions of outrage at their extravagances alienated many of the aristocracy. The willingness of Russians to talk of private scandals was incomprehensible to the tsarina, and the casual freedom with which people gossiped about the imperial family horrified her. "St. Petersburg is a rotten city, not an atom Russian," Alexandra once declared, indicating both her frustrations and her delusions.

Even Alexandra's entourage found her fussy and trying. The tsarina's behavior on the royal train caused particular discontent within and without. Rather than acknowledge the curiosity and presumed loyalty of the crowds at railroad stations, she would order the blinds drawn. As for the staff on the train, one of them succinctly stated: "We were all more gay and talkative when she wasn't there."

Russians were always complimented when foreign consorts of their tsars took an outward interest in the Orthodox Church. Alexandra's conversion to Orthodoxy, however, was deeply inward and assumed an alarming intensity, consistent with the wholeheartedness of her personality. For her, Orthodoxy became the only true religion, and ignoring many people's charitable, indulgent, and haphazard interpretation of this faith, Alexandra plunged enthusiastically into its ritualistic and theological aspect. She outdistanced even church officials with her interest in visiting sanctuaries, collecting icons, and discovering new saints. She became particularly receptive to mystics and fanatics. From religion Alexandra developed the self-assurance she could not find in society. She prayed only for guidance, unlike her fatalistic husband, who prayed for mercy.

In politics, as well as in religion, Alexandra became a convert and fanatic. For Alexandra, Russia came to mean the autocracy, involving a mystic equation between the tsar and the peasants, with the nobility and the intelligentsia a superfluous, if not harmful, quantity. She even lectured her grandmother: "Russia is not England. Here it is not necessary to make efforts to gain popular affection." To a young aristocrat who, wishing to avoid the army, avowed that he could best serve his country and the tsar as a private citizen, she rejoined: "But the Tsar is Russia!" And was it simple wife's pride or lofty fanaticism that lead the tsarina to complain so insistently to Repin about Nicholas' portrait in progress that Russia's greatest painter thrust palette and brushes at her in disgust?

In their personal relationship Nicholas and Alexandra maintained a perpetual romance. When apart, the royal couple exchanged letters daily or even more often, and these all contained expressions of the deepest affection, as did the advance entries Alexandra sometimes slipped into Nicholas' diary. "Thank you on my knees for all your love, affection, friendship, and patience," Alexandra once wrote, on another occasion declaring she loved Nicholas "as a man was rarely loved." In this attraction of opposites, the charmer of a man made up for his inhibited wife, at the same time respecting her as an authoritarian figure. They were boundlessly grateful to each other.

The comparative uneventfulness of the early years of Nicholas' reign was delusory; actually a tremendous ferment was going on in Russian society—economic, cultural, and political. Nicholas, however, remained largely unaware of the forces at work. The revolutionary and historian Trotsky declared that "between [Nicholas'] consciousness and his epoch there stood some transparent but absolutely impenetrable medium." After ten years Nicholas became involved in a war and then in a revolution at home, both of which were handled badly. The war of 1904 and the Revolution of 1905 were dress rehearsals for the later cataclysms, and Nicholas learned little or nothing from them.

But even Nicholas could not completely ignore the economic transformation that was going on in Russia. For more than a decade the young tsar had retained and given continuous backing to Witte, the minister of finance, the economic wizard who successfully promoted a kind of state capitalism. It was Witte who organized Russia's first census in 1897, revealing the nation as a potential giant with a population of nearly 130,000,000. It was Witte who, the same year, put Russia on the gold standard, gaining the confidence of the foreign money market. It was Witte who brought about the doubling of Russian railroad mileage, including the famed Trans-Siberian line, which opened that vast land to settlers, who came in the millions. Observing that the flow of peasants was a natural thing, the new tsar had for once obeyed his first impulse and ordered the authorities to assist, not persecute, the migrants.

During the 1890's Russia's industrial revolution occurred. Steel production, for example, almost quadrupled. Everywhere there were new or expanded factories: the heavy machine industries around St. Petersburg, including the huge Putilov works; the textile mills all about Moscow; the rich coal mines of the Donets (where Nikita Khrushchev began his working career soon after 1900); and the recently discovered oilfields of the Caucasus. From the Urals to Poland, Russia plunged into the machine age.

Philosophy and practical needs produced Russia's first organized political parties almost exactly at the turn of the century. They all were illegal, they all were persecuted, and they all flourished nonetheless. Drawing support from the Zemstvos and the professional classes, men like Paul

Miliukov started the journal *Liberation* in Germany in 1901 to preach representative government and property rights and, unknowingly, to prepare the way for the liberal party known as the Constitutional Democrats. Philosophic idealists, peasant Socialists, and anarchist terrorists were the main elements of the Socialist Revolutionaries (SR's), organized formally as a party at a secret congress in 1901 but actually the heirs of the Narodniks of the 1870's and of the assassins of Alexander II. Plekhanov and his bookish Marxism obtained a following, especially among city workers, and organizational structure followed through the efforts of Lenin (born 1870), Trotsky (born 1877), and Stalin (born 1879). These men and others brought about the launching of the Social Democratic Party in 1898, which was rich enough in ideas, if not numbers, to afford a split into right-wing and left-wing factions, Mensheviks and Bolsheviks, at their second congress in London in 1903.

Tsars can be forgiven for not spending their free moments studying philosophy, and Nicholas' police might be excused for not studying the substantial but easily obscured differences among liberals, SR's, Mensheviks, and Bolsheviks. All political activists were considered subversives, whether reformists or revolutionaries, whether laissez-faire economists or Socialists, and whether bomb throwers or peaceful propagandists. The police cannot be blamed for not recognizing a future foreign minister, a future war minister, and a future prime minister, respectively, when they arrested Miliukov in 1899, banished Trotsky in 1898, and sent Lenin off to Siberia in 1895. What *was* condemnable, however, was that Nicholas failed to appreciate the sheer numbers, sheer moral sincerity, and sheer influence of the opposition groups. The tsar was not sheltered or misinformed: There were detailed police reports twice a week that Nicholas conscientiously read and annotated. He chose stubbornly to go along with the fatuous assessment of Minister of the Interior Plehve who told the press that "the strength of the revolutionaries lies solely in the weakness of the police."

Quite aside from the newly hardened conspiratorial groups, there were increasingly open manifestations of discontent for Nicholas to ponder, but again he failed to understand. In the 1890's the Russian student movement at the universities in St. Petersburg and Moscow reached a pitch of political excitement. A student immolated herself as a protest against incarceration in Peter and Paul, and a riotous walkout occurred during opening-day ceremonies. The police replied by flogging demonstrators in the streets, and Nicholas simply ordered the immediate conscription of malcontents.

By 1900 Russia had acquired a new social class, the industrial workers or proletariat, numbering in the several millions. Already whole new sections of St. Petersburg to the north and to the south were known as worker suburbs, and the authorities found it increasingly difficult to keep groups of grubby types away from the Nevsky Prospekt, the boulevards, and the public gardens. Unions were illegal. The pressure to organize, however, was so strong that a police official named Zubatov suggested police-connected labor associations. The Zubatov unions, which became a pet project of the Grand Duke Sergius as governor general of Moscow, could not always be stopped from striking and rioting, and they were to backfire dramatically in time. Throughout Russia, as the new century advanced, spontaneous strikes involving hundreds of thousands of workers became a major problem.

Peasant unrest also flamed up anew, influenced less by the propaganda of revolutionaries than by the persisting hunger for land and bad harvests. In 1902, for example, the entire province of Poltava was given over to looting, arson, and the murder of landowners, causing troops to be called out and thousands of peasants to be arrested. Nicholas' response was a banal lecture to a mass of army recruits including these words: "One does not enrich oneself by pillaging the goods of others but by honest work and a life of obedience to the divine commandments."

To the growing unrest among the students, workers, and peasants was added the discontent of the non-Orthodox religious groups and the non-Russian nationalities, the latter amounting to about one-third of the population of the empire. Nicholas allowed himself many ethnic prejudices, and his reign saw new disgraces added to those perpetrated by his predecessors. Even Finns were driven into active opposition, Nicholas' personal dislike of this people negating the pleas and strictures of his Scandinavian mother. In the annals of religious oppression, a minor event of the early part of the reign was the emigration of 7,000 Dukhobors to Canada, another cause that stirred Tolstoy's eloquence. The major outrage of all, however, was intensified persecution of the Jews. In 1903, in a typical action, the police department forged and published the *Protocols of the Learned Elders of Zion,* a fabrication about ritual killing of child Christians and later a mainstay of Nazi anti-Semitism. In the same year there occurred the worst of the many pogroms that took place in southern Russia, the Kishinev Massacre, in which hundreds of Jews were killed or wounded during two days of rioting and lynching originally encouraged by the police and even joined in by the army units sent to restore order.

A new wave of assassinations soon confronted the regime. In 1901 the minister of education was gunned down by a student recently expelled from a university. The next year the victim was the minister of the interior, Sipiagin. His assassin was also a student but acted not as an individual but as a member of the SR terrorist group. Later a murder plot against the governor of Kharkov was successful, and a try against the governor of Ufa misfired. The tsar merely asked for more energy from his police.

In 1903 Nicholas went off to a remote village in the countryside. His mission, urged on him passionately by the tsarina, was the canonization of Seraphim, a local religious figure of true saintliness. A crowd of more than 100,000 people attended the ceremonies, and at one point a mob of zealots hoisted the tsar to their shoulders and carried him about in great fervor, trampling down members of the suite in the process. Nicholas returned to his capital convinced of the loyalty of all true Russians and humbly grateful for his popularity.

Blind to the real internal crisis, Nicholas devoted his prime attention to foreign affairs, and here, too, he let bad advisers eventually turn him on the road to catastrophe. One of the tsar's first acts was the reaffirmation of the alliance with France. In fact, in 1896, the newly crowned imperial couple made an unprecedented visit to republican France, enjoying a triumphant entry into Paris. The French put on a tremendous military review at Châlons; they invited Nicholas to lay the cornerstone of a new bridge in the center of the capital, then and now called le Pont Alexandre III^{ieme}; and they produced Sarah Bernhardt to give a reading in the Salon of Hercules at Versailles. In honor of the empress, the citizens of the Malakoff quarter (named after the French victory in the Crimea) petitioned, somewhat inaccurately, to be renamed Fedora-ville, and a movement was proposed to have all the children of the year named Olga after the tsar's firstborn.

The very year when Franco-Russian solidarity seemed a sure guarantee of peace in Europe, Nicholas let himself be temporarily enlisted in the Nelidov scheme, a reckless move in the Balkans that promised a futile and friendless war. "Scheme" was the only word for this idea of the Russian ambassador to the Ottoman Empire, Alexander Nelidov, to create incidents there to serve as a pretext for the landing of Russian troops at Constantinople to annex the straits. Nicholas, whose assent to this adventure was eager and unqualified, was eventually dissuaded by Witte and Pobedenostsev, the latter's first reaction being simply: "God help Russia!"

Another enterprise was an altogether opposite and worthwhile one—international disarmament. The tsar had been influenced by the scare book on future wars written by a Jewish railroad magnate—a somewhat incongruous person for Nicholas to listen to, except that his ideas were seconded by Witte, whose concern was primarily peaceful economic development, and by the war minister, who cynically realized that Russia could not afford at that juncture to match the improved equipment being introduced in the Austrian army. The Tsar of Russia became the main sponsor of the

First Hague Peace Conference of 1899, which unfortunately accomplished little beyond defining the rules of war, providing better treatment for prisoners, and outlawing the dropping of bombs from balloons for five years.

The Nelidov scheme and the Hague Conference marked the last signs of Russian interest in Europe for a period, as Nicholas' government turned enthusiastically and heedlessly into a forward policy in the Far East. Interest in this area began dramatically after the Sino-Japanese War of 1894–95, when Russia joined others to force Japan to give back one of her gains, Port Arthur, and allied herself, on economically profitable terms, with defeated China. The involvement deepened in 1898. Some German missionaries had been murdered by the Chinese, giving the kaiser the excuse to demand the port of Kiaochow as compensation. During a visit to St. Petersburg William II brought up the matter, and Nicholas later avowed that he could hardly refuse the request of a guest while out on a drive together. Accordingly, Germany annexed Kiaochow, and Russia helped itself to Port Arthur across the way, turning it into its major base in Asia. Britain, France, and Japan also gained during this battle for concessions.

"The Admiral of the Atlantic salutes the Admiral of the Pacific," the kaiser once wired the tsar after one of their seaborne meetings. The tsar's restrained reply was simply "Bon Voyage," but his actions suggested agreement. Indeed, the great Bismarck himself once said: "Russia has nothing to do in the West. She only contracts Nihilism and other diseases. Her mission is in Asia. There she stands for civilization."

When U. S. Secretary of State John Hay proposed in 1899 his Open Door policy regarding foreign commercial penetration in China, Nicholas' government refused cooperation, in the expectation of being able to carve off a large hunk of Chinese territory. The next fatal step came with the Boxer Rebellion of 1900, in which Chinese nationalists flailed out against all foreigners and even set about besieging the embassies of the great powers in Peking. The embassies were eventually rescued by an international relief column, the added and unnecessary Russian contribution being Russian occupation of all Manchuria.

Russian expansion in the Far East was viewed with increasing alarm by Japan, a country which, unlike China, had Westernized and armed itself with a vengeance in the brief period since it was opened by Commodore Perry in 1853. Japan was willing to negotiate, but its envoys were received icily by Nicholas, who went recklessly ahead with his own plans. Russia was not deterred even when Japan signed a military alliance with Britain in 1902.

In 1903 Nicholas ordered a halt to the evacuation of Manchuria by Russian troops, thereby breaking a previous promise. The same year he authorized an intensification of the activities of the East Asia Industrial Corporation, a private company financed by him, some generals, and court circles. His brother-in-law the Grand Duke Alexander Michaelovich was a major promoter of this adventure, which included infiltrating northern Korea with Russian troops disguised as lumberjacks. Finally, Nicholas established the viceroyalty of the Far East under Admiral Eugene Alexeyev, one of the most irresponsible of the expansionists, and thereby altogether removed Russian policy in that area from the control of the professional diplomats in the Foreign Ministry. Witte protested all these moves and was dismissed.

People later blamed Russia's misfortunes in the Far East on Nicholas' bad advisers, forgetting that the tsar himself was truly an adventurer, on a par with the worst intriguers in his entourage. Already in 1901 he had blithely confided to his brother-in-law that war with Japan was probably inevitable but that after five years Russia would be prepared for it.

With Russians already in Manchuria and Korea and with the tsar refusing to see the Japanese ambassador, Japan decided it had no alternative but to fight. On February 4, 1904, a sneak attack by the Japanese navy smashed the Russian squadron in Port Arthur. Nicholas received the news with his usual imperturbability on the way back from the opera. In his diary the next day he wrote: "Our losses are insignificant. . . . Everywhere there are touching manifestations revealing the unanimous enthusiasm of the people and their anger against Japanese insolence." Ignoring the fact that Russian bluff, bluster, and miscalculations had brought about the hostilities, Nicholas' generals and admirals looked to an easy victory.

The war 3,000 miles from Petersburg went badly for Russia from the outset, in part because of the tsar's failure to resolve command conflicts. As a result of the original surprise attack and subsequent naval encounters off Port Arthur, the Russian Far Eastern fleet was bottled up, and the Japanese landed troops in Korea at will. In May they defeated the Russian army on the Yalu River and then began a six months' land siege of Port Arthur.

At home a sensational event occurred in July, 1904—the assassination of the minister of the interior, Plehve, in broad daylight as he was going to deliver his police report to Nicholas. That the SR terrorist organization felt impelled to kill the hated minister was one thing, but that a police agent helped prepare the plot but failed to report it suggested that the government was as mad as it was oppressive. The emperor toyed with the idea of appointing another reactionary to the job (the man did get the post in 1916!) but was persuaded to placate public opinion by naming Prince Peter Sviatopolk-Mirsky, a liberal of integrity. Under Mirsky's benevolent eye, the press became critically patriotic, political parties organized more openly, and professional groups grew openly demanding of reform. Uncomfortable in the face of all this, Nicholas could only gamble on a big success in the war.

The guns of the Peter and Paul Fortress boomed forth triumphantly on August 12 of that summer; the 301 salvos were not for a victory, however, but in honor of the birth of a long-sought male heir, the Tsarevich Alexis. The war news did not improve, and in early September, 1904, a ten-day battle in Manchuria, while not the knockout blow the Japanese hoped for, culminated in a major defeat for the Russian army, which retreated northward. In October the emperor expressed the heartfelt wish personally to join his forces in Manchuria, but his advisers dissuaded him.

The year 1905 opened with bad omens, minor and major. During the ceremonies for the blessing of the waters on the Neva ice, a signal gun from the Peter and Paul sent a live shell into the Winter Palace, nearly injuring the royal family; the emperor avoided this residence ever after. Real disaster occurred on January 22, a day ever after known as Bloody Sunday. Nearly 150,000 men from the Putilov works were currently out on strike, and political agitators proposed that a procession carry a petition to the tsar asking for better labor conditions and a constitution. The bizarre situation was that the man forced to assume leadership of the protest march was Father George Gapon, a convinced antirevolutionary but also the organizer of the largest of the police-inspired labor unions. On the given day thousands of workers converged on the Winter Palace, singing hymns and carrying icons and portraits of the emperor. Ordered to halt, the petitioners marched on, and the police and Cossacks began to fire on them and the bystanders packed into Palace Square. The massacre left hundreds of dead, and Nicholas II, who was actually at Tsarskoe Selo that day, never after escaped the odium of being "Bloody Nicholas," enemy of the masses.

Mirsky resigned as minister of the interior, to be replaced by a bureaucratic nonentity named Alexander Bulygin, whose first idea was to have Nicholas give a tea for selected worker delegates in order to extend to them his pardon. In reality, a revolution had begun. The next major event in the drama was the assassination on February 17 of the Grand Duke Sergius, governor general of Moscow at the time of the Khodinka field disaster and still in charge of the troops in the old capital. A powerful bomb killed Nicholas' uncle and brother-in-law in his carriage as he was entering the Kremlin, and pieces of the body of the most unpopular Romanov of his day were gathered up subsequently by his wife on the roofs and battlements of the citadel. The Grand Duchess Elizabeth insisted on visiting her husband's assassin to give him her forgiveness, which he refused, and the government denied her plea for leniency. Again, it was later revealed that a police agent was conversant with the plot.

More bad war news came. At Mukden, Japanese and Russian armies, numbering in the several hundred thousands, fought one of the bloodiest battles in history, after which the Russians retreated. With no victories to bolster his regime and in the face of a rising tide of strikes and protests, Nicholas at last resorted to concession: A rescript of March 3 called for the maintenance of the autocracy but instructed Bulygin to prepare a plan whereby the laws might be discussed by the worthiest persons. This pledge of a consultive Duma might have satisfied enough people the previous December, but now liberals demanded universal suffrage and radicals called for insurrection. Congresses of lawyers, doctors, Zemstvo workers, peasants, trade unionists, and even churchmen met openly to air their increasingly political demands. Strikes involved half a million workers, the most notable single crisis being a general strike in Warsaw following May Day riots. All through the countryside, the spring planting over, the peasants were burning, killing, and seizing land.

Late in May the government's last hope evaporated: The Russian Baltic fleet, which had been sent around the world, was destroyed off Japan. When the Russians appeared through the dawn mists in the Tsushima Strait on May 27, the Japanese had all the advantages of rest, near bases, electrically fired guns, telescopic sights, and the latest signaling equipment. In a completely one-sided engagement, all but three of the Russian ships were destroyed, captured, or interned. Nicholas II received the news of the Tsushima disaster while he was playing tennis; he shrugged and resumed his serve.

Two shipboard events the next month promised more trouble ahead. A successful mutiny occurred on the battleship *Potemkin* in the Black Sea, when the crew, influenced only to a degree by Socialist agitators, killed or forced overboard their officers. Failing either to subvert the rest of the fleet or to link causes with the insurrectionary mobs in Odessa, the *Potemkin* made its way to Rumania and internment, a historic first in the demoralization of the tsar's armed forces. Far away to the north in the Baltic Sea, Nicholas was cruising on the imperial yacht when there was a seemingly chance encounter with the yacht of William II off Björkö, Finland. "Willy" presented a German-Russian alliance for "Nicky" to sign, and he signed it almost secretly. The Russian foreign minister, astonished to learn of a pact that contradicted the Russian-French Alliance, had the Björkö Treaty nullified, but the diplomatic world had been treated to a clear example of the emperor's weakness and incompetence.

Negotiations to end the war in the Far East began in August at Portsmouth, New Hampshire. Japan was exhausted militarily and financially, while Russia, stronger in the long run, desperately needed a respite to deal with the internal chaos. President Theodore Roosevelt, acting as mediator, swung from an anti-Russian viewpoint to the stance of moderating the extreme Japanese demands for territory, indemnity, and naval limitations on its enemy. Witte, whose wise counsels were ignored before the war, was the chief Russian negotiator, and he returned to St. Petersburg in September to be lionized and made a count for securing a settlement regarded as nearly miraculous. Russia ceded any rights it had in Korea, Port Arthur, and southern Manchuria and gave up southern Sakhalin Island, but no indemnity and no disarmament were demanded, and the essential realism of the arrangements was indicated by the fact that they lasted forty years.

Neither the peace treaty nor limited political concessions served to stay the revolutionary tide. Granting self-government to the universities in September merely provoked more student demonstrations and more clashes with the police. In October a printers' strike in Moscow and then a railroad walkout caused a chain reaction of labor actions culminating in Russia's first general strike, with 1,000,000 workers out in the streets and all essential services brought to a halt. The tsar at Peterhof was cut off from telephone, postal, and telegraph communication with the world except through military and naval facilities. Two destroyers stood by to take the imperial family to England if necessary. The deepening of the civil conflict was apparent in the appearance of the first soviets—strictly class organizations of workers directed against both government and property. The St. Petersburg Soviet, with Leon Trotsky playing a key role, contested the regular municipal authorities for three months. The chaos in the city streets, however, would have been a manageable inconvenience except for another factor: The peasants, with the harvest in, resumed their violence in the countryside, until half the districts of Russia were under martial law.

By the end of October there were two harsh alternatives for Nicholas II, as he later described them to his mother: first, "to find an energetic soldier and crush the rebellion by sheer force," meaning "rivers of blood" and in the end being only "where we had started," or, second, "to give the people their civil rights, freedom of speech and press, also to have all the laws confirmed by a State Duma—that, of course, would be a constitution." The decision to avoid civil war was not easily taken. The Grand Duke Nicholas was approached by the emperor with the offer of the job of supreme military dictator, but this popular general, always excitable and currently influenced by liberals, grabbed his revolver and brandished it at his own head, shouting that he would shoot himself if Nicholas did not grant a constitution. For this, the grand duke was ever after regarded with suspicion by the empress, who had Nicholas join her in long hours of prayer in the name of somehow saving the autocracy. Witte, likewise never forgiven, was a decisive voice in persuading Nicholas to act positively, and the new era began when Witte was invested with the powers of a prime minister, Russia's first. On October 30 appeared the famous October Manifesto "on perfecting the order of the state"; it granted civil rights, a broad electoral franchise, and a Duma with legislative powers. This famous document, dated the seventeenth (Old Style), appeared over the plain signature Nicholas, who in later state papers was to be styled "supreme" and "sovereign" but no longer "absolute." Russia had a constitution or the promise of one —roughly two centuries after Britain, a century after the United States and France, a half century after Austria and Prussia, and a decade and a half after Japan. The triumph of the forces of light in Russia was far from complete, however. Only two weeks later, on November 14, Nicholas' diary contained this fateful entry: "We have got to know a man of God— Gregory—from the Tobolsk Province." Nicholas' tragedy was that he would be remembered more for Rasputin than for the October Manifesto.

XIX.
Nicholas II: Between Wars and Revolutions

1. Ungracious Constitutionalist

FOLLOWING the Revolution of 1905, the Romanov dynasty had its great opportunity to shake off its complete dependence on the military, the bureaucracy, and the nobility and to create a monarchy on the British pattern, above politics and enjoying sentimental popularity. For this metamorphosis Nicholas II seemed to offer hope. In the evaluation of the British ambassador, the emperor possessed "the gifts perfectly fitted for the role of constitutional monarch—a lively intelligence, a cultivated spirit, assiduousness and methodicalness in work, to say nothing of an extraordinary natural charm." Put negatively, Nicholas showed in the first decade of his reign that he did not have the firmness and decisiveness successfully to play absolutist like his father. The table was set, but the guests did not partake of it, to use Prince Golitsyn's phrase concerning 1730.

The surge of revolution, allowed to proceed as far as it had, refused to die out. Millions of people wanted more radical concessions. Trotsky, to dramatize this, tore up the October Manifesto in the streets. Indeed, this piece of paper hardly satisfied the land hunger of the peasants, who continued to riot throughout Russia well into 1906. There were more strikes and more mutinies, culminating in December, 1905, in an armed uprising of thousands of workers in Moscow under the leadership of Socialists in the local soviet. The government, which kept control of the Nicholaevsky Railroad, sent off the famed Semenovskoe Guards for the work of bloody suppression. In the end concession, repression, and exhaustion combined to halt the violence of the masses. Among the forces of repression were groups of vigilantes known as the Black Hundreds. Once cowed, now revengeful, these right-wing extremists went about doing in suspected radicals in the name of the old slogan "Orthodoxy, autocracy, and nationality." Mistakenly seeing these know-nothings and bigots as a genuine expression of patriotism, Nicholas publically accepted a membership in one of the Black Hundred groups, thereby offending loyal but moderate people.

The new prime minister, Witte, who viewed the Black Hundreds as "thugs and scoundrels," was not a radical or even a liberal, just a realist. He once declared that he had accepted the need for a constitution "in my head," but "as for my heart . . ." he could only spit. His services to his sovereign were tremendous. The defeated army was brought back from the Far East without major incident. Essentially on the basis of his personal prestige, Witte secured a large loan from the French bankers, these supposed republicans agreeing that their Russian ally's monarch needed independent financial means in order to deal with the Duma. Then Witte saw to the writing of a constitution giving the executive the maximum of power and the legislature the minimum. For his efforts, Witte was abruptly dismissed in April, 1906, by the emperor, apparently now piqued that he had made any concessions. A colorless bureaucrat named Ivan Goremykin became the new prime minister, his main qualification being his conviction that his function was simply to take orders.

The meeting of the First Duma took place on May 10, 1906, in St. George's Hall of the Winter Palace, the assembly later transferring its sessions to the Taurida Palace. Nicholas II and the entire imperial family marched in great state to the opening ceremonies, at which the glittering grand duchesses and supercilious grand dukes stared down the somberly dressed delegates while the emperor read a less-than-inspired address in which the hope for a general amnesty was disappointed. The master of the court said: "The deputies? They give one the impression of a gang of criminals. . . . What wicked faces! I will never again set foot among these people." Young Prince Felix Yusupov confined himself to remarking that no room in the palace "had ever seen such a mixed crowd of queerly dressed people." These inauspicious reactions of the courtiers remind one of the irascible Duke of Wellington's saying of the reformed British House of Commons after 1832 that he had never seen so many "bad hats," to which someone's telling rejoinder was "nor so many good heads." In like manner, the men at whom the emperor was being encouraged to sniff his nose were, in fact, the cream of the Russian intelligentsia.

The membership of the First Duma, compared to later ones, was on the radical side, a situation for which Nicholas blamed Witte unfairly. On the extreme left there were a number of Socialists (including Marxist Social Democrats, but not peasant Socialist Revolutionaries, Russia's greatest party having boycotted the elections). The largest single bloc in the Duma was Miliukov's Cadets (Constitutional Democrats), professors and members of the middle class, who thought 1905 was just a good start. To their right were Alexander Guchkov's Octobrists, the very name of these true conservatives symbolizing that they accepted the changes of 1905 and little more. At the far reactionary extreme were various groups lumped together as Nationalists. The Duma as a whole sought real power and more reform. The government saw things differently, and Prime Minister Goremykin went out of his way to express his general contempt by waiting several weeks to submit the first piece of legislation for the Duma to act on, a bill to construct a laundry at Dorpat University. A threat by the Duma to investigate a recent pogrom alarmed the Black Hundreds, and Nicholas found a land distribution project totally unacceptable. Just over two months after its summons the First Duma was locked out and declared dissolved. The perpetrator of this coup was not the timid Goremykin but a new prime minister, Peter Stolypin.

For the next five years Nicholas II peevishly tolerated the devoted and competent services of this Russian Bismarck, a man essentially conservative but also practical and confident of his abilities to dominate a parliamentary regime. A burly, booming-voiced, bearlike person, Stolypin was the one provincial governor in 1905 who had distinguished himself for his capacity to handle revolutionary mobs, making wise concessions on some occasions and shaking rioters by the scruffs of their necks in other circumstances. He was to show great courage again just a month after his appointment as head of the government, when an SR bomb exploded in his summer residence, splattering ink all over him and maiming one of his children for life. The regime's reply to violence was in part more violence: Field courts-martial in the fall produced more than 500 executions and left the phrase "Stolypin necktie" as an expression for noose. Stolypin, however, was too much of a statesman to confine his energies to repression. Using emergency powers, he promulgated a program of agrarian reforms with which his name will always be associated. The Stolypin laws, anathema to Lenin and other radicals because of their very success, sought to isolate "the sober and the strong" among the peasants and to make them into a class of petty capitalists by facilitating hereditary land tenure (as against periodical redividing of a village's land) and even by promoting consolidated farmsteads on the American model (as against peasants all living side by side along the road and far from their scattered strips of land). In terms of the statistical changes in Russian landholding patterns that the Stolypin program produced in only ten years, one of the great ifs of history is what another decade without war and revolution would have produced in the way of social stability.

The emperor was advised by any number of people to end the constitutional experiment altogether. Nonetheless, Stolypin insisted on holding elections in February, 1907, for a new Duma, which, to his consternation, proved even more radical than the first. Although between the two fires of right and left, Stolypin boldly dissolved the Second Duma in June and prepared for a third, this time unconstitutionally changing the electoral law. In the subsequent rigged elections the vote of 1 landowner was worth that of about 26 peasants or of 540 city workers. The Third Duma, meeting in November and lasting to 1912, had a large majority of progovernment rightists, a big bloc of neutral Octobrists, only fifty Constitutional Democrats, and a handful of Socialists. The Octobrist leader, Guchkov, while not joining the cabinet, agreed to cooperate with Stolypin if the prime minister would observe constitutional procedures. Executive and legislature cooperated fruitfully, for example, in extensive educational reforms, which, if financed properly, would have put every Russian of school age into school as of 1920. (The comparative figure was 37 percent in 1907.)

More dear to the emperor's heart was the Duma's interest in army reorganization, including taking the initiative in the introduction of machine guns. Nicholas II was able to say eventually to Stolypin, "This Duma cannot be reproached with an attempt to seize power, and there is no need at all to quarrel with it."

The cooperation of monarch and Duma received a setback in early 1908, when Guchkov publically called on the Romanov grand dukes to give up their various sinecures, with patronage powers. For the empress, this was simply an attack on the royal family, just as she interpreted Guchkov's omission of the word "autocrat" from the address to the throne as an attack on her husband. She declared to Nicholas that Russia's Tory of Tories was an enemy. Witte, always ready to spite his successor, Stolypin, was among those who persuaded Nicholas that the policy of consulting the Duma in army affairs was a serious diminution of his prerogatives as sovereign. By late 1909 the emperor had swung around to the view, expressed in a letter to his mother, that the problem was getting money "without the Duma," adding that "we will do it one way or another—no fear."

The possibility of a strong prime ministership ended in September, 1911, when Stolypin was gunned down by an assassin during a gala opera performance in Kiev in the course of a royal visit to that city. Nicholas' description of the event to the dowager is interesting:

> During the second interval we had just left the box, as it was so hot, when we heard two sounds as if something had dropped. I thought an opera glass might have fallen on somebody's head and ran back into the box to look. . . . Women were shrieking and directly in front of me in the stalls, Stolypin was standing; he slowly turned his face towards us and with his left hand made the sign of the cross in the air. Only then did I notice that he was very pale and that his right hand and uni-

form were blood-stained. He slowly sank into his chair and began to unbutton his tunic. . . . People were trying to lynch the assassin. I am sorry to say the police rescued him from the crowd. . . . Then the theatre filled up again, the national anthem was sung, and I left with the girls at eleven. You can imagine with what emotions.

The court was less than bereaved by the loss of Stolypin, the empress going so far as to say that he had offended God. Stolypin had once predicted to Guchkov that he would be murdered by a police agent, and at the outset of the Kiev visit he noted that the elaborate security precautions for the emperor did not extend to his ministers, remarking, "We are superfluous." It gradually came out that the assassin had indeed been playing a scandalous double role as a revolutionary and as a police agent, but Nicholas blocked an investigation.

The new prime minister was the competent Count Vladimir Kokovtsev, formerly in charge of Finance, a conservative willing to work with the Duma. In an interview with the empress, Kokovtsev noted that Stolypin had died for his sovereign. Alexandra rejoined that Stolypin had "overshadowed his sovereign" and added pointedly that Kokovtsev would do well not to make the same mistake. In the fall of 1911 Nicholas was already discussing ways to curb the free press, and the Duma as well, with the ultrarightist minister of justice, for one of the peculiar limitations of the Russian constitutional system was that each minister was responsible only to the emperor and could work behind the back of the prime minister and cabinet. In 1912 Kokovtsev needed great persuasion to get Nicholas to thank the Third Duma for its work at the completion of its term. An equally conservative Fourth Duma was elected in the fall of that year.

By 1912 almost all the Russian public had come to accept the Duma as a fact of life. That year was the centenary of the Battle of Borodino, a reminder of that highpoint of the national identification of ruler and ruled during Napoleon's invasion. The official celebrations were elaborate and grand, but Nicholas deliberately did not invite representatives of the Duma. Among other things, family affairs centering on Rasputin had come as a new wedge between the emperor and his people.

2. Loving Father

There are hundreds of photographs to be seen of Nicholas II and his family. Even in the candid shots, the tsar always appears poker-faced behind his beard and mustache, but his look is direct and serene. The tsarina invariably seems frozen, although her sheer beauty of features and firmness of will come through to the viewer. Whether portrayed formally or not, their four daughters are all loveliness and unaffected simplicity; some might say insipidity. The sickly Tsarevich Alexis is singularly winning in every photograph: Wistfulness mingles with boyish determination as we see him being carried about in his sailor suit or trudging alongside his father at a review.

There are scarcely any photographs suggesting that the tsar and his family mingled with the populace at large. Moreover, Nicholas avoided the classes, as well as the masses. Society, high or smart or both, saw little of him, and he thus deprived himself of one of his greatest weapons—his overwhelming personal charm. Nor did the royal couple pose or associate much with their relatives. Nicholas, his wife, and his children were an extremely close-knit family who lived in virtual seclusion from everybody.

The imperial family's main place of residence was Tsarskoe Selo, whose elegant local railroad station lay several miles out from downtown St. Petersburg. For Nicholas, Tsarskoe Selo meant not the lavish Grand Palace of Elizabeth or the luxurious pavilions beloved by Catherine the Great but rather the relatively small Neoclassic Alexander Palace, which under the hand of Alexandra took on the look of an English country mansion. The most exotic touch about the imperial apartments was the quartet of colorfully dressed Negro guards. Center of all the family's activities was Alexandra's mauve boudoir, where not only all the furnishings but even the flower arrangements were keyed to the shade of violet.

When at Tsarskoe Selo, the emperor and empress seldom went visiting. Occasionally an evening might be spent with the dowager at Gatchina or with Nicholas' sisters, Xenia and Olga, at their palaces. The mansions of the well-born or well-placed in and about Tsarskoe Selo did not know the royal presence. One exception was a little house near the Alexander Palace that was the home of Anna Vyrubova, a daughter of a court official who made herself one of the empress' few confidantes. "I thank God for at last having sent me a true friend," wrote Alexandra of Vyrubova, after Nicholas' wife for more than a decade had waged hostilities with Russian society, which now was rankled at the preeminence of the mousy Vyrubova. It was at Vyrubova's house that the fateful meeting of the rulers with Rasputin took place.

After being at upland Tsarskoe Selo the months of the late winter and early spring, Nicholas and Alexandra often spent a few weeks in May at the Palace of Peterhof, enjoying its seaside atmosphere, but their greater delight was the period around June, when they lived on their yacht, the *Standart,* and spent long idle days cruising around the Finnish islands, occasionally going ashore for informal picnics and other excursions. The empress unbent as much as she was able to in the ship's company, and there are even movies of the grand duchesses dancing with young naval officers. In 1907 the whole family almost came to grief when the *Standart* struck a rock and nearly foundered (the revolutionists, for once, could not be blamed). The yacht was a favorite place to entertain foreign royalty— Kaiser William was jealous of its size and wanted Nicholas to give it to him as a present—but this was not frequent. The great royal family concourses of the days of Alexander III were not continued under his son, so Nicholas' contacts even with his exact peers were limited.

In August the family went off to the sumptuous royal hunting lodge at Spala, Poland, traveling in the specially appointed imperial train with its distinctive blue cars with golden double eagles (actually two matching trains were used in order to foil terrorists). September saw another progress by train, this time southward to the Crimea and the estate at Livadiya, where by 1911 Nicholas had finished transforming Alexander II's wooden palace into a gleaming white limestone marvel of informal luxury. Here the children were at their happiest playing in the gardens and romping in the Black Sea surf with their father. Nearby Yalta was the only place where Alexandra might be seen out for casual shopping. In the Crimea more than anywhere else, Nicholas was thrown into contact with his relations, all of whom had estates there.

St. Petersburg's Winter Palace was royally occupied only for a short season after the New Year. There might be dancing evenings for the older princesses, but the main function was the grand ball at which the emperor entertained more than 3,000 guests, following doggedly the tradition of previous reigns. There was little chance that the tsar and tsarina would meet interesting people: Artistic or political notoriety counted no more than sheer family standing if one was not of an appropriate grade in the military or civil service.

If Nicholas resigned himself to a routinely somber life with his wife, he at the same time found great pleasure in daily contacts with his children, to the point that they became his favorite company. The emperor easily played both the father and the comrade and was a sage disciplinarian even while indulging a taste for humor and horseplay reminiscent of his father and his children.

The four daughters seemingly grew up all of a piece in their healthiness, simplicity, and radiant good humor, but yet each developed some individuality. The eldest, Olga, born in 1895, came to be most like her father, to whom she was singularly devoted, and she was considered the most Russian for her physical vigor, willfulness, and sense of humor. She had considerable talents in painting, playing the piano, and singing and was more bookish than the others. When she was barely in her teens, the foreign minister began pressing for a match between her and Crown Prince Carol of Rumania (later of Madame Lupescu notoriety), but following a visit to Constanta, Olga received her father's promise to leave her free to choose her own husband, her mother readily agreeing in view of her dislike of foreigners.

The second daughter, Tatiana, was very much her mother's child. In fact, she came to be known among the other girls as "the little mother" or "the governess," for she took it upon herself to look after them as well as after her favored parent. Two years younger than Olga, she was taller and more stately than her sister. Little accomplished except for her piano playing, Tatiana grew up to be the most conscious of her position.

Maria Nicholaevna, who was born in 1899, gave promise of being the great beauty of the family. Plump and open in her friendliness as a child, she was readily nicknamed *le gros toutou* (the big bowwow). Her girlish physical strength (she could lift her tutor high in the air) was forgotten as she developed into an appealingly voluptuous young woman. Lazy and unstudious, she had some talent as an artist.

The youngest daughter, born in 1901, was named Anastasia, which was a favorite name among modern Romanovs, who were delighted with medieval memories such as that of Ivan the Terrible's beloved wife. This spirited child was a madcap and something of a tomboy. Her playfulness included a great talent for mimicry. Yet she rarely laughed herself and her shyness hid a wistfulness, revealing that she often lived in her own little world. Gray-eyed and brown-haired, Anastasia developed physically rather rapidly, but she was gawky and intellectually indifferent.

The four grand duchesses made it easy for people to keep their names in order by their habit of sending out joint letters and signing them O.T.M.A. All observers noted their great devotion to one another. They were allowed few companions their own age, in accordance with the empress' general distrust of Petersburg society. After being brought up à la English on camp beds and with cold baths, the girls had few airs. Friendly critics had to admit that the girls never quite seemed to grow up; one close court official observed that they talked like perpetual ten- or twelve-year-olds.

Olga and Tatiana, known as the Large Pair, were to have their coming out late in 1914. In 1911 the sixteen-year-old Olga had been given her first formal ball at Livadiya, at which time she received her first diamonds and pearls. The 1914 season opened with a party for the two princesses given by their grandmother, the dowager; on this occasion Alexandra left at midnight, but Nicholas stayed on to four thirty.

The entire family picture had changed in August, 1904, with the coming of a male heir, Alexis. In fact, the birth of the tsarevich has been called "the event which more than anything else determined the later course of Russian history" by Sir Bernard Pares, on-the-spot observer and leading British historian of Russia. The years of waiting for a male baby had put a great strain on Alexandra, already unpopular in society. Alexis' birth she attributed directly to the intercession of St. Seraphim, canonized by Nicholas the year previously, and her growing religious mysticism was given another boost. Within six weeks of his birth Alexis was found to be a hemophiliac.

Royal hemophilia was a forbidden subject at the turn of the century, although now it is common knowledge that women are the carriers and men the victims of it and that Queen Victoria was responsible for introducing hemophilia not only to the British dynasty, but to those of Spain, Germany, and Hesse as well. Genetic genealogy eventually established that an uncle, a brother, and a nephew of the Empress Alexandra had already perished from the disease. For the tsarevich as for others, hemophilia meant that his blood did not clot properly, and accordingly, the slightest bruises as a toddler could produce ominous dark swellings and eventually huge blood sacs, or hematomas, several inches in size. External scratches could be bandaged easily, while bleeding in the mouth or nose might assume near-fatal proportions. The worst thing was damage to joints, causing blood to accumulate internally, to the point that Alexis could not move an elbow or knee. Recovery from such crippling bouts meant months of treatment of Alexis' affected limb in heavy iron casts and mudpacks.

Life for the royal family came to revolve entirely around the ups and downs of the heir as he grew from golden-curled babyhood to auburn-haired boyhood. According to a tutor, when Alexis "was well, the palace was transformed as if bathed in sunshine." Hemophilia, however, was a peculiarly fickle disease in the frequency and intensity of its attacks. The child might die any day.

All the guilt for the tragedy of her son Alexandra took herself. Her own recurring heart attacks, headaches, and nervous ailments (like sciatica) date from his birth, according to Vyrubova. The dowager began to write Nicholas about his wife and "her ailing and always incapable of taking part in anything." A doctor spoke of Alexandra's "progressive hysteria." The empress spent hours on end in solitary prayer in a special chapel near her boudoir. "God is just," she once declared, and it was clear that she expected a miracle such as the doctors could never be able to offer her with regard to her son's health.

The miracle came in the person of the notorious holy man Rasputin. On many occasions after 1906, Rasputin's presence served to tide Alexis over frightful crises when he might be convulsed with pain, his parents in tears, and the doctors in despair. No one will probably ever know just how Rasputin succeeded. Was it quack drugs or homespun remedies? Was it hypnotic willpower? Was it fortuitous intervention when Alexis was due to improve anyhow? Whatever it was, Rasputin had "incontestable success in healing," as a hostile court official admitted, or in the words of a nurse, "call it what you will, he could really promise her her boy's life while he lived." Once Rasputin shocked the doctors by laying his dirty cloak over their instruments by way of blessing them, but Alexis got well. Another time he cured Alexis just by speaking to him on the telephone.

One nurse was to write that Alexis came between Alexandra and Nicholas, in the sense that the empress became blind to all but her son's interests. The full situation still remains clothed in riddles and innuendos. A head valet interviewed after the death of the imperial family muttered ominously about their "punishment for a terrible sin." The postrevolutionary Prime Minister Alexander Kerensky wrote in the most recent of his many histories that "for reasons I am not free to disclose, the Tsar felt that he had to give into Alexandra Feodorovna with regard to the heir apparent." One must simply accept Pares' generalization that "the nursery was the center of all Russia's troubles."

Despite his disabilities, Alexis grew up to be a lively, spirited lad. When he was five, the tsarevich was assigned two *Standart* sailors, one named Derevenko, to hover over him and see that he avoided any tumbles. The burly seaman and the cherubic boy were often photographed together, for the sad fact was that there were long periods when Alexis was so weak that Derevenko had to carry him about in his arms. There was lavished on Alexis a child's dreamworld of toys, including the most elaborate miniature castles, factories, and ships, all operated mechanically so that he could not hurt himself. Of course, what Alexis really wanted was something like a bicycle, but this was denied him (once he scooted out on a borrowed wheel during a military review, which promptly broke up as Nicholas and all the soldiers sought to capture the boy). His English tutor, Pierre Gilliard, soon detected a tendency to secretiveness approaching cunning, and received the parents' permission to let Alexis romp about more with other children for its psychological benefits despite the great physical risks involved.

Alexis became unquestionably handsome with a full head of straight brown hair and sparkling blue eyes. When he neared adolescence, he was of necessity thin, but he was tall for his age and well built. Gilliard spoke of "the treasures of his nature," particularly remarking the inborn sympathy for suffering in Alexis. As for mental abilities, the tsarevich had curiosity and imagination, but he was no great student, his schooling being often interrupted by illness. Once, inspecting a photograph of himself with his dog, Alexis commented that the dog looked more intelligent. Rasputin predicted that Alexis would be much healthier after he reached thirteen. As he neared that age, the tsarevich developed a companionable interest in all of the tsar's activities.

Admirable as a father, Nicholas was a complete failure as head of a dynasty. He isolated himself from the members of the imperial family at large, almost without exception, all the while fretting over the Romanov dignity. The privileges, often undeserved and unrequited, accorded Romanov grand dukes were to be a source of political headaches for Nicholas, but their marital scandals were even more painful. During all the political crises of the reign Nicholas found little consolation or counsel from the imperial family, mostly because he refused to ask.

As of the turn of the century there were about sixty Romanovs to be contended with. To be precise, Nicholas' male relatives included one brother (Michael), four uncles (Vladimir, Alexis, Sergius, and Paul), four first cousins (Vladimir's Cyril and two others, Paul's Dmitri), ten uncles of of the second degree or sons of great-uncles (two Nicholaevichi, three Constantinovichi, and five Michaelovichi), and nine male cousins of the third degree (sons of the uncles of the second degree and titled, since Alexander III, merely princes, not grand dukes).

Nicholas' two sisters, Xenia and Olga, proved sufficiently modest and unassuming to keep his confidence and to win Alexandra's friendship, even while remaining close to the Dowager Marie. They were proper and unpolitical. The Grand Duchess Xenia's life revolved around raising her children, while her husband, the Grand Duke Alexander Michaelovich, dabbled in social and financial affairs, being something of a confidant of his brother-in-law. Their six sons were suitable playmates for the tsar's daughters, while their daughter, Irene, married the mysterious young Prince Felix Yusupov in 1914. The Grand Duchess Olga was even more retiring than her sister after marrying her relative Prince Peter of Oldenburg in 1901. Childless herself, Olga took her role as aunt seriously and insisted on being allowed to treat Nicholas and Alexandra's four daughters to their only outings and parties in the capital city.

One of the last tombs set up in the Peter and Paul Cathedral is inscribed GEORGE ALEXANDROVICH (TSARSKOE SELO 1871–1899 ABBA TUMAN), thus commemorating Nicholas' brilliant younger brother who had died of tuberculosis in the south of Russia. The youngest brother, Michael, was brought up as the baby of the family of Alexander III, and he repaid being thoroughly indulged by being thoroughly good-natured. As late as 1905, when Michael was twenty-seven, even Alexandra could refer to him as a delightful child. His education hung lightly on him, as did his military duties. The grand duke's great delight was collecting those novelties of the day, automobiles. A fast but absentminded driver, Michael once overturned a car in which he and Olga were speeding to Gatchina, but both escaped injury.

Michael was never named tsarevich as might have been expected in the decade before Alexis' birth, but almost all his lifetime the grand duke was looked on as just a heartbeat or two removed from being Russia's ruler. Opinions of his abilities varied widely, often reflecting some prejudice of the observers. His brother-in-law the Grand Duke Alexander wrote after the Revolution that Michael's "whole-hearted simplicity of manner" made him a "favorite of his family, of his fellow officers, and of all his countless friends," adding that "he possessed a well-organized mind and would have succeeded in any branch of the service." Witte gave special instruction in political economy to Grand Duke Michael, professing to see in him "great abilities" and particularly admiring his "straightforwardness." An unfavorable view of Michael was expressed by Count Vassili, who dismissed him as "a meek young man, one of those indifferent beings who are sorry to be put in responsible positions."

Whatever his potentialities, Michael enjoyed no influence with his brother whatsoever, even before romantic escapades put him into complete disgrace. When the grand duke was twenty-three, his near elopement at Sorrento with one of his sister's ladies-in-waiting had been a warning of scandal. Five years later, in 1906, Michael was passionately declaring his intention to marry a twice-divorced commoner, and his horrified sovereign and brother was driven to declare: "I will never give my consent." The lady in question, Natalia Sheremetevskaya, was a Moscow lawyer's daughter who had recently been married to a captain in the Guards regiment of which Michael was commander. Michael's choice was, indeed, a beauty, but hostile society called her simply a political intriguer. Eventually the couple were driven to take the drastic step of going to live abroad, where a son, named George, was born in 1910. Then in July, 1912, when Michael and Natalia were in residence in Berchtesgaden, Germany, they secretly slipped across the border into Austria and were married in the Orthodox church of Vienna. Michael's wire reached Nicholas at Spala, where the imperial family were experiencing the worst crisis to date with Alexis' hemophilia. A distraught Nicholas wrote the sympathetic dowager: "He broke his word, his word of honor. How in the midst of our boy's illness and all our trouble could they have done such a thing." Actually, it was exactly because Alexis' death would make Michael successor to the throne and deprive him of the chance of marrying his mistress that he took the step. Nicholas realized this and added that this selfish calculation on his brother's part "revolts me more than anything else."

Nicholas' first reaction was that Michael's action "must be kept absolutely secret," but soon the whole world knew that the Grand Duke Michael Alexandrovich was living in London with his morganatic wife, who was eventually accorded the title Countess Brassov. Not until the war was Nicholas' brother permitted to return to Russia, but Natalia was never received at court.

Nicholas' eldest uncle, the Grand Duke Vladimir, was a kindly but loud and eccentric *grand seigneur* with the strongest opinions equally on politics, cuisine, and ballet. "He almost struck terror in Nicholas," wrote Mossolov, and realizing this, Vladimir deliberately stayed out of state affairs, contenting himself until his death in 1909 with twice-yearly visits to Paris and sponsorship of the arts in Petersburg (he was an original backer of Diaghilev). The grand duke's self-imposed effacement was not exactly matched by the behavior of his grand duchess, the equally overbearing and irascible Maria Pavlovna. The former Princess of Mecklenburg-Schwerin never forgot that her family stood nearest the throne after Alexis and Michael. After an unsuccessful effort to be social mentor for the young Empress Alexandra, Maria Pavlovna found it suited her more to be critic and rival of the court at Tsarskoe Selo. Her brilliant parties became the most persistently vicious source of gossip about everything Nicholas' friendless wife did do or did not do. Nothing better describes the abilities and animosities of the Grand Duchess Vladimir than the occasion in 1907 when she represented the Romanovs at a dedication of a monument to Alexander II in Bulgaria. After merely a few minutes' briefing about her hosts, Maria Pavlovna performed faultlessly for several hours of ceremony and conversation. Upon being complimented by a Russian official, she retorted: "One ought to know one's job. You may pass that on to the Grand Court."

The Vladimirs' three children proved without exception to be irritants to their cousin on the throne. The twenty-nine-year-old Grand Duke Cyril returned something of a naval hero of the Russo-Japanese War and promptly contracted the most outrageous marriage imaginable. It was terrible enough that he was wed abroad without the tsar's consent to a divorced woman. His chosen mate, the Grand Duchess Victoria Melita of Saxe-Coburg, was his first cousin (such unions are forbidden by the church), and she had deserted as consort none other than the Empress Alexandra's brother, Ernest of Hesse. Indeed, it had been at the wedding of "Ernie" and "Vickie" that Nicholas had proposed to Alexandra. On his return to the Russian capital, Cyril went to his parents' house at 8 P.M., only to find himself leaving for abroad again at midnight under Nicholas' sentence of dismissal from the navy, banishment forever from Russia, and the loss of his income. This dire punishment of Cyril provoked his father to threaten to resign all his posts, and soon the emperor bowed to this and other family pressures, writing the dowager: "After much thought, which in the end gave me a headache, I decided to take advantage of the name-day of your grandson and I telegraphed Uncle Vladimir that I would return to Cyril the title which he had lost." It was not until 1909 that the empress' former sister-in-law dared appear in St. Petersburg society, but then Victoria Melita rapidly established herself as a sparkling complement to an ambitious husband.

As for Cyril's brothers, the older one, the Grand Duke Boris, was noted only for his indolent and dissipated life as a bachelor in and about the capital until he suddenly roused himself to request the hand in marriage of the emperor's oldest daughter, Olga, then eighteen. Alexandra's understandably disgusted rejection of this "half-worn blasé . . . man of thirty-eight" understandably rankled Maria Pavlovna. The youngest grand duke,

Andrew Vladimirovich, was rated "gifted, intelligent, and a hard worker" by the court doctor, but he, too, hardly stood a chance of being a political counselor of the tsar in view of the fact that he openly boasted a mistress, who, incredibly, was the very Matilda Kshessinska of Nicholas' youthful dalliance.

The Grand Duke Alexis, Nicholas' second oldest uncle, avoided the trouble of having wife and children, but his profligacy caused scandal and even more so his utter incompetence as grand admiral during the recent war. "His was a case of fast women and slow ships," was the comment of a relative. Forced to resign his posts, Alexis went off to titillate Paris night-clubs until his death in 1909.

The most insufferable of the grand dukes, Nicholas' uncle Sergius, had been removed from the scene by a terrorist's bomb in 1905. The Grand Duchess Elizabeth, his ill-treated widow and Alexandra's sister, remained in Russia, and the childless "Aunt Ella" became increasingly cherished by any number of her younger relatives as the most patient, generous, noble, and sainted creature on earth. "All gifts were hers," wrote an admirer. After disposing of her properties in the capital, the grand duchess bought land in the Ordenka quarter of Moscow and had built the Convent of Martha and Mary, a hospital operation of which she became mother superior. Although the pearl-gray robes of the order were designed by one of the chic artists of the day, she adopted rigorously ascetic living habits and undertook nursing the worst unfortunates herself. Some Romanovs chose to criticize her for lowering the dignity of the dynasty, but society generally accepted her genuine conversion to Orthodoxy in its aspects of humility and service, this being marked as in contrast with the empress' preference for the mystical aspects of the faith. It was unfortunate that the thoroughly level-headed "Aunt Ella" chose not even to try to influence her sister and the court.

The tsar's youngest uncle, the Grand Duke Paul, was only eight years older than his nephew, but he too largely threw away any chances of becoming Nicholas' confidant. In the previous century Paul had rather indifferently married Princess Alexandra of Greece, his cousin, and he had two children by her before her early death. In 1902 at Leghorn he married again, this time the former wife of an aide of the Grand Duke Vladimir. Confronted for the first time with the prospect of a grand ducal alliance with a divorced commoner without his consent as sovereign, Nicholas had reacted sharply and prophetically, writing his mother:

> I had a rather stern talk with Uncle Paul, which ended by my warning him of all the consequences his proposed marriage would have for him. It had no effect. . . . How painful and distressing it all is and how ashamed one feels for the family before the world. What guarantee that Cyril won't start at the same sort of thing tomorrow, and Boris

and Serge [Sergius] the day after. And in the end, I fear, a whole colony of members of the Russian Imperial family will be established in Paris with their semi-legitimate and illegitimate wives. God alone knows what times we are living in when undisguised selfishness stifles all feelings of conscience, duty, or even ordinary decency.

Paul's subsequent defiance was punished by banishment and the loss of his titles and revenues. The uncle duly took up residence in Paris, each year dutifully showing his continued loyalty to his nephew by attending the name day services for the emperor in the impressive Russian Orthodox cathedral in the northwest of the French capital. In time Nicholas relented and restored Paul to his privileges, but it took several more years before the wife, newly created Countess Hohenfelsen by the King of Bavaria, was allowed to cross the frontiers (she received the Russian title Princess Paley after the outbreak of the war). Settled in a newly built mansion at Tsarskoe Selo, Paul's wife might have been completely accepted at court but for her association with the intrigues of the Grand Duchess Maria Pavlovna. As for the grand duke and his influence, some considered him a voice of political enlightenment, whereas others said he had no well-thought-out ideas.

"Nobody had an easier, more brilliant debut in life than he," wrote his sister of the Grand Duke Dmitri, Paul's son by his first wife. Dmitri not only became known as an elegant and popular officer in the Horse Guards, he also enjoyed the particular affection of the emperor and empress, virtually living in the Alexander Palace all during the years of his father's banishment and accompanying the sovereigns everywhere. When he came into his fortune, he acquired a magnificent palace on the Neva and was a member of the smart set that included Prince Yusupov, who, indeed, had to win out over his friend in gaining the hand of Princess Irene. The younger sister of Dmitri, Maria Pavlovna (not to be confused with her aunt by the same name), wed Prince William of Sweden in 1908, but she became bored with Stockholm, and she secured the dissolution of her marriage by the Swedish Council of State and the Russian Holy Synod, in spite of the fact that she had borne a son, Lennart, to the man who went on to gain considerable fame as a poet and explorer. There were two daughters (subsequently the princesses Paley) by Paul's morganatic marriage and a son, Vladimir (born out of wedlock in 1896). This "Volodia," who was beloved as a young man by his half brother and sister, early gained a reputation as a brilliant poet and intellectual light of Petersburg.

Of the tsar's collateral cousins, as considerable in importance as in numbers, the Nicholaevichi were distinguished especially in the person of the Grand Duke Nicholas (the younger). Sheer ability had made "Nicholasha" the top commander in the army, and this towering man with his weather-beaten face, steely eyes, and neatly pointed beard was a popular, as well as imposing, Romanov. Having rejected his own dictatorship in favor of the constitution of 1905, the grand duke was to display rather mercurial political convictions in later years, but basically his was a one-track military mind. He was an influence on the emperor, but neither a steadying nor an enlightened one. His brother, the sickly Grand Duke Peter Nicholaevich, stayed more in the background. If for nothing else, the two Nicholaevichi would be remembered for their wives, both princesses of Montenegro, who earned the sobriquet "the Black Pair" for their dabblings in the occult and their sponsorship of Rasputin.

The Constantinovich cousins of the tsar were far enough removed from any real power to make themselves critics of the whole royal setup. Their mother, who married into the Romanovs back in the era of Alexander II, stayed alive until 1911, presiding over the palace at Pavlovsk, insisting on fresh supplies of damask for the Directoire furniture there, and shunning electricity as contemptuously as she did the grand court three miles away. Constantine Constantinovich, ten years older than the tsar, was a noted writer of essays, short stories, and poems, and his signature "K.R." was widely respected. As president of the Imperial Academy of Sciences, Constantine was credited with being an original sponsor of Ivan Pavlov, and he was also hailed as a particularly progressive inspector general of military schools. The grand duke detested politics, however, and wanted to be left alone with his writers, scientists, and cadets, to say nothing of his large family of six sons and two daughters. He felt that some grand dukes had real capacity for leadership and should be given it, all the while they were to be subject to the severest penalties for neglect of duty.

His brother Dmitri Constantinovich, on the other hand, insisted that members of the imperial family should be treated like anybody else, insofar as starting at the bottom and promotion were concerned, but that command positions should be denied them, since the tsar's dignity was always at stake. "We are all grouped around the throne in order to facilitate the tasks of its occupier," declared this commonsensical, well-educated bachelor grand duke, who refused high responsibility himself out of principle and out of a timidity "beyond imagining." Eventually named state stud master, Dmitri was to complain: "I should eagerly have accepted the appointment if it only meant looking after horses. . . . I am afraid I shall never get on properly with officials."

The numerous breed of the Michaelovichi, once known as the wild Caucasians, was headed by the Grand Duke Michael Nicholaevich until the death of the venerable president of the Imperial Council at the age of seventy-seven at Cannes in 1909. The passing of Nicholas' surviving great-uncle was regarded as an "irreparable loss" by the court doctor, who admired this patriarch's peacemaking abilities. His eldest son, Nicholas, dubbed Philippe Égalité for his radical views by his fellow officers, went on to shock Parisians by being the one grand duke who preferred academia to Montmartre (his biography of Emperor Alexander I won him election to the French Academy). It was said of "Nick-Mish" that he would have made a good president of the Third Republic he admired so much or that at least he should have been named ambassador to Paris or London. As it was, this much older namesake of the tsar was denied responsibilities, and he fretted his years away in his club criticizing the regime with increasing vociferousness (his willingness to gossip was, perhaps, his basic disqualification, especially with the tsarina). Rated as lacking practicality by some, the grand duke was credited with a great deal of political common sense by Kerensky.

There was no question of wasted abilities in the case of the second Michaelovich, Michael, who married morganatically and had been living grandly at Kenwood in London ever since the 1890's. The third son, George, made a good career for himself in the Horse Artillery and married respectably a Princess of Greece. Considered by Pares "the most level-headed of the not untalented grand dukes of the branch of Michael," Grand Duke George showed the emperor's favor by being his chief hander out of medals, but that was about all. It was the younger Alexander Michaelovich who made himself brother-in-law to the emperor, as well as his cousin, by marrying the Grand Duchess Xenia in 1894. Of profoundly conservative views, Alexander preferred to be social companion rather than gadfly to Nicholas. Briefly he dabbled at the post of minister of the merchant marine, especially created for him, and he credited himself with giving a boost to Russian military aviation after having witnessed Louis Blériot's crossing of the English Channel. Unlike his Constantinovich counterparts, Alexander Michaelovich maintained that grand dukes should head all important departments of government. The difficulties inherent in this use of the Romanovs were illustrated by the case of the fifth and youngest Michaelovich brother, Sergius, who, as inspector general of Russian artillery, was accused of showing a partiality for the Schneider-Creusot munitions works because of his financial interest in it, and in time he received much of the blame for wartime unpreparedness.

With so many Romanov uncles and cousins at hand, it was perhaps inevitable that some should be involved in unsavory affairs. It is difficult to assess how much they affected the regime with corruption and incompetence. "Always parasites, often harms" was a French military attaché's evaluation of the grand dukes generally. Looking at the era in the retrospect of several decades, the last surviving grand duchess, Olga, mused that for the dynasty at large, "little mattered except the unending gratification of personal desire and ambition." As for the "appalling marital mess in which the last generation of my family involved themselves," such a "chain of domestic scandals could not but shock the nation."

Lacking the patriarchal authority displayed by Alexander III, Nicholas failed to use his winning charm in dealing with his relatives, generally avoiding frank discussions with them. Such fitful punishments as were visited on errant grand dukes were usually blamed on the puritanism and jealousy of the empress.

If there were black sheep Romanovs, there were also many talented ones —historians, poets, art patrons, science buffs, educators, and military experts. However, the emperor availed himself little of their advice or support. In the view of one observer, "the only grand dukes who were in a position to exercise any influence over the Tsar's decisions were his great-uncle Michael, Nicholas Nicholaevich, his brother-in-law Alexander, and his uncle Paul Alexandrovich." As for the others, including his own brother, they "saw the sovereign no more than two or three times a year and then in conditions that made political conversation almost impossible."

3. Friend of Rasputin

Society reporters, historians, economists, and poets will never agree on what was the essence of Russia before 1914. In part, Russia was tens of millions of peasants, legally free since Alexander II, more property-conscious since Stolypin, but still obsessed with the landowners' acres across the road. Russia was hundreds of thousands of railroad workers, coal miners, printers, and bakers who thought more in terms of wage levels and slum conditions than of their recent rural roots. Russia was the land of the Great Russians, but it was also an empire of Ukrainians, White Russians, Finns, Poles, Georgians, Uzbeks, and Jews. Russia was division upon division of conscript soldiers mechanically cheering the tsar while silently cursing their officers, who sometimes sported such titles as Ensign Count so-and-so or Lieutenant Prince so-and-so. Russia was the politicians of the Duma, Michael Rodzianko, Guchkov, Miliukov, and that new Socialist orator Kerensky. Russia was the Revolution in exile or in prison, Stalin in Siberia, Lenin and Trotsky abroad. Russia was the writers and dancers and painters of St. Petersburg and Moscow, so avant-garde that they looked more to themselves than to the West. Russia was Romanov grand dukes and Rurikovich princes ogling *premières danseuses* and cuddling gypsy singers on their laps. Last of all, perhaps, Russia was a tsar and tsarina and five children living in old-fashioned comfort and seclusion at Tsarskoe Selo, receiving visits from an unkempt religious fanatic.

The man who was to make and unmake Russian cabinets was born about 1871 in the village of Pokrovskoe in Tobolsk Province, which is in Siberia just beyond the Urals. His name was simply Gregory, son of Efim, until he later gained the surname Rasputin, possibly from a local place-name but probably from the Russian word for "dissolute." The father was a horse dealer, and the son was later put down as a horse thief. More certain is that Gregory was a rowdy, hard-drinking young man notorious for his sexual exploits. Then something of a change took hold of him after he came into contact with the extremely heretical and vigorously persecuted sect of Khlysti, or spirit wrestlers, whose secret rites included fanatic penitences and whippings, all ending in frenzied erotic orgies. Soon after this exposure Gregory disappeared, probably one step ahead of an investigation of his personal life ordered by the local bishop. Almost certainly he made a pilgrimage to Jerusalem and traveled as far afield as Mesopotamia and the Balkans. Returning to Russia, the man now called Rasputin became a starets, or self-appointed man of God who practiced various forms of self-denial, indulged in soothsaying, and expected support from peasants and princes alike. Probably Rasputin had enjoyed the hospitality of most of the great shrines in Russia before he turned up in St. Petersburg in December, 1903, a stocky, bearded, raggedly dressed, and foul-smelling figure notable for his steely, piercing gray eyes and his glib tongue about what a great sinner he was.

Rasputin was first received by the neophyte monk Illiodor at the religious academy, and through him he met a superior there, Theophan, a saintly man and onetime confessor to the empress. An important religious personage who came to champion the fast-talking penitent was the Bishop of Saratov, Hermogen. Later Rasputin made a convert of the Grand Duchess Militza. The Grand Duke Nicholas made Rasputin's acquaintance through his sister-in-law and was captivated when the holy man cured his ailing dog. The chain leads through these royal cousins to Anna Vyrubova, who began entertaining Rasputin frequently at her little house in Tsarskoe Selo and introduced him to Nicholas and Alexandra in November, 1905.

Rasputin was not the first religious quack to attract the attention of the granddaughter of Queen Victoria. In 1900 during a visit to France, Alexandra had taken up with a certain "Dr." Philippe, a spiritualist and faith healer discovered, again, by the Grand Duchess Militza. Later, when a police official ruled that Philippe could not be licensed in Russia, Alexandra told Nicholas that the tsar could do anything, and forthwith Philippe came to St. Petersburg and the offending bureaucrat was sacked. In time Philippe was holding séances at the palace and invoking the spirit of Alexander III. Once he mysteriously gave Alexandra a bell with which to ward off bad advisers. The Frenchman was sent back to Paris in 1904, having involved himself too much with politics, but never to be forgotten was his telling the empress: "You will someday have another friend like me who will speak to you of God." In due course Rasputin appeared and developed his hold over Alexandra with his success in controlling Alexis' hemophilia.

As Rasputin became established in St. Petersburg circles, his sex life became more and more an open scandal. The tales of his seductions, past and present, began to get into the press, which printed confessions of nuns and maids and hinted about debutantes. Even the police could not prevent the royal protégé from exposing himself in restaurants or organizing sex parties in public baths. There was no question of Rasputin's promiscuity. His chief crony said Rasputin's problem was that he had "too many offers." As for Rasputin's wife back in Pokrovskoe, her enigmatic comment was that "he had enough for all." The reports of the debauchery met only with disbelief from the empress, whose Victorianism simply excluded dirty stories and whose hatred of the police made her discount their evidence as malevolence. She once naïvely wrote her husband: "They accuse Rasputin of kissing women, etc. Read the Apostles; they kissed everybody as a form of greeting." Alexandra was not moved, even when things got close to home. The tsarevnas' nurse, Tyutcheva, complained that Rasputin went in and out of the girls' quarters unannounced; she was simply dismissed, although Nicholas did put a stop to the bedroom visits. Later another nurse claimed that Rasputin attacked her sexually, but for her trouble she was declared insane and obviously unfit for further service.

Rasputin did have an extraordinary ability to mask himself in innocence and piety, effortlessly getting up from some group bacchanal to play holy man on the telephone to the palace. His two-facedness is really the whole root of the Romanov tragedy, for it led to a vast mutual misunderstanding and misconfidence between the imperial family and the Russian people. The empress saw in Rasputin only the guarantor of her son's health, a role the Russian people knew nothing of, since the tsarevich's disease was kept secret. Alexandra could not comprehend the public's hatred of her miracle worker whom they knew only as a debauchee with mysterious ties, possibly sexual for all they knew, with the foreign-born empress.

Aside from the royal couple, hundreds of people in St. Petersburg society were taken in by a man who dressed, talked, and smelled like a peasant. Even more strange was that Rasputin lost no chance to insult and humiliate his patrons. His language was foul, and his manners were unspeakable. He prided himself on being a sort of Robin Hood, demanding large sums from his rich visitors and just as casually giving the money away. He also exacted gifts of sex, all through the mumbo jumbo that carnal union with him was not sin but the first step toward repentance and purification. By way of explanation of this, one biographer put it that "women found in Gregory Efimovich the fulfillment of two desires which had hitherto seemed irreconcilable, religious salvation and the satisfaction of carnal appetites." His insolence knew no limits, even among people who might seriously help or hurt him. To Illiodor he once said: "The Tsar has washed my hands and you. . . ."

One person not fooled by Rasputin was Prime Minister Stolypin. As early as 1906 the emperor had suggested Rasputin's services for Stolypin's daughter crippled by the terrorist's bomb. At the ensuing interview, Stolypin claimed that Rasputin tried to hypnotize him but succeeded only in filling him with revulsion. Later, when the notoriety of the man became insupportable, Stolypin ordered Rasputin to leave the capital, and he was packed off to Pokrovskoe, where he bemoaned his fate to Vyrubova, the emissary of the furious empress. In Kiev the day before Stolypin's assassination, Rasputin was an interested observer of the prime minister's riding by, muttering darkly that "death is driving behind him."

Late in 1911 Rasputin was cornered at a meeting with his original patrons, the monk Illiodor and Bishop Hermogen, who were now thoroughly hostile to him. In reply to general charges of defiling the church and to a specific count of molesting a nun, Rasputin was led to cry out: "It is true, it is true, it is all true," after which he was smitten by the bishop's cross, cursed out, and made to promise complete continence. Rasputin thereupon had an interview at the palace, and there soon followed the order that Hermogen and Illiodor retire to monasteries, the first bowing to his fate after being denied a trial before bishops by Nicholas, while the latter escaped to wander about spreading his disgusting knowledge of the holy man.

The Duma tried to investigate Rasputin early in 1912, after Guchkov's Moscow newspaper published a piece blasting the Holy Synod for the "shameful comedy" of tolerating "that cunning conspirator against our Holy Church, that fornicator of human souls and bodies—Gregory Rasputin." After this, "hanging was too good" for Guchkov in the empress' view. The president of the Duma, Rodzianko, exchanged apprehensions with the dowager about the crisis, at which time she wistfully and truthfully said of her son: "He is so pure of heart that he does not believe in evil." Nonetheless, Rodzianko persisted in securing an interview with Nicholas and to Rodzianko's surprise, Nicholas authorized a complete investigation and later studied the juicy police report carefully. The prime minister, Kokovtsev, was then authorized to talk to Rasputin and, surmounting the usual hypnotic effort, got his promise to leave. The denouement was prefigured in the next encounter of the prime minister and the empress: She cut him dead. The press and the investigators, not Rasputin, were the ones punished.

If the opposition to Rasputin had been confined to the radical press or even to Duma circles, it would not be surprising that Nicholas and Alexandra ignored it. In fact, an increasing number of enemies of the holy man were to be found among the church, the police, and the bureaucracy. Most of the imperial family were also alarmed. The Dowager Marie made no secret of her disgust, even predicting in tears that "my poor daughter-in-law does not perceive that she is ruining both the dynasty and herself." The Grand Duchess Elizabeth left her nunnery to remonstrate with her sister, while the Grand Duke Nicholas swore not to see the monk again.

Despite such widespread opposition to him, Rasputin kept his hold. Reports that he used arcane drops to obfuscate his royal patrons can be discounted for lack of evidence. He did take lessons in hypnotism, in 1913, but his teacher was soon deported, according to the responsible police official, a friend turned enemy. The obvious and most important thing was that Rasputin continued to be the answer to the empress' prayers regarding the heir. His general political views and stance, however, were also basic factors in keeping her confidence and Nicholas'.

Rasputin was a professional peasant, so to speak. With the imperial couple, Rasputin never dropped the mask, treating them as fellow peasants, kissing them unaffectedly, and addressing them directly with all sorts of earthy wisdom. To a perplexed member of his suite Nicholas once explained that Rasputin was "just a good religious, simple-minded Russian. When in trouble or assailed by doubts, I like to talk with him and invariably feel at peace with myself afterwards." One particular reason the emperor turned not to the finest minds in Russia but to an illiterate ex-horse trader was that Rasputin played on Nicholas' distrust of the Russian nobility.

Rasputin's political prejudices were real, not merely self-serving echoes of what his royal patrons believed. He was antiwar to an extreme, he had vague notions of giving the landowners' land to the peasants and their mansions to the educational system, and he was genuinely concerned about toleration of Jews and other minorities. The prejudice which struck the most responsive chord was his blind faith in the autocracy. "Why don't you act as a Tsar should?" he would say, and Nicholas would regain confidence that his will counted for everything and that the real Russian people were entirely loyal to it. Privately, Rasputin had his reservations about the particular autocrat on the throne, but he counted on the wife. "The Empress is a very wise ruler," he once observed, "but as for him . . . well, he is a child of God." Alexandra, perhaps, did not see herself as the "second Catherine" that Rasputin said she could be, but she certainly saw her role as that of bolstering a hesitant husband. And all three were definitely on common ground when Rasputin vilified the Duma. One specific and consequential result of the relationship of this triangle of pious absolutists was the blocking of meaningful church reform. "There is an anointed Tsar," Rasputin intoned in final reply to the proposition that a patriarch once more be consecrated and the subservience of church to state be modified.

In the fall of 1912 the tsarevich had a close call with death that served to ensure Rasputin's preeminence at court forever. While the imperial family was vacationing at Spala, Alexis slipped and fell on the gunwale of a boat, and what at first seemed a minor injury turned into eleven days of horror with the boy's leg doubled up against his chest as he lay in the cruelest pain. "Mama, help me. Won't you help me?" he cried for hours on end to the helpless Alexandra, even at one point asking her, "When I'm dead it will not hurt any more, will it, Mama?" The last sacraments were administered to the heir, but then Vyrubova produced a cable from Rasputin: "God has seen your tears and heard your prayers. Do not grieve. The Little One will not die. Do not allow the doctors to bother him too much." Perhaps Alexandra's new confidence was passed on to her son, for his recovery was immediate, although it was twelve months before he could walk again.

The year 1913 was dominated by the Romanov tercentenary. Among the many commemorative materials to be produced by Russian scholars and artists is the most striking set of stamps issued by prerevolutionary Russia, a series of portraits of all Romanov monarchs, major and minor, good and bad. Fabergé's jeweled Easter egg for that year was decorated with all the portraits on the outside and, for its inner surprise, contained a little globe with maps of the royal domains in 1613 and 1913. Somewhat ironically, the celebrations emphasized the personal glories of the autocrats, not the fact that a representative assembly in 1613 had raised up an untried dynasty in a time of great national stress. During the year the imperial family made pilgrimages to the original Romanov estate on the Volga and to the Ipatiev Monastery where Michael had accepted the throne. There were impressive ceremonies in Moscow, but the general political situation was tense enough for some observers to remark on Nicholas' brave composure in riding into the city 20 yards ahead of his escort and on the anxious hush that fell over his entourage until the Kremlin bells announced the tsar's safe arrival. The empress felt otherwise. Her prejudices were confirmed by the popular acclamation, and she berated the ministers for "frightening the Emperor with threats of revolution," when "we need merely to show ourselves and their hearts are ours."

Rasputin was much in evidence everywhere during the tercentenary, leading to a contretemps in the Kazan Cathedral of St. Petersburg when Rodzianko found him sitting among the seats reserved with great difficulty for members of the Duma. The burly Duma president encountered the usual hypnotic look of greeting, and then, in his own remarkable words: "I suddenly became possessed of an almost animal fury, the blood rushed to my heart, and I realized I was working myself into a state of absolute frenzy. I too stared straight into Rasputin's eyes, and, speaking literally, felt my own starting out of my head. . . . 'You are a notorious swindler,' I said." Forthwith, Rodzianko seized Rasputin by the collar and forcefully evicted him. This drama was really as meaningless in the short run as the cheers for the dynasty in 1913 were in the long.

Kokovtsev was unexpectedly dismissed as prime minister in January, 1914. A last royal interview, in which this uninspired but honest official defended himself, ended with Nicholas exclaiming: "You are right and I am wrong," after which the tsar embraced the official and exclaimed: "Friends part like this." The only explanation anyone could offer was that the empress was taking her revenge for Kokovtsev's attitude on Rasputin. The new head of the cabinet at what proved to be a critical time was "His High Insignificance" the seventy-four-year-old Goremykin, who had held the job briefly and ingloriously in 1906. No one doubted that all ministers held their posts on sufferance from Rasputin.

The Duma debates in the spring of 1914 were stormy, the opposition now including Guchkov's Octobrists, and the main demand was for the resignation of the most reactionary and unpopular ministers, notably the minister of justice, Ivan Shcheglovitov. On July 1 that year Nicholas unexpectedly summoned the cabinet to Peterhof and proposed that the Duma be done away with. All the ministers were fearful of such a coup, even Shcheglovitov getting up to say that it would be disloyalty on his part to countenance what was sheer madness. "Quite enough," the ever-floundering Nicholas interjected. "Clearly, we must drop the question." Three days before this meeting the Archduke Francis Ferdinand had been assassinated in Sarajevo, while, two days before that, Rasputin had been stabbed, critically but not fatally, at his home in Pokrovskoe by a fanatic woman disciple of Illiodor.

It was the unlikeliest of times for the Russian emperor to be listening to the counsels of darkness. One can tick off any number of triumphs of Russian enlightenment in the era before 1914, and the real truth is that the nation was undergoing a frenzy of creativeness in many fields that promised to make the golden ages of Catherine II, Nicholas I, and Alexander II seem pallid by comparison. That the intellectual upsurge escaped Nicholas II is part of his tragedy.

Name almost any of the arts and sciences, and Russia was abreast or ahead of the rest of the world. Pavlov led in behaviorist psychology, and Alexander Popov was a dominant force in electrophysics. In music, Igor Stravinsky's *Rite of Spring* was performed in Paris in 1913 and produced the riotous reception that heralded something massively new and important. Russian philosophy ranged from Lenin's reinvigoration of materialism in the revolutionist's consequential general writings to the idealistic, religious views of neo-Slavophiles such as Sergius Soloviev and Nicholas Berdyaev.

Maxim Gorky, the thundering proletarian novelist, was at his peak before the war, but he was perhaps overshadowed by a whole group of writers dealing in morbidity, sensualism, and perversion, the most celebrated of whom were Michael Artsybashev, Leonid Andreyev, and Fedor Sologub. The Empress Alexandra might well feel that Petersburg's purveyors of erotic sensationalism were just another sign of the wickedness and decadence of the capital, but these writers were the precursors of a whole modern genre. To the number of experimental novelists could be added a wide spectrum of noted avant-garde poets under such varied banners as Symbolism, Imagism, and Futurism.

Russian painting threatened to oust Parisian art as the most influential. Some historians now credit Vasily Kandinsky with the first nonobjective drawing in 1910, and in addition to this young master, there were the rising stars of Marc Chagall, Alexei von Jawlensky, Paul Tchelitchew, Casimir Malevich, and Tatishchev, not to mention the more traditional locally famed painters Ilya Repin and Serov.

The names Michel Fokine, Sergius Diaghilev, Anna Pavlova, and Vaslav Nijinsky are enough to establish the fact that Russian ballet was at its zenith. The sensation of the last prewar season was Nijinsky's appearance in an unusually revealing costume, the dowager empress' horrified glare and exit from her box, and the subsequent dismissal of the incomparable dancer from the Imperial Ballet. The Dowager Marie may have been a prude, but at least she was not home in her palace listening to a religious quack.

XX.
Nicholas II: Disaster and Doom

1. 1914

A S EUROPE blundered into the First World War in 1914, Nicholas II
and Russia fully shared in the war guilt and no country and no
dynasty paid a heavier price. Yet the tragedy might have been confined to the ghastly casualty lists. The war brought a unity of tsar and people unparalleled since 1812, and thus it represented an opportunity for the
Romanov ruler to lead his country not only toward victory but also toward
political and social sanity. Nicholas II threw away this chance, just as he
had many others.

The considerable complicity of the Serbian government in the assassination of Francis Ferdinand on June 28 was only dimly suspected at the time,
thus rendering Austria's resolve to crush Serbia unreasonable. Kaiser William's so-called blank check of July 5, promising to back any action, was
also unreasonable. Historians not adhering to the anti-German-Austrian
side can say that it was just as irresponsible and aggressive for Nicholas to
declare later in the month that "in no case would Russia remain indifferent
to the fate of Serbia." Moreover, France was quick to give its unquestioning support to its Russian ally. The solidarity of the two powers was proclaimed during a visit of President Raymond Poincaré and Premier René
Viviani to St. Petersburg from July 20 to July 23. While these French visitors were at sea on their warship for the return home, Austria presented
Serbia with a forty-eight-hour ultimatum regarding investigation and punishment of the June 28 criminals. Even though Russia advised compliance
with the ultimatum, except for one point compromising Serbia's sovereignty,
Austria declared war on its Balkan neighbor on July 28.

Nicholas ordered partial Russian mobilization on July 29, and the focus of world attention swung to St. Petersburg. False reports of a general Austrian mobilization on the Russian border later that day led the tsar to direct general Russian mobilization, but this order was countermanded in view of the hostility it excited in Germany, which also had borders with Russia. The crucial moment came in the afternoon of July 30, when the chief of staff prompted Foreign Minister Sergius Sazonov to represent to the tsar that an effort to mobilize only on the Austrian frontiers would wreck any subsequent endeavor to mobilize on all frontiers. To back down generally, the foreign minister declared, would mean the loss of two centuries of hard-won influence in the Balkans and would condemn Russia to "a miserable existence on the sufferance of the Central Powers." Heartsick and, as ever, hesitant, Nicholas signed a general mobilization decree once more. The chief of staff promptly announced that his phone had gone out of order, precluding another change of mind at the palace.

The following day Germany demanded that Russia demobilize on their common frontiers within twelve hours. Behind this ultimatum were some broad calculations of German diplomats: rightly, that Russian army reforms would not be complete until 1917; wrongly, that the recent outbreaks of hostility between the throne and the Duma and the revived wave of strikes indicated an inability, if not unwillingness, of Nicholas' regime to fight. The German military strategists' insistence on getting the jump on the enemy soon superseded the deliberations of the civilians. A declaration of war was delivered by the German ambassador on August 1. The old diplomat was so upset that he left behind two documents, one announcing hostilities because of noncompliance with the ultimatum, the other declaring war in any case.

Loyal hearts were gladdened, even amazed, by the patriotic outburst in Russia. The day after the declaration the imperial family assembled at the Winter Palace and enthusiastically applauded Nicholas when he went out on the balcony to read word for word the pledge of Alexander I to fight on until not a single enemy soldier remained on Russian soil. There were many thousands gathered below in the same huge square where the tsar's Cossacks had mowed down the demonstrators of 1905. On the present occasion the people cheered and wept, finally kneeling en masse on the pavement and singing "God Save the Tsar." Later in the month the scene was repeated in Moscow. The tsar and all the uniformed grand dukes descended the Red Staircase of the Kremlin to attend a ceremony of blessing in the Uspensky Cathedral. The tsarevich was too sick to witness the excitement in Petersburg, and he had to be carried in Moscow.

Such little opposition to the war as there was came largely from the right wing. Elder statesman Witte in futile letters and conversations indicated his willingness to let Serbia go down the drain rather than stay the economic progress which he saw as the only hope to avert revolution. None other than the war minister, Vladimir Sukhomlinov, was upset at the prospect of fighting Germany, which he saw as the chief buttress of the principle of autocracy. "Let Papa not plan war, for with war will come the end of Russia and yourselves, and you will lose to the last man," wired Rasputin, as he recovered from his wound at Pokrovskoe. He was later quoted as saying: "If only that hussy hadn't poked me with a knife, there would never have been any war at all. I should not have permitted it." Rasputin eventually returned to St. Petersburg in the fall of 1914. The imperial couple accepted his phone calls and saw him at Vyrubova's house, but his antiwar strictures neither moved nor alienated them.

The liberal members of the cabinet were cheered by the prospect of war alongside the Western democracies. The Duma, which met on August 8, was unanimous in its patriotism, men of all parties joining in an informal sacred union in support of the war. Conservatives and moderates hastened to associate themselves with the city and provincial Zemstvo committees, which were authorized to set up nationwide organizations to further the Red Cross and other home-front mobilization activities. Prince George Lvov was most prominent in this work. The fiery leader of the Constitutional Democrats, Miliukov, was outspoken in his conviction that only unity and firm resolve to win the war mattered now. The left-wing Kerensky wanted to make concessions from the regime a precondition of Duma support, but even he went along with the idea that defense came first and democratic Socialism later, the same reasoning that lined up German Socialists behind *their* government. The illegal Socialist Revolutionary Party dropped its appeals for terrorism and peasant anarchism. The Mensheviks stopped their strike agitation. Only the Bolshevik Party came out against the war, all the while complaining of the social patriotism rampant among its followers; the arrest of its leaders later in the year drew virtually no protests.

People said that Nicholas personally was transfigured by the coming of war, while the tsarina at his side breathed hostility and contempt for Germany and her royal relatives there. Yet the imperial couple remained essentially unmoved by their new popularity, as they had by their unpopularity before. Two years later the president of the Duma was to complain that the government had no long-range view of Russia's future and that it was frightened by the unity of the people. Almost from the outset Nicholas' bureaucracy jealously threw obstacles in the way of the initiatives taken by the Zemstvos.

In a bow to anti-German hysteria the tsar promptly authorized the changing of the name St. Petersburg to the more Russian-sounding Petrograd, a name the city kept for ten years. The regime banned the manufacture and sale of liquor for the duration. Nicholas was personally zealous about temperance, but eventually he laid his government open to the charge that it struck down the drinking pleasures of the poor, all the while tolerating genteel imbibing by the rich.

Nicholas' first impulse was to assume command at the front, but he was persuaded by his ministers that he was indispensable in the capital. The post of commander in chief went instead to the popular Grand Duke Nicholas Nicholaevich. All the Romanov grand dukes rallied to tsar and fatherland, some, like Nicholas' brother Michael, ending a period of banishment and disgrace.

The Romanov ladies were soon involved in the war effort, too. The Dowager Empress Marie, blithely vacationing in Germany that July, had to face hostile mobs outside her Berlin hotel and nearly had her train stopped before she made the safety of Denmark, along with the Grand Duchess Xenia and the newlywed Yusupovs. The old lady insisted on being in Russia for the duration, living in Kiev. Meanwhile, the Empress Alexandra undertook the management of close to 100 hospitals around the capital, first enrolling with her daughters Olga and Tatiana in a two months' training course. The Catherine Palace at Tsarskoe Selo was converted to a hospital. Friends of the empress were to insist that she did not shirk the most menial and arduous of hospital duties, such as taking amputated limbs from the hands of surgeons and removing bloody, vermin-ridden bandages. Critics were to picture her and her daughters dallying, gloves on, with only the most select officer patients. Many a cute story was to be told of this or that grand duchess humbly and faithfully attending some truculent casualty, only to have her identity given away, at which point the soldier would dissolve into tears and apologies. Less romantic and perhaps equally fanciful is the tale of the imperial lady who asked a heavily bandaged patient if he needed anything, only to have him point to the bedpan. Something of the reality of it all is to be found in a letter of Alexandra to her husband: "I had wretched fellows with awful wounds—scarcely a man any more, so shot to pieces, perhaps it must be cut off as so black, but hope to save it— terrible to look at—I washed and cleaned and painted with iodine and smeared with vasoline and tied them up and bandaged all up . . . a young nurse (girl) I sent out of the room."

Germany had thrown its main armies against Belgium and France on August 3, bringing Britain into the war the next day. The kaiser's summary of German strategy was "lunch in Paris, dinner in St. Petersburg." Russia had previously promised its French ally to take the offensive within sixteen days with an army of 700,000. Counting on a knockout blow in the West, the German strategists had deployed only small defense forces east of Berlin. A Russian army under Paul Rennenkampf duly invaded East Prussia, but it failed to come to the aid of another force under Alexander Samsonov moving north from Poland. Samsonov committed suicide after his army was annihilated by the German generals Paul von Hindenburg and Erich Ludendorff in the great Battle of Tannenberg (August 23–30). The disaster was attributed to a personal rivalry of the two Russian commanders going back to the Russo-Japanese War, when they had had a fistfight, prompting the observation that if the Battle of Waterloo was won on the playing fields of Eton, the Battle of Tannenberg was lost on the station platform of Mukden. The German generals, using simple divide and conquer tactics, now turned on Rennenkampf's army and drove it from East Prussia after the Battle of the Masurian Lakes (September 6–15). At about the same time on the western front, the French stopped the German thrust at Paris in the celebrated First Battle of the Marne. Insofar as the Russians had panicked Berlin into reallocating troops west to east, they had helped save Paris and the whole Allied cause. Reckless and ill managed as the Russian drive into East Prussia had been, it had its chivalrous aspect. Now and later Nicholas II never hesitated to meet what he considered his obligations of honor to his allies.

The Russian defeats in the north were compensated for by tremendous successes in the south on the Austrian front. After repelling an Austrian drive into Poland, the Russian armies turned and drove hard into Galicia, capturing Lemberg in early September. Later the tsar was to decorate the Grand Duke Nicholas with the Order of St. George, reserved for generals who conquered whole provinces.

In October the Germans struck in the center at Russian Poland, forestalling renewed Russian plans to aid France and taking some of the pressure off Austria. A battle was fought on the outskirts of Warsaw before the enemy fell back. The Russians were too exhausted to turn the German retreat into a rout, although some Russian units ranged westward as far as German Silesia. The tsar's army still had high morale, but it was desperately short of cannons, rifles, and even bullets. Casualties of 1,000,000 meant the loss of one-quarter of the army by the end of 1914.

2. 1915

Nobody in Europe had expected a long war. Now the first winter of the conflict ground on drearily, without much fighting east or west, but with the prospect of great sacrifices ahead. Russia hardly noticed a desultory three-day Duma meeting in February. Public attention was more aroused in March by the hanging of the traitor Miasoyedov; as late as February this high officer had been vouched for by the war minister, Vladimir Sukhomlinov, all the while he was passing secrets to Germany, to say nothing of his carrying on with his patron's wife. With this scandal still rankling in his heart, Nicholas left for the front in early March, admittedly cheered by two things: He had been given a blessing by Rasputin, and Witte had finally died, the father of Russian industrialization denouncing the war as a stupid adventure to the end.

The Allied strategy in 1915 was to hit the Central Powers by the back door, so to speak. The Ottoman Empire, which joined the German and Austrian side in November, 1914, offered a tempting target for large Allied armies that otherwise would be bogged down in the hopeless stalemate of trench warfare in France. Britain and France launched operations against the Dardanelles in February. Russia was to send troops south from Odessa if the demands of its increasingly victorious push forward in Galicia were not too distracting. In March Russian troops swept into Przemysl, capturing 120,000 Austrian soldiers, and by early April they had reached the Carpathian divide, controlling all but one of the passes leading into Hungary. Even Ludendorff could not help admiring the "supreme contempt for death" of the onrushing Russian cavalry squadrons. Nicholas, who tirelessly visited every sector of the front, toured captured Galicia and slept in Emperor Francis Joseph's bed in Lemberg.

Allied hopes rose further in the spring of 1915, when it became apparent that Italy was coming in against the Central Powers. Italy's entry into the war was the background for feverish diplomatic dealings culminating in the secret treaties of London, which provided for the partitioning of the enemy countries. Among other things agreed to by Britain and France was that Russia should control Constantinople after the war. Nicholas' greed was not limited to the straits; privately he talked of taking German and Austrian Poland and even bits of Silesia and East Prussia. The spring peace feelers from Austria were contemptuously ignored, while the empress starchily rejected a plea for negotiations from her own brother, the Grand Duke of Hesse. Her intense patriotism unfortunately remained largely unknown to a Russian public ready to believe the worst. (One nasty story that went the rounds told of Alexis' being perpetually upset at home because his father cried when the Russians lost and his mother when they won.)

At the beginning of May a German army bucking up the crumbling Austrians on the Galician front broke through the Russian lines in a surprise offensive that netted the enemy almost 200,000 prisoners. The Germans had shifted a majority of their divisions to the eastern front, and their superior artillery was telling. By June the Russians had lost all their gains. At headquarters Nicholas II fretted helplessly, while the volatile Grand Duke Nicholas was in tears on occasion. Meanwhile, the Allies had been stymied in their Dardanelles campaign, both the naval thrust and the troop landings at Gallipoli offering little promise of further success.

The surprising first response of the tsar to the defeats was to liberalize the regime and to rally the country around it. He assented to the creation of a Central War Industries Committee, in which government officials were to work in cooperation with private bankers and businessmen. The efforts of this organization and the extragovernmental activities of the Zemstvos, city Dumas, and cooperatives under the direction of Prince Lvov were really to save the Russian war effort, providing all the indispensables from medicines to heavy munitions. In June, 1915, Nicholas won further applause by dropping the four most unpopular ministers, including the war minister, Sukhomlinov, a devious incompetent who as late as the fall of 1914 had assured France's Marshal Joseph Joffre that Russia had no shortage of arms.

Concessions to public opinion were the opposite of the empress' ideas of winning the war. At the time of the ministerial crisis she began lecturing her husband in letters to the front. "If you could only be severe, my love," she wrote, adding "they must learn to tremble before you." A few days later her words were: "Be more autocratic, my very own Sweetheart." Then she reverted to the ominous Rasputin theme: "Our Friend's enemies are ours." Actually, the holy man had been somewhat in disgrace with the tsar. In April he had left his imperial patrons ostensibly to go pray at the shrines of Moscow, but once there he proceeded to make the most obscene spectacle of himself to date in the old capital's leading restaurant, shouting to the outraged patrons that he could do the same things in the palace in front of the "Old Girl." The police, who had to take the drunken, raving lecher away, made a full report which was relayed to Nicholas by the assistant minister of the interior. For his zeal this official was complimented and befriended by the tsar all that summer, only to be abruptly fired from his post early in September.

The German offensive shifted from Galicia to central Poland in July, and Warsaw fell on August 4. Total Russian losses of killed, wounded, and captured now approached 3,000,000. "In a year of war the regular army had vanished," wrote General Alexis Brusilov, observing that Russia was now using its huge reserves of untrained manpower. "We have no weapon except the soldier's breast," wrote a private to his family, a homely acknowledgment of the fact that some soldiers went into battle without rifles. Retreat on a grand scale began that summer on the whole eastern front and lasted to September, when a line roughly from Riga to Tarnopol was held. All Poland and part of Lithuania had been lost. That it was a relatively orderly retreat, not a disastrous collapse, was attributed to the dogged skill of the Grand Duke Nicholas.

The news of September 5, 1915, was received with incredulity in the capitals of the world: The tsar announced that he was replacing the grand duke as the Russian commander in chief. Allies and enemies alike had admired the giant general's ability, and many of Nicholas' ministers had earnestly begged him not to take over headquarters in Mogilev. Even conservatives feared that the absence of the tsar's authority in the capital would open the home front to the worst sort of intrigues and the unchecked influence of Rasputin, but the empress felt that the grand duke was overshadowing her husband. (She made much of the report that "Nicholasha" once jocularly referred to himself as Nicholas III.) As for Rasputin, he had not forgotten that at the beginning of the war he had proposed to visit headquarters to hang some icons there and had received the grand duke's return wire: "Come and I'll hang." The grand duke accepted the new turn of events without protest and went off to take charge of the Caucasus front.

The prime minister tried to resign and was refused. Eight cabinet members sent a collective letter of protest, but they were told, in effect, to mind their own business and to stay at their posts in the capital, even though the empress now regarded them as "fiends worse than the Duma." Generally, however, Alexandra was ecstatic about the turn of events. When Nicholas arrived to take over headquarters, he was greeted with her letter ending: "Sleep well, my sunshine, Russia's saviour." Some months later she boasted of the crisis to him as the time when "I fought for you even against yourself."

In effect, Nicholas had made Alexandra co-ruler in September, 1915. The empress consulted Rasputin in everything, and his political ascendancy, which began in 1911, became complete. That the ex-coachman meddled in everything is evident from Alexandra's letters to her husband: Rasputin had his own ideas about taxes; he had a plan to deal with the food situation; he wanted so-and-so for the highest office of the church; he considered an advance on this front timely; and he was projecting arrangements for a triumphal entry of Russian forces into Constantinople. Always there was his hand behind appointments and dismissals, from the cabinet down. "He likes our friend" became a constant refrain in the empress' messages, indicating that a new political favorite was on hand. There could be no fuller admission of Rasputin's hold on Alexandra than when she let slip to her would-be autocrat husband the awesome generalization "We must always do what he says."

Rasputin, after years of effort, got a man named Alexis Hvostov appointed minister of the interior. However venal and right-wing, Hvostov was patriot enough to realize soon that his patron was confiding state secrets to probable German agents during drunken evenings. The loss of Britain's most celebrated soldier, Lord Kitchener, whose warship was torpedoed on his way to Russia, may even have been a direct result of a Rasputin indiscretion. Incongruously, it became Hvostov, the holy man's protégé, who first seriously planned to murder him, but it was the minister, not Rasputin, who lost his position.

In December, 1915, when the tsar and his son were making a trip back to headquarters, Alexis banged his nose on the train window, and the seriousness of his hemorrhaging made the tsar decide to return to Tsarskoe Selo. Rasputin was phoned, and his mere appearance at the palace sufficed to make the tsarevich stop bleeding. Could it matter to the distraught empress that her miracle man was involved a month later in another vile orgy which became public knowledge because it ended in a brawl?

The government crisis of late 1915 ended the self-imposed political silence. Even many conservatives in the Duma now joined the old opposition forces to form a Progressive Bloc demanding a cabinet that enjoyed the confidence of the country and an end to police persecution of trade unions, Poles, Jews, and the organs of self-government. Their agitation was in vain.

Others regarded the political situation as so critical that drastic action was required. In the highest circles there was talk of removing the empress to a convent and sending Rasputin to Siberia or even of deposing the emperor and proclaiming a regency for Alexis. A leading fighter pilot concocted a wild scheme to bomb the tsar's train but did not go through with it.

Ironically, almost the very day Nicholas made his fateful decision to become commander in chief a scarcely noticed meeting of extreme Socialists took place in Zimmerwald, Switzerland. The majority of the handful present came out for immediate peace without indemnities and without annexations. A bitter minority led by Lenin could not get support for their extreme slogan to "Turn the imperialist war into a civil war"—that is, to utilize the fighting to begin social revolution.

By this time the eastern front had become virtually stalemated. The tsar had enough sense not to interfere with the military dispositions of his able chief of staff, Michael Alexeyev. Nicholas was merely an attentive bystander—an avid reader of all the dispatches, a devotee of military maps, and an amiable companion of his fellow officers over a cigarette—when he should have been ruling in Petrograd.

3. *1916*

In January of the third year of the war the major belligerents were confidently perfecting plans for new offensives. Russia was no exception. Nicholas' representatives promised a great push westward at a conference of the Allies at Chantilly in December. The tsar's generosity in committing his army was not utter foolhardiness, for in the past several months Russia's military posture had improved sharply, thanks to the efforts of the new war minister, General Polivanov, in training troops and of Guchkov's Central War Industries Committee in rounding up munitions. The chief British military observer reported that the morale of the Russian troops seemed remarkably high in view of the losses of the past year. Spirits were further lifted by the news of the successes of the Grand Duke Nicholas against the Turks on the Caucasus front, and in February, Admiral Alexander Kolchak's fleet made the Black Sea so much a Russian lake that he was able to mine the Bosporus. Yet there was increasing feeling that Russia's soldiers were being ill served by their government.

If Goremykin's dismissal as prime minister in February caused everyone's happy surprise, his replacement, Boris Stürmer, produced a reaction of shock and horror. The tsar's choice, in whom Nicholas said he had "unlimited confidence," was a reactionary, an adherent of Rasputin, a hater of the Duma, and an opponent of the war. According to the British ambassador, Stürmer was untrustworthy and motivated only by ambition. His French colleague was even more outspoken, calling the new prime minister "low, intriguing, and treacherous." Later, people were to look back to Stürmer as the beginning of the end. The cabinet ceased to function as a body. Stürmer and the others reported individually to the empress' mauve boudoir.

His habitual waverings of intention led the tsar to visit the Duma unexpectedly that February and to hail its members as representatives of his people for the first time. Cynics were to say that Stürmer simply needed a royal escort to escape being booed. In March, Nicholas made matters even worse by dismissing the cabinet official who commanded most confidence, General Polivanov, the man many credited with nothing less than the restoration of the Russian army. Polivanov's willingness to work with the Central War Industries Committee was one factor that set Rasputin and, in turn, the empress against him.

In the west the great Battle of Verdun had been in progress since February. As this slaughter moved into the hundreds of thousands, Nicholas again generously came to his ally's aid. A major push began in June, taking the name of the Brusilov Offensive from the highly energetic, hard-hitting general who was in charge of it. The artillery, so laboriously accumulated by Polivanov, proved decisive. In a few days the Austrian army was reeling back, and by August the Russians had broken through a 260-mile line. Germany had to transfer many divisions from the west to bolster her ally. Although 450,000 prisoners were taken, Russian losses approached 1,000,000.

Both the Duma and Russia's allies were distressed by the abrupt sacking of Sazonov as foreign minister in late July. Sazonov had worked out a scheme promising autonomy to the Poles, and Nicholas had approved this effort to win back their allegiance. Then the empress appeared at headquarters and quoted Rasputin to the effect that Nicholas should not give up "baby's rights"—that is, the tsarevich's future title of King of Poland. The detested Stürmer took over Sazonov's post. He soon made the disastrous error of pushing Rumania into the war, ignoring Sazonov and Alexeyev's predictions that the new Balkan ally would be more a liability than an asset. The Rumanians brashly invaded Hungary only to be thrown back, and by December a German army was occupying Bucharest. Instead of helping the Brusilov Offensive, Stürmer's move brought it to a grim close.

The capping political outrage perpetrated by the empress and Rasputin was the appointment of Alexander Protopopov as minister of the interior in September, 1916. Unlike virtually all his predecessors, Protopopov made no efforts to disassociate himself from the holy man, who, for his part, pointed to the palm of his hand and said, "That's where the power is now."

The rule or ruin policies of the regime stirred increasing anger and sorrow in all sections of society as Russia entered its third winter of war. The strike movement assumed alarming proportions again, and in October war-weary soldiers had joined a strike in the capital, firing on the police and retreating only before a large force of Cossacks. Food shortages were producing long queues and ugly crowds.

There were warnings to Nicholas from his mother and from the British ambassador. The Grand Duke Nicholas Michaelovich showed up at headquarters with a carefully written memorial asking his cousin to "protect yourself from constant systematic maneuvers that people are attempting by the intermediary of the wife you love." The grand duke's brother wrote from the south: "I can tell you everyone asks for the dismissal of Stürmer and a responsible ministry to protect you from the deceits of the Ministers. . . . I am sure the Lord will help you to meet the universal wish and avert the imminent storm which is coming from the interior of Russia." Once again Petrograd salons and clubs buzzed with talk of coups, of forcing the tsar to send his wife away or of proclaiming Alexis.

The fifth session of the Duma began in November, and that body was electrified by a speech of Miliukov not only castigating Stürmer but also hinting that the empress was party to German intrigues. Reciting the mistakes and abuses of the past years, the Cadet leader kept shouting, "What is this—stupidity or treason?" The empress demanded Miliukov's arrest, and publication of the speech was confined to secret presses.

Stürmer was dismissed late in November, his fault lying not in his unpopularity but in the loss of the empress' trust. The new prime minister, Alexander Trepov, was regarded as an extreme conservative but at least as an honest one. His loyalty was clearly to the tsar, not Rasputin, but after a few days he realized his position was impossible, and he tried to resign. Refused, he attempted desperately to bribe Rasputin to stay out of his way, and this attempt failed too. The Duma, not unpleased with Trepov, resumed its hostile posture when it was made plain that Minister of the Interior Protopopov would stay in the cabinet. Nicholas wavered, even begging Alexandra not to "drag our Friend into this," but she insisted on keeping Rasputin's henchman.

The Duma session of December was marked by an unexpected and ominous emotional outburst from one of the hitherto unquestioningly monarchist deputies, Vladimir Purishkevich. Russia's most lugubrious orator called for sounding the bell from the Tower of Ivan the Great to arouse the country against the unscrupulous Gregory Rasputin, whom he called a destroyer of the dynasty as surely as Gregory Ostrepev had brought on the Time of Troubles 300 years before. Purishkevich threw out such potent catchwords as "dark forces," "ministerial leap-frog," and the "infamy of Russian life."

Toward the end of the year the Grand Duchess Elizabeth left her convent in Moscow to have it out with the empress. Upon the mention of Rasputin, Alexandra angrily ordered a carriage for her sister, who left never to see her again. "She drove me away like a dog," "Aunt Ella" moaned. "Poor Nicky. Poor Russia."

In fact, just when *all* others were having second thoughts, the empress was emerging more hysterically unyielding than ever. Her most forceful letters to the tsar came that December. "Draw the reins in tightly, which you let loose. . . . Russia loves to feel the whip. . . . I have had no sleep, but listen, to me, which means Our Friend." The most striking of her outbursts ran: "Be the Emperor, be Peter the Great, Ivan the Terrible, the Emperor Paul—crush them all under you. Now don't you laugh, naughty one. . . . Send Lvov to Siberia. . . . Miliukov, Guchkov, and Polivanov also to Siberia. . . . I kiss you, caress you, long for you, can't sleep without you, bless you." To this Nicholas replied: "Tender thanks for the severe written scolding. . . . Your poor little weak-willed hubby."

High life went on in Petrograd. At the ballet on December 6 Kshessinska danced in the *Pharaoh's Daughter,* a celebrated performance of hers during which she shot arrows at a boy playing a monkey in the treetops. The young performer, George Balanchine, was presented to the tsar and tsarina afterward and given a silver box with candy in it.

On December 30, 1916, rumors of the murder of Rasputin were everywhere, from the Alexander Palace to the meanest slums of the capital. Actually, the existence of a conspiracy to rid Russia of its holy devil had been an open secret in Duma circles for a month. The chief conspirator was no less a person than the tsar's nephew-in-law, Prince Felix Yusupov. The twenty-eight-year-old heir to the largest fortune in Russia (more than $500,000,000), Yusupov in his recent youth had alternated between living in the most princely quarters imaginable at Oxford and making frequent appearances in St. Petersburg nightclubs dressed convincingly as a woman. When he married the Grand Duchess Xenia's daughter Irene in the last months before the war, his bride had entered on the tsar's arm. A belated enlistee in the armed forces, Yusupov was an old drinking companion of another of the conspirators, Grand Duke Dmitri Pavlovich, first cousin to the tsar and in recent years such a favorite in the royal household that he addressed Nicholas as Uncle. Reportedly favored as a husband for the tsar's oldest daughter, the twenty-six-year-old grand duke had a safe military position and enjoyed frequent leave from headquarters. (Alexandra was alarmed at Dmitri's drinking and had once written her husband: "Order Dmitri back to his regiment. Town and women are poison for him.") The third leading plotter was Purishkevich, the Black Hundreds man turned Rasputin hater, whose recent blast on the Duma floor Yusupov had listened to with delight. A doctor was also enlisted in the conspiracy as an expert on poisons.

Rasputin was lured to Yusupov's great palace on the Moika Canal on the night of December 29, the prince having already had social contacts with the holy man through Vyrubova and others. Possibly the prospect of meeting Princess Irene was the lure, although in actuality Yusupov's wife was in the Crimea. Knowing this, the empress tried to warn him against the rendezvous, as did Protopopov. There is some evidence that Rasputin had become fatalistic about his life. A letter by him predicting violence at the hands of royalty and consequent ruin for Russia was later produced by his friends, and at his last meeting with Nicholas, Rasputin had said ominously: "Today *you* bless *me.*" Nonetheless, he allowed himself to be conducted into the newly refurbished cellar apartment in the mansion and found himself alone with Yusupov, while upstairs there were sounds of a party going on as the other conspirators played "Yankee Doodle" and popular ballads on a phonograph. An elaborate bric-a-brac cupboard fascinated the holy man into relaxation.

The scheme was to poison Rasputin with cyanide of potassium contained in almond cakes and in wine. Eventually he availed himself of both offerings, but nothing happened. (It has been demonstrated by pathologists that the stomach of about one person out of twenty does not secrete the hydrochloric acid which is necessary to combine with ingested cyanide to produce the hydrocyanic, or prussic, acid that, absorbed by the blood, stops the oxidation process in the tissue cells and produces almost instant death.) Frantic, Yusupov consulted his colleagues and came back with a revolver. Rasputin hazily asked him to play the guitar, and the ex-transvestite performer was able to oblige him. Then Yusupov aroused Rasputin's interest in an icon, and, while the holy man was crossing himself, the prince shot him near the heart. Leaving the apparently lifeless body on the fur rug,

Yusupov went off to arrange an alibi with his friends. Upon his return to the cellar, Yusupov was suddenly confronted with an aroused Rasputin, who proceeded to chase him up the stairs. Purishkevich caught up with Rasputin in the courtyard and felled him after several shots. Yusupov battered at the corpse some more with a heavy object, and then Rasputin's body was loaded into Dmitri's automobile. The conspirators did a sloppy job of dumping the victim off a bridge into a canal, where he was found on January 1. The presence of water in the lungs indicated that death came only from drowning.

Rasputin was buried in the park of Tsarskoe Selo on January 3 in the presence of an agitated Alexandra and a worried Nicholas, who had hurried back from headquarters. This final solicitude of the royal couple disgusted a group of the imperial family, who, in turn, alienated the tsar and his wife by presenting an unprecedented joint letter asking for pardon for Yusupov and Dmitri. Among the signatories were the Grand Dukes Paul, Nicholas Michaelovich, Michael Michaelovich, the Grand Duchess Maria Pavlovna, and several of her sons. "It is given to nobody to occupy himself with murder," scribbled Nicholas on the margin of the document. Most of the Romanovs involved in this affair never were allowed contact with their sovereigns again. "The disintegration of the family could not have been more complete," wrote the court doctor.

The press was forbidden to publish the news of Rasputin's murder, but everyone knew, and some people went out of their way to salute and even kneel before Yusupov's palace, where the prince had been put under house arrest. Not everybody rejoiced, however: Soldiers were heard to mutter that the one peasant like themselves who had gained access to the tsar had been done in by the privileged, who were let off for their crime. Prince Yusupov was eventually exiled to his estates, while Grand Duke Dmitri was posted to the Caucasus front, a step which may have saved his life when the Revolution came.

Aspects of the Rasputin case have been live questions fifty years after his death. In 1934 a movie about the holy man featuring all the Barrymores was subject to a libel suit brought by Princess Irene, whose objection was that sexual relations between him and her were hinted at. She won, but not so her husband when he sued CBS in 1965 for invasion of privacy after a television presentation of the murder, apparently conceived on the presumption that *all* the principals were dead. The lengthy court proceedings in New York still left unsettled the question of whether the prince deliberately used his wife as bait. What did come as a surprise was Yusupov's going back on all the patriotic motivations he had paraded in his several books on the murder and declaring that only Rasputin's sexual depravity infuriated him.

4. *1917*

The assassination of Rasputin did not bring the expected palace revolution. No Romanov led a march on Tsarskoe Selo. The tsar, who stayed away from headquarters for the next two months, appeared apathetic but immovable. The ex-Prime Minister Kokovtsev was alarmed at his sovereign's "mirthless smile" and "expression of helplessness." The empress' mauve boudoir now became even more the center of the government of the Russian Empire. The chief telephone of the palace was in this room, and here Nicholas transacted affairs, while she often sat at her desk staring at the royal portrait above it—incredibly, a portrait of Marie Antoinette. Visitors noticed that when Nicholas granted an interview in the nearby audience chamber, it seemed as if someone else were listening from behind a curtain, and indeed, Alexandra did avail herself of a secret passageway and a hidden couch.

The colorless prime minister, Trepov, was finally allowed to resign early in January, to be replaced by the virtually unknown Prince Nicholas Golitsyn, whose experience in government was confined to administering one of the empress' charities. The poor man tearfully pleaded old age, inability, and ill health, but Nicholas insisted on the appointment, which had the effect of putting more power in the hands of the minister of the interior, Protopopov, who was rumored to be trying to recall the spirit of Rasputin via séances. After other cabinet changes, Russia found itself with a government of unknowns, except for a hated few. "We are wasting our time," exclaimed the chief British military representative at a meeting with fumbling Russian officials.

In mid-January British Ambassador George William Buchanan spoke plainly to Nicholas again, warning him as a friend of the dangers that were approaching. In answer to a plea to regain his people's confidence, the tsar riposted about the people's regaining *his* confidence, and afterward the eavesdropping empress angrily demanded the ambassador's recall. At a subsequent New Year's reception, Rodzianko pointedly refused Protopopov's hand, apologized to Nicholas for his rudeness in the palace, and then went on to report that the "gravest upheavals may be expected." Nicholas clutched his head and mused: "Is it possible that for twenty-two years I have tried to act for the best, and that for twenty-two years it was all a mistake?" Rodzianko's none-too-gentle reply was: "Yes, Your Majesty, for twenty-two years you have followed a wrong course." About this time Rodzianko was summoned to a meeting with the Grand Duchess Maria Pavlovna and her sons, and the loyal politician was shocked and had to protest his official capacity when she told him that the empress had to be done away with.

Shortly afterward the emperor instructed the minister of justice to draw up a manifesto dissolving the Duma, but then, just as vaguely, he let drop this bold plan for a coup. The Duma did meet, after a delay of a month, on February 27, and Miliukov and Kerensky vied in denouncing the regime, all the while offering no plan of action.

March 7 (February 22 Old Style), Wednesday: Nicholas decided to return to his duties at headquarters, a step urged on him by the Grand Duke Michael, who wanted to get his brother away from the influence of the empress. Earlier, in an interview with Prime Minister Golitsyn, the emperor had promised to appoint a responsible ministry, only to tell him before leaving that he had changed his mind. Protopopov tried to persuade Nicholas not to go but got only his promise to return in a week, as well as signed but undated documents providing for the proroguing or dissolving of the Duma. The departing emperor showed annoyance at the details of the troop redeployment on the capital, but the garrison commander, Khabalov, assured him that the soldiers would "do their duty" in case of trouble. Elsewhere that same day the director of the huge Putilov ironworks locked out 40,000 workers.

March 8, Thursday: On his way to Mogilev, Nicholas sent a message to Alexandra: "Feel again firm but very lonely." She soon made reply: The children had come down with measles, first Olga, then Alexis, and next Tatiana. Meanwhile, 100,000 workers were out on strike in Petrograd. Socialist orators stirred up crowds with speeches in honor of Women's Day. People clamored for bread, with a few shouting for the overthrow of the autocracy. There were scuffles with the police and some looting.

March 9, Friday: The police and army units in Petrograd were unable to stop concerted mobs of people from crossing the Neva bridges and demonstrating on Nevsky Prospekt and in front of the Taurida Palace, where the Duma was in session debating the food situation. Bakeries were being sacked everywhere. Nicholas wired Alexandra that she had better let the other two grand duchesses catch the measles also.

March 10, Saturday: The number of strikers continued to swell, and masses of students joined the demonstrators. No newspapers appeared, but red flags did. The troops were listless or friendly toward the crowds. A Cossack was cheered when he cut down a policeman. A dense throng in front of the Nicholaevsky Station was fired on in an area now honored as Uprising Square. The Duma went home after scheduling its next meeting two days hence. The cabinet tried to resign. Alexandra wrote her husband in annoyance of the "hooligan movement" in the streets, composed of "boys and girls" who ran about because the weather was unseasonably warm. Somewhat more realistic about the situation he was trying to assess from several hundred miles away, Nicholas phoned General Khabalov at 9 P.M.: "I command that the disorders in the capital shall be stopped tomorrow as they are inadmissable at the heavy time of war with Germany and Austria."

March 11, Sunday: Despite Khabalov's warning posters, the crowds reassembled and were systematically fired on. The leading force in the daylong repression was the training unit of the Volnsky machine-gun battalion. In despair, Rodzianko telegraphed Nicholas regarding the "anarchy" and the need for a "new government . . . without delay . . . may the blame not fall on the wearer of the crown," he pleaded. Nicholas' reaction in words to an aide was: "This fat Rodzianko has written me some nonsense, to which I will not even reply." Troops were ordered to the capital, and Golitsyn was authorized to dissolve the Duma, the official notice being antedated one day.

March 12, Monday: "It's a lovely morning. We'll go for a run in the car." It was Alexandra on the phone to a friend. From the early hours, leaderless mobs controlled the streets of Petrograd. Shots were exchanged with policemen firing from rooftops. All political orators were cheered good-naturedly. Beginning with none other than the training company of the Volnsky machine-gun battalion, the garrison units mutinied one by one, including the elite Guards regiments. By afternoon General Khabalov had fewer than 2,000 loyal men, and they were holed up in the Winter Palace. Thousands of civilians and soldiers milled in and about the Taurida Palace, where the Duma members continued to meet despite the order for their dismissal. "I don't want to revolt," moaned the ever-loyal but now-weary and frightened Rodzianko. "Take the power. . . . If you don't, others will," an even more conservative politician rejoined. Rodzianko's temporizing was perhaps fatal for law and order. Not until late in the day did the Duma set up a Provisional Committee to rule. Already down the corridor in the Taurida leftists had once again organized the Petrograd Soviet, which became an immediate rival for power. Elsewhere in the city the tsar's cabinet met under Golitsyn, but it did little more than tell Protopopov to go into hiding. The Grand Duke Michael, in attendance at this meeting, was asked to take charge of the troops and was commissioned to phone the tsar with a request for a responsible ministry. He succeeded in getting through to headquarters and was told to wait an hour, at which point General Alexeyev rang back to tell him to do nothing but wait for the tsar, who was coming to take charge. Calls also got through to Tsarskoe Selo, where the empress, calm in face of all the reports, insisted on remaining because her sick children could not be moved.

March 13, Tuesday: In the early hours General Nicholas Ivanov set off from headquarters toward the capital with one battalion of war heroes. An earlier plan to move in four regiments from the front had been abandoned. At the station platform he conferred with Nicholas, who was going on another train by another route, and the tsar concurred when Ivanov indicated that an attack on a completely hostile Petrograd was out of the question. That morning Khabalov's loyal force entrenched in the Winter Palace was forced to disperse when threatened with the guns of the Peter and Paul Fortress, newly captured by the revolutionaries. A handful of officers barricaded in the Astoria Hotel was now all that remained of the old regime in Petrograd. The Duma Building was again a crowded madhouse serving as a prison as delegations of soldiers kept bringing in ex-ministers to be dealt with. Kerensky's authoritative "Don't dare touch that man" probably saved a sniveling Protopopov from a lynching, but generally there was little decisiveness shown by the Duma. Rodzianko did phone the empress advising her to flee, but she found it impossible to get the imperial train. Without anyone's order, trucks with revolutionary soldiers descended on Tsarskoe Selo that day, and the empress could hear rifleshots in the town. Only a small force, mainly of officers, remained on guard, and fearing attack, they actually took up firing positions. Alexandra and her eldest daughter went out into the freezing night to provide their defenders with tea and other comforts. In Switzerland, Lenin received his first news of the Petrograd events with utter disbelief, having declared but weeks before that his generation would not see the Revolution.

March 14, Wednesday: General Ivanov's small force got through to Tsarskoe Selo, but he and the empress were soon confronted with the news that the tsar's train had been blocked near Dno by order of the Railroad Committee of the Duma. The Grand Duke Paul was summoned to the palace to give advice and ended up lecturing Alexandra that she should sign a constitutional draft that he had just drawn up in conjunction with the Grand Duke Michael. She refused to do anything, even though the number of riotous soldiers at Tsarskoe Selo was increasing and Ivanov decided to evacuate his battalion. The tsar's train, diverted westward, reached Pskov that evening. Everyone at hand remarked Nicholas' extraordinary self-possession in the crisis: He shaved, he ate, he got reports, he talked, and he slept just as always. Later he communicated with Rodzianko in Petrograd and offered him the prime ministership, but the Duma president replied that it was too late.

The Duma itself could not agree on the composition of a new government, and the Petrograd Soviet was issuing its own orders to the garrison. Sporadic shootings continued in the capital. Grand Duke Cyril at the head of the Navy Guards created a minor sensation by swearing allegiance to the Provisional Committee; his breaking his oath to the tsar was a necessary move if he was to retain any control over his command, he later explained.

March 15, Thursday: The Provisional Committee finally agreed in the early hours of the morning to ask the tsar's abdication, and about 5 A.M. Alexander Guchkov and Basil Shulgin left on a special train to Pskov to accomplish this. That morning Nicholas had already signed a manifesto appointing a responsible ministry and had ordered the halt of troop movements from the front. Before noon the tsar received the results of a poll of the chief commanders that had been arranged by Alexeyev: All five generals, including Brusilov on the southwestern front and the Grand Duke Nicholas in the Caucasus, advised his abdication and a regency. No one held out any hope for a counterrevolution.

Nicholas pondered the situation looking out the window of his railroad car and then turned toward his breathless staff to announce: "I have decided that I shall give up the throne in favor of my son Alexis." A document providing for the succession of "Alexis II" and the regency of Michael was drawn up by midafternoon. In the interval before the arrival of Guchkov and Shulgin, Nicholas had a long consultation with his personal physician, who advised him that the tsarevich's disease was incurable. Accordingly, when the Duma delegation arrived at 10 P.M. Nicholas had ready a new document abdicating not only for himself, but also for his son. The text ended: "May the Lord God help Russia! NICHOLAS." The spontaneous February Revolution had overthrown Nicholas II at the cost of about 1,300 casualties.

"You will understand the feelings of a father," Nicholas said simply as the emissaries from Petrograd were made comfortable in the sitting room of the imperial train. Actually, Nicholas' action was illegal by strict application of Paul's 1797 Succession Law, whereby a rightful heir would have to renounce the throne for himself. The ex-Foreign Minister Sazonov was to write: "I shall never forgive him for abdicating for his son," and many at headquarters feared for the monarchy.

Nicholas still had to name a new government. He indifferently agreed to the suggested choice of the popular Red Cross head. "Oh. Lvov? Very well, Lvov." Shulgin was beside himself with mixed pity and respect, blurting out: "Oh, Your Majesty, if you had done all this earlier, even as late as the last summoning of the Duma. . . ." Nicholas replied with characteristic vagueness: "Do you think it might have been avoided?" Throughout this momentous transaction Nicholas was entirely controlled, even charming and solicitous of the ease of his visitors. His staff on the train appeared almost indifferent, but one officer with a frustrated sense of the dramatic was to snort later that "he had abdicated from the throne of Russia as if he were handing over a squadron."

In privacy late that night Nicholas wrote in his diary: "All around treachery, cowardice, and deceit." Indeed, he found himself a virtually deserted man, isolated even from his wife. The scores of members of the Romanov dynasty had been entirely out of contact with him—many of them known to be hostile, some of them helplessly sympathetic, but virtually all alienated in some degree. The ex-tsar began that night to make plans about retiring with his immediate family to the Crimea. At Tsarskoe

Selo the ex-tsarina was having her wires to her husband returned with the printed notation "Address of person mentioned unknown," and there was no heat or electricity.

March 16, Friday: The provisional government was announced, with Lvov prime minister and with the Octobrist Guchkov, the Cadet Miliukov, and the Socialist Kerensky in the cabinet. The Petrograd Soviet, which controlled the masses, accepted the middle-class regime but would not join it. The news of Nicholas' second abdication caused consternation among the ministers. "Grand Duke Michael's accession is impossible," exclaimed Rodzianko, recalling the boos any mention of the monarchy caused in the crowds. Ironically, that special bugbear of the empress, Miliukov, argued most passionately for retaining the dynasty as Russia's rallying point. Meanwhile, Guchkov and Shulgin had arrived back with the abdication at Petrograd's Warsaw Station, but their triumphant reception by thousands of railway workers turned into a near lynching when they attempted the proclamation of Michael II.

Later that morning Michael was waited on by members of the new government, after they had overcome their scruples about awakening him at his residence at 10 Milliony Street. Already he had received a wire from the ex-tsar addressed, surprisingly, "To His Majesty the Emperor Michael." As the frail-looking grand duke listened in his armchair, Lvov and Rodzianko advised against his accession, after which Miliukov made an emotional plea for acceptance, to be seconded quietly by Guchkov. After conferring in private with the first two and being told there was no guaranteeing his safety, Michael came back to announce in tears that he would accept the throne only upon invitation by a constituent assembly. This abdication, the last by a Romanov, was formally drawn up in the children's schoolroom nearby.

Later in the day the Soviet Executive Committee demanded the arrest of the tsar and of all the dynasty (possibly it was the Bolshevik Vyacheslav Molotov who made the motion). They were assured by Lvov that the tsar was friendless and the others harmless. It was agreed that Nicholas could return to headquarters to say good-bye, then proceed to Tsarskoe Selo to join his sick children, and eventually leave the country.

The empress had been informed of the abdication by the Grand Duke Paul and a court official, and she proudly proclaimed that her husband had done as he did only to preserve his coronation oath.

The most moving moment of Nicholas' leave-taking at Mogilev occurred when he said good-bye at the train platform to his mother, the dowager, who had rushed up from Kiev. She blamed the abdication on Alexandra and bestowed more tears than comfort on her son, whom she was never to see again. Nicholas' last message to "the troops which I so fervently love" exhorted them to "submit yourselves to the Provisional Government," to keep up discipline, and to regard peace talkers as traitors.

Despite threats, Nicholas in company with a delegation of the provisional government arrived at Tsarskoe Selo on the morning of March 22 without incident. All his suite made their farewells to him at the train station, only Prince Basil Dolgoruky choosing to stay with his master. When he drove up to the Alexander Palace, Alexandra rushed out and embraced her husband passionately. He broke down when they were alone together. Later Nicholas went out for his afternoon walk in the park, only to find his path blocked by six guards, who roughly told him, "You can't go there, Mr. Colonel." Technically, the ex-tsar was under arrest, but it was for his own safety. Sometime after midnight the royal prisoners heard a bawling party of soldiers exhuming Rasputin's body and burning it near the palace.

While Nicholas dreamed of retirement at Livadiya, the provisional government decided that the former imperial couple should be sent off via Murmansk to England, which was an allied country, a monarchy, and the home of Alexandra's sister. King George V offered asylum through Ambassador Buchanan on March 23. Germany even was reported willing to guarantee passage of a British cruiser to fetch the ex-tsar. An immediate departure was impossible, however, because the children now had smallpox. The soviet was opposed to Nicholas' going, but as it turned out, it was not the Russians who backed down on the project but the British. Prime Minister David Lloyd George feared British worker demonstrations against the former autocrat and the Labour Party's making political capital of the situation. Accordingly, the king instructed Buchanan to announce April 10 that "His Majesty's Government does not insist on its former offer of hospitality to the Imperial family," and later that summer the offer was entirely withdrawn by the tearful ambassador. Nicholas took calmly his unwelcome in the country that hitherto had been haven for all the deposed.

In the first weeks after the fall of the tsarist regime the Russian press indulged itself in a frenzy of sensationalist speculation about Rasputin and the imperial family. Vyrubova was even driven to submit to a health examination to prove officially that she was a virgin and thus dispel some of the worst stories going around. An investigatory commission under the minister of justice, Kerensky, probed into Romanov affairs. At one point Kerensky required that Nicholas and Alexandra be separated to prevent them from corroborating evidence. They could take meals together in the presence of an officer, if they spoke only Russian, not their usual English. Nothing whatsoever was found to indicate that the former emperor or empress had anything to do with Russia's enemies or that they had even toyed with the notion of a separate peace. Thus assured, Socialist Kerensky became the self-appointed chief protector of the royalty at Tsarskoe Selo, endeavoring to silence press gossip and parrying all efforts of the soviet to harass them. On his first personal interview with Nicholas and Alexandra at the Alexander Palace late in March, the court chamberlain, Count Paul Benckendorff, escorted him into their presence with all the old ceremony. The fallen tsar put the rising politician of the hour at ease with a handshake and chitchat. Led in to meet Alexandra, Kerensky succeeded in dispelling her usual chilliness, backed by the additional conviction that he was some sort of revolutionary ogre. In the succeeding weeks she came to trust him completely, as did her husband. There is something pathetic about Nicholas' belated appreciation of Kerensky expressed in these words: "He is a man who loves Russia and I wish I could have known him earlier because he could have been useful to me."

Life at Tsarskoe Selo eventually settled into a not unpleasant routine for the royal prisoners. They had free run of the palace and a portion of the grounds. The soldiers' lounging about without their belts and smoking offended Nicholas' military sensibilities, but the family also found some humor in catching sentries asleep or at ease in gilded chairs borrowed from the palace. Generally, the ex-tsar tried to be affable with his captors, responding with a smile to either "Your Imperial Majesty" or "Citizen Romanov." Once when an officer refused his outstretched hand, Nicholas could utter only a surprised "But, my dear fellow, why?" Alexandra kept her composure, even when an antagonistic soldier plopped himself down on her blanket on the lawn; he put all sorts of sharp questions to her and then suddenly arose, shook her hand, and said: "Alexandra Feodorovna, I was mistaken about you." The daughters suffered no indignities. The twelve-year-old tsarevich suffered the most, perhaps: His sailor Derevenko unaccountably turned from compliant protector to a bullying tyrant; some guards taunted him by putting their bayonets into his bicycle spokes; and his toy gun was taken from him, to be returned broken. Alexis found diversion in showing movies to his family, using a camera given to him by the Pathé Company.

Kerensky noted that Nicholas seemed to be relieved at no longer being tsar, as if for twenty-three years he had acted only out of a sense of duty. As simple master of a home, Nicholas appeared supremely content, and he threw himself into such practical activities as cutting trees for firewood, shoveling the last snow, and planting a kitchen garden. In the evenings he enjoyed reading to his family or playing cards. The guards' leaders were encouraged to join in the entertainments. The ex-tsar "was an encouragement to us all," wrote Gilliard the tutor, whom Nicholas began to address whimsically as "dear colleague" after the two of them set up a school for the family.

The difficulties of the provisional government increased as the months wore on. Lenin returned to Russia in April to denounce the war as a "shameful imperialist slaughter," speaking from the balcony of the Matilda Kshessinska mansion which the Bolsheviks had appropriated for their headquarters. Widespread anti-imperialist sentiment forced the ouster of Miliukov from the Foreign Ministry for advocating the annexation of Constantinople and other of the former war aims. Discipline in the army was the greatest problem. Nicholas continued to follow military events with avid interest, and he ordered a memorial mass at the launching that summer of the Brusilov Offensive, another effort to take the pressure off the Allies, who were reeling from the mutinies in France and the Italian disaster at Caporetto. The Russian drive collapsed within a few days, and there followed the desperate Bolshevik-led riots in Petrograd known as the July Days. During the uproar the Kronstadt sailors, radical of the radical, nearly made a march on Tsarskoe Selo. Kerensky emerged in control of the situation, replacing Lvov as prime minister.

Kerensky now decided that the imperial family's safety urgently required their removal to a remote place. His plans were kept secret even from most of his cabinet, and the royal prisoners had little to go by except his advice that they pack warm clothes. On the night of August 13 he arrived to supervise the departure personally. The Grand Duke Michael was allowed to come for a farewell, but he and his brother found few words, as usual. There was a long wait before the promised train was released by the railroad men, some of whom later had second thoughts and tried to stop the journey. The tsarina was so ill that she had to be lifted into the car. They left on the fourteenth, the locomotive flying a Japanese flag and the coaches' curtains being drawn at every stop. Nicholas noted in his diary that service on the train was excellent, and he was pleased that he was allowed a half hour stop daily to take his constitutional.

The train headed not southward, as hoped, but eastward toward Siberia, with Tobolsk the destination since Kerensky considered this city a safe haven and, perhaps, a revengeful reminder of tsarist oppressions. After reaching Tyumen at the end of the line in the Urals on the evening of the seventeenth, they were transferred to the steamer *Rus* before the eyes of a crowd of diffident citizenry. During the river journey they passed Pokrovskoe, Rasputin's hometown, but the empress merely looked on this as the fulfillment of a prediction and as a good omen. Tobolsk, lying some 700 miles east of Moscow, was reached on August 19, but they had to stay on the ship another week before the governor's house in the city was fit to receive them. The mansion was comfortable but small, forcing several of the suite to live elsewhere. The local authorities, who were Mensheviks and Socialist-Revolutionaries, put no obstacles in the way of the going and coming of the doctor, tutor, and servants, and thus correspondence with the outside was easy. Nor was any effort made to stop nuns from bringing food or passersby from respectfully crossing themselves. The limited garden area available was a disappointment to the family, but they were permitted to go across the road to the church, which was presided over by none other than Hermogen, the bishop who had run afoul of Rasputin but who now could not have been more sympathetic to the arrivals.

The ex-empress began to send off letters to Vyrubova, letters full of religion, resignation, and some defiant hope. "I shall live on memories which no one shall take from me. . . . After a year I think the Lord will have pity on the country. . . . You know that it is impossible to tear the love out of my heart—and for Russia too, in spite of the black ingratitude to the Emperor which breaks my heart." Alexandra's health was a great difficulty: Her heart condition came back, and the chilliness of the house added to her discomfort. "I feel so old, oh so old," she wrote, but she turned to knitting socks for Alexis, for "all his are in holes."

There was talk of rescuing Nicholas and his family. Monarchists in Petrograd and Moscow sent money and emissaries. Unfortunately, one of the go-betweens was a Lieutenant Boris Soloviev, a mysterious political chameleon who had married Rasputin's daughter. He probably pocketed for himself much of the cash and even turned people over to the authorities if they did not obey him implicitly. The ex-empress was convinced, however, that there were 300 "good Russians" at Tyumen ready to serve her. Actually, the objects of rescue were themselves the obstacles. The government hoped to send them out of the country via Japan, but, as Gilliard recorded, Nicholas "insists on two conditions which greatly complicate matters: he will not hear of the family being separated or leaving Russian territory."

The commandant of the guards at Tobolsk was the same Eugene Koblinsky who had been appointed by Kerensky to this job at Tsarskoe Selo. A twice-wounded war veteran, Koblinsky fell victim to Nicholas' charm and was in turn described by the tsar as "my last friend." His pleasant regime was curbed after the arrival of two political commissars, vindictive revolutionaries, from Petrograd. These men were astonished to find Nicholas and his children playing cards with their guards, and the latter were now encouraged to be distant and disrespectful.

Kerensky's regime was overthrown on November 7 by Lenin and the Bolsheviks under the slogan "Peace, land, and bread," which summed up all the frustrations of war-weary soldiers, property-deprived peasants, and hungry city people. Mobs invaded the Winter Palace, and the ministers of the provisional government were packed off to join the tsarist officials in the Peter and Paul. The bloody February Revolution, which was shown to be a virtually unanimous rejection of the Romanovs, was overtaken by the bloodless October Revolution, which proved to be a declaration of class struggle to the death. The news of this most cataclysmic of events in the twentieth century took about two weeks to reach Tobolsk, and an even longer time elapsed before the second revolution was reflected in the local government. "I then for the first time heard the Tsar regret his abdication," wrote Gilliard.

The reports that Lenin and Trotsky had initiated peace negotiations became the greatest worry of the imperial couple. *"Who* are the traitors?" exclaimed Nicholas ironically. Alexandra wrote: "What an infamy! That the Lord God should give peace to Russia, yes, but not by way of treason with the Germans."

With the irony typical of the revolutionary days in Russia, less than a week before the Bolshevik take-over, the bells of Tobolsk had rung out to hail the anniversary of Nicholas' accession. Bishop Hermogen indiscreetly had prayers for the imperial family read on December 5, and other services were sung in the traditional manner. Forthwith, the family was forbidden to attend church in Tobolsk, and few Russians saw them ever after.

5. *1918*

The new year brought increased privations. The ex-tsar's monetary allowance was cut, so that servants had to be dismissed, and in February the family was put on soldiers' rations. The guards took matters in their own hands and voted 100 to 85 that Nicholas' officer's epaulets be removed. He made clear his distaste at giving up the colonel's insignia he had received from Alexander III (never having taken higher rank) but then dissuaded the disgusted Koblinsky from quitting. Kerensky's last commissars were chased away as not being radical enough, as were the friendlier guards. A snow mountain that Nicholas had built for his children to toboggan on was ordered demolished after the adults used it to wave good-bye to those departing. With no snow pile to play on, Alexis took to sliding down the stairs inside, promptly injured his groin, and began to suffer the worst hemorrhaging since the Spala crisis of 1912, this on top of having just recovered from the whooping cough.

Three hundred miles southeast of Tobolsk lay the city of Ekaterinburg, a mining center which had become the most rabidly Bolshevik enclave in the Urals. The Ekaterinburg Soviet twice that spring sent detachments to seize the imperial family, but each time they were scared off by the rival local forces.

On April 22 Basil Yakovlev, a direct emissary from Moscow (to which, a month before, Lenin had once more transferred Russia's capital), arrived at Tobolsk. Dressed in a naval uniform, Yakovlev was able to order the guards about authoritatively but yet treated Nicholas with prerevolutionary courtesies. He appeared particularly upset that Alexis was in such ill health. On April 25 he announced that Nicholas must leave with him the next day for Moscow, taking whomever he chose along. What was this man—ardent Bolshevik, would-be rescuer, or German agent? The ex-tsar tended to dismiss the idea of the Bolsheviks putting him on trial in Moscow, but he was more afraid of the intrigues of the German Ambassador Wilhelm Mirbach, who seemed all-powerful in Russia ever since the peace treaty had been concluded. "What they want is that I should sign the Treaty of Brest-Litovsk, and I will sooner let them cut off my head than do that," Nicholas declared. Alexandra's sense of doom increased, and to Gilliard she confessed that "for the first time in my life I don't know what to do." She then decided to accompany her husband and Yakovlev, even if this meant the heartbreak of leaving her desperately sick son in Tobolsk. The court doctor, optimistic that somehow they were going to England, packed his tennis flannels.

The next day Nicholas, Alexandra, Maria, and a small suite set out in carts in charge of the considerate but enigmatic Yakovlev. The trip over bad roads and frozen rivers was miserable. The last change of horses was made at Pokrovskoe under the very windows of the Rasputin house, with his family inside looking on. After reaching Tyumen, the group entrained in the opposite direction from Ekaterinburg, only to be halted by Red Guards. Despite Yakovlev's protests and even calls to Moscow, the imperial party ended up in the hands of the Ekaterinburg Soviet, their strange protector disappearing. A hostile crowd at the railroad station screamed, "Show us the Romanovs," but the royal party was safely installed in Ipatiev House, a pleasant enough mansion built originally for an engineer and recently surrounded by a high palisade.

The separation of the family was mercifully short. Alexis was well enough to sit up early in May, a fact observed by a rough new Bolshevik commissar who dismissed the guards commandant Koblinsky. The youngsters were transported by steamer and train to Ekaterinburg on May 24. The tsarevich, who never walked again, was carried about by a faithful servant, while the grand duchesses floundered about in the slush with their own luggage. The two tutors and the lady-in-waiting Baroness Sophie Buxhoeveden were sent off when they reached the station. The first night of the reunion at Ipatiev House the grand duchesses had to sleep on the floor.

Rumors of rescue plots began again. The situation became especially tense when the Czechoslovak Legion seized the Trans-Siberian Railroad and marched westward toward the Urals (the Bolsheviks had tried to disarm these former prisoners of war from the Austrian Empire who were on their way to join the Allies via Vladivostok). Worker meetings in Ekaterinburg talked of killing the imperial family before they could be liberated. On June 27 Nicholas wrote in his diary: "We spent an anxious night, and kept up our spirits fully dressed. All this was because a few days ago we received two letters, one after the other, in which we were told to get ready to be rescued by some devoted people, but days passed and nothing happened, and the waiting and uncertainty were very painful."

Ipatiev House was now under the command of a commissar named Alexander Avdeyev, a lout who thought nothing of reeling about drunk in the ex-empress' presence or of leaning between the imperial couple to help himself from the common bowl they were now reduced to eating from. He also insisted that the girls keep their doors unlocked and even posted sentries outside their lavatory. Graffiti, such as crudely obscene drawings of Alexandra and Rasputin, appeared on the lavatory walls. One by one the servants were dismissed. Yet Nicholas was to write of Avdeyev as one "who treats us well." The grand duchesses tried to keep up their good spirits, never ceasing their girlish chatter and on occasion attempting to drown out with hymns the raucous sounds from the guardroom below. Not all the guards were hostile. One of them, formerly a tsar hater, admitted in his diary a change of heart about Nicholas: "I got the impression he was a kind, simple, frank, and talkative person." As for the empress, he found her "a haughty, grave woman . . . exactly like a Tsaritsa." Except for Maria, he found the grand duchesses insipid.

Late in June the chief Bolshevik leader in Ekaterinburg, Isaiah Goloshchikin, went off to Moscow to see Jacob Sverdlov, the nominal head of the Bolshevik regime. Upon the former's return, Avdeyev was dismissed, charged with thievery of the royal family's possessions—not without justice. "I am sorry for Avdeyev," Nicholas put in his diary, later writing of his replacement, Jacob Yurovsky, that "this specimen pleases us least of all" (the last entry, July 10). Yurovsky was a converted Jew from Tomsk who had essayed various careers as clockmaker, photographer, and medical expert before joining the Bolsheviks. All the guards were once again changed at Ipatiev House, the new lot including only two Russians, with the rest vaguely described as Letts. (If these included German-speaking ex-prisoners of war, it would explain the Heine poem later found on the walls in German: "Belshazzar was that night done to death by his servants." Now the family was forbidden even to look out the windows, and a guard almost shot Anastasia for not heeding this at first.

Yurovsky and Goloshchikin, newly returned from another trip to Moscow, were observed by peasants on July 12 poking about an abandoned mineshaft at the Four Brothers, a spot named for a grove of trees in a forest 14 miles from Ekaterinburg. Two days later a priest visited the imperial family in Ipatiev House and found their former cheerfulness dissipated into listlessness and resignation. On July 16 Yurovsky told them not to go to bed that night, and in the evening he came to order them to assemble in the half basement. Nicholas carried Alexis down, and three chairs were found for the parents and son, while the grand duchesses, Dr. Eugene Botkin, a male and a female servant, and the dog made themselves comfortable on cushions on the floor. Yurovsky reappeared with several guards and read a brief order for their execution from the Ekaterinburg Soviet. Nicholas barely uttered a protest before a volley of revolver shots cut loose. The soldiers used bayonets to dispatch the last victims, who tried to shield themselves with the cushions.

XXI.

The Romanovs Since the Revolution

1. The Quick and the Dead

THE Romanovs were wiped out selectively in Soviet Russia, in the case of both past memories and of living persons. At the Cathedral of the Archangel Michael in the Moscow Kremlin the tourist today may leisurely contemplate the blackened brass coffins of the first Romanov tsars among the similar tombs of the Muscovite rulers of the Rurikovich line. Alexis' vaulted apartments are preserved in all their medieval magnificence, as is Fedor's impossibly giant cannon. Lenin early handed down the dictum that the treasures of the past must be preserved. The imperial eagles did permanently come down from the Kremlin spires, but the Soviets have conscientiously restored the glories of the royal citadel, in contrast with the two centuries of neglect it suffered under the last tsars.

Thanks to Peter the Great, the tombs of succeeding Romanovs must be sought out in Leningrad, in the Cathedral of the Peter and Paul Fortress north across the river from the Winter Palace. Here the visitor is usually hurried by the guide across the smallish nave of the building to the right front, where in the place of honor are the white marble sarcophagi of Peter the Great and his lowborn consort and successor, Catherine I. Nearby is the pulpit from which the excommunication of Tolstoy was read, and this *cause célèbre* inspires all the eloquence of Intourist intellectuals. The royalty-minded tourist may take the chance to slip away and inspect the other tombs—of course, one may simply come to the cathedral for a private tour. In front of Peter's tomb are those of his niece Anna Ivanovna and of his daughter Elizabeth. Behind Elizabeth's coffin are those of the more celebrated Catherine II and of her murdered husband, Peter III, the presence of whose remains in the cathedral is due solely to the whim of an unhappy son and another Romanov unfortunate, Paul I. Paul's tomb occupies the front-left area before the altar, and grouped around the mad ruler, who actually resired the dynasty, are the sarcophagi of his sons Alexander I and Nicholas I.

Moving back toward the entrance of the Peter and Paul on the left side one encounters the tomb of another Pavlovich, the Grand Duke Constantine, who helped cause the Decembrist crisis of 1825. Next comes a sarcophagus inscribed Alexander Alexandrovich, reminding one that Nicholas II had a brother who died in infancy. Beside it is the coffin of his younger brother George, who died of tuberculosis in 1899; this is the most recent Romanov tomb in the museum. Beyond are the unharmonious reddish granite tomb of the assassinated Alexander II and the sarcophagus of the last ruler memorialized in this place, Alexander III. In the very front of the building are a scattering of tombs of lesser nineteenth-century grand dukes, notably Michael Pavlovich and Nicholas Nicholaevich (senior). Twentieth-century Romanovs did not exist as far as the monuments in Peter and Paul would indicate. Guides fail to mention that several grand dukes were shot in the very shadow of the cathedral in 1919. As for Nicholas II, he has almost become an unperson. One place his likeness is to be found on public display is as the slight but presiding figure in the huge Serov painting of the Council of State in 1903.

A forefinger of the last Empress of Russia is reputedly preserved in a vial lying in a vault of a New York bank. The remains of the victims of the tragedy of July 16, 1918, were dug up at the bottom of the mine shaft at the Four Brothers after the White armies captured Ekaterinburg on July 27. The executioners had tried to burn everything with gasoline, and no bone fragments were positively identified afterward. Among objects found were buttons of the tsar, jewelry of the tsarina, Alexis' belt buckle, corset stays corresponding in number to the women victims, and the virtually intact body of the pet dog. An exhaustive investigation by the White-employed lawyer Nicholas Sokolov included interrogation of some of the guards on duty at the time of the execution, and Sokolov's reconstruction of the finale at Ipatiev House was borne out by a later Soviet inquest by P. M. Bykov.

Lenin's Moscow government at first denied responsibility for the murder of the tsar and his family in face of the ensuing international uproar, and it even went so far as to frame, try, and execute some Socialist Revolutionaries for the crime. Subsequently, it became known that Sverdlov had interrupted a session of the Council of People's Commissars to announce Nicholas' death and that Lenin then coolly moved that the reading of the new health law be continued. Trotsky, absent from the capital at the time, on his return to Moscow asked Sverdlov about the tsar's fate and was told that "we decided it here." Trotsky concluded that a correct decision had been made, writing in exile in the 1930's, "The severity of this summary justice showed the world that we would continue to fight on mercilessly, stopping at nothing . . . there was no turning back." Ekaterinburg was in time renamed Sverdlovsk after the first titular president of the Soviet regime, and the *Sverdlovsk* in turn was the name of the Soviet cruiser on which Khrushchev received the last tsar's cousin Queen Elizabeth II at Portsmouth in 1957. Ipatiev House became a local Bolshevik museum, with the shot-up basement room left as it was, until about a decade ago when visiting reporters were informed that the storage of documents there made entry impossible.

Nicholas, Alexandra, and their children were not the first or the last Romanovs executed. More than a month before, on June 12, the Grand Duke Michael had been lured from his hotel room and shot in a wood outside Perm. The morganatic wife of the tsar's brother, Countess Brassov, escaped abroad and lived until 1952. Her son, George, Count Brassov, died in a car crash in 1931.

The Soviet government moved a group of Romanovs to the Ural town of Alopaevsk in June, 1918. Most prominent among them was the Grand Duchess Elizabeth, the tsarina's widowed sister. "Aunt Ella" had refused Kerensky's plea to move into the Kremlin and that of her former admirer, the kaiser, to return to Germany. Instead, she stubbornly kept her hospital-nunnery going, on occasion lectured hostile mobs to their knees, and even browbeat the Bolsheviks into giving her supplies. In the end she was arrested and transported, along with several of her nuns, young Prince Vladimir Paley, the Grand Duke Sergius Michaelovich, and the princes John, Constantine, and Igor Constantinovich. On July 17, the day after the secret murders at Ekaterinburg, a few hundred miles to the south, the prisoners were loaded into carts and driven to an abandoned mineshaft, into which they were thrown one by one, followed by a hail of heavy debris. That some of the victims lingered on was suggested by the fact that peasants heard hymn singing from the bottom of the pit, and the belated rescuers found the head of one of the young Romanovs bandaged with "Aunt Ella's" handkerchief. Eventually, the poet "Volodia" Paley was reburied in Shanghai, while the remains of the grand duchess were brought all the way to the Russian shrine in Jerusalem, where miraculous cures have been attributed to them.

The general excuse for the unceremonious slaughter of the Romanovs in the anarchic Urals region was the possibility of their deliverance by approaching White armies. Six months later, with Russia in the grip of mutual class terrorism, the Bolshevik government ordered the deliberate shooting by firing squad of several imprisoned Romanovs in the courtyard of the Peter and Paul Fortress of Petrograd. The victims of January, 1919, included the surviving brother of Alexander III, the Grand Duke Paul (who was on a stretcher at the time he was shot), the grand dukes George and Nicholas Michaelovich (the latter clutched his Persian cat to the end), and Prince Dmitri Constantinovich (who prayed for his executioners). Gorky had appealed to Lenin unsuccessfully to spare the life of his fellow author, the Grand Duke Nicholas.

Of fifteen Romanov grand dukes living in 1917, only eight survived the Revolution, and the fate of the leading Romanov women was proportionately the same. The most distinguished survivor was the Dowager Empress Marie, who in May, 1917, had left riot-torn Kiev for the royal estates in the Crimea. Here she was joined by her daughter Xenia, the Grand Duke Alexander, their six sons, and the Yusupovs. Also in the party was the tsar's other sister, the Grand Duchess Olga, and her new husband, Colonel Koulikovsky, a cavalry officer she had married during the war after deserting her first husband, the Prince of Oldenburg. Such was the crazy chaos of that summer of 1917 that some of the men in the group were able to travel back and forth to Petrograd and Moscow to look after their properties, especially the ladies' jewels. Conditions were also such that there were nasty run-ins with the revolutionary authorities in the Crimea, in which situations the imperious dowager usually faced down her tormentors in grand style. After the Bolshevik Revolution, familiar rivalries arose among local governments, with the Yalta Soviet, for example, standing out in its determination to execute all Romanovs. The safety of the dowager's party was temporarily assured when the Treaty of Brest-Litovsk was signed and German troops took over the whole area, not that the Russian royalty would show any friendliness to the ex-enemy. Throughout the summer of 1918 the dowager steadfastly refused to accept the reports of the murders of her children as anything but Bolshevik lies. The Armistice of November, 1918, ending World War I meant the evacuation of the Germans, and once again the Crimea became a battleground of Reds and Whites. On April 7, 1919, the commander of the British fleet at Sevastopol called on the dowager and represented to her that her refusal to leave Russia would mean not only her own death but the sacrifice of her devoted family as well. The next day the Empress Marie boarded the HMS *Marlborough,* having secured a British promise to evacuate all refugees, and she sailed away to England, after enduring the final heartbreak of waving good-bye to a shipload of cheering young Russian officers going off to make a last stand for the White cause.

The Empress Marie was received joyfully but privately, almost surreptitiously, by the British royal family at a London train station, and she was afterward installed in Mansion House with her sister, the Queen Mother

Alexandra. The Grand Duchess Xenia was given a small mansion, Wilderness House, in which to raise her large family. The story was told of one of Xenia's servants that she fell on her knees and kissed the coat of King George V, whom she mistook for his look-alike cousin Nicholas. Xenia had been preceded to the West by her husband, who wished to make his voice heard at the Versailles Peace Conference, but the Grand Duke Alexander experienced rude shocks at the indifference of the tsar's former allies to the fate of Russia and the Romanovs. (The cousin and brother-in-law of Nicholas II had greater personal success on the American lecture circuit in the 1920's preaching Tolstoy and counterrevolution.)

Members of the families of the late tsar's uncles and cousins soon joined the exiles in the West. The Grand Duchess Vladimir had spent harrowing days in peasant disguise in the Caucasus during the Revolution. Having proudly refused rescue by her Rumanian relatives, she found herself fleeing Russia with her sons, Boris and Andrew, on a crowded refugee steamer to Venice. In Switzerland she was greeted by her Greek royal relatives, who were then also political exiles, including the eleven-year-old future Duchess of Kent. The onetime brilliant leader of St. Petersburg society stepped from her train a ragged scarecrow of a woman, and Maria Pavlovna died soon after in 1920. Her eldest son, Cyril, and his wife had escaped from the north of Russia to Finland, where their only son, Vladimir, was born in August, 1917, in a humble cottage. His brother Andrew at last married the mistress he had shared with the tsar, Matilda Kshessinska, in Cannes in 1921. (Later she was to conduct a ballet school and is still living in Paris as of this writing.)

Princess Paley also escaped to Finland with her daughters, and there they learned of the separate tragedies befalling the father, the Grand Duke Paul, and the son, Volodia. Their half brother, the Grand Duke Dmitri Pavlovich, made his way from the Caucasus front to Persia and did service in the British army before he reached London. His sister Maria Pavlovna, her marriage to the Swedish prince terminated, had married a Guards officer, Colonel Putiatin, just before the Revolution and with him endured a perilous journey from Petrograd to Odessa and finally to Rumania, leaving an infant son behind forever with her parents-in-law. (In her memoirs this Romanov lady was to note her stupefaction at finding the imperial waiting room closed when trying to entrain from the capital in 1917.) The younger Grand Duchess Maria, who eventually divorced her second husband also, lived in straitened circumstances in London and was briefly associated with Chanel in Paris before she came to make a new career in America. Princess Irene Paley at nineteen married the couturier Lucien Lelong in 1927 and later wed an American. Her sister Natalia, a tsar's granddaughter, married another Romanov, Prince Fedor

Alexandrovich, a great-grandson of a tsar. They had a daughter and a son, Prince Michael Romanov (not to be confused with the self-styled Mike Romanov of Hollywood fame).

Both the tsar's Nicholaevich cousins survived. The Grand Duke Nicholas had been named commander in chief again after the abdication, but upon his arrival in Mogilev, he learned that anti-Romanov feeling was running too strong to allow such an eventuality. In due course, Russia's first soldier made his way from the Crimea aboard a British warship. The Grand Duke Peter Nicholaevich, his wife, a son, Roman, and two daughters all reached safety. The Constantinovich line suffered heavily in the executions, but some princes escaped, notably Gabriel, who in turn sired a son, Alexander. Three Michaelevich grand dukes were dead, leaving Alexander (Xenia's husband) and Michael, who had no escape problems, since from the 1890's he had been a fixture of London eccentric society, as well as the father of a boy nicknamed Boy and two daughters Zia and Nada. A daughter of George Michaelovich, Xenia, was another Romanov to marry an American, William Leeds, while her sister Nina wed Prince Paul Chavchavadze (they currently live on Cape Cod).

A truly exotic leftover from imperial days was the Princess Yurievskaya, the morganatic wife of Alexander II, who for years was leader of the Biarritz social set. Used to twenty servants and her private railroad car, the old lady died in 1920, fortunately, some said, for all her money was gone. Her son, Prince George, "Gogo" as a child, had died in 1913. Catherine Yurievskaya, his sister, having married Prince Bariatinsky, found herself a widow in 1911 with houses in Russia, Italy, and Bavaria, as well as two sons. Subsequently, this tsar's daughter wed Prince Serge Obolensky, who subsequently married Alice Astor, who subsequently married three others. In the 1920's the princess turned to a career as a concert singer, boasting such accompanists as ex-King Manuel of Portugal and Dmitri Tiomkin. Obolensky, who could claim descent from Rurik in the thirty-third generation, partied with the Duke of Windsor in the 1930's, served in the OSS in the 1940's, and became a celebrated hotelman in the 1950's. (His special sword dance was a feature of society functions until a decade ago.)

2. The Real and the Unreal

The harried remnants of Russian royalty and aristocracy after 1917 took up residence in Paris, London, and New York, some drifting eventually to obscure country places. The stories of hard-up princes and counts becoming waiters and taxi drivers are familiar enough. (The author's late mother, years before this book was conceived, used to tell of her experience with a Russian butler in Paris in the 1920's: He appeared one evening in the box next to hers at the Opéra wearing his court uniform and decorations; he ceremoniously presented himself at the interval to kiss her hand; and he resumed serving madame's breakfast the next morning without comment.)

Prince Yusupov, to whom London was already familiar ground, appeared to have entered exile with the most liquid assets. His high style of living and his being in a position to help his fellow refugees financially were to be hailed by some, resented by others. Yusupov's willingness to write in detail about the Rasputin murder rankled the Grand Duke Dmitri, who kept his pledge of silence. Generally, however, the Russian *émigrés* showed much social solidarity and went about setting up welfare organizations for the unfortunates which exist to this day in major capitals. Some of the exiles, naturally, turned to the politics of revenge and restoration.

The great excitement of August 31, 1924, for Russians abroad at least, if not for the world at large, was the proclamation in France of Cyril Vladimirovich as "Emperor of All the Russias," and at the same time there was a new "Tsarevich," his son Vladimir. The late tsar's first cousin was not unfamiliar with causing public sensations: first, as naval hero in 1905; soon after, as the new husband of Victoria Melita, who had scandalously divorced the tsarina's brother; and then as the first grand duke to swear allegiance to the provisional government of 1917. The senior male Romanov in the direct line, Cyril felt justified as early as 1922 in announcing himself as "Protector of the Russian Throne." As "Emperor," Cyril went about issuing manifestos and creating titles in the old manner just as if he were surveying the Neva from palace windows. In time, there were angry protests in some *émigré* circles that Cyril was financing his "court" by hawking orders and decorations, such as selling the Imperial Order of St. Nicholas Thaumaturge to former Russian soldiers in New York for only $3. That Cyril's "Empress" was a sister of Queen Marie of Rumania was a more certain solution to money difficulties.

The political ideas of "Emperor" Cyril were as strange as some of his past actions. He appeared to believe that propaganda, rather than action, would regain him the throne of his ancestors, and he made sure that copies of his manifestos found their way to the hands of Red army officers. Originally, he advocated a restored monarchy without disturbing the soviets in their regional authority, but later in the 1920's he became enamored of Italian Fascism and the possibility of realizing the corporate state in Russia. His estate at St.-Briac on the coast of Brittany became a miniature re-creation of the Mussolini regime, with which he established diplomatic relations. Fascist salutes were blended in with traditional Russian royal etiquette and ceremony. The attitude of two other Romanovs prevented Cyril from rallying more than part of the *émigré* community to his standard. The dowager was indifferent and the Grand Duke Nicholas actively hostile.

The dowager found her position in London intolerable after her sister Alexandra became somewhat dotty (she retired to Sandringham, where she died in 1925). Hvidore Palace in her native Denmark was made available to her, and here the Empress Marie set up court in 1923 amid mementos and with a modest number of retainers, including a devoted old Cossack. Money was a real problem for the former first lady of Russia, who had salvaged only a small box of her best jewels, with which she would not part. There were reports of financial run-ins between her and her nephew, Christian X of Denmark, such as the time a messenger of the king chided her for having so many lights on, upon which Marie ordered her footman to turn every light on. Eventually, her British relatives came to her rescue, settling 10,000 pounds a year on her from their private incomes and providing her with an overseer to make sure that she did not squander it away on every importunate Russian who showed up at Hvidore, as hundreds did. The dowager remained unshakable in her belief that her sons and grandchildren would turn up alive, and thus she simply ignored her nephew Cyril's pretensions. Her intimates saw her become increasingly petulant and pathetic, but to Russian exiles she was the *grande dame* of the good old days, and when she died at eighty-one in 1928, the outpouring of devotion was tremendous.

In exile, the Grand Duke Nicholas Nicholaevich never dropped his ramrod military bearing, and it did not hurt his prestige any that he refused to mix in behind-the-scenes *émigré* political intrigues. When Cyril proclaimed himself, the "legitimists" found the grand duke a brick wall of nonrecognition and opposition. His own program for Russia was nothing more fancy than the restoration of law and order, and he surrounded himself with ex-officers who talked boldly of a military reconquest of Russia. Probably, a majority of Russian *émigrés* stood by "Nicholasha," many wishing him to declare himself Nicholas III. When the late tsar's cousin died in 1928, French authorities allowed a magnificent official tribute, accompanied by whooping parades of Russian veterans, in honor of a former Allied commander in chief.

There was some stir in the tabloids in May, 1938, when "Emperor" Cyril's younger daughter, Kira, married Louis Ferdinand, son of the former Crown Prince of Germany, Frederick William (himself the grandson of a Russian grand duchess). This heir of the Hohenzollerns, who had once worked at a Ford plant in Detroit for $35.50 a week, was currently living in Nazi Germany as a technical adviser to Lufthansa. Some read political significance in the union of the German and Russian royal families, albeit both deposed, and the marriage was lavishly celebrated first in civil and Orthodox ceremonies at Cecilienhof Palace in Potsdam and then in a Protestant rite at Doorn before the ex-kaiser and fifty members of royalty.

"Cyril I" died a worn and disillusioned man that same year in the American Hospital in Paris, leaving his London-educated son the empty title. A supporter and adviser of both the father and the son claimants was the Grand Duke Dmitri, who had married an American woman, Audrey Emery, in Biarritz in 1926 and duly secured her elevation to the title Princess Ilynsky, only to be divorced from her later. A son, Paul, Prince Ilynsky, was born to this match. Dmitri, sometimes a champagne salesman but more usually a dashing figure in international social circles, died in 1941 in Switzerland, the last true grand duke.

Back in the 1920's, when Cyril, the dowager, and Grand Duke Nicholas were rival centers of attention, the major Anastasia case burst into *émigré* sensibilities and politics. The prevalence of lost princes and princesses, even tsars, in Russian history deterred few from taking seriously the possibility that the woman in question was the miraculously saved daughter of Nicholas II. Nor was this Anastasia the first such claimant. Virtually from the day of the murder of the imperial family there had been self-styled survivors. Gilliard interviewed and exposed a supposed Alexis in Siberia. Other Alexises showed up, notably one in Baghdad, and there were not a few reports that even Nicholas II had been sighted walking about.

The most persistent claimant to being the youngest daughter of the tsar had shown up in Germany as a refugee from the East early in 1920. After a suicide attempt, she spent some time in an asylum, suffering from amnesia and delusions of persecution, and here she confided her real identity to a nurse and later to a police inspector, who in turn alerted Russian exile groups. Her story as it was pieced together—later to be published as a book, *I Am Anastasia*—proceeded from the contention that she had escaped the executioners' bullets at Ekaterinburg (there is general agreement on this detail) and that she also survived their bayonets. She was then spirited away in a peasant wagon, causing the Bolsheviks subsequently to make frantic searches for the missing corpse (a Swedish Red Cross official in the area at the time swore to this fact as late as 1952). Anastasia's alleged rescuer was a Red Guard named Alexander Tchaikovsky, who proceeded to take his charge westward the thousands of miles across war-torn Russia to safety in Rumania (it is difficult to see why they did not seek haven with the White armies approaching Ekaterinburg from only a few miles away to the east). While in Rumania, Anastasia bore a child to Tchaikovsky, and the shame of this, together with a general psychological upset, was her explanation for not revealing herself to her royal relatives there. Tchaikovsky disappeared, and when

Anastasia eventually found herself in Germany, she awoke to the possibility of seeking recognition from her aunt, Princess Cecilie of Prussia (who would have been with the tsar's children as late as 1912). During the late 1920's there was a complex series of secret and open interviews of the pretender with Princess Cecilie, Anastasia's paternal aunt the Grand Duchess Olga, and various other Russian and German court figures. Some persons, like Dr. Botkin's son and Lili Dehn, a friend of the empress, accepted her recollections of St. Petersburg, Livadiya, and Ekaterinburg as genuine and became her champions. Olga and also notably the Grand Duke Andrew tended to believe her at first and then changed their minds. There was never a confrontation with the dowager, as so poignantly has been presented in fictional treatments of Anastasia (the Ingrid Bergman movie, for example). Generally, the Romanovs refused to accept the "miracle," and people like the tutor Gilliard, who would have known Anastasia since she was four, went out of their way to denounce her as an impostor. After a visit to the United States in 1928, where her behavior was more distressing than titillating, her friends had her returned to Germany to live the life of a recluse, going by the name of Anna Anderson.

The crux of the Anastasia case was her claim to the millions of rubles she said her father had deposited just before the war in the Bank of England and elsewhere (she could not remember the name of the agent, although she had been told this magic word). Her supporters were to allege that sheer greed for this money on the part of the surviving Romanovs drove them coldly to snub her plea for their recognition and love. Scholarly investigators have come to discount the possibility that there was or is such a fortune at stake. There is evidence that the late tsar and tsarina had withdrawn whatever private funds they had abroad to subsidize hospitals and other wartime activities (a letter of Alexandra to her husband explicitly mentions one large withdrawal). German courts have consistently denied Anastasia's claims to Romanov funds there.

3. The Old and the New

A score of years and a few European wars after the French Revolution the Bourbons were restored to France, but World War II had no effect on Romanov fortunes, although some Russian exiles, probably a minority, had pinned their hopes on the Nazi conquest of Soviet Russia. Actually, Hitler had incredible plans to extirpate tsarist and Communist memories alike by leveling Leningrad and Moscow, and the invaders succeeded in bestially but systematically wrecking the imperial palaces they did occupy outside besieged Leningrad. Since the war, Soviet money has regilded and repainted Peterhof, Tsarskoe Selo, and Pavlovsk to a state they rarely, if ever, knew all together under the Romanovs. Livadiya Palace in the Crimea, spared, where the Tsarevna Olga had her first dance, was made newsworthy again when Roosevelt received Stalin and Churchill there during the Yalta Conference.

Since before the war the Romanov with the best claim to being head of the dynasty has been Vladimir Cyrilovich. As merely the great-grandson of a reigning tsar, Vladimir's title would properly be Prince under the old dispensation, but thanks to his father, he succeeded first to the dignity of Grand Duke and then that of Tsar. Vladimir has stayed out of the news and quietly celebrated his fiftieth birthday at St.-Briac in September, 1967. At this time his sister Kira died, leaving five children to her husband, Prince Louis Ferdinand, now head of the Hohenzollerns.

The last genuine grand duchesses of Russia died within months of each other in 1960. Xenia died in London in comfortable circumstances at the age of eighty-four, with her considerable family in attendance. Her equally unassuming older sister, Olga, passed away at eighty-eight, an invalid living with a Russian family over a barbershop in East Toronto. Olga had spent her exile in Copenhagen until 1948, when she retired to a farm in Canada with her husband, Colonel Koulikovsky. Her being invited to appear at a shipboard reception for Queen Elizabeth in 1959 startled her unsuspecting Canadian neighbors.

The Anastasia case revived in various ways after the war, the greatest spate of interest occurring in the 1950's with the Marcelle Maurette-Guy Bolton play (the authors gave Anna Anderson a share of the royalties), the Twentieth Century-Fox movie, and numerous magazine articles. In February, 1967, a Hamburg court ruled that Anna Anderson had failed to give sufficient proof that she was the tsar's daughter, in the latest development in more than thirty years of litigation involving Romanov monies (Mrs. Anderson has insisted she wants only recognition). At the same time the court did not endorse a counterclaim that Anna was actually a peasant from Poland, and the case will probably be appealed. For years the pretender was described to the world as a pathetic invalid living in a shack in the Black Forest and seeing only her doctor and lawyer. In the summer of 1968, however, Anna Anderson showed up in Charlottesville, Virginia, she soon after received recognition from her putative childhood playmate, Rasputin's daughter Maria, there on a visit, and at the end of the year she married a former history professor at the university, a longtime believer in her cause.

As of 1963 another Anastasia popped up, this one in Chicago. A lady, who for forty years had gone by the name Eugenia Smith, approached a publisher with a manuscript she said was written by her deceased friend, the Grand Duchess Anastasia, only to admit later that she herself was the author who showed extraordinary knowledge of the last years of the Russian court. Her version of miraculous survival involved being saved by a former officer, escape via Bukovina, marriage to a Croatian, and arrival in New York in 1922, after which she worked variously as a salesgirl, model, and wartime bombsight assembler. *Life* magazine took up her story, noting gravely that she stood up well under lie detector tests, but that handwriting experts demurred, as did a Harvard anthropologist who compared facial structures from old and new photographs. Mrs. Paul Chavchavadze, who was the Princess Nina and a playmate of Anastasia until they were both thirteen, interviewed Mrs. Smith and came away with a no to her claim, which soon after disappeared from press reports.

Almost simultaneously with the Chicago Anastasia case developed the Goleniewski-Alexis case. A small item in the New York *Times* for August 16, 1964, read: "A defector from Communist Poland who was an informant for the Central Intelligence Agency said last night that he was Alexei, the only son of Nicholas II, the last Czar of Russia." Colonel Goleniewski, whose valuable spy work the CIA has acknowledged without supporting his claim, maintained that the 1918 murder story was a complex Communist hoax and that the whole family escaped to Poland, the tsar dying only in 1924 and the tsarina as late as 1952, with *all* the tsarevnas still living. Allegations have been offered about a superconspiratorial Russian-international group protecting the royal family, a group related to Emperor Paul's Knights of Malta of 1798. The absence of traces of hemophilia and Goleniewski's fiftyish-looking age (Alexis would have been sixty in 1964) have been explained away. Apparently, a New York Russian priest reinforced the claim by registering Goleniewski under the name Alexis Nicholaevich Romanov, a fact for which the priest has never been forgiven by some exile groups. It was reported that Goleniewski and Eugenia Smith had an emotional recognition scene as brother and sister, only to disacknowledge each other later. Even *Pravda* got into the picture with a denunciation of Goleniewski's pretensions as involving his concern for an alleged $400,000,000 of Romanov funds in New York banks. The pretender lives with his wife and son on Long Island, and the last word on his case has certainly not been heard.

Romanov affairs are never long absent from the American press, as witnessed by the great interest shown in the Prince Yusupov suit against CBS concerning its Rasputin murder story on TV. The last tsar's nephew-in-law died not long afterward in his Auteuil, Paris, house on September 27, 1967, at the age of eighty-one, being survived by his wife and daughter, both named Irene. Incidentally, *Variety* and other journals occasionally do a piece on Maria Rasputin, who once created a great sensation when she showed up with a lion-taming act in New York in 1938.

Never long absent from the society columns are marriage notices involving Russian aristocrats, in which the parents are sometimes described as "formerly of St. Petersburg.". For example, a fine Rurikovich name came up with the wedding announcement of Prince Jean-André Sviatopolk-Mirsky in November, 1966, his grandparents being described as equerry and lady-in-waiting to the last tsar and tsarina. The next month one could read of the presentation of Princess Belesselsky-Belozersky at the Twelfth International Debutantes Ball at the Waldorf-Astoria.

Recent Romanov marriages include that of Prince Andrew, grandson of the Grand Duchess Xenia, to an American woman in San Francisco. Also in that city was celebrated the wedding of his cousin Marina Romanov to a New York man in January, 1967, the ceremony taking place in the Russian Orthodox Greek Catholic Church of the Nativity of the Blessed Virgin. A Sarah Lawrence graduate and a teacher at the Fifteenth Street School in New York, the bride was escorted by her father Prince Vasily Alexandrovich (a retired stockbroker), and she carried a lace handkerchief that belonged to her great-grandmother, the Dowager Marie.

It is easy in New York City to encounter Russian nobility, for example, at their church on Ninety-sixth Street and at numerous social functions. A tea dance the author attended at Delmonico's in the fall of 1967 was under the sponsorship of Countess Buxhoeveden, Prince and Princess Shcherbatov, Princess Volkonsky, and Prince and Princess Galitzine (the French spelling of Golitsyn). One of the ladies entertained with songs, among them "I Remember Yesterday," and the dancing included lively Russian folk steps. Perhaps the most fascinating thing the author learned was how to get around the United States' constitutional ban on the use of titles: Take Prince as a middle name. The Petroushka Ball at the Pierre Hotel to aid the Russian Children's Welfare Fund in January, 1968, was "under the patronage of Princess Vera of Russia."

A Romanov set foot once again in the Winter Palace and Kremlin in June, 1961, when Prince Alexander, a thirty-one-year-old London business executive, traveled in Russia with a tour group. This visit by a great-nephew of Nicholas II came off without a trace of alarm on either his part or that of the Soviet government. For the benefit of tourists generally, the Soviets have recently exhibited the royal jewel collection, including the coronation crown of Catherine the Great with its 4,936 diamonds and her scepter with the 199-carat Orlov stone. Foreign and *émigré* collectors of tsarist treasures have had to content themselves with some Fabergé creations going from $50,000 up. Imperial Russian bonds of a face value of $1,000 sell on the New York market at about $22.50.

Notes

I. Introduction

11. "To come and rule over us": Russian monks of the twelfth century compiled the first written histories. See Samuel H. Cross, ed., *The Russian Primary Chronicle* (Harvard Studies and Notes in Philology and Literature, Vol. XII, Cambridge, 1930). All quotations in the present book are from contemporary sources unless otherwise indicated.
12. "The rival of Constantinople": James Billington, *The Icon and the Axe* (New York, Knopf, 1966), p. 7. This is one of the most brilliant studies on Russia ever published.
14. A compilation of 1858: Prince Paul Dolgoruky, *A Handbook of the Principal Families of Russia* (London, James Ridgway, 1858). This work was published outside of Russia—originally in Paris—in part because of the author's aristocratically sniffy attitude toward the Romanovs.
14. Serge Obolensky, *One Man in His Time* (New York, McDowell, Obolensky, 1958).
16. "Land of Prus": V. O. Kliuchevsky, *The Course of Russian History,* trans. by C. J. Hogarth (New York, Russell and Russell, 1960), Vol. III, p. 62.
16. "Grand Prince Simeon": Anatole G. Mazour, *Rise and Fall of the Romanovs* (New York, van Nostrand, 1960), p. 11.
18. "The Russian land": Jesse D. Clarkson, *A History of Russia* (New York, Random House, 1961), p. 87.
19. "And the third stands": *ibid.,* p. 85.
19. "Ioann, by the Grace of God": *ibid.,* p. 86.
20. Kremlin: An excellent study is Arthur Voyce, *The Moscow Kremlin* (Berkeley, University of California Press, 1954). The present work is indebted to Voyce's descriptions, as well as his many fascinating maps and diagrams. A superior visual reconstruction of the Kremlin is to be found in Thomas T. Hammond, "An American in Moscow," *National Geographic,* Vol. 129, No. 3 (March, 1966), pp. 297–351.
23. "We have seen heaven!": Voyce, *op. cit.,* p. 35.

II. The Time of Troubles and a Change of Dynasty

28. "If you should do": Jules Koslow, *Ivan the Terrible* (New York, Hill and Wang, 1961), p. 3.
29. "As foreigners": *ibid.*, p. 5
29. "The ancestral rank": *ibid.*, p. 19. Ivan III had been hailed as tsar, but Ivan IV was the first to be crowned as such. The word is related, of course, to the Roman *Caesar*.
30. "My lord": *ibid.*, p. 25.
30. "Wise and of such holiness": *ibid.*, p. 25.
33. "Little heifer": Stephen Graham, *Ivan the Terrible* (New Haven, Yale University Press, 1933), p. 159.
33. "After the Tsaritsa's death": *ibid.*, p. 153.
33. "They defiled": Koslow, *op. cit.*, p. 224.
34. "A very beautiful": *ibid.*, p. 244.
35. "A sacristan": *ibid.*, p. 254.
35. "The Tsar is short": Kliuchevsky, *op. cit.*, Vol. IV, p. 14.
36. "Did all his life": *ibid.*, pp. 14–15.
37. "Harkened unto": *ibid.*, p. 18.
37. "Withering away": Robert Nisbet Bain, *The First Romanovs* (London, Archibald Constable, 1905), p. 39.
38. "In deep humility": E. M. Almedingen, *The Romanovs* (London, Bodley Head, 1966), p. 24.
41. "As God is my witness": quoted in Philip L. Barbour, *Dimitry* (Boston, Houghton Mifflin, 1966), p. 39. This exceptionally thorough and engaging work is the present author's main source on the whole Time of Troubles.
41. "Good Tsar": *ibid.*, p. 73.
41. "A parvenu": Kliuchevsky, *op. cit.*, Vol. IV, p. 28.
42. Dmitri the Self-styled: On the question of Dmitri's identity, see Barbour, *op. cit.*, Appendix D.
47. "The State appeared": Kliuchevsky, *op. cit.*, Vol. IV, p. 50.
48. "I do not like": Dolgoruky, *op. cit.*, p. 73.
49. "Let Michael Romanov": Bain, *First,* p. 40.
49. "Born Tsar": Kliuchevsky, *op. cit.*, Vol. IV, p. 62.
49. "Our Michael": *ibid.*, p. 63.

III. The Mildest of the Tsars: Michael

50. "With tears": Bain, *First,* p. 29.
53. "The Tsar's intentions": *ibid.*, p. 45.
53. "If these people": *ibid.*, p. 31.
56. "As the Tsar graciously makes": *ibid.*, p. 12.
58. "Picked up fortresses": *ibid.*, p. 55.
58. "God grant us": *ibid.*, p. 56.
58. "Lot of runaway thieves": *ibid.*, pp. 62–63.
58. "An honorable and glorious": *ibid.*, p. 65.
59. "We know": *ibid.*, p. 66.

IV. Tsar of the Good Old Days: Alexis

62. "I cannot": Bain, *First,* p. 101.
63. "You English": *ibid.*, p. 98.

63. "Now they listen": Almedingen, *Romanovs,* p. 60.
64. "Son of Satan": Mazour, *op. cit.,* p. 21.
64. "The sun never": Bain, *First,* p. 89.
66. "So vile": *ibid.,* p. 142.
66. "Elect and immovable": *ibid.,* pp. 129–30.
66. "You know": *ibid.,* pp. 130–31.
68. "A ravening bear": *ibid.,* p. 142.
68. "I know": *ibid.,* p. 147.
69. "Would she put herself": *ibid.,* p. 155.
69. "It is plain": *ibid.,* p. 156.
69. "Righteous mother": *ibid.,* p. 158.
71. "And this I tell": *ibid.,* p. 109.
71. "Wise in the Holy Scriptures": *ibid.,* p. 110.
72. "It is indecent": *ibid.,* p. 118.
73. "Contrary to all": *ibid.,* p. 118.
74. "I do not want": *ibid.,* p. 166.
74. "Little pigeon": *ibid.,* p. 185.
75. "The incomparable tsar": Billington, *op. cit.,* p. 148.
76. "A flight of screech owls": *ibid.,* p. 147.
77. "Cleverness": *ibid.,* p. 121.

V. A Struggle of Brothers and Sisters

81. "There is terror": Bain, *First,* pp. 161–62.
83. "I will put down": *ibid.,* p. 197.
83. "Come, come": *ibid.,* p. 198.
84. "I have heard enough": C. Bickford O'Brien, *Russia Under Two Tsars 1682–1689* (Berkeley, University of California Press, 1952), p. 31. In this unique and authoritative work on the period the author rates Sophia as very capable.
87. "For the Commander in Chief": Bain, *First,* p. 206.
87. "Never had there been": Clarkson, *op. cit.,* p. 185.
94. "The old she bear": Bain, *First,* p. 210.
95. "Would not be treated": *ibid.,* p. 214.
95. "That shameful": Kliuchevsky, *op. cit.,* Vol. V, p. 17.

VI. Greatest of Russia's Tsars and First Emperor: Peter I

99. "My Lord King": Bain, *First,* p. 224.
100. "This accursed hole": *ibid.,* p. 225. A map, pictures, and interesting details on Peter's grand tour are afforded in Constantin de Grunwald, "Peter and the West," *Horizon,* Vol. II, No. 1 (September, 1959), pp. 58–84.
101. "The Tsar is very tall": Bain, *First,* p. 228.
102. "He is a man of": Mazour, *op. cit.,* p. 144.
104. "Since nothing": Bain, *First,* p. 231.
104. "Take that icon": *ibid.,* p. 232.
106. "The shadow of doubt": *ibid.,* p. 237.
107. "There was no glory": *ibid.,* p. 246.
107. "Necessity now drove": *ibid.,* p. 247.
108. "Dressed-up dolls": B. H. Sumner, *Peter the Great and the Emergence of Russia* (London, English Universities Press, 1951), p. 59.

108. "Narva is avenged": Bain, *First*, p. 249.
110. "We of Astrakhan": *ibid.*, pp. 311–12.
111. "The power of Muscovy": Sumner, *Peter*, p. 64.
112. "A very hazardous affair": *ibid.*, p. 72.
112. "A very outstanding": *ibid.*, p. 73.
113. "Nothing was left": Bain, *First*, p. 273.
113. "Now by God's help": Sumner, *Peter*, p. 231.
114. "In case of my death": Bain, *First*, p. 278.
114. "To break": *ibid.*, p. 288.
116. "To bring the King of Sweden": *ibid.*, p. 297.

VII. A Son Undone by His Father: The Tsarevich Alexis and Peter

118. "I have taken": Bain, *First*, pp. 342–43.
119. "Sensible, upright": *ibid.*, p. 343.
119. "Your affectionately inclined": *ibid.*, p. 346.
120. "You are cleverer": *ibid.*, p. 348.
120. "Well, so long": *ibid.*, p. 348.
120. "My joy": *ibid.*, pp. 350–51.
121. "It must be": *ibid.*, p. 351.
122. "Wherever you go": *ibid.*, p. 352.
122. "My father says": Sumner, *Peter*, p. 102.
122. "Poisoning": Bain, *First*, p. 354.
122. "Before God": *ibid.*, p. 356.
123. "Melt the hard frozen": *ibid.*, p. 356.
123. "Our fatherly heart": *ibid.*, p. 358.
124. "If there had been no monks": *ibid.*, p. 358.
125. "You see what God": *ibid.*, p. 361.
125. "Do justice": *ibid.*, p. 362.
126. "The Almighty": *ibid.,* p. 366.
127. "That the Tsar should not grow": Sumner, *Peter*, p. 116.
127. "Most apprentices": Bain, *First*, p. 301.
128. "Why should we quarrel": *ibid.*, p. 372.
128. "To the illustrious": Sumner, *Peter*, p. 173.
129. "Those who buried": *ibid.*, p. 154.
130. "That there are few": *ibid.*, p. 162.
131. "The Tsar pulls": *ibid.*, p. 134.
131. "How many": *ibid.*, p. 124.
131. "You will pay": *ibid.*, p. 135.
131. "It is a vain thing": *ibid.*, p. 134.
131. "For learning is": *ibid.*, p. 149.
132. "Inasmuch as it is": Bain, *First*, p. 392.
134. "Thus children": *ibid.*, p. 394.
135. "I give all to": *ibid.*, p. 399.

VIII. The Dynasty in Disarray: Catherine I, Peter II, Anna, and Ivan VI

145. "Always had one foot in the air": R. N. Bain, *The Pupils of Peter the Great* (London, Archibald Constable, 1897), p. 123.
146. "Was so feared or obeyed": *ibid.*, p. 128.
146. "I will see": *ibid.*, p. 129.
147. "You see, I am at last": *ibid.*, p. 132.

147. "My dear Andrei Ivanovich": *ibid.*, p. 139.
148. "What am I to do": *ibid.*, p. 148.
148. "Thus died a princess": *ibid.*, p. 149.
149. "The Tsar is dead": *ibid.*, p. 160.
151. "Would you not do well": Kliuchevsky, Vol. V, p. 200.
151. "Here, in the streets": *ibid.*, p. 198.
151. "May God grant": *ibid.*, p. 199.
152. "What, were not these same Punkti": Bain, *Pupils*, p. 175.
152. "The banquet was spread": *ibid.*, p. 177.
153. "Few murkier pages in Russian history": Kliuchevsky, Vol. V, p. 222.
155. "Like a troop of cats": *ibid.*, p. 274.
156. "I cannot express how magnificent": Bain, *Pupils*, p. 195.
157. "Seek out for me among the poor gentlewomen": *ibid.*, p. 279.
157. The Ice Palace incident is described in detail, with even an illustration, in a little-known but brilliant work on the early days of the new capital: Christopher Marsden, *Palmyra of the North* (London, Faber and Faber, 1942), pp. 97 ff. This work is an account of architecture and ambience.
159. "Duke, Duke, my heart is sad": Bain, *Pupils*, p. 316.
160. "It is not too much to say": R. N. Bain, *The Daughter of Peter the Great* (New York, Dutton, 1900), p. 36.
160. "I should give your lordship": *ibid.*, p. 44.
161. "Come, my sister": *ibid.*, p. 57.

IX. The Good-Hearted Empress: Elizabeth

163. "She already had": Bain, *Daughter*, p. 134.
164. "I have a veneration": Marsden, *op. cit.*, p. 118.
164. "Tell Count Osterman": Bain, *Daughter*, p. 47.
164. "Too fat": Marsden, *op. cit.*, p. 130.
165. "Truly, Madam": Bain, *Daughter*, p. 54.
165. "My children": *ibid.*, p. 56.
166. "To what party": *ibid.*, p. 59.
167. "God and Her Majesty": *ibid.*, p. 65.
167. "Poor child": *ibid.*, p. 58.
168. "Written not with ink": *ibid.*, p. 135.
168. "Your Majesty may": *ibid.*, p. 142.
168. "Universally beloved": *ibid.*, p. 143.
169. "Do but love me": *ibid.*, p. 149.
171. "Frivolous and dissipated": *ibid.*, p. 113.
174. "She only got": *ibid.*, p. 89.
174. "A masculine habit": *ibid.*, pp. 153–54.
180. "Like the fruits": Marsden, *op. cit.*, p. 179.
180. "She could not look better": *ibid.*, p. 139.
182. "If this lasts": Bain, *Daughter*, p. 214.
183. "Well, your Excellency": *ibid.*, p. 240.
183. "Avoid in the future": *ibid.*, p. 258.
183. "So our campaigning": *ibid.*, p. 262.
183. "Must not be surprised": *ibid.*, p. 275.
183. "I will not survive": *ibid.*, p. 276.
184. "I am always": *ibid.*, p. 289.
184. "Hazarding our army": *ibid.*, p. 294.

184. "We will not conceal": *ibid.*, p. 306.
185. "Her Imperial Majesty": *ibid.*, p. 310.

X. Romanov St. Petersburg and Rastrelli's Palaces

183. This chapter is greatly indebted to Marsden, *op. cit.*
183. "The most abstract": Billington, *op. cit.*, p. 417.
190. "Small, far from handsome": Marsden, *op. cit.*, p. 113.
195. "The house": *ibid.*, p. 199.
197. "The completest triumph": *ibid.*, p. 228.
197. "The interior": *ibid.*, p. 229.
199. *"Un décor"*: *ibid.*, p. 244.

XI. A Husband-Wife Scandal: Peter III and Catherine

202. "I see that your Serene Highness": R. N. Bain, *Peter III, Emperor of Russia* (London, Archibald Constable, 1902), p. 11. Bain in his earlier work described Peter III as "this poor cretin" (*Daughter*, p. 191), but two years later he wrote of him sympathetically as "so hastily dismissed as a mere cretin."
204. "Extremely thrifty": Zoe Oldenbourg, *Catherine the Great,* trans. by Anne Carter (New York, Random House, 1965), p. 4. Of the many biographies of Catherine II, this recent one is particularly useful, especially for Catherine's early years.
204. "My father": Catherine II, *The Memoirs of Catherine the Great,* Dominique Maroger, ed. (London, Hamish Hamilton, 1955), p. 25.
204. "The little girl is impertinent": Oldenbourg, *op. cit.*, p. 7.
205. "Good-looking, well-mannered, and courteous": Catherine II, *op. cit.*, p. 33.
206. "Opera, comedy, poetry": *ibid.*, p. 54.
206. "It is incredible": Oldenbourg, *op. cit.*, pp. 57–58.
206. "I blushed": *ibid.*, p. 63.
207. "Since I can find": *ibid.*, p. 69.
207. "My daughter": *ibid.*, p. 79.
208. "Unrecognizable": Catherine II, *op. cit.*, p. 86.
208. "I decided to humor": *ibid.*, p. 89.
209. "How amused the servant": *ibid.*, p. 99.
209. "I told myself": Oldenbourg, *op. cit.*, p. 103.
209. "Was nothing but a boy": *ibid.*, p. 110.
209. "I saw that she": Oldenbourg, *op. cit.*, p. 110.
209. "Instructions": Bain, *Daughter,* pp. 188–90.
210. "Methinks, I was good for something else": Oldenbourg, *op. cit.*, p. 160.
212. "You will soon see how much I love": Catherine II, *op. cit.*, p. 208. As late as 1907 it was forbidden to publish this passage in Russia.
212. "As handsome as the day": Oldenbourg, *op. cit.*, p. 151.
212. "A miserable little necklace": Catherine II, *op. cit.*, p. 228.
213. "In the maddest hilarity": Oldenbourg, *op. cit.*, p. 179.
213. "She had a dazzling fairness": *ibid.*, p. 178.
213. "Well, there he is": *ibid.*, p. 184.
214. "I don't know how": *ibid.*, p. 192.
214. "I set myself to write": *ibid.*, p. 201.
216. "The rightful possession": Bain, *Peter III,* p. 40.

216. "I did not think": *ibid.*, p. 40.
217. "The vivacity of his disordered": *ibid.*, p. 103.
217. "This magnanimous act": *ibid.*, p. 46.
217. "Discreet as:" Catherine II, *op. cit.*, p. 88.
218. "Presently they would get up": Bain, *Peter III*, p. 102.
219. "What is there": *ibid.*, p. 101.
220. "It was then": Oldenbourg, *op. cit.*, p. 239.
220. "See, though, how unhappy I am": *ibid.*, p. 185.
221. "The first acts": Bain, *Peter III*, p. 69.
221. "Your Majesty surely": *ibid.*
221. "You give an example:" *ibid.*, p. 71.
222. "The general discontent": *ibid.*, p. 111.
222. "If the Russians": *ibid.*, p. 117.
224. "Deliver your message": *ibid.*, p. 154.
224. "Didn't I tell you": *ibid.*, p. 154.
224. "I can't do it": *ibid.*, p. 157.
224. "I am your Gosudar": *ibid.*, pp. 159–60.
225. "I hereby renounce": *ibid.*, p. 162.
225. "For fear of the scandal": G. P. Gooch, *Catherine the Great and Other Studies* (New York, Longmans, Green, 1954), p. 20.
225. "Matyushka, most merciful sovereign": Bain, *Peter III*, p. 171.
225. "They will never believe me": Oldenbourg, *op. cit.*, p. 250.
226. "I had him opened": Gooch, *op. cit.*, p. 20.

XII. The Brilliant Empress: Catherine II

228. "In that case": Oldenbourg, *op. cit.*, p. 271.
229. "The trouble is": Catherine II, *op. cit.*, p. 356.
230. "One cannot say": Oldenbourg, *op. cit.*, p. 265.
230. "I took the first": *ibid.*, pp. 319–20.
230. "Not to hasten": *ibid.*, p. 272.
230. "Do not make me a king": *ibid.*, p. 273.
231. "He lacks nothing": Gooch, *op. cit.*, p. 39.
233. "A genius": Oldenbourg, *op. cit.*, p. 311.
233. "An excellent": Gooch, *op. cit.*, p. 41.
234. "You are so busy": *ibid.*, p. 42.
234. "The wittiest of men": *ibid.*, p. 52.
234. "She is crazy about him": George Soloveytchik, *Potemkin* (London, Thornton Butterworth, 1938), p. 86. This work has been an invaluable source for quotations from correspondence.
235. "The strange basis": *ibid.*, p. 101.
236. "My master and tender spouse": *ibid.*, p. 102.
237. "Hoped to be a support": Oldenbourg, *op. cit.*, p. 324.
237. "The outlines are good": *ibid.*, p. 323.
237. "Beyond price": Gooch, *op. cit.*, p. 51.
237. "We are clever": Oldenbourg, *op. cit.*, p. 324.
238. "The only articulate ideologist": Billington, *op. cit.*, p. 217.
238. One project, never fulfilled: See Voyce, *op. cit.*, p. 61 and *passim*.
239. "O Tempora": taken from Leo Wiener, *Anthology of Russian Literature* (New York, Putnam's, 1902), Vol. I, pp. 272 ff.
241. "Our Mother who art": Billington, *op. cit.*, p. 272.

241. "If I possess": Gooch, *op. cit.*, p. 59.
241. "There is no God": Billington, *op. cit.*, p. 272.
241. "Every peasant": Oldenbourg, *op. cit.*, p. 117.
241. "For God's sake": Gooch, *op. cit.*, p. 70.
241. "The ninth and spirit": Oldenbourg, *op. cit.*, p. 341.
241. "You work only on paper": *ibid.*, p. 340.
241. "Liberty, soul of things": *ibid.*, p. 256.
242. "Your genius": Gooch, *op. cit.*, p. 67.
242. "The extent of the empire": *ibid.*, p. 93.
242. "Interest": Billington, *op. cit.*, p. 221.
243. "Peace is essential": Oldenbourg, *op. cit.*, p. 257.
243. "A mind infinitely more masculine": *ibid.*, p. 204.
247. "We can make a prince": *ibid.*, p. 297.
248. "Le Marquis de Pugachev": Gooch, *op. cit.*, p. 95.
250. "Governments established": Oldenbourg, *op. cit.*, p. 333.
251. "Unclouded": Marsden, *op. cit.*, p. 564.
252. "I have come back": Gooch, *op. cit.*, p. 53.
252. "I have had": *ibid.*, p. 52.
252. "I shall remain": *ibid.*, p. 99.
252. "Puppets of a few": *ibid.*, p. 100.
252. "I am awaiting": Oldenbourg, *op. cit.*, p. 343.

XIII. A Father Undone by His Son: Paul

257. "You have already": Constantin de Grunwald, *L'Assassinat de Paul Ier, Tsar de Russe* (Paris, Hachette, 1960), p. 35. Translations by John Bergamini.
258. "Everywhere my wife": *ibid.*, p. 40.
258. "I swear": *ibid.*, p. 40.
259. "Poodle": *ibid.*, p. 51.
259. "I am reaching": *ibid.*, p. 55.
259. "The most honest": *ibid.*, p. 61.
260. "The air of coming": *ibid.*, p. 62.
260. "You are a ferocious": *ibid.*, p. 79.
260. "Have I said": *ibid.*, p. 183.
260. "He will be": *ibid.*, p. 88.
260. "He must change": *ibid.*, p. 88.
260. "We are lost": Gooch, *op. cit.*, p. 36.
260. "The most singular": Grunwald, *Paul*, p. 67.
261. "Since there is no longer": Grunwald, *Paul*, p. 96.
262. Koutaissov. An amusing anecdote about his origins is to be found in Dolgoruky, *op. cit.*, pp. 124–25.
262. "I know that": Grunwald, *Paul*, p. 97.
263. "Invented ways": *ibid.*, p. 87.
263. "Know that no one": *ibid.*, p. 154.
264. "I tremble for him": *ibid.*, p. 74.
264. "Our way of life": *ibid.*, p. 11.
265. "See that young hairdresser": *ibid.*, p. 156.
266. "The dear children": E. M. Almedingen, *The Emperor Alexander I* (London, Bodley Head, 1964), p. 29.
267. "My father": Grunwald, *Paul*, p. 120.

267. "One could only await": *ibid.*, p. 189.
268. "Do you see": *ibid.*, p. 154.
268. "Russians have always fought": *ibid.*, pp. 118–19.
269. "I accord you": *ibid.*, p. 135.
270. "Worthy of the heroes": *ibid.*, p. 138.
270. "The duty of all those": *ibid.*, p. 142.
271. "I am like": *ibid.*, p. 177.
271. "Sire, you have": *ibid.*, p. 177.
272. "It is impossible": *ibid.*, p. 178.
272. "Sire, I hold": *ibid.*, p. 10.
272. "This is one of the happiest": *ibid.*, p. 12.
272. "You are all": *ibid.*, p. 13.
273. "We are among": *ibid.*, p. 17.
273. "In a short time": *ibid.*, p. 192.
274. "No, no, I will not at all agree": *ibid.*, p. 198.
274. "That's enough": *ibid.*, p. 201.
274. "The common misfortune": Alexander Kornilov, *Modern Russian History from the Age of Catherine the Great to the End of the 19th Century* (New York, Knopf, 1943), Vol. I, p. 58.

XIV. The Enigmatic Tsar: Alexander I

276. "I breathe peacefully": Kornilov, *op. cit.*, Vol. I, p. 96.
276. "To rule over his people": Leonid I. Strakhovsky, *Alexander I of Russia* (New York, Norton, 1947), p. 45.
277. "I cannot": Almedingen, *Alexander I*, p. 60.
278. "I do not trust": Strakhovsky, *op. cit.*, p. 63.
279. "The great and almighty": *ibid.*, pp. 104–5.
279. "The despotic form": Almedingen, *Alexander I*, p. 109.
280. "The autocracy": Constantin de Grunwald, *Le Tsar Alexandre II et Son Temps* (Paris, Berger-Levrault, 1963), p. 184. Translation by John Bergamini.
280. "Last night": Almedingen, *Alexander I*, p. 629.
281. "If Alexander": Strakhovsky, *op. cit.*, p. 62.
281. "Alexander's character": *ibid.*, p. 62.
282. "How long do": *ibid.*, p. 68.
282. "An insolent nincompoop": *ibid.*, p. 68.
282. "The chief enemy": Almedingen, *Alexander I*, p. 98.
283. "I hate the English": *ibid.*, p. 100.
283. "I shall be": Strakhovsky, *op. cit.*, p. 77.
283. "I have just seen": *ibid.*, p. 80.
283. "God has saved": *ibid.*, p. 80.
283. "Great and beautiful": *ibid.*, p. 81.
284. "St. Petersburg": *ibid.*, p. 82.
284. "The possession of Constantinople": *ibid.*, p. 82.
284. "What could he do": *ibid.*, pp. 88–89.
284. "Deaf to what": Almedingen, *Alexander I*, p. 116.
285. "In five years": Strakhovsky, *op. cit.*, p. 132.
286. "He did not sit": *ibid.*, p. 122.
286. "I will not lay down": *ibid.*, p. 123.
286. "In Russia": Almedingen, *Alexander I*, p. 132.

286. "I am ready": Strakhovsky, *op. cit.*, p. 114.
286. "For God's sake": *ibid.*, p. 126.
286. "The public want": Almedingen, *Alexander I*, p. 136.
287. "This will not decide": Strakhovsky, *op. cit.*, p. 135.
288. "Nothing is easier": *ibid.*, p. 141.
289. "Entered their walls": Almedingen, *Alexander I*, p. 150.
289. "It will be sufficient": Strakhovsky, *op. cit.*, p. 151.
289. "You would have thought": Almedingen, *Alexander I*, p. 153.
290. "This should never": *ibid.*, p. 162.
290. "Human gratitude": *ibid.*, p. 160.
290. "To submit oneself": Strakhovsky, *op. cit.*, p. 165.
291. "I could never": *ibid.*, p. 167.
291. "Sublime mysticism": Almedingen, *Alexander I*, p. 171.
292. "My intention": Strakhovsky, *op. cit.*, p. 163.
292. "Free institutions"; Kornilov, *op. cit.*, Vol. I, p. 193.
293. "Victor": Strakhovsky, *op. cit.*, p. 169.
293. "Not unto us": Almedingen, *Alexander I*, p. 155.
294. "I will not hide": Strakhovsky, *op. cit.*, p. 196.
294. "I was able to understand": *ibid.*, p. 96.
295. "The army": Kornilov, *op. cit.*, Vol. I, p. 174.
295. "It was from this time": Strakhovsky, *op. cit.*, p. 171.
296. "I was able to observe": *ibid.*, p. 172.
296. "I simply devoured": *ibid.*, p. 131.
296. "He inquired": *ibid.*, p. 182.
297. "No longer able": *ibid.*, p. 205.
298. "Rejoice, the evil": *ibid.*, p. 200.
298. "I have joined in": Almedingen, *Alexander I*, p. 209.
299. "I think I am pregnant": *ibid.*, p. 85.
299. "I have decided": *ibid.*, p. 184.
300. "I want to abdicate": *ibid.*, p. 187.
300. "The household took heart": *ibid.*, p. 214.
300. "I think that": *ibid.*, p. 216.
301. "Where can one find a refuge": Strakhovsky, *op. cit.*, p. 226.
301. "Do not worry": *ibid.*, p. 232.
302. Morganatic widow: Obolensky, *op. cit.*, pp. 219–20.
303. "I confess the story": Almedingen, *Alexander I*, pp. 229–30.

XV. The Iron Tsar: Nicholas I

307. "What will Europe": Nicholas V. Riasanovsky, *Nicholas I and Official Nationality in Russia, 1825–1855* (Berkeley, University of California Press, 1961), p. 33.
308. "Not by impertinent": Kornilov, *op. cit.*, Vol. I, p. 236.
308. "Sot and a bully": Almedingen, *Alexander I*, p. 118.
309. "I do not like war": Riasanovsky, *op. cit.*, p. 37.
309. "His greatest merit": *ibid.*, p. 37.
310. "God has given": *ibid.*, p. 17.
311. "The slightest negligence": *ibid.*, p. 12.
311. "One true delight": *ibid.*, p. 8.
311. "God, I thank": *ibid.*, p. 9.
311. "Here there is order": *ibid.*, p. 1.

311. "The native beauty"; Marquis A. de Custine, *Journey for Our Time*, trans. by P. P. Kohler (London, Arthur Barker, 1951), p. 96. This is an abridged edition of the original 1843 work.
311. "A tone of voice": *ibid.,* p. 109.
312. "Nicholas I was": Riasanovsky, *op. cit.,* p. 2.
312. "Smile of civility": *ibid.,* p. 9.
312. "He poses": Custine, *op. cit.,* p. 107.
312. "The Czar of Russia": *ibid.,* p. 96.
312. "How remarkable really": Riasanovsky, *op. cit.,* p. 11.
312. "Everything must proceed": *ibid.,* p. 184.
313. "I shall myself be Minister": *ibid.,* p. 46.
313. "You should know": *ibid.,* p. 42.
313. "This young lady": *ibid.,* p. 199.
313. "In ceaseless activity": *ibid.,* p. 195.
313. "We reached Bobruisk": *ibid.,* p. 200.
314. "Today Nicholas visited": *ibid.,* p. 202.
314. "Orthodoxy, autocracy": *ibid.,* p. 74.
314. "In the manner of a peasant": *ibid.,* p. 15.
314. "God rewarded me": *ibid.,* p. 14.
315. "God himself commands us": *ibid.,* p. 96.
315. "Most annoying": *ibid.,* p. 187.
316. "Serfdom . . . is an evil": *ibid.,* p. 210.
317. "To withdraw little by little": *ibid.,* p. 230.
317. "Happy in spite of themselves": *ibid.,* p. 11.
318. "Mental dikes": Kornilov, *op. cit.,* Vol. I, p. 281.
319. "The person of Emperor Peter": Riasanovsky, *op. cit.,* p. 114.
320. "In the style": Kornilov, *op. cit.,* Vol. I, pp. 239–40.
320. "Divine star": Irakly Andronikov, *The Last Days of Pushkin* (Moscow, Foreign Languages Publishing House, 1956), p. 129 and *passim*.
320. "A pity I must die": *ibid.,* p. 109.
322. "I abhor the Greeks": Riasanovsky, *op. cit.,* p. 239.
322. "Traitor to the King": *ibid.,* p. 256.
323. "He is stern and severe": *ibid.,* p. 264.
323. "Here the comedy": Riasanovsky, *op. cit.,* p. 257.
324. "Insolence, recognizing": *ibid.,* p. 5.
325. "One tender look": *ibid.,* p. 223.
325. "The quiet of the graveyard": *ibid.,* p. 219.
325. "This is deplorable": *ibid.,* p. 39.
326. "Now nothing is left to me": *ibid.,* p. 265.
327. "Not handing over": Kornilov, *op. cit.,* Vol. II, p. 3.
327. "I wanted": Riasanovsky, *op. cit.,* p. 35.
328. "The chief fault": *ibid.,* p. 266.

XVI. The Reforming Tsar: Alexander II

330. "Predilection for the good": Kornilov, *op. cit.,* Vol. II, p. 4.
330. "The parade ground ideals": *ibid.,* p. 4.
330. "One of the happiest": Grunwald, *Alexander II,* p. 28.
330. "I have seen": W. E. Mosse, *Alexander II and the Modernization of Russia* (London, English Universities Press, 1958), p. 33. The present chapter is particularly indebted to this short but brilliantly comprehensive work.

331. "He is tall": Custine, *op. cit.*, pp. 28–29.
331. "What will become": Grunwald, *Alexander II*, p. 29.
331. "We don't have to": *ibid.*, p. 31.
333. "With the aid of the Divine": Kornilov, *op. cit.*, Vol. II, p. 10.
334. "Our Angel Tsar": Stephen Graham, *Tsar of Freedom* (New Haven, Yale University Press, 1935), p. 55.
334. "It would be better": Kornilov, *op. cit.*, Vol. II, p. 10.
334. "Well-intentioned": Mosse, *op. cit.*, p. 43.
334. "Young tigress": Grunwald, *Alexander II*, p. 209.
334. "I am more than ever": Mosse, *op. cit.*, p. 51.
335. "It is necessary": Grunwald, *Alexander II*, p. 79.
335. "Thou hast conquered": Kornilov, *op. cit.*, Vol. II, p. 22.
335. "Greatly doubted": Mosse, *op. cit.*, p. 62.
335. "No Notables": *ibid.*, p. 67.
335. "Yes, if the nobility": Grunwald, *Alexander II*, p. 82.
335. "Sire, don't be intimidated": *ibid.*, p. 83.
335. "You do not know Panin": Kornilov, *op. cit.*, Vol. II, p. 39.
335. "This I desire": *ibid.*, p. 43.
336. "For in reality": Mosse, *op. cit.*, p. 81.
336. "The unlimited interference": Kornilov, *op. cit.*, Vol. II, p. 46.
336. "Formerly we kept": Sidney Harcave, *Russia* (Philadelphia, Lippincott, 1964), p. 284.
336. "Forged freedom": Kornilov, *op. cit.*, Vol. II, p. 66.
337. "There will be": Mosse, *op. cit.*, p. 80.
337. "Our motto is": Kornilov, *op. cit.*, Vol. II, p. 84.
337. "Science and the experience": Mosse, *op. cit.*, p. 86.
337. "At the thought": Graham, *Tsar of Freedom*, p. 119.
337. "Fast, just, and merciful": Kornilov, *op. cit.*, Vol. II, p. 103.
338. "The most radical": *ibid.*, p. 103.
338. "Oppression": *ibid.*, p. 104.
340. "Smash right and left": *ibid.*, p. 90.
341. "To the people": *ibid.*, p. 208.
341. "The summons": *ibid.*, pp. 73–74.
341. "Their paternal": Grunwald, *Alexander II*, pp. 186–87.
341. "He would be ready": *ibid.*
342. "How unlucky I am": *ibid.*, p. 108.
342. "In the hands of": Graham, *Tsar of Freedom*, p. 122.
343. "At your Majesty's command": Mosse, *op. cit.*, p. 136.
343. "Russians agree": Grunwald, *Alexander II*, p. 174.
343. "The Emperor is": Mosse, *op. cit.*, p. 137.
343. "Vaporous": Grunwald, *Alexander II*, p. 197.
344. "Wife before God": Mosse, *op. cit.*, p. 137.
344. "Don't forget": Grunwald, *Alexander II*, p. 214.
346. "Sincere entente": *ibid.*, p. 58.
347. "The Tsar is very powerless": Graham, *Tsar of Freedom*, p. 188.
348. "I am a Russian": Mosse, *op. cit.*, p. 149.
349. "Tormentingly anxious": Graham, *Tsar of Freedom*, p. 227.
349. "Would to God": *ibid.*, p. 253.
349. "We don't want to fight": *ibid.*, p. 191.
349. "Flattery and falsehood": Kornilov, *op. cit.*, Vol. II, p. 294.
351. "God has saved": Mosse, *op. cit.*, p. 167.
352. "Gogo, would you care": Alexander, Grand Duke of Russia, *Once a*

Grand Duke (Garden City, Garden City Publishing Co., 1932), p. 51.
352. "It is the happiest": Grunwald, *Alexander II,* p. 347.
354. "There need only": Mosse, *op. cit.,* p. 171.
354. "I am so happy": *ibid.,* p. 172.

XVII. The Last Autocrat: Alexander III

358. "Unshakeable belief": Alexander A. Mossolov, *At the Court of the Last Tsar* (London, Methuen & Co., 1935), p. 3.
359. "He glowered": Almedingen, *Romanovs,* p. 272.
359. "Why can't": *ibid.,* p. 272.
360. "As a citizen": Mazour, *op. cit.,* p. 165.
361. "In a country": Max M. Laserson, *The American Impact on Russia* (New York, Macmillan, 1950), p. 202.
361. "As wax before the fire": Billington, *op. cit.,* p. 440.
362. "Russia has become powerful": Harcave, *Russia,* p. 310.
362. "Power and truth": *ibid.,* p. 310.
362. "To end at once": Mazour, *op. cit.,* p. 118.
363. "Children of coachmen": Harcave, *Russia,* p. 310.
363. "Rise, gentlemen": *ibid.,* p. 316.
364. "The Western Border": *ibid.,* p. 323.
364. "Cottage industry": Bernard Pares, *The Fall of the Russian Monarchy* (New York, Knopf, 1939), p. 47.
364. "Crushed by his position": Mazour, *op. cit.,* p. 168.
367. "We are an immense": E. E. P. Tisdall, *Marie Feodorovna, Empress of Russia* (New York, John Day, 1957), p. 149.
367. "She was a charmer": *ibid.,* p. 123.
368. "Because the Emperor": *ibid.,* p. 123.
371. "Hereditary hysteria": Mossolov, *op. cit.,* p. 87.
373. Grand Duke Alexander: See bibliography.
374. "A man of the world": Alexander, *op. cit.,* p. 138.
375. "I cannot find": *ibid.,* p. 139.
376. "Silly, obstinate": Tisdall, *op. cit.,* p. 72.
377. "One of those": Alexander, *op. cit.,* p. 84.
378. "[He] prefers": Mazour, *op. cit.,* p. 167.
378. "Russian nobles": Harcave, *Russia,* p. 311.
378. "Means of preserving": *ibid.,* p. 316.
381. "Child-like interlude": Billington, *op. cit.,* p. 437.

XVIII. Nicholas II: Unhappy Beginnings

384. "I guess you are": Alexander, *op. cit.,* pp. 24–25.
384. "Deathly pale": *ibid.,* p. 59.
385. "I am astonished": Constantin de Grunwald, *Le Tsar Nicholas II* (Paris, Berger-Levault, 1965), p. 4. Translations by John Bergamini.
386. "It truly bothers me": *ibid.,* p. 8.
386. "He so much loses himself": *ibid.,* p. 8.
386. "But do you know": *ibid.,* p. 27.
386. "Irresistibly attracted": *ibid.,* p. 10.
387. "Palaces and generals": *ibid.,* p. 12.
388. "Thirty-two years ago": Noble Frankland, *Imperial Tragedy* (New York, Coward-McCann, 1961), p. 16.

388. "She looked": Pares, *op. cit.*, p. 35.
388. "The whole world": *ibid.*, p. 35.
388. "I lack words": Grunwald, *Nicholas II*, p. 24.
389. "Sweet child": Pares, *op. cit.*, p. 37.
389. "I never saw": Grunwald, *op. cit.*, p. 18.
389. "Greatest bliss": *ibid.*, pp. 28–29.
389. "Long hours": *ibid.*, p. 27.
390. "I feel that": Pares, *op. cit.*, p. 38.
390. "That the voice": *ibid.*, p. 56.
390. "The senseless dreams": *ibid.*, p. 57.
392. "A charm that attracted": *ibid.*, p. 31.
392. "His usual simplicity": *ibid.*, p. 31.
392. "A rare kindness": *ibid.*, p. 31.
392. "I have never": *ibid.*, p. 31.
392. "Nicholas II was a miniaturist": Grunwald, *Nicholas II*, p. 50.
392. "His force of will": *ibid.*, p. 61.
392. "Hesitant and dilatory": *ibid.*, p. 61.
392. "The source of all the misfortunes": *ibid.*, p. 62.
393. "Triumph over the tsar": *ibid.*, p. 68.
395. "St. Petersburg is a rotten city": Frankland, *op. cit.*, p. 32.
395. "We were all more gay": Grunwald, *Nicholas II*, p. 99.
395. "Russia is not England": *ibid.*, p. 82.
395. "Thank you on my knees": Pares, *op. cit.*, pp. 55, 126.
397. "The strength of the revolutionaries": Grunwald, *Nicholas II*, p. 116.
398. "One does not enrich": *ibid.*, p. 120.
399. "God help Russia": Pares, *op. cit.*, p. 63.
400. "The Admiral of the Atlantic": Grunwald, *Nicholas II*, p. 124.
400. "Russia has nothing to do in the West": Pares, *op. cit.*, p. 167.
401. "Our losses are insignificant": Grunwald, *op. cit.*, p. 135.
404. "To find an energetic soldier": Pares, *op. cit.*, p. 89.
405. "We have got to know": *ibid.*, p. 137.

XIX. Nicholas II: Between Wars and Revolutions

406. "The gifts": Grunwald, *Nicholas II*, p. 61.
407. "In my head": Pares, *op. cit.*, p. 86.
407. "The deputies": Frankland, *op. cit.*, p. 29.
407. "Bad hats": Prince Felix Youssoupoff, *Lost Splendor* (London, Jonathan Cape, 1954), p. 61.
409. "This Duma": Pares, *op. cit.*, p. 109.
409. "Without the Duma": *ibid.*, p. 151.
409. "During the second interval": *ibid.*, pp. 124–25.
410. "We are superfluous": *ibid.*, p. 124.
410. "Overshadowed": *ibid.*, p. 125.
411. "I thank God": Robert K. Massie, *Nicholas and Alexandra* (New York, Atheneum, 1967), p. 150.
413. "The event which ": Pares, *op. cit.*, p. 132.
414. "Her ailing": Massie, *op. cit.*, p. 153. Massie, with a similar tragedy in his own family, treats Alexis' hemophilia in great detail. For a scientific study of the extent of the disease in all royal houses, see Victor A. McKusick, "The Royal Hemophilia," *Scientific American*, XX (August, 1965), pp. 88–95.

414. "Progressive hysteria": *ibid.*, p. 153.
414. "God is just": Pares, *op. cit.*, p. 133.
414. "Incontestable power": *ibid.*, p. 138.
414. "Call it what you will": *ibid.*, p. 138.
415. "Punishment for a terrible sin": Alexander Kerensky, *Russia and History's Turning Point* (New York, Duell, 1965), p. 158.
415. "For reasons": *ibid.*, p. 162.
415. "The nursery was the center": Pares, *op. cit.*, p. 16.
415. "The treasures of his nature": Massie, *op. cit.*, p. 136.
416. "Whole-hearted": Alexander, *op. cit.*, p. 141.
417. "Great abilities": Mossolov, *op. cit.*, p. 95.
417. "A meek young man": Tisdall, *op. cit.*, p. 168.
417. "I will never": Massie, *op. cit.*, p. 233.
417. "He broke his word": *ibid.*, p. 234.
417. "Must be kept absolutely secret": *ibid.*, p. 234.
417. "He almost struck terror": Mossolov, *op. cit.*, p. 76.
418. "One ought to know": *ibid.*, p. 79.
418. "After much thought": Massie, *op. cit.*, p. 232.
418. "Half-worn": *ibid.*, p. 371.
419. "Gifted, intelligent": Mossolov, *op. cit.*, p. 96.
419. "His was a case": Alexander, *op. cit.*, p. 140.
419. "All gifts were hers": *ibid.*, p. 140.
419. "I had a rather stern": Massie, *op. cit.*, pp. 231–32.
420. "Nobody had": Marie, Grand Duchess of Russia, *A Princess in Exile* (New York, Viking, 1932), p. 71.
421. "We are all grouped": Mossolov, *op. cit.*, p. 84.
421. "I should eagerly": *ibid.*, p. 85.
421. "Irreparable loss": *ibid.*, p. 74.
422. "The most level-headed": Pares, *op. cit.*, p. 374.
422. "Always parasites": Grunwald, *Nicholas II*, p. 86.
422. "Little mattered": Massie, *op. cit.*, p. 231.
423. "The only grand dukes": Mossolov, *op. cit.*, p. 97.
424. "You will someday": Pares, *op. cit.*, p. 131.
425. "Too many offers": *ibid.*, p. 142.
425. "He had enough": *ibid.*, p. 145.
425. "They accuse Rasputin": Massie, *op. cit.*, p. 202.
425. "Women found": Rene Fülöp-Miller, *Rasputin: The Holy Devil* (New York, Viking, 1928), p. 207.
425. "The Tsar has washed": Pares, *op. cit.*, p. 145.
426. "Death is driving": *ibid.*, p. 143.
426. "It is true": *ibid.*, p. 146.
426. "Shameful comedy": *ibid.*, p. 147.
426. "He is so pure": *ibid.*, p. 148.
426. "My poor daughter-in-law": Massie, *op. cit.*, p. 218.
427. "Just a good religious": Pares, *op. cit.*, p. 139.
427. "Why don't you act": *ibid.*, p. 151.
427. "The Empress is": *ibid.*, p. 401.
427. "There is an anointed": *ibid.*, p. 151.
427. "Mama, help me": Massie, *op. cit.*, pp. 173–74.
428. "God has seen": *ibid.*, p. 176.
428. "Frightening the Emperor": *ibid.*, p. 227.
428. "I suddenly became": Pares, *op. cit.*, p. 156.

428. "You are right": *ibid.*, p. 157.
429. "Quite enough": *ibid.*, p. 157.

XX. Nicholas II: Disaster and Doom

431. "In no case would Russia": Harcave, *Russia*, p. 450.
432. "A miserable existence": *ibid.*, p. 451.
433. "Let Papa not plan war": Pares, *op. cit.*, p. 188.
433. "If only that hussy": Kerensky, *op. cit.*, p. 165.
434. "I had wretched": Massie, *op. cit.*, p. 309.
436. "Supreme contempt": Pares, *op. cit.*, p. 228.
437. "If you could only be severe": *ibid.*, p. 251.
437. "In a year of war": *ibid.*, p. 232.
437. "We have no weapon": *ibid.*, p. 232.
438. "Come and I'll hang": *ibid.*, p. 250.
438. "Friends worse": *ibid.*, p. 276.
438. "Sleep well, my sunshine": *ibid.*, p. 274.
438. "I fought for you": *ibid.*, p. 323.
438. "We must always do": *ibid.*, p. 300.
440. "Unlimited confidence": Pares, *op. cit.*, p. 318.
440. "Low, intriguing": Massie, *op. cit.*, p. 335.
441. "Baby's rights": *ibid.*, p. 341.
441. "That's where the power is": Kerensky, *op. cit.*, p. 170.
441. "Protect yourself": Pares, *op. cit.*, p. 390.
441. "I can tell you": *ibid.*, p. 390.
441. "What is this": *ibid.*, p. 391.
442. "Drag our Friend into this ": *ibid.*, p. 393.
442. "Dark forces": *ibid.*, p. 397.
442. "She drove me away": *ibid.*, p. 420.
442. "Draw the reins": *ibid.*, p. 397.
442. "Tender thanks": *ibid.*, p. 398.
443. "Order Dmitri": Massie, *op. cit.*, p. 354.
443. "Today *you* bless": Pares, *op. cit.*, p. 404.
444. "It is given to nobody": *ibid.*, p. 410.
444. "The disintegration of the family": Mossolov, *op. cit.*, p. 74.
445. "Mirthless smile": Massie, *op. cit.*, p. 365.
445. "We are wasting": Pares, *op. cit.*, p. 434.
445. "Gravest upheavals": *ibid.*, p. 424.
446. "Do their duty": Harcave, *Russia*, p. 478.
446. "Feel again firm": Pares, *op. cit.*, p. 438.
446. "Hooligan movement": Frankland, *op. cit.*, p. 91.
446. "I command": Pares, *op. cit.*, p. 442.
447. "Anarchy": Kerensky, *op. cit.*, p. 193.
447. "This fat Rodzianke": Harcave, *Russia*, p. 478.
447. "It's a lovely": Massie, *op. cit.*, p. 406.
447. "I don't want to revolt": Pares, *op. cit.*, p. 451.
448. "Don't dare touch": *ibid.*, p. 454.
449. "I have decided": Massie, *op. cit.*, p. 394.
449. "You will understand": Pares, *op. cit.*, p. 467.
449. "I shall never forgive him": Massie, *op. cit.*, p. 400.
449. "Oh. Lvov": Pares, *op. cit.*, p. 468.
449. "Oh, Your Majesty": *ibid.*, p. 468.

449. "He had abdicated": *ibid.,* p. 472.
449. "All around": *ibid.,* p. 1077.
450. "Grand Duke Michael's": Kerensky, *op. cit.,* p. 214.
450. "The troops": Pares, *op. cit.,* p. 472.
451. "You can't go there": Massie, *op. cit.,* p. 421.
451. "His Majesty's Government": *ibid.,* p. 429.
452. "He is a man": *ibid.,* p. 432.
452. "But, my dear fellow": *ibid.,* p. 432.
452. "Alexandra Feodorovna, I was mistaken": *ibid.,* p. 433.
452. "Was an encouragement": Pares, *op. cit.,* p. 474.
454. "I shall live": *ibid.,* p. 481.
454. "I feel so old": Massie, *op. cit.,* p. 457.
454. "Insists on two conditions": Frankland, *op. cit.,* p. 121.
454. "My last friend": Pares, *op. cit.,* p. 486.
455. "I then for the first time": Massie, *op. cit.,* p. 456.
455. "*Who* are the traitors": Pares, *op. cit.,* p. 488.
455. "What an infamy": *ibid.,* p. 488.
456. "What they want": *ibid.,* p. 489.
456. "For the first time": Frankland, *op. cit.,* p. 144.
457. "We spent an anxious": Pares, *op. cit.,* p. 494.
457. "Who treats us well": *ibid.,* p. 495.
457. "I got the impression": Massie, *op. cit.,* p. 486.
457. "I am sorry for Avdeyev": Pares, *op. cit.,* p. 495.
457. "This specimen": *ibid.,* p. 495.
457. "Belshazzar": *ibid.,* p. 496.

XXI. The Romanovs Since the Revolution

461. "We decided it here": Massie, *op. cit.,* p. 496.
461. "The severity": *ibid.,* p. 497.
467. Anastasia: See bibliography.

Bibliography

ALEXANDER, GRAND DUKE OF RUSSIA, *Once a Grand Duke*. Garden City, Garden City Publishing Company, Inc., 1932.

ALEXANDROV, VICTOR, *The End of the Romanovs*. London, Hutchinson & Co., Ltd., 1966.

———, *The Kremlin*. New York, St. Martin's Press, 1963.

ALMEDINGEN, E. M., *The Emperor Alexander I*. London, The Bodley Head, 1964.

———, *The Emperor Alexander II*. London, The Bodley Head, 1962.

———, *The Romanovs: Three Centuries of an Ill-fated Dynasty*. London, The Bodley Head, 1966.

ANASTASIA, *I Am Anastasia; The Autobiography of the Grand Duchess of Russia*, translated by Oliver Coburn. New York, Harcourt, Brace, 1958.

ANDRONIKOV, IRAKLY, *The Last Days of Pushkin*. Moscow, Foreign Languages Publishing House, 1956.

BAIN, R. N., *The Daughter of Peter the Great: A History of Russian Diplomacy and of the Russian Court Under the Emperor Elizabeth Petrovna, 1741–1762*. New York, E. P. Dutton & Co., Inc., 1900.

———, *The First Romanovs (1613–1725): A History of Moscovite Civilization and the Rise of Modern Russia Under Peter the Great and His Forerunners*. London, Archibald Constable & Co., Ltd., 1905.

———, *Peter III, Emperor of Russia: The Story of a Crisis and a Crime*. London, Archibald Constable & Company, Ltd., 1902.

———, *The Pupils of Peter the Great: A History of the Russian Court and Empire from 1697 to 1740*. London, Archibald Constable & Co., Ltd., 1897.

BARBOUR, PHILIP L., *Dimitry*. Boston, Houghton Mifflin Company, 1966.

BENCKENDORFF, COUNT PAUL, *Last Days at Tsarskoe Selo*. London, William Heinemann, Ltd., 1927.

BILLINGTON, JAMES H., *The Icon and the Axe: An Interpretive History of Russian Culture*. New York, Alfred A. Knopf, Inc., 1966.

BING, EDWARD J., *The Letters of Tsar Nicholas and Empress Marie*. London, Ivor Nicholson and Watson, Ltd., 1937.

BLACK, CYRIL E., *Rewriting Russian History: Soviet Interpretations*. New York, Vintage Press, 1956.

BOTKIN, OLEG, *The Real Romanovs, as Revealed by the Late Czar's Physician*. New York, Fleming H. Revell Company, 1931.

———, *The Woman Who Rose Again*. New York, Fleming H. Revell Company, 1938.

BUXHOEVEDEN, BARONESS SOPHIE, *The Life and Tragedy of Alexandra Feodorovna, Empress of Russia*. New York, Longmans, Green & Company, 1930.

B. W., *Russian Court Memoirs, 1914–16*. New York, E. P. Dutton & Co., 1916.

CATHERINE II, *The Memoirs of Catherine the Great*, Dominique Marget, ed. London, Hamish Hamilton, 1955.

CHAMBERLAIN, WILLIAM HENRY, *The Russian Revolution, 1917–1921*. New York, The Macmillan Company, 1935.

CHARQUES, R., *The Twilight of Imperial Russia*. New York, Oxford University Press, 1965.

CLARKSON, JESSE D., *A History of Russia*. New York, Random House, 1961.

CROSS, SAMUEL H. (ed.), *The Russian Primary Chronicle* (Harvard Studies and Notes in Philosophy and Literature, Vol. XII). Cambridge, Harvard University Press, 1930.

CUSTINE, A. DE, *Journey for Our Time*, edited and translated by P. P. Kohler from 1843 work. London, Arthur Barter, Ltd., 1951.

DOLGOROUKY, PRINCE PAUL, *A Handbook of the Principal Families in Russia*. London, James Ridgway, 1858. Originally written in French.

FLORINSKY, M. T., *Russia: A History and an Interpretation*. New York, The Macmillan Company, 1953.

FRANKLAND, NOBLE, *Imperial Tragedy: Nicholas II, Last of the Tsars*. New York, Coward-McCann, Inc., 1961.

FÜLÖP-MILLER, RENÉ, *Rasputin: The Holy Devil*. New York, Viking Press, Inc., 1928.

FUNK, V. V., AND NAZAREVSKI, B., *Histoire des Romanov 1613–1918*. Paris, Payot, 1930.

GERHARDI, WILLIAM, *The Romanovs*. New York, G. P. Putnam's Sons, 1939.

GOOCH, G. P., *Catherine the Great and Other Studies*. New Lork, Longmans, Green, & Company, 1954.

GRAHAM, STEPHEN, *Ivan the Terrible*. New Haven, Yale University Press, 1933.

———, *Tsar of Freedom: The Life and Reign of Alexander II*. New Haven, Yale University Press, 1935.

GREY, IAN, *Catherine the Great: Autocrat and Empress of All Russia*. London, Hodder & Stoughton, Ltd., 1961.

———, *Peter the Great: Emperor of All Russia*. Philadelphia, J. B. Lippincott Company, 1960.

GRIBBLE, FRANCIS, *The Comedy of Catherine the Great*. New York, G. P. Putnam's Sons, 1912.

GRUNWALD, CONSTANTIN DE, *L'Assassinat de Paul Ier, Tsar de Russie.* Paris, Hachette, 1960.

——, *Le Tsar Alexander II et Son Temps.* Paris, Berger-Levrault, 1963.

——, *Le Tsar Nicholas II.* Paris, Berger-Levrault, 1965.

——, *La Vie de Nicholas I.* Paris, Calmann-Lévy, 1946.

——, *La Vraie Histoire de Boris Godunov.* Paris, A. Fayard, 1961.

HAMILTON, GERALD, *Blood Royal,* Isle of Mann, Times Press, 1964.

HAMMOND, THOMAS T., "An American in Moscow." *National Geographic,* Vol. 129, No. 3 (March, 1966), pp. 297–351.

HARCAVE, SIDNEY, *Russia: A History,* 5th ed. Philadelphia, J. B. Lippincott Company, 1964.

——, *The Years of the Golden Cockerel: The Last Century of the Romanov Tsars.* New York, The Macmillan Company, 1968.

HINGLEY, RONALD, *The Tsars from Ivan the Terrible to Nicholas II (1533–1917).* New York, The Macmillan Company, 1969.

KANN, PAVEL, *Leningrad: A Short Guide.* Moscow, Modern Foreign Language Publications Series, 1959.

KATKOV, GEORGE, *Russia 1917: The February Revolution.* New York, Harper & Row, 1967.

KENNAN, GEORGE, *Siberia and the Exile System.* New York, The Century Company, 1891.

KERENSKY, ALEXANDER, *Russia and History's Turning Point.* New York, Duell, Sloan and Pierce, 1965.

KLIUCHEVSKY, V. O., *The Course of Russian History,* trans. by C. J. Hogarth. New York, Russell and Russell, 1960. 5 volumes.

KORNILOV, ALEXANDER, *Modern Russian History from the Age of Catherine the Great to the End of the 19th Century.* New York, Alfred A. Knopf, Inc., 1943. 2 vols.

KOSLOW, JULES, *Ivan the Terrible.* New York, Hill and Wang, 1961.

LASERSON, MAX M., *The American Impact on Russia—Diplomatic and Ideological, 1784–1917.* New York, The Macmillan Company, 1950.

LEROY-BEAULIEU, A., *L'Empire des Tsars.* Paris, 1881.

LIEPMAN, HEINZ, *Rasputin and the Fall of Imperial Russia,* trans. by Edward Fitzgerald. New York, Robert M. McBride Co., Inc., 1959.

McKUSICK, VICTOR A., "The Royal Hemophilia." *Scientific American* (August, 1965), pp. 88–95.

MARIE, GRAND DUCHESS OF RUSSIA, *Education of a Princess: A Memoir.* New York, Viking Press, Inc., 1930.

——, *A Princess in Exile.* New York, Viking Press, Inc., 1932.

MARSDEN, CHRISTOPHER, *Palmyra of the North: The First Days of St. Petersburg.* London, Faber and Faber, Ltd., 1942.

MASSIE, ROBERT K., *Nicholas and Alexandra.* New York, Atheneum, 1967.

MAZOUR, ANATOLE G., *Rise and Fall of the Romanovs.* New York, D. Van Nostrand Company, Inc., 1960.

MOOREHEAD, ALAN, *The Russian Revolution.* New York, Harper and Brothers, 1958.

MOSSE, W. E., *Alexander II and the Modernization of Russia*. London, The English Universities Press, Ltd., 1958.

MOSSOLOV, ALEXANDER A., *At the Court of the Last Tsar*. London, Methuen & Co., Ltd., 1935.

NABOKOV, VLADIMIR, *Speak Memory*. New York, G. P. Putnam's Sons, 1966.

NARYSHKINA, ELIZAVETA, *Under Three Tsars*. New York, E. P. Dutton & Co., Inc., 1931.

OBOLENSKY, SERGE, *One Man in His Time: The Memoirs of Serge Obolensky*. New York, McDowell, Obolensky, Inc., 1958.

O'BRIEN, C. BICKFORD, *Russia Under Two Tsars 1682–1689: The Regency of Sophia Alekseevna*. Berkeley, University of California Press, 1952.

OLDENBOURG, ZOE, *Catherine the Great*, trans. by Anne Carter. New York, Random House, Inc., 1965.

PALÉOLOGUE, MAURICE, *Alexander Ier, un Tsar Enigmatique*. Paris, Librairie Plon, 1937.

PARES, BERNARD, *The Fall of the Russian Monarchy*. New York, Alfred A. Knopf, Inc., 1939.

POLIAKOFF, V., *The Tragic Bride: The Story of the Empress Alexandra of Russia*. New York, Appleton-Century-Crofts, Inc., 1927.

RADZIWILL, PRINCESS CATHERINE, *The Royal Marriage Market of Europe*. New York, Funk & Wagnalls Company, 1915.

REED, JOHN, *Ten Days That Shook the World*. New York, Random House, Inc., 1935.

RIASANOVSKY, NICHOLAS V., *Nicholas I and Official Nationality in Russia, 1825–1855*. Berkeley, University of California Press, 1961.

RICHARDS, GUY, *Imperial Agent: The Goleniewski-Romanov Case*. New York, Devon-Adair, 1966.

ROSS, MARVIN C., *The Art of Karl Fabergé*. Norman, University of Oklahoma Press, 1965.

SAINT PIERRE, MICHEL DE, *Le Drame des Romanov*. Paris, Robert Laffont, 1967.

SALTUS, EDGAR, *The Imperial Orgy*. New York, The Modern Library, 1927.

SCHAKOVSKOY, PRINCESS ZINAIDA, *La Vie Quotidienne à Moscou au XVII Siècle*. Paris, Hachette, 1963.

SCHERMAN, KATHERINE, *Catherine the Great*. New York, Random House, Inc., 1957.

SCHUYLER, EUGENE, *Peter the Great*. New York, C. Scribner's Sons, 1884.

SETON-WATSON, HUGH, *The Decline of Imperial Russia*. New York, Frederick A. Praeger, 1952.

SOLOVEYTCHIK, G., *Potemkin: A Picture of Catherine's Russia*. London, Thornton Butterworth, Ltd., 1938.

STRAKHOVSKY, LEONID I., *Alexander I of Russia*. New York, W. W. Norton & Company, Inc., 1947.

STRONG, PHIL, *Marta of Muscovy: The Fabulous Life of Russia's First Empress*. Garden City, Doubleday & Company, Inc., 1945.

SUMNER, B. H., *Peter the Great and the Emergence of Russia*. London, The English Universities Press, Ltd., 1951.

———, *Survey of Russian History*. London, Gerald Duckworth & Company, Ltd., 1947.

THOMSON, GLADYS SCOTT, *Catherine the Great and the Expansion of Russia.* New York, The Macmillan Company, 1947.

TISDALL, E. E. P., *Marie Feodorovna: Empress of Russia.* New York, The John Day Company, Inc., 1957.

TUCHMAN, BARBARA W., *The Proud Tower: A Portrait of the World Before the War: 1890–1914.* New York, The Macmillan Company, 1966.

VALLOTTON, HENRI, *Catherine II.* Paris, Fayard, 1955.

———, *Pierre le Grand.* Paris, Fayard, 1958.

VASSILI, COUNT PAUL, *Confessions of the Tsarina.* New York, Harper and Brothers, 1918.

VORRES, IAN, *Last Grand Duchess: The Memoirs of Grand Duchess Olga Alexandrovna.* New York, Charles Scribner's Sons, 1965.

VOYCE, ARTHUR, *The Moscow Kremlin: Its History, Architecture, and Art Treasures.* Berkeley, University of California Press, 1954.

VYRUBOVA, ANNA, *Memories of the Russian Court.* New York, The Macmillan Company, 1923.

WALISZEWSKI, KASIMERZ, *Le Berceau d'une Dynastie, les Premiers Romanovs, 1613–82.* Paris, Plon-Nourrit, 1909.

———, *Paul the First of Russia.* Philadelphia, J. B. Lippincott Company, 1913.

———, *The Romance of an Empress: Catherine II of Russia.* New York, D. Appleton & Company, 1894.

WILSON, COLIN, *Rasputin and the Fall of the Romanovs.* London, Arthur Barker, Ltd., 1964.

YOUSSOUPOFF, PRINCE FELIX, *En Exile.* Paris, Plon, 1954.

———, *Lost Splendor.* London, Jonathan Cape, Ltd., 1954.

Index

– – – – – Limit of Romanov Russia, 1613

———— Limit of Romanov Russia, 1913

(Country boundaries shown as of 1913)

N O R W A Y

S W E D E N

F I N L A N D

KARELI

North Sea

DENMARK

GREAT
BRITAIN

NETHER-
LANDS

London

Amsterdam

BELGIUM

LUX.

Paris

F R A N C E

HOLSTEIN

Kiel

Copenhagen

MECKLEN-
BURG

*Baltic
Sea*

Nystadt

Hango

Helsinki

Stockholm

Vyborg

Narva

Reval

ESTONIA

Peter
INGRIA

Novg

Psk

*Lake
Peipus*

LIVONIA

Riga

Libau

Mitau

COURLAND

Tilsit

LITHUANIA

Vilna

Königsberg

EAST PRUSSIA

Grodno

Danzig

POMERANIA

Stettin

G E R M A N Y

Berlin

Kunersdorf

Posen

POLAND

Warsaw

Brest-Litovsk

Elbe R.

Rhine R.

SAXONY

HESSE

Leipzig

Jena

Dresden

Oder R.

SILESIA

GALICIA

Cracow

Dniester

Prague

BOHEMIA

Austerlitz

Danube

BAVARIA

Vienna

River

SWITZER-
LAND

Budapest

A U S T R I A - H U N G A R Y

MOLDA

Trieste

Belgrade

Buchares

WALACHIA

I T A L Y

SERBIA

Danube

Riv

MONTENEGRO

Plevn

BULGAR

Sofia

Corsica

Rome

*Adriatic
Sea*

Adrian

Sardinia

Aegean S